REPRINTS OF ECONOMIC CLASSICS

THE KING'S CUSTOMS

VOL. I

GEOFFREY CHAUCER.

Controller of the Custom and Subsidy of wool, fells, and hides, in the port of London, 1374 to 1386. (Area of control: London to Tilbury.) Controller of Petty or Aliens' Custom in the port of London, 1382 to 1386.

Frontispiece.

THE KING'S CUSTOMS

VOL. I

AN ACCOUNT OF MARITIME REVENUE & CONTRABAND TRAFFIC IN ENGLAND, SCOTLAND, AND IRELAND, FROM THE EARLIEST TIMES TO THE YEAR 1800

BY HENRY ATTON & HENRY HURST HOLLAND

WITH A PREFACE BY F. S. PARRY, C.B.
DEPUTY-CHAIRMAN OF THE BOARD OF CUSTOMS

REPRINTS OF ECONOMIC CLASSICS

AUGUSTUS M. KELLEY · PUBLISHERS
NEW YORK · 1967

First Edition 1908

(London: John Murray, *Albemarle Street W*, 1908)

Reprinted 1967 by

AUGUSTUS M. KELLEY · PUBLISHERS

LIBRARY OF CONGRESS CATALOGUE CARD NUMBER

67-21884

PRINTED IN THE UNITED STATES OF AMERICA

by SENTRY PRESS, NEW YORK, N. Y. 10019

PREFACE

'GREAT is the glory, for the strife is hard,' should justly be the verdict earned by this very welcome attempt to investigate the dark backward and abysm of a most interesting branch of Revenue history. The task of retrospective research, always difficult, is rendered doubly so in the case in question through the scarcity of ancient departmental records, a scarcity attributable to the fact that the central Customs Office, with untold documentary treasures, perished in the Great Fire of London, and that a similar catastrophe occurred early in the nineteenth century. The registers and letter-books kept at the out-port custom-houses have in most instances been abandoned to moth and mildew, and those that have survived furnish pathetic testimony of the extent of the loss sustained. But at last, despite all difficulties, two members of the staff have merited the gratitude of all tariff students by producing that long-desired work, a popular history of the Customs. It is in no sense an ordinary departmental record, prepared during office hours and at the public expense, like Chisholm's great Blue Book of 1869 on the Public Income and Expenditure, or the more recent official 'History of the National Debt.' The work is purely a private venture; the credit and the responsibility alike rest with the authors, as in the case of any ordinary history. They have not attempted to compile a masterpiece of antiquarian lore, but to do that which, perhaps, is just as difficult—viz., to assort the results of research in correct sequence, and then relate them with due conciseness, moderation, and simplicity. In short, their object has been the production of a direct narrative of Customs legislation and procedure, from the earliest periods of our history to the present day.

Few will deny the need for a popular history. The general ignorance on matters concerning the department is amazing. Quite recently a well-known periodical, edited by an equally well-known public man, produced an article entitled 'Baffling H.M. Customs,' in which the modern British customs officer was represented as detecting and seizing 'badly fitted bodices that contain hundreds of yards of Point de Venise and Honiton, waistcoats that bulge in the wrong place so as to hide bags of unset gems, even top-boots specially made for smuggling jewellery and gloves,' besides watches, silks, etc. Not a single article mentioned is liable to duty in this country!

Any true history of the Customs is essentially an obituary notice of Prerogative. It must show the Civil List, at first the provision for all the national expenditure (Navy, Army, and Civil Service), dwindling slowly into little more than the Privy Purse—the King's 'customary' privileges shrinking and vanishing under the assaults of Parliament—the King's 'customers' gradually becoming the servants of the nation—and the popular attitude towards the revenue official undergoing corresponding modifications. Once the bugbear of the public, in the end he becomes its trusted guardian and provider, collecting the national dues with as little trouble to the payers as possible, and in many instances rendering valuable assistance to merchants and shipowners.

To a member of the Board of Customs contemplation of these changes suggests consideration of one most attractive among the many interesting points of a narrative such as this—the ancient *internal* history of the department. The mediæval customs officer was exempt from practical *Customs* control. The great officials (often sinecurists), who were appointed by royal patent, were responsible only to the King's treasurer and to the barons of the Exchequer. Parliament occasionally thought fit to intervene by the cumbrous method of legislation, but there is no great reason to suppose that the mediæval customs officers were more immoral than the average men of the period. The issue of various restraining statutes does not necessarily prove that they systematically abused their powers, but rather that Parliament took advantage of derelictions to assert itself in the only way then possible. The evidence for the prosecution has come down to us; we know but little of the evidence for the defence. It is hard to learn how far the barons of the Exchequer exerted themselves to enforce discipline, but there is no doubt that they exercised a rigid scrutiny of accounts at the periodical days of payment. Often the King's Treasurer, the Chancellor, and the barons of the Exchequer were bishops; the mediæval Civil Service was largely officered by incumbents of Crown livings, and mediæval churchmen were notorious for their tenacity in money matters. 'The Exchequer officers,' says Camden in his 'Remaines concerning Britaine,' 'were extorters in the time of King Henrie the 4th, otherwise Henrie Bell, Collectour of the Custome (as he stiled himself at that time) would never have written a riming long Satyr against them, which beginneth thus:

> O Scacci Camera, locus est mirabilis ille,
> Ut referam vera, tortores sunt ibi mille.
> Si contingat ibi temet quid habere patrandum,
> Certe dico tibi cœtum reperire nefandum;

and concludeth in this manner:

> O sic vexate tortoribus et cruciate,
> Non dices vere propter tales Miserere.'

The system of administration was bad. Complaints against customs officers were treated as complaints against the Exchequer, or in later Tudor times, when the President overshadowed the whole of his colleagues, as complaints against the Lord Treasurer, the final hearer of appeals and framer of verdicts. An effort to establish more direct responsibility was made by the Long Parliament, but their system of temporary committees can scarcely have been adequate, for blame could easily be shifted to the shoulders of a previous committee. A more satisfactory method was introduced after the Restoration. A permanent Customs Board was instituted, and thenceforward for any sins of omission or commission specific persons could be—and were—pilloried, the primary requisite of good administration.

Another century had to elapse before Adam Smith laid the foundation of the modern theory of taxation, and Burke and Pitt purged the antiquated Exchequer, and established the modern system of Treasury finance. Almost another century passed before the slow Anglo-Saxon mind realized the justice of Burke's pregnant text: 'A teasing Custom House and a multiplicity of perplexing regulations ever have and ever will appear the masterpiece of finance to people of narrow views.'*

The fascinating annals of the smugglers (the 'Sea-Cocks,' after whom was named the country-seat of a modern Chancellor of the Exchequer, at once their enemy and prey) require no introduction. Yet another matter is worth passing comment—the very close connexion which has always been maintained between H.M. Customs and H.M. Navy. From the first the welfare of the Fleet has depended upon the efficiency of our Service. In days of old the merchants' natural disinclination to meet the demands of the King's Customers was mitigated by the knowledge that the King in return would protect 'such as pass on the seas upon their lawful occasions' (as the Prayer Book still puts it) from the violence of foreign foes and of the pirates who used to swarm in the narrow seas.

* 'Observations on a Late State of the Nation.' (The slip is Burke's.)

It was expressly for the needs of his Navy that the King first imposed tunnage and poundage. It was distinctly laid down that the proceeds 'soient entierement appliez *sur la salve garde de la meer* et nul part aillours' (5 Rich. II., stat. 2, cap. 3). The merchant who paid was vitally interested in 'the Navye of this Realme and the multitude of the shippes of the same, which to-fore this tyme hath been not onely a greate defence and suertie to this Realme of Englande in tyme of warre, but also a high commoditie to all the subjectes of the same *for transporting and conveyance of merchantdises in and from this Realme*' (23 Henry VIII., cap. 7); and again, 'the guarding and defending of the seas against all persons intending or that shall intend the disturbance of your said Commons *in the intercourse of trade* and the invading of this your Realm' (12 Chas. II., cap. 4). The practice of appropriating specific taxes to specific purposes has passed away, but Customs revenue still supports Naval expenditure, and when the latter increases, the former usually follows suit.

Like the great sister service under the White Ensign, ours of the Blue Ensign and Crown has gradually 'suffered a sea-change' into something which would certainly appear strange to the Norman collectors. Posted, as we of the Customs are, at the gates of the Mistress of the Sea, to watch the ebb and flow of trade, every generation burdens us with fresh responsibilities. The receipt of custom, which was everything with the old riming collector, is but one, though still most important, among many other Customs duties. Mercantile Marine work, the registration of ships, the collection of Light dues, the administration of the Merchandise Marks and Quarantine laws, other duties connected with wreck, Alien Immigration and the public health, and the collection and record of innumerable statistics—labours of which several other departments of Government reap the benefit and credit—all these fall to us to execute, and over all the Treasury stands, Argus-eyed, where once stood the Norman Exchequer. But, however much the conditions of Customs service have altered, its essentials remain. We can look back with some pride upon centuries of public service ; we may hope loyally that in the future—

STET FORTUNA DOMUS CUSTUMARIÆ.

F. S. PARRY.

INTRODUCTION

In compiling this treatise we have followed a settled and perhaps peculiar plan. Aiming at the production of a sustained narrative, we have when practicable opened each chapter with a statement of the more important Customs statutes. In dealing with the eighteenth century, a period prolific of contraband, we have opened with accounts of the 'tariff Acts,' and followed with sketches of the laws intended to prevent smuggling. We have found it impossible, in this small volume, to specify every Customs statute, but we have done our best to display those which have appeared influential and interesting.

To avoid undue complication, we have put a brief statement of the older history of the Scottish Customs directly ahead of our account of the Union between England and Scotland. The older Irish revenue history has been treated in similar fashion; the account appears at the end of the volume, and extends to the period immediately preceding the Union between England and Ireland.

Realizing that a mere enumeration of tariffs and restrictions would be exceedingly uninteresting, we have striven to clothe the skeleton with selections from the immense mass of Customs incidents available. For the more antique we have sampled the Rolls, the works of Hale and Rymer, and Mr. Hubert Hall's scholarly treatise on the older Customs. For the period subsequent to the accession of James I. we have used the collection of Treasury Papers (an almost exhaustless mine of reference on Customs matters) the State Papers, and the files containing the correspondence between the Admiralty and the important office of maritime revenue in Thames Street (not without amazement at the huge share taken by our venerable department in every sphere of ancient procedure). For information as to actual Customs 'practice' during the eighteenth century we have relied upon the outport Letter Books extant, and the 'Memoranda' left by that industrious and learned Commissioner of Customs, Sir William Musgrave. The Letter Books and Memoranda contain much interesting matter—matter which we think few except practical customs officers are competent to interpret for the benefit of the reading public.

These last-mentioned documents the Honourable Commissioners have placed at our disposal, and we take this opportunity of thanking them most cordially for their kindness. As a matter of course, the whole of our work has been done either outside official hours or during the annual leave allotted us, and this has rendered the grant of convenient access to the quaint old 'documents of practice' an inestimable favour.

We shall be grateful if readers can inform us whether there are any records extant—other than the 'Revenue documents'—that furnish evidence upon the following matters (*vide* pp. 449, 459, 462):

1. The grant to Raleigh of 'over-length cloth customs,' and whether the same disproves to any extent the prevalent idea that he lavished his own means on the equipment of privateers.

2. The collection of Plantation customs by Washington's ancestor.

3. The endowment of Congreve with *two* Customs offices.

THE AUTHORS.

CONTENTS

LIST OF ILLUSTRATIONS

THE KING'S CUSTOMS

CHAPTER I

THE DOMAIN OF CONJECTURE—THE PERIOD OF PARTIAL ILLUMINATION—EDWARD I.—EDWARD II.

To 1327

THE older English revenue historians and lawyers, while admitting their inability to furnish exact information as to the most ancient form of English 'Customs,' were unanimously of opinion that impositions upon maritime commerce had existed 'from time immemorial.' Even the compilers of Revenue handbooks cautiously supported this contention, and with good reason. Customs taxation must have been coeval with the earliest oversea traffic, for the maintenance of such traffic must have depended upon royal protection, and it is certain that the protectors would be rewarded by tribute.

It is matter of general knowledge that the Phœnicians traded with Britain long before Cæsar's invasion, and that there was frequent commercial intercourse between the southern Britons and the Gauls; but there is no record of customs levied, either in kind or the rude coinage then current. Yet the time-honoured conjecture recurs. Trade could only have been carried on with the sanction of the maritime chiefs, and sanction would not be given gratis.

Commerce increased and became regular under Roman rule, the imports being munitions of war, and goods, such as wine and spices, which could not be produced in

Britain; the exports lead, tin, wool, hides, horses, and cloth. Inland taxation was comprehensive and severe, for the chief object of Roman aggression was revenue. It is unlikely, with such ingenious inquisitors in power, that maritime commerce escaped exaction, but the Roman rates of duty and methods of collection in Britain are quite beyond discovery.

The Saxon system of taxation was quaint and characteristic. The king had his occasional 'feorm' or method of purveyance, under which goods were appropriated for the maintenance of the royal household. Purveyance was conducted by the reeves, each of whom controlled a district and held a monthly court. The thanes were subject to the martial and picturesque tax of 'heriots,' an exaction of arms and armour from each estate on its holder's decease. The king also profited by fines paid in condonation of deeds of violence. There were three immutable taxes—the 'bryg-bot,' for repairing roads and bridges; the 'burg-bot,' for equipping fortresses; and the 'fyrd,' for maintaining soldiers and mariners. The maritime districts were assessed in 'ship-geld' for the repair and maintenance of war-vessels. The 'Dane-geld' was at first a special 'ship-geld,' afterwards a standing tax to provide means of repelling invasion, later still a collection to furnish tribute.

The absence of any allusion to 'Customs' in the records and legends of the Heptarchy may be due to the fact that during the earlier centuries there was little English commerce. The triumph of barbarism on the Continent paralyzed merchant navigation, and the Saxons seem to have taken kindly to a pastoral life, the rich soils and sheepwalks of the southern and midland districts supplying them plentifully with corn, wool, and flesh. The cities left by the Romans may have existed as centres of homely handicraft, but the southern ports retained little of their ancient trade. Fugitive traffic occasionally enlivened them, being no doubt made subject to slight port dues, or occasional levies in kind by the maritime reeves.

Commerce increased with the advent of the seventh century. There was a little trade with the Levant, principally conducted by Italians, and occasional traffic with the south-western cities of Europe, the route being across the Channel and then overland. A message from Charlemagne to one of the Saxon kings is quoted in the records, conveying assurance of protection to English pilgrims visiting Rome, and stipulating that such as were merchants should pay the usual custom upon their wares. It may be concluded that the Saxon monarch extorted a similar acknowledgment when the pilgrim-traders returned.

The depredations of the northern pirates discouraged traffic during the succeeding centuries, yet English traders were occasionally adventurous; witness Athelstane's grant of thaneship to every native merchant who had made three voyages to the Levant. Queenhithe was the London mooring-place for 'aliens' (foreign merchants). Some of the revenue historians quote certain dues levied in the port of London on corn, ale, and herrings, erroneously describing them as 'customs.' At the time mentioned it would be neither profitable nor necessary to import corn and ale, and the duties obtaining on those commodities must have been city tolls levied at exportation. The tax on herrings was undoubtedly a local levy on fish caught on the coast and brought to London. The same writers quote a local levy upon charcoal, brought by river from the forests of the Kentish Weald, as a customs tax upon 'coal,' and specify as 'customs' the London impositions upon craft and water-borne timber. The error in regard to the last-quoted article appears strange when the immensity of the contiguous Kentish forests is taken into consideration, and the fact that two centuries later, according to Fitz-Stephen of Canterbury, the country to the north of London was for many miles densely wooded.

It is likely that the Saxon kings rarely or never exacted maritime dues in coin. But there is good reason to assume that they made levies in kind upon foreign cargoes, and that such levies were not systematic, but imposed in cases of royal need. The charters and rolls of the earlier Norman period contain allusions to Saxon levies upon sea-borne merchandise, notably upon wines—allusions which, though perhaps not absolutely corroborative, should not be overlooked. These will be quoted in their proper sequence.

William I. instituted startling changes in the system of taxation. His inland exactions were immense and grievous, and it is inconceivable that maritime commerce escaped. The Norman coinage seems to have resembled the Saxon, but evidence is in favour of the assumption that until the establishment of the Court of Exchequer during Henry I.'s reign the amount of silver available was so small, and the exactions were so vast, that most of the taxes were collected in kind, the amounts of goods taken being merely *computed* in coin figures. Therefore it is likely that the early Norman 'customs' took the form of purveyance or 'prisage.' It may also be assumed that when the Conqueror and his successor 'prised' merchandise they prised extensively, and made the more valuable cargoes special subjects of operation.

During the period extending from the accession of Henry I. to the promulgation of Magna Carta most of the royal impositions were answered in coin. The maritime exactions may be specified as Prisage, the Maltolte, and Ancient custom. By customs Prisage must be understood the appropriation of a portion of merchandise at or before landing or shipment. This was extensively practised, the goods being usually taken by the Chamberlain of the City of London, ostensibly for the use of the king's household. At intervals prises were made of foodstuffs, and, as England was an agricultural country, it may be concluded that these prises were in most cases of goods intended for exportation. Wine, of which there seems to have been a steady and abundant supply, was *systematically* prised at import. The Chamberlain had power to taste all wines, to select the most suitable, and to use wine from the unprised casks to fill those taken. There were two kinds of Prisage. The regularized appropriation was a tun from every ten when the cargo prised amounted to ten and was less than twenty tuns. If the cargo amounted to twenty tuns or more one tun was taken before and one behind the mast. Cargoes of less than ten tuns were exempt.* (A sum, stated as 20s., was paid to the merchant as 'freight' upon each tun taken.) This method was called 'rightful Prisage,' and appears to have been cheerfully submitted to. The other kind, known as 'evil Prisage,' was simply 'pre-emption.' The Chamberlain or his deputies enforced it under sanction of the king's special writ, empowering them to arrest all incoming wines at a certain port for a period, to 'buy' as much as the king needed at 'the king's price' (usually much below the market rate), and then release the rest upon payment of a 'fine.' This form of imposition was extremely distasteful to merchants. The kings frequently took much more than they really needed, and then made presents of wine to their favourite churchmen and courtiers, sometimes even to servants of the household. Occasionally, too, they became traders, and sold wines, both of rightful and evil Prisage, in the open market. Most of the records of prises and pre-emptions refer to 'Gascon wine.' For a long period all French wine went under that appellation. 'Gascon' was plentiful and cheap, despite the royal impositions.

The 'Maltolte' was an occasional heavy tax in coin upon merchandise, and was enforced at the larger ports by 'customers' or collectors. (It is likely that the collectors at this period were not permanent officials.) At remoter ports the levy was usually made by the sheriffs or port-reeves. The Maltolte, though not a systematic duty, was in most cases accounted for at the Exchequer, but now and then its proceeds were intercepted by the king.

* Exempt by popular interpretation of the unwritten law, but, as will be subsequently shown, the Exchequer barons of a later period insisted that under certain conditions cargoes of nine tuns might be prised.

There was one systematic tax in coin, the 'Ancient Custom' upon exported wool, wool-fells, and leather.* Some commentators quote 1275 as the earliest date of this levy, because its conditions were then fully expressed in an Act of Edward I., but it is probable that the Act in question merely *ratified* a long-standing tax. The exact rates prior to 1275 are unknown, but they may have been reaffirmed by the rates mentioned in Edward's Act, which were as below:

	£	s.	d.
On every sack of wool exported (28† stone of 14 pounds)	0	6	8 (half a mark).
On every 300 fells (skins with the wool on)	0	6	8 ,, ,,
On every last of leather (240 hides) ..	0	13	4 (a mark).

Certain taxes upon exported lead and tin, and upon imported cloth and wax, are also quoted as 'Ancient Custom,' but it is not clear that these were regularly levied, and it is safer to apply the term solely to the taxes on wool, fells, and leather. It is evident that Ancient Custom existed long prior to the date of the historic conference at Runnymede, for Magna Carta expressly provided that only 'the old and rightful customs' should be taken of foreign merchants. 'The old and rightful customs' could not have signified

* English wool had for many years been supreme in quality, and was eagerly sought after, especially in the Flemish markets. Most of the carrying trade was in 'foreign bottoms'; indeed, the 'aliens' appear to have dominated the export wool trade down to the end of the fourteenth century. Each race of foreign traders had its guild or mercantile society, and the societies were extremely powerful and enterprising. The principal alien traders were the Hanse merchants, who appear to have been popular in England, both with kings and people, for they were allowed easy rates upon their merchandise, their interests were protected by charter, and their transactions were rarely resented by the barons and burgesses. Next in importance were the various Italian guilds, known afterwards as the Friscobaldi of Florence, the Ricci of Lucca, etc. The Italians were disliked, on account of their skill in 'forestalling' (cornering), and the sinister powers which they often acquired by lending money to royal personages. The Venetian merchants were especially unpopular, being renowned as incorrigible usurers, arrant cheats, and subtle foes of English commerce.

† In Edward III.'s reign made 26 stone.

Prisage, or the unpopular and erratic Maltolte. The words could only have applied to an ancient and easily borne tax collected in coin—in short, to the 'Ancient Custom.'

It would seem that, though the kings made frequent levies upon merchants' goods and purses, there was no comprehensive arrangement of ports and places of collection. Some of the ports were 'farmed' by the principal burgesses, who paid a certain sum yearly to the Crown, and collected their 'customs' and port dues together. Occasionally the greater part of the collection was farmed by one or more of the foreign trading guilds; indeed it has been stated on excellent authority that during the middle of the thirteenth century the Hanse merchants farmed the entire customs of England.

The Act of 1275,* reciting the rates upon wool, fells, and leather, applied to England, Wales, and Ireland;

* '*De Nova Custuma Lanarum, Pellium, et Coriorum, in Originali Anno* 3. *Regis F. R. H.*

'A la novele custume, ke est graunte par tous les graunz del realme, par la priere des comunes des marchaunts de tout Engletere, est purveu, ke en chescun conte, ou la grem'ore vile ou port est, soient eslut deaus de plus leaus e plus pussaunz, ke averont une pece de un seil en garde, en un, ke sera assigne par le roi, avera un autre pece, e seront jurez, ke leaument resceveront et responderont des deniers le roi, c'est asavoir de chescun sak de laine demi mark, e de chescun treis cent peauls ke funt un sak demi mark, e de chescun last de quyre un mark, ke isceront hors del realm, ausi bien en Hyrlaund en Wales come en Engletere, de denz fraunchise e de hors. Estre ceo en chescun port, ou nefs pount issir, seront deus prodes hommes jurez, k'il ne sufferount a issir laynes peaus ne quyrs sanz leattre overte a la seel, ke sera au chef port en le counte. Et s'il est mil ke autrement sen isse hors del realme, ausi bien il perdra tous les chateus k'il a, e sun cors sera a la volunte le roi. Et pur ceo ke ceste chose ne pouv tost estre per furing, est purveu, ke le roi enveie ses lettres a chescun vesconte per tout le realme, e fait crier et defendre par touz les contes, ke nul, sor forfeture de son cors e de touz ses chateus, ne face mener hors de la terre laynes peaus ne quyres avaunt la feste de la Trinite en cest an, et adunkes par lettres overtes od le seaus si com est andudroe encime autrement sir les avantdites forfetures. Et le roi ad graunte de sa grace, ke touz les seigniorages, par quy porz laynes ou quyres isteront, averont les forfetures quant eles deviendront, chescun en sun port, sauve a roi demi mark de chescun sak de layne e des peaus, e un mark de chescun last de quyres.'

but it is probable that so far as Wales was concerned this was a mere assumptive declaration of authority. Sir Matthew Hale, from whose illuminative treatise on the older English Customs the specimen of the Act given below is quoted, states that many 'merchant strangers' were fined for infringing its provisions. It will be observed that the imposition was called 'Nova Custuma,' but this may only imply that the duties were levied at a new rate intended to be permanent, and may even be held proof that there *was* an earlier custom on wool. Later it will be shown that when higher rates were levied, and described as 'Subsidy,' this 'new Custom' of 1275 came to be called 'Ancient Custom,' and retained that title during many years. Indeed Hale, and several other ancient writers, were inclined to believe that there was a customs duty on wool, hides, and fells long prior to 1275. No doubt they were correct, for what other regular duties could the Hanse merchants have farmed? And it is plainly shown in the Patent Rolls that the Lucca guild farmed the customs from the beginning of the reign, which proves there were standing customs prior to 1275, and affords good reason for concluding that they existed prior to 1272.

The collection of the 'new Custom' on wool, etc., was entrusted to the Lucca merchants. The Rolls display several 'writs *de intendendo,*' empowering them to collect it, and to search for goods concealed, both in England and Ireland. In 1279 their accounts were checked by the Chancellor, who was assisted by the Archdeacons of Dorset and Durham. The period brought under audit extended from Easter, 1272, to Michaelmas, 1279.

It has been generally held that Edward's Charter of 1278, announcing that the barons (burgesses) of the Cinque Ports were free of Prisage on their wines, was the first grant of such exemption, but there is good reason for believing that the Cinque Ports had been exempted from Prisage by previous kings. A brief examination of Edward's Charter may be of service. It commenced with the usual formula: 'Edwardus, Dei gratia, Rex Angliæ,

Dominus Hiberniæ, et Dux Acquitaniæ, Archiepiscopis, Episcopis, Abbatibus, Prioribus, Comitibus, Baronibus, Justiciariis, Vicecomitibus, Præpositis, Ministris, et omnibus Ballivis et Fidelibus suis, salutem,' and proceeded to state confirmation to the barons of the Cinque Ports of all their liberties and freedoms, 'as they and their ancestors have had in the times of Edward' (the Confessor), 'William I., William II., Richard I., John, and Henry III., *which we have seen*.'* 'We forbid lest any unjustly disturb them or their merchandise.' 'We have also granted them of our special grace that they have "utfangtheff"' (power of trying felons for offences committed within the ports, even if the felons were captured elsewhere). The barons were also freed from service on assize or 'recognition' outside the ports, even though they owned lands in the districts in which such proceedings were held. Then came the exemption from Prisage. 'Et quod de propriis vinis suis de quibus negotiantur, quieti sint de recta prisa nostra: videlicet, de uno dolio vini ante malum, et alio post malum' ('And that of their own wines for which they trade they be quit of our rightful Prise: that is to say, of one cask of wine before the mast, and another after the mast'). Then came exemption from wardships, with an explicit avowal that Edward's ancestors had granted similar exemption. 'Our *aforesaid confirmation* of the liberties and freedoms aforesaid, and other our *grants following*, we now have made to them of our special grace.'

Although the direct statement that there had been prior exemption may to some readers of the Charter appear to apply specially to wardships, others will agree that it included all 'the liberties and freedoms' previously enumerated, or, to put matters more clearly, all the exemptions.

* In 1678 Jeake, the annotator, stated that in the records of Rye there was a document announcing that the Cinque Ports were enfranchised by Edward the Confessor, and that Edward I. granted a *Charter of Confirmation* in 1278. 'Whatever became of these old charters,' said Jeake, 'I cannot say, but it seems they were extant at the time Edward I. granted his Charter. It is likely length and tract of time hath worn them out.'

For this statement follows: 'That the barons and their heirs for ever may have all the liberties and freedoms aforesaid, as the charters aforesaid do reasonably testify.'

But there is convincing testimony elsewhere. In the Close Roll, 1 Edw. I., Membrane 5, appears a royal mandate to the mayor and bailiffs of Southampton, directing them to forbear prisage on certain wines belonging to Cudel and de Sere, barons of the Cinque Ports, till the king shall arrive in England, as the said barons claim that they and their fellows of the Cinque Ports have been quit of Prisage 'time out of mind.' Edward's Charter was dated at Westminster, June 17, 1278. It may be assumed, therefore, that the Cinque Ports burgesses were exempted under the previous charters, and the extreme antiquity of Prisage becomes almost a matter of certainty.

The audit of 1279 did not in any way loosen the hold obtained by the Lucca guild upon the customs, but it may have tended to convince the Exchequer barons that some systematic check upon collection was necessary. In 1282 a royal mandate was sent to the maritime sheriffs, enjoining them to appoint in each port 'two of the better and more faithful men' to collect the 'new Custom.' It is not apparent whether these new officials actually collected the duties and handed them over to the Lucca merchants, or whether the merchants collected under supervision by the officials. It is probable that the latter course was adopted, for Edward continued to borrow extensively from the Italians, and they in return were granted many privileges. They did not always go free with their booty. There is record of a commission of oyer and terminer in 1282, touching certain persons in Kent who had been charged with harbouring an outlaw named Bushe, with a large sum of the 'king's Custom' which the said Bushe had stolen from the merchants of Lucca.

The Prisage of Wine was taken out of the hands of the City Chamberlain, and put under the control of the king's

Butler or Wardrobe Chamberlain.* The supply of wine was large, and 'Gascon' was cheap. At one period the king fixed the maximum retail price of Gascon wine in London at 4d. a gallon (say about 4s. in modern money). The vintage had been deficient, and 4d. was considered a high price. Later one Peter de Denhull acknowledged owing the king's Pantler six tuns of wine (about 1,500 gallons), value £13 10s.—barely 2¼d. a gallon. Again the king, after debate with the Gascon merchants, fixed the maximum retail price of French wine in London at 3d. a gallon; in Oxford at 3½d. Rhenish was dearer, the price being usually about 5d. a gallon. It should be borne in mind that the gallon was about one-seventh less than the modern measure.

Although Edward I. made assignments of the custom to people and societies from whom he had borrowed money or received supplies, it does not appear that he

* A few extracts from the Wardrobe Account may be interesting:

'From Adam de Rokesle, the king's Butler, for 135½ tuns of wine, the same being wine purchased, prisage wine, and wine remaining after the withdrawal of Matthew de Columbar (a previous Chamberlain), sold by the said Adam at various prices, etc. - - £293 13 9'

(This sum was profit upon wine bought at the king's price and afterwards sold, wine prised with an allowance of 20s. a tun as freight and afterwards sold, and wine on hand in the royal cellars—also sold.)

'From the same, for monies from fines of sundry merchants coming with wines to various ports, in order that there should not be taken from them two tuns of wine of prisage in accordance with the custom of the realm, etc. £23 16 0'

(This sum was made up of money paid to escape ordinary prisage.)

'From the same, for ten tuns presented to the king by the burgesses of Yarmouth, and sold to the same burgesses at the price of 40s. a tun - - - - - - - £20 0 0'

(It is likely that the burgesses had taken the wine as prisage for the king, and, the king's cellars being overstocked, the Butler left the goods with the burgesses and accepted £20 instead.)

spent much on his private pleasures. His household expenses were anything but extravagant; but he was a born warrior, and it may have been necessary for the maintenance of government that warlike employment should be provided for the barons. Sudden and effective war meant expeditious borrowing, expeditious borrowing meant unbusinesslike methods of discharge. Edward became heavily responsible to the inhabitants of certain towns in Aquitaine, for goods supplied to his troops. The mayors of the towns in question were put upon the English custom at intervals, but neither in this reign nor the next did they obtain full recovery. Edward also became a debtor of John, duke of Brabant, and his attempts at payment may have made the duke's subjects wish that the debt had been forgiven. For the king invited Brabant merchants to trade to England for wool, promising them safe-conduct and various privileges, and when they became involved in business he laid the Maltolte upon their purchases. Then he put the duke upon the wool custom, and also allowed him to buy and export a large quantity of wool *duty-free*.

A short review of the position provides further enlightenment. The carrying trade was to a large extent in the hands of Italians, the most unscrupulous usurers of the period. Most of the wine consumed in England, and therefore made liable to Prisage and occasional impositions in coin, came from France, yet frequently at each of the larger ports the actual owner of the custom was a merchant of Lucca, Pisa, Florence, or a provost of Aquitaine. Extortion and smuggling must have been rife, especially as the assignees' proceedings were 'checked' by officials who received but nominal salaries, and who were either aliens or Norman-English.

In 1303 Edward issued his famous 'Carta Mercatoria,' reiterating the provisions of Magna Carta with regard to the privileges of merchant strangers, but prohibiting the 'aliens' from selling anything by retail except 'mercery.' Their wines were freed from Prisage, and their merchandise from purveyance except at trade price. In recognition of exemption from Prisage they were called upon to pay a tax called 'Butlerage' of 2s. per cask (afterwards levied at 2s. per tun) upon all wines they imported. This tax was to be paid in 'pence' (cash) within forty days after the wines were landed. It is probable that the aliens at once took to importing their wine in tuns, the tun being the largest convenient package, and that consequently the butlerage came to be collected on every 252 gallons, irrespective of size of cask.

Carta Mercatoria also prescribed a tax of 2s. upon every 'scarlet' and every cloth 'dyed in grain'; 1s. 6d. upon every cloth mixed with grain; 1s. upon every cloth without grain; and 1s. upon every quintal of wax, imported by aliens. This was likely to please the English cloth manufacturers, who appear to have been unable to compete with the Flemings in making the more valuable and showy kinds of cloth. The aliens had also to pay an *ad valorem* duty of 3d. in the £1 upon all other imported merchandise, and specially high rates upon wool exported. Thus amended, the wool duties stood as below:

Denizens.	*£*	*s.*	*d.*	*Aliens.*	*£*	*s.*	*d.*
Upon every sack of wool	0	6	8	The same sum and an additional quarter-mark ..	0	10	0
Upon every 300 fells	0	6	8	The same sum and an additional quarter-mark ..	0	10	0
Upon every last of leather ..	0	13	4	The same sum and an additional half-mark ..	1	0	0

The 'King's Weight,' or standard scale, was directed to be placed in every market town and fair, to secure the proper weighing of articles in which the aliens dealt. Goods bought in the realm by aliens and exported paid 3d. in the £1 value. Wine which had been imported by aliens might not be exported without royal licence, but other aliens' merchandise which had paid poundage on importation might be exported duty-free. It was maintained that in paying these special duties the aliens made due acknowledgment of the privileges granted them by Magna Carta, of the protection promised by the king, and of his guarantee, by establishing an accessible standard scale, that English goods bought by foreigners would be correct as to weight. The third part of this contention was justifiable, but the first and second may be dismissed as mere sophistry. Magna Carta had provided that aliens should pay 'only the ancient Custom.' This Edward considered, and rightly, a great boon, but he destroyed the privilege whilst claiming reward for maintaining it. As for the 'protection,' one has but to scan the Rolls to find what royal protection meant.

To return to Carta Mercatoria. Denizens' wines were still liable to Prisage, except those imported by the chief burgesses of the Cinque Ports. Merchandise imported by denizens was duty-free; the only legal impositions upon their foreign trade were Prisage, Pre-emption, and the ancient Custom outward. Soon after the promulgation of Carta Mercatoria Edward summoned a colloqium at York, and attempted to cajole his subjects into accepting the same duties as the aliens, but without avail.

The extra Carta Mercatoria duties on aliens' goods became known as 'the new Custom,' and were made a separate branch of receipt. At the larger ports special collectors were appointed to manage them, and one may often fall across references in the records to an official who was 'collector of Ancient Custom,' sometimes called 'the great Custom,' and to another at the same port who collected 'the new Custom,' sometimes called 'Aliens' Custom,' and at other times 'Petty Custom.' This means that the first collector accounted for the custom on denizens' wool, etc., outwards, and for that portion of the wool custom, paid by aliens, which was the rate prior to Carta Mercatoria, while the other collector accounted for Butlerage, the aliens' special duties on cloth and wax, the aliens' poundage on imports and exports, the quarter-mark extra on wool and fells, and the half-mark extra on leather.

On the accession of Edward II. the Customs revenue was saddled with the expense of a gigantic outburst of conviviality. The Seneschal of Gascony and the Constable of Bordeaux were directed by royal mandate to provide 1,000 casks of French wine for the coronation festivities. It is probable that the casks were all tuns, but an equal proportion of tuns, pipes, and hogsheads would give a total of about 150,000 gallons, from which we may conclude the courtiers, and perhaps many of the London citizens, drank his Majesty's health deep and often. The sagacious Friscobaldi of Florence paid for the goods, and took an exhaustive pull at the Customs revenue in return.

In 1308 the king's Butler was directed to provide, out of the new custom on wine,* 600 tuns (over 150,000

* Certain new instructions were issued to the king's Butler. Below is a summary from the Wardrobe Account.

The Butler was directed, when carrying out mandates of preemption, to buy the wines 'honourably,' giving no cause of slander, and disturbing the merchants as little as possible. He was to bring all wines taken, whether of *recta prisa* or *mala prisa*, to the place appointed by the Wardrobe Treasurer, and then deliver them into the custody of the chief Butler of the Household. He was to furnish an account in triplicate, specifying the number and description of the casks, the merchants from whom the goods had been taken or bought, and the charges of conveyance, etc. One of these accounts was to go to the chief Butler of the Household, one to the Clerk of the king's Cellar, and the king's Butler was to retain the other. The Clerk of the Cellar had to account to the king's Butler for the price and charges, and to the Butler of the Household for the way in which the wine was put to use. After the wine had been set up, and allowed time to 'settle,' it was to be viewed by the Knight-Marshal of the Hall, who was to inspect each cask and taste the wine therein. If the wine were found good, the prise charges were to be entered in the Butlery Roll, and allowed for as the goods were consumed. If the wine in any cask were found 'corrupt,' the head of the cask was to be knocked in and the wine spilt. The king's Butler had to bear the loss.

gallons) of Gascon for the army in the north. (By 'new custom' was meant 'Butlerage'). Some of the casks were sent to Berwick, the rest to Carlisle.

The king seems to have contracted debts in the blithest spirit, to have reposed great confidence in the resources of maritime collection, and to have been a mere tool in the hands of the Genoese and Florentine financiers. In 1308 the Italian guilds controlled the entire custom, and in the following year the king allowed them to assess their own export transactions at the ancient Custom rates. While enjoying the benefit of 'denizens' duties,' the Italians charged with aliens' duty 'such natives as were willing to pay.' The barons and commons detested the foreign assignees, and attempted to checkmate them by lowering or repealing duties. Thus king and legislators pulled different ways.

In 1310, while the Italians held the customs, the king considered the long-standing claims of the Aquitaine mayors, which were still undischarged, though the Frenchmen had been quartered on the customs at intervals. He allowed them to levy a special tax on imported wines. Then he still further complicated the collection of revenue by assigning 'the aliens' Custom of England' to certain Gascon merchants to whom he owed £3,254, for wines

---

(Prised and pre-empted wines were frequently deposited at various provincial towns whenever the king travelled, so that if he stayed a few days at any place he and his courtiers might be well supplied. When he left, the king's Butler took possession of any wine that was unconsumed, and removed it to some other place advised, usually to Westminster. Sometimes, by the king's order, it was given to the townsmen as largesse. The king's Butler's charges for such transactions were directed to be allowed.)

The purveyors and the king's Butler's deputies at the outports, etc., were enjoined to send all their wines to the appointed places of deposit as soon as possible after they collected them. Sometimes, if it were not convenient to send them, they were empowered to sell, answering to the king for the moneys received. (Chaucer's grandfather was assistant to the king's Butler, and collector of aliens' custom on wine. In 1308 he was charged with misbehaviour to some of the Gascon merchants. He appears to have succeeded in clearing himself, but it is possible the instructions quoted were issued in consequence of the charge.)

which his Butler had pre-empted. As the Butler certainly bought at less than the market price, the sum represented about 1,500 tuns! The Court and its purlieus must occasionally have been flooded with wine.

In 1311 a statute was issued abolishing all new imposts, including the Carta Mercatoria duties, which were decried as having been levied without the barons' consent, and against the spirit of Magna Carta. The ancient Custom and Prisage were retained, and aliens' and denizens' duties thus made similar. It was also enacted that the customs should be 'kept and received by denizens, not by aliens'; that the collectors of the ancient Custom should pay regularly at Easter and Michaelmas, answering for every ship, the quantities of wool carried, the ports of charge, and the owners of goods; and that the issues of all customs should come direct into the Exchequer. Merchant aliens who had held the customs were to be detained with all their goods, till they rendered full account to the Treasurer and barons of the Exchequer. But the Italian experts were soon released by royal writ, the king announcing that they were prepared to render the account required. Soon after they were again arrested on account of pressure brought to bear by the barons, and their goods impounded. Yet the king continued to apportion sums out of the customs to his court favourites, to intercept moneys for his private expenses, to grant his servants small bites at the wool duty, and to send his providers of knick-knacks to the Customs for their money. The queen bought trinkets from a Genoese, and the seller went on the Boston custom for pay. A soldier asked for his wages; the king sent him to the Customs. Frequently a paltry debt to a tradesman was discharged in the same way. The queen was put on the Southampton custom for £4,000, part of a large debt. Harassed as the Southampton custom was just then, the queen must have had but a poor chance of recovering. In the end the king revived all the imposts, and arranged for the Ballardi of Lucca to farm the customs. It is likely that he accepted secret loans and bribes from all the Italian syndicates in turn, and repaid with close writs that enabled them to batten upon Commerce.

An extraordinary riot over revenue matters took place during this reign. The citizens of Bristol, who had previously been allowed to collect their own customs and answer for them through the port-reeve, resented the appointment of a governor, empowered to act as collector. Despite the king's writ, they continued the ancient system. It is recorded that they shut the governor up in his keep, and afterwards seized two of the king's justices who had been sent down to investigate matters, and threw them into prison. An army was dispatched to invest the town, but the valorous rebels appear to have treated the attack with contempt, and easily maintained their position. In the end the Bristol citizens were outlawed, and not till then did they make submission, agreeing to render an account of the moneys illegally collected, and to pay a heavy fine.

In Edward II.'s time London was the most considerable port. Southampton ranked next, then Boston, then Sandwich. The principal ports for shipment of wool were London, Boston, and Southampton. Southampton and Sandwich imported much French and Levant wine. English shipbuilding was on the mend, but most of the wine and wool traffic was still conducted in foreign bottoms. The method of computing a vessel's capacity was to estimate her stowage in 'tuns of wine.' Most of the English vessels were of the Cinque Ports, and used in both commerce and war. The fleet of the Cinque Ports consisted of ships, galleys, barges, cutters, and 'cogs.' The vessels of Yarmouth were mostly cogs, those of Dartmouth, Poole, and Fowey barges and 'balingers.' And it must be stated that these last were often used in intercepting and plundering the vessels of the aliens. In Edward's day, and for centuries after, the English of the West Country were eminent as wreckers and pirates. If a foreign ship happened to lie becalmed off the coast of

Dorset, Devon, or Cornwall, lucky were her company if in the night a galley did not come alongside, and a dozen desperadoes leap aboard and carry off the choicest of her cargo. If a foreign ship went ashore on one of those picturesque strands, down came a gang of whooping country-folk, who stole everything they could lay hands on, and stripped such unfortunates as escaped the sea. The character bestowed in Kingsley's novel upon the rugged fellow who brought tidings of the Armada would have fitted many a mediæval mariner of 'Dertemouthe' or 'Fowy.' 'If he has not left his manners behind, look out for your pockets, gentlemen all! He's manners enough, and very bad ones they be, when he com'th across a quiet Flushinger.'

LIST OF AUTHORITIES.

Saxon taxation: Anglo-Saxon Chronicle.

Ancient system of collection: Hubert Hall's 'History of the Custom-Revenue.'

Act relating to 'Nova Custuma': Hale, quoted in Hargrave's 'Law Tracts.'

Assignments, pre-emptions of wine, etc.: Patent Rolls, 8 Edw. I., m. 28; 14 Edw. I., m. 19; 16 Edw. I., m. 13; 10 Edw. I., m. 17*d.*; 1 Edw. II., p. 1, m. 18; 1 Edw. II., p. 2, m. 3; 11 Edw. II., p. 2, m. 27; and Close Rolls, 10 Edw. I., m. 5; 17 Edw. I., m. 6*d.*; 22 Edw. I., m. 2; 1 Edw. II., m. 2; 5 Edw. II., m. 21; 5 Edw. II., m. 30; 5 Edw. II., m. 3.

Carta Mercatoria: Hale, quoted in Hargrave's 'Law Tracts' as Carta, 31 Edw. I., No. 44.

Prisage routine, etc.: Tate's Transcript, quoted by Professor Furnivall.

Bristol riot: Hubert Hall's 'History of the Custom-Revenue.'

Legislation: Ordinances, Edw. II., c. 4, 5, 8, 10, 11

CHAPTER II

THE 'SUBSIDY' OF WOOL, AND OF TUNNAGE AND POUNDAGE

1327–1422

In the early part of Edward III.'s reign the barons dealt sternly with the alien merchants and the unsatisfied assignees. The mailed guardians of the young king temporarily prohibited the exportation of wool, in order to benefit the English cloth industry. By a charter granted in the first year of the reign, the citizens of London were made free from Prisage.

Many of the Italian merchants having gone home, and taken their riches with them, there was a scarcity of coin throughout the realm, and this the barons attempted to remedy. The customs searchers were instructed to rummage for money sterling carried on board foreign-going ships. Persons going abroad were forbidden to take more coin than would cover their reasonable expenses, and the statute even directed that the innkeepers at the various ports should be sworn to search their guests.

As soon as the king shook himself free of restraint, it became apparent that a foolish spendthrift had been succeeded by an audacious man of business. In spite of the repeated protests of Parliament and the native merchants, he proceeded to extort, in addition to the wool custom sanctioned by Carta Mercatoria, a special impost of 40s. on each sack of wool, 300 wool fells, and last of leather, urging as pretext the needs of his 'great business.' This kind of 'Maltolte' had been occasionally used by previous kings, notably by Edward I. in 1297; but never had it been applied with such savage persistency as in this reign of the third Edward. The king repeatedly promised that when the period specified for continuance of the impost should expire he would take no more than the time-honoured customs—at any rate, of denizens. But in no case did he keep his word.

This imposition upon the richest product of English agriculture continued to the end of Edward's reign. Sometimes it was taken at the 40s. rate, sometimes at a rate even higher. Sometimes the rates were the same upon wool, fells, and leather; sometimes the leather rate immensely exceeded that on wool and fells. The impost was accompanied after a period by a duty upon exported cloth,* a tax totally against the old export revenue doctrine, for it had always been held a justification of the wool tax that it benefited the native cloth industry by making English wool dear in the Continental markets. Yet, when the cloth tax was petitioned against, the king merely made answer that cloth was justly liable to taxation, it being a product of wool. Not only did Edward increase rates, he actually, at one period of his reign, instituted a gigantic system of pre-emption or evil prisage of wool, arresting exportation of the article, buying to the amount of 20,000 sacks at his own price, selling at contract price to merchants, and at once compelling the merchants to pay the Maltolte on their purchases. Worse even than the Maltolte were the extortions of the king's buyers, who charged the wool-producers heavy fees, and the tricks of the farmers of customs at various ports, who exacted for their own benefit extra duties as 'loans to the king.' Through the whole of this reign the commons and wool-producers protested and petitioned against the unjust officials, and the arbitrary imposts enforced by them.

* The impost was 14d. per 'short cloth' upon woollens exported by denizens, 21d. on woollens exported by aliens. The various cloths 'dyed in grain' were rated proportionately Though a mere arbitrary levy, the cloth tax became 'perpetual.'

It would be tedious to specify the fluctuations of the Maltolte, or 'Subsidy,' as it was called towards the end of the reign. The rates quoted below may be taken as something near averages :

	Denizens' Duties.			*Aliens' Duties.*	
	Sack of Wool, or 300 Fells.	Last of Leather.		Sack of Wool, or 300 Fells.	Last of Leather.
	£ *s.* *d.*	£ *s.* *d.*		£ *s.* *d.*	£ *s.* *d.*
Maltolte	2 0 0	4 0 0	Maltolte	2 0 0	4 0 0
Ancient Custom	0 6 8	0 13 4	C. Merc. Duties	0 10 0	1 0 0
Total	2 6 8	4 13 4	Total	2 10 0	5 0 0

(It must be taken into account that towards the end of the reign the tax was levied on 240 fells instead of 300, and that for a long period denizens were forbidden to export wool.)

Occasionally Edward's senators tried to ease the burdens of the nation by juggling with the incidents of the wool industry. They set themselves to organize a national 'Staple' of wool, fells, and leather.* Newcastle, Bristol, Chichester, Exeter, Carmarthen, Dublin, Waterford, Cork, and Drogheda were named as ports where goods might be weighed, inspected, and sealed, for exportation or for coastwise transport. Several inland towns were also made places of staple, and each was linked with an adjacent port, to which all its stapled

* Previously the great centres of staple seem to have been Bruges and Middelburg, places where various kinds of imported goods were inspected, and then passed as reliable articles of trade. The antiquity of staples is proved by a document in the Record Office, included in State Papers, Elizabeth, 1561. It states that the Company of English Merchant Staplers was a corporation before Calais was English, the Staple being kept at 'various places beyond the sea, till by King Edward removed to Calais.' It is apparent, too, that stapling towns for certain products had existed in England long prior to Edward's reign.

goods had to be sent. York was linked with Hull, Lincoln with Boston, Norwich with Yarmouth, Westminster with the port of London, Canterbury with Sandwich, and Winchester with Southampton. At the 'staple ports' wool for exportation was weighed, inspected, and sealed, in presence of the customs officers and the Mayor of the Staple. At the 'staple towns' it was weighed, inspected, and sealed, by the Mayor of the Staple, and the outward custom paid. Then the goods were advised to the linked ports, and on arrival they were examined and reweighed by the customs officers as a check. It is not exactly apparent how long the English Staple endured. Later in the reign the Staple went to Calais, then back to England, then to Calais again.

Edward's 'needs' continued to increase, and his sinister knack of 'business' soon provided him with a new source of revenue, the levy of 'Tunnage and Poundage,' at the rate of 2s. a tun upon all imported wine, and 6d. in the £, value upon *all* merchandise except wine, fresh fish, and 'bestial' inward, and exported wool, fells, and leather. The new duties were practically thrust upon Parliament, with a demand that they should be sanctioned for a brief period. The Commons repeatedly reaffirmed them. They were destined to become 'perpetual,' and to play, centuries later, a tragic part in English history.

The minor customs incidents of the reign are not without interest. The Archbishop of York claimed restoration of his ancient right of prisage in the Humber waters. The Exchequer barons granted the request, but later the grant was revoked, and the king renewed prisage in Hull.*

The long-standing debt to the Aquitaine mayors was discharged, the Mayor of London and another com-

* The Archbishop claimed that his predecessors had held power of prisage under a charter granted by the Saxon king Athelstane, and affirmed by Henry III. Edward I.'s Chamberlain, Matthew de Columbar, dispossessed the Archbishop of 1283 (Close Roll, 1 Edw. III., p. 1, m. 11).

pounding with the creditors for about half the sum claimed as due, and then going on the Southampton custom. Afterwards the new assignees complained that they had been unable to realize the amount of their advance, and were put upon the Staple at Winchester.

Towards the end of the reign several farmers of customs and their deputies were dismissed for fraud, and two of them imprisoned.* The statutes testify that there was much extortion. One statute declared that the king's Butler and his deputies had misbehaved in prisage, taking more wine than the king needed, keeping the best for themselves and giving the worst to the king, extorting gifts from merchants, and occasionally conniving at escape from prise. Another statute regularized the fees of the alnagers or cloth-measurers, who had oppressed merchants. It also recited the regulations as to gauging of wine at importation,† and expressed profound suspicion of the good faith of the gaugers. Another statute stipulated that no vessel might be held forfeitable 'for a little thing uncustomed.' Evidently some of the officers had strained the law to their own profit, and seized vessels for trifling irregularities which were probably the result of oversight.

Richard II. was granted his predecessor's customs—viz., the subsidy of wool, fells, and leather—over and above the Carta Mercatoria duties on aliens' wool, wine,

* The case most notable was that of Richard Lyons, who was a farmer of customs, and 'one of the king's council.' He was arraigned before Parliament during 51 Edw. III., and committed to prison. His estate was also seized. Richard II. pardoned him. After Lyons' death Richard reaffirmed the pardon, so that the dead man's estate, which was considerable, might be disposed of. (See Patent Rolls, 5 Rich. II., p. 2, m. 13.)

† It appears that wines had been gauged on importation even prior to the imposition of 'Butlerage' in Edward I.'s reign. It may be interesting to experts to know that the gauging was mere 'dipping' to find the 'wet,' with an occasional measurement as check upon the standards of tuns, butts, pipes, etc. The gauge fee was a penny a cask, and Mr. Hall points out that this was not a gauger's perquisite, but was paid into the Exchequer.

and merchandise, and the new subsidy of 'tunnage and poundage.'* (Prisage and the Ancient Custom were of course immutable perquisites.) The provision which attached to Edward's tunnage and poundage was re-affirmed—viz., that the duties should be applied solely to 'keeping the sea.' (Sir Matthew Hale, in his treatise on Customs, has called the tunnage and poundage a convoy duty. At one period during this reign the collectors of customs were instructed to deliver their takings direct to the admirals of the fleet.) The rates of tunnage and poundage, after several fluctuations, became fixed at 3s. a tun on wine, and 12d. in the £, value upon merchandise. The method of estimating the value of goods for poundage was peculiar, and no doubt conduced in many cases to fraud. The collectors fixed the rate by conferring with the merchants who owned the goods, the merchants, if required, furnishing invoices from their factors.

Both officers and traders received occasional warning by statute. It was enacted that alnagers sealing faulty cloth should be imprisoned during the king's pleasure, that customs officers should not own or be concerned in shipping, and that their patents (writs of appointment) should endure during the king's pleasure only. The Clerk of the Market of the King's House (purveyor) was warned not to stay longer in one place than the legal contingencies of purveyance rendered necessary, and not to ride with more than six horses.† Merchant strangers were forbidden to buy from other aliens to sell again within the realm. Another act defined the lawful refuse of wool (Cot, Gare, and Villein), and provided that the 'cocket' or clearance for wool outward should be in the owner's name. It was also enacted that all West-Country

* 5 Richard II., s. 2, c. 2, refers to a grant of the wool duties by a previous Parliament. No doubt the tunnage and poundage were collected from the beginning of the reign, but Hale is of opinion they were not ratified by Parliament till the issue of 10 Richard II., c. 18 (an Act that has not survived).

† The purveyors, while travelling on their unpopular duty, were allowed to impress horses for carriage and transport.

cloth should be exposed for sale open, as merchants who had bought it by the bale and taken it abroad had been in danger of their lives from the incensement of buyers who had found the bales deceptive.

The wool trade provided cause for many writs, assignments, special licences, and royal interventions. The Staple was temporarily removed to Calais, but at the end of the reign came back to England. There appears to have been no little intrigue used, both in England and across the Channel, to gain possession of the stapling privileges.* Frequently the king granted licences to merchants of Newcastle to buy the rough wool of the counties north of the Humber, and ship it unstapled to Flanders and other places. There was a twofold excuse for such transactions. In the first place, the northern wool was of inferior quality, and thus rarely up to staple standard; in the second, it was held that the privilege encouraged exportation from the northern shires, and thus prevented the smuggling of wool across the Scottish border. Whenever such exemption was allowed, the king demanded, in addition to the custom, the sum of 19d. per sack, which was the amount of the stapling fees imposed upon other wool.

One or two instances of exemptive licence will illustrate this. A Bristol merchant was allowed to ship northern wool from Carlisle to Bristol. He had to attend personally at the Exchequer, so that he might give bond to pay the outward custom on the arrival of the goods at Bristol, and to export the consignment within a specified period. In 1393 an unusual transaction was licensed; a large quantity of Welsh wool was brought overland to Southampton, the outward custom paid there, and the goods shipped free of staple to Genoa.

* Occasionally, when the Staple was at Calais, the customs revenues accruing were applied to the maintenance of the English garrison, the duties being secured by bond, entered into with the English collectors of customs at the time of shipment. The moneys were collected when the goods arrived at Calais, and disbursed by the Mayor and Masters of the Calais Staple. The Mayor and Masters were English wool merchants, mostly of Lincolnshire.

The king equalled Edward II. in irresponsible extravagance, and incurred debts with great recklessness, flinging many of his semi-private liabilities upon the overburdened customs. He owed one Janyn, a Lombard, a sum amounting to over 10,000 marks, and, being also heavily in debt to the Mayor and Commonalty of London, divided the cocket or clearance seal of the port of London betwixt Janyn and the City Fathers, with the stipulation that if Janyn failed to collect the 10,000 odd marks within a reasonable time he might dispose of certain jewels, pledged with him by the king. Later other jewels were pledged with the Bardi of Florence, the Treasurer of the Exchequer formally handing them over. Later still ' a royal crown ' was pledged with the Mayor and Commonalty of London. The Treasurer and chamberlains were directed to deliver it, enclosed in a sealed coffer, and the mandate provided that if the debt for which it was security were not discharged before the following Easter the City officials might deal with crown and coffer as they pleased.

Yet the king, or perhaps some astute official acting as prompter, could execute a sharp business transaction when opportunity arose. In 1393 the royal sergeant-at-arms was sent into the counties north of the Humber, on the specious pretext that certain merchants had covenanted to lower the price of wool by stopping purchases. The emissary was directed to ' buy for ready money ' all the outstanding stock of wool, to ship it in certain vessels which had been forfeited to the Crown, and to press mariners. This was a notable commercial feat. The wool, which was free of the Staple, was really bought ' at the king's price,' the ships were prize, the provisions for them were pre-empted, the sailors were pressed.

The gradual enlightenment of the king's advisers on the matter of contraband traffic is worth notice. In 1387 the mayor of Bristol was directed to investigate as to English smugglers entering the Severn, and running goods into Wales. Inquiry was also made as to smuggling from the eastern ports to Middelburg. In 1390 it was discovered that extensive smuggling was practised off the Wight, and from the unguarded coasts of the north-west of England. A controller of customs was thereupon appointed for Cumberland. Investigation was extended to Yorkshire, Devon, and Cornwall, and in the end the whole realm was by implication indicted. Both aliens and denizens took part in the illicit trade. During part of the reign the exportation of wool was vested in aliens only, and then such denizens as smuggled wool outward were liable under two counts—defrauding the revenue and infringing the exportation laws. The whole kingdom was racked by lawlessness; indeed the contempt of maritime law prevailing was as nothing compared with the turbulence of the 'foresters' in the woodland shires of York, Nottingham, and Leicester, where there was a continual succession of raids upon parks, warrens, and manor-houses.

This reign is remarkable for the number of pardons granted for acts of riot, violence, wrecking, piracy, and smuggling. In some cases the writs of oblivion appear to have been granted at intercession of wealthy nobles or influential churchmen, in others the reasons of grant are undiscernible. Recital of a few instances will afford readers an opportunity of judging.

The mayor of Southampton, assisted by a body of citizens and *the collector of customs*, illegally imposed port dues upon vessels lying at Fareham, a place exempt 'from time immemorial.' The dues being disputed, he seized and carried off a quantity of merchandise, which he sold in Southampton for his own profit. He also heavily forestalled provisions and other goods. The Crown pardoned him and his associates.

A Lincolnshire merchant was indicted for carrying corn into Scotland, contrary to the statute that prescribed the minimum price at which corn might be exported. Pardoned.

A Hampshire smuggler who had carried uncustomed wool to 'the king's enemies' (the French) was pardoned.

Over two hundred defendants, mostly wool-merchants of Lincolnshire and the Midlands, who had been convicted of frauds in the weighing of wool, were pardoned in a batch.

One Geoffrey Blake, Irish merchant, impeached at the Exchequer for having, with the assistance of certain of his countrymen, defrauded the revenue at Bristol, was pardoned at intercession of his kinsman, a church dignitary.

One instance of scrupulous dealing may be quoted. A German trader approached the king, pleading that the Hanse merchants had expelled him from their guild because he had paid the king of England *more custom than was necessary.* The king admitted this incomprehensible Teuton to the privileges of a denizen, and the Mayor of London made him a freeman of the City.

Aliens had a parlous time, especially when cruising on the Cornish coast. When wrecked they were stripped, beaten, and their goods appropriated. Often their vessels were seized whilst cruising, on the pretext that they were owned and manned by 'the king's enemies.' When they petitioned the king for restitution he ordered a commission of inquiry. Usually the goods could not be traced. Occasionally the sheriff secured them, and the king restored them to their owners, charging double custom or a heavy fee for his trouble.

During this reign the 'scheme' of revenue ports was frequently exemplified in the various patents of office. The coast, from Berwick to Chepstow, was divided into customs districts, each district having as centre a 'great port.' (The record during the early part of the reign made no mention of Wales and the north-western maritime shires, and it is evident that such traffic as occasionally took place in the creeks and rivers from Land's End to Carlisle enjoyed immunity from customs supervision.) The districts were set out as below :

Great Ports.	*Extent of Districts.*
Newcastle.	Berwick to Scarborough.
Hull.	Scarborough to Grimsby.
Boston.	Grimsby to Wisbech.
Lynn.	Wisbech to Blakeney.
Yarmouth.	Blakeney to Ipswich.
Ipswich.	Ipswich to Tilbury.
London.	London to Gravesend.
Sandwich.	Gravesend to Dover.
Dover.	Dover to Winchelsea.
Chichester.	Winchelsea to Portsmouth.
Southampton	Portsmouth to Melcombe, including the Wight.
Exeter.	Melcombe to Bridgwater.
Bristol.	Bridgwater to Chepstow.

At each great port was stationed a 'customer' or collector, with a 'controller' as check. (The larger ports had two collectors and a controller.) The patents appointing collectors stipulated that they should reside at their places of employment. The controllers kept duplicate accounts. There were also officers called 'searchers,' who supervised the actual landing and shipment of goods, and 'tronours,' who performed the weighing of wools, etc.

The salaries of the collectors were small. Their patents empowered them to pay the controllers' salaries out of the takings, but the sums thus paid were merely nominal, and it is evident that both collectors and controllers were allowed to levy fees. The searchers appear to have had no pay except fees, and grants out of forfeitures and seizures.

Occasionally a port was 'farmed,' the king granting a lease of the takings for a specified period, and the farmers paying a lump sum in anticipation. But it seems that the collector and controller remained in office even while the farm was in force, to check the proceedings of the farmers' deputies. The following is a fair rendering of an agreement between king and farmers :

'Between the King and A——, B——, C——, and

D——. The King leases to A—— and his fellows all the custom of wool, wool-fells, and hides that may be shipped in the port of E—— from Easter next unto Easter following, they paying to the King — marks, and grants to the said A—— and his fellows that the customers, weighers, and controllers in the said port shall be appointed with their free assent : And that all issues of the said custom in the port of E—— shall be delivered unto F—— and G—— as the attorneys of A—— and his fellows, and that the customers shall account with the said attorneys for the receipt of custom from Easter next unto Easter following, and shall be discharged by the said attorneys of their account towards the King : And the King wills that the passage of wool, wool-fells, and hides shall be open in the said port from Easter next unto Easter following, and if the said passage be by the King restrained abatement shall be made in rent of farm in order with such time as restraint shall continue.'

The subsidy of wool and the tunnage and poundage varied occasionally as to rate during Henry IV.'s reign, but for the greater part of the time they were as follows : Tunnage, 3s. ; poundage, 12d. ; wool exported by denizens, 50s. ; by aliens, 60s. ; leather—denizens, £5 per last ; aliens, £5 6s. 8d. A penny in Henry's time was worth about a shilling in modern money. Thus, the tax may, in our coinage, be stated as about 20d. a pound on denizens' wool, 24d. a pound on aliens', and, roughly, as 5s. on every hide of leather. The restrictions involved bore heavily upon the producers, and if, as the older economists claimed, they fostered the English cloth industry, the fostering was a costly and not altogether advantageous process.

In an early year of Henry's reign it was enacted that alien merchants should furnish security to the customs collectors that all money received for foreign goods should be expended in the purchase of English commodities. It was also provided that all goods should be shipped or unshipped at the great ports, not at creeks. To prevent forestalling, it was enjoined that aliens should sell their wares within three months of landing. This last statute was soon repealed, provision being made that all aliens' merchandise should be sold, not carried out of the realm. Petition was tendered that aliens should be debarred from acting as collectors of customs. The king agreed, stipulating that the customs officers should be courteous to Italian merchants.

The revenue officials were enjoined to live at their towns of employment, and later the injunction was reaffirmed, with the significant addition that customs searchers might not employ deputies, and that all customs officers should answer upon oath for their remittances. The searchers were forbidden to take money of shipmasters by way of 'welcome' or 'farewell,' or to entertain merchants and mariners. Later still it was enacted that no common innkeeper should be a controller or searcher.

The king's stipulation that the Italian merchants should be courteously treated was perhaps made with a view towards his own accommodation, for he afterwards gave the Genoese merchants permission to export wool duty-free for a period, in discharge of loans which they had advanced him. Henry did not borrow so extensively and recklessly as his predecessor. His wars with Scotland were probably expensive, for in 1401 he directed the collectors of Hull, Boston, and Lynn to send money direct to the Earl of Northumberland and Harry Percy, in aid of the keeping of the Scottish marches.*

There were many complaints from merchants as to the improper taking of duties. The grant of 50s. and 60s. on denizens' and aliens' wool respectively had been intended to include the 'Ancient Custom' of 6s. 8d., but at some of the ports the collectors took the 50s. and 60s. rates as

* This grant to the Wardens of the Marches appears in the Rolls more than once.

subsidy rates only, and afterwards collected the ancient and the aliens' Custom. Several petitions were tendered, complaining of unfair practices used by alien merchants, and the king consoled the petitioners by imposing for one year double poundage upon aliens' goods.

It is evident that in spite of the enormous rating of wool, etc., the out-turn of the customs was unsatisfactory. For instance, at one period of the reign certain merchants of the Cinque Ports were allowed the proceeds of the tunnage and poundage, and a fourth of the wool subsidy, on condition that they furnished a defensive fleet. A certain sum was to be advanced at once, but the amount was not forthcoming, so the whole arrangement lapsed. The deficiency in the revenue was popularly attributed to extensive smuggling by aliens, whom the native merchants charged with systematic evasion of both wool and cloth duties. It appears that the aliens evaded the cloth tax by 'making up' woollens, and exporting them in the form of garments, paying only the outward poundage. The native merchants, in calling attention to the falling off in the revenue receipts, quoted the return during the latter part of the previous reign, stating that then the proceeds of the custom and subsidy of wool were £160,000 a year net. This was a gross exaggeration, and the petitioners may reasonably be suspected of a desire to harry their foreign competitors, and thus secure for themselves a larger share of the outward carrying and trading. But the statement must have had effect, for it was enacted that garments made of wool should be liable to custom as well as poundage.

The Genoese and Venetian traders were unpopular during this reign. The Venetians appear to have been enterprising folk, and they were ably assisted by their skilful and far-seeing senators, whom the Venetian ambassador in England kept posted on matters of trade, on the impositions made by kings and customers, and on the doings of the Venetian 'Factory.'

The Guild of St. Thomas à Becket, which afterwards

became famous as 'The Merchant Adventurers of London,' received a charter in 1404. To the efforts of this powerful and enterprising syndicate may be ascribed much of the English agitation against foreign traders, which many years later culminated in the Navigation Acts and the mercantile dominance of England. But there were other irritating influences, for which the aliens were clearly responsible. For instance, towards the end of Henry's reign certain London ships in the Morocco trade were captured by Genoese pirates, and Henry granted the aggrieved shipowners permission to make reprisals on Genoese commerce. He also extended favourable consideration to a petition that 'proper persons' should be employed as customs collectors, not such as were 'hosts to aliens.'

The subsidy was taken by Henry V. at the following rates: 43s. 4d. denizens' wool and fells, 60s. aliens'; 100s. denizens' leather, 106s. 8d. aliens'; tunnage 3s.; poundage 12d. (According to Hale, the grant was made during 1 Henry V., and for life during 3 Henry V.)

In 1414 the Venetian Senate limited the loading-time of its fleet in England to fifty days. All goods were to be shipped by the forty-sixth day, and it appears that the captains were held responsible if there were any delay through the outward duties not being paid. There was a Venetian 'Council of Twelve' in London, for regulating affairs of trade. The English customers were exceedingly strict with the Venetians, and if any duties were unpaid as the sailing-time approached they removed the sails and rudders, thus effectually preventing the vessel's departure.

Henry renewed Carta Mercatoria, and the privileges granted by Edward I. to the traders of the Hanse.

The salaries of the customs collectors and controllers throughout England during one year of this reign are stated as amounting to £547 only, and the total Customs revenue, including customs, subsidy of wool, and tunnage and poundage, to just over £40,000. Thus it is evident that the officers were allowed to charge many fees. It must be borne in mind that during the continuance of the fee system no official statement of net revenue could convey even approximate information as to the actual amount extorted from the public.

It should be stated, too, that the returns furnished by various ancient writers, even of the net payments into the Exchequer, will rarely stand the test of comparison. The sums occasionally quoted by interested people who approached the throne with petitions were often flagrantly unreliable. The safest conclusion is that at the large ports, especially at London, collection was in a way systematic, and that at the small and remote ports the collectors did much as they pleased. It is practically certain that the Customs net revenue up to the end of Elizabeth's reign rarely approached £100,000 per annum. Of course the comparatively great value of money in mediæval times must be taken into account.*

LIST OF AUTHORITIES.

Legislation.

Wool: 11 Edw. III., c. 1; 14 Edw. III., s. 1, c. 21; 27 Edw. III., s. 2, c. 1; 13 Rich. II., s. 1, c. 9.

Coin: 9 Edw. III., s. 2, c. 9, 10, 11.

Cloth: Hale, 'Pars Tertia,' Hargrave's 'Law Tracts'; 13 Rich. II., s. 1, c. 11; 11 Hen. IV., c. 7.

---

* Mr. Hall furnishes many illuminative statements of the returns of certain duties, usually London returns. These must be accepted as quite authentic, but it is noticeable that he rarely attempts to estimate the *total* yield. No doubt after profound consideration, he makes the guarded statement that during Edward III.'s reign it may have been about £60,000 per annum. Sir William Petty, writing during Charles II.'s reign, avowed that he had come to the conclusion that the old returns of revenue were frequently, sometimes wilfully, misstated, to the great prejudice of speculators who relied upon them, and farmed the customs at rates founded on the Exchequer figures. If this remarkable statement be correct, it would seem that Mr. Hall's reticence should be applauded. It is to be wished that at least one other writer had been equally cautious.

Officers: 25 Edw. III., s. 5, c. 21; 3 Rich. II., c. 2; 14 Rich. II., c. 10; 13 Rich. II., s. 1, c. 4; 1 Hen. IV., c. 13; 4 Hen. IV., c. 20; 4 Hen. IV., c. 21; 11 Hen. IV., c. 2.
Wine: 27 Edw. III., s. 1, c. 4 and 8.
Ships: 38 Edw. III., s. 1, c 8.
Merchants: 5 Hen. IV., c. 9; 6 Hen. IV., c. 4.
Ports, etc.: 4 Hen. IV., c. 20.

Incidents.

Assignments: Patent Rolls, 6 Edw. III., p. 2, m. 1 and 5; 7 Edw. III., p. 1, m. 4; 5 Rich. II., p. 2, m. 25; 6 Rich. II., p. 1, m. 36; 2 Hen. IV., p. 2, m. 7.
Special licences: Patent Rolls, 16 Rich. II., p. 1, m. 7; 16 Rich. II., p. 3, m. 23*d.*; 9 Rich. II., p. 2, m. 39.
Prisage and pre-emptions: Close Rolls, 1 Edw. III., p. 1, m. 11; Patent Rolls, 16 Rich. II., p. 3, m. 23*d.*
Frauds: Patent Rolls, 10 Rich. II., p. 2, m. 23*d.*; 14 Rich. II., p. 2, m. 44*d.*; 15 Rich. II., p. 1, m. 20*d.*; 5 Rich. II., p. 1, m. 13; Hubert Hall's 'History of the Custom-Revenue.'
Pardons: Patent Rolls, 1 Rich II., p. 2, m. 6; 1 Rich. II., p. 4, m. 31; 19 Rich. II., p. 1, m. 30; 19 Rich. II., p. 1, m. 14 and 15; 19 Rich. II., p. 1, m. 34.
Reprisals: Fœdera ('De Reprisalia').
Venetian trade: Calendar Venetian State Papers, 1414 and 1419.
Mercantile privileges: Fœdera ('De Confirmatione pro Mercatoribus').
Revenue: Fœdera ('Declaratio Prosicuorum Regni et Onerum Supportandorum').

CHAPTER III

THE PERIOD OF VAGARIOUS IMPOSTS AND PETTY PROHIBITIONS

1422–1603

HENRY VI. received the wool subsidy and custom as below:

Denizens: 33s. 4d. wool and fells, 100s. leather.
Aliens: 53s. 4d. wool and fells, 106s. 8d. leather.

(Hale states that the wool duties were granted by a statute of 1 Henry VI., but in the Patent Roll of 1423 there is allusion to an ordinance 'by advice of Council,' specifying the rates on aliens' wool.)

Considering the length of Henry's reign, the revenue statutes quotable are few. One Act defined the measures of wine in cask according to the ancient standard—a tun, 252 gallons; a pipe or butt, 126; a tertian, 84; a hogshead, 63—stating that of late the casks had been imported at smaller sizes 'through device and subtilty.'

It appears that the Danes had a staple for fish. In the eighth year of Henry's reign English merchants were enjoined not to trade in the Danish king's dominions, which included Denmark, Norway, Sweden, and Iceland, except at the fish Staple of Bergen.

It was announced that uncustomed goods were frequently smuggled through Wales and into England.

Patents empowering the holders to receive sums out of the revenue, or to levy impositions, were directed to continue during the king's pleasure, not 'for life.' Certain holders were exempted, mostly royal or titled personages, and the commonalties of privileged cities such as London and Winchester. The tunnage rate on 'sweet wines' (Madeiras, Muscadels, etc.) brought by aliens was doubled, and so was the poundage upon tin exported by aliens. The Act of 1454, granting the subsidy for life, appears to have contained the first constitutional grant of the outward cloth duties, which duties, through the growth of the English cloth manufactures, were fast becoming important items of revenue.

The customs officials were directed to give warrants, instead of the usual 'tallies,' in respect of duties taken. In default merchants were empowered to sue, and the penalty in case of conviction was fixed at £10, half to go to the plaintiff. The statute stated that by withholding receipts many officers had embezzled duties and escaped Exchequer proceedings, the merchants concerned having no vouchers to show. The statute prohibiting customs officers from owning ships or acting as merchants, factors, or wharfingers was reaffirmed, and made applicable to officers' deputies. A special Act was issued condemning extortions practised by certain 'water-bailiffs, controllers of the search, and searchers,' particularly by those employed at the notorious ports of Fowey, Plymouth, Dartmouth, and Poole. These enterprising officials had 'by distress and arrests' made heavy impositions upon merchants, both native and foreign. (It is to be presumed that the foreigners suffered most.) A general writ of trespass was issued, empowering the injured merchants to sue for £40 each, and to take the whole as damages if successful. If they failed to sue, any 'liege person' might take action on their behalf, receiving half the penalty if he won his case, the other half to go to the Crown. The full details of the roguery practised are not exactly clear to him who merely reads the Act, but it almost seems that the officers, after fleecing the merchants most unmercifully, levied certain taxes of their own devising upon the ship's fittings.

The Staple* was at Calais during this reign. The usual exemptions by licence were granted to merchants of the north of England, for wool of Northumberland, Westmoreland, and Cumberland only. The Italian merchants were often licensed to ship wool unstapled to their own countries, it being provided that the goods should go by the Straits of Morocco (Gibraltar), *and not overland.* This seems to imply that there was still trade by the Channel and then overland to the Mediterranean.

It is apparent that the custom taken at the Staple fell off during Henry's reign. It is likely that this was due to the increased English manufactures, which provided a new market for the raw material. It was better for the producer to take a low price in England than to subject his goods to the burdensome outward expenses, and to risk of storm and piracy. The king's advisers seem to have attributed the falling-off to other causes, for they enacted that all wool or fells placed in remote places near the coast, except under indenture for legal exportation, should be forfeitable.† The desire of the English to dominate the trade had previously been made manifest in a petition that the export of live sheep to Flanders might be prohibited, as it improved the breed of Flemish sheep to the loss of English trade. The request had been acknowledged by prohibition of export, except under royal licence or to the Staple. Occasionally privilege was

* It is possible that the maintenance of the Staple at Calais instead of in England may have assisted in the prevention of smuggling, for no wool would be received at the Calais Staple unless 'cocketed' in England, and secured by bond as to duty. Thus smuggled wool could not well be run directly across Channel into the parts of France subject to England, for the Masters of the Calais Staple, during such time as they held exclusive stapling privileges, kept a sharp watch upon all vessels arriving on the adjacent coast. Whether the Staple were in England or Calais, the smugglers could scarcely have cleared the whole amount of the custom, for they would have to sell their wool unsealed. Its quality would therefore be unattested, and the buyers would offer a low price, and refuse to believe that the goods were of the English counties south of the Humber.

† In 1427 a Commission had inquired into the unlading and lading of uncustomed goods on the coast of Sussex, and as to non-residence of officials.

granted to certain Welsh wool-producers to have their goods stapled at Carmarthen, the duty collected there, and the goods shipped via Bristol without further charge.

The yearly expenses of the king's household were stated as 10,000 marks—quite a moderate sum. 2,000 marks were appropriated towards this end from tunnage and poundage, 5,000 from the wool subsidy, and the rest from the Welsh revenues, the revenues of the Mint, and Wardships. But the king contrived to burden himself with debts, and his creditors, among whom the Bishop of Winchester and the Florentine and Venetian guildsmen were conspicuous, were frequently allowed to dabble in the customs receipts. Other curious assignments appear in the records. For instance, the Justices of the King's Bench were quartered on the Hanaper and the Customs for 180 marks each yearly, besides £5 6s. 11¼d. 'and the sixth part of a halfpenny' for a furred robe every Christmas, and £3 6s. 6d. for a lined robe every Whitsuntide.

In 1450 Dutch and Flemish wares were prohibited for a period, the Netherlanders having prohibited English cloth.

There was much bartering and adjusting of commercial privileges between England and foreign states. A treaty betwixt Henry, the Master-General of the Teutonic Knights of Prussia, and the Consuls of the Hanse towns, renewed all commercial privileges granted between England and the Almains concerned during the previous hundred years, and provided that the duties and customs formerly prescribed should remain on the ancient footing.* The treaty does not appear to have been rigorously observed on either side. The Venetians' trade with England must have been on the diminishing scale, for the Senate enjoined that its London factory should not be called upon to expend more than £20 per ship in corrupting

* About this time the Hanse merchants began to lose their trade, which gradually passed into the hands of the English and Dutch.

the English collectors.* An amicable understanding seems to have existed between Henry and the king of Portugal. The latter was frequently granted licences to ship large quantities of English goods.

English merchant enterprise was manifested by the sudden emerging into importance of a company that in after years gained a firm grip of the export cloth trade, and commanded powerful legislative support. The Society of St. Thomas à Becket, extending its operations with immense vigour, entered into formidable competition with the Hanse traders. A 'great ship' belonging to one Taverner, of Hull, entered the Thames, and the king seems to have taken special interest in her. He granted a licence, empowering her to carry outwards 'all kinds of merchandise, either aliens' or denizens',' bringing back 'such goods as were most needed in England,' and named her *The Grace-Dieu.*

The southern English maintained their reputation as wreckers and pirates, and Spanish commerce in particular suffered terribly from their depredations. The Rolls furnish numerous records of their lawless doings. It appears they did not confine their excursions to the English side of the Channel. Below is quoted a complaint in Chancery presented by certain Breton merchants :

'To the revend Father in God, Bysshop of Bath & Chauncellor of England.

'Besechith mekely John Bonodyn and Aleyn le Bihous, proctours and attornez of Gyan de Garne, Piers Bourdyn, John le Peyntor, Guyllam Maner, Piers Guyllam, Piers Tourell, Piers Duryan, and Richd. Kerbouter, merchauntes of Vennes† in Britaigne, that where the seide

* Bribing them to put a low value on goods for poundage. The 'loading period' was made ninety days instead of fifty, with an extra fifteen days for clearing through the Custom House. It would seem that the London customs men held, with their whilom controller Chaucer, that it was impossible to work 'bothe wel and hastilie.'

† Vannes in Brittany.

merchauntes, late beyng possessours and owners of a schipp called *Seint Gillian*, de Vennes in Britaigne, with divers marchaundisez, godes, and moneys beyng in the seide schipp, to the value of vjM crounes, the which yn a sedule to this bill annexed specially appearith, beyng on the costes of Britaigne yn the moneth of Octobr the XIX yere of the reigne of Kynge Herry the Sixte, saylinge toward the coste of Burdeux, having at that tyme the safe-conducte of the Erle of Huntyngdon, then beyng lieutenant of Guienne, and under the Kynges pees of Englond made and p'claymed betwene the Kynge of Englond and the Duke of Britaigne, yn way of marchaundise toward the port of Burdeux, fast by the entrynge into the ryver of the seide port, unto such tyme that the seide schipp and godes within the seide moneth of Octob'r there were taken by IIJ balyngers of were of the counte of Cornewayll : That is to sey, on balynger cleped the *Cristofre* of Trerewe,* and thereof Wolfe maister and Sr Ramfray Arundell and Sr John Trerys, Knyghtes, owners and vitallers : Another balynger cleped *Ihu* of Peryn in Falmouth, and thereof John Jetard maister and the seide Sr Ramfray Arundell, Knyghte, owner and vitaller : And the thrydde balynger cleped the *Flour de la Mare*, and th'of John Treehowe maister and the forseide Sr Ramfray Arundell owner and vitaller : And by another balynger yn their copeney as yet unknown : The seide safe-conducte and trewes natwithstondyng : And afterwardes the maisters and mariners of the seide balyngers ladde the seide schipp and godes into the ryver of Jerand,† and there dispoiled the seide godes and sold the seide schipp with grete pt of the seide godes to maister John Tregoran, clerke, Robt Maundeson of Hull, Edmond Mathewe, and Peter Gyles : The which, knowyng the seide schipp and godes soe to be dispoiled and robbet upon the see, bought the seide schipp and godes, and ladde the seide schipp and godes to the porte of Hulle within the roialme of Englond, and kepith the seide godes

* Truro.

† Gironde.

agenst gode feith and concience : The which mat's youre seide besechers bien redi to p've by resonable p'ves, lyke as it plese youre g'cious Lordschipp that they schall doe : Wherefor hit plese youre g'cious Lordschipp tenderly to consider this p'misses, and to graunte severall writtes of suppena directe to the seide mysdoers to appere afor you at a certain day to aunswere to the p'misses, and th'upon to restore youre seide besechers to the seide schipp and godes, as gode feith and concience askith and requirith, for the love of God and yn wey of charyte.'

One of the records may appear almost incredible. It should be stated that in Richard II.'s time, when the outlaws of the north Midlands made themselves busy in plundering the estates and abodes of the rural landowners, they were sometimes headed by desperadoes who in the subsequent writs of inquiry were described as 'priests' or 'abbots.' Yet the account of such doings in Richard's time, up in the 'lawless shires,' scarcely prepares readers for the statement that in Henry VI.'s reign the abbot of St. Augustine's, Canterbury, aided by 'other evildoers,' boarded a French vessel off the Isle of Thanet, and appropriated ship and cargo.

Edward IV. received the subsidy on wool, etc., at the following rates : Denizens' wool and fells, 33s. 4d. ; aliens', 66s. 8d. ; denizens' leather, 66s. 8d. ; aliens', 73s. 4d.* He also received tunnage at 3s., with an extra 3s. on sweet wines imported by aliens, and poundage at 12d. in the £1, with an extra 12d. on aliens' tin outward. All the above for life. Thus the total rates levied would be—

	Denizens.			*Aliens.*		
	£	*s.*	*d.*	*£*	*s.*	*d.*
On every sack of wool and every 240 fells outward	1	13	4	3	6	8
On every last of leather outward ..	3	6	8	3	13	4

* Hale states tunnage and poundage granted by an Act of 3 Edw. IV., but he is unable to give the date of the wool grant.

(The ancient Custom, and the Carta Mercatoria duties on aliens' wool, should be computed with the subsidy, and the whole of the wool and leather duties outward will thus come into the rate.)

	Denizens.			*Aliens.*			
	£	*s.*	*d.*	£	*s.*	*d.*	
On every tun of wine imported, except sweet wines imported by aliens	0	3	0	0	3	0	(tunnage)
		—		0	2	0	(butlerage)
				0	5	0	
On every tun of sweet wines imported by aliens ..		—		0	3	0	(tunnage)
				0	3	0	(impost)
				0	2	0	(butlerage)
				0	8	0	
On every £1 value of merchandise imported or exported by denizens or aliens, except wool, fells, and leather exported by denizens or aliens, cloth exported by denizens, tin exported by aliens, wine imported by denizens or aliens, and imported fresh fish or bestial	0	1	0	0	1	0	
		—		0	0	3	(C. Merc. duties)
				0	1	3	

(Double poundage on tin exported by aliens. The cloth duties were maintained.)

Edward's parliaments appear to have busied themselves in defending native handicraft against foreign competition. They prohibited many articles of foreign manufacture, and granted extensive powers of search, to the end that the goods might be confiscated if found within the realm. 'The Liberties of Great St. Martin's' were exempted from the operations of this statute.

It was enacted that cloth unfulled in England should not be exported.

English archery having decayed through the scarcity of bowstaves, it was enacted that aliens should bring four bowstaves with every ton of merchandise. (The best foreign bowstaves came in the ships of Venice, but of course they were not Venetian produce.) It was provided that he who defrauded the king of tunnage and poundage should answer with body and goods.

It was also enjoined that no Scottish merchandise should enter England except by way of Berwick or Carlisle, and that no English goods should be sold into Scotland except at those places.

Edward seems to have made a less rigid estimate of official responsibilities than some of his predecessors, for he repeatedly relaxed by writ the provisions of the statute forbidding customs officers from acting as merchants, keeping taverns, and being interested in shipping. At the same time he or his advisers must have thought that a show of supervision was desirable, for 'Controllers of the Scrutiny'—*i.e.*, surveyors of the searchers—were appointed at various ports. A special surveyor was appointed at Poole, his district including Exeter, Bridgwater, and the irreclaimable ports of Fowey and Dartmouth. Special surveyors were appointed at London, with power to supervise all the revenue officials of the port, to examine books and memoranda, to rummage merchandise, and to arrest and imprison offenders. Previously a Commission had sat to inquire into extensive frauds at Bristol and Southampton, and the conduct of the officers there, and another Commission had investigated frauds in Devon and Cornwall, and accusations against the officers of taking bribes, being interested in merchandise, keeping taverns, and neglecting their duty.

The Staple was at Calais, and a portion of the wool custom and subsidy there collected was granted to the mayor and burgesses as usual for the maintenance of the garrison. At one period of the reign they expended a great sum in repairing the fortifications of the town, and were allowed to ship wool duty-free from England, giving security that a portion of the proceeds should return in the form of coin or plate, and thus be expended in the mother-country. There were many grants of duty-free shipment to creditors of the king, and to commonalties of towns that had incurred expense in repairing fortifications.

The increasing importance of English merchants rendered them useful as lenders, and they frequently made advances to the Crown. The Genoese and Florentines figured occasionally as royal creditors, but by no means to the same extent as of old. In 1471 the former were given exceptional privileges in discharge of a royal debt. The Florentines were quartered for a time on the London, Southampton, and Sandwich customs. Yet it is apparent that maritime commerce and the profitable business of financing the king were being gradually wrested from their original holders. A few of the royal obligations to English merchants and corporate bodies may be advantageously noted.

The king whilst at Calais borrowed £40 from one Sapcote, and allowed him to deduct half a mark from the duty on every sack of his own wool, shipped at Ipswich, up to the amount of the debt. (The deduction was of course made at Calais, where the duties were paid.) A quantity of woollen cloth was allowed shipment duty-free, in satisfaction of a royal debt due to English creditors. In 1478 the king acknowledged a debt of over £12,000 to the City of London.

In spite of the havoc wrought by the wars of the Roses, the extinguishment of many noble and wealthy families, and the reduced importance of others, the importation of wine was extensive, and it was found necessary to appoint one of the royal yeomen as deputy purveyor, 'the Chief Butler being fully occupied.' That English commerce in general was increasing is proved by the mention of Plymouth and Chester as rising ports, and the increase in the staff of London controllers. The port of Sandwich appears to have been prosperous. A petition sent to the king many years later by the burgesses of this ancient town alluded to the condition of Sandwich during Edward IV.'s time, stating that the port then had ninety-five ships, and yielded about £17,000 yearly in customs. The statement was no doubt an exaggeration, yet probably the petitioners were right in naming this as the summertide of Sandwich's prosperity.

The price of wine in England had slightly increased, Gascon occasionally selling at £4 a tun. The following goods were plentiful in the London markets : anise, cummin, worm-seed, wax, alum, grains of paradise, ginger, cloves, mace, cinnamon, rhubarb, scammony, spikenard, senna, turpentine, dyers' grains, zedoary, almonds, rice, dates, euphorbium, stavesacre, cassia, nutmeg, pepper, mastic, frankincense, litmus, and woad. In the early part of the reign the Commons petitioned Edward to investigate the manufacture of cloth, stating that 'through fraud and deceit' in the making English cloth had ceased to be asked for in foreign markets, and much foreign cloth was imported into England ; but undoubtedly the Commons were either scheming or misled, and the movement was really inspired by some of the English manufacturers, who desired that their foreign rivals might be hampered by restrictions. There is every reason to believe that the English cloth industry was swiftly gaining ground. The returns of export revenue show it, for they indicate a steady decrease in the return from wool, and a corresponding increase in that from cloth. Much more reliable than the revenue returns are the records of wrecked and plundered ships, from which it may be seen that foreign woad was a large item of almost every import cargo.

It is likely that the fostering of manufactures, which had been conducted for many years with a ruthless disregard of the interests of agriculture, had made sad inroads upon the rich old English rural spheres of existence. Not only had the strain of the wars of the Roses been borne by the rural population, but the burden of this commercial conflict, victory in which meant the enrichment of hundreds of smug burgesses, and the transformation of thousands of sturdy peasants and shepherds into dejected weavers.

Besides the merchants bred, many of the country nobles were possessed by the frenzy of trade. One instance of knightly traffic is worth observation. William, Lord Herbert, fitted out a vessel called *The Gabriel*, and sent her abroad for merchandise. On her return she was cast away on the coast of Ireland, and the king by writ relinquished claim upon the wrecked goods. These matters, and the hints in the statutes as to the decay of English archery, indicate a growing change in English life, a change no doubt prophetic of wealth, yet to a certain extent destructive of national manhood. It must be admitted that the change *was* slow, and that the old rural industries died hard, for foreign potentates and noblemen, even in Edward's day, made large purchases of sheep and oxen in England under special licence from the king, and there is record of a Dorset gentleman who owned 14,000 sheep.

There was one peculiar industry that showed no sign of decay—piracy. It is highly necessary to devote a few paragraphs to the doings of the west-country adventurers, and Edward's reign is most suitable to the purpose, for no other period furnishes so many instances, and its revenue and piratical records intermingle in peculiar fashion. In many cases the king put the aggrieved parties upon the custom of the ports most convenient, and thus piracy became more disastrous to the revenue than direct smuggling, for the merchandise stolen was run to prevent identification, and its value afterwards taken from the outward custom.

For one case of piracy or wrecking on the eastern coast there were a score on the south-western. This was in a small part due to the circumstance that the vessels traversing the English Channel carried cargoes specially attractive, and principally to the peculiar instincts of the Devon and Cornish coast-dwellers. In most cases the malefactors were of Dartmouth and Fowey, the latter port being simply a nest of pirates. The sheriff of Cornwall seems to have had a busy time, for writs were continually issued, empowering him to make inquiries and arrest offenders. Inquiries may have been made, but for record of arrests one searches in vain. Perhaps 'Henry Bodrugan, knight,' and his partners, did not exert themselves much even in investigation, for year after year

Fowey continued to send forth companies of industrious buccaneers to intercept the alien merchant, laugh at the safe-conduct the king had granted him, 'grievously maltreat' his agents and mariners, and appropriate his goods. In some cases the ship was taken as well, and the crew and passengers put ashore, their bones sore with trouncing and their pockets empty. The unfortunate foreigners then made their way to London, and unfolded their burning grievances to the king's advisers—gentlemen, it may be conceived, not particularly interested in the sufferings of their fellow-countrymen, much less those of a crowd of 'beggarly, forestalling aliens.' Lack of space forbids quotation of more than a few cases, yet these may cause readers to marvel that foreign merchants ever ventured into English waters.

John Heavey and Denis Lane, Irish merchants, having been legally customed and cocketed in Ireland, were 'sailing towards England,' and off Winchelsea they met one William Mather in his balinger, who promptly seized both ship and cargo.

Two Gascon merchants loaded a ship with wine, and set sail for England. They held a safe-conduct from the king, and the wine was intended to provide ransom of certain prisoners. Hardy mariners of Fowey encountered them, villainously maltreated them, appropriated the letters of safe-conduct, took ship and cargo, and *sold* the wine at Fowey.

In 1462 belated inquiry was made into the case of *The Katherine* of Bayonne. It appeared that while she lay at anchor off St. Ives *on Christmas Eve* a gang of Cornish pirates carried off her cargo.

Certain mariners of Sandwich boarded *The Pink* of Middelburgh, jocosely stating that they acted under authority of the earl of Warwick, and despoiled her of cargo and rigging.

In 1463 a Spanish vessel was wrecked on the Wight. Her crew came safely to land, and her cargo as safely into the hands of the islanders.

In 1467 the balingers of John Rawleigh or Raleigh, Walter Cock, and Ralph Mercer, Devon worthies, made up to six Flemish merchant ships which were 'sailing upon the sea,' and took from them wine to the value of 4,330 crowns of gold. The king, as in the previously quoted cases, directed that restitution should be made. Probably by the time the sufferers reached London and made plaint, and the writ travelled down to the west country, most of the wine had disappeared, for no restitution was made except the usual grant of customs. The king then issued orders to arrest the delinquents, but it does not appear that anyone was arrested, and it is likely that in bonny Devon the whole affair was regarded as an exquisite joke. Perhaps the king, in his secret soul, was not overmuch offended. Later an order was issued to arrest certain Cornishmen, who had helped themselves to the goods of Breton merchants. The thieves could not be found. It should be mentioned that one of them was the vicar of St. Keverne, and his share of the spoil had been three tuns of wine.

Yet the harvest of the Channel was but imperfectly gathered till John Wilcock, skipper of *The Barbara* of Fowey, went forth. From February in 1468 to the Tuesday following Whitsun in the same year he plundered sixteen foreign vessels, mostly laden with the produce of the Gascon vats, and conveyed the spoil to Fowey.

Fowey continued her aggressions, and in 1474, Commissions being found useless, a royal writ was issued to arrest all masters, mariners, possessors, and victuallers of ships, *and all pirates*, that did inhabit there. 'They have committed great depredations upon merchandise' —thus ran the royal fulmination—'and do not heed the king's mandates, but daily do worse.' The specification of 'masters, mariners, possessors, and victuallers' appears superfluous. 'Pirates,' one might think, would have included all the folk of Fowey, not excepting the revenue officers of the district, for it is impossible to conceive that these latter would be ignorant of what was going on, or able to collect much custom *for the king* in the turbulent little port they supervised. In 1476 the Fowey blades were again busy, as though mandates were things of nought.

These west-country feats provoked occasional retaliation, but, as is usual in such cases, the real culprits did not suffer; indeed it may be assumed that few aliens would venture to attempt reprisal upon the shipping of Fowey. Worthy and innocent English traders suffered. About the time when the English Exchequer paid a large sum* to the merchants of Castile as part compensation for damage done them by west-country pirates, and put them on the English custom for further reimbursement, one Payne, a merchant of Bristol, went with a ship to Spain. He and his partner, with the ship and cargo, were captured by Castilian privateers. The two merchants succeeded in escaping to England, and appealed to Edward, who gave them letters to the Spanish king. Twice they visited Castile with no advantage, each time on their return appealing to Edward. They made a third essay, and, being unable to obtain audience, they nailed a written protest to the Castilian monarch's chamber door. For this act of justifiable effrontery Payne's partner was put to death. Payne escaped, and once more laid his case before Edward. The dilatory monarch, who had good reasons for avoiding a quarrel with the Castilian king, put the Bristolian upon the custom of Sandwich, Southampton, and Bristol for 3,600 golden crowns, of which 2,000 were to be reckoned compensation for loss, and 1,600 expenses of travel. It is doubtful whether Payne ever realized the sums.

In 1482 'convoyers or wafters' were stationed off the English coasts, to protect commerce and the fishing industry.†

* The sum paid down appears to have been for piracies committed during the time of Henry VI., and the further sum assigned from the customs was to cover transactions during Edward's reign.

† The fishermen had to contribute towards the expense (Patent Rolls, 22 Edw. IV., p. 1, m. 2).

Edward made many grants of prised wine to the Church, occasionally stipulating for the benefit of prayer. At the beginning of his reign he saddled the customs of London, Hull, Ipswich, and Boston with his deceased father's debts, directing the account to be specialized in the Exchequer memoranda, 'that the soul of the departed may soar to Paradise.'

Richard III.'s accession was signalized by vindictive edicts against aliens and their manufactures. The wording of these statutes illustrates vividly the antipathy of the older English to races (such as the Italians and Jews) who followed none but the inevitably crooked occupations of traffic and usury. It was stated that many merchant strangers, especially of Italy, had warehouses at the larger ports, in which they stowed their goods until prices were intolerably augmented; that though allowed to buy English goods and sell them within the realm at pleasure they did not employ their ultimate profits within the kingdom, but conveyed them oversea; that they acted in colonies and made secret bargains, and that they came to London in numbers as artificers and usurped the manufacture of native goods, instead of taking to laborious occupations such as those of ploughing and carting.* It was accordingly enacted that the Italians should sell by gross only, not by retail; that all aliens should sell within eight months of importation, or remove their goods oversea; and that alien artificers should not practise their callings in England. The almost incredible statement followed that bowstaves had risen in price to £8 per 100, and it was enjoined that aliens should bring ten bowstaves with each butt of malmsey. (This was levelled against the Venetians, who through their control of the

* Before readers blame the old English overmuch, let them bring to mind the doings of the Italian guildsmen in the days of the Edwards, and attempt to imagine what would have happened in Venice, if a body of London merchants had contrived to collect the Venetian customs.

Levant trade had opportunity of obtaining good bow-staves, and who were especially obnoxious.) It was further stated that malmsey had gradually risen from 50s. a butt of 126 gallons to more than twice that rate, and that the butts had come to hold 108 gallons only. Therefore it was prescribed that all casks of wine should be carefully gauged on importation, and the old standards maintained.

Another statute provided that no merchant stranger should bring into the realm girdles, wrought harness, points, leather laces, purses, pouches, gloves, knives, pins, shears, hangers, andirons, scissors, tongs, cupboards, grid-irons, fireforks, locks, keys, hinges, spurs, garnets, painted glass, painted paper, painted cloth, beaten gold, beaten silver, saddles, saddletrees, stirrups, boots, buckles, wire, hawks' bells, etc., the whole produce of the crafts of many classes of artificers being specified.

The first of these statutes was not destined to endure, and need only be regarded as an expression of national impatience. The great trading cities of the blue inland seas had tried similar expedients and failed, and down to the present day it has not been made evident that such edicts are likely to succeed.

There is not much more to be said with regard to Richard's short reign, except that he seems to have been able to trust Italian merchants to a greater extent abroad than in his own kingdom. He appointed Strozzi, a Florentine, English consul at Pisa, allowing him for his trouble 'one-fourth of one per cent.' out of the value on all English goods carried thither.

In 1484 the king's mother was allowed to ship a quantity of wool duty-free, to provide her with a specified sum, and it is worth notice that the duty thus remitted was computed at the aliens' rate. In the same year Richard presented the prior and canons of Carlisle Cathedral with two tuns of Gascon wine from the prisage of Hull, desiring them to pray for the king and queen during life, and for their souls after death.

Duties were as in the preceding reign.

Henry VII. received the usual subsidies 'for life.' The Act of the previous reign against Italians and other aliens was revoked in deference to a request made by the Italian merchants, and it appears that the king granted the Italians temporary remission of a portion of the extra wool duties outward. It was enacted that wine of Gascony and Guienne might only be imported in ships manned by English, Welsh, or Irishmen. This Act also extended to woad from Toulouse. The pretexts furnished were the encouragement of the English shipping industry, and the due maintenance of the navy.

It was enjoined that aliens who had been made denizens should still pay aliens' customs, and that all foreign goods carried coastwise from port to port in England should be advised to the collectors stationed at the ports of discharge, and their unlading certified.

The old Act providing that aliens should employ their takings in purchasing English goods, and the Act of Edward IV. prohibiting exportation of unfulled cloth, were reaffirmed. Provision was also made that no woollen cloth might be exported unless barbed, rowed, and shorn. It was also enacted that no 'common officer' of a town should act as collector of customs.

The Venetians, who had previously engrossed the Levant trade, found that English merchants were interfering extensively in that branch of commerce, and heavy duties were imposed upon English shipments from Candia. In retaliation the English Parliament laid a duty of 18s. per butt on malmsey brought to England in alien shipping, and at the same time fixed the selling price of malmsey at a rate which the Venetian ambassador, in a statement to the Senate, declared ruinous to Venetian trade.

There seems to have been a desire on the part of both king and legislators to foster English commerce, and to open up new channels of traffic. The Merchant Adventurers of London, whom success had made more arbitrary and enterprising than ever, fomented hostility to foreign traders by every means within their power, and there can be no doubt that at this time the famous merchants known in London as Men of the Steelyard had lost much of the outward wool and cloth trade.

The arrangement made by Henry with the Cabots evinced astuteness and enterprise. In return for his substantial encouragement of their great venture, which brought about the discovery of Newfoundland, the king stipulated for one-fifth of the proceeds of the voyage, but at the same time he allowed them freedom from all customs duties on such goods as they brought back.

An Act was passed prohibiting the exportation of horses, except by royal licence, and the exportation of mares of a value exceeding 6s. 8d. It was provided that all entries of foreign goods should be in the name of the real owner.

Meantime many members of the public found as much reason to complain of the growing importance of the newly strengthened trade syndicates, and the villainies of certain native manufacturers, as of foreign competition. Two statutes of the reign, though not applying directly to revenue matters, illustrate this in striking fashion. It may be as well to furnish a summary of their provisions, to show that fraud inhabits the very arteries of trade, and that often when a nation is spurring itself into bitterness against a rival's methods it may have good reason to mend its own.

One was the Act rendered necessary by the practice of that arrogant company previously mentioned, which had come to be widely known as 'The Fellowship of Mercers and Merchant Adventurers of London.' They had originally levied an entrance fee of half a noble on each novice who joined their society. But this had been increased, 'contrary to every Englishman's liberty, of their own incharitable and inordinate covetise,' to £20. The Act abolished the fee.

The other statute revealed the existence of an ingenuity almost modern, and brought into relief the artifices of 'certain denizens,' who occupied themselves in preparing fustians which had been imported unshorn. Instead of operating 'with the broad shear,' they for purposes of expedition used an instrument that 'broke the ground' of the fustian, and to conceal the effect they 'sleeked' and singed the article, and then dyed it. Said the statute, 'The poor serving-men find that their fustians endure four months instead of two years.' Thus it will be seen that not only was expedition aimed at, but an enduring increase in the demand for fustians.

During the latter part of the reign the collection of custom and subsidy of wool was assigned to the Calais Staple for sixteen years, £10,000 odd of the receipts to go to the Calais Treasurer for the garrison and defences, and the rest to be accounted for at the Exchequer, subject to a small grant to the London 'customers' or collectors (probably as a formal acknowledgment) and the payment of certain fees.

Henry VIII. was granted the perquisites of his predecessor for life. (The impost on sweet wines imported by aliens was later made 6s. 8d. per butt by order in Council. The king seems to have obtained almost arbitrary powers in the regulation of trade, especially the trade in foreign wines, and his method of altering and increasing wine imposts was copied by more than one of his successors.)

Henry VII.'s statute as to entering of foreign goods was repealed, and it was provided that 'one Englishman might enter for another Englishman, and one alien for another alien.' Edward IV.'s Act, by which all who defrauded the revenue of tunnage and poundage were made answerable with body and goods, was reaffirmed, and made to endure during the king's life.

The penalties applying to customs officers who delayed the sealing of valuable imported cloths were increased, and the officers made liable to a fine of £20 if they extorted fees for such service.

The exportation of Norfolk wool was prohibited, in

order to secure a plentiful and ready supply to the Norwich cloth manufacturers. This was but one of many instances in English history, of the yeoman being hampered for the weaver's benefit. 'The Act of Apparel' was another concession to cloth, providing that no man not ennobled should wear woollen cloth, unless it were of the make of England, Wales, or Berwick.

In the tenth year of his reign Henry by charter exempted the burgesses of Southampton from Prisage, except to the extent of five tuns yearly, which had previously been allotted from the port prisage to various abbeys in the locality. Later the charter was affirmed by statute. (It is evident that the five tuns were taken even after the Reformation, for the final remission was not formally announced till 1608. It is likely that they were appropriated by the usurpers of the abbey lands.)

Many Englishmen had established themselves in Flanders and other countries and there sworn fealty, yet they continued to trade with England as denizens, thus gaining the advantage of preferential customs duties. It was enacted that they should be made to pay aliens' customs on all goods landed by them in England. The Merchant Adventurers of London and the English ambassadors were instructed to make inquiry as to all such English residents abroad. It is likely that the first-named had part in inciting the issue of the Act, and that, as many of their own agents lived abroad, they exercised their powers of inquiry with great circumspection.

A grant previously made to the citizens of York, that they might ship northern wool under the ancient privileges secured to the merchants of Newcastle, was annulled, it having led to the enrichment of a few of the citizens only, instead of to the advantage of all.

The privilege of exporting wool seems to have been the subject of many mercantile intrigues. The quantity of fells exported was still considerable, in spite of the persistent attempts to foster the cloth industry.

The Acts of Richard II., intended to confine the shipment of merchandise as far as practicable to English vessels, and the Act of Henry VII., restricting the importation of Gascon wine and Toulouse woad to English bottoms, were recited, with the significant statement that in spite of their provisions the navy had decayed, and it was apparent there would soon be few expert English mariners. Therefore it was enacted that the statutes quoted should be sternly observed. The retail price of French wine in England was limited to 8d. a gallon, and that of sweet wine to 1s. The enactment was to endure till the end of the next Parliament.* The next Parliament provided that the king might by proclamation or letters patent repeal or make void the restrictions upon French wine. (This appears to have been construed into a grant of power to the king to alter or levy imposts upon wines, and both he and his successors seem to have taken full advantage of the mysterious extension of prerogative.)

It was found that much leather was being exported uncustomed, especially from the south-western counties. Sworn 'tellers' and packers were stationed at the principal ports, and their fees stated. Leather conveyed from inland towns to the coast for shipment was to be advised to the officers.

An Act was passed regulating freights, which contained the interesting stipulation that owners of ships outward-bound from London should advertise the dates of sailing by affixing written statements 'to some post in Lombarde strete, there to remain for the space of seven days.'

The terms of some of the licences granted to English merchants to import French goods during time of war with France are rather instructive. One was granted late in the reign to George Lazenby, London grocer,† the

* Towards the end of the reign the provisions were relaxed, import prices having risen (34-35 Hen. VIII., c. 7).

† In olden times 'grocery' as a tariff and trade term had a wide significance, comprehending an immense number of articles, and the appellation 'grocer,' now usually bestowed upon a petty tradesman, often signified a wealthy and distinguished merchant.

cargo being wine, woad, canvas, and prunes. He had to import the goods in an English ship, or a ship of a friendly nation, to pay the ordinary custom and 13s. 4d. a ton besides, and to leave a copy of his licence at the Custom House when making entry. Another licence to a London merchant to import French wine stipulated that the king should have part of the cargo at a figure lower than the London market price. A licence granted to a Dutchman to import a mixed Dutch and French cargo described the goods as 10 tons plaster, 35 cases Normandy glass, 2 vats prunes, 28 dozen skins, 200 ells canvas, 1 empty vat with curious drinking-glasses, and 9 iron pots.

In 1546 a licence was granted to export certain packages of spikenard free of outward duty. They had formed part of the cargo of 'a great Venetian ship,' which had been seized for use by the English during the war.

In 1547 two Paris merchants brought a quantity of jewels to London, in order that the king might make selection and buy. But the king was sick unto death when they arrived, and the arrangement fell through. The merchants made a few sales in other quarters, and were directed to pay custom on the wares sold. The rest they were allowed to export duty-free.

Edward VI. received his predecessor's subsidies, the tunnage rates being 3s. (6s. on sweet wines imported by aliens, including Hanse merchants) and 12d. per aum on Rhenish. The poundage was 12d. on all merchandise imported or exported by aliens or denizens, and 12d. extra on wrought tin or pewter exported by aliens. Wool and fells by denizens paid £1 13s. 4d., hides £3 6s. 8d.; wool and fells by aliens (including aliens who had been made denizens by letters patent) £3 6s. 8d.; hides £3 13s. 4d. Goods shipped by denizens in caracks or galleys paid aliens' duty. The Hanse merchants' ancient rights of freedom from inland toll were affirmed. Besides these there were the Carta Mercatoria poundage on aliens' merchandise, the butlerage on aliens' wines, and the special impost on sweet wines brought by aliens (6s. 8d. per butt, levied by order in Council of Henry VIII.'s reign).

It was enacted that there should be no purveyance of victuals and provender for the king's household, except at market price and by owner's consent.

Certain Admiralty officers having made grievous exactions in money and kind from English vessels coming with fish from Ireland, Iceland, and Newfoundland, such exactions were forbidden under a penalty of treble the value of the amount extorted.

The exportation of 'white ashes' was forbidden, they being useful in the making of soap and saltpetre, and the scouring of wool.

Wool was plentiful in England, but forestallers and engrossers* kept the price up. It was enacted that none should buy wool except for private use, or directly for use in the weaving of cloth for sale, except members of the Calais Guild, who might buy for shipment to the Staple. Aliens might not buy any of a season's wool prior to the Feast of Purification (February 2) in each year. Owners of wool were to sell within twelve months of shearing. Merchants of Newcastle dealing in northern wool were exempt.

The customs grants were the same as usual when Mary ascended the throne, the tunnage and poundage being specified as applicable to the defence of the realm and the keeping of the sea. A 'Book of Rates,' furnishing the values of merchandise for poundage, was issued. It was expressed in this document, according to a decree of the Lords of Council, that the existing rates on woollen cloths outward were too little. It appears that four 'short cloths' could be made out of a sack of wool. (A

* 'Forestalling': buying goods on their way to market, or contracting to buy before the goods were ready for delivery.

'Engrossing': buying corn in the field, fruit on the tree, etc.

'Regrating': buying at public sale and re-selling in same market, or within a specified distance—in short, buying with no purpose save to 'turn over.'

short cloth was 28 yards in length, and weighed 64 pounds). It was decreed that each short cloth exported by denizens should pay 6s. 8d. (double if by aliens).*

Henry VIII.'s Act, fixing the sale price of foreign hats, caps, and bonnets of woollen, was recited, and amended to the effect that customs collectors were to apprise the mayors of towns as to such importations, and on an appointed day each collector in presence of the mayor concerned was to sell the goods publicly at no more than the price specified, and hand the proceeds to the importer. Not more than a dozen articles were to be sold to any one person.

Corn, victuals, and wood being at a great price, were for a period forbidden exportation except by licence.

It was enacted that commissions for purveyance should be expressed in English, and endure for six months only. Purveyors were to give a 'docket' to the High Constable for all goods taken, and he was to submit it to the sessions justices, who were afterwards to send it to the king's steward.

In 1554 the burgesses of Southampton were by letters patent given a notable concession. They had represented that the trade of the port had fallen off, the merchant strangers no longer bringing their Levant goods and sweet wines to Southampton as of old, but landing them at creeks and remote places in Sussex and Kent. It was accordingly enjoined that all sweet wines brought by aliens should be landed at Southampton, so as to revive the customs receipts of that port, and enable the burgesses to fortify the town and repair the sea bank as they had formerly done. The grant brought little benefit to the city, although made perpetual in 1571, for it appears that it became the practice to issue licences to enable the aliens to discharge at other ports. At first the issue of a licence

* The cloth duties remained at this rate till about the middle of James's reign. It seems that the denizens' cloth duty was by Mary's Rate-book made exactly equal to the denizens' wool duty, minus the ancient custom. Thus, 4 cloths at 6s. 8d. = £1 6s. 8d. The wool duty was £1 13s. 4d., made up of subsidy and ancient custom. The ancient custom was 6s. 8d. *Hale* (doubtful.)

of this kind was made to appear a great favour, as, when the Venetian ambassador made suit upon one occasion to the Privy Council that one of his country's ships might be allowed to discharge her cargo of malmsey in the port of London, the transaction was allowed 'for this time only.' It appears that there was a special 'Southampton duty' on sweet wines, for it was stipulated that the owners of this particular cargo should present the Southampton burgesses with four butts of malmsey, in recognition of the privilege granted of discharge in London. No doubt the expense and trouble of obtaining licences, with the alternative of confinement of discharge to one port, hampered the Venetians, and assisted the English merchants in gaining possession of the Levant trade.

In 1558 an impost was laid by order in Council upon all French wine imported. It was at the startling rate of 26s. 8d. a tun, and the collectors were ordered to take security for this duty, or to exact the duty, before the wines were landed. It was accompanied by an impost of extra poundage upon all French goods. It is evident that this tax caused consternation amongst importers, and that the officers had some difficulty in collecting it. On August 4, 1558, it was directed that the London officers responsible should be called upon for the impost on wines discharged in the port under their survey. One Fisher was the receiver, and he was summoned before the Council for being in arrear. My Lords gave him a fortnight's grace. At the end of the fortnight he appeared before the Council. His books were inspected, and found incomplete. He was ordered to put them right, to pay into the Exchequer a sum of £1,500 which he confessed he had retained, and to produce the receipt to the Council. Then he was called upon to find security in £5,000 for the speedy rendering of a full account.

A few days later the Council sent peremptory directions to Bristol that the officers should enforce payment of the impost, as 'we meane not to alter or change.'

During the following month the Council were apprised

that certain merchants refused to land their Spanish wines on account of the increased duties. (This seems to show that the Southampton duty on sweet wines was being imposed at all ports.) My Lords replied that the merchants might take their wines whither they pleased, but they should not be allowed to land them till they had given security for payment of the duties.

It will be perceived that the imperious Tudors took full advantage of the provisions of the Act of 26 Henry VIII., c. 10, empowering them to levy on wines by patent or order in Council. Indeed, during the period between the passing of that statute and the issue of James I.'s 'Book of Rates' in 1611, the variations of the wine duties are extremely puzzling, and the commentators, not excepting the careful and industrious Hale, seem to have regarded the duty actually collected on wine as mere matter of conjecture.

At the beginning of Elizabeth's reign the exportation of tallow, raw hides, and leather was forbidden for a period. When this Act determined, the price of boots, shoes, etc., increased, so the law was again put in force.

The hours during which cargo might be discharged and shipped were fixed by statute, and the limits of ports defined. It was enacted that the owner or master of every ship from foreign ports should furnish a full report of cargo, and that a declaration should be made of all goods shipped outward. In consequence of extensive smuggling, customs collectors were instructed to provide deputies at all creeks and remote places within their respective districts.

The provisions of Richard II. and Henry VII.'s Acts as to natives importing goods only in native ships were repealed, it having been found that foreign princes in defence made similar rules. But goods shipped in foreign ships by denizens were still liable to aliens' duty.

Elizabeth received the grants and customs that had been allowed at her sister's accession, and the proceeds of the impost on French wine and wares levied by Mary (this last not specified in the Act).

Coastwise traffic in English goods was restricted to ships owned by denizens, captained by Englishmen, and with at least three-fourths of the mariners English. Attempts were made to encourage English sea-fishing by freeing exported English fish from outward poundage, and prohibiting the importation of foreign fish. The latter provision had to be repealed, fish, especially herrings, reaching a great price. Denizens were then allowed to import herrings in English square-rigged ships, paying subsidy. (A trade appears to have sprung up in English-cured fish, principally with France, Portugal, and Italy.) Later the restrictions were relaxed, and aliens allowed to export English fish in English ships, and to import foreign fish at will, paying such customs as were charged on English fish abroad.

Foreign harness, etc., were prohibited, to encourage the decaying native industries.

The prohibition of the exportation of live sheep was revived, and embellished with terrific penalties. It was provided that he who offended should be imprisoned for 'one whole yere without bayle and maynepryse, and at the yere's ende in soome open Market Towne in the fulnesse of the Market on the Market Daye have his lefte hande cut off, and that to be nayled up in the openest place of suche Market.' This punishment was to be accompanied by forfeiture of goods.

The grant to the port of Southampton of the exclusive landing of Levant wines brought by aliens was made perpetual in 1571. (As before stated, the grant brought no great benefit to the town, for by the beginning of the next century the English Turkey Company had succeeded in dominating the Levant trade, especially the trade in sweet wines. Being an English company, it could carry wines into any English port.)

English vessels from foreign, on their arrival in English ports, were made to pay a tonnage tax, to be applied to the repair of Dover harbour. This was collected by the Customs, and paid into the Exchequer as a special account, the Exchequer handing over the moneys in instalments to the mayor of Dover.

The importation of logwood was prohibited, the article being held to produce a fraudulent dye. Later the provisions of the Act were strengthened, offenders being made liable to the pillory.

An Act was passed ordering that all casks imported for the use of brewers were to be gauged and marked by 'the masters and wardens of the Art and Mystery of Coopers,' as it had been found that beer had been sold in casks fraudulently marked as to content. The Act did not apply to casks imported by strangers and intended to be filled with beer for exportation, or to casks intended for shipment to Scotland.

In 1591 a new impost was levied on French goods, at the rate of 3s. a tun for wine and 3s. a ton for other merchandise. This was really a convoy duty, and the proceeds were devoted to 'waftage'—*i.e.*, the maintenance of war vessels to defend the merchant fleets that periodically visited Bordeaux.

On February 20, 1593, the Council sent notices 'to the officers of all the Custom-houses,' commencing thus: 'Whereas her Maiestie of late time to her exceeding great chardge hath bin often occasioned to send over into Normandie divers troupes of souldiers to the aid of the French King: Forsomuch as by dailie experience yt falleth owt that manie of these souldiers do indirectly withdraw themselves'; and then instructing the officers to rummage all vessels arriving from France, and detain any deserters they might find.

On June 17, 1593, a letter was sent from Whitehall to the Lord Mayor of London, alluding to a practice, which appears to have existed for some time, of referring disputes on questions of mercantile assurance to a board of merchants chosen yearly by the City worthies, 'and by oathe enjoyned to attend and determyn these cawses according to equitie.' The Council directed the Mayor and aldermen to elect three merchant strangers to serve on the board. (Thus it would appear that the system of assuring ships and cargoes is of ancient origin.)

The importation of wool-cards was prohibited, in the interest of the cardmakers of London, Bristol, Norwich, Coventry, etc.

The Merchant Adventurers of London having repeatedly complained of their foreign trade being hampered by the Hanseatic League, and all attempts at adjustment having failed, the Privy Council abolished the privileges so long enjoyed by the Leaguers, so far as the German sections of the League were concerned, but intimated that the merchants of Polonia (Poland) might still trade in England. The German traders were ordered to depart, and the customs searchers of London and Gravesend were directed to satisfy themselves, before the Germans embarked, that all outstanding obligations had been discharged. In 1600 the Lord Mayor of London was directed to seize the famous 'Steel Yard' (the London depot of the Hanse traders), which stood in the place now occupied by Cannon Street Station. The Steel Yard was made a naval storehouse.

On September 16, 1600, it was conveyed to 'The Adventurers on the Voyage intended to the East Indies' that the queen highly approved of their design. On October 26 they were encouraged by the Council to proceed with their fitting-out 'with all expedicion and possible speede.' 'Otherwise,' wrote the energetic councillors, 'you maie muche prejudice yourselves by your staggering and delaies.' It appears that some of the promoters were not quite as adventurous as their title implied, for on January 11, 1601, the Council threatened to commit them to prison unless they speedily made good their deposits.

This syndicate was the foundation of the celebrated

East India Company. The first fleet left in 1601, and the Council at once proceeded to urge the Adventurers to bestir themselves in preparing a second.

It appears that the ancient system of adjudicating upon assurance disputes was fast falling out of favour, despite the interest taken in it by the Council in 1593. An Act was passed providing that the Lord Chancellor should in future appoint Commissions to deal with such matters. Each Commission was to consist of an Admiralty judge, two doctors of law, two common lawyers, the Recorder of London, and 'eight grave and discreet merchants.' Litigants had power to appeal to the Court of Chancery.

Enterprising reformers, anxious to increase the customs receipts, and at the same time secure valuable offices for themselves, seem to have been plentiful in Elizabeth's day. 'The humble petition' of three citizens of London, dated 1568, is an example of the suggestions tendered:

'We crave your hyghnes to have our service in tryall to bryng your highnes great gayne, whereas we know your maiestie to be deceaved £3,000 or £4,000 by the yere in coustome and subsidie inwarde onlie of the porte of London, by merchant straungers dwelling alongst divers the keys.' The petitioners stated that they would ask for no reward until they had increased the revenue of the port. They described themselves as men who had been long accustomed to deal with merchandise, and went on to state that whilst £100,000 worth of silks and haberdashery were imported yearly only £30,000 worth paid duty; that by reviewing the books at the Exchequer they had found that scarcely any duty was taken upon goldware and silverware, etc., yet such goods were extensively imported; that the landing-waiters had each a fee of £4 a year only, yet could afford to pay large sums to obtain their offices; that many of the said waiters, who before taking office had been poor and in debt, had mysteriously become men of substance; and that while, according to the law, all costly and fine goods were to be examined at the Custom-house Quay, many aliens bribed the officers to allow them to take such wares to private quays, where they were entered as coarse goods and paid little poundage. Whether the statement was wholly credible cannot be ascertained. Possibly it was true ; undoubtedly it was not disinterested.

Two years later one Needham wrote a pamphlet on the same subject, and sent it to the Lord Treasurer. It commenced with a statement that the writer ' thought it his duty justly and truly to open to his Honour such notes and knowledge as by his service and travel he had gathered during ten or twelve years, devoted to searching how to reform such abuses, deceits, and disorders as were used all England through against the queen's Majesty, both by the officers of customs and by merchants and shippers, and how they might be redressed, and her Highness justly answered of her rights and duties.' He continued that the said officers, their clerks, and their ' clerks' clerks,' wronged many honourable merchants by imposing novel duties, delaying cockets, and not observing the proper hours of employment, and that ' by long sufferance ' the officers, with many merchants, and many of the watermen, were ' nestled and grown into a disordered liberty,' so extremely profitable that they could not be reformed except by severe measures.

Later one Thomas Ferrers threw down his soiled gauntlet in challenge of corruption, stating that if he could but be granted a certain lucrative post he would advance the customs receipts by several thousands a year, besides keeping all coin and bullion within the realm. If he failed in the attempt he would relinquish the office, and never be a suitor again.

A collector who was unable to meet his creditors' claims attributed his condition to ' having served without corruption, and dispatched the merchant without expectation of reward.' He pleaded that he had paid a vast sum for his collectorship, and that if he were deprived of his office his creditors would close upon him and take everything he had. In the proceedings on this case it was suggested that the defendant's dismissal should be kept as secret as possible, as public cognizance of such cases was undesirable, and it was urged as partial extenuation of the offence that an officer who had to give an unreasonable sum for his appointment could scarcely be expected to behave properly.

A pamphlet produced in 1601 by the secretary to 'The Merchant Adventurers of London' contained a broad allusion to the privileges once enjoyed by the Hanse merchants, to their preferential customs, and the unfair advantage which they had till recently secured in trade. (Be it noted that the Merchant Adventurers had for over a century been busily undermining the Hanse men, and had captured most of their business.) It also complained of 'the great fraternitie, familiaritie, kindness, and inward friendship between the officers of her Majesty's Customs and strangers,' and hinted that there was a sinister reason for this good understanding. Apparently the same kindness had not been extended to the Adventurers, for the tone of the document hereabout soared into rhetoric. 'Let these customers, while they warn other men, be wise and warned themselves also, lest by too much leaning unto and favouring of such strangers they prove in the end bad customers to her Majesty, and consequently corrupt and unnatural members of the State.' It further complained that the aliens had tried to bring the trade of the Adventurers 'to confusion,' but hinted that the Adventurers expected to survive, 'even though these odd customers' might assist the aliens to the fullest of their power. Then it pointed out the immense benefits conferred on the revenue by the Adventurers, calling attention to the fact that they paid their duties in lump sums yearly, instead of 'by driblets and small parcels.' It even tried to palliate the special impositions made by them upon cloth, both in England and abroad, and other incidental charges which they levied upon goods, urging that these surtaxes were systematically collected by skilled overseers, who were thus rendered able to furnish the English Customs with valuable information upon trade matters and upon customs due. It compared the dealings of the Society with those of other companies, greatly to the Adventurers' advantage, stating that they were not like other merchants, who shipped their goods at remote places, 'in covert manner, hugger mugger,' for the Adventurers shipped all their goods at London and the other great ports—ports at which, it was insinuated, the officers were well paid, and therefore not easily corrupted.

In the concluding statement of the Adventurers' recital there was undoubtedly a delicate hint to the 'well-paid' officers at the great ports that it might be advantageous to extend a few special facilities to the Society.

The average amount collected annually as customs during Elizabeth's reign may be stated with something like confidence as about £80,000. One account for thirteen years renders an average of over £70,000, another for ten later years (perhaps more reliable) gives an average of nearly £94,000. The first appears in Stow's 'Survey,' the other in the State Papers of the reign of Elizabeth (1602).

LIST OF AUTHORITIES.

Legislation and Incidents.

Wine: 2 Hen. VI., c. 14; 1 Hen. VII., c. 8; 7 Hen. VII., c. 7; 26 Hen. VIII., c. 10; Acts of Privy Council, April 17, 1558; September 23, 1558; October 19, 1558.

Frauds: 20 Hen. VI., c. 7; 11 Hen. VI., c. 15; 28 Hen. VI., c. 5; 12 Edw. IV., c. 3; Patent Rolls, 6 Hen. VI., p. 1, m. 28*d.*; 6 Edw. IV., p. 1, m. 4*d.*; 13 Edw. IV., p. 2, m. 21*d.*; Act 1 Rich. III., c. 13; 11 Hen. VII., c. 27; 27 Hen. VIII., c. 14; 2-3 Edw. VI., c. 6; 31 Eliz., c. 8.

Subsidies: Hale (quoted in Hargraves' 'Law Tracts'); 1 Hen. VIII., c. 20; 1 Edw. VI., c. 13; 1 Mary, s. 2, c. 18; 1 Eliz., c. 20.

Staples: 8 Hen. VI., c. 2.

Assignments: 31 Hen. VI., c. 5; Patent Rolls, 2 Hen. VI., p. 3, m. 13; 2 Hen. VI., p. 3, m. 6; Ordinance of 18 Hen. VI.; Patent

Rolls, 2 Edw. IV., p. 2, m. 11; 1 Edw. IV., p. 4, m. 20; 11 Edw. IV., p. 1, m. 11; 2 Edw. IV., p. 1, m. 19; 18 Edw. IV., p. 1, m. 8; 1 Edw. IV., m. 23; 1 Rich. III., p. 4, m. 6; 1 Rich. III., p. 2, m. 20; Act 19 Hen. VII., c. 27; 21 Hen. VIII., c. 17; 23 Eliz., c. 6.

Special licences: Patent Rolls, 1 Hen. VI., p. 3, m. 13; 5 Hen. VI., p. 2, m. 19; Acts of Privy Council, October 17, 1545; June 21, 1545; January 18, 1546; March 3, 1547.

Cloth: 31 Hen. VI., c. 8 (Hale); 7 Edw. IV., c. 3; 4 Hen. VIII., c. 6; 6 Hen. VIII., c. 1; 'Book of Rates' (Mary).

Wool and Sheep: 14 Hen. VI., c. 5; 3 Hen. VI., c. 2; 6 Hen. VIII., c. 12; 5-6 Edw. VI., c. 7; 8 Eliz., c. 3.

Protective measures and prohibitions: 28 Hen. VI., c. 1; 3 Edw. IV., c. 3 and 4; 12 Edw. IV., c. 2; 22 Edw. IV., c. 8; 1 Rich. III., c. 9; 1 Rich. III., c. 11; 1 Rich. III., c. 12; 3 Hen. VII., c. 9; 3 Hen. VII., c. 12; 14-15 Hen. VIII., c. 4; 22 Hen. VIII., c. 8; 23 Hen. VIII., c. 7; 2-3 Edward VI., c. 26; 1 Mary, s. 2, c. 11; 1-2 P. and Mary, c. 5; 1 Eliz., c. 10; 14 Eliz., c. 4; 18 Eliz., c. 9; 1 Eliz., c. 13; 5 Eliz., c. 5; 5 Eliz., c. 7; 23 Eliz., c. 9; 39 Eliz., c. 11; Acts of Privy Council, 1591-1592; Act 39 Eliz., c. 14.

Venetian trade: Calendar Venetian State Papers, 1444 and 1456.

Mercantile arrangements and privileges: Fœdera ('De Confirmatione Appunctuamentorum inter Regem et Magistrum Pruissiæ'; 'Pro Rege Portugaliæ'; 'Super quadam Navi, quæ ex Concessione Regis de Causa Magnitudinis, Nominetur Carraka'); Patent Rolls, 5 Edw. IV., p. 1, m. 21; 20 Edw. IV., p. 1, m. 1; 20 Edw. IV., p. 2, m. 9.

Piracy: Chancery Rolls; Patent Rolls, 4 Hen. VI., p. 2, m. 19*d.*; 1 Edw. IV., p. 1, m. 15*d.* and 5*d.*; 2 Edw. IV., p. 1, m. 21*d.* and 20*d.*; 7 Edw. IV., p. 2, m. 4*d.*; 8 Edw. IV., p. 1, m. 8*d.*; 9 Edw. IV., p. 2, m. 17*d.*; 14 Edw. IV., p. 2, m. 15*d.*; 21 Edw. IV., p. 2, m. 8 and 16.

Wrecking: Patent Rolls, 3 Edw. IV., p. 2, m. 11*d.*

Consular appointment: Fœdera ('Pro Laurentio Strozzi').

Officers: Patent Rolls, 1 Edw. IV., p. 1, m. 7; 13 Edw. IV., p. 1, m. 13; 18 Edw. 4, p. 1, m. 10; 20 Edw. IV., p. 2, m. 20; Act 3 Hen. VII., c. 8; Acts of Privy Council, September 13, 1558; and of 1591 and 1592.

Preventive: 11 Hen. VII., c. 14; 3 Hen. VII., c. 8; 1 Hen. VIII., c. 5; 1 Eliz., c. 11.

Merchant Adventurers: 12 Hen. VII., c. 6.

Southampton Privileges: Davies' 'History of Southampton,' Act 22 Hen. VIII., c. 20; Acts of Privy Council, July 20, 1556.

Freights and assurance: 32 Hen. VIII., c. 14; Acts of Privy Council, 1593; Act 43 Eliz., c. 12.

Purveyance: 2-3 Edw. VI., c. 3; 2-3 P. and Mary, c. 6.

Schemes of reform: State Papers, Eliz., 1568; Stow's 'Survey'; State Papers, Eliz., 1575; Wheeler's 'Treatise of Commerce.'

CHAPTER IV

THE PERIOD OF PROCLAMATIONS AND ORDINANCES

1603–1660

FEW historians have had a good word to say for James I., and all agree that he was not popular with his English subjects. The latter circumstance deserves consideration, for the English have usually been inclined to make liberal allowance for kingly deficiencies. It is possible that the principal causes of his undoubted unpopularity were his industry in augmenting taxes, his disdain of constitutional methods of imposition, and the Stuart facility in getting rid of an immense amount of money without having anything to show for it.

As soon as he was familiar with the English throne he turned his attention to the Customs revenue. Consulting his personal antipathies, he laid an astounding impost upon tobacco, amounting to 6s. 8d. a pound 'over and above the custom of 2d. hitherto paid.' Then, dissatisfied with the return of the outward subsidy, the cloth duties, tunnage and poundage, the aliens' Custom, and the wine imposts, he with the assistance of Robert Cecil altered the values of most goods liable to poundage, making startling additions to Mary's rates. The new list was issued, James probably furnishing the preamble. 'We let you wit,' said he, 'reasonable and indifferent values and prices ought to be paied unto us.' The public, much to James's chagrin, stigmatized the new imposts as monstrous, and the high rating of currants led to the celebrated Bates case. Bates, a dealer in goods from the Levant

1.

2.

3.

4.

5.

6.

ANCIENT CUSTOMS SEALS (SILVER).

1. Fowey, in the port of Plymouth (Royal Arms ; date, prior to 1603).
2. Dartmouth, in the port of Exeter (Royal Arms ; date, Stuart period).
3. Lyme Regis, in the port of Poole (Fleur-de-Lys and letters 'C.R.,' probably Charles I.) : Controller's Seal.
4. Spalding, in the port of Boston (Portcullis and 'G.R.,' probably George I.).
5. Poulton, in the port of Chester (Rose and Crown and 'G.R.,' probably George I.). : Comptroller's Seal.
6. Ramsey, Isle of Man (Arms of England—being three lions passant-guardant—and 'G. III. R. 1765) : Collector's Seal.

From 'Seals in the Board Room,' by H. V. READE, Assistant Secretary of Customs.

To face p. 72.

(then called a 'Turkey Merchant'), being assessed on a parcel of currants at the old poundage plus the new impost, refused payment of the latter. The case was tried at the Court of Exchequer in 1606, Bates pleading that the impost was illegal, it being levied without the sanction of Parliament. The judges decided in favour of the Crown, ruling that the king was entitled to levy imposts at will.

In 1609 appeared a fresh list of imposts, many of them doubling the rate, and logwood, long prohibited on account of its use in the manufacture of fraudulent dyes, was—'so much the better to suppresse and hinder both the bringing in and use thereof within the Realme'—admitted at a heavy value rating; the king thus proposing to profit by the toleration of fraud. Numerous petitions were presented against the new schedule, in spite of the many assurances it contained that the public benefit was dearer to James than the prospect of gain. It is evident that he found it prudent to temporize.

In 1611 he brought out his final 'Book of Rates,' dedicated to Cecil, and fervently commended to all revenue officials.

In his preface to the new book James described the method by means of which the assessments of 1609 had been made. 'Certain of our counsell conferred with the principal merchants.' (He had in 1604 used the old plea to justify a special tax on exported cloth—viz., that he was entitled to profit by the shipment of manufactured as well as of raw wool.) He proceeded to explain that in his schedule of 1609 he had exempted the following goods from the new impost inwards:

Corn, fish, cheese—viz., merchandise of sustenance.

Naval requisites, arms, and ammunition—munitions of defence.

Wax, hides, and tallow—merchandise usually transhipped.

Cotton, silk, and hemp—raw material of handicraft.

Gold, silver, and jewels—articles of enrichment.

'Yet,' he went on, 'some of those whom reason cannot satisfie continue their complaints.' He affirmed:

1. That the law of Nature incited every man to prefer his own people.

2. That most foreign articles were vain and unprofitable, and should be kept out by impositions.

(This had to some extent been the opinion of more than one of his predecessors, but they had adopted the expedient of *prohibition.* Elizabeth had prohibited logwood; James had allowed that 'vain and unprofitable' article to be imported, and had profited by the grant. And it is unlikely that he contemplated closing a fruitful channel of revenue by shutting out a large portion of foreign merchandise.)

3. That the Crown had previously lost through the undervaluing of foreign goods, which was a matter against the national welfare.

(Be it noted that James had previously stated that foreign goods were vain and unprofitable, yet here he insisted that their values had often been understated.) He withdrew the obnoxious privilege he had so recently granted to logwood. 'Wee desire not to make profit by disgrace.' The list ended with an order to all concerned to observe the provisions of his 'Book of Rates.' 'On pain of our heavie indignation and displeasure, and as they will answer the same at their uttermost perill.'

Below are specified most of the articles 'raised' in value by the new list:

Argal (crude tartar deposited by wine-lees, and used in dyeing), ashes of soap or wood, bombasin (a twilled fabric of silk and worsted), buckram (coarse linen stiffened with gum), caddas (tape or lint riband, used in dressing wounds), camlet (thin woollen stuff, sometimes mixed with silk), candle-wicks, carpets of certain kinds, cochineal, drugs of certain kinds, flax (wrought), fustian, galls, groceries, grograin (coarse fabric of silk and mohair), gum, hemp (dressed), hides (tanned), hops, indigo, latten (ornamental brass), linens of certain kinds, madder, oil (except train oil), onion seed, pans of certain kinds, plates of copper, plates of earthenware, printing paper, quicksilver, serge, silk (wrought), starch, steel, succades, sturgeon, tapestry, thread (except crossbow thread), vinegar, wainscots, wood of Brazil, woad* (the plant).

Beaver wool was raised in value immensely, the impost upon it being fivefold. Mary's value for pins had been 4s. per 12,000 ; James added 10s. ; total, 14s. The value of wrought flax was more than doubled, and that of leaf tobacco quadrupled.

	Subsidy Value.			*Impost Value.*			*Total Value.*		
	£	*s.*	*d.*	£	*s.*	*d.*	£	*s.*	*d.*
Tobacco, leaf, per pound ..	0	6	8	1	0	0	1	6	8

(Thus the poundage was raised from 4d. to 1s. 4d.)

	£	*s.*	*d.*	£	*s.*	*d.*	£	*s.*	*d.*
Tobacco, manufactured, per pound	0	10	0	1	0	0	1	10	0

(Thus the poundage on manufactured tobacco was trebled, being raised from 6d. to 1s. 6d.)

Even if the subsidy value be taken as the real value, and James's impost rate as an utter overcharge, it is evident that tobacco was dear.

French wool was admitted at the old rating ; Polonia wool was surtaxed. Flemish soap escaped the impost ; Venice soap was charged. Muscovy leather and Muscovy yarn were specially surtaxed.

The subsidy value given for oranges and lemons was 6s. 8d. per 1,000. Bowstaves were valued at £4 per 120, quails at 4s. per dozen, ' sucking-bottles ' at 5s. the gross. Dripping-pans and frying-pans were subjected to the impost, warming-pans escaped.

Sugar was classed as white, panellis, candy, and muscovado. There was no loaf sugar.

The only export goods raised in value were bays, lead, and tin. Woollen cloth paid a special tax as of old, instead of poundage. The impost on uncast lead outward was two and a half times the subsidy rate, and on

* ' Woad ' : a plant with four petals, yielding a permanent blue dye.

unwrought tin double. (Merchant strangers exporting unworked lead or tin of course paid twice as much as denizens.) Bays manufactured at Barnstaple escaped the impost ; other bays were charged. All exported goods, except those specified above and beer, remained at the old values for poundage.*

The tunnage rates, as settled by James's list, stood as below. The exact wine duties during the latter part of Elizabeth's and the early part of James's reign are difficult to specify. The statute that granted James his original subsidy is explicit enough, yet its rates do not agree with those quoted as ' subsidy rates ' in James's book. There appears to have been a ' composition tax ' levied in 1609 on all wines imported into London, and a smaller composition tax on certain wines imported into Southampton and Bristol. These extra taxes may have been surtaxes charged on account of the special facilities for unshipment, sale, etc., at the ports mentioned, or mere adaptations of the old wine imposts.

James's tunnage rates were as below :

Duties for Wines brought in by Englishmen.

Gascon and French wines, and all other wines of the growth of the French King's dominions.	Brought into the port of London, the tun.	Subsidy, 3s. Impost, 42s. Composition, 15s.	60s.
	Brought into any of the other ports, the tun.	Su sidy, 3s. Impost, 37s.	40s.
Rhenish wine.	Brought into any port, the aum (42 gallons).	Subsidy, 12d. Impost, 8s. 8d.	9s. 8d.

* By 1 Jas. I., c. 25, it had been enacted that corn might be shipped oversea when the price in England did not exceed a specified sum (26s. 8d. a quarter for wheat, 14s. for barley, 15s. for rye). The outward custom was 2s. a quarter on wheat, and 1s. 4d. on other grain. By 3 Jas I., c. 11, beer might be exported when the price of malt did not exceed 16s. a quarter. The reasons for allowing exportation of beer were quaintly expressed. It was stated that the merchant navy would thus be increased, because one shipload of barley might be brewed into four shiploads of beer ; also that the brewing trade would be made prosperous, and 'divers Port Townes greatly comforted and relieved.' The duty outward was 1s. 6d. a tun (custom) and 8s. 6d. (impost).

Wine	Port	Duties	Total
Muscadels, Malmseys, and all other wines of the growth of the Levant.	Brought into the ports of London, Bristol, or Southampton, the butt.	Subsidy, 1s. 6d. Impost, 20s. 4d. Composition, 2s. 6d.	24s. 4d.
	Brought into any of the other ports, the butt.	Subsidy, 1s. 6d. Impost, 20s. 4d.	21s. 10d.
Sacks, Canaries, Malagas, Madeiras, Romneys, and Hollocks.	Brought into the port of London, the butt or pipe.	Subsidy, 1s. 6d. Impost, old, 18s. 6d. ,, new, 7s. 6d. Composition, 2s. 6d.	30s.
	Brought into Bristol or Southampton, the butt or pipe.	Subsidy, 1s. 6d. Impost, 18s. 6d. Composition, 2s. 6d.	22s. 6d.
	Brought into any of the other ports, the butt or pipe.	Subsidy, 1s. 6d. Impost, 18s. 6d.	20s.
Bastards, Teints, and Alicants.	Brought into the port of London, the butt or pipe.	Subsidy, 1s. 6d. Impost, old, 17s. ,, new, 7s. 6d.	26s.
	Brought into any of the outports, the butt or pipe.	Subsidy, 1s. 6d. Impost, 17s.	18s. 6d.

Duties paid for Wines brought in by Strangers.

Wine	Port	Duties	Total
Gascon or French wines, and all other wines of the growth of the French King's dominions.	Brought into the port of London, the tun.	Subsidy, 6s. Impost, 42s. Composition, 15s. Butlerage, 2s.	65s.
	Brought into any of the other ports, the tun.	Subsidy, 6s. Impost, 37s. Butlerage, 2s.	45s.
Rhenish wines	Brought into any port, the aum.	Subsidy, 12d. Impost, 8s. 8d. Butlerage, 4d.	10s.
Muscadels, Malmseys, and all other wines of the growth of the Levant.	Brought into the ports of London, Bristol, or Southampton, the butt.	Subsidy, 3s. Custom, 6s. 8d. Southampton duty, 10s. Impost, 20s. 4d. Composition, 2s. 6d. Butlerage, 12d.	43s. 6d.
	Brought into any of the other ports, the butt.	Subsidy, 3s. Custom, 6s. 8d. Southampton duty, 10s. Impost, 20s. 4d. Butlerage, 12d.	41s.

Sacks, Canaries, Malagas, Madeiras, Romneys, and Hollocks.	Brought into the port of London, the butt or pipe.	Subsidy, 3s. Impost, old, 18s. 6d. ,, new, 7s. 6d. Composition, 2s. 6d. Butlerage, 12d.	32s. 6d.
	Brought into the ports of Southampton or Bristol, the butt or pipe.	Subsidy, 3s. Impost, 18s. 6d. Composition, 2s. 6d. Butlerage, 12d.	25s.
	Brought into any of the other ports, the butt or pipe.	Subsidy, 3s. Impost, 18s. 6d. Butlerage, 12d.	22s. 6d.
Bastards, Teints, and Alicants.	Brought into the port of London, the butt or pipe.	Subsidy, 3s. Impost, old, 17s. ,, new, 7s. 6d. Butlerage, 12d.	28s. 6d.
	Brought into any of the outports, the butt or pipe.	Subsidy, 3s. Impost, 17s. 6d. Butlerage, 12d.	21s. 6d.

Note that for such wines as shall be landed in any of the outports, and afterwards brought to London, there is to be paid	For every tun of Gascon or French wines	20s.
	For every butt or pipe of Sacks, Canaries, Malagas, Madeiras, Romney, Hollocks, Bastards, Teints, and Alicants	7s. 6d.

NOTE.—The Southampton duty on Levant wines imported by strangers was paid at all ports.

An arbitrary impost of 3s. 4d. per short cloth was levied on exported woollens. This tax became known as 'pretermitted customs.' (The explanation of the title may perhaps be found in Sir Matthew Hale's suggestion that the impost was recommended by certain officious collectors, who represented to the king that 3s. 4d. too little had been charged in the old subsidies, through misapprehension as to the ancient Custom on wool being included in the wool tax.)

The yield of the Customs in 1610–11 (during publication of the new list) is stated by Mr. Hall as £137,000. In 1613 it appears to have been £148,000.

Cecil died in 1612, and James, deprived of his great financial pilot, seems to have adopted a policy of taking all he could, both by customs and inland impositions. After Cecil's death, one Cranfield was appointed Surveyor-General of customs, and, if some of the statements of Customs revenue may be credited, the returns increased enormously. But the accounts are dreadfully conflicting (one writer puts the return of 1623 at £323,000, an incredible sum, considering the misappropriation that prevailed).*

In 1616 it was proclaimed that the merchants of London had gone beyond their rights in disputing the officers' fees prescribed in the 'Book of Rates.' They were enjoined, if they desired to benefit by an abatement of 5 per cent. on duties, promised to all who paid the duties promptly, to render unto Cranfield, 'our faithful and well-beloved servant . . . Surveyor-General of Customes great and small, Subsidies, Imposts, and Impositions throughout the Realm . . . such fees as have heretofore been allowed to the holder of the office.' (The order when issued contained a table of fees, but this is now missing.)

In 1620 James, by means of one of the proclamations to which he was so hopelessly addicted, prohibited the planting of tobacco in England. The proclamation stated that the king disliked the weed, and that its use was hurtful to both body and mind, but that he considered it wiser to allow importation of the evil article, 'with many other varieties and superfluities coming from beyond sea,' than to tolerate its growth within the realm. All persons having tobacco to the amount of 10 lbs. or upwards in their possession were to bring the goods to the Hawk and Pheasant, Cornhill, to be sealed and marked. Officers were empowered to search for and seize any tobacco withheld. Certain historians have attributed the issue of the proclamation to a motive far different from that announced by James, and accused him of a desire to engross profits, he having assumed pre-emption of all Plantation tobacco, and made its importation subject to special licence.

In 1622 a Commission was appointed to inquire into the

* See also the paragraph as to a Commission in 1622.

cause of a sudden falling off in Customs receipts. The matters submitted for consideration were many and puzzling. The Commissioners were directed to inquire why the price of wool had fallen, how the cloth laws might best be systematized, and whether joint-stock companies were beneficial. The old craving for coin inspired the putting of a couple of time-honoured questions—viz., whether the exportation of English goods might be regulated so as to ensure an ample return of bullion, and if it would be wise to compel foreign merchants to expend their takings within the realm. Another question, as to how foreign ships might best be kept from carrying English goods, was no doubt vaguely expressed, the subject intended for consideration being the best means of securing English dominance in the carrying trade. (This matter was destined to be dealt with thirty years later, by men much wiser and more determined than either James or his counsellors.) Then came a brace of questions which have been debated upon many times since, and are even at the present day subjects fruitful of discussion.

1. 'Whether an excess of imports over exports may be held disadvantageous?'

2. 'Whether such excess may be prevented?'

It appears that the customs receipts in 1621 were less by £30,000 than in 1613.*

The method of compiling total values of imports and exports at this time was to multiply the customs poundage receipts inward and outward respectively, less the extra aliens' Custom under Carta Mercatoria, by twenty. Then an estimate was made of the values of such goods as were not subject to poundage—the tunnage, wool, and cloth Customs totals, with other incidentals, being used. Then an amount was added for 'goods run.'

In 1624 James by proclamation forbade the use of any tobacco not Plantation-grown. He had previously secured

* Yet, according to one statist, in 1623 the customs yield exceeded that of 1613 by £175,000! If this be correct, the labours of the Commission were crowned with success.

pre-emption of all Plantation tobacco. But afterwards, when it suited him to do so, he granted licences at heavy rates for occasional importations of Spanish tobacco.

The celebrated Hanger Prisage case, by means of which the conditions governing exemption of London citizens from Prisage were clearly laid down, was decided during the early part of James's reign. 'Prisage,' said the judges, 'is a duty which the kings of England by themselves or their officers have taken from time immemorial.' They decided that Prisage was not legal until after bulk was broken (unloading begun), and that they who imported wine for private use were 'naturally Prisage-free.' 'The Prisage of Wines,' continued the judges, 'is a Flower of the Crown,' and they defined such qualities of citizenship as secured exemption. A freeman not in residence was liable to Prisage. A freeman resident, yet not a householder, was liable. A resident and householder, yet not a freeman, was liable. Those exempt were freemen holding houses and residing within the City, and if even they imported wine for sale the goods were not free of Prisage unless they were the sole property of the importers, and intended for sale to none but citizens for the use of citizens. Sex of importer no bar.

Charles I. came before his Parliament with two decided disqualifications—a pile of debts left by his accomplished father, and a reputation for high-handedness. War with Spain was contemplated, and the royal needs were urgent. The attitude of Parliament was discouraging, and highly incensed the king. Then began that venomous struggle between the Crown and the people's representatives, in considering which most readers find their sympathies distracted with the varying aspects of the contest, now inclining to the king, now to the champions of those who contributed towards the support of the realm (at the same time enriching the farmers of taxes and their subordinates.) The Parliament of 1626 was also averse to granting money, and desirous of impeaching the king's favourite, Buckingham. Charles dissolved it.

It must be admitted that the conduct of the Parliaments was rather unreasonable, especially in avenging upon the king his father's debts and antics, but it has always been the English way to endure overlong and then resent in stubborn fashion. It is possible that many of the more thoughtful amongst the better classes, and nearly all the merchants, were tired of Stuart rule. The king was apt in furnishing pretexts for quarrel, and perhaps a large number of his most influential subjects were determined that quarrel should be. Indeed this is almost rendered clear by the action of the third Parliament.

It contained a host of implacable economists, and announced its true character by formulating the Petition of Right, and stating that no supplies would be granted until the claims of the petition were met. Charles by an ungracious acknowledgment obtained temporary supplies, but in 1629 he was again protesting. The Commons countered by charging him with infringing the Constitution. It appears that the king's officers had met with opposition in collecting his arbitrary levies of tunnage and poundage, and certain refractory merchants had been imprisoned. He declared that the recusants had been incited by the action of Parliament, and ordered the House to confirm the tunnage and poundage. 'I do not desire it out of greediness,' said he. 'I must be instant with you; proceed with this business. . . . You must not think it much if I finding you slack shall give you further quickening.' But quickened the stubborn assembly would not be. Charles dissolved it, and for eleven years governed without a parliament.

It should be noted that the Commons, in reproaching the king, referred with unmistakable resentment to James's arbitrary increases of poundage. Undoubtedly the imposts rankled in the commercial mind, and the poor suffered by the inflation of prices. This may explain the rigid adherence of the mercantile class to the Parliamentary cause during the subsequent hostilities.

Charles's needs soon became urgent, and he revived in full the system of farms and assignments. The proceeds of the old imposts were divided amongst royal favourites and royal creditors, the names 'Hay,' 'Montgomery,' and 'Murray' figuring side by side in the grants with 'Pindar,' 'Wolstenholme,' 'Dawes,' and 'Jacob.' Pindar, Jacob, and Dawes seem to have been in the thick of affairs. At one period they farmed the entire customs, and were allowed to keep back from the rent a huge sum which they had advanced or disbursed. Pindar was a collector of customs as well as a farmer. Jacob was receiver of tobacco duties. Dawes was a distinguished pluralist, collector of customs, surveyor of customs, and clerk of the Rolls.

In 1635 was published a new 'Book of Rates,' extending the impost on poundage to many articles left untouched by James, and here and there adding special imposts. The new scheme had many other unfavourable points. For instance, payment of duty was demanded *before entry*. Prisage was instituted on imported groceries, with heavy composition fees, and additional tunnage was levied on wine at outports. The poundage on Barbadoes tobacco was reduced to 6d., on Virginian to 4d.; on Spanish roll tobacco it was raised to 2s.

While thus juggling with the Customs, the king raised money by many other arbitrary expedients. The obnoxious ship-money tax was in full swing. Two years later Hampden's case was tried in the Exchequer, and a majority of the judges decided in favour of the Crown. The soap, glass, and other manufactures were vested in syndicates, that paid large sums to the king for their privileges, and then made the public pay excessive prices. (In 1630 Charles had renewed his father's prohibition of tobacco-planting in England, prohibited all foreign tobacco unless imported under royal licence,* and copied his father in pre-empting all Plantation tobacco. In 1631 appeared the grotesque 'Licentia Thome Badger Militi et aliis pro exportatione Canum,' providing that Sir Thomas Badger and Thomas Potts, Masters of Harriers, and Sir Timothy Tyrrell, Master of Buckhounds, should enjoy sole privilege of exporting 'hounds, beagles, and hunting-dogs.' Indeed, it would seem that any company that tried the king with a purse might obtain almost any unfair privilege that could be asked for. The Merchant Adventurers of England obtained the power of levying monstrous fees on all desirous of becoming members of their society, and threatened to increase the rates after a specified period had elapsed.) In 1636 proclamation was made that the monopoly of retailing tobacco, which had been vested in a patentee, was being infringed by 'divers vagrant pedlars,' who made it a practice to 'carrie tobacco upp and doune in packs, . . . and sell and retail the same to the damage of the pattentee.' It was enjoined that such hawkers might be arrested, and dealt with as rogues and vagabonds. Mayors, bailiffs, constables, etc., were ordered to 'bee ayding and assisting unto ye said pattentee' in repression of the irregular traffic.

The celebrated Long Parliament met, voted tunnage and poundage and the wool duties for a brief period, and then impeached as 'delinquents' a number of farmers and officials. It is apparent that the rest did not pay much regard to the ominous proceedings, but continued when practicable to collect unwarranted dues for the king and intolerable fees for themselves, for later Parliament, while renewing tunnage and poundage for a limited period, enacted that if any officer continued the collection beyond the date specified, *or collected any illegal customs*, he should be liable to the provisions of the Statute of Præmunire. The act of grant stated that farmers had taken duties not

* See the Proclamation, 'That our Subjects may not unthriftely vent the solid commodities of our owne kingdoms, and return the proceed thereof in smoak.'

sanctioned by any parliament, and that this had been proved on examination before the House and by confession of certain of the culprits. The tunnage granted was the ancient rate of 3s. only; 6s. on sweet wines brought by aliens. Thus the wine imposts enduring from the times of Mary and Elizabeth were practically condemned as illegal. Plantation tobacco was freed of all duty except 2d. a pound.

The revenues sanctioned were continued again and again for brief spaces of time, as though purposely to exasperate the king. All grants of tunnage and poundage by letters patent (assignments, etc.) were annulled, and it was stipulated that no forfeiture for breach of the laws relating to tunnage and poundage should hold unless the act of grant had been proclaimed. Meanwhile the Customs revenues were being most improperly collected, the officials at certain ports scraping up what they could for the king, others conforming outwardly to the new regulations, yet collecting little. Others no doubt there were who did the best they could for themselves, yet went hourly in dread of the formidable Parliament and the Act of Præmunire.

The last rumble before the storm was a mutter at Westminster that the nation was drifting fast into debt for naval expenses. Then, while swords were being secretly sharpened for the inevitable conflict, Parliament made public certain of its recent dealings with the king in the matter of tunnage and poundage. The ordinance of disclosure accompanied a new 'Book of Rates,' and was a terse and ably-expressed document.

It stated that fifty-two ships of war were in commission, and that a debt of £200,000 had been incurred on behalf of the navy; that a bill of tunnage and poundage and the annexed 'Book of Rates' had been sent to the king; that the king did not acknowledge them; and that he gave no audience to a commission sent to move him in the matter.

It alluded to an Act passed for the relief of captives taken by Moorish pirates, under which Act all merchants importing or exporting goods were required to make entry of them promptly and correctly. It reiterated the injunction, and enjoined the customs officers at all ports to vigilance in enforcement.

It admitted that, as the Bill for tunnage and poundage had not received the royal assent, none was bound to obey it, yet payment of the duties therein expressed was invited as a loan for national purposes at 15 per cent. It continued that, though the king had the Bill in his possession, he was not competent to ratify it, except by his patent, declared in the Upper House in full presence of Lords and Commons.

The ordinance pledged both Houses to secure and confirm to all who paid duties in advance the 15 per cent. allowance before perfecting the subsidy in question or any future subsidy, and provided that all delinquents should be charged with full arrears.

It assured the officers of customs that they would be acting legally in obeying its instructions, and that ample provision would be made for their security.

(It alluded afresh to the Act for the relief of Moorish captives, under which all merchants were called upon for an advance of 1 per cent. on their contemplated revenue transactions to meet urgent necessities under the said Act, and stated that such as had not complied would be held liable, but the definition of the liabilities consequent was by no means clear.)

It empowered collectors to allow the 15 per cent. as a defalcation upon all duties paid under the provisions of the ordinance. They were to make monthly return of all moneys received, and the returns were to be sent to William Toames, Surveyor-General of Customs, who in turn was to furnish an abstract to a committee of members, appointed by the full House. Copies of the Bill and 'Book of Rates' were to be sent to every port.

It may be concluded that this ordinance was the guarded expression of a profound and subtle scheme. The Bill was void, yet Parliament, by publishing its provisions, secured to the party of revolt the power of taxing most of the goods imported. London was with the Parliament men, and in case of hostilities would be the stronghold of their cause. As soon as war broke out Parliament would, for revenue purposes, be able to control the ports of Boston, Yarmouth, Lynn, Ipswich, London, Dover, Sandwich, and Southampton. The king would be restricted to the remoter and smaller ports, and be compelled to raise money by impositions upon the inland towns. The allowance upon duties paid appealed powerfully to the commercial mind. It is noteworthy, too, that for the first time in history Parliament took the revenue officers into its confidence, indirectly adjuring them, the London officers especially, to do their best to support constitutional liberty.

The Bill to which the ordinance alluded was also remarkable. It affirmed:

1. That no national charges on merchandise, inward or outward, could legally be made without the full consent of Parliament, except as provided (*vide* 4).

2. That grants made by Parliament were not immutable, but might be altered even by the parliament that made them.

3. That all such grants to the king were made solely that he might defend the seas.

4. That the 'old customs' were the king's own. It recited them as the 'ancient Custome upon wool,' Prisage, Butlerage, the Carta Mercatoria duties, the ancient duties on the exportation of corn and grain, the duties of 3 James I. upon the exportation of beer, and Elizabeth's 'licence duties' upon the exportation of leather, tallow, and hides. It then proceeded to give the rates and define the incidence of the 'old customs,' and certainly went astray, for it quoted Edward I.'s Carta Mercatoria duties on aliens' wool, etc., outwards as being 'the ancient wool Custom' rates; it stated Prisage as obtaining upon *every* vessel bringing ten or more tuns of wine; and it described Butlerage as a 'fraight.'

The Bill prohibited the importation of currants. (This was against the Venetians.) It continued the officers' fees at the legal scale, hinting that they might soon be regulated by Parliament. In the accompanying 'Book of Rates' appeared concise rules for the guidance of merchants and officers. Below is a précis :

1. All masters of ships from foreign ports were directed to report, furnishing a full account of cargo. If they proceeded to other English ports to complete discharge, the collectors at such ports were to be furnished with an account of all goods previously discharged.

2. The privileges previously extended to certain merchants by the late farmers were to be extended to all other merchants.

3. Casks of wine much reduced by genuine leakage were to be admitted duty-free. Wine ' gone corrupt, fit only to distil into hot waters ' (spirits), ' or to make vinegar,' received the same privilege. Twelve per cent. was to be allowed for ' leakage ' on all wines duly entered.

4. Aliens were to pay the same poundage inward as denizens, except on lead, tin, and woollens, and the Carta Mercatoria duties as well. On lead, tin, and woollens they were to pay double poundage, and the Carta Mercatoria duties. They were to pay double customs outward on native manufactures of wool, and on all other goods outward the usual poundage plus the Carta Mercatoria duties.

5. Wine imported and afterwards exported was to be available for drawback of the tunnage paid at import, less 20s. per tun withheld from denizens and 25s. from aliens.

6. Foreign wool imported and duty-paid was not available for drawback if afterwards exported, but might be shipped free of the outward custom, if the shipping and cocket fees were paid, and the goods exported in English bottoms.

7. Other goods duty-paid inward and exported were available for drawback of half the inward duty, if exported within a specified time.

The hours and places for unlading and shipping were defined. The landing and shipping officers were to give attendance between 6 a.m. and 6 p.m. in summer, and from sunrise to sunset in winter, *if actually required.* Officers neglecting to attend when duly notified were made liable to a fine of £5, part of the fine to go to the merchant aggrieved.

The indoor officers at outports were to attend from 9 to 12 in the morning, and from 2 to 4 in the afternoon. Those in London were to attend from 9 till 12, and in the afternoon were to help at the waterside, 'an able clerk' remaining within 'to attend the book.' The merchants were to be dealt with in fair rotation. Officers who showed favour with a view to extort gratuities were to be punished.

Emphatic reference was made to the table of fees ratified by Parliament, and it was announced in plain terms that if an officer exceeded he was to be dismissed.

The searchers of outward-bound ships were warned not to detain any vessel beyond a specified time (three tides at Gravesend, one tide at the outports).

Certain privileges of slight defalcation in entry outward of cloth, long enjoyed by the merchants of York, Hull, Newcastle, and Exeter were confirmed.

The rates mentioned in the Book were not to entrench on any dues such as package, scavage, balliage, portage, or on any local custom dues levied by cities and ports upon aliens' merchandise for the upkeep of quays, harbours, etc.

It will be perceived that the Parliament extended consideration to the convenience of merchants, and was determined to see that the officers did their duty fairly and efficiently. Gentlemen appointed by royal patent, and accustomed to partnership with the employés of revenue-farmers, would probably scan the new regulations with disapproval.

Two years later, when the land resounded with conflict, Parliament issued another ordinance, continuing its

'Book of Rates.' It appears that a Committee of members supervised publication of the Book, with the ordinances and bill appertaining.

The ordinance of 1644 appointed Samuel Avery, Richard Bateman, Charles Lloyd, Christopher Pack, and Walter Boothby Commissioners of Customs, and referred to 'the late Commissioners' (the dispossessed farmers). It reaffirmed that the officers would be protected, and held accountable to Parliament only, and stated that in future schemes of tunnage and poundage provision would be made, not only for indemnifying merchants who might make advances, but for the security of collecting officers. It gave elaborate instructions as to dealing with seized goods. The account of all such goods was to be kept by a London officer, and the proceeds of the seizures were to be divided between the Treasury and the seizer. All proceedings against revenue defaulters were to be in the Court of Exchequer.

The allowance of 15 per cent. was withheld from payments upon imported tobacco. The prohibition of currants was repealed, and one-third of the proceeds of the currant duty appropriated to the maintenance of the garrison of Gloucester.

The Parliamentary Committee appointed to deal with naval business was notified of all customs after collection, and its order became the Commissioners' discharge. The customs officers were enjoined to be vigilant in the performance of their work, to conform closely to the 'Book of Rates,' and to obey Parliament and its committees. (The printer of the volume containing the 'Book of Rates,' Bill, and Ordinance was specified, and granted monopoly of publication. The price of the volume was fixed at 2s. 6d.)

Nearly all the values for poundage were increased, for the Parliament had no sustained source of revenue except the customs of the south-eastern ports. Spanish and Venetian goods were heavily surtaxed, as may be seen by the following comparison with the rates of 1635 and 1611 :

1635.	£	s.	d.	1642–4.	£	s.	d.
Total tunnage in London:				Tunnage in London:			
Levant wines imported by Englishmen—Venetian Cargo (the butt) ..	1	14	4	The butt	2	5	0

1611.	£	s.	d.	1642–4.	£	s.	d.
Total value at which rated for poundage:							
Spanish tobacco, leaf, per pound ..	1	6	8	Value for poundage	3	0	0
Total poundage ..	0	1	4	Poundage	0	3	0

(Tobacco from the English Plantations was rated extremely low—value, 3s. 4d.; duty, 2d.)

The rating of several articles was doubled. For instance:

1611.	£	s.	d.	1642–4.	£	s.	d.
Aqua vitæ (per hogshead)	4	0	0	Aqua vitæ (per hogshead)	8	0	0
Poundage ..	0	4	0	Poundage ..	0	8	0

Outward Rates for Poundage.

1611.	£	s.	d.	1642–4.	£	s.	d.
Tallow (the cwt.) ..	1	0	0	Tallow (the cwt.) ..	2	0	0
Poundage ..	0	1	0	Poundage ..	0	2	0

The Parliament believed in rigid protection. During its control of the revenue there was no attempt at reducing the tariff, although strenuous and highly successful retrenchment of public expenditure was practised whenever opportunity arose. The martial Puritans had no love for foreigners; their political motto appears to have been: 'England for the English, and England against the world.'* (Cromwell was much more disposed to toleration, both religious and racial, than the shrewd

* See preamble to the Commonwealth Act of 1656, c. 5: 'Forasmuch as the prosperous estate of all islands is maintained by a just endeavour and care that the exportation of native commodities overbalances the importation of foreign commodities.' 'The balance of trade' was a serious consideration with the old Puritans.

and fierce sectaries who followed, admired, and bitterly suspected him.)

The 'Book of Rates' furnishes evidence that a sugar-refining industry had sprung up in England. In the 1611 Book there was no mention made of refined sugar. In the 1635 Book 'refined sugar in loaves' was listed at an extremely high rate for poundage, but the item did not appear in the outward list. 'Refined sugar in loaves' appeared amongst the imports in the 1642–4 Book, and was almost the only item standing at a lowered value.

Value for Poundage Inward.

	1635.			1642–4.		
	£	*s.*	*d.*	£	*s.*	*d.*
Refined sugar in loaves (per cwt.) ..	21	6	8	17	0	0

Apparently the refining of sugar in England had lowered the value of the foreign article. In the 1642–4 Book's *export* list appeared :

Value for Poundage Outward.

	£	*s.*	*d.*
Sugar (coarse), having paid custom inward, refined, and made into loaves and exported (the cwt.) ..	2	0	0

The Parliament's Ordinance and 'Book of Rates' were to endure until a specified date in 1647. Meantime additional funds were raised by an Excise duty, levied on the 'first buyer' of certain foreign commodities. Wine was included, and, to make sure that the tax should be diverted from the importer, the retail selling price was fixed at 14d. per quart for Spanish wine and 8d. for French, a higher price than had previously obtained. Excise duties were also placed upon beer, ale, and spirits, produced in England. The standards for wine-casks were recited thus : Tun, 252 gallons ; pipe or butt, 126 ; puncheon (anciently called 'tertian'), 84 ; hogshead, 63 ; tierce, 42 ; quarter-cask, 31½.

Messrs. Towle, Langham, Foot, Kendrick, Cullum, Evans, Lamot, and Claxton were appointed Excise Commissioners. Mr. Faulconbridge was made controller, and Mr. Bond auditor. The oath to be taken by each Commissioner ran as follows :

'You shall swear to be faithful and true in your place of Commissioner of the Excise during the time you shall be a Commissioner, according to the Ordinance of both Houses of Parliament in that behalf made. You shall according to your knowledge execute the same diligently and faithfully, having no private respect to yourself in prejudice of the Commonwealth. You shall make and deliver a true account of all your receipts and disbursements to such Auditor or Auditors as is or are or shall be from time to time appointed by the Houses of Parliament according to the said Ordinance : so help you God and the contents of this Book.'*

The operations of the 'New Impost,' as the Excise was called, were for a time restricted to London and the neighbouring districts, but as the Parliament gradually wrested control of the various counties from the king, they were extended to England, Wales, and Berwick. At first there was much evasion by 'roomaging and removing of goods,' and the New Impost was received in no friendly spirit by the nation, especially as extensive powers of search were granted to the officers. The professed reason for the tax was that the eastern ports, which were friendly to the Parliament, would by their contributions of tunnage, poundage, etc., have borne the bulk of the expense of the war, had not this new method been applied to the inland counties, many of which had at first taken the part of the king. The Ordinance instituting the tax described it as a 'New Impost, whereby Malignants and Neutrals may be compelled to pay proportionate parts of the charge for the preservation of the Kingdom.' Yet it does not appear that Parliament,

* Later the wording of the oath was altered, each Commissioner being required to vow allegiance to the Commonwealth.

though capturing county after county, called upon any of them for arrears.

The only foreign goods exempt from Excise duties on sale were bullion, corn, victuals, arms, ammunition, and ordnance. (Thus it seems that the revenue maxims of the Parliament were the same as those of James I., whom the leading men of the new school held a blundering tyrant.) Goods imported for private use were liable. Barter counted as sale. There was no escaping the tax. More remorseless exacters of dues never lived than the stern and incorruptible English Republicans. But they accounted honestly for the moneys they collected, and used them to the best advantage.*

The next Ordinance worth note was that of 1646, which freed export trade between England and the Plantation of New England and the West Indies of all duties.

In the same year the Act granting Tunnage and Poundage was renewed.

The exportation of wool was prohibited in 1647.

In 1651 the Rump passed its momentous Navigation Act, stipulating that no merchandise of Asia, Africa, or America should enter England except in ships built and owned by Englishmen, navigated by English captains, and manned by crews of which more than the half part were Englishmen. Such merchandise as came direct from Europe, and was in ships of the country of shipment, was excepted. Fish might not be imported into or exported from England unless it had been caught by English fishermen.

This, of course, was a deliberate attempt to provoke a quarrel with the Dutch, and gain an opportunity of

* In 1649 Parliament, in one of its Acts, described the New Impost as 'the most useful and indifferent' (fairly apportioned) 'levy that can be laid upon a people.' The tax brought in a deal of money, and at the time Parliament was in great need. The King had been beheaded, the Rump was in power, and executive government had been entrusted to the strongest body of men that ever ruled a nation—the famous Council of which Bradshaw was president and Milton foreign secretary.

making England supreme as a carrier of goods. Nothing in history is more remarkable than the resoluteness of this Parliament, unless it be the efficacy of its measures. It had dethroned the king, tried him as a common criminal, and beheaded him as a traitor. Through its wonderful general and peerless soldiers it had shattered the opposition of Scotland, and been able to strike enduring terror into the hearts of the Irishry. Withal it had an eye to the ports and the ocean beyond them, and had resolved to stake the existence of the Commonwealth upon a novel and tremendous venture.

It seems that the Dutch at once realized the danger at hand. They sent an embassy of remonstrance, but it was received coldly. The Commonwealth demanded—

1. A sum as damages for fishing carried on by the Dutch in English waters.
2. Cession of the Spice Islands.
3. Compensation for an outrage upon Englishmen at Amboyna.
4. Satisfaction for the murder of Dr. Dorislaus, Parliamentary Envoy at the Hague.
5. Reparation for damage caused to English shipping by the Dutch.

The third and fourth items of demand were reasonable ; the rest could be granted by no self-respecting nation. The sum claimed for damages to shipping was really an outrageous item, yet there is good reason to believe that, had it been instantly paid, fresh demands would have been made. Parliament had but one object—to shatter the power of the Dutch.

'A fair fight, and the winner has the world's trade,' was the watchword on both sides when Blake and Van Tromp began their tremendous struggle. But during that brief and glorious space in her history, that commenced with the rise of Cromwell and ended with the death of Blake, the best of England gave England counsel and fought her battles, and England could not lose. The destruction of the Dutch fleet, and the death of its heroic commander, fixed the rule of the seas beyond successful challenge. The damage sustained by Holland was irreparable. Within two years she lost almost all her ships of war, and several hundreds of her merchantmen. She was made to 'pray and pay.' The English East India Company received notable concessions, and the Stuart cause was left for the time destitute of both support and hope. The Channel Islands and the Colonies had been forced to renounce it; Scotland and Ireland had been bludgeoned into submission, and now even the stubborn Dutchmen were compelled to condone the execution of 1649.

In 1652 tobacco-planting within the realm was prohibited.

In 1653 Barebone's Parliament issued an Ordinance continuing the Customs until 1658, and provided that there should be no drawback of subsidy on goods which had been taxed at sale or altered in quality and afterwards exported. It was also provided that the pay of the Commissioners of Customs should take the form of 'poundage upon receipts'—1d. on every 20s. of net customs money.

In 1654, Barebone's Parliament having vacated office, a unique Ordinance was issued. Perhaps the grave Commissioners had been scandalized by the ribald outcry of Billingsgate, Fresh Wharf, and the Wool Dock, or some of Cromwell's men may have visited the Custom-house at mid-day. Below is the Act:

'An Ordinance empowering the Commissioners of the Customs and others for the better suppression of Drunkenness and prophane Swearing in persons employed under them.

'Whereas several persons such as Carmen, Porters, Watermen, and others who are employed upon the Keys* as also upon the River of Thames in Ships, Boats, and Lighters, and in Thames Street and other Streets and Lanes adjacent within the City of London, for shipping

* Quays.

and unshipping, packing, carrying, craning, and removing Goods and Merchandise, are very ordinarily drunk, and do also Prophane and Blaspheme the holy name of God by Cursing and Swearing, to the great dishonour of God, the scandal of the Professors and Profession of the Gospel among us, and of the present Government : For the preventing whereof, Bee it Enacted by His Highness the Lord Protector, by and with the consent of his Council, that the Commissioners of the Customs for the time being bee and are hereby authorised and required to take care that the Laws of this Nation against Drunkenness, Swearing, and Cursing bee put in execution against all such persons as shall bee guilty of the crimes aforesaid : And for that purpose shall and hereby have the Power and Authority of Justices of the Peace within the said places : And every Officer and Officer's Deputy and Deputies of the Commissioners of the Customs, having a Commission whereby they are deputed and authorised to bee Officers and Deputies under the hand and seals of the said Commissioners, shall have and hereby have power and are authorised to apprehend and attach and in safe custody to bring before the said Commissioners, or anyone of them sitting at the Customhouse in London, every person or persons whom they shall see to bee Drunk, or shall hear to Swear, Curse, and Blaspheme the holy name of God as is aforesaid : And shall have power, and hereby have power to execute, any power or powers, authority, or authorities in this case which by Law any Constable may or ought to exercise or use, although the said Officer or Officers have no particular warrant of the Commissioners aforesaid for apprehending any of the offenders for the offences aforesaid, as in the like cases are usually issued unto Sworn Constables by Justices of the Peace upon the like occaysions : And all persons whom any of the said Officers shall require to bee aiding and assisting unto them for the apprehending and bringing before the said Commissioners any such offenders are hereby required to bee aiding and assisting unto them therein accordingly : And in case of refusal such punishment and proceedings shall bee had and awarded against them as by Law may bee and ought to bee upon every person that shall refuse to bee aiding and assisting to any Sworn Constable or Constables when required thereunto.

'*Friday, June 30th,* 1654.

'Ordered by His Highness the Lord Protector and His Council, that this Ordinance bee forthwith Printed and Published.

'HENRY SCOBELL, *Clerk of the Council.*'

It will be observed that Cromwell's councillors did not 'imitate the honourable Romans in brevity'; their ordinances were elaborate as sermons. It is possible that the language in Thames Street then may have been as bad as that used there at the present day. If it were, the proclamation may almost be excused, though it is certain that if the customs men tried to carry out its provisions they had little time to collect and safeguard the revenue.*

In an Ordinance fixing the retail prices of wine, French wine was listed at 7d. a quart, Rhenish at 12d., Spanish at 18d. Tunnage and poundage were continued, applying to Scotland and Ireland as well as England. Certain Spanish goods were surtaxed, thus :

	Additional Tunnage.			
	£	*s.*	*d.*	
Spanish wine imported by subjects ..	1	10	0	per tun.
" " " " aliens ..	2	0	0	"

	Additional Duty.			
	£	*s.*	*d.*	
Spanish 'raisins of the sun,' by subjects ..	0	3	0	per cwt.
" " " " strangers	0	3	9	"
Other Spanish raisins, by subjects ..	0	1	6	"
" " " strangers ..	0	1	10½	"

* A letter from the Commissioners to Thurloe shows that the officers performed other incidental duties. The water-guard men seem to have acted as political detectives, and to have detained passengers suspected of being 'malignants.'

'Now is come into our hands a letter of the officers at Gravesend, signifying that there are divers persons come in there out of a ship,' etc.

Certain capital revenue regulations were initiated during the periods of the Parliament and the Protectorate. It was directed that foreign goods carried by lighter from a ship lying in the stream were to be accompanied by a 'lighter-note,' made out by the officer boarded on the vessel. The lighter-note was to be the warrant for the landing of the goods. The landing-waiters were to check the entry and out-turn of the goods by it, and inquire into any discrepancy. An Act of the Protectorate instituted what is now known as 'The King's Warehouse,' but which in the preamble was called 'His Highness's Warehouse.' One such place was to be maintained at every port of consequence. All fine goods or small packages, on arrival in port, and all goods remaining undelivered from vessels within twenty-eight days of their breaking bulk, were to be removed to 'His Highness's Warehouse' for safety, at owners' charges. The keeper of each warehouse had to provide 'good bond,' and was held responsible to owners for the safety of the goods in his custody.

The penalty for making incorrect entry of goods was fixed at £10. Smuggling was made punishable with a fine of treble the value at issue, and forfeiture of the goods. No proceedings were to take place until the seized goods had been warehoused and registered. (It would be extremely difficult to improve upon any of these regulations.)

Steps were taken to farm the revenue. (According to Thurloe, Cromwell had always favoured the idea.) A committee was appointed to contract, it being provided that none of the committeemen should be concerned in the farm, or deal in the commodities taxable. The Customs Commissioners were directed to practise similar abstention. Thus the Great Revolt, which at its outset was marked by bitter persecution of revenue-farmers, may be said to have expired amid requests for tenders.

Two rather interesting cases were tried in the Exchequer during the period of the Protectorate. In 1656 the Attorney-General proceeded against one Shirt, for prisage on nine and a half tuns of wine. The court were of opinion that Shirt imported his goods is small parcels purposely, to elude prisage, and that when such intent appeared any quantity between nine and ten tuns was subject to prise.

In 1658 a bill was presented in the Exchequer against Samuel Mico, 'for discovery of the truth' in connexion with a charge of his having bribed Hawes and Oldenham, 'officers of customs and excise,' to allow him to import 290 casks of currants into the port of London, in a ship called *The Christopher*, without paying the custom due. Mico demurred, pleading that if he answered the charge he might be made to accuse himself of smuggling. He was defended by Hardres, a celebrated Exchequer lawyer. Hardress commenced with an appeal to 'the Law of God,' and ingeniously twisted St. Paul's reply to Tertullus into a contention that the Apostle considered himself not bound to answer to his own peril. He also instanced Christ's silence when interrogated by Pilate. After these illustrations of what 'the Law of God and the God of Law' allowed 'in cases of crime,' the indefatigable pleader appealed to the 'Law of Nature,' and then unwound a mighty chain of ordinary legal precedents. This case is well worth reading, as a specimen of the methods used by ancient pleaders.

LIST OF AUTHORITIES.

Legislation and Incidents.

Imposts: Fœdera ('Commisssio pro Tabacco'), 'Book of Rates,' 1611; Hale ('Hargrave's 'Law Tracts'); 'Book of Rates,' 1635 and 1644.

Protective measures and prohibitions: Fœdera ('Proclamatio super abusu Herbæ Nicotianæ'; 'A Proclamation concerning Tobacco'; 'A Proclamation for the Utter Prohibiting,' etc.); Commonwealth Acts, 1648, 1651 (Navigation Act); 2 of 1652.

Officers: Treasury Papers, 1615-1616.

Commissions of Inquiry: Fœdera ('De Concessione speciali directa Domino Presidenti et aliis concernente Negotium Lanæ').

Prisage (Exchequer trials): Bohun, Hardres.

Excise duty: Commonwealth Ordinance, July 22, 1643, and others.

Wine: Commonwealth Acts, October 9, 1643, 8 of 1656.

British tunnage and poundage: Commonwealth Act 9 of 1656.

Revenue-farming: Commonwealth Act 31 of 1656.

Preventive: Commonwealth Act 9 of 1656.

Long Parliament's grants to Charles I.: 16 Chas. I., c. 8, 12, 22, 25, 29, 31, 36.

Frauds (Exchequer trials): Hardres.

CHAPTER V

THE OLD SUBSIDY, AND ITS EARLIEST OFFSHOOTS

1660–1707

A CLEVER revenue historian of the time of the Georges, after enumerating most of the taxes imposed from the accession of Charles to the death of Anne, confessed that he had omitted some, which, 'like noisome meteors, made their appearance for a year or more, and then vanished.' As a similar method will be applied in this treatise, it may be well to quote his excuse, which ran as follows : 'These we have forborne to mention, because we believe that the reader will be as heartily tired of reading, as we are of collecting and writing, such a disagreeable scroll as that we have now given. Let him consider what kind of people they must be who are to pay these taxes, and on account of these taxes are made liable to an infinite number of pains, penalties, and hardships.'

The thing most intolerable in connexion with Charles's revenue business was not the extent of the impositions—at least so far as the Customs revenue was concerned—for his Parliaments were not much more extortionate upon maritime commerce than those of the Commonwealth had been. It was the conspicuous failure of the levies to realize the sums intended. The financial officials were always in straits, even though the peerless army had been disbanded.

It appears that the duties remained in farm up to the latter end of 1671.* During July of that year an under-

* It is curious that about the last official act of the Farmers was the issue of a code of regulations (the 'Index Vectigalium') for the guidance of officers.

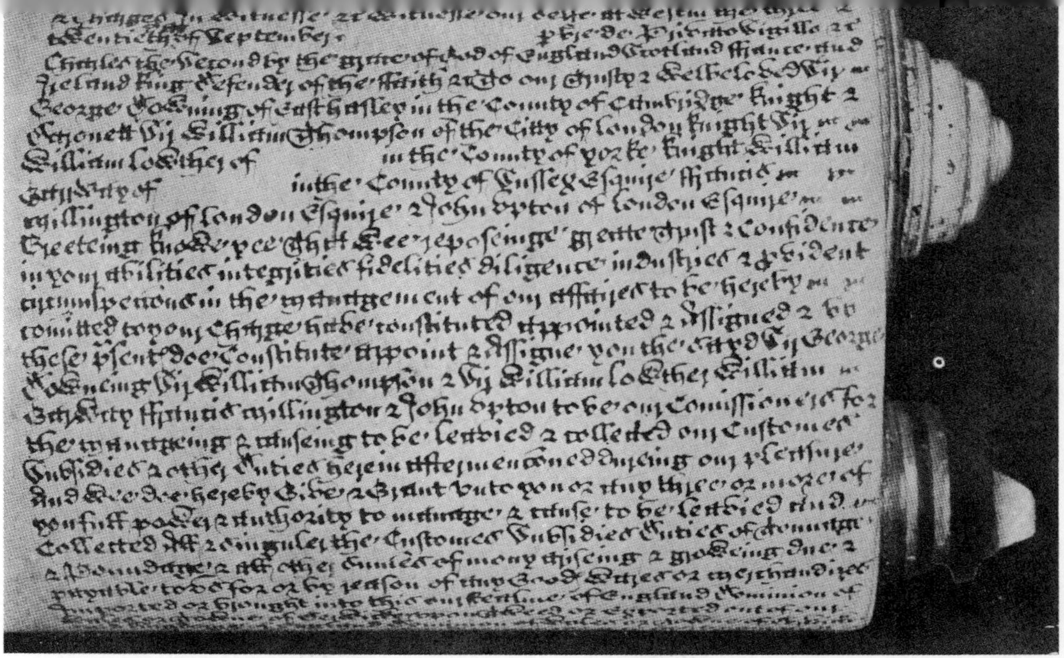

Charles the Second by the grace of God of England Scotland France and Ireland King Defender of the Faith &c To our trusty and welbeloved Sir George Downing of East Hatley in the County of Cambridge Knight and Baronett Sir William Thompson of the City of London Knight Sir William Lowther of in the County of Yorke Knight William Garway of in the County of Sussex Esquire Francis Millington of London Esquire and John Upton of London Esquire Greeting Knowe yee that Wee reposeing great trust and confidence in your abilities integrities fidelities diligence industries and provident circumspections in the management of our affaires to bee hereby committed to your charge have constituted appointed and assigned and by these presents doe constitute appoint and assigne you the said Sir George Downing Sir William Thompson Sir William Lowther William Garway Francis Millington and John Upton to bee our Commissioners for the manageing and causeing to bee levied and collected our Customes Subsidies and other Duties herein aftermentioned dureing our pleasure And Wee doe hereby give and grant unto you or any three or more of you full power and authority to manage and cause to bee levied and collected all and singuler the Customes Subsidies Duties of tonnage

Section of M. 1*d*. Part 2, Patent Roll 23 Charles II., showing Preamble of Document installing Sir George Downing and others as Commissioners of Customs in 1671.

(During the same year instructions were given to the Remembrancer of the Exchequer to proceed against the lessees of a Customs farm which expired in 1667, the said lessees being in debt to the Crown for a large sum.)

The Commission begins at 'Charles the Second by the grace of God,' and contains nearly 5,000 words. The lines above 'p · bre · de Privato Sigillo' ('by writ of Privy Seal') conclude M. 2*d*. on same Roll, a document furnishing instructions to Lord Ranelagh and others, who farmed the Irish Revenue.

To face p. 104.

taking was entered into by Lord St. John and others to farm the customs upon all goods exported and imported, except the temporary imposition upon wine and vinegar, the temporary duty of 5s. a ton upon French shipping, the customs upon bullion, smalt, saffers, salt, timber, glass, potashes, and logwood, the Coinage duty, and such duties as were 'usually exempt from farming.' The farmers advanced £140,000, and undertook to pay a rent of £480,000 per annum. They were to pay the rent in monthly instalments, and to meet all debentures on goods duty-paid and afterwards exported. They undertook 'not to clogg the markett towards the end of the tearme.' The farm was to endure five years, and to commence on September 29.

Later they made another advance, and obtained permission to farm the imposts on wine and vinegar as well as the permanent duties. By September, 1671, they had advanced in all £226,000, and a Privy Seal warrant of that month directed the Exchequer officials to pay the interest upon the loan out of the forthcoming customs receipts, and to arrange for paying off the principal by instalments. They were also bidden to hold themselves in readiness to pay to Lord St. John and his associates in the lease such other sums as 'the king by Sign Manuall may appoint as gratuities in respect of their surrendering their farm.'

Thus it appears that the farm had been cancelled. On September 27, 1671, just two days prior to the date on which the lease should have come into effect, Commissioners were appointed to manage the Customs revenue. The patent (23 Chas. II., p. 2, m. 1*d.*) is too long to be reproduced *in extenso*, but a brief account may be of interest.

The Commissioners named were Sir George Downing, Sir William Lowther, Sir William Thompson, William Garway, Francis Millington, and John Upton. Downing had originally been an Exchequer Teller. (Pepys was his clerk in 1659.) He was made a baronet in 1663, and thenceforward was occasionally employed in adjusting the disposal of the customs takings.* Sir William Thompson and Garway had been employed as Commissioners of Accounts.† The new Commissioners were granted salaries of £2,000 per annum. Robert Sherwin ‡ was made Secretary—salary £400 ; and Richard Prowse Solicitor—salary £300.

The Commissioners were empowered to collect the subsidy and imposts, to appoint inferior officers by nomination, etc., from the Treasury or Exchequer, to remove or displace them by similar warrant, and to take security for their good behaviour ; to authorize the Receiver-General and the outport collectors to expend customs money for 'incidents' ; to administer oaths on customs matters ; to board and search vessels by day or night, and to search warehouses, etc., by day. Admiralty officers, Justices, Sheriffs, etc., were directed to assist them. They might grant Portage Bills,§ administer the Acts in encouragement of shipping, and compound petty seizures. Certain farming privileges previously allowed

* 'Thence to the Treasury Chambers, and there all the morning, to my great grief, put to do Sir G. Downing's work of dividing the customs for a year between the Navy, the Ordnance, and Tangier,' (Pepys, March 22, 1669). (Large loans had been taken on the customs in 1669, and Downing had spoken to Pepys in despair of being able to do no more out of the revenue than pay the interest. Thus it would seem that the seeds of national indebtedness were sown long before the time of James II. or William III.)

† Garway and Sir William Thompson overhauled Pepys' account in 1666. Says Samuel : 'Sir W. Coventry says Garway is a man not well used by the Court, though very stout to death, and hath suffered all that is possible for the king from the beginning.' Sir William Thompson was elected for the City, March 19, 1661. Says Pepys in 1666 : 'Capt. Cocke tells of Garway and those people what they object as to the mal-administration of things as to money. But they mean well, and will do well.' Pepys quotes a statement of revenue based on their calculations. There is an item of £2,390,000 collected and not accounted for. Says Pepys : 'So what has become of all this sum ?' Garway is also quoted as speaking against the maintenance of a standing army.

‡ 'Mighty strange to find myself sit here in committee with my hat on, while Mr. Sherwin stood bare as a clerk' (Pepys, January 17, 1665).

§ Sums of money as rewards to shipmasters for reporting their cargoes correctly.

and not determined were to endure till end of lease, and the Commissioners were to supervise the importation of the goods appertaining. They were exempted from answering for any deficiencies in the duties of Customs, etc., except such as were results of 'voluntary and particular misfeazance.'

Later* a Receiver-General was appointed, at a salary of £1,000. He was to keep separate accounts of the standing customs and temporary imposts, to pay in the moneys every Monday, and to furnish the Treasury and Board every Tuesday with a statement of the cash in his possession. The Treasury might demand an account every six months, or more frequently if necessary.

Several other important offices were 'erected.' For instance, Giles Dunster, John Man, and George Blake were made 'Surveyors Generall in all Ports and Creeks throughout the Realme.'

The institution of responsible officials in the place of mere speculators had been first ventured upon by the Long Parliament (*vide* p. 90). That the step was not taken earlier in Charles II.'s reign than 1671 may have been due to a desire to satisfy the outstanding claims of men like Wolstenholme and Jacob. There can be no doubt that the change was highly judicious, yet it might have been made much more effective had it not been thought fit to duplicate some of the existing offices. It seems that new collectors were appointed at many of the ports, yet the old 'customers,' with their 'controllers' and 'searchers,' were allowed to retain their offices as sinecures. When the 'patents' lapsed, other favourites were appointed, and the extraordinary system of having one set of officers to do the actual work, and another set of officers who were merely pensioners upon maritime trade, continued for more than a century.

* During the eighteenth century the system of accounting for cash lapsed, and the accounts became extensively muddled. The offices of Surveyors-General were abolished before the end of the seventeenth century, and revived during the eighteenth.

The arrangement of ports, etc., was as below :

Head Ports.	*Members.*	*Creeks.*
Berwick-on-Tweed	Nil.	The East Marches, Holy Island, Blyth Nooks, Alnmouth, Seaton Delaval.
Newcastle-on-Tyne	Shields Sunderland Hartlepool Stockton Whitby	with Middlesborough.
Hull	Scarborough Bridlington Grimsby	,, Gainsborough.
Boston	Nil	Saltfleet, Theddlethorpe, Mumby Chapel, Wainfleet, Fosdyke, Spalding.
Lynn	Nil	Cross Keys and Heacham.
	Wells	with Burnham.
Yarmouth	Blakeney.	
	Southwold	,, Lowestoft and Walberswick.
	Aldeburgh	,, Dunwich and Orford.
	Woodbridge	Nil.
Ipswich	Colchester	,, Harwich, Manningtree, Wivenhoe, and Brightlingsea.
	Maldon	,, East Mersea, West Mersea, Burnham, and Leigh.
London	Nil	Gravesend.
Sandwich	Rochester	with Queenborough.
	Milton.	
	Faversham.	
	Dover	,, Whitstable, Margate, Ramsgate, and Deal.
Chichester	Hythe	,, Folkestone.
	Rye	,, Romney, Lydd, and Winchilsea.
	Hastings	,, Pevensey.
	Lewes	,, Seaford and Newhaven.
	Shoreham	,, Brighton.
	Arundel	,, Selsey.

Head Ports.	*Members.*	*Creeks.*
Southampton ..	Portsmouth	with Emsworth.
	Cowes	,, Newport and Yarmouth.
	Nil	Lymington and Christchurch.
Poole	Nil	Wareham and Swanage.
	Weymouth	with Lulworth and Portland.
	Lyme Regis	,, Charmouth and Bridport.
Exeter	Nil	Axmouth, Exmouth, Lympton, Sidmouth, Powderham, Topsham, Seaton, Starcross, and Teignmouth.
	Dartmouth	with Totnes, Torbay, Brixham, and Salcombe.
	Barnstaple	,, Bideford, Appledore, and Clovelly.
	Ilfracombe	Nil.
Plymouth	Nil	Stonehouse and Saltash.
	Loowe.	
	Fowey.	
	Falmouth	with Truro, St. Mawes, and Penryn.
	Helston.	
	Penzance.	
	St. Ives.	
	Padstow.	
Bridgwater ..	Minehead	Nil.
Bristol	Nil	Uphill and Pill.
Gloucester ..	Nil	Severn from Bridgnorth to King's Road.
Cardiff	Swansea	with Chepstow, Newport, Penarth, Aberdare, Newton, Neath, and South of the Burry.
Milford	Pembroke	,, North of the Burry Llanelly, Carmarthen, Tenby, and Haverfordwest.
	Cardigan	,, Liskeard and Newport.
	Aberdovey	,, Aberystwith.

Head Ports.	*Members.*	*Creeks.*
Chester	Carnarvon	with Barmouth and Pwllheli.
	Beaumaris	,, Amlych and Holyhead.
	Conway	,, Mostyn, Bagillt, Birkenhead, Neston, and Hilbree.
	Liverpool	,, the south shore from the Red Stones, also Frodsham and Sankey Bridge.
	Poulton	,, Preston and the Wyre.
	Lancaster	,, Grange.
Carlisle	Whitehaven	,, Milnthorpe, Ravenglass, and Workington.
	Nil	West Marches.

The legal landing and shipping places in London were Brewer's Quay, Chester's Quay, Galley Quay, the Wool Dock, Custom-house Quay, Porter's Quay, Bear Quay, Sub's Dock, Wiggon's Quay, Young's Quay, Ralph's Quay, Dice Quay, Smart's Quay, Somers Quay, Lyon Quay, Botolph Wharf, Hammond's Quay, Gaunt's Quay, Cox's Quay, and Fresh Wharf. At these wharves all goods might be landed or shipped. Billingsgate was approved only for fish, salt, victuals, fuel, fruit, and the shipment of English building material. Bridge House, Southwark, was approved for corn for the provisioning of the City.

The goods allowed to be discharged 'in the stream'—*i.e.*, from vessels moored in the river—were iron, deals, and timber. These could be unladen between Westminster and Limehouse Dock, and the duties on them had to be paid prior to unshipment. The goods that could be *loaded* in the stream were horses, coal, beer, stone, corn, grain, and fish taken by denizens. Custom outward to be paid and cocket issued prior to shipment.

The officers levied fees upon merchants, masters, etc., for all revenue transactions of accompt, receipt, indenture, and declaration. Below appear a few of the authorized fees :

	£	s.	d.
For taking report of an English ship from the East Indies or beyond the Straits	0	2	6
For taking report of an English ship from Spain, West Indies, and the Plantations	0	2	0
For taking report of an English ship from other countries, including Scotland and Ireland ..	0	1	0
(Foreign ships paid double.)			

Custom Inward.

	£	s.	d.
For issuing a warrant to a Freeman of London ..	0	1	4
For issuing a warrant to any other merchant ..	0	2	0
For issuing a Bill of Sight	0	2	0
For any special employment	0	2	6
For issuing a certificate for foreign goods proceeding coastwise	0	1	0
For issuing a bond of any kind	0	0	6
To the collector for an oath	0	0	2
When goods were short entered to the amount of over 5s., they were sent to the King's Warehouse, and the warehouse-keeper charged per package for checking them on receipt ..	0	0	2
For a transire or let-pass for coastwise goods ..	0	0	6

Custom Outward.

	£	s.	d.
For the outward entry of a ship going beyond the Straits	0	4	0
For the outward entry of a ship going to other foreign parts	0	1	4
For the outward entry of a ship going to an outport in England	0	0	5
For the clearance of a ship outward	0	2	6
For endorsing a warrant or licence	0	0	8
For a cocket issued to a Freeman of London ..	0	1	8
For a cocket issued to any other merchant ..	0	2	6
For a cocket for goods going duty-free (having been duty-paid inward)	0	1	8
For a cocket for a ship going foreign and calling at an English outport	0	3	0
For a certificate for goods shipped duty-free on Treasury warrant	0	3	6
For a debenture for repayment of any part of outward custom	0	2	0
For a licence for a foreign ship to take beer as stores	0	2	0

There were many other clerical fees. The landing, shipping, and searching officers also charged fees on almost all transactions supervised by them. The landing and shipping officers' fees were usually taken in gross upon a number of transactions, and afterwards divided among the officers concerned. The searchers took large fees for rummage and final clearance of vessels outward.

The systems of assessment and collection were slovenly and imperfect, and the preventive regulations were erratically administered. There were no docks in England for merchantmen; vessels unloaded and took in cargo at the 'legal quays'; and when there was a glut of shipping, which often occurred, the ships had to lie off until berths were vacant. In special cases they were allowed, notwithstanding the regulations previously quoted, to discharge into lighters, when the document called a 'lighter-note,' instituted in the Commonwealth time, was found useful.

The gauging of wines, etc., was unreliable in the extreme. The gaugers used callipers to ascertain the lengths of casks, but the bung diameters were merely taken by perpendicular measurement. The contents were cast by the pen, and a set of tables first published by Henry Phillips in his 'Mathematical Manual,' and reprinted in the 'Index Vectigalium.' The method gave tolerably correct results as regarded computation, but there seems to have been considerable confusion upon the important matter of allowance for irregularities in shape. Worst of all, if the gauger checked his work by actual measurement it was likely that the measure used was incorrect, for the standard vessels were unreliable.*

The old gaugers relied upon the 'gauging-rod,' or dip-rod, a cumbrous and uncertain tool. It had a line of

* This was conclusively proved in 1688. One Wybard asserted that the standard 'wine and spirit' gallon measure in the London Guildhall was too small by seven cubic inches. On May 25, in the Guildhall, in presence of the Lord Mayor, the Commissioners of Excise, the King's Astronomer, and 'other ingenious gentlemen,' Mr. Shales of the Excise filled a brass vessel of 224 cubic inches 'with clear water,' and emptied it into the standard measure, which it exactly filled. Thus Wybard's assertion was proved correct, for the standard should have contained 231 cubic inches.

inches for showing the perpendicular diameter, a line for 'contenting' casks by diagonal measurement, and no less than eight additional lines for finding ullages of various kinds of casks 'by the dip.' These lines were adapted to standard casks only, 'as made by the London coopers,' and had been constructed by the primitive method of measuring successive wine gallons into the standard casks, inserting the rod, and 'marking off' the spaces covered by the liquid. The rods were thus marked for tuns, butts or pipes, puncheons, etc. There were separate rods for gauging ale, etc., the ale gallon being larger than the wine gallon (282 against 231). As the foreign-made casks were of irregular shape, and often wide of the standard contents, the results of such 'gauging' must have been perplexing to the retailer, especially when, as was often the case, the gaugers used an incorrect gallon measure to regulate their 'contenting' of casks, and a correct quart was used in measuring the goods for sale.*

In 1660 a subsidy, destined to become *perpetual* as 'The Old Subsidy,' was granted Charles for life, and the grant was accompanied by the issue of a new 'Book of Rates.' The tunnage duties therein expressed were almost similar to those levied by the Commonwealth. The wine duty for London was higher than for outports, and, as of old, when wine duty-paid at an outport was removed to London it was liable to the extra duty. The poundage was 1s. in the £1 value upon all goods imported and exported, except as below:

* In 1683 Thomas Everard, an excise officer, by an adaptation of the logarithmic scale, constructed a sliding-rule for computing gauges. It was of boxwood, 1 foot long, 1·2 inches broad, and 0·75 inch thick, and was an ingeniously devised and useful instrument. It is likely that as time went on the gauging became more accurate, for an excise handbook of the middle of the eighteenth century states that many of the customs officers of the port of London were extremely expert in cask-gauging.

English-taken fish, and fresh fish and bestial imported. The latter had always been duty-free.

Sheep's wool, imported. This was made duty-free in aid of the manufacture of cloth.

English fustians and garments, exported. These were made duty-free to encourage manufacture.

Woollen cloths, or 'old Draperies.' These were free of poundage, but paid a special tax of 3s. 4d. a cloth if exported by English; 6s. 8d. if by aliens, and the aliens also paid Carta Mercatoria duties.

English beer, exported. This also paid a special tax. If exported by English, it paid 2s. a tun; if by aliens, 6s.

The ancient regulation prohibiting the exportation of corn when above a specified price in England was maintained. So was the ancient Custom upon English wool, English lead, and English tin—exported by English—but aliens paid double duties on those articles, and the Carta Mercatoria duties as well. The aliens also paid double outward poundage on all goods exported by them which had been manufactured from English material, or produced in England.

The general tendency of the rates was decidedly against the foreigner. Below are a few items of illustration:

	Rate for Poundage.				*Poundage.*		
	£	*s.*	*d.*		*£*	*s.*	*d.*
Spanish tobacco, inward, per pound	0	10	0		0	0	6
Hops, inward, per cwt.	15	0	0		0	15	0
Woollen cloth, inward, per yard (made up)	8	10	0		0	8	6
Aqua vitæ, inward, per hogshead ..	4	0	0		0	4	0
Loaf sugar, inward, per cwt. ..	17	0	0		0	17	0
Plantation tobacco, per pound ..	0	1	8		0	0	1
Hops, outward, per cwt. ..	1	10	0		0	1	6
Woollen cloth, outward, by English, per yard	(Special tax)			(about)	0	0	1½
Aqua vitæ (English spirits), outward, per hogshead, by English	2	0	0		0	2	0
Loaf sugar, outward, per cwt., by English	0	10	0		0	0	6

It is interesting to note that goshawks were valued at £3 6s. 8d. each, and falcons at £4.

An ox outward was valued at £6 13s. 4d., poundage 6s. 8d. Among the skins specified in the outward list were those of the coney, kid, hare, fox, dog, cat, swan, squirrel, and badger. The list also had as separate items Sheffield knives and London knives.

Oranges and lemons inward were valued at 20s. per 1,000, poundage 1s. Ordinary apples were valued at 4d. per bushel, pippins at 1s. Eggs were 1s. 8d. per 120, poundage 1d.

With a few exceptions, the poundage was almost similar to that imposed during the time of the Commonwealth.

Besides the subsidies inward and outward, there was granted a tax which afterwards was known as 'The Additional Duty,' and which became perpetual in a later reign. It took the form of an added tunnage on wine, and an added poundage of 6d. in each £1 value upon all wrought silk other than that of the East Indies, and all linen except Irish linen and calico; also an extra 1d. per pound duty on Plantation tobacco. The added tunnage was to be paid within nine months after importation, the added poundage within twelve, and these postponed duties were to be secured by bond, entered into when the goods were landed. Thus the extra duty was for a space forborne, as all the duties on bonded goods are forborne at present until clearance from warehouse.

In 1662 the One per Cent. Inward and Outward duties (also destined to endure) were granted. These were vague imitations of the Long Parliament's tax for the relief of Moorish captives. They were levied upon goods brought from or taken to the Mediterranean beyond Malaga in English ships with less than two decks, and carrying less than sixteen guns with two men to each gun, and were intended to stimulate the use of vessels capable of resisting the Moorish pirates. (This tax was included in the 'Act against Frauds,' quoted later.)

These, with one or two temporary imposts, were the only important customs granted during Charles's reign. The Coinage Duty, a special tunnage of 10s. on foreign wine, beer, and vinegar, and 20s. on foreign spirits, although collected by the Customs, may scarcely be considered a customs tax, for the proceeds went to the maintenance of the Mint. It is necessary at this point to abandon tariffs, and approach matters even more important.

The most momentous statutes of the reign were those dealing with navigation and the Plantation trade. Under the Act 'for the Encouragement and increasing of Shipping and Navigation,' passed in the year of Charles's accession, many classes of goods were made liable to aliens' Custom, even if imported by denizens, unless in English-built ships, with English masters, and three-fourths manned by English mariners, and brought direct from the places of growth or manufacture. By 'English-built' was meant built and owned in England, Ireland, or the Plantations; by 'English mariners,' the king's liege subjects from the same dominions. Several subsequent statutes amended and explained this Act, and the main provisions then stood as below:

Goods might not be taken from Asia, Africa, or America to England or Ireland except in 'English ships' that were 'English manned,' and direct from the place of growth or manufacture. Sugar, tobacco, ginger, cotton, indigo, and woods used in dyeing, all which were entitled 'enumerated Plantation goods,' might not be put on board ship in the Plantations,* except for landing at other Plantations, or direct carriage to England. If intended for a foreign port they were to be brought to England, landed, and then reshipped for their destination. Ship-masters

* When the word 'Plantations' is used without qualification such as 'Spanish,' French,' etc., it must be taken to mean 'English Plantations.'

proceeding from England or Ireland to the Plantations had to enter into bond before an English or Irish collector of customs to bring their Plantation goods to England direct, and if they entered a Plantation port from foreign to load cargo they had to give similar security there before shipment. European goods for the Plantations were to be first brought to England, landed there, and reshipped, except victual, horses, and *servants*, from Scotland or Ireland. Similar exemption was granted to wine of Madeira and the Azores laden at places of production, and goods laden at ports south and east of the Cape of Good Hope. These excepted goods might go to the Plantations direct, if the regulations as to English shipping and mariners were complied with. The Plantation governors were to take oath to provide to the best of their power for the due observance of the Navigation and Plantation laws. Foreign ships might only bring goods to England direct from the countries in which such ships were built. They were excluded from the Plantation trade. Coastwise traffic in England and Ireland was to be in " English " ships, with " English " mariners.

It is to be hoped the above account of these important regulations is understandable. The main points of their subsequent history will be duly indicated, but it must be clearly understood there will not be space in which to explain fully all their meanderings. Readers will perceive that they were inspired by the Commonwealth Act of Navigation, and that two ideals were steadfastly kept in view, one being permanent English dominance at sea, the other the establishment of England as 'a universal Staple.' It cannot be denied that these ideals were realized.

Yet even at the outset colonial merchants, especially those located in the American Plantations, were dubious, and later the American colonists came to regard the complicated restrictions as intolerable. Their goods were rendered dear in foreign markets, for some one had to assist in bearing the expense of the extra journey, and of the unnecessary unshipment and relading. Frequently vessels from the Plantations, which might have performed the direct voyage to Europe in safety, were cast away on the storm-swept English coast, while attempting to reach Cowes, Bristol, or London, in order to land their cargoes. This of course tended to a great extent to prevent the colonists from trading with Europe, and gave England almost a monopoly of Plantation traffic. The Acts bore hard upon Ireland, too, for all Plantation goods carried thither had first to be turned over in England. It remains substantial matter of debate whether the subsequent triumphs of England in naval war, which were hugely assisted by this method of making a large number of her sons familiar with the sea, and the vast increase in her carrying tonnage and oversea trade, were or were not discounted by the gradual impoverishment of Ireland, and that irremediable disaster, the severance of England from the thirteen mighty Provinces. There remains one thing to be said in favour of the old legislators. Whilst striving to 'corner' trade and shipping, they did not altogether forget their duty towards national manhood.

Parliament continued to exert itself in attempts, not always wise or well-directed, to regulate industries. It bountied the woollen manufacture at the graziers' expense by prohibiting the exportation of wool. Ireland and the Channel Islands were included by the prohibiting Act, but it was provided that they and England might trade with each other. The provisions soon had to be strengthened. 'Owling,' or smuggling of wool outward, became a common practice, especially in Kent and Sussex.*

Foreign bone-lace, cutwork, embroidery, etc., were prohibited, and, still further to assist manufacturers, expor-

* It appears that the French Government secretly encouraged this illegal traffic, being desirous of destroying the English woollen industry.

tation was encouraged by repealing the aliens' double outward custom on English products, and making the rate the same as with denizens, except with respect to coals.

Meanwhile, as these measures impoverished the agriculturists, Acts had to be passed 'in Encouragement of Tillage.' The poundage outward on horses and cattle was reduced, and an impost levied on imported sheep and cattle. The duty on foreign corn was increased. It would seem that not only did the legislators believe that an Act of Parliament was as direct an instrument of enduring benefit as a fine harvest or a favourable trade-wind, but that they conceived that two such instruments might be made to work in different directions without friction.

An Act was passed in the early part of the reign prohibiting the blending together of wines of various countries, and the adulteration of wine. The adulterants quoted were cider, perry, honey, sugar, molasses, raisin juice, herbs, and *flesh*. The people of England must have been sadly deficient in discrimination if their palates were not sufficient protection against such grotesque ingredients of fraud. The mixing of wine with isinglass, brimstone, and lime was forbidden. It is scarcely conceivable that merchants would use such articles as 'adulterants.' Isinglass has generally been deemed a valuable agent in 'fining'; brimstone and lime, one might reasonably conceive, could only have been used in the cleansing of foul casks.

The celebrated 'Act against Frauds,' issued soon after the Restoration, seems to have been drafted, so far as its preventive provisions obtained, after comprehensive study of the Long Parliament's ordinance of 1644, and certain other Commonwealth enactments. It allowed only three days for vessels in transit between Gravesend and London (to prevent smuggling in the middle reaches). At all outports vessels from foreign were to go direct to the place of unlading. Masters were to report their cargoes on oath. Small parcels were to be placed in the King's Warehouse for security. Wharfingers, carmen, porters, watermen, etc., dealing with uncustomed goods, were made liable to heavy penalties. Aliens under twenty-one years of age were forbidden from entering goods as owners. Sight and sufferance entries were to be promptly perfected. Mail-boats were not to carry merchandise unless specially privileged. Goods were not to be carried coastwise without sufferance and cocket, and a certificate of their being landed in the kingdom was to be furnished within six months. Scotch goods were to be customed at Berwick or Carlisle. The officers were enjoined not to show partiality to merchants.

C. 7, of 25 Car. II., forbade the Plantations dealing *with each other* without first bringing the goods to England, unless certain duties were paid at shipment, and accounted for to the English Commissioners of Customs. The Plantation officers might take these dues in kind if money were not forthcoming.

During this reign there were immense inland impositions, and the odious tax of 'Hearth Money'—a duty upon chimneys—was instituted. The importation of fat cattle from Ireland was prohibited. (This last Act was diligently evaded, and the importers frequently mixed a few English bullocks with the smuggled 'runts,' so that if the herd were seized they might be able to enter action for damages. In 1680 it was enacted that in all such cases the English cattle should be forfeited as well as the Irish.)

Amongst the Treasury papers preserved in the Record Office there is a terse and lucid statement, dated 1680, which deals with the revenues collected during the latter part of Charles II.'s reign. From this it appears that the net yield of the customs in the port of London, for the year ending Lady Day, 1680, was £554,964, and in the whole of the outports £136,941; total, £691,905. This was called the 'net' because it represented the sum remaining after debentures, etc., had been paid. But there was a charge of about £46,000 for 'management,' so the amount paid to the Exchequer may be taken as about £646,000. During a year and a half, ending Michaelmas, 1680, the Treasurer of the Navy received out of the customs about £476,000. But it appears that loans had been taken in anticipation of customs receipts, and out of the 'Loans on Customs' the naval Treasurer had received about £234,000 more. It appears that ordinarily the navy cost about £350,000 yearly. The year and a half quoted had been a time of stress. The military expenses were about £200,000 a year. The king's allowance for household expenses, as settled in 1667, was £90,000 a year. Perhaps, after all that has been said, Charles was not so very extravagant. £90,000 was not a great allowance for household expenses, but it appears that his servants' wages were often overdue.

In 1662 the Attorney-General proceeded in the Exchequer against a merchant, for the double custom on certain goods imported 'contrary to the new Act of Navigation.' The defendant demurred, pleading that the goods were forfeitable under the Act granting the subsidy of tunnage and poundage, and that if he paid the double custom demanded his goods might afterwards be seized. The Court overruled the demurrer, stating that after the Attorney-General had 'informed' upon a penal law no further proceedings could be taken.

During the same year a similar action was entered with regard to a quantity of Asiatic spices imported from Holland. Verdict for the Crown, but the defendant pleaded in arrest of judgment that it had not been particularly stated in the charge that the goods were 'not of the growth of Holland.' The quibble was successful.

In the same year it was reaffirmed that when an importer brought several parcels of wine in different ships, such parcels being each of nine and under ten tuns, his goods were liable to Prisage, unless proof were furnished that at time of lading there was not room on board for more.

In 1663 Sir William Waller, who farmed the Prisage and Butlerage of England, took action against Giles Travers, a London citizen, who had imported wines at several outports, and had raised the novel plea that as London citizens were exempt from Prisage such exemption obtained on their wine even if not imported into London. Hardres defended Travers, and displayed wonderful skill in twisting plain statements into puzzling conclusions, and furbishing up old records.

He quoted several singular charters of the City of London in support of his contention that wide discrimination should be made between the charter freeing London citizens of Prisage and that granting exemption to the 'barons' of the Cinque Ports. It appeared from his statement that there were charters allowing—

1. That in the City of London a man might be arrested for debt before the debt became due.

2. That a beadle, by mere virtue of his office, had power to search a house for suspicious persons.

3. That an executor might pay a debt on a simple contract prior to a debt secured under bond.

In discriminating between the charter exempting London citizens and that exempting the Cinque Ports barons, he insisted that the latter was granted because the Cinque Ports defended the realm, but the former for advancement of London trade. He claimed that the City of London was 'the Heart and Epitome of the whole kingdom, the King's Chamber, the Merchants whereof fill his Coffers by their customs paid,' and that the privilege of exemption from Prisage, being annexed to the *goods* of the citizen, obtained in every English port into which such goods might be brought for landing.

It was urged for the plaintiff that exemption had never before been granted to a London citizen except for wine imported into London. Hardres replied that complete exemption had been intended by the granter of the charter, and that 'non-user' could never destroy the validity of a grant. Therefore he claimed that London citizens were Prisage-free *per totam Angliam.*

The barons decided in favour of the plaintiff, Sir Matthew Hale, Chief Baron, making a special point of the fact that he had found, by consulting the Red Book of the Exchequer, that in the days of the Edwards exemption from Prisage throughout the realm had been occasionally granted for limited periods to certain guilds of merchants; that in all such cases it had been particularly stated that such exemption was *per totum Regnum;* and that had Edward III. intended to make the London citizens Prisage-free throughout the realm that provision would have been fully expressed in the charter.

It appears that during the Plague of 1665 the foreign trade of the port of London was terribly hampered. Defoe discoursed upon this, stating that all the 'extraordinary' (temporary) officers of customs were dismissed. This is borne out by Pepys' remark that in November, 1665, Sir G. Carteret was amazed to find the Upper Pool 'so empty of boats,' and the Custom-house quays deserted.

Defoe stated that the trade from London to the Levant was stopped for a time, as soon as tidings of the plague's ravages in London reached the Mediterranean ports. The statement may have been correct, for during the seventeenth century the Mediterranean coast-dwellers were frequently visited by the ghastly disorder, and they who are thus afflicted rarely miss a chance of imposing restrictions upon folk who suffer occasionally.

But much of Defoe's history of the Plague was mere opportunist journalism. For instance, he asserted that the eastern ports, profiting by the isolation of London, exported immense quantities of goods to Holland. Yet Holland and England were at war. He also stated that during the height of the disorder the ships lay in tiers from the Pool 'down the river as low as Gravesend.' Yet that extremely keen-eyed observer, Samuel Pepys, spent much of the autumn of 1665 upon the river, and failed to record anything of the kind.

It is apparent that the Excise revenue suffered severely. It was let to a host of speculators, and the records for this period contain many copies of requests for remission of rent. In the next great lease a clause appeared, providing that allowance should be made if the plague revived.

The account of this reign would be incomplete without a further reference to the immortal diarist. Pepys found time, amid all his gossiping and prying, to converse occasionally with Sir Philip Warwick, historian and economist. Warwick appears to have considered the assessments made by the Long Parliament and Commonwealth more effective than those made by Charles's advisers. In this he was of course correct, but his estimate of the amounts raised by the Parliament and Protector may be discounted. The country was cheaply governed during the interval between the death of one Charles and the accession of the other, no matter what Sir Philip might think—cheaply and effectively; its army and navy then, compared with the forces during Charles's reign, were luminous items of instructiveness.

Warwick even went so far as to coach Pepys upon the balance of trade. It is doubtful whether at this point Pepys did not become muddled—perhaps his own record of the argument was not correctly stated—but the old slyboots dismissed the matter with the pregnant remark, 'Though I do not remember the argument, yet methought there was a great deal in what he said.'

Sir Philip appears to have been a kind of amiable and self-elected oracle at the Treasury. He worried Pepys a deal with figures, yet to the end Samuel held him a good man; and no doubt he was, for he would not talk even statistics on a Sunday. Yet on the death of the Lord Treasurer in 1667 Pepys mournfully remarked that the slowness and remissness of the illustrious deceased had gone as far to undo the nation as anything else that had happened, which would indicate that Sir Philip's advice had either not been taken, or had been taken with disastrous results.

Pepys, as the world knows, though an industrious official, was not over-scrupulous. He not only pocketed bribes, but defrauded the revenue more than once.* While on important public business at Gravesend he bought a quantity of smuggled goods at 'a blind ale-house,' and afterwards philosophized over the smugglers, the evils of smuggling, and other incidental matters. His dealings with prize goods were extremely crooked. One of his little hauls was temporarily seized by the customs officers, and the constable left in charge, no doubt realizing that Pepys was wide-awake, made a subtle proposal, a proposal which Pepys was merely too shrewd to accept.

Several imposts on foreign merchandise were levied during the short reign of James II. One took the form of an increase of the tunnage rates on wines and vinegar, the proceeds of the extra duty being appropriated to 'weighty and important occasions' and repairing naval ships. The Prisage, which for some years had been given to royal favourites, was by this Act shorn of much profit, the holders being made to pay an abated duty upon their prised goods.

The second impost was upon tobacco and sugar, Plantation tobaccos and sugars being preferentially treated. The new duties might be postponed if bond

* It is evident that such matters were thought little of in olden days, yet at certain periods corruption reached such a pitch that it was found necessary to issue special enactments. For instance, see 33 Hen. VI., c. 3—a statute aimed expressly against Exchequer officials.

were given for their payment within a specified time. The proceeds went to the supply of the king's 'weighty and important occasions,' and the discharge of debts due to the late king's servants and family.

The third was upon silks, linens, calicoes, and spirits, to endure for a period of five years. The collecting officers were enjoined to keep a special account of the proceeds, and pay them into the Exchequer weekly. Loans were invited up to £400,000, in anticipation of receipts, interest being guaranteed at 8 per cent. per annum, payable quarterly. Thus was established a seductive and deadly precedent, and from this period the 'funding' of taxes became fashionable. Whence of course England's National Debt, that seems likely to endure as long as England herself.*

Charles II.'s Act 'for the Encouragement of Tillage' was amended, it being provided that the price of corn, in accordance with which the inward duty on corn lapsed or fluctuated, and the exportation of corn was permitted or prohibited, should be stated by the justices in the counties at the quarter sessions, and by the City Fathers in London twice a year. The prices thus fixed were to be advised to the various collectors of customs.

It is noticeable that the preventive statutes up to this period frequently contained references to extensive smuggling. These became more frequent as the tariff grew more complicated, but the illicit traffic did not attain full development till the time of George II. The account must tarry till that picturesque period is approached, when there was a systematic and permanent traffic in contraband, sympathized with by the bulk of the population of the maritime counties.

'The Glorious Revolution' occurred in 1688. The first Parliament, which was to a large extent composed

* The impost appears to have produced only £93,000.

of self-elected members, did one good thing by abolishing the 'Hearth Money' tax. Having thus commended themselves to the nation, the legislators proceeded to grant money without stint. All Charles and James's revenues, except Hearth Money, were temporarily continued for William's benefit. The proceeds of James's three imposts were appropriated thus : £60,000 to satisfy the outstanding claims of Charles II.'s unpaid servants, £600,000 from the residue to reward the United Provinces for having provided England with a king, and the rest towards the subjugation of Ireland and the war with France.

(In 1689 tunnage and poundage were formally granted, and a loan of £500,000 invited upon the proceeds.)

Special commissioners and officers were appointed to carry out the Act prohibiting the exportation of wool, and it was ordered that wool taken coastwise entered at the intended port of shipment before being brought within five miles of the coast. A central account of all wool carried coastwise was instituted at the London Custom-house. The exportation of wool from Ireland was limited to traffic between the principal Irish and the western English ports, so that there should be less opportunity of running Irish wool to the Continent.

French goods, and foreign spirits such as brandy and *aqua vitæ*, were prohibited during continuance of the war with France. The excise duties on tea, coffee, and chocolate, levied on the goods *after infusion*, were repealed, and a customs tax substituted, to be paid at time of landing. Foreign 'thrown' silk was prohibited, except Italian silk, imported in accordance with the Navigation Act.

'The impost of 1690,' granted upon fifty-five articles of foreign merchandise, came into force on Boxing Day. The articles made liable were linen, silks, and calico, besides many classes of goods extensively used in manufactures—goods such as unwrought iron, raw silk, steel, and wool, together with such absolute aids towards comfortable existence as soap and candles. With most of the fifty-five articles the impost took the form of an addition to the poundage. The provisions as to the rating of various kinds of paper were remarkably complicated.

The Board of Customs informed the Treasury that the privateers brought in many French prizes, but that the customs officers, who were supposed to take an account of the goods, were often not allowed to go on board until the privateers' crews had helped themselves freely to the best of the captures, while the collectors, having to appoint extra tidesmen to look after the wounded and captives, had no time left in which to do their ordinary revenue work. The Treasury promised to appoint special commissioners and tidesmen to look after the privateers and their prisoners, but a long time elapsed ere the promise was fulfilled.

During the war in Ireland many Irish protestants fled to England, carrying their goods and effects with them. In most cases the Treasury allowed them to land and remove the goods and effects duty-free. The collectors on the western coast of England were often directed to furnish sums to the Commissioners of Transport, to be used in conveying Dutch and Danish mercenaries to Ireland.

The tobacco manufacturers of Bristol complained to the Board of the customs method of deducting 5 per cent. from the drawback payable on tobacco manufactured into roll and exported, the said deduction being intended to account for the addition of moisture during manufacture. They used the ancient plea that if the Customs continued the method the trade would leave the country. The Board, in forwarding the application to the Treasury, advised that full drawback should be taken on 'the bright fair kinds,' admitting that after importation the merchant had to cut away the stalk and abandon it, thus losing much of the weight he had paid duty on. But they insisted on continuing the deduction with regard to 'the darker kind.' Later they relented, and advised that full drawback should be allowed in all cases.

An English frigate, after a desperate engagement, in which her captain and sailing-master were killed, had captured two French men-of-war that were engaged in convoying sixteen merchant ships, and brought the captains prisoners into Plymouth. The customs collector took charge of them, and during the night they escaped from his custody by filing through an iron bar, and appropriating a small boat which lay in the harbour. It was stated in the report that the frigate would have captured the whole fleet of merchantmen if darkness had not come on.

During 1689 the Board of Customs received hundreds of applications for appointment to the office of landing-waiter at London, although there were only thirty such situations in the port. All the applicants were nominees of influential persons, and had been referred to the Board by the Treasury. Shortly afterwards a Treasury minute conveyed to the Commissioners the king's expressed opinion that many customs situations had been traded. The Board replied that they were 'greately sencible' of the aspersion, and reminded the Treasury that by law anyone who bartered an appointment was held incapable of public office. They insisted that under their method of appointing landing-waiters strict selection was practised, each Commissioner taking his turn in nominating a candidate, and the appointment being discussed by a full Board. The king then intimated that it would be better if a majority of the Commissioners undertook to nominate.

In 1690 certain Irish Jacobites who had escaped to England made an attempt to take ship at Dover for France, but were detected. It was found that the Dover surveyor of customs had assisted in trying to secure their escape, and he was thrown into prison with them.

Many detentions of cargoes under the Navigation Act took place, but the Act was not tyrannically enforced.

Most of the detentions were of goods of one European nation brought in the ships of another, and in such cases the parties concerned petitioned the Treasury, and were usually let off with an injunction to compensate the detaining officers. Occasionally an English captain would arrive with Asiatic goods, and a crew consisting mainly of aliens. Then the goods he brought became liable to aliens' duties; but the captain might obtain remission if he proved that he left England with an English crew, that sickness and death had reduced their number, and that he had been compelled to engage foreigners.

A petition for a customs appointment in Dorset reached the Treasury, and they referred it to the Board. The Board recommended it to be 'sunk,' stating that since the prohibition of commerce with France there had been little genuine trade on the southern English coast. So little custom was taken at the Kentish ports that the officers' salaries had to be paid out of the London receipts.

The Archbishop of Dublin asked the Treasury to let him have an officer to inspect certain goods which he was about to send from London to Ireland, stating that if this were not done the officers at Chester would charge exorbitant duties, 'making every pair of shoes, not cobbled, new.'

The Receiver of the 4½ per cent. duties in the Leeward Islands informed the Board that he could not send his account and the proceeds* of collection to England for lack of convoy, and because the rate of exchange on bills from the West Indies was 15 to 20 per cent.

During this reign many heavy inland impositions were made, including a huge excise impost and a searching poll-tax. Most of the taxes had been 'funded,' and the national indebtedness swelled daily. Fiscal schemes, and devices towards borrowing, were the standing topics of parliamentary debate.

* Duties collected chiefly in kind.

The eleventh Act of 1690 expressed alarm. ‘Whereas many great revenues, sums of money, and provisions, have been expended, granted, raised, and assigned, since the 5th November, 1688, on which day the king landed in England. . . .’ Thus ran the preamble. A commission was appointed to take account of the revenues from lands, firstfruits, fines, forfeitures, subsidies, and imposts, and of the nation’s ships, goods, and stores. The Act stated that large sums had been granted for the navy during James’s reign, yet the ships had neither been repaired nor properly maintained. This may have been a suggestion that James or some of his officials had carried off the money, or it may have been designed to avert responsibility, for it is certain that great peculation was practised during William’s time. The contracts were often made at 50 per cent., in some cases at 100 per cent., above the market price.

The prohibition of commerce with France having been evaded by the bringing in of French cargoes falsely described as prizes, and by the agency of gangs of armed smugglers, an Act was passed which among other preventive provisions contained clauses amplifying the powers of the magistracy, and authorizing sessions justices to deal summarily with smuggling cases. In 1691 the exportation of munitions of war to France, and the taking passage thither, were made acts of high treason. Exporters of merchandise to France were made liable to the Statute of Præmunire. In spite of these prohibitions an immense amount of wool was run, principally from Romney Marsh, and the revenue sloops on the Kentish coast were quite unable to cope with the desperate and well-armed smugglers.

A miller of Cheltenham planted a field with tobacco. The excise officers destroyed the crop, and the miller was fined £360. He approached the Treasury, pleading ignorance of the law, and the fine was remitted.

A spy who had been sent by the English Government to France returned, and accused Abraham Hough, a customs officer stationed at Margate, of having sent information to the French, by means of which the mission of espionage was frustrated. He denounced Hough and several other customs officers as Jacobites, and expressed a hope that there were 'none of that kidney on the Board of Customs.' The Treasury exculpated the officers.

The Bristol collector of customs, suspecting collusion between some of his officers and the Bristol merchants, employed a spy to watch proceedings, and discovered many flagrant irregularities. The officers concerned were fined £500, and compelled to exhibit themselves publicly in Bristol during Assize time, and to display a paper declaring the nature of their offences.

It appears that the officers exerted themselves to obtain custom upon wrecked goods, and thus frequently came into collision with the proprietors of 'droits.' The Lord Warden of the Cinque Ports complained that the collector at Deal had forcibly taken wreck from the custody of the Admiralty sergeant, and held it till the duties were paid. But both the Board and the Treasury upheld the collector.

In 1692 the Commissioners wrote the Treasury that much of the clandestine carrying out of coin and bullion, and the illegal importation of East India goods from Holland, was conducted by officers of the navy.

The officers of customs at Whitby sent news that five French privateers had chased an English vessel into Robin Hood's Bay, and had held the master captive till he sent to Scarborough for £200 as ransom. The privateers had been observed hovering for some time, and it was thought they were on the look out for an opportunity of carrying Jacobites to France.

News came from 'down West' that a French privateer of twenty-eight guns had engaged an English ketch of ten guns, which was carrying a cargo of pressed men to the fleet. The ketch was captured, and the Frenchmen put ashore her cargo, consisting of 106 victims of the press. This privateer had captured five English merchantmen within sight of Padstow.

James, Lord Mordington, petitioned 'the King's Most Excellent Majesty' as follows: 'A seizure of silks, muslins, and other things prohibited by law, was made lately in the cuntrey in a Coach-and-Six, and the same was carried into your Majestie's warehouse [in] London in the custody of Mr. Isaacson, booke-keeper of the said warehouse, and are to be condemned Thursday next, and One Hundred Pounds only to be returned into Your Majesty's Exchequer: wherfor your Petitioner humbly prays Your Majesty wd. be gratiously pleased to grant him an order for your Majestie's share in kind, by which your Majesty will preserve yr. Petitioner, his Lady, and childring, from sterving, at present not having bread,' etc. 'Granted—to send to the Commissioners of the Customes, to know at what value these things are appraised, and how much the king's part comes to.'

A sheaf of charges against the collector of Bristol reached the Treasury, with a letter signed 'Ambrose Williams.' The papers were referred to the Board. (The Commissioners then furnished a general statement on the matters involved, and referred to a recent special survey of the port of Bristol.)

There were nineteen charges, dealing with receipt of bribes and presents, composition of frauds, appropriation of officers' seizure awards, receipt of a sum of £100 from a merchant concerned in the cargo of a ship called *The Constant Love* (as acknowledgment of services rendered in obtaining removal of an embargo), neglect to destroy a crop of English-grown tobacco (in consideration of a present of fifteen guineas), illegal release of a vessel detained under the Navigation Act (recompense, a pair of silver candlesticks), *impolite behaviour towards the Patent Officers of the port*, etc.

The Board reported at great length upon the matter. 'Ambrose Williams,' they stated, 'is a person unknowne to us, and, tho' enquired after, not to be found.' As to the affair of *The Constant Love*, they had summoned the merchant named as briber, a 'Mr. Gardiner, of good reputation,' and he had furnished denial upon oath. As to the English-grown tobacco, they had found that the collector was absent from the port at the time quoted, and they had failed to obtain corroboration with regard to the bribe of fifteen guineas. In short, after spending much time in investigation, 'the said severall persons being heard face to face,' they had decided to 'support' the collector. They ended by referring to a mass of enclosed 'testimony, which,' said they, 'is quite opposed' (conflicting).*

The following is a copy of a statement sent by the Board to the Treasury, with reference to disputes as to interest due on duties in arrear:

'*The State of the Account between the Officers of the Customs and the East India Company.*

'The East India Company are Debtors to their Ma^{ts}. for the Interest for forbearance on severall Entrys, made up from ye times of their first Entring at Sight to the placing the Same to Acco^{t}. in ye King's officers books, The Summe of :

	£	s.	d.
	5,428	10	2
'The said Comp^{y} pretend that by reason that they paid in severall considerable Summs of money in part for the duties on their Said goods, severall months & days before ye quite P'fecting their said Entrys (which indeed wee doe find they did) that they are overcharged in that Acco^{t} of Interest† ye Summe of	663	18	6
	4,764	11	8

* The collector had previously been instrumental in discovering extensive frauds, and securing the pecuniary punishment of certain officers concerned (*vide* p. 130).

† The Customs had charged the Company interest on duties

	£	s.	d.
	4,764	11	8
'And more that they say is due to them for the Interest on Severall Tallys, which was not allowed them, this Acco^{t} being depending, ye Summ of	1,492	10	4
	3,272	1	4
'There is likewise due from the Said Company for their Duties on the last 4 Shipps ye Summe of—Estimate—	45,000	0	0
which they have not fully p'fected, because they would have allowance for Damage on tea, as they pretend, because at ye Sale they had not for ye whole anything considerable more than what ye same was sold for.*	48,272	1	4
'And they make another pretence: That a certaine Commodity they formerly past as floretta Yarne, at 8 p.c. value, is upon a better information a Raw Silk: But this is but a bare pretence, because Raw Silk is charged but with 5 p. cent. for this new Duty of Impost, when as Floretta Yarne, being a manufacture, is Lyable to 20 P. Cent.			
'Of which Summe of	48,272	1	4
according to this own Acco^{t} they have paid and promise to speedily pay in ye remainder, or one ½ thereof as ye last week and ye other within one month after: Yet for all that promise of their Govern^{or} Sr. Thom^{as} Cook: They have in fact paid not one penny more'	20,000	0	0
	28,272	1	4

From the above it seems that the Company were either in straits, or conscious of the undoubted fact that the customs accounts were in a muddled condition.

Later the Board complained afresh, and furnished, in place of the previous 'Estimate' of duties due, what purported to be an exact account.

---

overdue. From this charge, and the total of the duties, the Company claimed a deduction on account of duties paid in advance, and of interest due on outstanding tallies.

* This means that the Company claimed to have made little profit by sale of the tea, the goods being damaged by salt water, and the Customs having failed to make allowance for the said damage.

'CUSTOM HOUSE,
'31st August, 1692.

'TO THE RIGHT HON[BLE] THE LORDS COMMRS. OF THEIR MATYS. TREASURY.

'*The Commrs. for managing and causing to be Leavied and collected their Maties. Customs, Subsidy, and other Dutys.*

'The said Commrs. (after many disappointments in the daies wherein the Committee of the East India Company have promised to satisfy their demands of such sums as appeare to bee due to their Maties. from that Company, as well from the Customs and Imposts on the Entryes of their ffoure Last Ships, as upon Accomp[t] of Interest for the time wherein they failed of their former payments) thinke it their duty to lay before their Lordpps. (in the paper thereunto annexed) the present state of that Account, as it was adjusted by the Patent Officers to the 17th Currant, and since sent to the Govern[or] of the Company, without further satisfaccon than a promise of payment, which has hitherto proved ineffectuall: Humbly submitting it to their Lordpps. that such speedy and effectual Remedy may bee taken upon the Bonds they have entred into upon this Occasion as to their Lordpps. shall seeme meet.

'C. GODOLPHIN.
G. BOOTHE.
J. O. WERDEN.
ROBERT SOUTHWELL.
ROBERT CLAYTON.'

They annexed a statement as to separate amounts due upon the cargoes of certain vessels belonging to the Company 'for sights* yet unperfected.' It appears that the following sums were owed and overdue:

* 'Sights': the entries 'upon sight,' sometimes called 'entries upon view.' These were documents permitting the Company's officials to 'view' the cargoes upon landing. An account of the goods was then taken by both Company and Customs, and the Company were expected to 'perfect' each sight within a specified period, and pay the duty.

	£	s.	d.	£	s.	d.
Upon the cargo of the *Princess Anne* (Captain Maurice)				15,200	15	8½
Upon the cargo of the *Josiah* (Captain Gayer)				13,334	19	10
Upon the cargo of the *Royal James and Mary* (Captain Buck)				9,106	4	0½
Upon the cargo of the *Defence* (Captain Heath)				10,384	6	8
				48,026	6	3
As interest at 6 per cent. on the respective sums from the dates on which they were payable: £802 3s. 11d., £686 2s. 0d., £467 0s. 8d., £532 11s. 8d.				2,487	18	3
Arrears of interest upon other cargoes, incurred before November 1, 1690 ..				5,175	5	7
Paid in part of this account	23,272	1	4			
Interest to be forborne on account of above payment	419	4	7			
	23,691	5	11			
Moneys due ..	31,998	4	2			
	55,689	10	1	55,689	10	1

At the foot of this account the Commissioners added the significant statement:

'Besides ye Customes for Tea and all Dutys for their China Ware in the *Defence*, for which wee had noe value to compute ye same by.'

(This statement is difficult to understand,* but it would almost seem that the Company had succeeded in landing, viewing, and disposing of the greater part of the *Defence*'s cargo without the cognizance of the customs officers. For it appears from a general study of the records that at

* It is by no means safe to draw confident deductions from statements such as the above. The Commissioners themselves were often misled as to the true condition of affairs with regard to sums due, many of the clerical officers being vastly in arrear with their work. The clumsy methods of expression adopted by certain members of the secretarial staff, and the grotesque fashion in which they stated matters of accompt, render the documents extremely puzzling to the direct thinker.

this time the duties were not levied as percentages on the gross prices at the sales.)

A petition reached the Treasury from Mary Jones, daughter-in-law to the late collector of Lyme Regis. She stated that when the duke of Monmouth landed in England he took by force £200 from the Lyme Regis customs receipts. Her husband, who had succeeded his father as collector, had been ordered to make good the loss, and, dying shortly afterwards, had left his estate burdened with the charge. The Board reported favourably upon her petition, and the Treasury granted it. There were other customs charges on the estate, and the Board seem to have thought that this remission would enable the widow to pay them.

Another huge impost was laid upon many foreign articles, some being surtaxed by rate, others by direct additions to duty. This tax, which became historic as 'The Impost of 1692,' was appropriated to 'the king's extraordinary occasions.' The odious increases in the salt poundage commenced with this Act. The tunnage on French wine was increased, and an additional 25 per cent. *ad valorem* laid on other French goods.

During the time of the Commonwealth an ordinance had been issued against the false packing of butter and cheese for exportation. Its provisions had been practically reaffirmed by a statute of Charles II., but afterwards the control of the export trade in butter and cheese had been dominated by the Cheesemongers' Society of London. This syndicate, under pretence of enforcing the Act, frequently sent its agents to the various ports, where they behaved in arbitrary fashion, 'to the great oppression of farmers.' William's parliament prohibited the unfair preferences and extortionate actions of the London agents, and directed shipmasters to forbear the practice, previously common, of refusing shipment to goods uncontrolled by the meddlesome Society. Factors were enjoined to put their own seals upon all their packages of butter and cheese, and were made responsible for the quality of their goods.

Later there were several enactments of prohibition, affecting foreign 'hair buttons' and the importation of brandy in casks of less than 60 gallons. This latter was to prevent the bringing in of small casks for running. The foreign silk stuffs known as 'alamodes and lustrings' were subjected to close supervision on importation, the motive announced being the protection of the English silk manufacturers.

The Act of 1692, for the encouragement of privateering, appears to have had a disastrous effect upon the French mercantile marine, which at this time was harried unmercifully by scores of privateers, mostly hailing from the southern English ports.

A tonnage duty was imposed upon shipping, two-thirds payable by the importers of goods, one-third by the shipowners. The proceeds of this tax, together with those of certain existing customs and excise duties, were to be kept apart, and used to guarantee a loan from the public. In connexion with this loan a famous national institution came into existence, the sum of £1,200,000 being subscribed by a corporation, to be called the 'Governors and Company of the Bank of England.'

In 1694 additional poundage was levied upon spices and pictures, and the duties on tea, coffee, etc., were increased. The first part of this grant afterwards became one of the standing branches of revenue, under the name of 'The Spice and Picture Duty.' The right of customs officers to 'overtime' for attendance beyond the legal hours was recognized under this Act the Commissioners of Customs in London and the collectors at outports being directed to fix the amounts that merchants should pay.

About this time many requests to be employed in lucrative offices reached the Treasury, and many seductive proposals of reform. In the latter one curious point of similarity obtained. The success of the schemes was made to appear a direct consequence of the employment of the schemers. It will be as well to quote two or three.

One William Culliford, ex-Commissioner of Irish Revenue, asked to be made a surveyor-general of customs, and on being reminded that the post had been abolished, requested a London surveyorship, with a yearly grant of £500 in excess of the ordinary salary, and a commissionership when one became vacant. It would seem that he based his claim upon the fact that one George Cruffe, a customs officer out of employment, had shot him 'with two bullets,' and that he still carried the bullets in his body.

An enthusiastic reformer submitted a scheme, arranged under six heads thus :

1. That any officer who succeeded in getting a superior convicted of fraud should be rewarded with the superior's office. (The Board of Customs replied that this was impossible, as an illiterate tidesman might thus become a surveyor.)

2. That the practice as to compounding seizures should be amended. (The Board answered that the proposer appeared to know little of Exchequer practice.)

3. That shipmasters should be prosecuted for falsely reporting cargoes. (The reply was that this was the practice.)

4. That a surveyor-general of outports should be appointed. (The Board replied that they did better by sending experienced men occasionally.)

5. That the number of officers should be reduced.

(The Board stated that they had recently increased the staff, on account of loose management by the previous Commissioners.)

6. That the offices of such customs patentees as employed deputies should be abolished, especially that of the head searcher at Gravesend. (It was answered that there was no head searcher at Gravesend, and that all patent officers whose salaries were paid out of the Exchequer were empowered to employ deputies.)

The author of this proposal seems to have retired discomfited.

An enterprising person, named William Carter, appears to have directed his energies partly to the suppression of owling, and partly to the conspicuous advertisement of his abilities. In a petition to 'My Lords of the Treasury' he claimed to have brought about the capture of thirty owling shallops within a period of fourteen months. He also wrote a pamphlet upon the prevention of wool smuggling, embodying a scheme of exact account and supervision of all wool produced in England—a scheme which, if carried into effect, would certainly have brought about a rising of the English yeomanry. Both Board and Treasury soon displayed signs of being tired of Mr. Carter; but he persisted, repeatedly asking for grants of money in order that he might effect captures, and painting lurid pictures of the doings of the Kentish owlers. He succeeded in obtaining advances amounting to several hundreds of pounds, but in the end the Treasury repulsed him.

Then came forward Lord Lanesboro and his coadjutor, Onesiphorus Albin. They started with a statement that the aliens' duties were not properly collected, and that the ancient statute, providing that aliens should expend a moiety of their takings within the realm, was not enforced. They raised the old cry that aliens were usurping English trade, and tagged it with a hint that this would continue until Lord Lanesboro and Onesiphorus Albin were provided with extensive powers of supervision.

Their proposals were referred to the Board, and the

Board countered effectively by stating that the system of compelling aliens to expend their takings in England had lapsed since Charles I.'s time, and that aliens had since taken little part in the carrying trade. They also made cheerful comparison between the existing state of English commerce and its condition in days of yore. 'Then,' said the Board, 'there was no East Indian or Plantation trade, and such trade as existed was mostly in Aliens' hands.' They opposed the employment of extra officials at high salaries, stating that such appointments could only be justified by the multiplication of restrictions, and that too many restrictions were unfavourable to commerce. 'The freer and more easy trade is in any place, the more it flourishes.' A remarkable statement, surely, for a Customs Board to make.

The brace of reformers returned to the charge with a proposal to farm the aliens' duties. This scheme was also referred to the Commissioners, who reported against it, asserting that since Charles II. abolished the customs farm in 1671 it had been the general opinion that farming should not again be resorted to. (The Commissioners appended and approved a report of the Board of 1679 on a similar application. This report suggested that the impositions upon aliens should not be enforced too strictly, and propounded as a query 'whether the king in point of his customs as well as the Trade of the Kingdome is not a greater gainer by the not too Troublesomely collecting the Dutys upon Aliens.')

Onesiphorus made a third attempt single-handed, going back on his previous proposals, and graciously admitting that it would be unadvisable to let any portion of the customs to farm. Still, he was desirous of having a finger in the pie, and offered to advance a substantial sum for the use of the Crown, to be repaid out of the aliens' customs. So far as can be gathered, nothing came of this, and it is probable that the applicant turned his energies into other channels.

Applications of the kind were not always directed

towards obtaining appointments in the Customs, for in 1691 a gentleman who had been surveyor of Greenwax approached My Lords, asking to be restored to his office. He said that since his discharge he had employed all his means in detecting ministerial and official corruption, and had thus got into debt. He wound up with the following plaintive appeal: 'If My Lords will do nothing, please let me know it, that I may hide from my creditors till Parliament meets.'

It was directed that all 'molten silver' exported should be stamped.

In 1696 French goods were again heavily surtaxed, the tunnage on French wine and vinegar being increased, a heavy tunnage laid upon French brandy, and an additional 25 per cent. *ad valorem* on all other French goods. This last was to endure for twenty-one years, but it eventually became one of the permanent branches, under the title of 'The second 25 per cent. on French goods.' Parliament had succeeded in establishing many incitements towards smuggling, but none so stimulating as this.

The exportation of stocking-frames was prohibited, and their removal or sale within the kingdom made subject to registration by the Wardens of the London Framework-Knitters' Society.

An Act was passed to allow the importation of plate and 'battered money for coining purposes,' and, to defray the expenses of coining, an impost, at varying rates of 20 and 25 per cent. *ad valorem* in excess of all previous duties, was laid upon foreign paper, vellum, etc.

Cap. 28 of 1696-1697 prescribed the methods of receiving and accounting for moneys paid into the Exchequer. (This is not Customs history, but it is as well to furnish a précis of the Act.)

Moneys received, whether as loans or revenue, were to be counted and weighed by the Tellers. They were to record the amounts and particulars on slips of parchment, which were to be thrown down the Pipe into the Tally Court, whence the tallies of receipt were issued. The Tellers were to be charged with the sums, and to hold the cash till authorized by debenture from the Auditor of Receipt to make disbursement. The Auditor-General's authority for issuing debentures was to be the king's order under the Great Seal, or an order under the Privy Seal, or an Act of Parliament. (A statement of the condition of the loan Funds was to be displayed constantly in the Auditor-General's office.)

The money received in the room above was to be kept in chests under three locks, one key being held by the Tellers, one by the Clerk of Pells, and one by the senior Deputy-Chamberlain who struck the tallies of receipt. At the end of each day the key-holders were to assemble in the Court of Receipt, and the Tellers to produce the day's takings, made up in bags. The Chamberlain and the Clerk of Pells were to weigh the bags as an approximate check, ticket them, and put them into the chests. Then each key-holder was to lock the chests with his own key.

The debentures issued below by the Auditors of Receipt were not to be paid till the following day. Then the key-holders were to assemble in the Court of Receipt, unlock the chests, take out sufficient money to discharge the account, and lock the rest up again. The amount thus withdrawn was to be left with the Tellers.

The Auditor of Receipt was to make an exhaustive survey every twenty-eight days.

Additional duties were levied for a period upon Scotch coal, and upon English coal carried coastwise, the Customs to collect the same, and appoint meters and weighers.

Duty was to be paid before breaking bulk, on the quantity of coal reported. If by measurement or weighing the cargo were found to exceed the quantity reported, the amount in excess was to be duty-paid by 'post entry.'

An added subsidy of tunnage and poundage on imports was granted for a period, to aid in furnishing an allowance for the king's household. This was subsequently continued, and made permanent as 'The New Subsidy.'

It was enacted that cases and dial-plates of English-made clocks and watches should not be exported without the 'works' appertaining.

The law as to foreign alamodes and lustrings was amended. Their importation was restricted to the port of London, and even into London they might only be imported by special licence from the Commissioners of Customs.

An additional duty was levied on whale-fins, etc., the cargoes of the English Greenland Company paying only one-half of the new rates. This became a permanent impost, and powerfully protected the Company's trade.

The minimum legal weight at which packages of tobacco might be imported was fixed at 224 pounds net. Smaller packages were forfeitable. This, like the previously quoted regulation as to the legal content of spirit casks, was intended as a check to smuggling.*

An additional 15 per cent. *ad valorem* was levied on muslins and similar goods of the East Indies. The 'value' to which the rate applied was the gross price realized at sale. This also became a permanent impost, as 'The 15 per cent. on Muslins.'

The wearing of East India silks and stuffs was prohibited. Their importation was restricted to London, where they might be landed and warehoused for exportation only. When thus exported they paid half the old subsidy rate outwards. Officers were deputed to inspect the East India Company's books and stock at stated

* Even at the present day there is a 'legal limit' as to minimum size of imported casks of spirits, and 'weights' of tobacco.

periods, and to prepare an account for each session of Parliament.

Meanwhile the Flemings, finding that their export trade suffered on account of the prohibition of foreign lace and cut-work under Charles II.'s Act, had prohibited English woollen manufactures. The English Parliament in response directed that the English prohibition of lace, etc., should cease three months after cancellation of the Flemings' prohibition of English woollens. Then Parliament repealed all duties upon English woollen manufactures outward, and provided that the ancient aulnage duties on cloth, which had been granted by Charles II. to the duke of Richmond and his heirs, should cease *on expiration of the grant in* 1724.

The collectors of customs at the outports were often in difficulties, the claims for bounties on exported corn frequently exceeding the amounts of official moneys available for their discharge.* They were therefore directed by an Act of 12-13 William III., when short of funds, to give each claimant of corn bounty a certificate of the amount due, which he might produce, with the debenture, to the Receiver-General of Customs in London, who might then pay the bounty out of the London moneys. It is not clear whether the claimant might employ an agent to do this, and probably many country merchants who exported small quantities would forego their claims rather than travel to London for their money, and risk being called upon to 'Stand and Deliver' on the way back. For at this time the roads swarmed with daring highwaymen, so that a special reward of £40 was offered by statute to anyone who arrested a road thief. (The highwayman's horse, pistols, and money, if unclaimed, became the property of his captor.)

In 1701 the minimum tonnage for vessels bringing foreign spirits was fixed at 15 tons. The trade in contraband spirits was steadily increasing. It should be

* The bounty system on exported corn was first instituted in 1689.

explained that the only real customs duties on foreign spirits were the old subsidy poundage, the impost on brandy, the French duty, and the Coinage; but in addition to these there were heavy excise duties which, being payable on landing, were usually collected by the customs officers, although paid into the Excise account.*

Whilst diligently stiffening the import tariff, Parliament had lightened the taxes here and there upon native products. They had made Irish flax, hemp, and linen duty-free on importation. They had reduced the outward custom on English tin, and to balance this had increased the duties upon drugs imported in English ships, which under the Old Subsidy had enjoyed preferential rating. They had remitted the outward duty on English sail-cloth and bone-lace, and, as a necessary consequence of the bounty system, the outward duties on corn and bread. They had allowed a temporary drawback of the excise duty upon English malt, and prohibited foreign malt during the period.

Yet they had found time to complicate still deeper the provisions of the Plantation Acts, enjoining that ships lading or unlading at the Plantations should be subject to the Customs rules and searches as obtaining in England, and granting the Plantation customs officers powers accordingly. It had been thought that Plantation goods which had paid custom at the Plantations† might be exported thence without being first brought to England. Parliament made the matter clear by forbidding anything

* There was an additional duty payable upon foreign salt at landing, which was not really a customs duty, though collected by the customs officers. There were continual changes in the collection of many duties. Even the French duty on spirits was by 6 Geo. II. made an excise duty. An exact record of all these changes would only mystify readers. Some of the more advanced economists of the time ascribed the complications in collection to the villainy of legislators, whom they accused of wilfully creating hundreds of unnecessary offices, with no other object than the increase of their own political influence and scope of patronage.

† These would be goods carried from one colony to another (see p. 118).

of the kind. All commercial laws previously made *in the Plantations* were declared repugnant to the English Plantation Acts. The Treasury and the Commissioners of Customs were jointly empowered to appoint the Plantation customs officers. All ships trading with the Plantations were to be registered by the English collectors of customs, unless colonial-built, when they were to be registered by the chief Plantation revenue officer. The exportation of wool from the Plantations was forbidden.

The Navigation Act was strengthened. Masters of vessels going to the Fisheries (Newfoundland and New England) were ordered to carry a certain proportion of 'green men'—viz., men who had never been at sea as mariners. The collectors of customs were to obtain each master's declaration upon oath as to this, before allowing fishing-vessels to leave England. This was a laudable device towards increasing the stock of English mariners.

'The 4½ per cent. duties' passed quite under control of the Commissioners of Customs. These duties had been granted to Charles II. upon all 'dead commodities' exported from Barbadoes. They were usually collected in kind, and from the time of grant up to the ninth year of William's reign had been farmed. The goods collected under this tax, which since its institution had been extended to the whole of the Leeward Islands, were from the time of cession sent to London by the collectors of the islands, and stored in a separate warehouse. They consisted principally of sugars, and these were distinguished in the official memoranda as 'the King's sugars.' Two officials, the 'Husband' and a Controller, supervised the warehouse. Thrice a year the 4½ per cent. goods were put up to auction. The sales (afterwards advertised in the 'London Gazette') were without reserve, and if any parcel of goods failed to realize the value at which the collector had invoiced it the collector was surcharged.

Throughout the reign great exertions were made to put down 'owling.' Every owner of sheep living within ten miles of the coast in Kent or Sussex was required to furnish an account of his wool within three days after shearing. No inhabitant of Kent or Sussex, within fifteen miles of the coast, might buy wool without entering into bond not to export it. The price offered for English wool on the Continent must have been immensely higher than that obtainable in England, to induce the Kentish and Sussex men thus to brave the formidable penalties of the law forbidding exportation.

The inland impositions during William's reign were certainly severe : some of them appear grotesque. Not only were there taxes upon heads and windows, but *direct* impositions upon marriages, births, and burials. The tax upon widowers and bachelors, though it lacked the doubtful dignity that enshrouded most of the ancient impositions, was perhaps excusable, for the war had made marriageable men scarce. But what of the tax upon tobacco-pipes, 'for carrying on the war with France,' and the tax on hawkers and pedlars (collected by the most corrupt set of officials known to English history), which was appropriated to paying the interest of the transport debt incurred in the reconquering of Ireland ?

It is almost terrible to contemplate the progress of the taxes during this reign. They followed each other like billows sweeping in on a lee shore, and the silence with which the people regarded their advance is quite unaccountable. War and taxation, and the shouldering of their grievous results upon Posterity, were the chief objects of legislative energy. Be it noted that the war, which was begun with the avowed object of keeping out the Stuarts, soon became a mere crusade in defence of Dutchmen. Certain pamphleteers of the time did not scruple to express their opinion that the piling-up and subdividing, the re-sorting and re-complicating, of imposts, were the results of ministerial design—a threefold design : to favour the Dutch at the expense of English commerce, to provide opportunities for stock-jobbing and commissions, and to increase the ministers' powers of patronage. The first point of supposition was probably unfounded ;

the second and third seem plausible. Anyhow, it is evident that such religious and political advantages as accrued from the Glorious Revolution were extremely expensive benefits. The finger of the sedate little Dutchman was thicker than the loins of the Stuarts.

Anne's first Parliament was soon at work in the prevention of salt smuggling. Customs officers were empowered to board vessels ' hovering off the coast ' with salt cargoes, and compel them to come into port and unlade. It was enjoined that all foreign salt should be imported in bulk.

In 1703 additional tunnage and poundage were granted, at one-third the rate of William's ' New Subsidy.' This became a permanent branch of revenue as " The $\frac{1}{3}$ Subsidy.' The importation of woollen manufactures was prohibited.

The Commissioners of Customs issued a quaint order, providing that one of their number should attend daily at the Bench Office in the Long Room of the London Customhouse, ' to ensure solemnity.' The ' Bench Officers ' were the higher indoor clerical patentees, and their deputies were very lazy fellows. The Board also decided that the recommendation of successors to vacant officerships in the outdoor branch should be vested in the Commissioner who might happen to be ' in the Chair ' at the Board Room when such vacancies were first made known.* Previously each Commissioner had held his own bunch of ports, and nominated successors to vacancies in his own district.

A Treaty of Commerce had meanwhile been concluded between England and Portugal, by which the Portuguese engaged to admit ' for ever ' the woollen goods of England, and the English to admit the wines of Portugal at such rates that the duty demanded on them should never be more than two-thirds that taken on French wines. The latter provision was to endure whether peace or war obtained between England and France. The English

* The Commissioners occupied the Chair week about.

preference of 'Port' set in with the ratification of this treaty.*

Additional tunnage and poundage were granted, at two-thirds of the Subsidy rates, on all foreign wines, and on all other foreign goods with a few unimportant exceptions. This became permanent as 'The ⅔ Subsidy.' Thus it may be stated that on nearly all foreign goods the duties were three times as much as those granted in 1660. The special imposts on numerous articles must also be taken into account, and the tremendous 'French duties.'

In 1704 an additional impost was laid on spice, pic tures, drugs, coffee, tea, chocolate, chinaware, white calico and muslins, Indian dimity, and other cotton manufactures. This became permanent as 'The Additional Spice and Picture Duty.'

A petition in duplicate reached the Treasury, one copy being addressed to the Queen, one to the duke of Marlborough. It was from the merchants of London, stating that some of the customs 'landing-waiters' (officers who took account of goods at landing) were Frenchmen, that French goods were not properly excluded, and that the landing-waiters made it a practice to work several ships at once, so as to gain all the fees with a minimum amount of trouble. Soon after, whether on account of the petition or no doth not appear, the Board of Customs directed the London landing-waiters to desist from wearing swords while on duty.

In 1705 the Commissioners, realizing that 'solemnity' was as necessary in the Board Room as in the Bench Office, directed that an 'instrument' should be provided with which to keep order. (The records are blank as to the nature of the instrument.) Later the Lord Treasurer

* Said the blunt and heroic Borrow, in 1833: 'The English, who have never been at war with Portugal, who have fought for its independence on land and sea, and always with success, who have forced themselves, by a treaty of commerce, to drink its coarse and filthy wines, are the most unpopular people who visit Portugal.'

acquainted the Board that a person recommended for the post of collector of Milford was quite ignorant of customs work. After some discussion of this the Lord Treasurer announced his determination that none should be appointed to a collectorship 'unless bred up in customs business.' In the following year the Board enjoined that none should be appointed a 'tidesman' unless able to write. (The tidesmen were employed in boarding, rummaging, and watching ships, and tallying goods out and in.)

Before ending this chapter, a few extracts from a treatise published by one Charles Davenant, LL.D., may be profitably quoted. Davenant appears to have been at one time Commissioner of Excise. Why he left that department does not appear, but there are occasional bursts of peevishness in his book which seem to indicate that he would not have objected to return, if things could be made comfortable for him. He was dreadfully bitter against the Excise Commissioners, and never missed a chance of girding at them. Shortly after he published his treatise he was an Inspector-General of customs in London, and considered an authority upon revenue matters. He was a shrewd and observant man, but his 'tables of revenue,' like most of such statements, should be viewed with caution, despite his opportunities of consulting with the Receiver-General. He must have been a plucky and outspoken person : few, even now, would dare to attack the chiefs of an important department, to accuse them openly of incompetence and favouritism, and to suggest that their duties should be handed over to farmers.

Davenant charged the ministry with being hopelessly under influence of 'the wretched projectors and contrivers of deficient funds,' and with having under such influence formed funds in anticipation of the proceeds of various taxes, whilst having no definite conception of what the taxes would realize. He ridiculed the practice of conferences between high revenue officials and merchants. 'There is hardly a Society of Merchants,' said he, 'that would not have it thought the whole prosperity of the kingdom depends upon its single traffic. And at any time when merchants come to be consulted their answers are dark and partial, and when they deliberate in assemblies 'tis generally with a bias, and a secret eye to their own advantage.' (That this statement was true as the light of heaven no man of the world can conscientiously deny.)

He likened the financiers of the period to the corrupt ministers of Spain, who by their fostering of "funds" had devoted the greater part of the Spanish revenue to the payment of interest, and paralyzed and ruined a nation once lordly and invincible. He boldly stated that it was often to the advantage of corrupt officials that the nation's affairs should be entangled, even as unjust stewards might thrive under encumbered masters.

He denounced the system of encouraging the formation of funded duties which barely realized the interest, and left the principal a burden on the coming years, and declared that a multiplicity of fund-holders meant ruin to the rural interest, causing moneyed people to congregate and abide near the centre of stock-jobbing. He enunciated the unchallengeable proposition that it could never be for the enduring public benefit that one class should obtain an immovable hold upon the goods produced by the rest. He recommended economy, peace, and strenuous application to the discharge of liabilities, as the surest means of making the new usurers 'quit their hold.' (Better economic doctrine had never been preached, and it would have been well for modern England if Davenant's sermon had taken effect. But sound doctrine can only take root in sound minds, and at the time most Englishmen who could read and write had gone mad on stock-jobbing, and held that the world might be made rich, not by productive effort, but by merely juggling with the counters of wealth.)

It is foolish to believe that because an outspoken man is inspired by a sordid motive there can be no truth in his utterances. The most luminous and inspiring truths have been spoken by disappointed self-seekers. Readers may therefore applaud Davenant's doctrine, and assess the integrity of his motives by what comes after.

He attacked the Commissioners of Excise, and furnished most disconcerting statistics. He accused the Commissioners of having for years neglected to visit their officers, of discharging efficient gaugers to gain opportunity of installing favourites, and of engaging certain collectors who embezzled £25,000. He stated that there were men on the Excise Board whose fortunes made them above their work, and whose ignorance of revenue matters rendered them incapable of doing it, and showed that in spite of the huge increases in the excise rates the revenue was not so large as when Dashwood farmed the duties in 1680. He insisted that a regulated and judicious system of farming would be better than management by an incompetent Board, as the farmers would at least encourage energetic collection, and would not spend days in wrangling across a table 'over My Friend and Thy Friend.'

Among the many quaint hints furnished, one was conspicuous—viz., that the English disliked a variety of new duties, though they might answer with alacrity impositions with which they were acquainted, especially if not called upon to render the same "in dry money, out of the course of trade." (It is strange that so acute an observer failed to note that whenever a tax on commodities is altered someone who has an aptitude towards forestalling gets a splendid chance of plundering the public.)

Some of Davenant's figures may be interesting to modern observers of Commerce. For instance, he stated that the imports from the Plantations reached the annual value of £950,000, and that about two-thirds of these were re-exported. He displayed prophetic anticipation of a future American revolt. 'Wise countries never teach their colonies the art of war.'

In short, his treatise contained, amid many ingenious

statistics and some vagarious expressions, a deal of good material, and it may be read with profit even by the economists of the present day.*

LIST OF AUTHORITIES.

Permanent branches of revenue: 12 Car. II., c. 4; 14 Car. II., c. 11; 18-19 Car. II., c. 5; 2 W. and M., c. 4; 2 W. and M., s. 2, c. 4; 4 W. and M., c. 5; 5-6 W. and M., c. 20; 6-7 W. and M., c. 7; 7-8 Wm. III., c. 20; 9 Wm. III., c. 13; 9 Wm. III., c. 23; 9 Wm. III., c. 45; 11 Wm. III., c. 3; 7-8 Wm. III., c. 31; 8-9 Wm. III., c. 25; 2-3 Anne, c. 18; 3-4 Anne, c. 3; 3-4 Anne, c. 18.

Temporary imposts: 14 Car. II., c. 10; 1 Jas. II., c. 3; 1 Jas. II., c. 4; 1 Jas. II., c. 5; 1 W. and M., c. 10; 1 W. and M., c. 28; 1 W. and M., s. 2, c. 6; 8-9 Wm. III., c. 7.

Preventive measures: 12 Car. II., c. 25; 14 Car. II., c. 11; 2 W. and M., s. 2, c. 14; 10 Wm. III., c. 10; 12-13 Wm. III., c. 11; 9 Wm. III., c. 40; 1 Anne, c. 15.

Frauds: Treasury Papers, June 29, 1691 (on May 16, 1691).

Accounts: 2 W. and M., s. 2, c. 11; Board's Report to Treasury, August 31, 1692; 8-9 Wm. III., c. 28; 12-13 Wm. III., c. 10.

Exchequer trials: Hardress.

Departmental incidents: Treasury Papers, May 7, 1689; January 23, 1691; May 24, 1689; June 10, 1689; June 28, 1689; August 22, 1689; August 23, 1689; September 4, 1689; September 17, 1689; September 19, 1690; November 20, 1691; June 11, 1692; June 13, 1692; November 12, 1692; February 10, 1705; Sir William Musgrave's 'Memoranda.'

Protective measures and prohibitions: 12 Car. II., c. 18; 15 Car. II., c. 7; 12 Car. II., c. 32; 14 Car. II., c. 18; 14 Car. II., c. 13; 25 Car. II., c. 6; 25 Car. II., c. 7; 18-19 Car. II., c. 2; 25 Car. II., c. 2; 1 Jas. II., c. 19; 1 W. and M., c. 32; 1 W. and M., c. 34; 2 W. and M., c. 9; 3 W. and M., c. 13; 4 W. and M., c. 7; 4 W. and M., c. 10; 4 W. and M., c. 5; 6-7 Wm. III., c. 7; 7-8 Wm. III., c. 20; 9 Wm. III., c. 28; 9 Wm. III., c. 43; 11 Wm. III., c. 10; 11 Wm. III., c. 11; 11 Wm. III., c. 20; 7-8 Wm. III., c. 39; 8-9 Wm. III., c. 34; 11 Wm. III., c. 3; 7-8 Wm. III., c. 22; 10 Wm. III., c. 16; 10 Wm. III., c. 14.

Establishment: Patent Rolls, 23 Car. II., p. 2, m. 1*d.*; 'Pepys' Diary'; 'Book of Rates,' 1671; 'The Royal Gauger'; 'Index Vectigalium.'

Privateers: 4 W. and M., c. 25.

Highwaymen: 4 W. and M., c. 8.

---

* 'Davenant's book is highly saucy . . . it was and is a hint to show everybody where they should be angry.'—*Matthew Prior to Stanyan:* 1700.

CHAPTER VI

THE SCOTS' CONTRIBUTIONS, AND THE GROWTH OF SMUGGLING

1707–1727

As this chapter opens at the period when the Act of Union between England and Scotland was planned and executed, a curt sketch of Scottish revenue history will not be out of place. There is nothing in the Scottish statutes to indicate that the customs returns were important, or that Scottish oversea trade, prior to the Union, was extensive or profitable. Ancient Scottish history undoubtedly contains elements of picturesqueness, even of grandeur. Many of the quaint statutes, notably those regulating the 'walpinschawingis,' the maintenance of bale-fires, the affairs of the Border marches and the Highlands, and the cleansing and safety of the old thatched cities, are deeply interesting. It is possible that the true Customs history of the rugged old land has not up to the present been comprehensively exhibited, despite the skill and industry of Scotsmen in research and compilation. No elaborate statement of Scottish revenue matters may be attempted here; merely a rough précis of the more striking details. The task of amplification must be left to Scotsmen born, of whom there are many eminently capable, who may be referred encouragingly to the preamble of one of the Scottish Acts, worded thus: 'This nation hath continued now upwards of two thousand years in the unaltered form of our monarchical government, under the uninterrupted line of one hundred and eleven kings.'

In olden days there was no love lost betwixt Scots and English. Most of the Scottish revenue Acts were worded resentfully against the Southrons, and one or two of the English Acts disparaged the Scots. Overland traffic between the two countries seems to have been by mutual agreement confined to the narrow routes by way of Berwick and Carlisle (legal overland traffic, for there was occasional smuggling across the Border). There were other transactions which may scarcely be called 'traffic,' little ventures by the Scottish 'reivers,' by means of which English goods passed into Scotland, not only uncustomed, but without permission of owners. Sometimes these transactions were pushed beyond the bounds of endurance, and then a Norman king or a mail-clad Warden would come storming through the Debatable Land, with thousands of stalwart archers at his heels, each archer equipped with a six-foot bow and arrows of a cloth yard, and fire and sword would leave their traces across the hard, barren country, right up to the gates of Edinburgh. (The Scottish kings seem to have understood the Scottish deficiencies, for they were continually prohibiting the games of football and golf, and urging the country youth to practise at the butts.)

Most of the revenue laws were directed to the following ends :

1. The restriction or prohibition of English trade.

2. The confining of foreign traffic to the 'royal burghs,' or king's ports, such as Edinburgh, Dumbarton, etc. All these ports were on the south-eastern and extreme south-western coasts.

3. The compelling of foreign merchants to buy Scottish goods up to the amount of their Scottish takings.

4. The encouragement of the inbringing of bullion by Scottish merchants who had traded abroad.

5. The extensive importation of food material, and the discouragement of its exportation.

6. The establishment of a good understanding with the Flemings, who were the principal buyers of Scottish wool.

There appears to have been considerable doubt in the minds of most of the antiquarians who collected and transcribed the older historical records, as to the possibility of discrimination between the duties collected for the king and those levied as toll by the bailies of the various burghs. It appears that the privileges of the burghs were of extremely ancient origin. The dues collected by the bailies on merchandise brought in from the country were probably 'market impositions,' and in most cases they were levied after the goods had been sold.

It is doubtful whether the customs ratified by David I. were anything but burgh tolls on seaborne merchandise. A light tax was collected from each ship laden with corn or salt, and the cargo was subjected to trifling prisage. The tax was on the vessel, in account of her 'sett,' or privilege of riding at anchor in the haven. Each alien who brought wine, honey, or oil paid 'twal pennies' for his 'sett,' a duty of 4d. a tun on entry, and 4d. a tun on 'furth passing' (delivery). If his wine were 'tavarnyt' (sold to a taverner) the king had right of prisage. There were also slight taxes on 'fysschar schipps.' But it is inconceivable that these trifling money tolls were collected for the king, and it does not appear that the prisage of wine was at all extensive.

It is, however, quite evident that the king took custom on wool and skins outward, and that the origin of the tax, as in England, was immemorial. In the records appertaining to an ancient reign it is stipulated that the king shall have his dues of merchants passing by land and sea as in his father's day. Undoubtedly such wool as went by land to England was supposed to be customed before it passed Berwick, but it is unlikely that much went. The wool, it may with reason be assumed, would be of inferior quality —much like the 'rough wool' of the English shires north of the Humber. Yet there was a steady trade with Flanders, and it appears that David II.'s ransom was furnished out of the custom on Scottish wool, collected *in*

Flanders by certain Scottish burghers specially commissioned for that purpose.

In 1398 it was ordained that the statute made at Perth during the previous year as to the paying of custom upon English cloth imported, and upon Scottish cloth, butter, horses, and cattle, should be 'payit as it wes ordanyt in þe forsaid consail.' The burghers (of Perth ?) agreed to pay certain dues, stipulating that their 'fredomes' should be preserved, that they should pay no more for wool, skins, etc., outward than they had done in Robert II.'s time, and that they should be free of the impost on salmon (an export tax, usually applied with considerable rigour to salmon bought by English traders).

The first plain account appears at the opening of the reign of James I. (of Scotland). His export impositions on cattle, sheep, and horses were 12d. in the £1 value. Herrings paid 4s. per last if exported by Scotsmen, 6s. if by strangers. There was an export duty on skins, woollen cloth, and salmon, and an import duty of 2s. 6d. in the £1 on English goods.

In 1425 Scotsmen were forbidden to pass into Ireland without special licence. If any person thus licensed brought passengers with him on his return, they might not land till permitted by the bailie of the port. This was partly because many rebels against the Scottish king had taken refuge in Ireland, and partly to prevent incursions of 'the English Irishry,' who were held particularly dangerous. The statute explicitly stated that nothing was intended in rupture of the friendship that had long existed between Scotsmen and the native Irish.

James III.'s parliament decreed that none should trade oversea unless he were a burgess of a king's port, that craftsmen should not act as merchants, that no ship should be freighted without a charter-party, that each merchant carrying outward more than five lasts of goods should render one 'sack' to the 'Chaplains of the Nation,' and that if he carried five lasts only, or less, he should render half a sack. None was allowed to pass oversea as a merchant unless he carried at least half a last of goods.

The practice with regard to the bringing-in of victual by foreign merchants was as follows: The strangers entered their goods at the tolbooth of the port, and the prices were fixed by agreement between the merchants and the port officials. The king's household was served 'with the best' at the prices prescribed, and then the nobility had second choice. The remainder was sold to the common people. None might buy to sell again. As the port officials and the customs men frequently fleeced both merchants and 'common buyers,' it became necessary to proclaim the fixed prices at the market cross. (This Act applied particularly to Edinburgh.)

Unstable people were forbidden to trade abroad. Only 'famous and worshipful men' were allowed to take goods to Flanders.

Towards the end of the century there was much smuggling, especially at Leith, and it was enacted that merchants landing goods at places other than king's ports should lodge at the principal taverns, and the tavern-keepers were held responsible that the merchants' goods did not pass uncustomed.

It was found that the collectors frequently took custom for the king first and for themselves afterwards, and a statute was issued prohibiting this. 'Quha that dois in the contrare to be punist as an oppressour and brekar of the Kingis law.'

A few years subsequent to the disaster at Flodden an Act was passed stating that for many years the districts near the Border had been wasted and plundered by English 'thevis and trators,' and that food was therefore at a great price. It was decreed that no Scot should send oxen or sheep to England, or victual, fish, or salt, but such Englishmen as were granted safe-conduct by the Scottish king might enter the realm and buy, paying in 'gold and siluir.'

In the sixteenth century Scottish merchants trading

abroad were bidden to carry passports. Merchants going to Flanders had to produce their passports to the Scottish Conservator there stationed, and he was to keep the home Government informed as to their manner of trading, 'vnder þe pane of tinsale of his office.'

War with England being contemplated, all Scottish men of substance were ordered to furnish themselves with 'small artillery,' and all Scottish merchants from abroad to bring home two hackbuts each, with a supply of powder and metal. This was just before the battles of Halidon Rigg and Solway Moss.

James VI. (afterwards James I. of England) uttered many revenue decrees. He issued a 'Table' to his customs collectors (probably a rough 'Book of Rates'). He created three extra 'King's Ports,' one at Lochaber, one at Cantire, one at Lewis, and gave close attention to the doings of both merchants and officers.

One of the Acts issued during his reign foreshadowed so closely in its preamble the style of the 1611 English 'Book of Rates' Ordinance that one is inclined to think James dictated the preface, which stated that it was the practice in all countries to impose customs, especially upon strangers, and proceeded: 'It cannot be denyit bot his maiestie is a free prince of a Souerane power, haueing als grite liberteis and prerogatiues be the lawis of his realme and priuilege of his crowne and diadame as ony other king, prince, or potestate quhat-sum-euir.' It gave authority to the Auditors of the Exchequer to 'sett down the A.B.C. of the custum,' and to fix values (issue a 'Book of Rates'). The collectors were to 'uplift custum' accordingly at the rate of 12d. in the £1. The nobility might import or export goods duty-free.

At this time James was anticipating the event that was to make him monarch of a land where 'custum' was really worth 'uplifting.' He was in secret and constant communication with the audacious Cecil. Still the old spirit of hostility to English commerce was paraded. Another Act stated that English cloth was 'unproffitable, haueand onlie for the maist parte ane outwarde shaw [show] wantand the substance and strenth quhilk oftymes it appeiris to haue.' (It is likely there was some truth in this statement.) English cloth and English wares were accordingly prohibited.

In 1604, James being in possession of the English throne, certain Scottish Commissioners were appointed to confer with certain English Commissioners as to the best way of strengthening union betwixt the two countries. The preamble of the appointing Act ran : 'For sa mekle as it hes plesit his maist exellent Maiestie, acknawledging the unspeikable favour quhair-with the divine providence hath blissed him by the oft-wisched bot hardlie-expected cojunction of twa sa Ancient and lang discordent kingdomes . . . miracoulouslie accompleisched in the blude and persone of sa Rare ane Monarch.'

The eighteenth Parliament of this reign (1606) adjusted certain customs matters. The farmers of the Scottish customs were directed to keep a book of goods entered and shipped to England, and another of goods imported by sea from England. The English farmers were to keep similar books, and every year duplicates of the accounts thus taken were to be sent from Edinburgh to London, and from London to Edinburgh. It is evident that all shipments between the two countries were secured by bond, for the Act directed that the certificates in discharge of bonds were to be transmitted with the duplicates of account. Cockets for Scottish goods were to be granted to responsible persons only, 'not in poore menis names scarslie knawin in England.' Goods sent overland from either country were to be accompanied by certificates ; Scottish goods being certified by the farmers' deputies at Edinburgh, English by the farmers' deputies at Berwick or Carlisle. Goods might not pass by the waste lands (marches).

In 1641 it was enacted that the charge for taking a ship's report should not exceed 23s. 4d. Scots ; for issuing a cocket 40s. This was on account of extortions by collectors and report clerks. In the same year all 'extraordinary ' customs and imposts were declared illegal, and it was enjoined that goods which had been customed inward should be duty-free outward, ' as in England and Ireland.' It was also directed that the ' Book of Rates ' should be reformed. Many privileges were granted to ship-masters and merchants.

A system of Import-Excise was adopted in 1644, the duties being payable by the first buyer. Wine and tobacco were the principal foreign goods made liable. Certain inland duties were levied under the same Act. The rates were increased in 1649.

During the later years of the Commonwealth the Westminster Ordinance of Tunnage and Poundage applied to England, Ireland, and Scotland.

In 1661 a duty of 8s. Scots per gross was imposed upon foreign tobacco-pipes, to prevent money from leaving the kingdom!

In the same year a Scottish Navigation Act was passed. Its provisions were much the same as those of the English Act, except that ' Scots ' took the place of ' English ' in the clause dealing with the preponderance of mariners. English and Irish ships were to be accounted foreign, until the full benefit of the English Navigation Act should be extended to Scotland. The Act was not to apply to goods of Asia, Africa, America, Russia, or Italy, till Scottish merchants succeeded in establishing trade with those territories.

Later was issued a unique statute, providing that craftsmen might not import articles of the kind they manufactured. (Thus an armourer might not import swords, or a smith ploughshares.)

In 1663 certain merchants complained that the provisions of the Navigation Act were systematically infringed in the port of Glasgow by Dutchmen and other foreigners. The petitioners described themselves as on the verge of ruin, being unable to compete with their foreign rivals, who were encouraged and supported by many of the Glasgow people. Parliament enjoined that the Act should be enforced.

In 1689, at 'The Meeting of the Estates,' an embargo was put upon all vessels at the western ports, to prevent their passing to Ireland, and then being used to bring Jacobites to England and Scotland.

In 1695 it was found that the collectors of the import-excise of 6s. a pint on brandy had in some cases charged the retailers more than once. (Probably they had levied it on successive buyers of the goods, instead of confining it to the first retailer.) It was enacted that the tax should only be collected from genuine retailers, who were defined as 'Toppers,' keeping shops and taverns in which brandy was sold in small quantities for immediate consumption.

It appears that the distillation of rum from molasses was common in Scotland. The sale of this liquor was prohibited in 1695, on the pretext that it was 'a drug rather than a liquor,' and that its manufacture curtailed the distillation of spirits from malt, but in the following year the prohibition was repealed, as prejudicial to the Scottish sugar-refining industry. In 1698 the impost on brandy was transferred to the importer, and made a branch of the Customs.

Later Parliament reaffirmed prohibition of the exportation of wool, and forbade the importation of all foreign woollen manufactures. It also prohibited French wine and spirits, and all foreign silk and cotton goods, except goods of India and Persia imported in the ships of 'the Company of Scotland trading to Africa and the Indies,' plain stuffs for hoods and scarves, and materials for robes of ceremony.

These brief details may serve to illustrate the progress of the Scottish Customs revenue, previous to the Act of Union. The Articles of Union were agreed upon in 1705, by Commissioners nominated under the Great Seals of both countries. The Scottish Parliament ratified the Act early in 1706. It was provided that the two countries should be united on May 1, 1707, their armorial bearings conjoined, and their trade privileges made similar. Scottish ships were to be deemed British-built, provided that no foreigner shared in ownership. The ownership of Scottish vessels was to be attested to the Customs upon oath, and registers of shipping were to be kept at London and Edinburgh. The customs drawbacks, duties, prohibitions, etc., obtaining in England, were to be applied to Scotland. Patents and privileges were to remain undisturbed. The bounty on English corn, grain, meal, etc., exported, was to extend to similar Scottish goods. It was found necessary to add oatmeal to the list, and to provide that Scottish 'bere' should be rated as barley. Thus the English customs duties, together with the English system of Excise, in all their tangled and jumbled glory, were applied to a land in which the pound sterling meant a sum scarce sufficient to cover an English labourer's daily pay, and many a high-souled gentleman walked barefoot. Certain exemptions had to be made with regard to Scottish victual and salt, but they were temporary and trivial. The relative proportions of revenue were reckoned at something near the following figures :

	Customs.	*Excise.*
England	£1,350,000	£950,000
Scotland	£30,000	£33,500

The English coinage, weights, and measures were to be used, and a Mint was established at Edinburgh on the same lines as the London Mint.

The Parliaments were united, the Scottish members attending at Westminster, but Scotland was granted a separate Court of Exchequer at Edinburgh, with Exchequer barons as in England, and a separate Board of Customs Commissioners, also at Edinburgh, to control the Scottish customs. There was to be but one Privy Seal for the two countries. Scottish justices of the Peace were to be appointed under the Great Seal. The Scottish burghs retained their ancient liberties.

It is likely that the new scheme was viewed with sour

disapproval by the common people of both countries, and that, as usual, their wishes were not consulted. Scurrilous pamphleteers of the time did not scruple to express their opinion that the Scottish people suffered by the Union, being hit in their tenderest spot by the complicated English customs and excises.

After the Scottish customs had paid their share of the salaries of Exchequer and Session, and the expenses of collection, the net yield was but trifling. This was due to a trio of circumstances. Scotland was a poor country, not, like the Scotland of to-day, full of flourishing banks and roaring industries. The duties were loosely collected, and at some of the ports little or nothing remained after the 'salaries and incidents' had been paid. Lastly, there was quite an enormous amount of canny smuggling—smuggling not conducted in the brazen, whole-souled fashion that obtained in Kent, Sussex, Hants, and Dorset, yet quite as effective in diminishing the revenue. The returns increased as the years rolled on, and then they were saddled with the bounties granted to the Scottish herring fishery.

From Scotland to Liverpool. In 1709, the port having greatly increased its business, and the Liverpool Corporation having granted four acres of land to furnish space for a dock, of which there was much need, the port being dangerous to enter, it was enacted that the land in question should for ever be devoted to the purpose assigned, and that the Corporation might during twenty-one years levy certain tonnage dues on ships coming to Liverpool, the proceeds to be devoted to the construction and maintenance of the said dock. The limits of the port were defined as the Redstones, Warrington, and Frodsham Bridges. The Liverpool customs officers were directed to withhold clearance till the dues were paid.

Parliament granted an impost, which became permanent as 'The Duty on Candles.' Later appeared another, which became permanent as 'The Duty on Pepper and Raisins.' Then came 'The Duty on Coals,' which included seven different duties on coals exported, and this also became permanent. With this impost was bracketed 'The Additional Duty on Candles,' also destined to become permanent.

The plague being prevalent at the northern European ports, ships from the Baltic were made liable to quarantine. This appears to be the first instance of a quarantine Act being deemed requisite to confirm the usual proclamation. Maritime justices were directed to set a watch upon all ships thus detained. The immediate administration of the Act was vested in the Customs authorities. (The Commissioners each received £200 a year extra for supervising the quarantine duties.)

Other fresh imposts were levied, all fated to become permanent. They were 'The Duty on Hides,' an impost upon hides, skins, parchment, vellum, cards, and dice; 'The Duty on Hops,' an additional tax of 3d. a pound on foreign hops; 'The Duty on Soap and Paper,' an amazingly tangled bunch of varying additional rates and duties, applying to foreign soap, paper, millboards, pasteboards, scale-boards, and various kinds of foreign linen; 'The Additional Duty on Hides,' which varied with charming complexities the previous Hide Duty, and also embellished the rates on drugs and the duties on parchment, vellum, starch, tea, coffee, etc.; and 'The Duty on Sailcloth,' an additional tax of 1d. per ell on the foreign commodity. Then came 'The Additional Duty on Coals.' Beside these were one or two fugitive imposts, which need not be described.

It was enacted that officers of customs should assist in procuring aid for vessels in distress. They were empowered to demand assistance from any man-of-war or merchant ship available, and to take part in regulating claims for salvage. If salvage were not paid they might detain ship and cargo. In disputed cases they might nominate justices to decide matters at issue. They were allowed to participate in salvage awards, and some of them soon found this privilege lucrative. The Customs administration of this Act was, as a rule, vested in the collectors of ports. The Act, which was issued on account of 'barbarous wrecking,' was to be publicly read four times a year in all seaport towns.

In 1711 a remarkable interview took place at the Treasury, the parties being the Lord Treasurer, the Chancellor of the Exchequer, and the Board of Customs. His Lordship recommended the Commissioners to take great care of the revenue, especially of the tobacco duties. He stated that he believed many of the officers of customs to be 'faulty,' and expressed a hope that the Board would apprise him if he happened to instal anyone who was unfit.

In 1712 the Board instituted a fund for pensioning superannuated tidesmen. A 'Receiver and Controller' of the fund was appointed, and all moneys stopped from officers for misconduct were handed over to him.*

In 1713 an interesting case was tried in the Scottish Court of Exchequer. The English Prisage of Wine had been introduced into Scotland at the time of the Union, and appears to have been extremely unpopular. In the end a Scottish merchant named Gordon contested the legality of the imposition. He had imported a quantity of Spanish wine, and protested against paying the usual composition fee to the Prisage-holder, but he gave bond for payment if the decision went against him.

* During the infancy of the Superannuation Fund the allowance to pensioners was 1s. a day. Only 'preferable tidesmen,' who had served twenty-one years, who had no other means of subsistence, and were *over eighty years old*, were allowed to participate. The fund grew shaky in 1736, but was given a fresh start in 1741. In 1750 the Receiver, one Harrison, was charged with embezzling the moneys, and dismissed from the Service.

It was contended on Gordon's behalf that Prisage had not been provided for in the Act of Union, and that even in England it was merely 'an ancient usage indistinctly paid.' Sir James Stewart, the Advocate-General, appeared for the Prisage-holder. The judges were the Scottish Exchequer barons (Smith, Maitland, Clark, and Dalrymple). Their decree, summarized, ran thus :

'Prisage is an ancient prerogative, disposed at the time of Union in favour of certain subjects as a private right. It was never settled or established by any Act of Parliament in England itself, and there was no mention of it in the account of customs and duties given in by the English Commissioners at the time of Union, therefore it was not considered in the treaty.'

The barons accordingly directed that Gordon should be freed of his bond, and should 'go without day.' There was a good deal of rummaging amid the old records of English revenue in connexion with this case. Undoubtedly Gordon's courage deserved success, yet it seems likely a flaw might easily be found in the decision.

The official minutes of the London Commissioners of Customs show that the customs tidesmen employed on the Thames had rather a hard time. They were divided into two classes, 'preferable' and 'extraordinary.' Those in the preferable class were kept constantly employed, the pick of them in the Pool and on the quays, and a certain number of the seniors were stationed upon the sacred Customs wharf itself. These last were called 'piazza men.' The 'extraordinary' men were employed at a daily wage when required. The majority of the tidesmen were on 'boarding duty'—*i.e.*, kept in readiness at the London Custom-house, and drafted in bodies to Gravesend as required, to accompany ships from foreign up the Thames, and remain on board them as watchers till they were cleared. The records are full of curious things about these waifs of the river. There were at

Gravesend two taverns, at which the tidesmen were expected to lodge whilst waiting to be boarded. In times of fog or slackness the men often remained in these taverns for several days, and then the tavern-keepers were permitted to advance them money up to a specified amount. When news arrived of East Indiamen in the Downs a number of tidesmen were sent to Deal to be boarded on them. These men performed the journey from Gravesend to Deal on horseback, and were as merry on the way as Chaucer's Canterbury Pilgrims.

Once two of the tidesmen quarrelled, and one trounced the other. The Board fined the victor, and gave the fine to the beaten man. One afternoon a London tidesman went to sun himself upon the Tower Quay, lit his pipe, and made himself comfortable. The sentry on duty ordered him to put his pipe out ; the tidesman refilled it, and smoked harder than ever. The sentry summoned one of the guard, and the two soldiers attempted to enforce routine, on which the tidesman beat and overthrew them, and broke one of their firelocks. For this he was severely punished.

An extraordinary tidesman, being boarded on a ship in the Pool, neglected to apprise the river inspectors of the completion of the vessel's unlading. Why should he ? Her charge meant 2s. a day to him, and if he were cleared it might be a week or two before he was employed again. So he stayed on for eighty days after the vessel's discharge. The Board were extremely wroth with the careless inspectors who had permitted this, and made them pay the tidesman's wages out of their own pockets.

The tidesmen appear to have often suffered through the churlishness or inhumanity of shipmasters. They were in a way at the mercy of the captains of the vessels which they were deputed to watch, the captains being able to make things uncomfortable for them if they became officious. A master refused to allow his tidesman a place in which to sleep, and made him walk the deck for two days and two nights. The Board took the Solicitor-

General's opinion upon the matter, who decided that a prosecution would not hold. But the captain was not allowed to escape. There was a certain bounty called 'Portage,' which the Customs paid to masters of vessels from foreign, to induce them to make correct reports of their cargoes.* The Board made a practice of refusing this bounty when a master failed to report correctly, or otherwise misbehaved, and in the case mentioned they stopped it for 'obstinacy.' Once a master lost his portage for 'abusing' a tidesman, and another skipper's bounty was stopped because his tidesman's 'trunk' was stolen. One master gave his tidesman a dram, upon drinking which the unfortunate fellow went to sleep, and awoke no more. Apparently the case was not clear enough to warrant a prosecution, but the Board stopped the captain's portage.

The most interesting customs documents of Anne's reign are those kept at the Scottish ports, for they illustrate the effect of the Act of Union upon Scottish revenue practice. In 1708 the Scottish Commissioners of Customs were their Honours Dickson, Isaacson, Norman, Boyle, Rigby, Kent, and Fullerton. The collector and controller at Montrose were douce, earnest Scotsmen, rather overloaded with the responsibilities of the new system, and inclined to refer all doubtful matters to their Honours at Edinburgh. Their chief causes of worry were the drawback upon Scottish fish cured with foreign salt, and the high-handed proceedings of the Earl of Northesk, who was Deputy High Admiral, and looked sharply after his perquisites of wreck.

The Commissioners, whether they were Scotsmen or not, possessed in full the Scottish disinclination to rash-

* The captains of Danish and Norwegian vessels usually authorized the Customs to pay their portages to the ministers of the Scandinavian places of worship in London.

ness in giving advice, yet they were extremely desirous that there should be no chance of fault-finding by the English Treasury officials. They learned as fast as they could, meanwhile labouring to convince their subordinates that they would show little consideration if things went wrong. They received a deal of private information of contemplated smuggling, which information they promptly communicated to Montrose, with no result as regarded important seizures. Meanwhile the collector and controller lost no opportunity of informing the Board that it was impossible to protect the revenue in the Montrose district, especially in the neighbourhood of Arbroath, unless a few score soldiers were kept within hailing distance of the Custom-house.

The first question sent to the Board was to this effect: 'May the Admirall, who has salved goods from foreign, and taken a fifth as his share, be allowed to deal with them as he pleases? He reffuses to export the prohibited goods, and he claims the ballance clear of duty.'

This question the Board referred to the Lord Advocate, and his answer was a miracle of ambiguity. It ran thus: 'The wrecked goods in excess of the fifth part are not liable, being meer casualtie. It hath been thought that wrecked goods are not liable to duty.' He then vaguely hinted that the admiral was in error as to the fifth part which he had retained as salvage compensation, but his expression of opinion was by no means lucid.* Meantime the Board dexterously made it apparent that they desired the officers to give the 'Admirall' as little trouble as possible.

The officers were informed by the Board that Montrose merchants had entered French paper as Dutch, to avoid

* 3 Edw. I., c. 4: 'Where wreck belongeth to other than the king, etc.' It is evident that the Earl of Northesk had taken the wrecked goods as droits, and, the owners having afterwards claimed them, he had handed over four-fifths, and kept the other fifth as salvage dues. In the condition of the law then, he appears to have been entitled to his fifth duty-free. The Advocate seems to have misapprehended both the law and the circumstances.

the 'French duty.' Later they were cautioned as to certain large exportations of tobacco on drawback at Borrowstoness. 'It has been thought,' wrote the Board, 'the merchant will run these goods after shipment.'

The Commissioners received 'A Book of Opinions' from their London brethren, and, perusing it, came to think that the Lord Advocate had gone wrong in his decision as to wrecked goods.

The officers were still puzzled over the salted fish drawback, and after much correspondence between Edinburgh and London instructions reached Montrose that some of the fish shipped on drawback were to be measured, so that an estimate might be formed of the quantity of salt used in curing. The officers were to certify to 'the dementions,' measuring from the bone of the fin to the third joint of the tail. 'You have herewith,' wrote the Board, 'the printed form of a codd, which is printed out by the letters A and B, according to which you are to governe yourselves.'

The Earl of Northesk claimed the wrecked cargo of a ship, and the officers sent queries to Edinburgh as to what duties they were to charge him. The Commissioners replied that they hoped there would be no dispute. The officers claimed *duty* on all the spirits salved, and detained such of the goods as were 'prohibited,' meanwhile asking the Board for further instructions. Not a word of instruction was received, but the Board's Secretary sent an ambiguous letter, hinting that the Board did not approve of the officers 'cavilling with the Lord Northesque or his doers,' and desired no further trouble in the matter. It appears that the Earl had made complaint in the proper quarter that he could not get his droits duty-free.

In 1709 the Board, having received 'relyable information' that the Montrose officers did not enforce the maritime regulations and duties applying to aliens, and that brandy was being smuggled into the port '1,200 anchors' (ankers) 'at a time,' sent the collector and controller a letter of warning, that ended thus : ' If a punctuall complyance be not given hereto, others will be appointed to succeed you who will make it their study and care to perform the same.'

Soon after another letter arrived from Edinburgh, commencing : ' We have certayn information that there is a very wicked practice in your precincts.' This, it appeared, was getting drawback at shipment on fish cured with foreign salt, and afterwards unshipping the goods and presenting them for drawback again, and yet again. The officers were directed to mark the casks in future, and to cut off the tails of the fish !

The Board sent the following instructions as to the details required in sufferances for carrying wine and tobacco coastwise. ' Specify of wine the casks prick't, made up, and upon the turn, of tobacco the quantity wet, funk'd, and dry rotten.'*

News came that a ship from the Plantations had gone ashore on the Orkneys, and that the islanders had stolen her cargo, the most valuable part of which consisted of 17,000 deerskins.

The Board sent a disconcerting letter, apprising the officers that French wine was being sold freely in all the Edinburgh taverns, and that it was thought to have been run at Montrose or thereabout. Other disquieting tidings followed, to the effect that Scottish captains were in the habit of taking fish to Bilbao, and then shipping French wine with the purpose of running it into England and Scotland, and that it had come to be known that other mariners were in the habit of shipping drawback goods in Scotland, pocketing the drawback, and then running the goods into England.

Undoubtedly the good citizens of Montrose, and others residing in the district, were guilty of some of the illegal

* ' Pricked ' : spiled. ' Made up ' : landed at a low ullage, and made up to a specified ullage by addition of wine from other casks. For instance, the last cask of a consignment might be expended in making up several other deficient casks. ' Upon the turn ' : becoming sour. ' Funked ' : offensive to the smell.

acts they were confidentially blamed for. Extracts from the records of a later reign prove that most of the charges had good foundation.

We close our account of this reign with an enumeration of the Scottish ports, creeks, etc., from which it will be seen that a vast stretch of coast was left unguarded by the Customs. The north-western portion of Scotland was a stronghold of lawlessness, the wild Highlanders and fisher-folk distilling their own whisky, settling their quarrels in their own time-honoured way, and no doubt occasionally welcoming the arrival of Dirk Hatteraick or Will Watch. The customs stations most remote were Helmsdale on the east and Cantire on the west coast.

Ports.	*Members.*	*Creeks.*
Dunbar ..	Nil	Eyemouth, Coldingham, Cockburnspath, Skateraw, Tynninghame.
Preston-pans	Nil	North Berwick, Aberlady, Port Seton, Musselburgh.
Leith ..	Nil	Newhaven, Muirhouse Haven, Cramond.
Boness ..	Alloa	Queensferry, Blackness, Avon Water, Carron Mouth, Airth, Stirling, Clackmannan, Kincardine, Culross, Torryburn, Limekilns, Inverkeithing.
Kirkcaldy	Anstruther	Aberdour, Burntisland, Kinghorn, Dysart, West Wemyss, East Wemyss, Buckhaven, Methil, Leven, Largo, Elie, St. Monance, Pittenweem, Crail, Fife Ness, St. Andrews, Eden Mouth.
Dundee ..	Nil	Ferryport-on-Craig, Balmerino, Monifieth, Buddon Ness.
Perth ..	Nil	Earn Mouth, Inchture, Pow of Errol.
Montrose	Nil	Arbroath, Auchmithie, Lunan Water, Usan, Ferryden, Mathers, Johnshaven, Gourdon, Bervie, Tod Head.
Aberdeen	Nil	Catterline, Crawton, Dunnottar, Stonehaven, Skateraw, Findon Cove, Old Aberdeen, Newburgh, Slains, Boddam, Peterhead, Rattray Head, Cairnbulg, Fraserburgh, Rosehearty, Banff, Portsoy, Cullen.
Inverness	Nil	Garmouth, Lossiemouth, Burghead, Findhorn, Nairn, Alness, Cromarty, Portmahomac, Tain, Dornoch, Dunrobin, Helmsdale.

Thence the whole northern coast, with the western coast as far south as Knapdale, had no Customs supervision. The 'creek' most remote on the western coast was the Mull of Cantire.

Ports.	*Members.*	*Creeks.*
Campbeltown	Nil	Mull of Cantire, Carradale Bay, Claonaig Bay, Skipness Point, Tarbert, Kyles of Bute.
Port Glasgow		Toward Point, Dunoon, Holy Loch, Roseneath, Dumbarton, Kilpatrick, Scots Town, Partick, Renfrew, Erskine.
	Greenock	Gourock, Cloch Point, Inverkip, Skelmorlie.
Irvine ..	Nil	Largs, Portincross, Saltcoats.
Ayr ..	Nil	Troon, Dunure Castle, Turnberry Point, Girvan.
Stranraer	Portpatrick	Ballantrae, Bay of Cairn, Scar, Loch Float, Drumore, Glenluce.
Wigtown	Nil	Burn of Monreith, Isle of Whithorn, Newton Stewart, Creetown, Gatehouse of Fleet.
Dumfries	Kircudbright	Balmangan Bay, Balcary Bay, Entry of Ure, Eastside, Burbary Bay, Carse Thorn, Kelton, Cummer Trees, Annan, Entry of Sark.

The National Debt at the beginning of George I.'s reign amounted to several millions. The provision for the Civil List was at first less than that granted to Queen Anne, but it was speedily made up to £700,000 per annum, the extra money being yielded by 'The Aggregate Fund,' a new institution which combined several branches of Customs and Excise revenue, and two other inland duties.

The duty on coals in the port of London was charged with the maintenance of the ministers of fifty new churches. The churches had been built out of the proceeds of the same tax. 'The Duty on Wrought Plate' appeared, and became a permanent tax.

It was enacted that on account of frequent disputes between merchants and officers in dealing with wines found to be damaged, the ancient system of allowing the officers to remit the duty on damaged wine should be abolished, and that merchants should pay on all wines, good or bad, and receive an allowance out of the gross duties paid, or they might destroy the damaged wine, and be allowed a sum in compensation of freight charges.

Certain traders at once started manufacturing stuff, purporting to be damaged wine, in the Isle of Man, and bringing it to England so that they might destroy it, and gain an excessive 'freight allowance.' To combat this it was enacted that damaged wine might be warehoused with the Customs, and sold for 'distillation into spirits.'

In 1719 it was found that much tobacco entered for exportation to Europe and granted drawback had been run into Ireland. Ireland was accordingly made 'foreign,' as far as the drawback regulations obtained. (Later the Isle of Man was similarly dealt with.)

The Lord Warden of the Cinque Ports was directed to keep an eye upon the Deal, Dover, and Thanet pilots, who had used their pilot cutters for running goods.

'The New Duty on Apples' appeared (a tax of 2s. per bushel, which produced little revenue). It was probably intended to act as an instrument of prohibition. The tax on pictures, which, being included in the 'Spice and Picture' branch, had gained additional solemnity by being made 'perpetual,' was amended. In its new form it stood as follows:

	£	*s.*	*d.*
On every imported picture of 4 square feet or upwards	3	0	0
On every imported picture of 2 or less than 4 feet square	2	0	0
On every imported picture of smaller size ..	1	0	0

The *ad valorem* duty on foreign books was made a tax *by weight:* 14s. a cwt. on all bound books imported.

(Evidently the authorities had lost faith in the artistic and literary discernment of the landing-waiters.)

The Crown acquired tenancy of the Wool Quay near the London Custom-house, for the purpose of warehouse accommodation. This quay had in 1432 been left by William of Sevenoaks, a London 'grocer,' to provide and maintain a teacher of grammar in Sevenoaks, and for the benefit of the poor there. The bequest was confirmed by Queen Elizabeth, and made a fund to maintain a free grammar school and an almshouse. The Crown now agreed to pay the Wardens of Sevenoaks, who were trustees of the fund, a sum of £2,500, and an annual rent of £550.

The weighing and garbling of imported tobacco were made subjects of a statute, and it was provided that tobacco might not be imported stripped of the stem, and that drawback should not be granted on exported tobacco-stalk. (The clause prohibiting stripped tobacco inward was soon repealed.) Throughout this reign there were many statutes against drawback frauds, and many readjustments of the Preventive laws. A writer on revenue matters has aptly remarked that the Customs regulations of the period were extremely formidable, 'from their many exceptions, and exceptions from exceptions—their many regulations, and regulations of regulations.'

The clause in the Act of Union stipulating that the Customs of England and Scotland should be under two distinct Commissions was annulled, and one Commission granted for Great Britain. (This system lasted till 1742, yet the English and Scotch revenues were still collected separately, and administered at London and Edinburgh by members of the joint Commission.)

An additional 'Book of Rates' was issued. Since the grant of the Old Subsidy in 1660 many goods previously unknown had become articles of import, and as there was no mention of these in the old 'Book of Rates' their values had been declared by the importers on oath. The new Act furnished rates of value for a number of them, and provided that if any articles not enumerated in either the old or the new list were imported collectors should be empowered to check the values declared, and if they thought the goods were undervalued they might buy them at the value stated by the importer, and pay him the same plus an extra 10 per cent. and the amount of the customs duties on the goods. The collector might then warehouse the goods for public sale. When the goods were sold he was to draw back the money previously expended, and the surplus, if any, was to go to the Sinking Fund. What would happen if the goods failed to realize the amount paid by the collector did not appear in the context.*

The additional customs duties on tea, coffee, etc., were repealed, and the goods made subject to a heavy excise tax. The duty on snuff was amended. Meanwhile home-manufactured silks had been granted an allowance on exportation, and the poundage outward on many British manufactures and products abolished. The duties on Plantation tobacco had been slightly eased. Old rags, linseed, and drugs used in dyeing, had been made duty-free inward.

In 1721 the Customs and Excise Commissioners were called up to the Treasury together. There may have been a dispute as to precedence, for the Customs Minute Books exultingly announce that the gentlemen of the Customs were 'called in first.'

The Board decided that gaugers, before being certified

* Legend has it that sometimes the collectors were duped; for instance, that a merchant would bring in at one port a parcel made up of 'portions' of an unrated article, and at another port the corresponding 'portions,' and declare both parcels at trifling values. The collectors would be afraid to buy the goods for the Crown, fearing that they would not get their money back, and would therefore assess poundage at the rate declared. Then the merchant would combine the two parcels. It may be that Legend is a lying jade on this point, for the two 'Books of Rates' made up an exhaustive list between them, and the few kinds remaining unrated were not such as are specified in the tale.

to as competent, should prove that they were skilled in practical gauging as well as in 'working out contents in figures.'

A Treasury warrant was issued to provide £200 to furnish a regiment of soldiers with new shoes and stockings, to replace those worn out in chasing smugglers.

The Quarantine laws provided material for curious enactments by the Board. In 1722 it was enjoined that officers who in the prevention of smuggling boarded ships liable to quarantine need not perform quarantine in the same manner as the ships' companies. In the following year the Board granted the fishermen of Milton, Kent, a sum of money to compensate them for the loss of their oyster-fishing, which had been suspended while certain vessels performed quarantine in Stangate Creek.

The Weavers' Company of London approached the Board, and requested that officers might be appointed to seize 'prohibited apparel' under the Company's direction. The Board complied.

Captain Thwaites, commander of the East Indiaman *Carnarvon*, succeeded in smuggling 880 pieces of silk and 1,500 pounds of tea. Afterwards information was laid against Thwaites, and on inquiry being made it was found that he had gone abroad with his vessel. On his return in 1724 action was taken against him, but there being some delay he managed to get his effects on board, and would have evaded prosecution again had the Board not called upon the East India Company to stop his ship. He was fined £2,800, and applied to the Treasury that the fine might be reduced. His petition was referred to the Board, and they refused to entertain it, stating they had proof that Thwaites had corrupted several of their officers.

The ancient system of sending tidesmen to Deal to be boarded on East Indiamen arriving in the Downs was discontinued, as the tidesmen were often rendered unfit for duty by sea-sickness. It was provided that certain persons of Deal, well accustomed to the sea, should be boarded in their stead.

About this time the Commissioners of Customs did several strange things. They had a fit of economy, and restricted the Bench officers' yearly allowance of stationery to eight reams paper and 6,000 pens. They issued a self-denying ordinance, stating that 'in order to a frugal management of the Revenue and an example to officers' they would in future buy their own breakfast coffee, pay their own coach-hire, and purchase their own books and pamphlets, 'except the "Book of Rates,"' which had recently come out in new form under the editorship of Mr. Carkesse, Secretary to the Commissioners.

Jeremiah Gardener, an excise officer, being engaged on preventive duty at Blackstock, Suffolk, stopped a gang of smugglers who were carrying their venture inland, and demanded surrender of the goods. The smugglers replied with a volley of stones, upon which Gardener drew sword on them. They set upon him with cudgels, beat him cruelly, took his sword from him and cut off his nose with it, and left him lying in the road. Afterwards one of them returned with the intention of killing him. Gardener's affidavit on the matter stated that having crawled through a hedge he heard the smuggler pacing up and down the road searching for him, and that in the end the ruffian exclaimed, 'Ah, damn him, he is gone!' and then went off after the rest of the party.

During this reign both Parliament and the Customs Commissioners made desperate efforts to cope with smuggling, and to restrict the nefarious energies of corrupt officials. An Order in Council forbade the appointment of customs officers in ports near to their places of birth or recent residence. A process-server for wool frauds was appointed for Kent and Sussex. His salary was £120 a year, and he had to keep three horses and an attendant. Many riding-officers were appointed on the coasts of Kent and Sussex. Later, a few were appointed on the north-western coast, but most of these were subsequently removed to Essex. (Riding-officers are mentioned in the records as early as 1670.)

There was an immense amount of pilfering on London river, and the wharves and quays around the Pool were frequently harried by thieves. In 1716 three street-keepers employed by Christ's Hospital asked the Board of Customs to be allowed to watch the quays at night. The Board employed them, giving them 3s. 4d. a week each, and a reward of 5s. for every pilferer arrested and convicted.*

Disputes between customs and excise officers as to precedence in rummaging vessels were frequent. (The Excise had power to rummage afloat.) It was arranged that if a customs man were first on board he should be allowed to complete his work before an exciseman should search, and *vice versa*.

Meanwhile Parliament issued formidable acts of prevention. It was provided that vessels of less than 15 tons used in importing spirits should be forfeited, and that rum imported in casks of less than 20 gallons should also be liable to forfeiture. Goods found on a vessel in excess of report, and foreign goods taken in at sea by coasters, were made forfeitable. Vessels of 50 tons and under found 'hovering' on the coast might be detained till the master entered into bond to proceed on his voyage. Later the legal tonnage for ships used in importing spirits was raised from 15 to 30 tons, and it was provided that 'hoverers' found within two leagues of the coast might be compelled to enter port. In 1721 the tonnage for ships carrying spirits was raised from 30 to 40 tons, and on account of smuggling in large galleys, often rowed by twelve men or more, it was provided that any boat with more than four rowlocks found in the Middlesex,

* The subsequent history of this trio of thief-catchers should be instructive to all advocates of 'blood-money.' After a time their pay was increased, and they were directed to assist in pressing men for the navy. Later they were dismissed for conniving at frauds.

Surrey, Kentish, or Essex waters should be forfeited. Royal barges, ships' boats, and boats specially licensed, were exempt

The enactments aimed against operations from the shore were extremely severe. In 1719 it was enjoined that smugglers assembling to the number of eight or more, and 'hindering, beating, or wounding officers,' should be transported to the Plantations. In 1721 the number constituting 'an assemblage' was reduced to five. Smugglers were made liable to prosecution by 'capias,' directed to any magistrate convenient. On arrest they were to be called on to find bail for their appearance in the court from which the capias issued, and on appearing were at once to find security for the forfeitures and money penalties sued for.

The inducements held out to informers were alluring, and produced what at first appeared a huge outburst of sordid treachery. Most of the informations laid, however, related to transactions which had by lapse of time become immune from prosecution. In 1725 it was provided that in such cases the Crown might sue, but only for the duty involved, and that if the culprits were unable to pay the full rate the Treasury might effect composition. Action was to be taken in the Court of Record, London, for cases in England, Wales, and Berwick, in the Edinburgh Court of Exchequer for Scottish cases, and in the Dublin Court of Exchequer for Irish. The frauds on the Excise were as numerous as those on the Customs, though the quantity of goods involved was less. When excise officers made seizures the goods, if liable to inland duties, were held by the Excise, if liable to import duties they were handed over to the Customs. Officers of both customs and excise might detain goods *if they had suspicion* of their not having paid duty. The onus of proof that the goods had been customed lay with the owner, as it does even at the present day. (Officers might prosecute at their own charge, even if the Commissioners directed release of the goods.)

If officers entered into fraudulent understanding with importers they were liable to dismissal, and the owners of the goods to a penalty of treble value. Acquittal was promised to him who turned King's evidence. Yet the Act failed, and had to be amended.

The disposal of seized goods was regulated thus: Tea, coffee, and spirits were to be sold publicly at London and Edinburgh by the Commissioners concerned. A third of the proceeds was to go to the seizing officer; the rest, minus expenses, was to be paid into the Exchequer. All seized tobacco was to be sold *by the Customs*. If the goods, being tea or tobacco, did not fetch a specified price, they were to be destroyed, the officers still being rewarded. Seized ships and boats were to be destroyed, or used by the Customs in the prevention of smuggling.

This Act contained a clause aimed directly at the customs officers, who, being first dealers with a widely dispersed traffic, had special opportunities of acting collusively. It provided that every customs officer who made a seizure should apprise an excise officer within forty-eight hours, otherwise any other customs or excise man might reseize the goods. Seized goods were not to be removed without an excise permit. This was severe on the Customs, but another clause implicated the Excise, providing that any officer of that department who dealt in tea, coffee, or spirits should be fined £50 and dismissed. Informers who supplied evidence in such cases were to be presented with the fine.

The more the fox is hunted the cleverer he becomes, and mountains of law may not prevail against winds that are favourable, nights that are dark, and fraudulent folk who are active and resolute. While the Rolls teemed with provisos and penalties, the art of smuggling was carried to a perfection previously unknown. For a full century from this date the revenue staff failed conspicuously in prevention. The contestants were unevenly matched. The population of the southern and eastern coasts of England, and of the south-eastern coast of Scotland, furnished thousands of turbulent men, eminently fitted by Nature and inclination for the lawless trade. It must be borne in mind that the British lower classes, both maritime and inland, were an entirely different race to those of the present day. Hardship, blows, and rough company were their heritage. The mob was a many-headed monster to be fervently dreaded—a monster that endured patiently many grievous inflictions, yet occasionally manifested its true temper ; not as now, by processions and wordy tumult, but by wrecking palaces, burning jails, and defying musketry. He who would realize what even rustics of that day were capable of must read Somerville's 'Hobbinol'—read and believe, for the author scarcely exaggerates except in burlesque of an older literature of combat. Glimpses of the British sailor and longshoreman may be obtained in the pages of Smollett. Most of the men engaged in contraband dealing had known the roughest of the rough life then obtaining. They were the best sailors and watermen in the world—better far than the men of the Navy, many of whom had been pressed from various sedentary occupations.

Against these shrewd desperadoes were pitted the customs officers. Little in the way of watching, chasing, and capturing could reasonably be expected of the controllers, collectors, and searchers ; their training had been utterly unfavourable to anything of the kind. They had their fees to collect and their involved accounts to check, and such work rarely develops hardihood. The riding-officers were sometimes ex-cavalrymen, and had heard the rattle of cold steel, but these had little knowledge of the longshoreman's ways and wiles. Others were men who had been 'jobbed' into the force, and were more likely to make their rounds with as little trouble to themselves as possible than to court danger and unpopularity by being over-officious. The 'sloop system' of prevention (certainly as ancient as the 'Old Subsidy') was in some ways admirable, yet often spoiled by the method of equipment and manning. Some of the sloops were private ventures, the Crown paying the owners a sum towards maintenance and victualling, and in such cases it is conceivable that few risks would be taken with the vessels, and that petty seizures and savings on the allowances might be in vogue. The captains were not always men of sterling character, and sometimes informers were shipped as mariners. Anyone who has had actual acquaintance with the type knows that there is no more despicable character than your informer—a human rat with the nerves of a rabbit.

And the smuggler was quite a popular person. (Even now, when originality has been almost schooled and policed out of mankind, respectable folk, out of pure waywardness, occasionally attempt to defraud the revenue.) In the time of the Georges it was extremely profitable to live near the coast and be on confidential terms with one's neighbours. To be able to buy brandy at a third of the duty rate, and tea and tobacco at half-price, meant much to a man convivially inclined. And the liquor primed one the speedier, the tobacco was the more fragrant, the China leaf the more refreshing, that they were found in the outhouse at daybreak, and paid for at the back-door on the following night. Of course it was so. Stolen love is sweet; so is smuggled liquor.

To illustrate fully the severe and searching nature of the preventive regulations, the determination of a large section of the king's subjects to evade them at all hazards, the unreliability of some of the collecting officials, and the nature of the work thrown upon the Board and Treasury by the complicated tariff, it will be necessary to furnish specimens of official correspondence. It must be understood that only one bundle of papers, taken almost at random, will be dealt with, and the period of time covered by them is very brief. They date from January to July, 1720, and undoubtedly they do not represent the total correspondence during that period between Thames Street and Whitehall. (Only a curt summary will be given.)

1. The Lieutenant-General in charge of the Leeward Islands complains to the Treasury of misbehaviour by the collector of St. Kitt's. The complaint is referred to the Board of Customs, the accuser and defendant are brought face to face, and the Board report the result of the investigation, as below:

It appears that a Creole named Drascon made affidavit that the collector employed him to buy uncustomed goods on board a vessel discharging at St. Kitt's. The collector produced an affidavit made by another person to prove that the purchase was made merely to find out whether there were uncustomed goods on board, that the articles bought were condemned, and that the ship was seized. The Lieutenant-General then urged that the goods were condemned and the ship seized as the result of afterthought, merely to screen the illegal proceeding. But the collector replied that he would have seized the ship earlier had not the weather been so rough that he was unable to go on board.

Drascon also made affidavit that the collector sent him to 'the French islands' to buy wine and other goods, and transhipped the wine into a vessel for Europe, thus infringing the Navigation Act. The collector admitted trading flour for sugar. He pleaded ignorance of the law. He denied buying wine.

The collector was charged with offering to release a seized ship for 150 pistoles. He denied the charge.

He was further charged with commuting the 4½ per cent. duties of sugar in kind for a money payment, and charging a shilling a tierce more than the monetary equivalent. He replied that he allowed certain merchants, for their own convenience, to commute the duties in kind, and charged the extra shilling for his trouble, as he had to use the money received in buying other sugars to send home 'for the king.'

Report: The Board consider the first three charges not proven, but hold the collector blameable for commuting the duties in kind, and consider the practice likely to lead to fraud. They will warn the other collectors in the Leeward Islands.

2. The Board inform the Treasury that it has become a frequent practice to remove in boats goods which have paid duty, and to lure the officers into seizing them. Then action is taken for damages, and, as the case is tried in the county where it has occurred, the jury are partial, 'being generally people concerned in smuggling, who seldom fail of giving a verdict for the plaintiff.' The Board have therefore prepared a clause, which they beg may be submitted to Parliament, giving power to the Crown officers to claim that any such case may be tried 'in an indifferent' (disinterested) 'county.'

3. The Board having in 1715 submitted a schedule of values for certain goods as yet unrated in the 'Book of Rates,' and having received no word as yet that it shall be submitted to Parliament, suggest that certain of the articles scheduled may at once be rated for poundage, to counteract to some extent the existing 'evil practice of swearing goods at different values' (declaring unenumerated goods at insufficient values to escape a portion of the poundage).

4. The collector of Bridgwater has reported to the Board that a Hamburg ship went ashore near his port, and that 370 hogsheads wine, 98 puncheons brandy, 12 hogsheads prunes, 36 casks resin, 1 hogshead indigo, and 200 bags chestnuts, were salved, and secured under Customs charge. The master of the ship had no money wherewith to pay the salvage claims, and his agent applied for permission to sell a portion of the salved goods, and to convey them by sea to Bristol for that purpose. The rabble of the place prevented the shipment of the goods, broke into the Customs cellars, and helped them-

selves to several casks of wine and brandy. The Board offer a reward for the apprehension of the rioters, and order two revenue sloops to repair to Bridgwater and defend the goods and the officers.

Attached to the correspondence is a doleful letter from the agent at Bristol to Mr. Earle, M.P., requesting him to use his influence in getting troops sent to Bridgwater. '50 or 60 men carried off 6 casks brandy . . . . We would have searched for it, but 40 or 50 villaines with Forks, Shovells, etc., opposed us, Swearing Bitterly they would "murder every soul of 'em." . . . The constables and tythingmen are among the greatest offenders. . . . In this Deplorable case what shall I do ?' (He referred to the unfortunate foreigners, who had been treated with great inhumanity by the rabble.) 'We cannot leave them to be Devoured by Beares.'

The Board suggest a troop of soldiers be at once sent.

5. The Board submit several clauses, to be embodied in a Preventive Act, to this effect :

(*a*) Promising pardon and reward to such as give information as to the obstruction of officers.

(*b*) Providing that brandy ships shall not lie nor hover within two leagues of the coast.

(*c*) Providing that when a vessel is detained for smuggling her officers shall be imprisoned for six months.

Etc., etc.

6. A seizure of lace, muslin, and jewels has been made in a house. The owner of the house approaches the Treasury, stating that the muslin and jewels were left with him as pledges. The Treasury refer to the Board. The Board reply that they have returned the muslin and jewels, but will prosecute for the lace.

7. A London merchant approaches the Treasury. He imported 137 butts of raisins. The usual tare was 14 per cent. of the gross weight, but the customs officers insisted that 12 per cent. would be enough. The

importer then removed the goods to his private warehouse, being afraid that if tared on the quay they might be plundered. He still claimed the high tare, and asked the officers to go to his warehouse and tare one of the casks. They refused.

The Board report, upholding the officers. 'The permitting goods to be reviewed by officers after they have been out of their possession may be of ill consequence to the Revenue.' Therefore the importer must be content with the low tare.

(My Lords concur.)

8. Certain merchants approach the Treasury, praying an alteration in the method of paying drawback on exported cider and perry. (It was urged that the goods were sent abroad in small consignments so as not to glut the foreign market, that the drawback allowed was small, and the customs officials insisted on a separate debenture for each parcel shipped. This caused the merchants much trouble and expense. It was suggested that each merchant should take out one debenture per year, to cover his total annual shipment, and receive each year's drawback in a lump sum.)

Treasury refer to Board. Board report the patent officers and searchers are against the suggestion, as the method proposed will complicate their work.*

Minute : '*Read*.'

9. Mr. Gravener, dismissed from the collectorship of Ipswich, approaches the Treasury. Board referred to.

(Gravener stated he had taken certain sums of money from merchants for attending their shipments of bountied corn at sufferance wharves and at other than legal hours, and that he was entitled to charge for such attendance.)

The Board reply that he had charged 10s. for each corn debenture and 6d. on every last of corn exported, and

* The proposal appears to have been business-like and reasonable, but readers must bear in mind that the patentees charged fees on *each* debenture.

that when a certain merchant refused to pay Gravener detained his vessel. 'No such instructions have been given by us.' Some slight recompense is due in such cases to the officers who actually execute the sufferance, but the collector should fix the sum. He has no right to charge for his own attendance. 'He cannot be a judge in his own cause.'

(Gravener stated that the merchant in question trapped him by insisting upon a receipt, and then sent the receipt to the Board; also that the merchant had a spite against him, because Gravener's father had tried to get the river made navigable from Stow to Ipswich, which was against the merchant's interest. Gravener also reminded the Treasury that when the Board dismissed the collector of Exeter for a similar transaction My Lords reinstated him.)

The Board reply that since Gravener's dismissal other charges have been made. He has been accused of extorting 4s. for every entry of goods inwards, and of charging a sufferance, in which several merchants took part, to each individual merchant; also with executing one bond for several transactions, charging the expenses on each transaction, and pocketing the surplus; also with extorting 5s. each from the captains of all colliers entering and leaving the port of Ipswich.

10. The Board, having received information from the Scottish Commissioners of Customs that great frauds occur in connexion with the Isle of Man, remind My Lords of a similar report sent from Thames Street on 18th February, 1718.

Minute: 'To be read at a full Board.'

11. The Board report as to charges of management in the port of London, stating that since the adoption of the new system of allowing for damaged wine and tobacco two out of the eleven surveyors in the port have not been required, and may be dispensed with.

Minute: 'Read. To be reconsidered another time.'

12. Presentment by Board to Treasury:

'Mr. Stanhope having by his letter of 19th Novr. last signified to us that your Lord^{pps} did agree to the Prosecution of E. Curll, Bookseller, for reflecting on this Board in an adv$^{t.}$ of the publication of a pamphlet intituled "The Present Management of the Customs," in such manner as should be advised by Mr. Attorney Gen$^{l.}$, a Prosecution has been commenced against the said Curll accordingly: But he having since attended us, and being desirous to make his submission for his said offence: We are willing, if your Lord^{pps} have no objection, upon his making his submission, that the Prosecution be dropped.

'J. Stanley.
J. Pultney.
G. Walker.
G. D. Pringle.'*

Minute: 'Agreed to.'

(It may with safety be said that the above twelve papers are about a fair sample of the correspondence between the Treasury and the Board of Customs during the eighteenth century. Volume after volume might be filled with such matter—matter highly illustrative, not only of the revenue practice, but of the social condition of England—of the manners of the day, as well as of its customs.)

It is time to take a trip across the Border, to study a few incidents of Scottish smuggling; afterwards to renew acquaintance with the controller and collector of Montrose,

* This was the notorious Edmond Curll, whom Pope made a butt of in one of the most obscene pamphlets ever printed. According to Sir William Musgrave's 'Memoranda,' the advertisement in question appeared in the *Daily Courant*. Curll in his day published much scurrilous and indecent literature, and on one occasion was set in the pillory for his pains.

and the 'Bide-a-wee' Board at Edinburgh. First must be told the story of Dunbar of Thunderton.

In 1716, the collector of Inverness had a passage of arms with 'Dunbar of Thunderton,' Provost of Elgin County. It is evident that Dunbar, although a minister of the law, was not exactly a law-abiding person. Before describing the 'tuilzie' between him and the collector a letter must be quoted, sent previously to Dunbar by one William Sutherland, a merchant who frequently acted as agent in smuggling ventures.

'I have ventured to order Skipper Watt, how soon it please God he come to the firth, to call at Caussie, and cruise betwixt that and Burgh-head until you order your boats to waite him. He is to give half of what I have of the same sort with his last cargo, to any having your order. It's not amiss you secure one boat at Caussie as well as the Burgh boats. The signall he will make will be all sails furled except his main topsaile, and the boats you order to him are to lower their saile when within muskett shott, and then hoist it again: this, least he should be surprised with catchpoles. He is to write you before he sails from Bordeaux per Elgin post.

'WILLM. SUTHERLAND.'

This letter was sent in 1710, and there is reason to believe that between that date and 1716 Dunbar continued to deal with Skipper Watt, and with other importers and receivers of smuggled goods. In 1716 the customs tide-surveyor at Inverness heard of a run, and, acting upon the information, traced seven hogsheads of wine to the cellar of William Crombie, vintner, of Elgin. He detained the goods, and summoned 'Dunbar of Thunderton' to witness their seizure. That unreliable official attended, and he and the tide-surveyor placed their locks upon the cellar. The tide-surveyor then sent for Mr. Erskine, the Inverness collector, and told him what had been done; whereupon Erskine, naturally anxious to view the seized goods, went to the Provost, and asked him to assist in unlocking the cellar. Dunbar declined (this interview took place late at night), and it is evident that the collector and tide-surveyor then foolishly went home.

Whether Dunbar really retired to rest does not appear, but it is likely that if he did it was not to sleep. On the following morning Erskine and the tide-surveyor revisited the cellar, and found that the customs lock had been broken, the Provost's remaining intact. They sent for Dunbar, who calmly took off his lock and admitted them. The casks were still there, but instead of good red Gascon they contained 'coloured water.' Then came the trouble, and it is necessary to quote some of the correspondence appertaining.

'*27th April*, 1716.

'Alexander Erskine, collector of Customs att Inverness, protests against Archibald Dunbar of Thunderton, Provost of Elgine, for all damage and loss that happened to seven hogsheads of rede wine, imbezled without payment of duty, and seized by Alexander Cummine, tyd-surveyor att Inverness, in the cellar of William Crombie, vintner, in Elgine, one of the keys of the said cellar being in the possession of the said Archibald Dunbar, and delivered to him by Alexander Cummine fforesaid, which key he refused to me, the said Alexander Erskine, on the 26th. att night, and next morning the hanging lock of the said cellar, of which the collector had the key, was brock off, and the other lock, of which Thunderton had the key, was intire and close lockt up, which he himself opened, and upon tapping, the fforesaid seven casks was found with nothing in them but water a little colloured with wine, whereas they were all left by the said Alexander Cummine ffull of good and sufficient rede wine upon his delivering up the key to the said Archibald Dunbar, and thereffor protests that he shall be lyable in the ffull value of the fforesaid seven hogsheads of rede wine, conforme to eighteen pound per hogshead, and also protests against the fforesaid William Crombie, vintner, ffor the value of the said wine imbezled by him and taken in without paying the duty, and also carried out of his said cellar and the casks ffilled up with water.

'ALEXANDER ERSKINE, *Collector.*'

It would seem that Dunbar and Crombie had been in such a hurry to remove the precious goods, and substitute 'coloured water,' that they had failed to extend due consideration to the matter of adjustment. Otherwise, it may be conceived, they would have broken *both* locks; and thus diverted suspicion from the person most liable to be suspected.

The collector also applied to Dunbar for a warrant to search the town, and a constable to assist and protect him. Dunbar refused point-blank, making his case look blacker than ever. The collector entered another protest :

'Alexander Erskine, collector of Customs att Inverness, protests against Archibald Dunbar of Thunderton, Provost of Elgine and Justice of the Peace of the County of Murray, ffor refusing me a warrant to search such houses, kilns, barns, &c. of the town of Elgine and adjacent places in that county, and refusing to give me a constable to goe along with me to search ffor wine imbezled out of the cellar of William Crombie, vintner, in Elgine, and other uncustumed goods, confforme to a Write of Assistance produced to him.

'ALEXANDER ERSKINE, *Collector.*'

He then reported the matter to Edinburgh, and Charles Eyre, Solicitor for the Scottish Customs, went to work with a view of having the Provost exchequered. Readers may be inclined to think that Dunbar was in a perilous position, but there were ways of settling such matters. The Provost consulted one Ludovic Brodie, writer to the Signet, and Ludovic took the only promising course. He interviewed Eyre more than once. The matter in dispute was one of wine, and it followed that a considerable quantity of wine was consumed while they were threshing the matter out. Let Brodie's letter to Dunbar after the final interview proclaim Brodie's method, and the pleasing result:

'Your affair with the Exchequer has bein advysed, and the bills are ordered to be redelivered, you paying the officers' costs who seized the wynes. Now the costs to them, according to the rules of Court, will be but about three or four guineas, besyde what may be claimed for information-getting, as to which Mr. Erskin seems not to demand anything for himself, but to referr himself to your discretion. This matter has stood the most drinking (and also some considerable charges) that ever I drunk in any other, for tho Eyre be a gentlemanie prettie little fellow yet he drinks like a devil, and I have had many sore heads with him. Wyseman will not deny but I desired him to buy or make such a brydle as would please you: if you do not plague him with your tongue you are in wrong to yourself and me, for he would not lose ane hour's drinking for all the bussieness in the world.

'LUDOVIC BRODIE.'

Who 'Wyseman' was, and the meaning of the mysterious allusion to the 'brydle,' remain to be discovered, but it is possible Mr. Brodie wrote this with a wet towel around his head. The affair seems to have been adjusted in a manner likely to afford at least partial satisfaction to all concerned. Eyre had several rosy nights, Brodie ditto and got his 'charges.' Dunbar and Crombie got off with the good 'rede wine,' and the officers got their 'costs,' the collector probably coming off much better than the tide-surveyor. Dunbar, no doubt, was put to considerable expense, but it is probable the arrangement would lead to a comfortable understanding between Provost and officers, and that Skipper Watt would in future be able to run goods without fear of being 'surprised with catchpoles.' Small wonder that the returns of Customs revenue did little more than pay the cost of collection and the salaries of the judges.

In 1725 the collector of Montrose reported to the Scottish Board that the Montrose surveyor of customs had made a large seizure of brandy, etc., at Arbroath. The surveyor stated that finding that certain vessels, names unknown, had been 'hovering on the coast,' he procured a party of soldiers, went to Arbroath, patrolled the town all night, and in the morning searched and found the goods in question. The collector and controller in their report requested the Commissioners to use their influence towards procuring a detachment of soldiers to be permanently stationed at Arbroath. 'There are more goods run there than at any place on the coast.' Later a person named Dennison claimed that the seizure was due to private information furnished by him, and that he was entitled to a substantial share of the reward. This led to some very pretty fencing.

It was a practice amongst smuggling skippers, when freighting with contraband oversea, to obtain a bill of lading for Bergen, so that if whilst 'hovering' to run their cargoes they were driven by stress of weather into a British port they might produce the document, and thus account for having on board a thousand or so ankers of brandy which, being under the 'lawful content' of 60 gallons each, would be deemed illegal packages and liable to seizure. (At Bergen there was a Staple for all foreign goods taken into the Scandinavian realms.) Both the English and Scottish Boards were aware that this was usually mere fiction, for it had happened more than once that a 'hoverer' had put forward this plea in port and been allowed to depart for Bergen, but shortly afterwards had been driven again by storm into the same port or one adjacent, when it had been discovered that there was no brandy left on board, except a demijohn or two in the captain's locker, and an ullaged anker in the forecastle. So when Captain Hamilton of the revenue sloop captured a 'hoverer,' and brought her into Montrose with her illegal cargo, and the master produced a Bergen bill of lading, the collector and controller referred the matter to Edinburgh. The Board directed that the master's plea should be accepted, that he should be allowed to depart, and that two customs tidesmen should be put on board to keep him company to Bergen, to see the cargo discharged there. One may imagine the smuggler captain's disgust at this inquisitorial proceeding. He left with his two tidesmen, and in due course the tidesmen returned safe and sound, and stated that they had carried out their instructions. Then they put in an appalling bill for expenses, which caused much correspondence between Montrose and Edinburgh.

The collector and controller, in a later message to the Board, gave a doleful description of the state of affairs in their district : 'The boatmen along the coast and the country people favour and assist the smuglers in carrying on their smugling trade so much that it is almost impracticable to an officer to get any intelligence from them, and when any poor man happens to bring an information to an officer he is afraid (if discovered) of his life, or at least of being obliged to leave this part of the country.'

In transmitting their account of the balance in hand for the month of December, 1725 (after paying certain charges), the collector and controller asked permission to retain the money and pay the officers with it. 'The amount,' said they, 'of this month is seldom enough to pay the officers.' The amount in hand was £42 odd.

Early in 1726 the collector of Newcastle informed the Montrose officers that a ship of Arbroath had been driven by storm into his port, that she had a large quantity of brandy on board, and that the master held the usual papers for Bergen. A week later the vessel entered the port of Montrose, and on being rummaged was found to have nothing in her hold but seed and old iron. The Montrose officers reported the matter to Edinburgh, but the concluding portion of their statement was unlikely to encourage the Board to proceed further in the business.

'We have questioned the sailors, but they are better taught than to divulge anything, either of the running of the goods or any other passage of the voyage, notwithstanding all the civil and discreet offers we can make them, they being a set of ingrain'd rogues. The master had the assurance to deny positively that he was ever within Tynmouth Bar.'

The officers at Kirkcaldy seized an 'open boat,' containing 60 bushels of smuggled salt. The sole occupant of the boat was a sturdy rogue, said to be Thomas Watt of Johnshaven. Thomas Watt 'furiously assaulted' the Kirkcaldy officers, beat and overthrew them, triumphantly put to sea again with the goods, and escaped. The Board directed the Montrose officers to proceed to Johnshaven, and if possible arrest the valiant smuggler. The officers reported back to the Board the result of their efforts. They had been to Johnshaven, and failed to find Thomas, or his open boat, or his 60 bushels of salt. 'The only Watt in Johnshaven,' said they, 'is a shoemaker, and appears a poor silly fellow.'

Later one or two rather important seizures were made, in each case with the assistance of the military. The goods were kept for some little time in the warehouse of Montrose, and then sent per sloop to Leith for condemnation and sale, advised as to quantity, etc. The Leith officers examined them on arrival, and discovered the following discrepancies :

Montrose Advice.	*Leith Re-examination Account.*
1 butt brandy.	2 butts brandy.
73 full ankers brandy.	70 full ankers brandy.
1 ullaged anker brandy.	1 ullaged anker brandy.
25 full ankers geneva.	24 full ankers geneva.
1 ullaged anker geneva.	1 ullaged anker geneva.
A quantity of cocoa and treacle.	Largely deficient.
A quantity of tobacco.	38 pounds short of advice.
A quantity of coffee.	Slightly deficient.
A quantity of sugar.	Somewhat short.
A quantity of starch.	Largely deficient.
A quantity of currants.	7 pounds in excess of advice.
Four casks gunpowder.	No gunpowder.

The above are quoted from a Board's query on the matter. The collector and controller replied that possibly the goods had lost by leakage and drying during the voyage. They made no other attempt to account for the disappearance of three full ankers of brandy and one of geneva, for the transformation of one butt of brandy into two, or for the total evanishment of four casks of gunpowder. 'Never,' said they, 'were goods more carefully weighed and gauged, and shipped on the sloop that conveyed them. We can't understand it. We always have three locks on our warehouse.'

The balance for the Crown at the end of January, 1727 (after paying the quarterly salaries), was £2 19s. 10¼d.

The *Michael and Mary* of Holy Island was driven by storm into Montrose, and found to have on board a large number of half-ankers of brandy, a quantity of tea, and the usual Bergen bill of lading. The officers referred the case to the Board, and were directed to make the master enter into a 'hovering bond.'* The master complied. Seven months later the officers wrote to the Board, stating that having received no certificate of the landing of the goods at Bergen they still held the bond undischarged. No further correspondence on the subject is forthcoming, and it may reasonably be surmised that the sureties had absconded, and the vessel, with her rig and name altered, was 'hovering' again.

The balance for September, 1727, reached £182 odd, and the officers found themselves confronted with a new difficulty. They wrote: 'We cannot at present procure Bills on Edinburgh for remitting said balance.'

On October 6, 1727, a ship arrived from Philadelphia with 103 hogsheads of tobacco, legally entered for discharge at Montrose. This caused quite an official commotion. The sum due to the Crown at the end of the month was over £231. The officers asked the Board to allow them

* This was really a bond to refrain from 'hovering.' Convicted smugglers, on release, were often called on to enter into bond to refrain from smuggling, and this was called 'a smuggling bond.'

to keep a portion of this 'great balance' in hand, as the importer of the tobacco had given them to understand he would soon be exporting part of the goods again, and asking for drawback. Thus it would appear that there was no accommodation for bonding tobacco at Montrose, and the importer had to deposit the whole duty even on goods that were soon to be exported.

The Board sent information that one Gillespie of Arbroath was about to make an illegal shipment of wool. The collector and controller replied that they were sending 'a trusty tidesman' to assist the Arbroath tidesmen in seizing the goods. Lest the Board might become too sanguine of success, they added: 'Arbroath is so mobish a place that unless troops be quartered there it is almost impracticable to stop these frauds.' The trusty tidesman returned with news that the ships had left before he reached Arbroath.

Readers will no doubt have realized by this and previous quotations from the Letter Books that the Montrose officers were by no means equal to the exigencies confronting them. Later particulars will show that the exigencies were more formidable than they appear—that the collector and controller had reason to dread, not only the mob, but the magistrates.

Meantime the London Board had been kept busy, not only in devising schemes for the suppression of smuggling, but in dealing with complaints made by the public, in settling disputes between the customs officers and the excisemen, and in regulating the domestic economy of the Custom-house. The records are rich in amusing and instructive references, but here is space for a few only.

In 1714 a large fire broke out in Thames Street, which did great damage to the Custom-house.* The Commissioners laid a report before the Treasury, stating roughly the

* The Custom-house had been built after the Great Fire in Charles II.'s reign.

amount of the loss incurred, and of the expense sustained otherwise. The principal item of loss was the complete destruction of 232 hogsheads of sugar, which had been collected in the Leeward Islands as 4½ per cent. duties in kind, sent to London, and stored beneath the Custom-house. The value of these was stated as £2,780. 61½ gallons brandy and 18 gallons wine, being part of a seizure, had been distributed among the people who helped to put the fire out. The books and papers had been removed, but the Commissioners were unable just then to state the total expense of saving and housing them, or even the expense of temporary offices for the staff. But they uttered their minds upon the action of the Clothworkers' Company, who had allowed them the use of the Clothworkers' Hall as a temporary refuge, and charged at the rate of £500 a year for the accommodation. (During the earlier stage of banishment the Commissioners themselves put up at Garraway's Coffee House.)

The London merchants petitioned the Treasury, objecting to the many holy-days observed by the customs officers, especially Shrove Tuesday, St. Swithin's, Holy Cross, and Wednesdays of Easter and Whitsun. They also requested that one Commissioner should attend in the Bench Office at 9 a.m. to sign cockets. The Commissioners at once agreed, and stated that if the merchants had approached them the Treasury need not have been troubled with the matter.

In 1725 the Board decided to allow a bonfire to be made upon the quay on Coronation Day. 'But,' said they, 'being apprehensive that a large bonfire would endanger the shipping, we direct our Housekeeper to make a moderate bonfire, not exceeding 40 faggots. He may give some liquor to the watchmen and others to drink the health of his Majesty and the Royal Family, as usual on such occasions, but he may not suffer firebrands to be thrown about or any squibbs fired.'

In 1727 a customs landing-surveyor and an excise officer were deputed to investigate the gauging of casks in the port of London. On the second day of inquiry trouble arose, it being discovered that the customs and excise methods of gauging differed. The merchants seem to have preferred the customs method, for they united in a complaint against the delay caused by excise gauging. Of course it does not follow that the customs gauging was correct because it pleased the merchants.

The Board issued an order that Swedish religious books, ‘for the use of the Congregation in Pennsylvania,’ should be allowed to pass duty-free.

It was the practice, when a new foreign ambassador arrived, for the Treasury to issue a warrant directing the Customs to ‘extend every facility to the passing of his baggage.’ He was allowed a certain quantity duty-free, and the Commissioners usually required him to furnish a schedule of the goods, and declare above his signature that they were for his own use, nor would they allow him to *import* goods duty-free afterwards. In 1720 Baron Discow imported ‘a suit of cloaths,’ and the Treasury enjoined the officers to ‘use all civility and despatch consistent with law.’ The officers reported that the clothes were embroidered, ‘and cut out though not made up.’ The Board of Customs thereupon directed a prosecution.

The king had to pay duty on his customable goods. The royal baggage on arrival was removed under seal to Whitehall, and ‘the three senior land-surveyors’ attended to examine it. Stringent instructions were issued to collect all duties payable, and *two* officers had to be present whenever a package was opened. The Board in 1723 issued an order to the effect that His Majesty being expected to arrive from the Continent the river guard was to be strengthened ‘to prevent running of goods,’ and letters were sent to the chief officers of Kent and Essex, directing them to be extremely vigilant. When wine was imported for the king's use it was removed to Whitehall, being first entered on ‘a Bill of Sight,’ and officers were sent to gauge the casks and assess the duty. ‘The Secretary of State's box’ was examined at Whitehall after arrival from foreign in 1715, the officers being particularly directed to charge duty upon any customable goods they might find in it.

Nor were the Commissioners childishly trustful of each other. They directed that whenever a package arrived from foreign for one of them the landing-officer dealing with it was to remove it to the King's Warehouse, and the Warehouse-keeper was bound to furnish a report of the matter at once to the assembled Board. Most of the Georgian Boards of Customs appear to have been aflame with zeal.

It should be mentioned that in 1724 Lord Poulet, one of the Exchequer 'tellers' or receivers, was called upon to account for £4,191 14s. 6d. which had been stolen from his office in the Exchequer.* (The deficiency was made good out of the Sinking Fund in 1729.) It appears that the thieves broke through the roof, and forced the lock off the end of one of the chests, thus creating an aperture, through which they withdrew five bags of gold. Four of these, and a portion of the contents of the fifth, they carried off, and left the broached bag lying on the floor.

LIST OF AUTHORITIES.

Scottish revenues before Union: Assisa de Tolloneis; Custum Portuum; Assisa Regis (David); Acts of Robert III.; Scottish Acts, 1424, c. 19, 22, 23; 1425, c. 18; 1466, 1-4; 1478, 5; 1493, 12-17; 1535, 25-32; 1540, 11-12; 1567, 63; 1581, 12; 1597, 'Act anent the Custumes'; 1597, 23; 1604, 'Commissioun for the Vnion'; 1606, 'Act anent the Customes betuix Scotland and England'; 1641, 127-150; Convention of Estates, January 31,

* This appears to have been the only theft of Exchequer money since the romantic feat achieved by Richard de Pudlicote early in the fourteenth century. The undetected thief who got off with Poulet's takings was a mere trifler, compared with Richard. Not only did the latter carry off £100,000 worth of gold and jewels, but he was assisted in his exploit by many of the monks of Westminster Abbey, and several of the officials of the Palace. The robbery was performed at dead of night, and the Palace mason assisted Richard and his associates in breaking through the wall of the Pyx Room. Much of the plunder was not recovered till months after the robbery.

1644; 1661, 92, 277, 310; 1663, 8; Warrant of April 16, 1689; 1695, Act 32; 1695, 70; 1696, 7; 1698, 42; 1701, 8, 9, 13.

Liverpool: 8 Anne, c. 8.

Permanent branches of revenue: 8 Anne, c. 5; 8 Anne, c. 12; 9 Anne, c. 6; 9 Anne, c. 12; 9 Anne, c. 13. 10 Anne, c. 18; 10 Anne, c. 19; 12 Anne, c. 12; 13 Anne, c. 18; 1 Geo. I., s. 2, c. 23 (on 9 Anne, c. 17); 6 Geo. I., c. 11; 8 Geo. I., c. 20; 9 Geo. I., c. 19; 11 Geo. I., c. 7.

Quarantine: 9 Anne, c. 2.

Wreck: 13 Anne, c. 21.

Departmental incidents: Sir Wm. Musgrave's 'Memoranda'; Montrose Letter Books; Treasury Papers, July 16, 1727; Treasury Papers, vol. 261; Treasury Papers, January to July, 1719-1720; Customs Book, No. 15; Treasury Papers, vol. 252.

Establishment: Carkesse's Book of Rates, 8 Geo. I., c. 31; 9 Geo. I., c. 21.

Wine: 6 Geo. I., c. 12.

Frauds: 6 Geo. I., c. 21; 'Social Life in Former Days.'

Preventive Measures: 9 Geo. I., c. 21; 5 Geo. I., c. 11; 6 Geo. I., c. 21; 8 Geo. I., c. 18; 12 Geo. I., c. 28.

Temporary Imposts: 10 Geo. I., c. 10; 12 Geo. I., c. 26.

Protective measures and prohibitions: 8 Geo. I., c. 15.

CHAPTER VII

THE PERIOD OF FRANTIC RESTRICTIONS AND FEARLESS SMUGGLING

1727–1760

WHEN George II. ascended the throne, it must have appeared to some of his subjects impossible to invent many alterations in the tariff list. The latest 'Book of Rates,' although edited by the Secretary to the Customs Commissioners, had been an indescribable hotch-potch. Yet the revenue tables were to be rendered still more perplexing.

Imported wine-lees were made liable to duty as wine. Wine imported in bottle, or in casks containing less than 25 gallons, was prohibited, unless from the Levant. Lignum vitæ grown and shipped at the Plantations was freed of duty inward.

Amid uproarious rejoicing, the excise duty on home-made salt, and the customs surtax on foreign salt, were abolished. The collection of these imposts had been both inquisitorial and expensive, yet the pay of the collecting officers was continued for eighteen months from the cessation of the duties.

The bounty on British sailcloth was increased, and British gunpowder was bountied on exportation.

In 1732 the odious excise duty on British salt, and the customs surtax on foreign salt, were revived 'for three years.' Their renewal was tumultuously opposed, but the ministers were obdurate. The collectors were re-instated, as though the temporary remission had been a device towards securing them a holiday on full pay. (At the end of three years the duties were continued for seven years, and yet again, and yet again.)

To encourage British hat-makers, exportation of hats from the Plantations was prohibited, it being also provided that no plantation hatter should have more than two apprentices at a time, that no 'black or negro' should be taught the trade, and that no person in the Plantations should sell hats unless he had served full apprenticeship as a maker.

In 1729 the Customs Commissioners directed that goods of flotsam, jetson, and lagan were to be entered and duty-paid as though landed in the ordinary way.

In 1731 they directed that merchants who failed to enter their goods within the specified time should be sued for the duties payable.

It was found necessary to direct excise officers not to go beyond their stations to rummage vessels, and not to interfere with the customs rummagers.

The customs officers were instructed, when they suspected 'women of fashion' of carrying customable goods, to call in the services of a female searcher 'in whom they could confide.'

It appears that the eel-schuyts of Worcum, which may at the present day be seen lying in the Thames abreast of Billingsgate, plied between Holland and London in 1732. Duty was levied on the eels carried, at the rate of £3 a cargo.

The Custom-house Registers of 1732 stated the shipping belonging to the port of London as over 1,400 sail, navigated by nearly 20,000 men. 130 of the ships were from 300 to 500 tons, 83 from 200 to 300; the rest were under 200 tons, except one 'great ship' belonging to the South Sea Company, which was 750.

The Board of Trade informed Parliament that the Council of the American province of Massachusetts Bay, by passing an Act to encourage paper-making in the province, had seriously injured the British paper trade to the Plantations, that a duty recently levied by the State of New York upon imported negroes was undesirable, and that Plantation manufactures promised to compete formidably with those of Great Britain. Soon after more discouraging information was supplied. It was stated that large iron forges were being set up in New England, and that many ships built there had been sold to the French and Spaniards, being paid for in wines which were smuggled into the Plantations. Inquiries were made in consequence of these reports. The answers furnished were contradictory, every official questioned reporting according to the interests of his office.

The inland duty on coffee of the British Plantations was reduced from 2s. to 1s. 6d. a pound, and the goods were burdened with such a host of restrictions as to certificates, oaths of declaration, special markings, etc., that the planters would have been justified in resenting the remission.

To encourage the Plantation sugar trade, a duty was placed on all rum, sugar, and molasses imported into the West Indies from other parts of America, and all such goods sent from the 'other parts' to Ireland were to be landed in England during transit.

An alteration was made in the drawback on British refined sugar exported, leaving it as below:

	£	s.	d.
Rate during time of William and Mary	0	3	0
Increase during Anne's reign	0	1	0
Increase by this Act	0	2	0
Total drawback	0	6	0

Later the special 'French duty' on brandy from France was abolished, it having been extensively evaded by the importation of French spirits as Flemish, etc. Instead, an extra excise duty of 1s. per gallon was laid on imported 'single spirits' (spirits below a certain strength), and 2s. per gallon on 'double spirits.'

In 1736 the Board began to make arrangements for

the bonding of rum. Warehouses were to be provided at certain legal quays, the merchants interested to defray the cost, and the pay of the officers in charge. (Bonding was not legalized till 1742.)

The duty on arrack was amended. Previously arrack had been rated as an East Indian commodity, and its value for poundage had been the gross price paid at the East India Company's sales. The excise duties being payable as well, it had thus been rated higher than other foreign spirits.

The duty on woollen yarn from Ireland was abolished. The importation of books, written and printed in Great Britain, and reprinted abroad, was prohibited.

In 1739 the Stationers' Company undertook to pay the expenses incurred by the Customs in prosecuting importers of pirated books, and to reward the seizing officers.

In 1740 the Board enjoined that owlers should not be allowed to compound for penalties.

Rum and spirits of the Plantations were allowed to be deposited in warehouse on importation, the customs duty or Old Subsidy being first paid. Then bond might be entered into by the importer to pay the excise duties when he wished to deliver his goods for home consumption. The warehouses were to be supervised by the excise officers. The importers had to clear the goods within a specified time.

An additional tax was placed on foreign cambrics, and made a fund for bountying British and Irish linen. In 1745 'The Additional Wine Duty' was instituted, being an extra tunnage of £8 on French wine and vinegar, and £4 on other wine and vinegar. A loan of £2,000,000 was raised upon this tax, part to be by a lottery. During the reign there were about a dozen public lotteries in connection with national loans. And with all these lotteries and all this funding, Parliament issued statutes against private lotteries, stock-jobbing, horse-racing, gambling, and cursing and swearing.

French cambrics and lawns were prohibited importation, except if warehoused under bond to export within three years. The wearing of apparel made from these materials was also forbidden under heavy penalties.

The inland duties on tea, etc., were altered to 1s. a pound, and 25 per cent. of the gross price at the East India Company's sales. In 1746 'The Glass Duty' was established, being a bunch of additional duties on the various kinds of foreign glass. By 19 Geo. II., c. 27, it was provided that if a British ship arrived in a British port carrying foreign sails duty should be paid upon the sails. Later appeared 'The 1747 Subsidy,' an additional 5 per cent. poundage on all dutiable goods. The tremendous loan of £6,300,000 was raised upon it, and in connexion with this there seems to have been some tricky 'operating,' the courtiers and their friends trying to monopolize investment.

In 1748 a premium was granted upon Plantation indigo. By 22 Geo. II., c. 36, foreign embroidery and brocade were prohibited. In 1750 raw silk of the Plantations was made duty-free. A bounty was granted to British ships built for the herring fishery, being 30s. a ton per annum for fourteen years from date of building, provided they were decked vessels of from 20 to 80 tons. This act specified the limits of the herring-grounds, and the legal times of fishing. The Shetlands on the east and Cantire on the west were the northern limits. The fishing on the east was to commence not earlier than June 13, and the shoal to be followed not later than October 1. On the west coast fishing was to commence not earlier than September 1, and to end on December 31. The bounty money was to be paid out of the Customs revenue.*

Pig-iron from the Plantations was made duty-free, and bar-iron freed in the port of London only. (The latter privilege had soon to be extended to all British ports.) It was enacted that no mill for slitting iron, no plating forge to work with a tilt hammer, and no furnace for making steel, should be erected in the Colonies. (This

* In 1757 the bounty was increased to 50s. a ton.

Act, though passed by both Houses, was not put into execution.) The Irish parliament having bountied Irish sailcloth, and established a growing export trade, a duty equivalent to the bounty was placed on Irish sailcloth imported into Great Britain.

In 1752 two new permanent branches of customs were established—' The Duty on Linen Yarn,' and ' The Duty on Gum Senega.'

In 1758, it having been found that the owners of imported spirits which were liable to excise duties on landing frequently kept the goods on board ship for an unreasonable period, to postpone entering them for the Excise, it was enacted that such goods should be landed, entered, and the excise duty paid, within thirty days of importation, unless they were rums of the Plantations, in which case they might be bonded. The excise officers were permitted to take a sample not exceeding a quart from each cask, for the purpose of ascertaining the strength, and these samples were to be paid for by the Crown at the rate of 16s. a gallon. This last clause was soon found detrimental and repealed, and the official sample was limited to a half-pint without payment. The old practice of allowing the importer a duty-free sample of half a pint from each cask was reaffirmed.

In 1758 two of the Commissioners of Customs were directed to wait upon the duke of Newcastle, to discuss a scheme put forward by the Board of Trade for preventing revenue frauds in the Plantations. The Commissioners attended, but desired to be excused from considering the scheme, unless commanded to do so by the king, the Privy Council, or the Treasury. So the project was returned to the busybodies who had framed it.

During 1758 a royal licence was granted and a passport issued for the carrying of 800 bushels of oysters to France, ' for the Queen and Dauphiness.' This reads strangely, for at the time there was war between Great Britain and France. Besides, 800 bushels was a large order. Yet the record is clear on this point.

It was decided to employ a proctor at the Crown's expense to arrange for the appropriation of a quantity of Spanish silver, shipped by the collector of Charleston on board the *Winchilsea*, which vessel was captured by the French, and retaken by an English privateer. The amount originally shipped was 3,456 ounces, the amount restored by the privateer 1,736 ounces.

So many flagrant depredations were committed by British privateers that a committee of merchants was formed to inquire into the matter, and a customs solicitor was directed by the Board to attend the meetings, and render all assistance possible.

On account of an attempt upon the life of the Portuguese king, the officers of customs were directed to detain any Portuguese subject landing in Great Britain, and at once acquaint the Board. Later the order was qualified by an injunction that sailors need not be detained, and again to the effect that the order applied only to such Portuguese subjects as were 'scarred upon the cheek.'

Customs officers were directed to be vigilant in searching for escaped prisoners of war. If any were found they were to be sent 'to the nearest agent for such people.' The agents paid 10s. a head and expenses, in all cases of capture.

The quarantine regulations were strictly enforced. A man-of-war sent a boat's crew aboard a Levant trader to press seamen for the navy, and in consequence the man-of-war had to undergo quarantine.

It appears that tea was inspected as to quality. A quantity of tea from Deal (undoubtedly a contraband cargo seized) was ordered to be burned, it having been found 'dyed and adulterated.'*

Towards the end of the reign 'The Subsidy of 1759' was granted, another permanent branch, being additional poundage at 5 per cent. *ad valorem* upon many classes of merchandise, including tobacco, sugar, grocery,

* In 1761 a similar order was made in respect of a cargo seized at Exeter.

linen, paper, and spirits except rum. About this time appeared an Act allowing bonded Plantation rum a drawback on export of all the customs duties paid at landing, and remitting all the excise duties applying to such goods.

Undoubtedly at the end of this reign there was no citizen competent to act as a clearing agent for all classes of goods, and no customs official who thoroughly understood the whole of the Customs regulations.* The documents used in payment of duty were miracles of elaboration, with their numerous items of subsidies old, fractional, and new; of imposts, additional imposts, special duties, coinage duties, etc. The Plantation Acts bristled with exceptions and special provisions. The Coasting regulations were a monument of circumlocution. Every tax had a fringe of exasperating ramifications, even the Acts of bounty were clogged with bewildering formulæ.

The inevitable result of the huge burden of duties was increased smuggling, to combat which Parliament issued string after string of regulations, which we proceed to summarize. The first revenue law of 1729 was a concession to culprits, providing that in cases prosecuted by capias defendants might plead *in forma pauperis.* In 1732 an attempt at practical prevention was made. Three sixth-rate ships and eight armed sloops were sent to cruise in the Irish Sea, to prevent the exportation of woollen goods from Ireland to foreign parts. The captains were granted powers of search, and instructed to seize all vessels carrying Irish woollens not cocketed for the

* In 'The British Customs, with the Laws relating abridged and digested under Proper Heads,' a handbook compiled by Henry Saxby, of the Custom-house, London, which appeared in 1757, there are several remarkable paragraphs, conveying the author's declaration that all the previous compilers of similar handbooks had been guilty of many blunders. Specimens of the errors are given, and they are certainly flagrant. 'Although,' says Mr. Saxby, 'it is a disagreeable employment to animadvert on the errors of others, yet a just regard to improve and instruct necessarily requires that some few instances should be pointed out.'

stipulated western English ports.* In 1734 bitter penalties were prescribed against the landing of foreign hops prior to entry, and the carrying of foreign hops to Ireland without their being first landed in England.

The famous Act of Indemnity was issued in 1736. This was one of those odious revenue Acts peculiar to the time of the Georges, Acts which appealed to the baser villain. It indemnified all smugglers who might be mean enough to disclose their past offences, thereby implicating their comrades, and made the infamous process cheap and handy. (The plea of indemnity was to cost no more than 1s. 4d.) It provided against future offences by an enactment which for cold cruelty has never been surpassed. Persons pleading and subsequently offending were liable to prosecution for *both* offences, and if the offence quoted for indemnity carried the punishment of transportation the subsequent offence involved death without benefit of clergy. Three or more smugglers carrying firearms were punishable with transportation.†

* Later in this reign the privilege of importing Irish woollens was extended to every British port.

† The well-known Galley and Chater case furnishes a striking example of the deadly hatred felt towards revenue informers by the smuggling fraternity, of the fierceness and recklessness of many of the leading smugglers, and of the partiality and severity with which some of the judges interpreted the laws.

In September, 1747, a large quantity of tea was seized, and lodged in the Custom-house at Poole. On the night of October 6, 1747, a gang of armed smugglers attacked the Custom-house and carried off the tea. (Mr. Milner, later described by us as dismissed from the Service, was at this time collector of Poole, and was the first that gave evidence in the subsequent trial of Galley and Chater's murderers.)

The smugglers carried the tea inland, and on the way passed through Fordingbridge, Hants. One Daniel Chater, a shoemaker living at Fordingbridge, recognized a member of the gang named Dimer, and laid information at the Southampton Custom-house, in consequence of which Dimer was arrested and lodged in Chichester jail. It appears that one of the leaders of the gang, named Tapner, convened a meeting of the smugglers, and arranged for a night attack upon the jail, but, reckless as the men were, the arrangement fell through.

On February 14, 1748, the collector of Southampton directed one of the tidesmen of the port, named Galley, to accompany the informer Chater from Southampton to the residence of Major

Two or more armed smugglers carrying goods inland, or found within five miles of the coast with 6 pounds tea, or 5 gallons spirits not covered by permit, were to be deemed 'runners.' Persons 'lurking' within five miles of the coast were liable to be whipped and put to hard labour. Persons maimed in arresting smugglers were entitled to a reward of £50. Informers discovering two or more accomplices were entitled to £50 for each person convicted, and held free of their own offences. The law against 'hoverers' was strengthened, and the 'illegal limit' for transhipment of foreign goods at sea increased

---

Battine at East Marden. He gave them a letter which they were to hand to the Major. Battine was a J.P., and surveyor-general of customs for Sussex.

They set out on horseback, and on arriving at Leigh found it necessary to ask the way. Three villagers undertook to guide them, and brought them as far as Rowland's Castle. They all went into a public-house kept by a widow named Paine. Mrs. Paine became suspicious of Galley and Chater, and secretly apprised several smugglers living in the neighbourhood. The smugglers soon arrived, armed with whips, pistols, and knives, and managed to lure Chater out of the taproom. They proceeded to interrogate him as to his business, upon which the tidesman Galley came out and interfered. A fellow named Jackson struck Galley with his fist, and knocked him down. Then the gang took both the strangers into the house. Galley produced his commission, and announced that he was a king's officer. 'You a king's officer!' answered Jackson; 'we'll make a king's officer of you!'

Then the smugglers compelled the terrified men to drink, and it is likely they drugged them, for Galley and Chater fell asleep. Jackson and his comrades carried them into an adjoining room, and searched them. The letter was found, and it revealed that Chater was an informer.

The gang sat drinking for some time, and debating as to what they should do. First they decided to run both Galley and Chater across the Channel, and detain them in France, there being war at the time between France and England. Next they decided that the confederacy should subscribe for the men's keep, and detain them in England till Dimer had been tried. 'Then,' grimly suggested one of the gang, 'we will do unto them whatever is done to Jack Dimer.' But as the drink mounted they altered their minds, and resolved upon murder.

The ringleader Jackson went into the room where the men lay, and aroused them by slashing them with his whip. The poor fellows were driven into the road, and both of them tied upon one horse. It appears that many of the villagers came round, and some may have protested, for one of the gang drew a pistol, and

to four leagues from the coast. Revenue officers were privileged to oppose force to force, and entitled to bail if charged with maiming or killing offenders.

In 1745 a fresh Act of Indemnity was issued. In 1746 assembling to run contraband goods was made punishable 'by death as a felon.' Counties were made liable for offences committed within their limits. If goods were captured and afterwards rescued the fine on the county was £200. If an officer was beaten in the execution of his duty the fine was £40, if killed £100, but the county was held exempt if the offenders were convicted within

---

informed the spectators that if any man present uttered a word afterwards of the matter he would be sought out and shot down without mercy. Then away in the direction of Harting. It was already dark. The smugglers made one of the villagers lead the horse on which Galley and Chater rode.

As soon as they were clear of the village they made an onslaught, and lashed the two unfortunates in a shocking manner. Jackson was especially vindictive, and urged his comrades on with shouts of 'Lick them, damn them, cut them, slash them, whip them!' He was very bitter against Galley, and in the end the poor tidesman fell into the road, and died of his wounds. His body was thrown across a horse in front of one of the smugglers, and the maddened cavalcade went on till they reached a public-house at Rake, kept by a man whom they knew. They compelled this man to show them a place where they might bestow the dead body. He took them to a fox-earth some distance away. A hole was dug, and the mangled remains were buried. Chater was conveyed to Trotten, and the party put up at a house kept by a notorious smuggler named Mills. Chater, who had been treated most brutally, was chained up in an outhouse hard by. All the smugglers living near who had been concerned in the attack upon the Poole Custom-house were sent for, and a council held. It was agreed that Chater should be put to death.

The man Tapner, who had proposed to rescue Dimer, was one of the new arrivals. He led the others into the outhouse, and bade Chater betake himself to prayer. While the poor wretch was praying one of the gang kicked him, and Tapner drew a knife and slashed his victim across the face. They led him to a dry well, and Tapner put a rope round his neck and hurled him down. They let him hang for some time, then cut the rope, and he fell. Thinking he might still be alive, they flung earth and large stones upon him. Then they went back to the tavern, and fell to drinking again.

It is of course impossible to urge anything in extenuation of such abominable brutality, yet there seems to have been some unfairness in the charge made to the grand jury by Mr. Justice Foster, when several of the persons implicated in the above

six months. If an offender failed to surrender within forty days, and was afterwards captured, the person capturing was entitled to a reward of £500. Strong inducements towards official temerity were held out. If an officer seized goods, and they were afterwards released on action taken, the officer was exempt from costs, provided that the judge considered there was 'probable cause of seizure.' If an action for damages were won against a seizing officer, and the judge certified 'probable cause,' the plaintiff was entitled to no more than 2d. damages. This Act contained one provision which

---

crime were put on trial the following year at Chichester, at a special Commission of oyer and terminer, presided over by the duke of Richmond. Justice Foster commenced by stating that dangerous confederacies had been formed 'for robbing the Revenue.' Like Duncan Forbes of Edinburgh (*vide* p. 235), he invited every man of the jury to 'lay his hand upon his heart,' and ask himself in what smuggling differed from robbery. (Yet the prisoners were not on trial for smuggling, but for murder.)

Tapner was charged with 'choaking and strangling Chater with a rope (of the value of sixpence).' Old Mills and his son were charged with 'inciting, moving, stirring up, instigating, counselling, persuading, and procuring thereto.' (This was a matter of murder, and we think should have been as heinous a crime if committed upon a miller and a tailor as upon a tidesman and an informer.) Jackson, Cobby, Hammond, and Carter were also charged with murder and participation. It is not exactly clear why the learned judge should have delivered a long discourse upon smuggling, and the revenue laws recently issued. Yet thus did he; indeed, he spoke of little else. He stated that when armed persons were assembled for smuggling, and one of them killed a revenue officer, the whole assemblage were guilty of murder, though they went out but to smuggle. And if, in striving to kill a revenue officer, a smuggler killed one of his own comrades, the whole of the smugglers present (except, of course, the dead man) were liable for murder. Nor was this all. He insisted that all who had advised or persuaded the smugglers to go a-smuggling would also be liable for murder in the cases quoted. (Yet the men were not tried for murder committed whilst smuggling.)

There can be no doubt that the prisoners richly deserved hanging. They made little or no defence, and did not attempt to question the witnesses. They were sentenced to death, and, with the exception of the two Millses, their bodies were to be hung in chains. Jackson had been ill before the trial, and died soon after receiving sentence. The rest were hanged the day after trial. Two of them, Cobby and Hammond, preserved an aspect of sullen dejection. Tapner and Carter, when the hangman fitted the nooses, reached towards each other and shook hands. The Millses

smacked of forethought, considering the difficulty of securing seasoned sailors for the King. It allowed smugglers to indemnify past offences by volunteering for the navy.

In 1750, on account of extensive smuggling of candles, soap, and starch, a legal limit for packages was fixed (224 pounds). In 1751 the tobacco trade from the Plantations was burdened with a host of maddening restrictions which need not be enumerated. In 1753 it was discovered that on account of the higher London rates on wine there had been a deal of fraudulent carrying of wine by land from outports to the metropolis, and it was

---

displayed not the slightest concern. All the men were turned off at the same time. The younger Mills was the first one noosed, and the hangman took some time in noosing the rest. During this interval Mills, who appears to have been a dogged and stubborn wretch, watched the process with evident curiosity.

The bodies of Jackson and the Millses were buried in 'a hole' at the foot of the gallows. The rest were disposed of as follows:

Tapner's body was hung in chains on Rook Hill.

Carter's body was hung in chains on the Portsmouth Road.

Cobby and Hammond were exhibited in a fashion that reminds us of Tennyson's 'Rizpah.' They were suspended at Selsey Bill,

> 'That all the ships of the world might see them passing by.'

(Such a grim old England as it was!)

The most extraordinary point of the whole matter was that though the murders must have been known to many people, though the news must have travelled amongst the smuggling fraternity all over the south of England, the bodies were not recovered till several months after the crime. Undoubtedly this was due to fear of the smugglers, and it exemplifies clearly the power which a few armed and desperate men may wield over a scattered community.

The man Jackson was a notorious character. He was a native of Welsworth, Hampshire, and a smuggler of many years' standing. He professed the Catholic faith—if such a character may be held to have had any real religion. A relic was found on him after death, bearing this legend:

> 'Sancti tres Reges
> 'Gaspar, Melchior, Balthasar,
> 'Orate pro Nobis nunc et in Hora Mortis Nostræ.

'Ces billets ont touché aux Trois testes de S.S. Roys a Cologne. Ils sont pour les Voyageurs, contre les malheurs de chemins, maux de teste, mal-caduque, fievres, sorcellerie, toute sorte de malefice, et mort subite.'

enacted that 'outport wines' brought to London should pay the extra duty at the place from which they were removed. 'London' for the purposes of this Act included all places within twenty miles of the Royal Exchange. It was enjoined that velvets and silks imported should be sealed by the customs officers prior to delivery. The penalties of counterfeiting the seal were an hour in the pillory and a fine of £500. In 1755 the 60-gallon limit for casks of spirits was extended to all foreign spirits, even if reported for exportation. Tea above 6 pounds, imported in vessels other than those of the East India Company, was made forfeitable.

It should be mentioned that there were frequent riots to prevent the exportation of corn, bread being often dear. Throughout the reign there was much distress, and one of the latest freaks of Walpole's Parliament was a bloodthirsty Act against sheep-stealing, the offence being made punishable with death without benefit of clergy. Later, this cruel provision was extended to cattle-stealing.

The National Debt had been immensely increased, and the staff of tax-collectors had swelled into a small army—an army not overpaid officially, but tireless and insatiable in the collection of fees. Posts in the Customs and Excise were battled for with a fury that was intensely significant, and the sordid strife endowed all place-givers with far-reaching influence. It is probable that 20 per cent. of those able to read and write were either collecting taxes or clamouring to be thus employed, while most of the people with a few guineas to spare were on the look out for lottery results and dividends on public loans. Some of the more thoughtful writers of the period cherished forebodings of national bankruptcy. They had lost all faith in ministers, they suspected every professed patriot as a place-hunter. They referred to the pages of ancient history, and found warrant for their fears at every flutter of the leaves. Yet Britain was to sustain the rule of other Georges, to have vaster experiences of war and taxation; her debt was destined to assume proportions hitherto undreamt of, and to become impregnable as the everlasting hills, and yet she was to hold and even mend her place in the world. The croakers might have found solace in the contemplation of things around them. A magnificent record of naval and military achievements had been enrolled, the stock of illustrious poets, literary men, and inventors had been conspicuously augmented, and the lower classes, in spite of the imminence of famine, the press-gang, the stocks, the hulks, and the gallows, retained their old attributes of stubborn valour and broad humour. It was merry in England still. Even the tariff may not have been so dreadful in that day as it appears now to the student of Carkesse's 'Book of Rates.' The taxes may but have furnished food for laughter to that vast section of the community that never paid them.

It will be well to survey the regulations applying to Plantation commerce. Originally matters of revenue discipline in the Plantations had been left in a great measure at disposal of the surveyors-general stationed there. (Once one of these powerful officers forwarded to England a charge against a subordinate, and the Board made no inquiry. The officer accused was dismissed without being allowed to defend himself.) This method obtained up to 1740, and conduced to much injustice.

The Plantation collectors paid the wages of the inferior officers out of the receipts, but their own salaries were paid through their attorneys by the Receiver-General in London. The West Indian collectors submitted their accounts to the 'surveyor and controller' of Jamaica, the American collectors to the surveyor and controller of South Carolina. The surveyors-general were allowed a month to check the accounts, after which all the documents, with the moneys, were sent to London by the first available Government ship leaving. There appears to have been occasional difficulty in getting the accounts in, especially those of dead West Indian collectors, and in such cases the London Commissioners stopped the 'surveyor and controller's' salary till an attempt was made at clearing things up. In 1743 many frauds were detected in the Plantations, and one of the surveyors-general was dismissed.

The invoices furnished by Plantation collectors, which contained full particulars of the quantities, nature, and origin of goods shipped, accompanied the cargoes to which they related. When a Plantation cargo came to London, either for final unshipment or landing and reshipment for foreign, the invoices were sent to the jerquers at the London Custom-house. At an outport they went to the collector, and in either case if the out-turn did not correspond with the invoices the Board were at once apprised.

The doings of the East India Company at this period are extensively interwoven with Customs history. The Company's affairs were scrutinized closely by the Customs authorities, and there seems to have been need of vigilance, for the directors were always ready to exceed their charter privileges. In 1721 the Privy Council found it necessary to issue an order directing that the shipment of negroes by the Company, and the carrying of them direct to the Plantations, should be discontinued. In 1725 the customs officers employed at the Company's London warehouses complained of unfair dealings at the periodical sales. It appears that the system of 'sale by candle-inch' conduced to fraud. The Board amended the method of auction, and directed that no sale should be concluded until bidding had ceased. The Company's higher officials occasionally presumed upon the privilege granted of paying only half the duties at time of warehousing, and shipped goods thus partially duty-paid, claiming and receiving the full drawback. It was therefore provided that drawback should not be paid upon the Company's goods till the 'Collector Inward' had apprised the Receiver-General that the full duties had been rendered. The Collector was to endorse 'Secured' upon the debenture.

The Board distrusted the Company's maritime officials, and were never done with devising restrictions. As soon as it became known that an East Indiaman was in the Downs the official hive was astir, and great was the buzzing in the reaches of the Thames, and at the various legal quays. The ancient practice was to put eight tidesmen aboard in the Downs, to accompany the vessel to Gravesend. Later eight Deal men were used instead of tidesmen. In 1749 the practice was discontinued, and the vessel watched by a customs galley till she entered the Thames. The river officers were kept on the alert, and the Medway revenue sloops cruised in Sea Reach and the Lower Hope. At Gravesend 'head and stern boats' were posted, to guard the vessel by day and night. A tide-surveyor and eight tidesmen went on board, and at intervals during the night the tide-surveyor had to hail the head and stern boats, to ascertain whether their crews were keeping a good look out. Thus formidably occupied and beset, the vessel proceeded to her discharging place at Blackwall. (At the time there were no docks in London.)

The officers commenced to rummage as soon as the vessel was 'reported inwards.' All baggage and 'private trade' packages were unshipped into 'hoys,' and a special account of such goods was transmitted to the Customs Commissioners. The hoys were placed in charge of tidesmen, who accompanied them to the legal quays, where their cargoes were landed, and conveyed to the East India Company's 'private trade warehouses.' The keys of these warehouses were in duplicate, one being kept by the Company's warehouse-keeper, one by the customs officer in charge. By 'private trade' was meant goods brought on freight, and therefore not the

Company's actual property. The goods belonging to the ship's officers were put in the King's Warehouse.

The rest of the cargo was delivered into lighters from the ship, and each lighter was escorted by tidesmen to the quay where the goods were to be examined. After examination they were taken to the Company's warehouses in the vicinity of Crutched Friars, and the landing-waiters who had made up the account at examination delivered a duplicate of their list to the Company's warehouse-keeper, who at once entered the particulars in his ledger.*

Meantime the vessel was being watched, rummaged, and guarded,† as though her very ballast were gold-

* The Company made the customs landing-waiters a present of 30 guineas each ship.

† It may be instructive to compare the above with the following description of the methods used at the present time—to assume that a P. and O. steamer—say the *Macedonia*—arrives in the port of London, and proceeds straight to her berthing-place in Tilbury Docks. She has disembarked about two-thirds of her passengers, and landed most of their baggage, at Continental ports and at Plymouth. The rest go ashore directly she berths at Tilbury, or earlier by tender, and within an hour they and their baggage are clear of the Customs. A preventive officer and two or three 'rummagers' go on board, and collect the dutiable goods brought by the officers and crew. If the owners of these goods desire to pay duty on them at once, the duty is taken and the goods are cleared. The larger parcels usually go to the baggage warehouse, and are cleared there. But if any member of the crew desires to keep his dutiable goods on board, for use during the outward voyage, they are placed, free of charge, under customs seal in the ship's storeroom, and when the vessel gets to sea again the seals are broken and the goods restored.

After the preventive officer has dealt with the 'stores,' he and his assistants rummage the vessel, or such portions of her vast fabric as they think fit. Partial re-rummages are subsequently made at intervals.

The *Macedonia* commences discharging directly she is alongside, and her cargo is tumbled ashore or into lighters with amazing rapidity. The Customs warrant for landing is a copy of the vessel's report, stamped in the Custom-house, and transmitted to the landing-officers, but a perfect entry must be passed for each consignment of goods before they may be examined and delivered. The duty-free goods are usually examined by the customs officers soon after the entries for them are received. A number of packages are opened and inspected to see that the goods are in accordance with the entry, and thus each consignment is rapidly

dust. Each tide-surveyor employed reported upon his brother tide-surveyor's conduct, and all the reports went to the Commissioners. Each day the ship was overhauled from stem to stern, and the tidesmen who formed the watch were changed every week. As soon as a hold was cleared of cargo it was rummaged, and then placed under customs lock. Notices were posted on board, bidding all and sundry to beware of attempting fraud. Tidesmen stood constantly at the gangway, ordered to *search* every one who left the ship. The officers of excise came on board frequently, and, unmindful of the upturned noses of their customs brethren, rummaged to

---

cleared and delivered. The *actual tally* of duty-free goods, and of such goods as are liable to low rates of duty, is furnished to the Customs by the dock officials, or the lightermen who receive the packages.

The higher-rated dutiable goods, such as tobacco, cigars, spirits, etc., are removed under customs lock to 'uptown' bonded warehouses. These, and goods transhipped for export without examination, are the only articles *counted* by the landing-officers. Now, if we suppose the *Macedonia* to have come from India or Ceylon, about one-third of her cargo will consist of tea. This huge quantity of dutiable goods goes by rail or lighter under lock to the City tea warehouses, and the first customs account of it is taken when it is brought to the warehouse scale to be weighed.

If the vessel is urgently required to load, as fast as a convenient portion of each hold is emptied of cargo the space is inspected and cleared by the preventive officers, and loading commences. Thus import cargo may often be seen going out at one side of the hatchway while export cargo is going in at the other, and by the time discharge is completed about one-third of the export cargo is shipped. Loading is performed as expeditiously as discharging. All 'bonded goods'—viz., dutiable goods shipped from bond—are swiftly examined by the customs officers prior to shipment. The vessel's requisites in the shape of wine, spirits, tobacco, etc., for use of passengers and crew, are also shipped from bond, and placed under customs seals, to remain thus secured till the vessel gets to sea. Such of the outward passengers as join in London go on board. The moorings are cast off, the dock tugs are in attendance, and away she goes fully loaded, having been in port, say, three weeks only.

The *Macedonia* is over 10,000 tons, and has accommodation for about 500 passengers, yet the clearance of passengers' baggage, and the 'searches' of the vessel, do not occupy in all much above a day's work of three or four customs officers. Compare this with the tremendous parade of search and guard in George II.'s day, on an East Indiaman of about 500 tons.

the best of their skill. The Board's concluding instructions upon the matter of East Indiamen were worded thus : 'And when all this is strictly performed and complied with, the ship is to be deemed and declared duly cleared inwards.'

There was a customs as well as a Company's warehouse-keeper for the general warehouses, and customs locks were on all the doors and outlets. The lockers were selected tidesmen, and the two seniors reported confidentially on the conduct of their assistants. The excise officers had free access, and checked all accounts and deliveries of goods subject to excise duties. The Company's method of account of receipts and deliveries was dictated by the Board of Customs. The Board's instructions as to sampling were painfully elaborate, yet the sampling officers were bidden to apprise Thames Street if they thought additional precautions necessary. The periodical sales were conducted with imposing solemnity, and under supervision of an army of customs and excise officers. When deliveries of private trade goods were required, the Company's directors granted a 'sufferance,' and sent their own selected officers to assist the Customs in examining the packages and supervising delivery. When a ship's officer wished to clear his stores from the King's Warehouse he had to apply to the Board, furnishing a full account of his goods.

It might reasonably be concluded that with all these precautions, the import vessel in a way corked and sealed by the Customs, watched on all sides from the time she was first sighted till she left the mouth of the Thames six months later, her cargo surrounded by officers till it reached the warehouse, then constantly watched though under lock, and every one concerned in the business spying and reporting upon his fellows, not one wisp of herba silk, not one ounce of tea, not one curio in porcelain, could escape custom. Be it borne in mind that the Company's directors were as eager as the Commissioners to suppress fraud, that they employed many supervisors for that purpose, and issued instructions almost as elaborate as those we have quoted. But nothing good ever came of circumlocution. The records show that smuggling was rife ; even the captains were frequently unable to accompany their ships outward because Exchequer proceedings were pending against them. In 1748 a number of customs officers were dismissed for conniving at export frauds committed by the Company's officials. Complaints from merchants who bought at the sales were frequent, and in 1756 the Board announced their opinion that the regulations governing the water-guard practice had been rendered futile by the instrumentality of the very officers who should have carried them out. Often there was great confusion over the payment of drawback, the Company having received the full amount, yet having only paid a moiety of the inward duty. Once the Collector of London was cautioned for *paying* debentures, instead of merely certifying to the account and leaving actual payment to the proper officer —the Receiver-General.*

It scarcely appears that the Commissioners were to blame. They sat aloof in Thames Street, doing the best that Commissioners could do, but knowing none of their subordinates except the higher indoor officials, and these latter really seem to have been victims of circumlocutory dementia. Whenever they got news of fraud or carelessness at the quays, in the warehouses, the Thames reaches, or at the outports and creeks, they meted out punishment to offenders, and then issued a few pages of fresh regulations. Now it is perfectly true that there was never yet an elaborate regulation contrived that practical men could carry out. Thus it must have been with the codes of instructions. The landing-waiters, tide-surveyors, and riding-officers, whether practical men or not, read

* Undoubtedly the vicious fee system was responsible for this. Payment of a sheaf of debentures meant a few guineas in fees to the paying officers, and thus the spectacle was presented of one civil servant complaining bitterly because another had intercepted his work.

them, shuddered at the penalties prescribed against disobedience, and, realizing that to comply would be impossible, at once started to devise dodges.

By the Letter Books of Montrose, May, 1728, it appears the collector and controller transmitted to Edinburgh the report of Roderick Pringle, tidesman, as to his treatment by the people of Arbroath, and suggested that troops should be stationed at that turbulent port. 'Our tidesmen,' said they, 'are so terrified to go on duty at that place for the insults given them by the inhabitants that unless some troops be quartered in that town there is no preventing their continued practice of smuggling at the very shoar.'

In 1729 the Arbroath tidesman sent word to Montrose that a large quantity of tobacco had been run. The Montrose officers provided themselves with a military escort, proceeded to Arbroath, and after search found a small quantity of tobacco abandoned in an open place. The Arbroath tidesman stated that though the smugglers passed close by him he was not able to recognize any of them. 'It was dark,' said he, 'and they were disguised.'*

Great news at last. The officers, assisted by the military, made a large seizure, and captured twenty-nine horses and fifteen carts. These were condemned, and the collector put them up for sale. There were no bidders, so he disposed of them 'to certain people at the appraised price of £15.'

(The officers excused themselves in their report to the

* It appears that smugglers, after a run, frequently abandoned one package, so that the officers finding it might be pacified and return home. Of course this suited such officials as were not anxious to cross staves with a dozen scowling ruffians. A flaming report was usually furnished, and the formula, 'We followed the track of wheels and found,' etc., seems to have been much in favour.

Board by pleading that the animals and vehicles were 'sorry truck,' but the Board waxed wroth, and censured the collector.)

This seizure made the next cargo of seized goods sent to Leith quite a respectable freight, amounting to 3,015 pounds of leaf tobacco, nearly 2,000 gallons of brandy, 8 gallons of canary wine, and 154 gallons of white wine. Sharpened by the Board's censure, and mindful of what happened with the last consignment, the collector wrote : 'All the casks have been filled to prevent imbezilment, and the goods are put free of all charges on board the sloop. We have paid the pilotage out and in.'

Trade was evidently growing brisker. The balance for one quarter in 1729 was £548 7s. 6d. 'But,' wrote the collector and controller, 'there is drawback due on a quantity of tobacco, which will exhaust most of this ballance.' It seems as though they hated parting with money.

Early in October, 1729, the officers of excise seized a large quantity of brandy, and placed it in the King's Warehouse for security. Shortly afterwards the Board received the following letter from the collector and controller:

'CUSTOM HOUSE, MONTROSE,
'*11th October*, 1729.

'HONOURABLE SIRS,

'This morning betwixt the hours of twelve and two the door of His Majesty's Warehouse was broke open, and 107 ankers of Brandy which was seized by the Excise Officers and one of the Quarter Casks of Brandy formerly seized by our officers, carried away.

'At two o'clock in the morning when the Guard came to relieve the two Centry's that were placed at the Warehouse door they found the door open, the Centry's gone, their muskets lying near the warehouse, and one of their Beyanats lying broke before the door, and no person to be seen near the Warehouse nor in the Street. The Sergeant immediately went and acquainted the Commanding Officer, who with a party came to the Warehouse and found it in the above Condition, nor no account what was become of the Centry's, and no person to be seen on the Street save a maltman whom he sent to the Guard. Thereafter the Officer came and acquainted the Collector, and they together went to the Provost's house to demand his assistance, but could get no entrance, so we went round the Town, and finding everything quiet and no person to be seen sent some of the Souldiers to the Links to patroall, when they found the two Centry's lying tyed neck and heel. The Officer asked them why they had left their posts, they told him that Fourteen or Fifteen men had come upon them with Clubs and other weapons and had knocked them down and tyed them in the condition they were found, and afterwards dragged them to the Links where they left them lying, but that they knew none of them—this is all they could say. Our officers with the Souldiers kept patroalling round the Town till the morning to prevent as much as possible the Conveying any goods out of Town, and this morning the Collector and Surveyor acquainted the Collector of Excise with what had happened, and they together went to the Provost and desired a Warrant for a General Search of the Town, which he refused, telling us that it was not an ordinary thing, and that he could not do it without calling a Council. We told him that did not relate to his Council, and so took a Protest against him, upon which the Collector as a Justice of the Peace gave warrant to the officers of Customs and Excise to search everywhere where they had any suspicion, but when they began their Search the Provost sent a Town Officer and carried off the Constable, which oblig'd our Surveyor and the Supervisor of Excise to go to him and ask his reason for taking away the Constable. He said he was an inhabitant in the Town and he would not allow him to officiate, and gave it them as his advice to take care of themselves. Upon this the Collector appointed a new Constable, and they began their search again, and when they came to the house of Baylie Murison there arose a Mobb of a vast number of People, so that the Collector was obliged to go and read the proclamation against Riots. This is all we can inform your Honrs. just now, the post going off, but we are affraid of little Success by reason of the night's coming on and almost all the Inhabitants against us, however we shall take all imaginable care that no goods be conveyed out of Town till Munday morning, and your Honrs. shall be acquainted next post.'

There appears good reason to think that the searchers were ' there or thereabout ' when they were preparing to invade Bailie Murison's premises. Further particulars were furnished on the ' Munday.'

'CUSTOM HOUSE, MONTROSE,
'13*th Octr.*, 1729.

'HONOURABLE SIRS,

'We acquainted you by our letter of the 11th instant of our proceedings in relation to the Goods stolen out of the King's Warehouse. The Officers of Excise and Customs having demanded the Search of Baylie Murison's house and Shops he peremtorally refused, and called his Town officers to seize the Constable whom the Collector had appointed to act and carry him to prison, but the Souldiers protected the Constable, upon which the Mobb rose, but upon the Collector's reading the Proclamation the Baylie thought proper to call them to disperse. However this so terrified the Constable that he was ffrighted to act, not knowing whether a Single Justice's warrant upon such a juncture was sufficient for him. This with the night's coming on put a Stop to the Search, but upon application to the Commanding Officer he ordered Centry's to be placed upon the Baylie's house and Shops till this morning, when there was a Justice of Peace Court, where the Excise Officer who made the Seizure which was taken out of the King's Warehouse gave in a List of all the houses and places of this Town where he had Suspicion the Brandy was Lodged to the Court upon Oath as the Law required, but the Provosts of Arbroath, Brechin, and Forfar with the Provost of Montrose (who as we understand had called them for that end) overruled the Court and refused the Officer a warrant after he had given his Oath, upon which James Scott of Logy and the Collector as two Justices of the Peace Showed their Dissent by Entring their Protests, as did the Collector of Excise protest against the proceedings of the Court in this matter as Illegal. Upon this we gave over any further Search, finding it impracticable to do any manner of Good, and some of the Excise officers fearing their Lives. The Collector of Excise is to lay all this before his Board, and we must humbly begg leave to lay before your Honours that if some notice be not taken of this matter the Officers of the Revenue in this District will have a difficulty to make good any Seizures or to protect the King's Warehouse.'*

It is apparent that the collector and controller were trying to whitewash themselves. Finding that they were involved in a dispute on legal points, they had allowed caution to disarm them, even with the law undoubtedly on their side, and were puzzled to invent excuses. 'The Officers *of Excise* and Customs having demanded the Search' ('Excise' first), 'Some of the *Excise* Officers fearing their Lives.' Probably the excise officers appreciated to the full the exigencies of their position, yet it is certain that the two old customs gentlemen were in considerable fear, if not of their skins, at least of queries from Edinburgh. If they had but thrown legal consideration to the winds, and pressed forward, protected by the soldiers, to the search of Bailie Murison's house, they would have been able to furnish warrant for their proceedings in the shape of 108 full ankers. He who takes no chances makes few seizures of contraband.

* It does not appear from the Letter Books that any action was taken by the Board.

In 1730 the Secretary at Edinburgh discovered that certain ancient revenue bonds of Montrose remained undischarged, and directed the collector and controller to investigate the matter. They did so, and the parties concerned refused to acknowledge their indebtedness. It appeared that when the rebels seized Montrose in 1716 the customs staff fled, and the Jacobites thereupon appointed one Skinner to the office of collector. The bonds mentioned, which were for security of certain coal duties, fell into Skinner's hands, and he raised about £20 on them. When the rebellion was over, the original customs staff were reinstated. The collector and controller laid these particulars before the Board, and intimated that there was little hope of recovering anything on the bonds. 'For,' wrote they, 'Skinner is long dead, and was broke before he died, and his family live on charity.' The matter was allowed to lapse.

In June, 1730, the collector applied for ten days' holiday. He stated that he had had no leave since March, 1727, and only ten days then. It is to be feared that he was not a brilliant official, but he stuck to his desk.

On May 18, 1733, the collector of Inverness sent the following lugubrious letter to the Scottish Board:

'Yesterday morning some ill-disposed villains have carried away the Custom House boat across the ferry, and with saws and axes have cut her in two by the middle, left the one half on the beach, and disposed of the other to the waves.

'The execution of this is owing no doubt to common people, but the contrivance to greater heads, and that it has been premeditated appears by the tools they had provided themselves with to perform it.

''Tis hard to tell where this will end. The warehouse has been twice broke open, the boat destroy'd, the Expresses from the outports stopp'd, and the Letters taken away, a Person under suspicion of being an Informer dreg'd across the Firth and his ears cut out, and hints every day given to myself to take care of my life; in short, no part of the Face of the Earth is peopled by such abandoned villains as this Country.'

The letter proceeded in complaint that a promised revenue sloop had not appeared. 'I am in no small pain till she arrives, for I find the people here will stick at no kind of villainy whatsoever.'

This letter the Scottish Board transmitted to the Lords of the Treasury, and the covering report contained a remark which must have made my Lords stare: 'We confess we are not expecting a remedy. We are even at a loss how to propose the means.'

During the same year the English Commissioners of Customs apprised the Treasury of immense smuggling in Suffolk, Essex, Kent, and Sussex. Within twelve months 54,000 pounds tea and 123,000 gallons brandy had been seized, yet smuggling was steadily increasing. The cargoes were being run by 'well-armed gangs' of desperate fellows, who had succeeded in intimidating both sheriffs and customs officers. One hundred and six dragoons were asked for, to assist 185 already supplied.

In 1736 the famous Porteous Riots took place in Edinburgh. One Andrew Wilson of Pathhead had been concerned in many smuggling enterprises, which had involved him in prosecution and heavy fines. Hearing that the Kirkcaldy collector was at Pittenweem, and in possession of a large sum of public money, Wilson, with three comrades, broke into his lodgings and robbed him. The theft appears to have been almost publicly conducted, and the thieves walked off with the spoil without the slightest hindrance. Later they were pursued, the money was recovered, and Wilson and one of his comrades were arrested, tried, and sentenced to death. While in custody Wilson, who was a powerful and determined man, contrived and secured the escape of his accomplice.

Captain Porteous, the commander of the City Guard, by his extreme officiousness and brutality had become unpopular with the folk of Edinburgh, and his proceedings in connexion with Wilson's execution excited them to fury. It appears that the citizens manifested their sympathy with the culprit by disorderly conduct directly the ceremony had ended, and Porteous thereupon ordered his men to fire upon the mob. Several people were killed, and many wounded. Porteous was arrested, tried in the High Court of Justiciary, and condemned to death. Many of the more wealthy citizens signed a petition recommending him to mercy, and Queen Caroline, in the absence of George II. on the Continent, granted respite. This caused great indignation amongst the lower classes of Edinburgh, and on September 7, 1736, an armed mob broke into the Tolbooth, dragged Porteous forth, and hanged him. Erskine, the Solicitor-General, appears to have investigated the matter, and from the tenor of his report it is evident that there was little likelihood of the active participants in the deed being discovered. No one was punished except the mayor, who by an Act of 1737 was disabled from holding office. It seems that the mayor had been over-cautious upon the matter of summoning troops to protect the Tolbooth; anyhow, the indignant authorities in London made him a scapegoat.

While upon Scottish matters, an incident of 1744 must be narrated, though it breaks the sequence of affairs. During that year one William Gordon ran a cargo of brandy and tobacco into the harbour of Spey, and landed it at various places along the coast. The Scottish Board came to know of this, and applied to the local justices to take a 'precognition.' The justices refused, alleging that they might be compelled to interrogate witnesses who would turn out to be implicated. The Board thereupon consulted the Lord President of the Court of Session, who sent the chairman of the local bench a tremendously solemn letter, which is here quoted.

'DEAR SIR,

'The Christmas holydays, which have emptied the town and adjourned the Board of Customs, have prevented my being able to write to you on the subject of your smuggling as I once thought I should; but lest what I may write you after consultation with others should come too late for your meeting on the 15th inst., I have taken the part in the meantyme of dropping you this line.

'I have not been more surprised for a great while than when I heard that a majority of justices, at your last meeting, putt off the precognition on a doubt whether they lawfully could take information from the witnesses upon oath, and thereby, however innocent their intentions were, flung some cold water at least upon the enquiry.

'As to the doubt itself, I confess I am at a loss to guess on what it is founded: precognitions have at all times been taken on oath in Scotland, and hence the established practice in the Court of Justiciary of cancelling, at the trial, the oath formerly emitted on the precognition, before the witness emit his deposition in Court, if he desire it. No occult crime, however dangerous to the commonweal, or to the Crown, could be detected or punished, if witnesses were in the least backward, without a power, in those whose duty it is to enquire, to examine upon oath. And if the practice in English law is enquired into, no justice can commit, as they may in Scotland, upon a signed information only. The justice must examine the informant upon oath before he can issue his warrant, so that, as I apprehend the scruple is without any just foundation, I doubt not at your next meeting, after gentlemen have time to inform themselves duely, it will evanish.

'I cannot suffer myself to suspect that, considering

the notoriety of the mischief that smuggling does to this poor unhappy country, and the forwardness lately shewn, by all ranks of men, to express their detestation of it, and to bind themselves to one another and to the publick, by resolutions and engagements of honour, to discourage that villainous traffick, any gentleman or number of gentlemen, will in broad daylight, and in an open Court (whatever their connexion with, or tenderness for the unhappy smuggler be) be so impudently profligate as to attempt to screen the cutthroats of their country, and thereby expose themselves to the universal contempt and abhorrence of mankind. Such an attempt requires more than an ordinary degree of courage and wickedness ; the guilty person cannot hope to remain unknown, the minutes of the court must record his infamy, nor is it to be expected by him that the character, which by such practice he may purchase, shall remain confined to his own country ; the common post can, by an extract from the minutes, convey his fame to Edinburgh, from whence it may be communicated to the whole kingdom.

'Now, tho for these reasons I hope you will be unanimous at your next meeting, yet, if contrary to my expectations, and very much against my wish, the smugglers should find protection, and the national justice, as well as interest, should be defeated, I hope you will be so good as to transmit the minutes, distinguishing how each justice voted, besides furnishing me as a private gentleman with information who I ought to detest and avoid as a scoundrell. I may be able to inform my fellow-subjects, as far as that may be done within the laws, who they ought to look upon as enemies to their country. Other rebukes they may possibly meet with, but it is not necessary to speak of that at present. I write, you see, with great freedom, as I am very much in earnest, but what I have said are the dictates of my heart, and you are at full liberty to make what use you please of what I have wrote. This mean, shameful course to destruction must be prevented, or our unhappy country must be undone. Make my compliments to everyone who can lay his hand upon his heart, and say he does not deserve the title of Rascal, and believe me to be, &c.,

'DUNCAN FORBES.'

A few extracts from the correspondence between Thames Street and the port of Boston may be of interest. Readers must picture the long stretch of coast under supervision, extending from Grimsby to Wisbech, the flat, dyked country inland, the North Sea with its chances of a quick run from the Continent, and the large and thirsty agricultural population of the Fens eager for cheap brandy and geneva. Ardent spirits were much in demand in Lincolnshire ; they were thought potent against marsh-fever and ague, and medicine more pleasant to the Fenmens' palates would be hard to find. To gratify an inherited liking, and benefit the constitution as well, what more popular pastime can be conceived ? No wonder the smuggler was liked, encouraged, and screened, when he was both cheap provider and family doctor.

In the play performed betwixt Boston and Thames Street the leading *dramatis personæ* were the Commissioners, very affable on paper, extremely forbearing with errant officials, and ever signing themselves with the gracious old formula, 'Your loving friends.' They seem to have been heart and soul in the prevention of smuggling. They had one or two indefatigable spies on the Continent, who kept them well posted as to the lading of illegal cargoes. Their secretary was Mr. Carkesse, a gentleman with literary leanings, who had compiled the most maddening 'Book of Rates' known, and when information from the Continent reached Thames Street he transmitted it to Boston. The result as regarded seizures was not at all impressive. Some of the preventive men seem to have preferred interviewing informers after the fact to riding the bleak coast at night, and they sent on much information about ancient runs, a deal of which the Solicitor at London contemptuously dismissed as corrupt or inconclusive. Some of it, however, was manifestly sound, and showed that a large business was being done.

The collector and controller did nothing rashly. It may reasonably be assumed that they were of the average official type. They looked sharply after their fees, as most men in their position would. Once they quarrelled, and took to writing separate reports, till admonished by the Secretary.

A play is always the better for a whole-souled, persistent villain. The villain of the piece was Captain Jewell, commander of the revenue sloop. He appears to have been possessed by but two ideas. The first was that on that exposed Lincolnshire coast the weather was usually so rough that it was unsafe to put to sea; the second that his sloop needed extensive and expensive repair about once a quarter. The bills he sent in for repairs would almost have defrayed the cost of a frigate. When queried on these points he stoutly maintained the correctness of his charges, and on one occasion actually discovered that he had forgotten an item of expense. The commanders of sloops had to keep journals, and occasionally the Board sent for the documents and checked them. Jewell was never caught tripping in that respect; he had the gift of imagination, and could make startling records of work which had not been performed. It is likely that his journals were neat and well written, for he appears to have rarely ventured out into rough water.

The subordinate officers made many detentions of goods for informalities, for being brought coastwise without cocket, or with a cocket incorrect as to particulars, and other petty breaches of the regulations, and whenever, after due inquiry, such matters were cleared up, and found to have occurred otherwise than through official neglect, the parties in fault were directed by the Board to 'make reasonable compensation to the detaining officers for their trouble.' The amount of such compensation appears to have been settled privately between the detaining officers and the culprits.

Sometimes when seizures were made the London Solicitor informed the seizing officers that they might prosecute in the Exchequer at their own charge. This was usually ordered when the evidence was not conclusive. If the officers declined, the Solicitor sometimes directed prosecution 'at the Crown charge,' and in such case the officers were debarred from participating in the profits.

During 1733 the Board sent informations 'a many,' including news of a small Bridlington sloop loading contraband at Zealand to run between the Spurn Light and Bridlington, and of two Sunderland ships, one Whitby ship, two Newport ships, and one Chichester ship, loading tobacco and brandy at Dunkirk to run on the east coast. Boston failed to profit by the tidings.

In 1734 a quantity of silk was seized at Grantham by the excise officers, and handed over to the Customs at Boston. Samples were sent to Thames Street. Expert opinion was invited, and the goods were pronounced East Indian silks. The Solicitor directed that the goods should be formally seized by an officer of customs, and prosecuted in the Exchequer at the charge and for the benefit of the Excise.

Perhaps to stimulate Captain Jewell to action, H.M. ship *The Fly*, Captain Oates, was commissioned to cruise between Flamborough and Yarmouth, to prevent the exportation of wool from Lincolnshire to France, and the running of brandy and other goods. Captain Oates was directed to cruise diligently ; to visit all suspicious vessels, and in case of seizure take them to the nearest port and surrender them to the Customs ; to keep up correspondence with the Customs, not to search unnecessarily, to go into port only when necessary, to stay no longer than necessary, and to forward a copy of his journal once a month.

The officers seized *two and a half pounds* of tea *by information*, for that the retailer who owned it had offered it for sale without having an authorized room for the purpose, as required by law. The Solicitor directed as follows : 'If they have proof of this, let them prosecute under the Excise Act. If they have proof that the tea was run, let them also prosecute under the Customs at the King's charge. But if they have no proof, let them deliver it.'

The collector sent to London the annual account of Captain Jewell's seizures. The Board replied that the seizures were few and of small value, and asked if the sloop was often at sea with captain and mate on board, why more seizures were not made, and whether the sloop was really necessary. (That she was necessary there can be little doubt ; whether she was useful or not was easy to ascertain from the seizure list.) In response the collector and controller forwarded affidavits against Jewell, accusing him of embezzling seizures. He was directed to make answer in writing, and meantime the mate was put in command. The captain countered with an affidavit, stating that whilst trying to board a smuggling sloop he had been fired on. Evidently this cleared him, for he was soon in command again, and repairing his sloop. Soon the officers reported him for staying too long ashore. He was cautioned, and the collector was directed to ascertain whether he supplied his mariners with proper provisions. Mr. Carkesse urged the collector to be vigilant in his inspection of the men's food, hinting that it was possible to show good provisions at inspection and afterwards use bad.

Certain mariners on the sloop mutinied, and were discharged. The collector was instructed to have them pressed for the navy. (In equity it was Jewell who should have been pressed, but it is to be feared the navy would have found him not worth the trouble.)

In 1735 the Board directed the collector and controller to ascertain the course taken by smugglers in carrying goods overland from Lincolnshire to London, and in particular as to whether they passed by certain roads in Hertfordshire.

The collector asked the Board if he was to advance money to a troop of dragoons sent down to Lincolnshire to assist the officers. Answer: 'No. They will receive half the King's share of seizures made with their assistance.'

Repeated information was sent of vessels of Sunderland, Newcastle, Folkestone, etc., loading goods at Continental ports for running on the east coast. One message spoke of six Folkestone cutters, each cutter carrying twenty-five men.

The Solicitor at London reported on a case submitted by the Boston officers. A French vessel within the limits of the port had on board 400 half-ankers of brandy (illegal-sized packages) and she had illegally unshipped 80 gallons. He directed as follows: 'If the vessel were really within the port limits, seize the illegal packages, but not otherwise. Prosecute the runners of the 80 gallons at the Crown charge. The vessel may not be seized, as she is of the legal tonnage.'

In 1736 an officer stationed at Grimsby granted an informal permit for wool, and in consequence of the informality the collector at Hull detained the goods. The owner of the goods put in a claim against the Customs for £10 damages. The Board ordered the Grimsby officer to pay it.

The Board received information of extensive smuggling between Boston and Lynn, and, thinking it possible this was due to negligence on the part of the sloop captains, directed that the Boston sloop should call at Lynn once a week, and the Lynn sloop call once a week at Boston. This must have been hard on Jewell, a man with a taste for snug anchorage.

Later there came information that at Zealand were three collier ships which had discharged their cargoes, taken in goods for running, and overstowed them with ballast; a sloop that brought slates from Salcombe, and had freighted back with contraband; about twenty smuggling *galleys* from Kent and Sussex busy loading; and five other vessels full to the coamings specially for the Lincolnshire coast. The 'galleys' each carried ten men.

On July 31, 1736, the King's Warehouse-keeper in London, in transmitting a receipt for seized goods sent from Boston, endorsed the following memo on the document:

'We have hot sultry weather, which has thrown the populace into I don't know what sort of madness. For three or four nights past the Tower Guards and Militia have been up to prevent their Mobbing, which is not yet quieted. The popular resentment arises from the encouragement given to Irish labourers, who work for less money than the English.

'P.S.—Just shutting up the warehouse. Excuse haste.'

The collector and controller informed the Board that large runs were being made on the Lincolnshire coast by armed smugglers, whom the officers were powerless to oppose. The Board thereupon applied to the Admiralty, and two sloops were sent to assist the energetic and intrepid Jewell. Jewell at once took his sloop into harbour and started repairing her, and did not even employ his crew in watching the coast while this was being done. The Board received information of his proceedings, and censured him. They also censured the collector and controller for not looking after him.

Information reached the Board that goods for smuggling in England were brought from China to Sweden, shipped there by English Baltic traders, and afterwards run on the east coast. The collector of Wells apprised the Board that he had received information that the owners of a smuggling vessel recently seized at that port had bought another sloop and run a cargo between Boston and Lynn. The Board again censured Jewell, and directed the collector to examine Jewell's journal. The journal appears to have been quite in order.

In 1738 an order was issued that officers who made seizures with the assistance of the military were to furnish full particulars *on oath*, as complaints were made that the soldiers did not get their proper share of the seizure-money.*

Occasionally, in sending information of vessels loading contraband oversea, the Board furnished *the master's* name, but omitted the name of the ship. This appears to have been when the revenue spy who made the communication suspected that the ship's name would be 'painted out' on departure, or a misleading name substituted.

The Board sent information of a boat expressly built in London for running goods. Though of great length, she had apparently only four rowlocks (the legal number), but was contrived so that she might be readily fitted with twelve. This boat had been taken oversea on board a smuggling sloop that carried a numerous company. When loaded the sloop hovered off the English coast, and the boat, with her additional rowlocks shipped, was used to run goods from vessel to shore. Later was sent a formidable list of vessels clearing outward for France and the Netherlands, and expected to smuggle on their return. These all cleared within three days, so the traffic in contraband must have been enormous. Four of the vessels belonged to Scarborough.

The Board issued a fresh stock of journals, new instructions to all the officers, and urgent injunctions to the collector, controller, and Jewell, to play the man and try to cope with the smuggling. (A note of despair is apparent in their repeated references to the illegal traffic. It is significant that the seizures were trifling, and there was scarcely any seizing of wool outward, though at the

* In the affidavits relating to these seizures, at all ports, the deponents end by stating that there has been no private arrangement or collusion between them and the military.

time there was an immense yield of wool in Lincolnshire, and it is scarcely conceivable that smugglers so active and resolute in running goods inward would neglect the outward avenue of contraband.)

Fresh information arrived of four smuggling vessels, and another troop of dragoons was sent to Lincolnshire and quartered at Wisbech. The particulars of information were as follows :

'The *Thunderbolt* runs her goods at the Old Chapel, Lynn Channel, the *Ann and Mary* on the Lincolnshire coast, the *Sugar Droger* to the north of Lowestoft, and the Dutch schuyt with the English skipper on the coast of Suffolk.'

At this period there were four riding-officers for the Boston district—one at Saltfleet, one at Wainfleet, one at Fleet, and one at Surfleet Bridge. There were also two riding-surveyors and one riding-supervisor.

In 1739 a sloop was seized, but not by Jewell. The crew and master escaped. The brandy and tea on board were 'prosecuted to condemnation' in the Exchequer at the Crown charge, the sloop at the officer's charge. Certain other goods on board were prosecuted before the local justices. Soon after a riding-officer seized a horse loaded with tea, the rider escaping. The tea was prosecuted in the Exchequer at the Crown's charge, the horse at the officer's.

A smuggler in Lincoln jail turned approver, furnishing startling information. His name was Garrett, and he appears to have been a brazen and mercenary rascal. After implicating a number of people he informed Charlton, the officer in whom he confided, that he expected 'ten guineas down,' and if thus accommodated would give evidence of still larger transactions. The Solicitor in London advised that no reward should be tendered or even mentioned, and directed an inquiry into Garrett's character. The inquiry seems to have produced discouraging evidence, and the Solicitor promptly washed his hands of part of the matter, accepting the rest, and directing prosecutions. Below is a list of those against whom action was taken :

Jackson, an innkeeper of Hull, who had unshipped 515 gallons of brandy.

Bancroft, a tailor of North Somercoates ; Oliver, a mariner of Theddlethorpe. Each had been concerned in the unshipment of 300 pounds tea and 150 gallons brandy.

(Hubbard, a mariner of North Somercoates, had been concerned in both of the above transactions.)

Bancroft and Rossthorne, mariners of Saltfleet, who had unshipped 150 gallons brandy.

Baker, a mariner of Colchester, who had unshipped 400 gallons brandy.

Compton, a mariner of Hull, who had unshipped 250 gallons brandy.

Ombler, a mariner of Hull, who had unshipped 150 gallons brandy.

Burleigh, captain of the *Thunderbolt,* who had unshipped 3,500 pounds tea.

Bell, a mariner, who had unshipped 2,000 pounds tea.

Robinson, a mariner, who had unshipped 500 pounds tea.

The Solicitor's statement was interesting. He mentioned the grounds upon which smuggling *vessels* were liable to forfeiture. 'Carrying brandy and being below the legal tonnage ; carrying tea from a land where such tea is not grown.' Thus Burleigh's, Rossthorne's, and Robinson's sloops were liable to seizure—*when found*. The officers who might seize them should prosecute the sloops to condemnation in the Exchequer. If not prepared to do so, they must relinquish claim on the profits, and the Crown should prosecute. Hubbard's sloop was held not seizable, on a curious point. Since the date of the transaction quoted in the information she had been seized elsewhere for a more recent offence, and the Board had released her and accepted a sum of money from Hubbard in composition, he entering into bond to sin no more. Therefore his vessel was held not seizable, yet he was liable to prosecution. (The matter seems hard to understand, but thus said the lawyer.)

Soon after Garrett informed of one Patrick, keeper of the Spurn Head lighthouse, for unshipping 1,000 pounds tea. He also implicated the keeper of 'The Ferry in Lincolnshire opposite Holden Dyke in Yorkshire,' for 2,100 pounds tea. Then he asked again for ten guineas, promising that if he were given twenty he would implicate 'two men of fortune and estate,' who had lately run 1,600 pounds tea. All the above transactions took place within a limited period.

It is apparent that the excise officers did their work loosely. In 1729 an arrangement had been made between the two Boards that excise officers who seized spirits on the coast and placed them in customs charge should gauge and try the goods first, ledger the account, and obtain a receipt from the Customs. This had not been done, for in 1739 goods which had been thus handed over turned out at condemnation unaccountably different from the warehousing record, and on investigation it appeared that the excise officers had neither gauged nor tried them prior to deposit.

In 1740 Mr. Carkesse departed from his usual affable style, and addressed a few curt words of caution to the collector and controller, who had failed to make correct record of undischarged bonds for shipment of wool coastwise. They were directed to forward all bonds that had lain undischarged for six months. 'If you fail, you will be dismist. Your loving friend, CHAS. CARKESSE.'

Certain officers had been acting as appraisers of seized goods and ships, and in the usual fashion had appraised lightly. A reappraisement by trustworthy experts gave four times the officially appraised value.

Several smugglers arrested on Garrett's information were interviewed by officers, and became approvers. So many informations were forwarded that the Solicitor became restive. The officers began to strain the law in their eagerness to get awards. The Solicitor discovered suspicious interlineations in some of the affidavits sent, and some of the imprisoned smugglers accused officers of using threats to induce them to give evidence. The officers were warned by the Board to be extremely careful in seizing for forfeiture ships with prohibited or uncustomed goods. 'Proof must be very clear, or the officers may subject themselves to great damage.' Later came a momentous order. 'Seizures have been made without sufficient cause.' The collector and controller were directed to inquire fully into all circumstances connected with seizures, before taking the goods into warehouse, and if the officers were unwilling to prosecute at their own expense they were to be called upon to state why they refused.

Captain Jewell transmitted the usual bill for repairs to his sloop, and the Board sent it to be checked by a competent and reliable person. The expert's report was comic:

'It must be some extraordinary accident which the Captain hath not mentioned that could occasion such large Bills in so short a time after the Sloop's being rebuilt. In October, 1739, she lost the Crown £142 7s. 1d., a very large sum for so small a vessel, and so soon after to require £92 4s. 6d. for repairs only.' He then proceeded to query:

'1. The Joyner's Bill. 2. The Shipwright's Bill. 3. The Ironmonger's Bill. 4. The Cooper's Bill. 5. The Ship-chandler's Bill. 6. The Smith's Bill. 7. The Sail-maker's Bill. 8. Bread and cheese and beer for the workmen, amounting to £4 0s. 0d. 9. The Captain's own expence, £34 17s. 0d.'

'And if I am not mistaken,' he went on, 'the better part of the £10 charged for sails is charged twice.' Later he wrote: 'As much Labour and Materials charged for 1½ years wear and tear as would almost build the vessel.'

Jewell was directed to make his bill more reasonable. After a struggle he abated an item, and got his money.

Like most inefficient revenue officers, when he did come to be concerned in a seizure he wanted more than his proper share of profits. He charged his cabin-boy for a share at mariner's rate, evidently intending to pocket the extra award; but his rascality was discovered, and the Board directed him to compensate the boy *out of his own share.* It is extremely improbable that the boy got anything, except an extra cuff whenever Jewell bethought himself of the failure of his trick.

In 1742 a petition was sent to the Board by two wool-dealers of Spalding, stating that Spalding paid a deal of revenue, that there were officers stationed there who were competent to supervise the weighing and shipping coastwise of wool, and asking that the town might be relieved from paying the heavy travelling expenses charged by the collector and controller of Boston, who insisted on seeing all parcels of shipped wool. The petition commenced thus: 'We do most humbly request on the behalf of ourselves and our country,' and requested that the deputy at Spalding might view the weighing and shipping coastwise of wool, the collector and controller of Boston making heavy charges, and often causing delay. 'We already pay 10s. 6d. for coquet, and 6d. for a permit for every parcell of wooll, a charge very burdensome.

'We crave that we may not under pretences suffer such impositions, or be further obstructed in our honest lawfull employment.

'JOHN SKINNER, Senr.
JOHN SKINNER, Junr.'

The collector and controller fought stoutly for their fees, quoting the Board's instructions of 1728 that the principal officers should attend the weighing; but the Board, who seem to have been eminently reasonable and practical, directed that the deputies at Saltfleet, Wainfleet, and Spalding should attend the weighing, thus depriving the Boston gentlemen of their fees and travelling allowances, and relieving the wool-merchants of much expense and delay.

The stolid rascal in command of the sloop, though more than her value had been charged as repairs within three years, had the effrontery to suggest that extensive alterations were again necessary, and to inquire whether the Board would be disposed to grant a large sum for that purpose. An expert was sent to survey this mysterious vessel, and reported that she needed no repairs at all. The expert found her at anchor, as usual. The collector thereupon ordered Jewell to put to sea. Jewell apparently considered the weather too unsettled, and calmly remained in port, nursing his frail shallop. The long-suffering Board thereupon dismissed him, stating that he had made no seizures of consequence during the whole term of his employment. It will be remembered that he had been shrewdly suspected of starving his crew, had been detected in trying to cheat them of their shares in award, and that once his company had mutinied. Yet when he was dismissed his mariners voluntarily went with him.

The new captain wrote to the Board, stating that he could get no men unless increased pay were offered. So far from consenting, the Board told him they intended to withdraw an extra allowance for victualling granted to Jewell in 1730, provisions having become cheaper, and if this did not suit him they would lay the sloop up. The captain at once procured men.

Quarantine was strict. The plague was at Smyrna, and on the arrival of the Smyrna fleet a watch was kept at southern ports, to prevent persons quitting the ships as they passed along the coast. The Board sent word to all ports that a Dutch vessel from Messina, with plague on board, had attempted to enter Plymouth Sound. On being ordered to stand off the master refused, and was at once treated to a broadside. He then bore away to the south-east.

An extraordinary bill for expenses was put in by

George Hall, riding-officer. Hall had been entrusted with the task of carrying what he called 'caipases.'* His account commenced thus :

'George Hall, Riding-Officer of Boston, his Bill of Charges to take Smuglers with Caipases, as Followeth.'

He charged two days' travelling expenses, at 3s. 6d. a day, for going into Norfolk to inquire into the 'Scircumstances' of two proposed sureties. He then charged two days spent in 'carrying Caipases.' Then his own and another officer's expenses in travelling to the Isle of Ely, 'to try and take Richd. Turrington, but could not find him.' Then a day's expenses for going into Northamptonshire, 'to try to take Anthony Walgrave and John Burke, but could not find them.' Again the same, 'but could not meet with them.' On the next day he went home, 'after trying to take ditto, but could not.' The next day, invigorated by the caresses of his family, he with a comrade went to the Isle of Ely, 'to try to take Richard Turrington, but could not meet with him.' Then they went home, charging another day's expenses, 'after trying to take Richard Turrington, but could not.' Again off to Northamptonshire. 'Tried to take Anthony Walgrave. Lay at Peterborough all night.' The next day they 'went after ditto, but could not meet with him.' On the following day they went home, 'after trying to take Walgrave and Burke, but could not meet with them,' and sent in a bill for £5 7s.

The bill appears to have been drawn up by an amateur notary. Hall *printed* his signature in the corner.

A Treasury order was issued in 1745, directing the customs officers to stop and examine all vessels going to or coming from Scotland, and send the Board account of their cargoes, and to allow no arms or military stores to be shipped coastwise without the Board's consent. This was on account of the rising under the Young Pretender.

* Carrying writs of capias.

An excursion southward will be a welcome change. It appears from the Weymouth Letter Books, 1736, that the collector was in straits. He had been queried frequently for errors in his account, the officers' salaries were in arrears, and he was desperately striving to explain quite inexplicable matters. Referring to the 1733 accounts, he had to admit that the salaries and incidents for that year, 'though almost agreeing with the correct totall,' showed vast discrepancies 'in the severall branches,' and that scarcely any of the items agreed with the Controller-General's duplicate account.

Soon after he asked for leave, 'to settle urgent private affairs in Yorkshire,' and on his return was superseded. He wrote a letter to an official friend in London, and entered a copy of it in the Letter Book, evidently as his 'last speech and confession.' It contained certain vague 'explanations' of the errors in his accounts, and wound up thus:

'I had no intention of continuing here long, but I was injoyn'd to keep my design private, and therefore cou'd not be so free in communicating it to my friends. I am a little surpris'd that I hear nothing from the Gentleman appointed to Succeed me, and as I am an intire stranger to him I wou'd be glad if you cou'd inform me in what way the Gentleman hath been bred.'

The new collector took up his appointment. The staff of the port were as follows:

Warren Lisle, captain of the revenue sloop. (Lisle appears to have been a brilliant officer.)

R. Henley, riding-supervisor. (This gentleman was fifty-six years old, and was usually reported upon as one who took a deal of pains, and performed as much as could be expected from a man of his years.)

S. Templeman, land-surveyor (forty-six years old, and he and his two land-waiters were held 'very well quallified').

E. Tizard, tide-surveyor. (Tizard was sixty-seven, and efficient 'for a man of his years.')

T. Smart, tidesman and boatman; and H. Morrish, extra hand. (' In an advanced age, yet hail men.')

There were six riding-officers, and once the collector handed the following memo. to Mr. Henley: ' You are to acquaint your men that if they do not exert themselves in preventing Frauds in their Respective Districts, and perform their Duty's with great care and diligence, the Honourable Board of Customs will provide otherwise for the Service.'

There were also waiters and searchers at various creeks and places adjacent, and one of these, named William Randall, who was stationed at Abbotsbury, distinguished himself in a peculiar manner. He made a large seizure of tea near Bexington, and his account of the same was scarcely satisfactory; so the collector read him the Board's order of March 26, 1737, which provided that when a seizure was made and no one apprehended the seizing officer was to state full particulars on oath. Randall accordingly deposed that he found the goods concealed in certain hedges, that no person was near when he found them, that no boat or vessel was in sight, that no horses or carriages were near to the goods, and that he would be diligent in trying to discover the persons concerned. The tea was in fifty-eight oilskin bags (each two bags strung together and made up to resemble a mackerel-pot.) The collector was of opinion that the Sussex fish-buyers, who came into the county to procure fish for the metropolitan market, would have taken these goods to London.

In the following month the excise officer at Abbotsbury found 16 pounds of tea in Randall's house, and it appeared that this was part of the seized goods. Randall was then called upon to explain why he had kept the fifty-eight bags in his house during the whole of the night of seizure, instead of taking them direct to Weymouth and putting them in the warehouse. He replied that he left the tea in his wife's charge while he went to Weymouth to report, and bade her be careful ' not to embezzle the least quantity.' It would, he pleaded, have been dangerous to take the tea to the warehouse that night, as he had no assistance. The collector and controller in their report exonerated Randall, and put all the blame upon Randall's wife.

Mr. Carkesse sent twenty copies of the Act of Indemnity to Weymouth, and they were distributed thus: one to the mayor, one to each of the two bailiffs, one each to the land and tide surveyors, one each to the captain and mate of the sloop, one to Mr. Henley, one to each of his six officers, one to each of the two land-waiters, one each to two of the principal merchants, and the other two copies were kept in the Custom-house, 'for the upstairs officers or anyone wishing to peruse them.' Then the collector asked for six more copies, proposing to distribute them among 'the justices at large.'

Captain Lisle brought in *The Thomas*, of Galloway, with Irish wool and woollen yarn on board, intended for Nantes. As soon as the prize was moored her sailors ran away to avoid giving evidence. Two witnesses were procured from Ireland, who proved the shipment of the goods. The collector 'subsisted' them at 7s. a week each till the goods were condemned. Then he turned them adrift, and a few days later received instructions that proceedings were being entered against the master for the full penalty of £500. But the witnesses were not to be found, so the prosecution was abandoned.

One Colonel Horner, living near Abbotsbury, embarked in a smuggling transaction, of which the excise officers got wind too late to seize the goods, but not too late to serve a writ upon information received. The customs collector also went to work, and obtained vague information from the longshoremen who ran the goods for the colonel. They admitted bringing ashore four cwt. of tea and a cask of rum, and delivering the goods to the colonel's butler. 'But,' reported the collector, 'they refuse to make affidavit from fear of incurring the Colonel's displeasure. If suspena'd and compell'd to spake they will stand to what they have said.' The matter was left with the Excise Commissioners.

One Captain Cosart wrote to the Board, alleging that extensive frauds were carried on at Portland. The collector gave Captain Warren Lisle of the revenue sloop a reference, and the gallant skipper bluntly stated that he did not believe a word of the allegation. The collector and controller supported this denial, quoting Lisle's seizures, which had been numerous and important, and stating that if he had a reliable sloop 'he could not fail,' but that his vessel would not 'stay' in a head sea, and therefore he had to keep his boats 'continually on the Scout, which,' said they truthfully, 'is one of the hardest services in the Customs.' They also expressed their reliance upon the riding-officers, five of whom, stationed respectively at Lulworth, Portland, Wyke Regis, Langton, and Abbotsbury, had each two dragoons as reinforcement. 'The Ill-Success,' said the officials, 'the Kent and Sussex gang of smuglers have met with on this coast, hath we presume driven them hence, having not heard or seen any of them in these parts for some time.' They reported also that the weapons used by Lisle's crew were rusty and unfit through constant exposure, and that new equipment was necessary. (The crew numbered sixteen, and each man carried a musket, a bayonet, a cutlass, and a pistol.)

Captain Lisle complained to the collector that Jonathan Hatton, one of his crew, had left him and shipped on an Ipswich schooner. The collector and controller sent for Hatton, and 'with offers of friendship' pressed him to return, besides providing him with a new outfit of bedding, shirts, shoes, and stockings. After all this 'kindness' Hatton refused to return, 'pretending that he had been insulted on board the sloop. We prest him severall times, but he would not be prevail'd on to discover the offenders.' It is evident that Hatton was an informer who had been taken on board as a member of the crew, and had found the work too hard and dangerous to suit him.

During a period of twelve days Warren Lisle made three seizures, amounting to 486 pounds tea, 102 gallons brandy, 72 gallons rum, 50 pounds coffee, and 4,120 pounds tobacco.

The Board called upon the collector for a statement of the method of dealing with bountied stuff of silk and worsted at shipment. The reply ran thus: 'In all silk stuffs mixed with worsted yarn the officers see that the warp is all mixed or twisted with silk, or that at least two-thirds of the ends of the threads are of silk, and that the same be obvious and apparent to their view, and that the silk therein used (to the best of their skill) is double the value of the bounty paid on the exportation of the manufactures.'

In 1741 an officer named Weeks was prosecutor in a smuggling case tried by the local justices. The case broke down, and the justices directed that Weeks should be prosecuted for perjury. He was convicted, and the collector urged the Board to support him in an appeal, 'or we shall never be able to carry on a penall prosecution more in these parts. Weeks,' said the collector, 'has been imprisoned with no other design than to deter every man from giving evidence for the Crown in future.'

In 1742 Warren Lisle chased a smuggling sloop so fiercely that her crew ran her ashore at Abbotsbury and escaped, and the riding-officer there seized her before Lisle could board. The seizure amounted to 200 pounds tea, 16½ gallons brandy, 5½ gallons rum, and 990 pounds tobacco.

A Guernsey vessel arrived with a French subject on board, The collector put a tidesman to keep close watch upon Jean Crapaud, 'in order to see that he does not stir from his quarters to view the town, or make any observation to the detriment of our shipping, as we lay open and exposed to the assaults of privateers.'

On May 28, 1744, the collector and controller sent the following report to the Board:

'We beg leave to acquaint you that this day arrived here from France in a Small Boat James Prescott of

Rochester in the County of Kent, mariner and late master of the *Sea Ranger* sloop of the burthen of 60 tons or thereabouts, with William Bagner a Saylor belonging to the mentioned vessell, who in her passage from Bideford laden with Oats for acc[t] of Mr. Thomas Coxhead of Tower Hill London was taken this 9th inst. off of Bridport (on this Coast) by a French Privateer called *Le Subtil*, of 18 carriage and 6 swivell guns and 164 hands, whereof Joseph Fayle was Commander, and carried them into Sherbrooke* in France. Where after 12 days restraint in Prison these Two Men made their Escape, and by means of this Small Boat which they fortunately got Brought them safe here in Want of Everything for the support of Life. We have carefully examined the Boat and Men, and being fully sattisfied that what they relate are reall Facts we have let them go on their Lawfull occasions.'

A prosecution being entered against three smugglers, Beale, Elliot, and Chip, the collector intimated to the Board that it would be judicious to suspend proceedings. 'Chip is gone on board a Man-of-War, Elliot is delirious and often chain'd in his House, and Beale is so very Poore as hardly to have Bread to Eat.'

The Charming Molly arrived from St. Malo with 180 exchanged English prisoners on board. The officers rummaged her, and in certain artfully contrived places behind bulkheads found a large quantity of spirits concealed.

The Duke, a schooner of 40 tons, belonging to Cowes and bound for South Carolina, was captured 200 leagues west of the Lizard by a French privateer, carrying 20 guns and 200 men. The privateer captain put six hands on board to take the prize to St. Malo, and left with them one English sailor named White. The wind being south, and the weather thick, they failed to make the French coast. White persuaded them to let him navigate the vessel, and coolly brought her into Weymouth, where she was seized with her crew by the captain

* Cherbourg.

of the *Jamaica* sloop-of-war. The collector sent a flaming report to London, insisting that the customs tide-surveyor was the first to take possession of her.

During the entire period covered by the letters reviewed, the folk of Portland misbehaved sadly, plundering wrecks, assaulting and obstructing the customs officers, refusing to allow search of premises, and when proceeded against by the Exchequer disdaining to accept summons. The trouble was temporarily adjusted by the Portlanders paying the costs of the summonses, etc., and asking pardon of the officers in the public room of the Custom-house, Weymouth. A few days later certain sailors of the *Cholmondeley* revenue sloop came to Weymouth, and made affidavit that while attempting to seize goods run near Portland Castle the Portlanders 'grievously assaulted' them, and carried off the goods. In his report of this the collector stated: 'And we further beg leave to assure your Honours that unless some speedy and effectuall method be taken to putt a Stop to the audacious and insolent Behaviour of these Islanders, no officer may with safety enter that Island to Execute his office. And we have reason to believe that on any ships in Distress comming on Shoar in or near the Island of Portland no officer of the Customs will venter to lay out all night in order to protect and defend such unhappy Sufferers and Guard their Goods, for fear of being knock'd on the head with a volly of Stones from the Islanders.'

A vessel of Amsterdam went ashore at Fleet soon after. She was stated to be a West India trader, but as she appears to have had 'a deal of money' and little cargo on board, and to have carried 74 men and 24 guns, it is probable that she was a privateer. 'The Country People,' reported the collector, 'came down in Great Gangs and carry'd off what they could lay their hands on, in defyance of the officers.' Though the officers were badly beaten by the mob, they contrived to save some of the money. The conduct of the Dutch skipper and his crew was peculiar. They got ashore safe, but made no attempt to protect the officers in their efforts to save the treasure, nor did they lift a finger to help. Two of the sailors, while the mob were playing football with the officers' bodies, fought a duel on the shore with knives, which ended in one of them being mortally wounded, and then his comrades put him out of pain by beating him to death. The Dutch skipper made himself comfortable at a tavern adjacent, and when the officers went to tell him of their success in saving some of the money he blew a great cloud from his pipe, but no more. Not even a grunt of gratitude did he vouchsafe them, never a dram did he offer as 'medicine for their aching bones.'

A glance at the practice of the port of Cowes may be interesting. In 1749 the 'established' staff consisted of a collector, a tide-surveyor, two landing-waiters, and a riding-officer. There were also the following 'incidental' officers: a deputy-controller, three riding-officers, and two boatmen. There were thirteen tidesmen, all 'extraordinary'—viz., employed when required, at a daily wage. The total pay and 'allowances' of the staff (including the 'incidental' and 'extraordinary' hands, who appear to have been constantly employed) amounted to about £1,000 a year.

The port was fairly busy. The drawback transactions were extensive, and sometimes there was not enough cash in hand to discharge the debentures. The Plantation trade assisted in keeping the port lively, Cowes being a convenient place of call for Plantation ships bound for the northern Continental ports. These vessels, under the Plantation Act, had to unship their cargoes in England, and afterwards reship them for the final ports of destination.

Wrecks were terribly frequent. Unowned wrecked goods were claimed by the Earl of Portsmouth, governor of the island, but most of the wrecked cargoes were salved, and in such cases the collector, who under the Act of Queen Anne held considerable powers with regard to wrecked goods, did not fail to report himself to the Board as 'aiding and assisting to the salvage thereof.' By the Act quoted he was entitled to participate in salvage money, and no doubt he came in for many a bright guinea that way. The salvage claims were frequently disputed, and then the collector, by authority of the Act, nominated justices to decide. After the decision was announced it was usual for the owners to make application through the collector to the Board for permission to sell duty-free as much of the salved cargo as would discharge the award. In one case the skipper of a stranded Dutch vessel agreed with an islander named Ratsey for £200, to be paid down in case he got the ship off. Most of the cargo had been jettisoned, and Ratsey succeeded in his attempt, but the Dutchman proposed to delay payment until the total salvage was assessed on ship and goods. Ratsey entered a protest, and bided his time. Within a very short period the award was made, and the justices gave Ratsey his £200, with an additional *penny in the pound* as interest due for the time he had to wait, and £2 to compensate him for his trouble in protesting. This roused the collector's ire, and he complained to the Board that the additional sums were unfairly granted, but the Board seemed indisposed to interfere.

The four riding-officers covered the whole of the coast in their rides. Each ride extended about fifteen miles. There appear to have been few seizures during the early part of 1749, but the Board queried the collector as to whether he had heard anything of extensive smuggling in his district. He referred to the riding-officers and tide-surveyor, and their reports were on the whole re-assuring. Therefore he replied in the negative; but it is evident the Board had reliable information, for the revenue sloops began to muster thick around the Wight. This appears to have incited the officers to vigilance. A small seizure of rum was made, and the boat carrying the goods was seized as well. Some practical joker stole the boat during the night, and the collector reported the matter to the Board. The night after the report was sent on the boat was restored to her moorings, and the collector no doubt regretted his readiness with ink and paper.

The riding-officer at Niton saw two men landing a hogshead from a boat. He made for them, but they got the hogshead back into the boat, pushed off, and hailed him from afloat, asking if a couple of guineas would not be more in his way than a seizure. Said the collector suggestively in his report: 'They did not actually produce the money.' Finding the officer either too dull to apprehend their meaning or too virtuous to acquiesce, they put to sea again.

In 1751 the following letter reached the collector:

'SIR,

'One John Fleming has been so indiscreet as to take into his boat or wherry half-a-anchor of Gin, which some of your officers have seiz'd together with the Boat. As the Man has a Wife and Several Children, and the Boat his All, for want of which he must come chargeable to our Parish: We the officers of this Parish do Request the Favour of you to take the Man's Poverty and Family into consideration, and Order the Boat to be restor'd him, which will oblige many. Particularly

'Your most obedient Serv[ts].

'*Churchwarden*, WM. JOLLIFFE.

'*Overseers* { MARMADUKE BOOTFLOWER,
JNO. SKETCHLY.

'GOSPORT IN ALVERSTOKE PARISH,
'*2nd Augt.*, 1751.'

The collector reported favourably, and Fleming got his boat back. It appeared that Fleming had taken into his boat a female passenger from a passing Dutch ship, and the keg of gin had been thrown into the sea as a present.

One James Shotter was convicted of smuggling, and lodged in Winchester jail. His sons craved a composition, thus :

'*The Humble Petition of James Shotter and William Shotter.*

'Most Humbly Sheweth

'That your petitioners by supporting their Father with the Common Necessary's of Life during his confinement have expended all their substance and are reduced to the utmost Extremities that can possibly attend persons in such distressed Circumstances. That had not we his Sons out of our hard Labour now and then sent a small pittance to our Father he must long ago have perished through Want. That at the same time our poor Mother who is also very aged depends upon us entirely for her subsistence. That we have a very sensible and dutiful Concern for our unhappy Father, and were it in our power, of which God and all the World knows it is not, would willingly offer something by way of Recompence to the Government for his Great Offence. That we have hitherto lived in our Neighbourhood with the Reputation of Honest and Industrious Men. The Utmost we can do is to implore the Charity of well-disposed persons on the part of our distressed Father, and believe with their Assistance we may be able to offer to your Honours Twenty Pounds, if your Honours will be pleased to accept of that sum by way of mulct atonement for his past Offence.

'We humbly beg your Honours to take this our Petition into your Compassionate Consideration, and be pleased to let us know whether this offer in favour of our unhappy Father for whom our harts are bleeding will be accepted.'

It is to be hoped that readers will attribute the strained piteousness of this petition to its right source, the bad taste of the amateur notary. The collector's report stated that the Shotters were extremely poor, yet the official overcame the man, and a hint was inserted that a trifle was owing for expenses of prosecution. The Board thereupon claimed £30 as the lowest composition practicable. A genuinely pathetic letter from the old smuggler's wife announced that the £30 had been raised. Undoubtedly the money was made up by neighbours. The Crown and the lawyer were paid—even if an old dame's heart drops blood the lawyer must have his fee.

The commander of the *Savage* sloop was a man much unlike Captain Jewell of Boston. His name was Foley, and it is probable that he hailed from the Emerald Isle. He was a vigilant and successful officer, and made many huge seizures. Something of the sea-lawyer was in him as well; he was given to penning pompous dispatches, and seems to have imagined himself to be an extremely important person. Withal he looked sharply after Captain Foley's pecuniary interests, and no doubt spent much of his spare time in conning such Acts of Parliament as dealt with awards and shares in seizure profits. One of his seizures produced £524 odd on condemnation, and the collector paid one-third as captain and crew's share, upon which Foley nibbed a new quill and delivered himself of a bunch of quotations from the Act of Indemnity, proving beyond dispute that he was entitled to one-half the proceeds. He wound up thus:

'Pursuant to the Direction of this subsequent Act of Parliament . . . and if in Case it be doubted whether I am entitled to a Moiety or not I will readily submit the same to the decision of the Attorney-General, or any other person that shall be approved of by the Board of Customs, to whom I desire you will represent this case accordingly.'

Here is another of his messages:

'On the 10th inst. I cut my Cable in a Gale of Wind at Studland Bay, and gave chase to a Smugling Cutter called the *May Flower* of Rye, George Hemings Master, which I took about two miles to the southward of Christchurch Head, and found in her 250 small Casks of Rum and Brandy.

'I sent my master and seven men on board of her to Rummage her effectually, and he is to deliver her with all her furniture, to be proceeded against according to Law, which I desire you will communicate to the Board of Customs.

'I herewith send you a copy of the Orders my Master is under for your information.

'I desire you will order the Casks to be carefully Examined as soon as they are landed, and as they are Leaky to give me leave to start the Liquor into Iron-bound Hogsheads and Puncheons, which I will procure at my own Expence, for it will be a very Considerable Advantage both to the Crown and me.'

His orders to the master were explicit.

'Whereas the Smugling Cutter which was taken by me,' etc.

The wonder is how he managed to pen all this in a gale of wind, and how he came to write 'me' after 'the Crown,' and with a small 'm.'

There was a riding-officer, named Richard Rogers, who was for ever getting himself 'obstructed' and assaulted. Here is one of his affidavits :

'To wit : Richard Rogers One of the Riding Officers of the Port of Cowes in the Isle of Wight in the County of Southampton maketh Oath that on the 27th day of January last he had an Information that some Prohibited and Uncustomed goods would be lodged in the Dwelling-house of Henry Matthews, within the parish and Manor of Godshill in the Isle of Wight aforesaid, Schoolmaster.'

It appears from the rest of the affidavit that Rogers procured a writ of assistance and a constable, and approaching the suspected house met Matthews outside the door. Matthews demanded the name of the informer, and, failing to obtain it, put his back to the door, and announced that if Rogers would enter he must first prove himself the better man. He kept the officer at bay for some time, then stepped aside, and bade him 'Search and be damned.' On going into the room Rogers noticed that the back window had been removed. He searched, and found nought. Soon after Rogers' son, an alert youth of fifteen, told his father that while Matthews blocked the entrance several casks had been removed by the back window and put into the barn. Rogers thereupon made for the barn, calling upon the constable to follow, but that wary official promptly discovered that the barn was 'out of his jurisdiction,' and remained 'where he had a right for to be.' Matthews pursued Rogers, and seized him before he could enter the barn. Matthews' mother, an aged but spirited dame, also laid hands on the riding-officer, and assisted to drag him back 'into jurisdiction.' Rogers, who, like most of the other revenue officials, was a man of law rather than a man of hands, retired, and tendered affidavit.

Joseph Jerem, the constable, also made affidavit, and it is easy to perceive that evidence was dragged from Joseph Jerem against Joseph Jerem's will. He ended thus:

'The said Matthews left the place where he stood as aforesaid and bid the said Rogers search and be damned and thereupon the said Rogers went into the said room and when he came into the same said I see it is gone (or used words to that effect).'

But not one word from Joseph Jerem as to the assault outside the barn, that being 'outside his jurisdiction.'

It was not uncommon during the Georgian period—a period that opened many seductive avenues for mean knaves to wander in—for utterly unfounded information to be lodged against innocent people. In some cases this was done from motives of petty spite, in others to direct attention from the informer's own misdeeds. The following specimen was no doubt due to both incentives:

'Francis Morris of West Cowes Marriner and late Master of the *Prince of Wales* voluntarily maketh Oath that on or about the 22nd day of January, 1750, he did take on board the said vessel at Haverdegrace in France six Casks containing thirtysix gallons of brandy and Rum, one oil-skin bag containing fiftysix lbs. of tea, one cwt. of burnt coffee in bottles, and two dozen lbs. of Soap, for and on account of Frederick Todd of West Cowes, and by him the said Morris put on Shoar,' etc.

This fellow Morris was a lying and malicious rogue. It turned out that on January 16, 1750, he had actually cleared with a cargo of salt for Shoreham, and that he did not return to Cowes till March 15.

Captain Foley reported that the cutter seized would be useful to him as a tender, and pompously proposed his intentions : 'Firstly ; I will take the cutter together with all her materials, and victual and Man her at my own Expence.

'Secondly ; I will keep the said vessel in wear and tear during the time I shall be commissioned,' etc.

He continued to 'Thirdly,' and 'Lastly,' making it apparent that though rather circumlocutory for a sailor-man he was wide awake ; and in the end desired that his report might be laid before the Board, 'for their approbation and consent.' It is likely that about this time the gallant captain had to buy a new cocked hat, his head having become too large for the old one.

Later he again approached the collector. 'Having wrote to you on the 17th past, desiring you would report a proposal of mine to the Board of Customs : To which proposal I have not received any answer : I desire,' etc. In a postscript he commanded the collector to be expeditious in making up the seizure accounts. 'It will be an advantage both to the Crown and me.' But neither Board nor collector appear to have been much flustered by Foley's peremptory missives, even when it was announced that the Admiralty had directed him to bring to London the tea he had seized, amounting to 3,579½ pounds. He made known his intention of 'arriving at the Nore in about six days,' and no doubt it irked his valiant soul that he could not pass up the winding reaches as some of the old plate-ship plunderers had done, with sails of silk, with hautboys playing and kettle-drums resounding, and lower his flag in response to a salvo from the Tower guns.

The riding-officer Rogers had another barn-door experience. On information he went, with neither writ nor constable, to the house of one Sanders. Sanders was from home, the barn was locked, and Mrs. Sanders inclined to believe her husband had the key with him. Rogers hardened his heart, and broke the barn-door in. 'In an empty cask' within he found 227 pounds tea. For some reason or other the collector tried to screen Sanders, and wrote to the Board stating that he believed the man to be innocent. 'He is an inoffensive man, having scarcely common sense.' About this time Rogers' case against Matthews the schoolmaster was settled, Matthews paying five guineas as compensation.

During a terrible storm in January, 1753, the following ships went ashore on the Wight:

The Adrienne, of Bordeaux, laden with wine.

The Friendship, of Scarborough, laden with tobacco.

The Svend Hoolm, of Copenhagen, laden with staves and copper.

The Samuel, of Cork, laden with sugar, cotton, and ebony.

A Boston ship, laden with oil and turpentine.

A brigantine of Poole, in ballast.

A Dutch vessel, laden with wine and other merchandise.

All these became total wrecks. The Earl of Portsmouth secured thirty barrels of wine from the Dutchman, and these were put under Crown lock in Carisbrooke Castle.

Other wrecks were reported. The harbour was filled with vessels which had run in for shelter, and the collector was quite unable to provide tidesmen to watch on board of them. Soon after this Captain Foley returned to his cruising-ground, and signalized his arrival by a seizure of 1,823 pounds tobacco. The Crown warehouses were full to the very roofs with seized goods and wrecked goods, and the collector chartered private warehouses, and filled them up as well.

A vessel arrived from the Plantations, and her cargo was landed, the usual Plantation certificates were produced, and the goods reshipped on the vessel for Rotterdam. One of the parcels consisted of logwood, and this the master claimed as exempt from the restrictions upon Plantation goods, stating that it had been brought from Honduras to South Carolina to be put on board his vessel for Rotterdam. But he had no certificate of its place of origin, so the collector treated the parcel as Plantation produce, had it landed with the other goods, and demanded poundage on its reshipment. The poundage was paid, but the captain brought the necessary certificate next voyage, and got the money back.

Certain wrecked goods being liable to excise duties, the collector of excise desired to put them under excise lock. Full as the customs warehouses were, the collector of customs would not endure this encroachment upon his prerogative, but managed to squeeze them into the King's Warehouse. Then the excise officer attempted to put an excise lock on the King's Warehouse. The customs collector objected, and reported the matter to his Board. From which it may be gathered that rivalry between departments is no new thing.

The great Foley put his foot into it. Two of the customs tidesmen stopped Captain Foley's servant, who was carrying a package in the direction of his master's lodgings. The package contained six pounds tea. Foley wrote a flaming letter to the collector, stating that part of the tea had been bought of a grocer in Gosport, and that the rest was a present from brother officers. 'I was sending it to my lodgings to be dryed on a sheet, and I should be glad to be informed who were the officers that seized it.' The collector held on to the tea, and reported the matter to the Board. Foley's second letter on the subject was remarkably deferential. It does not appear that anything was done in the matter. But nothing could stop Captain Foley from making seizures. He pounced upon a parcel of coin, and got it forfeited as being illegally shipped for transmission to a foreign land. Directly after he made a great haul: 33 pounds tea, 37 pounds coffee, 264 gallons brandy, 90 gallons rum, 1,560 pounds tobacco, and 160 gallons wine.

An ancient longshoreman named Webster petitioned the Board from 'Winchester Goal.' ('Gaol' was usually spelt 'Goal' in those days, and indeed it was the inevitable goal of many.) The collector reported on the petition, stating that the petitioner Webster had served many years in the navy, and left with a very bad character; that since his discharge he had pretended to be a fisherman, but really had been at the bottom of most of the smuggling in the locality, being assisted by his two sons, lads of thirteen and seventeen; that the elder son had been smuggling ever since he was able, and was a most profligate young fellow; and that Webster had been heard to boast of being worth £700.

Rogers the riding-officer got into trouble again. He went with another officer to arrest one Dyer on a capias. Dyer's wife and daughter, assisted by two yokels, assaulted and obstructed the officers. Dyer escaped, but was afterwards captured with others, one of whom was Matthews the schoolmaster.

A customs boatman saw a fisherman 'take up' nine casks of wine, which had been attached to bags of ballast and sunk near the shore. The boatman would have seized the goods, but the wily trawler foiled him by announcing that he was about to take them to the Custom-house as wreck.

The three chief officers of the port had grown very keen after seizures. Mr. Godwin the tide-surveyor had returned 2,422 pounds of seized tobacco within the half-year, and Mr. Wilkinson the deputy controller 3,023 pounds, and the collector seems to have been anxious to distinguish himself as well. A sloop belonging to Dublin, and bound from Gothenburg to Oporto, put into Cowes, and it was discovered that she had fifteen tons of tea on board. By the letter of the law the goods were seizable, the tea being from a place not the land of its growth, the vessel not an East India Company's ship, and there appearing no likelihood of her having run in for shelter, as the weather had been fine for several days. Yet she could scarcely be deemed 'a hoverer,' for the tea was in chests each containing three cwts., and a hoverer would not have sailed into Cowes in fine weather and anchored near the shore. The three chiefs held council, and there is reason to think that they resolved to strain the law, being instigated thereto by the prospect of great gain, for if they succeeded in getting the tea condemned they would divide amongst them about £2,000. Anyhow, the collector sent Godwin to seize the tea.

The master of the sloop made no protest till the goods had been taken ashore and put under Crown lock. Then he came storming into the Custom-house, with witnesses to prove that on the previous night he had sent one of his crew to acquaint the customs watchmen with the nature of his cargo. His papers turned out to be correct, and it was found that he had entered harbour to obtain a new mast.

The collector at once penned a letter to the Board, and every line testified to the panic that possessed the writer. He described the circumstances under which he had made the seizure, using 'we' as often as possible, and making desperate efforts to thrust most of the responsibility upon Godwin. But in the end terror made him give himself completely away. He suggested in conclusion that perhaps a prosecution might hold, but stated that he and the others humbly relinquished their 'right title' to prosecute and their claim to reward, and surrendered said rights and profits to the Crown. He put the letter into the hands of his friend Mr. Gill, patent controller of the port, and Mr. Gill went express to London, crossing the Solent in the dark, chartering relays of post-horses, and running up a tremendous bill of expenses. Early on the following day Mr. Gill arrived at the London Custom-house.

The position was at once manifest to the shrewd gentlemen who sat in the room looking out upon the crowded river, and Mr. Gill was soon on his way back, carrying an order to the collector to release the goods, unless prepared to prosecute at his own risk. The collector sent back a doleful report. The master had refused to take the tea on board, and had communicated with the shipowners at Dublin. Mr. Godwin had made the tender of restitution, 'in presence of two witnesses,' but without avail, and had then retired, probably registering a mental vow never to seize tea again. The collector, in his letter, pleaded abjectly for protection, expressing a hope that their Honours would intervene. 'The master,' he wrote, 'seems quite litigious. We beg that you will defend us from damage, as we have done all in our power to avoid it.'

Later he wrote that he had personally tendered restitution, and had been repulsed. Again he wrote as to renewed tender, made 'in the most amicable manner,' yet again repulsed, although the new mast had been rigged, and the vessel made ready for sea.

Godwin, whose misdirected astuteness had been at the bottom of the bungle, collapsed under his manifold anxieties, and applied for a month's leave, 'to go to the baths.' And no doubt the collector prayed that the first bath Mr. Godwin took might end Mr. Godwin's tremors for good and all, and his chances of making any more seizures of 'tea in chests.'

Mr. Blennerhassett Grove, supercargo, arrived from Dublin, and allowed the tea to be put on board, 'but,' piteously stated the collector, 'he refuses to give any further indemnification.'

About this time there were many wrecks of tobacco cargoes, and when the wrecked goods were abandoned as unmerchantable the collector sent them to London for destruction. In May and June, 1755, he sent no less than 229,000 pounds of damaged tobacco, the freight per sloop amounting to £56 10s.

Mr. Godwin came back from the baths, and took to reporting tidesmen instead of seizing tea. He caught two unlucky fellows asleep when they should have been patrolling the deck and admiring the moonlit heavens. Richard Colebrook, charged with leaving his charge, going aboard another ship 'to drinking,' and being afterwards found asleep during his watch, answered thus, and his statement may have tickled the Commissioners:

'The charge I do not deny. I drinkt of a small mugg of Water, Sugar, and a little Rum * * * * to squench my thirst. To rest myself a little I set down on the main hatches where I chanced to fall on sleep. Gentlemen, if I am guilty of a Falt I must humbly ask Pardon. But Gentlemen, I was never the man to see the Government abused since I have been in the Employ, for I always act much to the Contrary, and I haterly wish I could serve it more.'

Michael Facey, charged with being found asleep on a hencoop during his watch, replied:

'I do hereby acknowledge that having a bad Legg I did set down on a Chest which was on deck. I very probably might take a Nodd, but was not sound asleep.'

(When an officer was accused the charge invariably concluded thus: 'To which matter you are hereby required to give a plain and distinct answer, avoiding all Scurrilous or Abusive Expressions.')

A poor wretch languishing in Winchester 'Goal' for smuggling wrote a manly and affecting letter to the Board. He stated that he was starving, and that his wife was begging in the streets, and added that he had served in the navy. He prayed to be allowed to volunteer for that service, and thus gain indemnity.

Mr. Godwin became more officious than ever. He cleared a Norwegian ship outward, and called upon the captain to pay duty on certain planks used for shoring the ballast. When the captain objected, Godwin seized the ship's dutiable stores (ten gallons brandy, which the skipper protested had been previously declared and passed). Godwin also reported that the Palatines (Germans), who shipped on the Continent for the Plantations, brought small kegs of spirits which they claimed were stores necessary for the voyage, and he suggested that the spirits should be landed and duty-paid before reshipment, as cargo for the Plantations. All this appears to have been pure litigiousness, to avenge himself by causing the collector trouble. The latter reported dead against Godwin in both instances.

A pilot wrote to the collector, stating that he conducted a Dutch vessel 'out of the Kneedles,' and the captain being short of money gave him a two-gallon jar of gin. This was seized from the pilot by the officers ashore, and they also detained his boat. He pleaded that the gin was for his own private use, he being 'troubled with the Gravel.'

In 1756 the collector, having allowed a year and a half to elapse, brought up the matter of the expense he had incurred in connexion with the abortive seizure of tea, and requested the Board to reimburse him. He furnished a statement, showing that he had paid in all £10 4s. 11d., which included Mr. Gill's posting expenses (£6 13s. 3d.) and an item of 5s. 2d. for 'nails and wood used in repairing the packages.' Unfortunately the records do not show whether he gained or lost his point, but it is evident he was not one to suffer tamely in pocket. Most of the memoranda in the Letter Books display the superior officials as sly fellows, ever on the look out for a chance of turning a penny, and regarding the Commissioners as champions pledged to stand betwixt them and the public whenever they might happen to overshoot the mark. It is improbable that either the controller or Godwin had subscribed to the expense, yet the collector thought it best to implicate them in the request for compensation.

'We hope your Honours will not let us be sufferers thereby.'

There was a new collector at Poole in 1758. His predecessor, Milner, had been dismissed for various malpractices, and had gone into partnership with a firm of Poole shipowners. Milner's dismissal had been mainly secured through the agency of the deputy controller, and it is plain that Milner and his new partners had resolved upon getting even with the deputy, if possible. Early in 1758 a sailor named Long, employed upon one of Milner's ships, furnished an affidavit, in which he stated that on coming into port he was approached by the deputy controller, who asked him if the captain had any brandy, and on being answered in the affirmative requested Long to obtain him five gallons at the cheapest possible rate. Long declared that he procured the brandy, and took it by night to the house of the controller's father. This affidavit, with the controller's reply, the new collector forwarded to the Board.

The controller stated upon oath that he did 'in a bantering way' ask Long if the captain had any grog left, and that his reason for uttering the jest was that the captain had been caught with 40 gallons. But the controller had to admit that his father *did* buy five gallons of brandy from Long, though without the controller's sanction. He declared that the whole business was 'mere trepanning,' and concluded thus: 'I now beg liberty to remark that this Long is a Brother-in-law to Glover (the Captain) who is in partnership with the late collector. They, in revenge for the discovery I lately made of Mr. Milner's malpractices, contrived this malicious Scheme against me, I being very creditably informed that they have given out that if this will not do they will endeavour to find out something else against me that I shall do, meaning to get me dismiss'd. So I find 'twill be necessary for me to exert myself against the late collector, by putting him in the Crown Office for collaring me in my office in the month of January last. Having proper witnesses to the Fact, which I thought to have lain before the Honourable Board, but was not willing to be troublesome.'

The Board very wisely took no notice of Long's affidavit, and the controller, perhaps with equal wisdom, took no proceedings against Milner for the 'collaring.' Milner, as will be seen further on, was an impudent and determined fellow, who stuck at nothing to cause his successor trouble.

The collector apprised the Board that four officers at break of day found in Bitman's Chine a great number of casks of spirits and bags of tea, with four of the crew of the vessel from which the goods had been run standing guard over them. One of the officers went to get horses and a wagon, and soon after a number of country people attacked the others, beat and bound them, and carried off the goods. Officers were sent in pursuit, but without success. The collector ambiguously stated: 'Should have gone myself, but the Heighth of Plantation work, and a sale at the Custom House.' A reward of £20 was offered for discovery of the offenders. One Robert Wilkins, of Sutton Mandeville, made an attempt at securing this by an affidavit, but his information was bald hearsay. He accused the following:

'Mark Chamberlain, who lives at John Goulding's at the New Inn within the Parrish of Downton, and goes by the name of "The old Man."

'Isaac Gulliver, who is very often at the same Inn.'

In 1759 the collector, the controller, and the tide-surveyor signed the following report to the Commissioners of Excise:

'We apprehend ourselves indispensably oblig'd in vindication of our Character to complain to your Honours of the unwarrantable Liberties taken lately by Mr. Thomas Ireland, the supervisor here, who in public company at Wimborne declar'd that he would make a Reformation in the Custom House at Poole. That he had been up in it, and mark'd out a place where he would have an office built, by which he should save £500 per annum to the Revenue. We beg leave to assure your Honours he never was in this office on any such account, and that if he had he would have been properly turn'd down stairs. He told Mr. Keay, a Common Brewer of Wimborne, that the officers of the Customs at Poole were Smuglers, "and considerable ones." We humbly apprehend these Declarations carry a very severe reflection upon us as Principal Officers of the Port of Poole, and tho' we are sensible he was very drunk when he made them we humbly submit to your Honour's Determination how far that is an excuse for a Charge of this Nature.'

They went on to charge him with extorting £6 from the Vestry of St. James's, Poole, as a contribution towards his land tax, and furnished a certified extract from the parish register in corroboration. Then they asked that he might be made to apologize 'in the Publick Papers.'

But the supervisor was ready with an answer. Whilst flinging back a few vague hints that reformation was necessary, and one especially nasty hint about an irregularity in the entering of rum, he contrived to put quite a different aspect on matters. He denied that he was drunk at Wimborne, and implied that the customs officers had on several occasions obstructed him in the performance of his duty. He admitted that the Vestry made him a grant of £6, but proved that it had not been paid. 'I disdain'd to receive it.'

This roused the customs men's ire. They may also have been enraged that the Board of Excise referred the matter to the excise collector of the district. They returned to the charge, sarcastically pointing out that the grant was *made*, and that it was hard to tell whether Mr. Ireland would have 'disdain'd to receive it,' seeing that their charge was formulated before the time of payment had arrived. But the affair, like that between the controller and Milner's gang, seems to have ended in nought.

Readers must not think too harshly of the customs men whose sayings and doings are quoted. It was a corrupt age. Holy offices were sometimes traded, parliamentary seats often, subordinate official posts universally, and where jobbery rules in public business it is bound to influence private character. Probably most of the corporation officials, military and naval contractors, political agents, attorneys, and churchwardens of the day, as well as the civil servants, were almost as honest as men could be who desired to live at a little above the ordinary standard of expenses.

A curious list appears in Sir William Musgrave's notes on this period. It seems that even smugglers were occasionally smitten with genuine remorse for their misdeeds, and made anonymous tenders of 'conscience money.' The list is not extensive. It includes but nineteen contributions, extending over a period of twenty-six years:

In 1731, £3. In 1734, 3s. In 1736, £3 3s. In 1737, £5 5s. In 1738, £600 and £120. In 1740, 20 guineas. In 1741, £58 10s. In 1743, £7 8s. In 1747, £100. In 1748, £1 2s. 6d. and £31 2s. 9d. In 1749, £3 3s. In 1754, £7 11s. 8d. In 1755, £30 and £3 17s. 6d. In 1756, £40 10s. In 1757, £25 and £4 13s. 6d.

It would be interesting to know what the 3s. signified. It may have been what some student of ancient revenue history conceived would be the reasonable duty on a tun of French wine. The subsidy tunnage on French wine was 3s. in Elizabeth's day, and the learned smuggler, having escaped George II.'s tunnage, which in London would be over £50, may have said to himself, 'Good Queen Bess's dues should be enough,' and sent in the Elizabethan tunnage. The 1747 contribution of £100 may have been a penalty, sent by some one who had on many occasions escaped it.

LIST OF AUTHORITIES.

Wine: 1 Geo. II., s. 2, c. 17.

Permanent branches of revenue: 3 Geo. II., c. 20; 5 Geo. II., c. 6; 6 Geo. II., c. 17; 7 Geo. II., c. 14; 15 Geo. II., c. 29; 18 Geo. II., c. 9; 19 Geo. II., c. 12; 19 Geo. II., c. 27; 21 Geo. II., c. 2; 24 Geo. II., c. 46; 25 Geo. II., c. 32; 32 Geo. II., c. 10.

Protective measures and prohibitions: 1 Geo. II., s. 2, c. 17; 4 Geo. II., c. 27; 4 Geo. II., c. 29; 5 Geo. II., c. 22; 5 Geo. II., c. 24; 6 Geo. II., c. 13 (same on 2-3 Anne, c. 9, and 9-10 Wm. III., c. 23); 12 Geo. II., c. 21; 12 Geo. II., c. 36; 18 Geo. II., c. 36; 22 Geo. II., c. 36; 21 Geo. II., c. 30; 23 Geo. II., c. 20; 23 Geo. II., c. 24; 23 Geo. II., c. 29; 23 Geo. II., c. 32; 33 Geo. II., c. 28.

Warehousing: 15 Geo. II., c. 25.

Puritanical measures: 7 Geo. II., c. 8; 13 Geo. II., c. 19; 12 Geo. II., c. 28; 19 Geo. II., c. 21.

Temporary imposts: 18 Geo. II., c. 26.

Excise duties: 31 Geo. II., c. 36; 32 Geo. II., c. 29.

Preventive measures: 5 Geo. II., c. 21; 7 Geo. II., c. 19, 9 Geo. II., c. 35; 18 Geo. II., c. 28; 19 Geo. II., c. 34; 23 Geo. II., c. 21; 24 Geo. II., c. 41; 26 Geo. II., c. 12; 26 Geo. II., c. 21; 28 Geo. II., c. 21.

Departmental incidents: Sir William Musgrave's 'Memoranda'; Montrose Letter Books; Treasury Papers, 1733; Boston Letter File; Weymouth Letter Books; Cowes Letter Books; Poole Letter Books; 'Social Life in Former Days.'

CHAPTER VIII

THE PERIOD OF FISCAL CHAOS AND COLONIAL DISRUPTION

1760–1787

In reviewing the progress of revenue legislation during the first half of George III.'s reign, it will be unnecessary to specify every trifling amendment and imposition ; only the more important alterations need be noted.

In 1763 additional tunnage was levied on foreign wine and vinegar, and the 'leakage' allowance was withheld except for wine imported direct from land of production. The latter provision was intended to counteract a practice which had become common of importing wine into the Channel Islands, coopering and filling the casks, and shipping them to the southern English ports, where the leakage allowance was claimed although the packages were landed full.

The duty on beaver skins imported from the Plantations was reduced to 1d. per skin, to encourage British hat-making. The outward duty was 7d. per skin.

Duties were laid on many articles imported into the American colonies. Much dissatisfaction ensued, but the imperial legislators took little heed. Wine landed in the Plantations was made liable to tunnage. Cockets were to be used for goods removed by sea from one colony to another.

The Plantation Acts had been evaded by masters calling at Great Britain with 'part cargoes' of goods from foreign, shipping a few packages of British goods, and then under cover of the certificates for the latter landing the whole in the Colonies. It was therefore enacted that clearance should not be granted to any vessel bound for the Plantations from a British port, unless the whole of her cargo had been *shipped* in Great Britain. Irish horses, linen, and provisions, Madeira wines, and salt from any country for use in Plantation fisheries, were exempt from this restriction.

The law against hoverers was extended to ships cruising within two leagues of the Plantation coasts. Government vessels that made seizures in Plantation waters were granted preferential awards. All Plantation revenue officers absent from their stations were ordered to return at once on pain of dismissal. The Treasury directed the American governors to support the American revenue officers in the discharge of their duties. Several of the higher Plantation officials were on leave in England. They were ordered to place themselves under instruction 'in the business of their respective offices,' and on certificate being made of their fitness they were to depart at once. Their instructors were those eminently unpractical gentlemen, 'the patent officers of the port of London.'

Hemp and undressed flax from the American Plantations were bountied on landing in England. The bounty was to be £8 a ton from 1764 to 1771, £6 from 1771 to 1778, £4 from 1778 to 1785. It was to be paid by the collectors at ports of importation. If in any case the money were not forthcoming from the port receipts the Receiver-General was to pay it. The bounty was intended to secure a liberal supply of hemp and flax for naval use, and the Naval Commissioners had power to pre-empt the bountied goods. The customs officers at ports of importation were to examine the hemp and flax and satisfy themselves as to the quality. If after bounty the goods were not pre-empted, they might be sold in ordinary trade. If they were exported the bounty was to be returned.

(A vessel from the Levant, with the Algerian ambassador on board, was quarantined at Stangate Creek in 1761. The ambassador contrived to send a letter to the Secretary of State, complaining of detention. This caused much consternation, for in law all concerned, from the post-office people to the aristocratic officials who handled the letter on receipt, became liable to be sent to the Kentish marshes and rigorously quarantined. Needless to say, for once the law was evaded.)

Both the patent and deputed searchers of the port of London were reminded of their responsibilities, the Board stating that there were great frauds in connexion with the shipment of goods. (Many of the patent men reaped huge harvests of fees, and employed deputies and clerks to do the work of their offices, the said deputies and clerks being sometimes paid by the Crown 'out of incidents.' Whenever work became brisk, the deputies clamoured for extra assistance, and for many, many years they rarely clamoured in vain.)*

The Treasury complimented Mr. Temple, surveyor-general for the northern district of North America, upon his successful enforcement of the laws against smuggling. The higher Plantation officials were directed to furnish the English Commissioners of Customs with full reports of the character and capabilities of subordinates, and particulars of all cargoes shipped and unshipped, and the English Commissioners were to supply the Treasury with quarterly abstracts of the reports. All newly appointed Plantation officers were to be instructed by the London officers prior to leaving England, and their pay was to be withheld till they took up their employment. (The Custom-house records refer to a serious riot at Rhode Island, in opposition to one Lieutenant Hill, who acted for the Customs there.)

* The Bench officers (patent officers who actually attended in the Long Room) seem to have caused the Commissioners a deal of trouble. They were constantly being reproached for absence, disorderly behaviour, insolence to merchants, and rapacity. Much of the apparent lenity of the Board towards them was due to the fact that most appointments were the result of weighty recommendation, and each censure uttered by the Commissioners might offend some lordly patron.

The privilege previously enjoyed by South Carolina and Georgia of exporting rice to places in the eastern hemisphere southward of Cape Finisterre, without unshipping the rice in Great Britain, was extended to shipments to American ports lying southward of Georgia.

(Various interesting orders were issued to the British customs officers. They were directed to be vigilant in searching foreign vessels, especially those windbound in the Downs, for British seamen fleeing from the press, and to detain and send to the Secretary of State all sealed letters found on ships from abroad.)

The Attorney-General decided that customs officers were not empowered to enter the dwellings of 'private gentlemen' in search of contraband lace and embroidery, as the law was only intended to apply to 'dealers.' He gave no opinion as to the immunity or otherwise of 'private' plebeians, no doubt thinking that none but 'gentlemen' need be suspected of harbouring lace and embroidery. He also decided that duty might not legally be abated upon goods damaged by accident, so long as the owners had power to claim upon persons legally responsible for such damage.

Curious illustration of the laxity obtaining in the higher Customs was furnished by a Treasury letter, enjoining all newly appointed officers to take up their offices *within six months* after appointment.

In 1764 the Chairman and Deputy Chairman of the East India Company attended at Thames Street, and conferred with the Board upon the prevention of smuggling.

The Board issued new instructions as to dealing with effects of foreign ambassadors, etc. Each ambassador was to furnish schedules in duplicate of the goods he imported. One document went to the River Inspector, who witnessed the unshipment and landing of the goods, the other to the officers who performed the actual examination. The ambassador's agent witnessed the opening and searching of the packages, which took place in the King's Warehouse. The allowance of duty-free wine was one tun for an ambassador, two hogsheads for an official of 'inferior character' (lower rank). If there were any discrepancy betwixt schedule and goods, or the quantity of wine imported exceeded the above quantities, the Board were apprised.

Certain landing-surveyors were granted £120 each, as reward for discovering that various linens had been undervalued, and for 'extraordinary pains in considering the Irish "Book of Rates."'

Parliament levied stamp duties in the American Plantations, on the pretext that the Colonies should contribute towards the expense of government and protection. The duties applied to almost all mercantile and legal agreements, to pamphlets, newspapers, almanacs, calendars, and advertisements, and to cards and dice. The stamp duty on cards was 1s. a pack, on dice 10s. *a pair.* On documents couched in other than English the duties were doubled. Heavy duties were laid on indentures of apprenticeship, and formidable penalties enjoined against unlicensed retailers of wine and spirits. These imposts were placed under the management of the British Commissioners of Stamp Duties.

An *additional* duty of 4s. per chalder was levied on coal exported from Great Britain to places other than Ireland, the Isle of Man, and the American colonies.

A bounty was granted to Plantation 'lumber' suitable for shipbuilding, to be paid on landing in Great Britain. Plantation coffee was favoured by remission of part of the excise duty, and Plantation iron was allowed to be carried to Ireland without unshipment in Great Britain. But these grants were spoiled by odious provisions as to bonds, certificates, and affidavits. The Plantation officers' fees, of which the colonists had complained, were directed to remain as settled by precedent, till they could be regulated by Parliament. They were never regulated.

The bounty on British refined sugar outward was raised to 14s. 6d. per cwt. for loaf and lump sugars, and 6s. 4d. for bastard, ground, and candy.

Foreign-made silk stockings and gloves were prohibited from importation into Great Britain. If seized they were not to be burned, but sold by candle-inch for exportation.

The Board ordered that if a surveyor of the river rummaged any boat leaving an East Indiaman during the night, he should then call the crews of the 'head and stern boats' to re-rummage her, and if the crews made a seizure he should be shut out from the award. Of course this was a reflection upon the efficiency of the river surveyors. The Board would scarcely have issued an order so subversive of ordinary discipline had there not been grim reason.

Several peculiar grants of public money were made by the Commissioners. The deputy consul at Ostend received £100 for transmitting intelligence of illicit trade. The son of the late collector of Beaumaris received a gratuity of £20, 'on account of his long attendance in expectation of being provided for in the Customs.'

The superior officers at Gravesend were cautioned by the Board against undue preference in 'boarding' tide-waiters (placing favourites as watchmen on comfortable ships). The Board also directed the tide-waiters not to take their wives on board!

It was provided that duties paid by the East India Company should be entered in the Exchequer books as a separate account.

The Board were directed by Treasury warrant to provide out of the customs £70,000, as purchase-money for the Isle of Man.

In 1766 the Plantation Stamp Act was repealed, and the next statute enrolled may be regarded as an expression of Parliament's displeasure at having had to yield to colonial disapprobation. The Act ran thus:

'Whereas several of the Houses of Representatives in his Majesty's Colonies and Plantations in America have of late against law claimed to themselves, or to the General Assemblies of the same, the sole and exclusive right of imposing Duties and taxes upon his Majesty's Subjects in the said Colonies and Plantations ; and have in pursuance of such Claim passed certain Votes, Resolutions, and Orders, derogatory to the Legislative Authority of Parliament, and inconsistent with the Dependency of the said Colonies and Plantations upon the Crown of Great Britain : May it therefore please your most excellent Majesty that it may be declared ; and be it declared by the King's most excellent Majesty, by and with the Advice and Consent of the Lords Spiritual and Temporal and Commons in this present Parliament assembled, and by the authority of the same : That the said Colonies and Plantations in America have been, are, and of Right ought to be subordinate unto and dependent upon the Imperial Crown and Parliament of Great Britain, and that the King's Majesty by and with the Advice and Consent of the Lords Spiritual and Temporal and Commons of Great Britain in Parliament assembled had, hath, and of Right ought to have, full Power and Authority to make Laws and Statutes of sufficient Force and Validity to bind the Colonists and People of America Subjects of the Crown of Great Britain in all Cases whatsoever.

'And be it further declared and enacted by the Authority aforesaid : That all Resolutions, Votes, Orders, and Proceedings, in any of the said Colonies or Plantations, whereby the Power and Authority of the Parliament of Great Britain to make Laws and Statutes as aforesaid is denied or drawn into question, are, and are hereby declared to be, utterly null and void to all Intents and Purposes whatsoever.'

Parliament continued to juggle with the Plantation trade, and issued a statute fixing legal ports in Jamaica and Dominique. This Act bristled with provisions as to single-decked ships, goods which might be carried, goods excepted for no apparent reason, methods of commerce in negro flesh and blood, and many other mysteries of traffic. It mixed up the commercial regulations of the

Colonies as a pestle blends ingredients, and was immediately followed by another statute that made confusion worse confounded. Attempts were afterwards made to explain and amend these perplexing Acts.

Three permanent branches were added to the British customs: 'The Duty on Exported Cambrics,' 'The Additional Duty on Italian Tiffanies, etc.,' and 'The Duty on East India Wrought Silk.'

The officers of the East Indiamen were told by the Board that if they were caught smuggling they would lose the privilege of importing 'private trade' goods. The customs 'lockers' employed at the Company's warehouses were enjoined not to accept food from the Company's officials, but to pay for it themselves and have their meals sent in.

More interesting grants. Mr. Venner, a surveyor, was given £65 as an encouragement to continue the compilation of a book called 'A Compleat View of the British Customs.' Two tide-waiters were given £5 each, as a reward for resisting 'frequent solicitations, and offers of bribes.'

The Board strengthened the Thames guard. (In 1770 they armed their London quay watchmen with cutlasses to prevent 'the frequent and daring attempts of the plunderers which infest the river.')

Corn became dear, and from 1767 to 1773 the exportation of corn, flour, and similar foodstuffs was prohibited. At certain stages of this period corn was allowed to be imported duty-free, and the privilege was occasionally extended to Plantation rice, sago powder, and vermicelli. 'Unenumerated' Plantation goods were allowed to be imported into Ireland.

Resident Commissioners* were appointed in the American Plantations, to relieve merchants from the delay

* The new appointments were dated from 1767, and the American collectors were ordered to make up and close their accounts to date. The London 'Plantation Clerk,' Mr. Henry Hulton, was made one of the new Commissioners. See Patent Roll, 7 Geo. III., Part 5, m. 11.

caused by sending their applications on revenue matters to London. (The American collectors were at one time directed to pay their moneys to the Paymasters of the Forces in America, and take bills upon the Paymaster of the Forces in Great Britain, who had to make good the amounts to the London Receiver-General of customs.)

The East India Company were in arrear for customs duties to the amount of £180,000. They applied for time, and were granted a month's respite, conditional upon their paying down 6 per cent. on the moneys due.

The Treasury had purchased the Isle of Man in 1765,* and in 1767 a scale of duties was applied to the island, as below:

British spirits imported into the island from England	1s. per gallon.
Plantation rum imported into the island from England	1s. 6d. per gallon.
French wine imported into the island direct	£4 per tun.
Other wine imported into the island direct	£2 ,,
Bohea tea from England	1s. per pound.
Green tea ,, ,, ...	1s. 6d. per pound.
Coffee ,, ,, ...	9d. ,,
Tobacco ,, ,, ...	2d. ,,
Corn and grain, bountied in Great Britain ..	10% *ad valorem.*
Coal from Great Britain or Ireland ..	3d. per chalder.
Foreign hemp, iron, deals, and timber ..	5% *ad valorem.*
All other goods which had received drawback on exportation from Great Britain	5% ,,
All other goods from Great Britain or Ireland	2½% ,,
All foreign goods not previously mentioned	15% ,,

All linen imported had to be shipped in Great Britain or Ireland, and all glass and woollens in Great Britain. As the tariff shows, tea, spirits, coffee, and tobacco, had to be shipped *in England*, and the amounts of these which might be imported yearly were: British spirits, 50,000 gallons; Plantation rum, 30,000 gallons; tea, 25,000 pounds; coffee, 5,000 pounds; tobacco,† 120,000 pounds. All shipments of these articles were to be licensed by the

* The island had been a notorious smugglers' rendezvous.

† The quantity of tobacco allowed was afterwards at a much smaller rate.

Board of Customs, carried in British-built ships, and landed in the port of Douglas.

Manx wool and woollens might only be exported to Great Britain. Manx vessels were to be deemed British-built. Manx fishing-boats were to be registered, and their masters were to enter into bond to refrain from smuggling. An annual impost of 10s. was laid upon every Manx fishing-boat, and out of the proceeds the Government undertook to provide prizes for industry, thus:

	£	s.	d.
To the owner of the boat making the first herring-catch of the season	5	0	0
To the owner of the boat fishing through the greatest number of nights	10	0	0
To the owner of the boat fishing through the second greatest number of nights	7	10	0
To the owner of the boat fishing through the third greatest number of nights	5	0	0
To the owner of the boat fishing through the fourth greatest number of nights	2	10	0
To the owner of the boat catching most fish ..	10	0	0
To the owner of the boat catching the next greatest number	5	0	0
To the owner of the boat making the latest catch of the season	5	0	0
To the admiral of the fishing-fleet for his trouble	5	0	0
To the vice-admiral of the fishing-fleet for his trouble	3	0	0
To the water bailiff	20	0	0
To the champion weaver	6	0	0
To the second-best weaver	4	0	0
To the champion spinner	5	0	0
To the second-best spinner	3	0	0
To the manufacturer exporting most linen ..	10	0	0

The legislators renewed onslaught upon the Plantations. They imposed duties in the American colonies upon glass, painters' colours, pasteboards, strawboards, millboards, 'painted paper,' tea, and the various stationery papers. The paper duties varied from 3d. a ream to 12s. The duty on tea was 3d. a pound. Undoubtedly these were intended to lead up to the imposition of taxes much more comprehensive, but their ultimate results were the loss to England of a bunch of magnificent colonies, and the addition of about £100,000,000 to her National Debt. Indirectly they were the means of shattering her unequalled military prestige, and thus strengthening the hands of her immemorial enemy.

The new Plantation duties were to be paid in sterling English money. Masters were to report and enter their cargoes in and out, and furnish 'ship's content' at clearance. Formidable powers of search were granted to the customs officers, and, to facilitate search for uncustomed goods, it was provided that the Supreme Court of each colony should be competent to issue writs of assistance. A drawback was granted on Plantation coffee exported from Great Britain, and drawback was withheld from chinaware shipped in Great Britain for America. This last provision the legislators, in the eccentric fashion that was fast growing usual with them, soon thought fit to cancel, stating that it had worked quite contrary to their anticipations.

There is not much interesting matter in the minor British customs records for the year under survey. The patent searchers of London were directed to refrain from taking extortionate fees, and from being uncivil to merchants. An annuity of £9,000, payable out of the proceeds of the 4½ per cent. duties, was settled on the King's brother, the duke of Gloucester.*

The clerks in the Receiver-General's office were censured for extorting fees *from officers* on paying them their salaries.

The Board improved the pay of the tide-waiters, 'to obviate the distresses they are under by being obliged to borrow money at an exorbitant rate of interest for the support of themselves and their families, and to prevent their being under the influence of the captains of those vessels upon which they may happen to be boarded.'

A Mr. Samuel Vaughan attempted to buy the reversion

* In 1795 it was found that the duties were insufficient to meet the many charges levied upon them, and the duke was placed on the Aggregate Fund.

of a clerkship in the Plantation Courts. It seems that the office had been previously traded, and the precedent thus furnished had encouraged Vaughan to put forward his application. But the Ministry disliked his political record, and the duke of Grafton, who was Chief Treasury Commissioner, ordered him to be prosecuted. This furnished the celebrated 'Junius' with an opportunity of which he took full advantage. He made public the particulars of an arrangement with Colonel (afterwards General) Burgoyne, by means of which the latter had been allowed to dispose of his patent office in the Customs to a Mr. Hine. Nothing in the famous 'Letters' is more remarkable than the malignant dexterity with which this counter-stroke was levelled. The *coup* was effective. The prosecution of Vaughan was dropped, and though Junius reiterated his statement the duke remained silent. We furnish a few quotations from Junius's charges and challenges in connexion with this matter.

Letter 33, addressed to the duke of Grafton: 'Come forward, thou virtuous minister, and tell the world by what interest Mr. Hine has been recommended to so extraordinary a mark of His Majesty's favour, what was the price of the patent he has bought, and to what honourable purpose the purchase-money has been applied. . . . Do you dare to prosecute such a creature as Vaughan, while you are basely setting up the royal patronage to auction? . . . It is indeed highly to your interest to maintain the present House of Commons. Having sold the nation to you in gross, they will undoubtedly protect you in the detail.'

Letter 34, to the same: 'I accused you of having *sold*, or permitted to be sold, a patent place in the collection of the customs at Exeter, to one Mr. Hine, who, unable or unwilling to deposit the whole purchase-money himself, raised part of it by contribution, and has now a certain Doctor Brooke quartered upon the salary for £100 a year. No sale by the candle was ever conducted with greater formality. I affirm that the price at which the place was knocked down* . . . was, with your connivance and consent, paid to Colonel Burgoyne, to reward him, I presume, for the decency of his deportment at Preston. . . . With what countenance dare you appear in the royal presence, branded as you are with the infamy of a notorious breach of trust ? With what countenance can you take your seat at the Treasury Board, when you *feel* that every circulating whisper is at *your* expense alone, and stabs you to the heart ?'

Junius then challenged the duke to attempt to clear himself by bringing the matter before the House of Lords, or the Court of King's Bench, and ended with one of those curt, diabolic taunts with which he usually finished off a victim. 'My lord, you dare not do either.'

The duke was impressed by this concluding blow, and *did neither*. Soon afterwards he resigned his position on the Treasury Board, and we cannot help thinking that the dreadful assault influenced his action. A writer, signing himself 'Justice,' took up the cudgels on the duke's behalf. We reproduce a part of his letter.

'A place in the Custom House at Exeter becomes vacant. Colonel Burgoyne asks it of the duke of Grafton —he gives it. The colonel says, "I cannot hold it myself; will you give it my friend ?" The duke consents—the colonel nominates—the duke appoints; "but," says Junius, "the colonel set it up for sale, and actually received a sum of money for it." Be it so—he took a gross sum for what was given him as an annual income; and who is injured by this ? If the duke of Grafton sold it, he is impeachable; if he gave it to be sold, he is blameable; but if his Grace did neither, which is the fact, he is basely belied, and most impudently and wickedly villified.'

This defence was rather clever; most pamphleteers of that day were clever. Yet it failed to convince. The duke had incited the attack on Vaughan, and then retired from it. Undoubtedly the duke had given the

* £3,500.

place to Burgoyne so that Burgoyne might sell it. Burgoyne had sold it. 'Justice's' plea fell flat, and the denouncer triumphed. It could hardly be otherwise, for such was the denouncer's mastery of his weapons that even a foul stroke seemed fair, and a fair hit was irresistible.

Early in the following year Junius bestowed a parting slash. He taunted the ex-minister upon his withdrawal from the prosecution of Vaughan, and then dismissed the matter in a few masterly sentences. 'Your Grace is afraid to carry on the prosecution. Mr. Hine keeps quiet possession of his purchase, and Governor Burgoyne, relieved from the apprehension of refunding the money, sits down for the remainder of his life, *infamous and contented.*'

In 1769 the Coinage duty was made perpetual. Excise officers in Great Britain were empowered to seize and detain horses and conveyances used in the carrying of foreign uncustomed goods. A bounty of £25 in every £100 value was granted to raw silk produced in the Plantations and brought *to London.* The grant was to decrease periodically during three terms of seven years each.

The Board fined the Collector Inwards of London and his controller £60 each for having paid too much drawback, and also compelled them to make good a deficiency in their accounts.

The Receiver-General's clerk paid the salary of the patent searcher of Milford, who was in London on leave. For this little service the clerk exacted a fee of 6s. The Board came to know, and compelled the clerk's employer to return the fee out of his own pocket.

In 1770, on account of the volume of business, the London Commissioners agreed to breakfast together at the Custom-house.

An extraordinary incident is recorded. One Thomas, a landing-waiter, bequeathed £100, to be applied to the Old Subsidy.

The undermentioned officers of other departments had seats in the Long Room of the London Custom-house :

The Collector of the Excise Office and his controller.
The Collector of the Salt Office.
The Receiver for the City of London.
The Receiver for the Turkey Company.
The Receiver for the Russia Company.
The Receiver for the Trinity House.
The Receiver for Lighthouses.

An ordinary 'weigher' named Stone was deputed by the Board to examine tobacco on shipment, and the Commissioners thought so highly of him that they accepted his opinions in preference to those of the searchers, and even hinted that the Registrar-General of Tobacco might do worse than follow the guidance of this undeniable expert.

A yacht (and later a barge) were fitted up for the London Commissioners. (The barge was manned by ten stalwart oarsmen, and when the Board went afloat the whole water-side gazed admiringly. During winter the yacht cruised against the Kentish smugglers, but on April 1 it had to be ready and spick and span off the Custom-house. The regulations as to precedence were quaint. 'The Commissioner whose holiday it was on Friday' might claim the yacht—not for Friday only: he might take her on the previous Wednesday morning, and enjoy her till the following Tuesday night. Thus it seems that 'Friday off' meant a week's holiday.)

Parliament repealed the new duties levied in the Plantations, in so far as they applied to glass, painters' colours, and paper, manufactured in Great Britain. The preamble of the repealing Act stated that the said duties on British goods had proved a great discouragement to commerce.

In 1771 the exportation of live cattle from Great Britain was temporarily prohibited, as imported cattle were duty-free for a period. 'White oak-staves' from the American Plantations were bountied, to encourage British cask-making.

In 1772 the East India Company's bond was put in suit, they being in arrear for duties owed eighteen months previously. Process was stayed on the usual deposit of 6 per cent. interest on the sum outstanding.

The London Controller-General was granted £190 a year to pay five additional clerks to bring up arrears, on condition that two years' arrears were wiped off per annum.

The Customs and Post-Office Secretaries were summoned to Whitehall, to confer with the Treasury upon a practice which had become common, of importing silks and lace through the foreign post. It was decided that goods thus imported were forfeitable.

A grant of £6 a year from the Customs to 'The Lecturer of Barking Parish' should be quoted.* (The London Custom-house was in 'the parish of Barking.')

The Board transmitted to the collectors certain instructions from the Admiralty with regard to the pressing of men for the navy. When men were taken from a merchant coaster by the captain of a man-of-war, the pressing officer had to put on board a sufficient number of trusty men from his own crew to assist in navigating the coaster to her destination. These had to leave the ship on her arrival in port, and present themselves before the collector of customs, who was directed to send them to another port to rejoin their vessel, or to maintain them until such vessel arrived. If they left by road to rejoin their ship he was to allow them 1d. a mile as travelling money; if they remained to await her he was to grant them 6d. a day as subsistence allowance. Moneys thus advanced were to be charged to and repaid by the Navy Board.

Great exertions were made to prevent the importation of infected animals, the cattle distemper prevailing

* This grant lapsed occasionally.

abroad. A copy of a letter from one Captain Fraser at Dunkirk to Lord Weymouth was sent to Southampton, in which it was pointed out that great quantities of eggs were shipped from France to the southern English ports, packed in straw which might have come from stables and outhouses occupied by diseased cattle. It was enjoined that all such straw should be burned.

The constables of seaport towns held 'press warrants,' enabling them to arrest such seafaring men as might be 'lurking about,' and hand them over to naval commanders. The collectors of customs were empowered to pay constables 20s. for each capture, with 1s. in addition to reimburse the constable, who had to give the last-mentioned sum as 'press-money' to each man taken. Moneys to be repaid by the Navy Board.

The Swedish Government required bills of health from every vessel arriving in Sweden, and the British collectors were empowered to grant such bills to vessels proceeding thither from Great Britain. One of these documents is annexed to a Southampton Letter-Book. It is quaintly worded, commencing thus:

'To all Christian People, To whom these presents shall come: We, the Ministers of the Most Serene Prince, Our Lord King George the Third,' etc.

The growing difficulties with the American colonists appear to have influenced the Commissioners, for they directed the English collectors to watch outward trade to the Plantations, and if a ship cleared in ballast for America to send full particulars to Thames Street 'by the very first post.'

It seems that at this time the customs officers did not try the strengths of imported spirits. The only customs duty on spirits was the Old Subsidy, the rest of the varying duties on 'single' and 'double' spirits being excise, yet the Customs in most cases collected them. It is likely that the excise officers tested the goods and assessed the rates, and the Customs took the money, but it is tolerably certain that the customs men always gauged the goods.

During 1772 the Commissioners of Excise suggested that their officers should be allowed to try the strength of all seized spirits sold, otherwise parcels of high overproof goods might be sold 'at a common price.' The Customs Board consented to allow the excisemen to sample and test one cask in five, 'but,' the document ended, 'they may not take the samples away.'

The duty on imported oak bark was reduced, to encourage the British tanning industry.

The East India Company were forbidden to build any new ships for oversea traffic till their total of shipping was reduced to 45,000 tons. (In the next year Parliament advanced the Company £1,400,000.)

A rigorous Act was issued against drawback frauds committed by Irish shippers, who entered goods for foreign, received drawback on them, and then relanded them, or ran them into Great Britain. Both drawback and ship were made forfeitable, and every person concerned was made liable to a penalty of treble the value of the goods. In all future cases of drawback shipments from Ireland both shippers and masters were to swear to the debentures, and if the goods were for Great Britain drawback was to be withheld till a certificate of landing was received.

The British system of bountying and customing corn, etc., was regularized in 1773. From January 1, 1774, when the price of middling British wheat reached or exceeded 48s. a quarter, the price of rye, peas, and beans 32s., the price of barley 24s., or the price of oats 16s., import duties were to cease on foreign corn and wheat-flour, except to the amount of 6d. a quarter on wheat, 3d. on rye, etc., 2d. on barley and oats, and 2d. a cwt. on wheat-flour. The price was to be estimated, as of old, in each county, and if the price at one port were at or above the specified rate, and at a port in another county less than the rate, corn imported at the first port might not be carried coastwise to the other. When wheat was at or above 44s., rye, etc., at 28s., barley at 22s., and oats at 14s., they might not be exported, but if under those prices they were allowed exportation, and bountied.

An additional duty was put upon foreign 'painted paper' (wall-paper, etc.).

The Board quoted a decision that goods shipped, and afterwards lost or damaged within the limits of a port, were not entitled to drawback.*

At this time the East India Company paid about £1,000,000 a year in customs and excise duties.

In 1774 appeared a statute, the preamble of which ran: 'Whereas dangerous Commotions and Insurrections have been Fomented and Raised in the Town of Boston in the province of Massachusetts Bay in New England by divers ill affected Persons, to the subversion of His Majesty's Government, and to the utter Destruction of the publick Peace and good order of the said Town, in which Commotions and Insurrections certain valuable Cargoes of Tea, being the property of the East India Company, and on board certain vessels lying within the Bay or Harbour of Boston, were seized and destroyed,' etc.

It proceeded to enact that all lading or unlading of goods within Boston Harbour, except stores for the troops or 'fuel for the inhabitants,' should be discontinued, and to endow the Admiral and the customs officers with power to compel any vessel nearing the coast to depart on penalty of forfeiture. It declared all charter-parties and bills of lading for goods to Boston void. The town was to 'make full satisfaction' to the East India Company, and 'reasonable satisfaction' to the revenue officers of Boston. (The difference between 'full' and 'reasonable' was not explained.)

The Act went on to state that when Boston had abased

* Observe the wretched lack of finality appertaining to legal decisions. In 1778 this opinion was set aside, and drawback allowed on goods shipped for Dublin and destroyed by fire before the vessel left Great Britain. In 1783 the Attorney-General decided that drawback might be paid on goods shipped, and afterwards damaged within the limits of a port, provided such damage was accidental, and the goods were thereby rendered valueless.

her mutinous crest, 'and not till then,' his Majesty would prescribe the limits of the port.

The Governor and Council of the State of New York were forbidden from assenting to any 'Act, Vote, or Resolution of the House of Representatives,' till his Majesty's troops had been supplied with necessaries as enjoined by statute.

The Act forbidding exportation of corn from Great Britain was temporarily relaxed, to allow of shipments to the Sugar Plantations (West Indies), to the Plantation fisheries (Newfoundland), and from Southampton to the Channel Islands.

The stock of tea in the East India Company's warehouses had grown so large* that sale within the specified time (three years from landing) appeared impracticable. The period was extended to five years, the Company being enjoined to keep the British market well supplied at a moderate price, otherwise the Treasury might withhold the privilege of exclusive importation of tea, and license other syndicates to bring tea from European ports.

Parliament issued a fresh statute against the disaffected colonists, providing that any person brought to trial for taking life in the maintenance of just authority might claim to be tried elsewhere than in the colony where the deed was committed.

Quantities of old and light silver coin of the realm, 'or coin purporting to be such,' were being brought into Great Britain. The practice was accordingly prohibited, and it was provided that such goods might be seized or searched for under Charles II.'s Act of Frauds. The standard of weight was 62s. to the pound troy, the standard of fineness 11 ozs. 2 dwts. pure silver, and 18 dwts. alloy.†

* Probably through stoppage of the trade with the American colonies.

† Compare these with the ancient standard, say, in Henry I.'s day, when the pennies were of pure silver, and 240 of them weighed a pound troy.

Parliament continued to apply restrictive and irritating legislation to the American Colonies. Originally the governors and their councillors had been appointed by royal patent, but in William and Mary's reign it was granted that the councillors might be chosen annually by the General Assembly. Parliament revoked this charter, and provided that the king should appoint the councillors by warrant, and that they should hold office during his pleasure. The governors were empowered to appoint judges, to make sheriffs without the Council's consent, and to forbid public meetings. Jurors were no longer to be elected, but appointed by the sheriffs. If the Colonies neglected to provide suitable barracks, the king's troops might be billeted upon inhabitants.

Several officers were sent from England to the West Indies, to investigate revenue matters, and their efforts secured the suspension of the collectors of Barbadoes and St. Vincent. The former was fined £1,500, and a cargo of sugar which he had collected under the 4½ per cent. duties, to send to England presumably for his own profit, instead of for deposit in the 'Husband's' custody for the Crown's benefit, was seized in transit. Both he and the St. Vincent collector were restored to duty, 'for a year on trial.' The bonds of several other Plantation collectors were put in suit, on account of large sums owing to the Crown.

The trade of the port of Liverpool had increased immensely. The Liverpool collector's bond for good behaviour was raised from £5,000 to £15,000.

The sum of £312 18s. 8d. was granted to pay expenses incurred by Emanuel Matthias, a revenue spy employed in collecting information on the Continent.

The port of Hull, which up to 1774 had been exempt from the laws* as to provision of legal quays, was deprived of the privilege, and empowered to provide a dock. The old Staiths, 'Thomas Walton's Shipyard,' and 'Rotten

* Elizabeth's Act, as amended by Charles II.'s Act of Frauds.

Herring Staith,' 'used,' quoth the Statute, 'from time immemorial,' were still allowed to be used for landing and shipment, on condition that they were fitted with proper quays.

A captain of a king's ship stopped a Newfoundland trader at sea, and overhauled her cocket. He found it to display an unratified erasure, and thereupon detained the ship. On inquiry being made, it was found that one of the London patent officers was responsible for the defect. What compensation, if any, was made to the shipowner and shippers may not be discovered in the records, but all the superior clerical officers known as searchers were called into the Board Room and admonished. The Attorney-General uttered an opinion upon the case, recommending that all erasures in customs documents should be made by drawing 'a strong line' across the superfluous item, the said line being ratified by the initials of the eraser and his check officer, 'agreeable to the ancient rules of the Court of Exchequer.'

Instructions were sent to all collectors that the brigantine *Industry* was on her way to England, conveying messages from the American rebels to sympathizers in England. Ships from the rebellious Colonies were to be closely searched for letters, and the Board were to be apprised of all vessels fitting out for America. The Plantation Acts were to be sternly enforced. Vessels going to America or the West Indies were to be rummaged closely, and the officers were to detain 'letters going to persons in the provinces actually in rebellion.' All persons coming from America were to be strictly examined, and their letters and papers sent to the Board. British officers carrying dispatches were exempt.

The old French duties, which had been continued in Quebec since its conquest by the British in 1759, were replaced by a new tariff. The French duties had been certain small levies on wine and spirits, and 3 per cent.

ad valorem on dry goods. The new duties were as follows :

Foreign spirits imported from Great Britain	1s. per gallon.
Foreign spirits imported from American Plantations	9d. ,, ,,
Foreign spirits imported from Sugar Plantations	6d. ,, ,,
British spirits	3d. ,, ,,
Plantation spirits imported from foreign ..	1s. ,, ,,
Molasses and syrups in British or Irish ships	3d. ,, ,,
,, ,, ,, other ships ..	6d. ,, ,,

The above duties were to be paid in sterling money, and the routes of importation were prescribed. The Receiver-General for the Provinces was to have custody of the receipts, which were to be applied towards defraying the expense of civil government, etc. Any surplus which might accrue was to remain with the Receiver-General, for disposition by Parliament.

Parliament recited the original conditions of Plantation trade—viz., that the Colonies should either export to each other, or send their goods to Great Britain, and should import via Great Britain (Irish linen, wine from Madeira and the Azores, and salt for the Fisheries, excepted). Then it forbade the disaffected provinces from trading with each other, or with the American Colonies that remained loyal. Thus they might only trade with Great Britain, Ireland, and the West Indies. Disaffection spread rapidly, and soon it was deemed necessary to apply the prohibition to the hitherto secure provinces of New Jersey, Pennsylvania, Maryland, Virginia, and South Carolina.*

* The Privy Council issued elaborate instructions to all newly appointed colonial governors. We furnish a précis. It must be understood that the instructions could scarcely be carried out in the American Colonies in 1775, but in the other Plantations they were rigidly enforced. Readers had best consider them as applying in full in the West Indies. These were the regulations of trade and revenue that a West Indian governor had to carry out:

1. The naval officers in charge of the various ports were to furnish security to the British Commissioners of Customs for the due observance of the Navigation and Plantation Acts, and to apprise the governor when this had been done. Custom-houses

The duty on rape-seed imported into Great Britain from Ireland for expressing oil was reduced, and it was enacted that 'rape-cake for manure' might enter duty-free. Raw goatskins from foreign were freed of duty for five years, to encourage the manufacture of 'red leather.' The duty on foreign earthenware was increased.

Most of the troops on the Irish establishment had been sent to assist in the war with the disaffected colonists, and it was enacted that clothing and accoutrements for their use might be shipped in Ireland at will, provided a certificate from the 'Chief Governor of Ireland' were produced at shipment. The bounty of 5s. a hogshead on imported flax-seed, provided in 1763 by the Irish Parliament, was supplemented by a similar grant from the British Parliament, to be paid by the English Receiver-General. This was to endure for two years.

---

might only be established at ports controlled by naval officers. The collectors were to reside at their places of employment.

2. No excuse for non-compliance with the provisions of the Navigation Act as to three-fourths British or Plantation seamen might be accepted, unless there had been loss from sickness, death, or foreign aggression, during the voyage. Spirits might not be exported from the Plantations to the Isle of Man.

3. William III.'s Acts prohibiting the exportation of wool, and the entrance into Plantation ports of foreign traders from places beyond the Cape of Good Hope, yet within the dominions of the East India Company, were to be enforced. If a foreign trader approached a port, the master was to be warned off, even if he pleaded distress; and if he persisted in entering the Customs might seize ship and cargo, unless he could prove that he was bound for a foreign West Indian Plantation, and then he might be 'relieved,' and sent away as soon as practicable. He might not land goods.

4. All certificates as to goods carried under the Plantation Acts were to be closely scrutinized, and the bonds cancelled within eighteen months. The naval officers in charge might admit no person to bond until the collector approved the sureties. A close watch was to be kept upon inter-Plantation traffic, to see that the goods were really carried from one Plantation to another, and not to foreign countries.

5. Every three months returns were to be made to the British Treasury and Customs of vessels trading in the province supervised, with lists of the bonds appertaining. Invoices were to be sent in triplicate of cargoes cleared outwards, one invoice to go to the Treasury, one to the Board of Customs, and one to the collector at the British port of discharge.

In 1776 all trade with the rebellious colonists was forbidden. Ships engaging in such traffic might be seized. If taken into American ports they were to be handed over to the customs collectors. The crews were to be pressed.

The Declaration of Independence was issued. Adam Smith's 'Wealth of Nations' appeared.

An extension of time was granted to the East India Company to dispose of their stock of muslins and calicoes, which had grown on their hands through stoppage of the Plantation trade.

The London Board tendered thanks to Sir John Frederick for his present of forty-four volumes of the Parliamentary Journals, and to Sir William Musgrave for his gift of 'a valuable collection of rare books.' One of the Board's solicitors made a compilation of the 'Laws of the Customs.' One thousand copies of this book were printed at the public expense, for the use of collectors

---

6. No European commodities might pass into the Plantations unless first landed in Great Britain. The cockets were to be inspected closely, it being thought that forged cockets were frequently used.

7. The collection of the countervailing duty on foreign sugar landed in the West Indies was to be supervised. Full particulars as to shipment and place of growth were to accompany all consignments of indigo from the Plantations to Great Britain, as the goods were granted a premium on landing. Planters and the public were to be informed of the regulations governing the legal weight of packages of tobacco. The sixpence per month from seamen's wages, for the support of Greenwich Hospital, was to be diligently collected.

8. The customs officers were to be supported and encouraged in the discharge of their duty, and allowed free access to the copies of the various Acts kept in public offices. Inefficient or neglectful officers were to be reported, and offending merchants prosecuted. In all trials as to ships, goods, or duties, the jurors were to be king's subjects, and this qualification applied to appointments of officials who served under the Treasury. If an official died, the governor might name a substitute ; the appointment to endure until confirmed, or until a new official was sent out by the home authorities.

9. Regular correspondence was to be maintained with the British Commissioners of Customs.

10. All Plantation by-laws repugnant to the Imperial Acts were to be made void.

and other officers. (In 1780 the author received £200 for his trouble.)

One of the London jerquers was charged with allowing his work to fall into arrear, paying many portages which he should have withheld, and acting corruptly in taking a fee of £200 for giving employment to a clerk. The first charge was dealt with by a severe reprimand. He was then surcharged to the amount of twenty-eight portages. He was acquitted of the charge of corruption, 'for want of proof.' Later the Board fined and censured him for neglecting to attend when summoned by them. He asked for leave 'to settle private affairs,' and failed to return. Dismissed.

The Board issued an order, that still remains in force, directing that officers going on leave should temporarily surrender their 'deputations' or 'commissions.' This was because certain officers while on leave had made improper use of the parchment scrolls.

In 1777 certain revenue cruisers under the command of Warren Lisle were supplied with carriage and swivel guns.

One Shafto, controller to the Receiver-General of Fines and Forfeitures, gave the Board much trouble. He had been allowed to levy 'poundage' on the awards made to seizing officers, and the Board thought fit to deprive him of this lucrative privilege, and grant him a salary instead. Mr. Shafto became indignant, and haughtily refused to accept the said salary. The Board therefore had it paid into the Exchequer. Shafto then demanded restoration of the power of levying poundage. The Board refused, and told him he would get no salary in lieu unless he 'made proper submission.' Shafto then memorialized the Treasury, and my Lords restored his right of poundage.

Meantime a new Receiver-General of Fines and Forfeitures had been appointed, at a fixed salary. As soon as this gentleman knew of Shafto's success he went to the Board, and demanded permission to levy poundage.

But the Board would not hear of it. Mr. Shafto went his extortionate way rejoicing, but the Commissioners had not finished with him. (In 1780 they caught him misbehaving, and stopped his poundage once more. In 1782 they caught him red-handed, and stopped his poundage for good and all; for they dismissed him, and then wrote the Treasury, suggesting that the office of controller of Fines and Forfeitures should carry no more poundage, so long as they remained in commission.)

The Admiralty granted commissions to privateers, empowering them to prey upon American commerce. Before proceeding to sea each privateer captain produced his commission to the collector at the port where the vessel fitted out. The collector thereupon inspected the vessel, and if he found her suitable for the work, and in accordance with the terms of her commission, clearance was granted.

The drawback on tea shipped from Great Britain to Ireland, which had previously been but a moiety of the duty paid, was made equal to the duty.

The captains of homeward-bound East Indiamen committed great frauds by unshipping tea, muslins, etc., into craft that met them at sea, and afterwards ran the goods at secluded places on the coast. Similar frauds were committed when the vessels left England, the runners meeting the East Indiamen in the Channel, and transhipping large quantities of foreign wine and brandy, which were thus conveyed to the East Indies without paying the usual British duties.

There was much fraud in connexion with drawback shipments generally, drawback bonds being illegally obtained, and the goods relanded after the drawback had been paid. It was therefore enacted that certificates of landing abroad should be produced for all drawback goods. The time allowed for production was six months if the goods went to Ireland or the Channel Islands, fifteen months if to any part of Europe, eighteen months if to Africa or the American Plantations, and thirty months if to ports within the boundaries of the East India Company's Charter. This provision was soon repealed, being found most inconvenient.

In 1778 extra tunnage was levied—£8 8s. on French wine and vinegar, £4 4s. on other wine and vinegar. This became permanent as 'The 1778 Wine Duty.' French, Spanish, and Portuguese wines were directed, on penalty of forfeiture, to be imported in casks not less than a hogshead.

Parliament attempted to conciliate the Americans. Cap. 12 of 1778 opened thus: 'Whereas Taxation by the Parliament of Great Britain for the purpose of raising a Revenue in his Majesty's Colonies, Provinces, and Plantations in North America has been found by experience to occasion great uneasinesses and disorders among his Majesty's faithful Subjects, who may nevertheless be disposed to acknowledge the Justice of contributing to the common Defence of the Empire, provided such Contribution should be raised under the Authority of the General Court or General Assembly of each respective Colony, Province, or Plantation,' etc. The Act continued that in future no tax should be imposed in North America or the West Indies, by King or Parliament, except such duties as might be necessary for the regulating of commerce, and that the net produce of these should be paid and applied for use of the colony in which levied.*

Cap. 13 was still more accommodating: 'For the Quieting and Extinguishing of divers Jealousies and Apprehensions of Danger to their Liberties and Rights, which have alarmed many of his Majesty's Subjects in the Colonies, Provinces, and Plantations of New Hampshire, Massachusetts Bay, Rhode Island, Connecticut, New York, New Jersey, Pennsylvania, the three Lower Counties on Delaware, Maryland, Virginia, North Carolina, South Carolina, and Georgia, and for a full Manifestation of the just and gracious Purposes of his Majesty and his Parliament, to maintain and secure all his Sub-

* A stillborn Act.

jects in the clear and perfect Enjoyment of their Liberties and Rights,' etc.

The king was empowered to appoint five Commissioners to treat with the Americans and inquire into their grievances. The Commissioners were enabled to order a cessation of hostilities, and to suspend the Act prohibiting Plantation trade and commerce, or any other Act relating to America which had been passed since February 10, 1763. They might also grant pardons and appoint governors. But the war was fated to continue to the bitter end.

Ireland's commercial fetters were eased. It was enacted that all Irish goods, except wool, woollens, cottons, hats, glass, hops, gunpowder, and coal, might be exported *direct* from Ireland to America or Africa, and that Irish cotton-yarn might enter Great Britain duty-free. The *full* privileges applying to British-built ships were granted to ships built in Ireland.

The East India Company's directors complained to the Board that the London customs officers did not attend at a sufficiently early hour, and requested that the landing-waiters might be ordered to work until two in the afternoon without going to dinner. (The Company's warehouses closed at two.) The Board granted this, subject to notice being given, so that the landing-surveyors could exercise close supervision.

The Board directed their Secretary to inquire closely into the antecedents of persons whom the Treasury might appoint to offices in the Customs, and to report if he found anything unsatisfactory, meanwhile withholding the commission of the grantee. (We are inclined to think that a stiffer-backed Board than this never sat around a carved table.)

An officer who had been dismissed applied to the Board to secure him repayment of certain moneys which he had lent to other officers, but all he got in reply was a reminder that trade amongst officials was against the rules laid down by the Exchequer.

The officers at Dover must have been either dull-witted or illiterate, for they were censured for admitting ostrich feathers to entry as French goods.

A Mr. Dwyer was appointed collector of a port in Jamaica. He entered into bond in the usual manner, received his commission, and proceeded to celebrate the occasion. The Commissioners revoked his appointment, and demanded return of his commission. Mr. Dwyer refused, and it was found that he had deposited the document as security for money borrowed. His bond was therefore put in suit, and the Board provided that in future, when a Plantation officer was appointed, his commission should be sent to the collector at port of appointment, and the newly made officer be told what ship it was going by, 'so that if he pleases he may accompany it.' It appears from the records that Mr. Dwyer's lapse occurred on March 17.

The captain of a privateer brought in a smuggling vessel which he had captured, and was told by the Board he might prosecute at his own risk, and if he got the sloop condemned he and his crew would receive two-thirds of her appraised value. Notice was sent to the collectors that this system should be adopted in all similar cases, and that privateer captains should be told that if they strained the law the Board would not protect them. (The Commissioners were always doubtful, and with good reason, of the honesty of bearers of letters of marque.)

That intrepid and vigilant seizing-officer, Warren Lisle, resigned his command—much, no doubt, to the delight of the Sussex and Hampshire smugglers. Why he resigned is not apparent. It is possible that he had gone a little too far, as such enterprising folk often do. Yet he may have resigned from other reasons, for we find by reference to the Treasury file that his son William was allowed to succeed him.

In 1779 the revenue cruisers on the south coast of England were manned and armed to the fullest extent necessary, and sent to the Downs, to await orders from the Admiral.

Up to this date small parcels of imported goods, the duty on which was less than 10s., had been allowed to enter free. The practice was discontinued.

Parliament levied a curious tax, being an impost of 5 per cent. upon *the produce* of all previous customs duties, import, export, and coastwise (after the usual discounts and allowances had been deducted). This was made permanent as 'The Additional Impost of 1779.' The produce of this tax, in the idiotic fashion then prevailing, was kept apart, and handed in separately, being appropriated to a fund for paying annuities and raising a lottery.

Certain provisions of the Navigation Act were explained by statute thus: All goods from Asia, Africa, or America, imported into Great Britain or Ireland, were to come direct. If raw goods were carried from Asia, Africa, or America, to Europe, and manufactured there, the manufactured articles, if brought to Great Britain or Ireland, were liable to forfeiture 'with ships and tackle.'

Cotton of the British Plantations, landed in Great Britain, was allowed to be exported duty-free, if carried in British-built ships.

Tobacco-planting was allowed in Ireland. The goods thus produced might only be exported to Great Britain, under the regulations applying to tobacco of the American Plantations. The Irish collectors were to deliver manifests with full particulars to all shipmasters conveying Irish tobacco to Great Britain, and send duplicates to the British Commissioners of Customs. On arrival at ports of unshipment the manifests were delivered to the collectors. The goods were liable to the same duties as Plantation tobacco. The packages were to be casks, chests, or cases, each containing not less than 450 pounds tobacco. The Act included Irish manufactured tobacco as well as Irish leaf.

In 1780 Irish trade to British Africa, British America,

and the West Indies, was placed on the same footing as British. It was enacted that goods might be exported from Great Britain and Ireland to any place in America that was under protection of the British arms. The Secretary of State was directed to apprise the British and Irish Commissioners* of Customs as to the ports thus available for trade, and the masters of ships proceeding thither were to enter into bond to land their cargoes at the places mentioned, the bonds being cancelled by certificates from the British naval officers in charge of the ports of destination. The trade was to be regulated by the British Commander-in-Chief in America.

The tunnage on French wine and vinegar was increased by £8, on other wine and vinegar by £4. This tax became permanent as 'The 1780 Wine Duty.'

Additional duties were levied upon foreign starch and hair-powder, and the exportation of copper was prohibited. The restrictions as to 'times and hours,' imposed by Charles II.'s and subsequent Acts upon the removal of wool by land, were repealed. These inquisitorial regulations had vexed farmers and wool-dealers, and played the mischief with the inland wool trade generally.

The public accounts were in a chaotic condition, and no department's books were more dolefully confused than those of the Customs, a circumstance that need cause no wonder, when the many divisions and subdivisions of duties, the bewildering discounts and allowances, the innumerable exceptions, and the absurd methods of entry and receipt, are taken into consideration. A Committee was appointed to investigate the national accounts, and to inquire into the management of the public departments.

That imbecile creature, Lord George Gordon, incited the lower classes of London to a series of outrages upon their fellow-countrymen. Many Catholic places of worship were plundered and burned, and those dreadful English Bastilles, Newgate, the Fleet, and the King's

* Note that there was a separate Board for Ireland (*vide* Chapter IX.).

Bench Prison, made heaps of smoking ruins. The rioters might have ended by burning London, but for the national failing. They proceeded to investigate the condition of the vintners' warehouses and vaults, and drunkenness overcame the ruffianism that had prevailed against stone ramparts and volleys of musketry.

During these riots great precautions were taken to protect the London Custom-house, and the 'Surveyor of Sloops' was directed to contract for 100 musquetoons for that purpose. The principal officials mustered their clerks, and enjoined them to be ready to defend the building if it were attacked. One of the said principals afterwards put in a heavy bill for expenses incurred, which bill the Board sent back, with the remark that the security of the gentleman's office was 'mainly his own concern.'

After the riots the Sardinian ambassador was allowed to import books and ornaments for his 'new chapel' duty-free. The old chapel had been destroyed by the rioters.*

During this year the Board cautioned the London jerquers, who checked the landing-waiters' books, against allowing their clerks to extort fees from the landing-waiters for passing their accounts.

The Board came to grips with one Wiggins, surveyor of baggage. Finding that Wiggins had various outside employments which interfered with his attendance at the King's Warehouse, they gave him a space of time in which to decide whether he would attend to his duties as a baggage officer, or resign the Customs and look after his other businesses. Wiggins took the full space allowed for consideration, and then went to the Treasury and

* See Horace Walpole's letter to Mann: 'Monsieur Cordon, the Sardinian Minister, suffered still more. The mob forced his chapel, stole two silver lamps, demolished everything else, threw the benches into the street, set them on fire, carried the brands into the chapel, and set fire to that. Poor Madame Cordon was confined by illness. My cousin Thomas Walpole dragged her, for she could not stand with terror and weakness, to his own house.'

obtained four months' leave. The Board refused to receive the Treasury warrant, stating that they had many times censured him for non-attendance.*

The baggage of the Lord Lieutenant of Ireland was 'allowed every facility' in transit from London to Dublin. Officers were sent to his London residence to inspect and seal all the packages, and the customs men at Chester and Holyhead were instructed to pass the sealed goods without further examination.

Mr. Lutwidge, surveyor-general, inspected the port of Liverpool, and found that the collector had allowed a large quantity of dutiable foreign corn to be delivered duty-free. The collector was surcharged £2,496.

The Receiver-General paid £470 into the Superannuation Fund, being fines levied upon certain outport collectors.

The Board surcharged their 'housekeeper,' Mrs. Bridget Kelly, with a sum which she had expended in purchasing certain newspapers which they had not ordered. They also discovered that the keeper of the Coffee Warehouse, *and one of his lockers*, rented a portion of the warehouse, and they bade the two pluralists decide within six months which they would resign, the warehouse business or the Customs.

In 1781 Mr. Temple, who as surveyor-general of America had been specially rewarded for ability, was called upon to make good a large deficiency in his accounts. 'Plead within a week, or be proceeded against'—thus ran the injunction.

The clerks in the Secretary's Office presented a memorial against the special promotion of an officer to 'Western Clerk,' an office previously deemed a standing perquisite of the secretarial staff. The two leading protesters were suspended, one for six and one for twelve weeks, and the others were fined, the Board telling them that if they desired promotion they had best qualify themselves by becoming acquainted, not only with the

* In 1783 he was compelled to resign his office.

routine of outer work, but with all branches of customs practice, especially with the history of the 'Customs Laws, so as to be able to remind the Board.'

Two Commissioners conferred with the Secretary for War upon the matter of employing troops to prevent smuggling *in the neighbourhood of Croydon.*

The officers at Margate were enjoined to be vigilant in preventing artificers from leaving England.

A parcel of coin, amount £52,000, was allowed to be exported to Barbadoes, to supply a relief fund, the island having been devastated by a hurricane.

The Customs employed several solicitors, each solicitor advising upon a certain class of bonds, or upon matters connected with a certain number of ports. They were paid large salaries, and received liberal allowances for clerks and messengers. They were also granted sums of money annually for rent of chambers outside the Custom-house, and for coals and candles used therein, it being assumed that they frequently took their outstanding work home. The Board refused to continue the allowances for chambers, coals, and candles, stating that many other customs officials carried work home, yet received no extra grants. They also reminded the solicitors that many eminent lawyers contrived to support themselves in affluence upon fees earned under stress of competition, and to pay the rent of chambers and offices as well, while the customs lawyers had offices in the Custom-house, and clerks free of expense. Then these iconoclastic Commissioners reminded the solicitors of the heavy fees that enriched them, and bluntly adjured them to put their hands in their own pockets, for that the Revenue should no longer be burdened with their chamber-rents, coal bills, and charges for candles of expensive mould and material. Then the Board sent for the 'Auditor of Law Expenses,' and bade him pay particular attention to his work in future, so that he might be able to satisfy them that the large sums disbursed on credit of his certificates *were really due!* And they directed him, 'for his own more ample information,' to study and précis the Minutes relating to his office.

A fleet of eighteen East Indiamen arrived. The Board at once employed 174 extra customs watermen.

Parliament abolished the confusing discounts* allowed on customs duties, and considerably relaxed the provisions of the Navigation Act. A heavy impost was laid upon foreign verdigris, and 'smalt blue' was made duty-free.

It was directed that the prices of corn, whether for bounty or duty, in Kent and Essex, should be regulated by the London price, which was to be published weekly in the *London Gazette*, and certified to by the collectors of London and of Kentish and Essex ports.

An additional duty of 1¾d. per pound was laid on tobacco, and of 4s. 8d. per cwt. on sugar. The proceeds of these imposts were to go to the Sinking Fund. British refined sugar was granted a handsome additional drawback on exportation, and tobacco an added drawback equal to the increase in duty.

In 1782 an additional 4d. per pound was levied on tobacco, and 8d. on snuff. The rate value for brandy was abolished, and the customs† duty on that article made £8 8s. per tun, which included the Coinage duty. The new duty was liable to the 5 per cent. impost on net proceeds. Additional duties were placed on salt and beeswax, and to crown the whole an additional 5 per cent. was levied on the produce of all duties, the previous 5 per cent. excepted.

It was provided, 'for the better securing the freedom of elections,' that no revenue officer should vote at parliamentary elections, under penalty of £100 and loss

* This rendered the old 'Books of Rates' useless, and Messrs. Frewin and Sims, of the Customs, were ordered to prepare a new 'Book of Rates.'

† The French duty remained, and it must be borne in mind that besides the customs duty on spirits there were nine different branches of excise duties. The total excise on 'double spirits' was nearly twice the excise on 'single spirits.' At most ports these duties were collected by the Customs.

of office, but officers might retain the power of voting by resigning their appointments prior to the date on which the Act came into force. Thus it is evident that Parliament did not wish to disconcert people whose votes were worth more than their offices.

An Act was passed empowering the king to treat with the Americans for peace, and to repeal by letters patent any Act relating to the American Plantations.

To prevent British ships from passing into the possession of the king's enemies, it was enacted that they might not be sold to persons residing abroad, without special licence for each sale, and that the master or owner of any British ship trading foreign should give bond not to sell his vessel to foreigners. If a British ship were sold to a British subject the old bond lapsed, and a new bond had to be entered into by the purchaser. The bonds were to be at the public expense.

There had been some misapprehension as to the application of the Tobacco-planting Act to Scotland, and the point in doubt was consequently made clear by statute. It appears that tobacco had been cultivated extensively beyond the Border. The Scottish supervision must have been very slack, for it was found necessary to provide explicit regulations as to the method of taking Scottish tobacco to account for duty. Future planting was prohibited, but the standing crops were allowed to be gathered. Each planter was to account to the nearest collector of customs for the tobacco grown by him or in his possession, furnishing the amount of the current crop within three months after gathering. The goods were to pay the same rates as Plantation tobacco, and they might not be removed to England except by sea.

It was enacted that no office newly granted by patent in the Plantations should be executed by deputy.

A large quantity of tea was stolen from one of the East India Company's London warehouses, and the Attorney-General decided that the Customs could not claim the duty involved, as the goods had not been exposed for sale. This appears a challengeable decision, for one of the conditions under which the Company were allowed to warehouse goods was that they should keep the goods in safe custody.

The learned gentleman had no scruples as to advising enforcement of the regulations, when he was asked as to the legal method of dealing with a crop of tobacco grown in Yorkshire. He advised that the excise officers should procure the co-operation of the local justices, and arrange for the destruction of the young crop, and that if the grower gathered it in spite of them the Customs Board should proceed against him for a penalty of £10 *per rod* of land from which the crop was gathered!

The Committee of Account queried the Board of Customs as to why the customs accounts were in arrear. The Board made a telling statement as to the difficulties they lay under in dealing with the patent officers. Thereupon my Lords of the Treasury stopped their previous practice of granting long and frequent holidays to the patentees, and decided to refer all future applications for leave to the Board of Customs.

The Board had for a long time been empowered to levy dues on vessels lying at Custom-house Quay, and the collection seems to have at first been leased to a high customs official. The system of leasing was discontinued, and they appointed a manager of the business, giving him 5 per cent. of the takings. The Margate hoys discharged and loaded at this quay, and the Board seem to have thought little of the Margate trade, for they instructed their manager to turn the hoys away if he could secure the custom of the Ipswich packets.

The Treasury directed the Board to prepare a scheme for consolidating the customs taxes. A committee was formed, consisting of the Solicitor, the controller-general's principal clerk, the deputy Collector Inwards, and the deputy Collector Outwards. They were instructed to begin by drawing up a list of such titles of goods, expressed in the old 'Book of Rates,' as had become obsolete. The Board spoke highly of their Committee, but informed the Treasury that, 'on account of the intricacy of the computations,' there was little chance of a scheme being got ready for the ensuing Session.

The Plantation collectors were instructed to procure 'good bills' for remittance of such balances as were not transmitted in kind or in bulk silver, and were told that if their bills were 'protested' they would be charged with the sums at issue, plus interest. It was arranged that whenever a Plantation collector was dismissed or removed for misconduct his successor should, before departing from England, be called into the office of the London controller-general, informed of his predecessor's irregularities, and cautioned against repeating them. The controller-general was to endorse the certificate of the new collectors' qualifications with a statement that this had been done.

Messrs. Frewin and Sims produced their new 'Book of Rates,' and each compiler was rewarded with £100. The book was published by Longman, and it seems to have sold well. In 1784 Longman paid £153 7s. 6d. into the hands of the Collector Inwards.

The Customs Committee appointed to arrange the consolidation of duties were directed to prepare a new 'Book of Duties and Drawbacks,' 'disregarding fractions.'* Thereupon Messrs. Frewin and Sims came forward, and stated that they had evolved a plan of consolidation. They were directed to proceed with it, and promised £500 each if the result were satisfactory

The Treasury and the Board had a dispute over the ex-collector of Rochester. That gentleman had been dismissed for misconduct. He contrived to incite the Treasury into reopening his case, and they called on the Board for a copy of the proceedings. The copy was sent, and accompanied by a manly and remarkable statement.

* The net duties in previous 'Books of Rates' had been carried out to minute fractions of a penny.

The Board declared that the ex-collector had not served with 'high integrity' for twenty years, as in his application to the Treasury he had stated, but had during that period been guilty of many gross irregularities. They described the official method of adjudicating upon such cases, and protested that they had always used great care in investigating them, weighing every point of evidence as closely as possible. The concluding portion of their statement deserves literal reproduction :

'The Commissioners cannot recollect a previous instance of the Treasury having influenced the decision of the Commissioners in these cases, and it is sincerely to be wished that the Treasury may in future adhere to so salutary a rule, because the Board, having no means of rewarding, if they are deprived of the power of punishing, will lose every kind of control over their officers, and the effect of such relaxation will be immediately felt at the Exchequer.'

The salaries of the customs boatmen were adjusted, the Board quoting a Treasury warrant of 1684-1685, which enjoined that the boatmen's pay should be 'a competent and congruous subsistence.' Under the new scheme it was made £30 a year in England, £25 in Wales.

A merchant's clerk apprised the Board of certain clandestine dealings contemplated by his employer. The information saved the Revenue £532, and the Board gave the informer £100.

The following is an exact copy of an order issued to the officers (as quoted in the memoranda) instructing them as to the approved method of distinguishing flour from starch on importation :

'Put it into a tumbler of water which if Starch will sink to the bottom and form a hard Substance, and if Flour will turn into Paste and may be drawn into a kind of string like doe* and further by Starch being much whiter than Flour.'

The 'Officers of the London Burning-Ground' were

* Dough.

fined for allowing a seized cutter to lie in 'the Condemned Hole' with her sails unbent.

In 1783 an extra tide-waiter laid information against certain customs officers who had connived at extensive smuggling from the *Rochford*, East Indiaman. He received a reward of £40, and was superannuated with a yearly pension of 16 guineas.

The Commissioners set to work to curtail the expenses incidental to the domestic management of the London Custom-house. They discovered that the official Housekeeper, Mrs. Kelly, had made a practice of claiming all the partly used candles and selling them, realizing private profit thereby to the amount of £150 a year. This was stopped, and boxes were provided, in which the candle-stumps were deposited every morning, and kept under lock till the receptacles were full. Then 'the Controller of the Housekeeper' had to weigh the candle-ends and return them to the chandler, who had to allow for them in his bill.

It appears that Mrs. Kelly received an allowance of £215 per annum, to enable her to keep twelve servants, but the notable dame had only kept eight, and one of these had been paid in candle-ends and broken victuals. She was ordered to keep the full complement of servants in future, and to pay them proper wages.

She was also told to refrain from selling the cinders, the Commissioners shrewdly suspecting that in such secret traffic coal might pass as well as the charred residue. All cinders were to be collected, 'and carefully used again.' The Secretary was ordered, no doubt much to his disgust, to direct the scavenger to clear the ash-hole every third day.

The Board's order upon these important matters was emphatic. It began: 'Notice is hereby given to the Housekeeper in the most solemn manner,' and proceeded, 'The Housekeeper surely cannot imagine that the same plea of precedent would justify collectors, who hold under the same sort of grant as herself, in converting the public money to their own use, and yet the loss is equal, whether officers deprive the Revenue of the money, or of the candles that cost money.' Of course this was simple and honest reasoning, and it is to be wished that such homely truths were oftener uttered. Yet the Board might have been a little easier with Mrs. Kelly. They need not have ended with: 'She would have been made sensible to her cost that her plea is inadmissible if the Board had ordered her to be prosecuted for her misdemeanors.'

Then the Commissioners went into the matter of 'chips.' The yearly charge for chips with which to light the fires was £28, and the Housekeeper admitted that only £14 worth had been used. She had also ordered 'mould candles' for use in her private apartments, and had unduly profited by charges for supplying pens, ink, and paper at the sales of condemned goods. She seems to have been a notable lady, with an admirable knack of here and there turning a penny. Though the grave gentlemen in the Board Room came down with more than Roman firmness upon her secret profits, it is evident they found her indispensable.*

The keeper of the King's Warehouse was charged with breaking open a package addressed to the Queen. Acquitted, but told to inform the Secretary whenever packages arrived for members of the Royal Family, so that the Secretary might apprise the Board of Green Cloth.

The landing-surveyors were told to enjoin their subordinates 'to behave soberly, civilly, and with good manners towards each other, as well as to merchants.'

* Mrs. Kelly was a great favourite. She merely supervised the deputy Housekeeper occasionally; indeed, her office was, in the main, a lucrative sinecure. Two or three years later the Commissioners increased her 'chip-money' from £14 to £55, and her allowance for cooking their breakfasts and furnishing attendance from £110 to £150. In 1798 her daughter, Miss Eleanor Kelly, was allowed to succeed her, receiving the full emoluments of the office. Miss Eleanor appears to have been an interesting lady, and to have infused considerable gaiety into the domestic arrangements of the Custom-house. It is even stated that she occasionally gave balls in the Long Room.

The Treasury appointed a collector at Senegambia. The Board returned the warrant, stating that the appointment was unnecessary.

There were three classes of 'searchers': the patentees, their deputies, and the 'deputed' or 'controlling' searchers. The last-named officers were appointed by the Board, while the patentees were of course granted their privileges by the Treasury, and employed deputies at will.* During 1783 the Board reminded the deputed men that they had no legal right to take any money as fees from merchants, except such 'satisfaction' as the merchants might give them for extra attendance, and that they were expected 'not to be a clog upon public business, but a check upon the patent officers and their deputies.' They were told to report at once to the Board any irregularities committed by the deputies or patentees, and that if they failed in this they would be deemed participators.

A large seizure was made in the house of the Bavarian Minister, and his secretary, Mr. Hellerhof, was prosecuted and committed.† One Burdett, an army officer, assisted in making the capture, and the Board rewarded him with 50 guineas. The customs men concerned also offered to

* The Board appear to have always grudged the Treasury officials their power of appointing patentees. Here is a passage in a letter on the subject, sent to the Treasury in 1694: 'But for Patent offices, the Com[rs]. have alwayes look't upon them as bountyes, in the hands of the Crowne or y[r] Lord[pps], being generally bestowed upon persones with power to execute by deputy, and therefore the Com[rs]. have alwayes been passive and easy in the transaction of these grantes, not thinking it became them to enter into consideration of the meritts or services for which they were bestowed.'

† It is likely that the real culprit was the Minister, Count Haslang. See Horace Walpole's letter on the Gordon Riots, 1780, which proclaims that Haslang had for many years been suspected of smuggling: 'Old Haslang's chapel was broken open and plundered, and, as he is a prince of smugglers as well as Bavarian Minister, great quantities of tea and contraband goods were found in his house. This one cannot lament, and still less as the old wretch has for these forty years usurped a hired house, and though the proprietor for many years has offered to remit his arrears of rent, he will neither quit the house nor pay for it.'

reward the gallant ensign out of their shares, but he declined, stating that he was satisfied with the Board's gift.

The Attorney-General's opinion was taken as to whether the Customs Board had authority to compel their patent officers to render obedience to orders issued for the public benefit. He remarked that proceedings might be taken to repeal the patents, which appeared to be 'a clog upon the administration of so large a branch of the public service.' Notice was sent to the patent officers that the Board would take proceedings if any future misconduct occurred.

The Bristol officers refused to clear a French vessel with goods for the United States. In this the officers appear to have been wrong. They were set right by a letter from the Privy Council, explaining that though under the old Acts vessels might not trade from Great Britain to the American Plantations, they might now trade from Great Britain to the newly recognized American Republic. Clearance was granted.

The Treasury directed that all loyalist refugees from the United States might land their effects in Great Britain free of duty.

It was provided that any person liable to a revenue penalty (sum less than £500) might clear himself by furnishing one seaman and one soldier. If the penalty were higher he might clear himself by providing two seamen and two soldiers.

The directors of the Bank of England approached the Board, complaining that large quantities of coin of the realm were clandestinely exported. The Board issued special instructions to the officers.

The *Wasp*, revenue lugger, Captain Beer, after a bloody and desperate conflict, captured a smuggling lugger called the *Cow*. The Board wrote *pleno jure* to Captain Beer and his crew, complimenting them upon their conspicuous gallantry.

The first-fruits of the labours of the Commission of

Public Account were made apparent in an Act that must have caused temporary discomposure in certain official circles. 'Whereas it appears from the Reports made by the Commissioners appointed to examine, take, and state the Publick Account of the Kingdom, that in the Receipt of His Majesty's Exchequer there are several useless, expensive, and unnecessary offices, and that the Emoluments arising from other of the offices in the said Receipt of Exchequer are become excessive, and that the mode of Paying the officers by Allowances, Fees, and Gratuities is inconvenient both to the Publick and to Individuals,' etc. It was directed that the offices of the Chamberlains, the Tally Cutter, and the Usher, should expire on the death, surrender, forfeiture, or removal of the holders.

A cheque receipt was to replace the tally method, on the death of the Chamberlains. There was a quaint provision as to the lapse of the Usher's office.* His successor had been named prior to the investigation, therefore he was to succeed to the vacant office when the Usher died, and keep it during life. The Teller's 'Second Clerks' were adjudged superfluous, but they were to retain office till their respective superiors' interest determined.

When the holders of the offices of Auditor of Receipt, Clerk of Pells, Tellers, or Chamberlains died or were removed, the 'Fees, Gratuities, Allowances, Perquisites, and Emoluments' were to be bestowed in paying the inferior clerks employed by the Auditor of Receipt, Clerk of Pells, and Tellers, who succeeded them. Any surplus left was to be divided thus: one-third towards the expenses of his Majesty's Civil Government; two-thirds to the Sinking Fund. The officers succeeding to the posts were to be paid salaries: good salaries. The Auditor was to get £4,000 a year, his Chief Clerk £1,000, the Clerk of

* Horace Walpole held the patent of this office. See his published statement, produced after the Committee queried him. Horace was also quartered on the London Collectorship Inwards (Customs).

Pells £3,000, his Chief Clerk £1,000, each Teller £2,700, each Teller's Chief Clerk £1,000. The rent-free houses previously allowed to the Auditor, Tellers, and Usher were to pass to the Crown as their tenants vacated office. The daily hours of labour in this venerable and picturesque Court were four in winter and five in summer. There were many holy days, and it is likely that about 800 hours per year would be considered decent attendance.

Much of the tobacco that during the previous year had been grown in Scotland was found not worth the duty, and the Scottish Commissioners were empowered to buy it for destruction, paying not more than 4d. a pound.

To encourage the cultivation of coffee and cocoa in the West Indies, the British excise duty on those articles was lowered by two-thirds.

In 1784 an additional duty was placed on candles, 'not of wax or spermaceti.' 'To encourage British Hat-making,' the exportation of hare-skins and coney-skins was prohibited, and foreign goat's-hair was made duty-free. Additional customs duties were levied on foreign tiles and bricks, and an additional excise duty on home-made bricks. The duty on imported wax was increased. An impost was levied on certain kinds of foreign paper.

Yet occasionally there were signs of a broader spirit moving in revenue matters. The vexatious Aliens' duties and the one per cent. Mediterranean tax were repealed. The 'Aliens' Custom' was about 480 years old, and the Mediterranean tax about 120.

A curious adjustment of the tea duty followed, it being changed to 12½ per cent. on the gross price paid at the East India Company's sales. The new duty was to be paid to the Company by the buyers. The Company were to make up the account within thirty days after conclusion of each sale, and pay the duty collected into the hands of the Receiver-General. The Company were enjoined to at once put upon the market 5,000,000 pounds of tea, and soon afterwards another 2,500,000 pounds, after which the sales were to be held at least every quarter. The goods were to be sold without reserve to the highest bidder, the bidding to advance at 1d. per pound. Maximum 'putting-up' prices were prescribed for the first four sales, as below:

Bohea, 1s. 7d. a pound; Congo, 2s. 5d.; Souchong, 3s. 3d.; Singlo, 3s. 3d.; Hyson, 4s. 11d.

After the four sales were completed the goods might not be *put up* at prices exceeding the prime cost, plus freight, importation charges, and lawful interest from time of landing. This seems an impracticable proviso, but be it remembered many parliamentary enactments of that day proved abortive.

The Company were to keep enough tea in stock for one year's public consumption, and to buy back at prime cost all sold tea left in warehouse. The reasons put forward for the change were the excessively high price of tea, and the success of smugglers.

To counterbalance the loss caused to the customs revenue by this reduction of the tea duty, that unpopular inland imposition, the window tax, was increased, and the additional moneys thus obtained were to go into the Customs Receiver-General's account. If the sum thus forthcoming more than made up the deficit, the surplus was to be paid back to the Excise. The duty on foreign coffee and cocoa was increased under this Act, and the previously existing inland duties upon those goods repealed. It is hard to see what good purpose was intended to be served by such abominable complications. The idea dominant with the disposers of revenue seems to have been to keep as many tills as possible, to have as many clerks as possible, and to toil unwearyingly in devising fresh methods towards obfuscation.

The two 5 per cent. imposts on the proceeds of duties were removed from West Indian rum for two years. Additional duties were then placed on raw silk imported, lead exported, on foreign hats and caps, and on gold and silver plate.

In spite of the Attorney-General's decision of the previous year, the patent officers continued to misbehave, and were censured by the Treasury.

The Commissioners conferred with the directors of the East India Company upon the prevention of smuggling, and certain sly tricks performed by the Company's warehouse officials, especially their conspiring to keep prices low at the sales of 'private trade' goods. The Board directed that when passengers landed at outports from East Indiamen their baggage should be sent under seal to the King's Warehouse in London, in order that assessment of the proper duties might in all cases be secured. About this time a Treasury warrant was issued, empowering the Company to import tea from Copenhagen and other Continental ports, to an amount not exceeding 3,000,000 pounds.

The searchers at Gravesend were censured for taking exorbitant fees, and charging 2s. 6d. as 'boat-hire' whenever they visited a ship.

A quantity of provisions arrived from Hamburg for the king, and the Treasury directed that they should be delivered duty-free. The indomitable Board declined, stating that no proper proof had been furnished that the goods were for the royal household, and that previously whenever the Board of Green Cloth had applied for such goods the duties had been demanded and paid. They referred the Treasury to 'the ancient usage,' as applied to King George I. on his arrival, and stipulated that if this were to be departed from, and the goods delivered duty-free, the officers of the royal household should send some responsible person to clear them, instead of a common broker. Strange Commissioners, indeed, were these Thames Street worthies—now haggling over chips and cinders, then standing to their guns with the pertinacity of the gallant and unconquerable sailors of the period, defying my Lords of the Treasury, and suggesting that the king should pay duty on his caviare and sausages!

In 1785 the riding-supervisor at Dartford stopped a messenger who was conveying dispatches from Dover to the Spanish Embassy at London, and treated him rudely. The officer was censured, and ordered to apologize to the Spanish ambassador.

Two officers made a large seizure of East India goods. The case went before the Exchequer barons, who allowed the prohibited articles to be exported, admitted the rest to entry on payment of the ordinary duty, and refused to allow the seizing-officers' expenses. But the Board, believing the officers to have been in the right, gave them as a reward the amount of duty received on the goods.

A number of officers were informed against for conniving at fraud. The Commissioners had a notice posted at the London Custom-house to the following effect: 'All persons making complaint against any officer of this revenue are desired to do the same in writing, and at the foot thereof to mention the place of their residence, in order that recourse may be had to them from time to time to substantiate the said complaints.'

The salaries of the following London officers were stopped from January 29 to July 6, their accounts being in arrear: the Collector Inwards and his controller, the patent surveyor, the patent surveyor-general, the Examiner in the Long Room, and all their deputies and clerks.*

The French ambassador complained of depredations committed on the French coast by English revenue cruisers. Two commanders were charged, and one of them was dismissed.

The East India Company owed £923,000 Customs duty, and deposited £400,000 to stay proceedings.

The various customs collectors were ordered to search all bays, rivers, creeks, inlets, and boatbuilder's yards,

* Of course the salaries were merely nominal. The Board could not stop the collection of fees.

within the limit of their respective surveys, and to seize all boats of illegal build thus found.

The London searchers were warned against absenting themselves from duty on trifling pretexts. The Board informed them that such conduct did not become officers who held such an important trust, and on whose certificates the Revenue disbursed annually over £2,000,000 in drawbacks and bounties.

The Solicitor for Bonds and Criminal Prosecutions 'obtained an order' from one Commissioner to defend 'Justice Addington' from an action. The rest of the Commissioners, on hearing of this slip, waxed furious, and ordered him never to act thus again, but to ask sanction of a full and competent Board, and warned him that if by acting otherwise he caused the Crown to be saddled with expenses they would make him pay them out of his own pocket.

The collector at Cape Breton, Newfoundland, was one Mr. Uncle. His controller, when error led the Lieutenant-Governor and Council of the colony to suspend his coadjutor, did take it upon himself to appropriate the fees of the office. The Board investigated the affair, restored the collector to duty, and suspended the controller till he returned Mr. Uncle's fees.

An appalling statute appeared, regulating the importation and warehousing of tobacco—a statute full analysis of which is neither practicable nor desirable. Only tobacco grown in Ireland, the British American Plantations, the United States, and the Spanish and Portuguese dominions, might be imported. The ports at which tobacco might be landed were specified: London, Bristol, Liverpool, Lancaster, Cowes, Hull, Whitehaven, Greenock, and Port Glasgow. Sampling regulations were introduced, and no doubt these were judicious, for they are in existence at the present time. All imported tobacco was to be warehoused.

A Commission was instituted, to inquire into the system of fees in public offices, to 'examine into abuses,' and to report as to possibilities of improved methods of business. The departments to be overhauled were the Treasury, Admiralty, Board of Ordnance, Secretary of State's Office, Paymaster of Forces' Office, Secretary for War's Office, Naval Treasurer's Office, Naval Commissioners' Office, Customs, Excise, Sick and Wounded Seamen's Department, Tax Commissioners' Office, Stamp Commissioners' Office, Salt Commissioners' Office, Postmaster-General's Office, Land Revenue Department, Woods and Forests, Hackney Coach Commissioners' Office, and Hawkers and Pedlars Commissioners' Office. It would be interesting to know whether the officials of the Sick and Wounded Seamen's Department levied fees,* and, if they did, who paid them.

For some reason not apparent to ordinary minds, Parliament thought fit to remodel the new tea duty. Instead of £12 10s. per cent., as enacted in 1784, it was made £5 per cent., and £7 10s. per cent., the first portion to be under the Customs, the second under the Excise.

In 1786 an additional duty was placed on foreign deals and battens.

It was enacted that all captains arriving from foreign ports should produce manifests, and when shipping goods on drawback enter into a personal bond not to reland them, and that no ships subsequently built outside the king's dominions should be deemed British. even although owned by British and British manned.

The four latest imposts on wine, amounting in all to £32 8s. per tun on French, and £16 4s. on other wines, were repealed, together with the two 5 per cent. imposts on proceeds (as far as these last applied to the four wine imposts), and in lieu an impost of £35 14s. per tun on French and £17 17s. on other wines was established, and placed under the Excise. The £35 14s. and £17 17s. were, of course, in addition to all duties levied on wine up to 1745.

* They did, and some of the fees seem to have been for peculiar services.

About this time the legislators began to shake the revenue items this way and that. Certain customs branches went to the Excise, and certain excise and stamp duties to the Tax Commissioners.

For the present adieu to the tariffs. As the opening of the next chapter will show, things had become utterly unendurable to the public. But it appears that the British commercial mind had for years been pondering a return to simple methods, and the consolidation of the Customs was at hand.*

The rest of the administrative history of the period covered by this chapter is principally connected with official derelictions. Here are a few for the year 1786.

It being found that a cargo of barley transhipped for London had been charged with the 'low' duties when it should have paid 'high,' the Collector Inwards (Sir Banks Jenkinson) and his controller were surcharged with the difference.

The London collector of coal duties and his controller were suspended, and all their clerks dismissed. The controller was told to occupy himself during suspension in learning the duties of his office.

Instructions were issued to collectors that when receiving seized goods from the captains of revenue cruisers they were to make each captain furnish a certificate that he had thoroughly searched his own vessel, the Board having reason to apprehend that seized goods were frequently embezzled by the sailors.

The collector, the deputy controller, the deputy searcher, and the tide-surveyor, at the port of Chepstow, were dismissed in a batch. Dismissal also overtook the commanders of the revenue cruisers at Poole and Yarmouth. A number of London officers were dismissed for conniving at frauds on board East Indiamen. During the period from 1760 to 1787 the Commissioners used the

* Towards the end of 1786 Messrs. Frewin and Sims produced schedules of rates for the new scheme, and it was ordered that the Inspector-General should be supplied with an account of the gross produce of the customs duties.

broom strenuously. They were lenient with subordinates who had committed trifling errors, but once they got a fair hold of a hardened sinner they made an example of him.

It must be understood that only such cases of dismissal have been quoted as illustrate the habits of the time, and the exigencies of revenue administration.* It appears that the Commissioners of the period were conscientious and independent, and that nothing would have suited them better than to have power to dismiss most of the insufferable patentees, to abolish the wretched fee system, and to render the 'Book of Rates' understandable by ordinary men.

Before passing to purely preventive matters, mention must be made of a few strange incidents connected with the Superannuation Fund. The Fund had become a permanent institution. All the officials contributed to it, and it was enriched by grants out of fines, special awards, etc. Only such officers as had reached the age of sixty, and had subscribed for ten years, could be pensioners, and if after they became pensioners it was found that they had other means of subsistence they were at once struck off the list.

In 1776 a pensioner living at Hull was struck off, it having been found that he had 'an estate of £100 per annum.' In 1780 a pensioner (of course over sixty years old) was struck off because he had joined the army, and during the same year another venerable scapegrace was disqualified because he had taken service on board a privateer. In 1784 John Partridge, a native of Deal, was struck off for having become a leader of smugglers, 'frequently going as Captain on board the smuggling shallops.' In 1785 a pensioner living at Poole was dis-

* During the last six weeks of 1772 the Commissioners dealt with seven successive cases of smuggling by officers of the East India Company, connived at by customs officials. During the first nine months of 1773, they adjudicated upon fifty-eight similar cases. Many officials were dismissed, and many others saved themselves by treachery.

abled from further benefit because he had 'sold the king's sails.' All which goes to show that the Customs service produced some hardy veterans.

During the period covered by this chapter the senators exercised themselves frequently in devising schemes for the prevention of smuggling. These must be dealt with as briefly as possible. The 'legal tonnage' for vessels carrying spirits and tobacco was increased, and the restrictions with regard to hoverers were intensified. Ships from foreign, entering the port of London, were prohibited from being moored 'at the back-doors of masters' houses,' or near riverside taverns, while waiting to go alongside the legal quays.

In 1778 the Board of Customs made a strange proposal to the East India Company. They suggested that the pilot-boat which was sent out to meet each homeward-bound East Indiaman should carry 'a complete crew' for the vessel, and that the original crew should be removed from the ship and put ashore. All this was to be done before the vessel entered the lower reaches of the Thames. They insinuated that by constant practice the relief crews would become extremely skilful in navigating East Indiamen 'through the narrow channels of the river,' and that this would be of advantage to the Company. Then they revealed their real motive, hinting that the method suggested might put a stop to 'the atrocious smugling' that prevailed. But the Company, probably conceiving that their pilots, not their mariners, were responsible for the safe navigation of the Thames, declined to entertain the proposal.

In 1779 a biting statute was issued, in consequence of smuggling by 'gangs of daring and dissolute persons armed with offensive weapons.' It made ships forfeitable for having on board brandy in illegal packages, or when, not being over 200 tons, they carried any *goods* which became forfeitable. The Act against boats with more than four rowlocks, which applied to the south-eastern counties only, was made to include all boats with more than six oars in the other counties, tow-boats of Bristol excepted. Excise officers were granted still wider powers of seizing goods afloat, and justices were enabled to fine jailers for allowing smugglers to escape. Smugglers were made liable to be pressed for the army as well as the navy. All foreign thread lace was to be stamped by the Customs at the end of each piece, and was forfeitable if found unstamped.

In 1781 out came an Act levelled against fraudulent traders rather than hoverers and runners. It provided that a ship's captain caught smuggling should be liable to forfeit his wages to the shipowner, and pay the ship-*owner* treble value of the goods seized, besides paying the Crown penalties. If mates or seamen were caught, the shipowner might sue them for 10s. a pound for all tea smuggled, and 10s. a gallon for spirits, besides keeping back all their wages, and if the offence were committed during time of war he might then send them aboard a king's ship for three years. (Well might Sir Samuel Romilly say, 'I have examined the codes of all nations. Ours is the worst, and worthy of the Anthropophagi.')

In 1784 it was enacted that a ship should be forfeitable for hovering within four leagues of the coast for the purpose of running goods. Boats built for running and found hovering were made forfeitable, even with no cargo on board. Vessels found 'within the limits,' carrying weapons beyond two carriage-guns of 4 pounds calibre, and two muskets to every ten men, were made forfeitable, Government vessels and ships from 'distant places' excepted. Any person shooting at a revenue vessel or officer, or wounding an officer, was made liable to 'death as a felon, without benefit of clergy.' Revenue cruisers might fire upon vessels that refused to bring to. Many other severe provisions were included in this Act.

Yet, in considering these terrific statutes, it should always be borne in mind that they were carried out by other than twentieth-century methods. Such laws would indeed be terrible now, when men have forgotten how to defy danger and endure pain, and the law is unerring in pursuit of criminals. The bark of the old statutes was worse than their bite. The skill of the smugglers increased as the penalties became more formidable. Many of the contrabandists were desperate fellows, and their determination in combat was so great that the officers usually shirked an encounter. Then the justices around the coast were often inclined to favour the free-traders—men whom they had in youth fished, sailed, and played with. Even if convicted, the smuggler might make an attempt at compounding, and the Treasury officials were often willing to accept part of the money penalty, rather than lose all. True, the smugglers might be pressed, but many of those who were sent aboard men-of-war succeeded in escaping, and were soon back at the old trade. It does not appear that the grim laws were plied viciously. The customs solicitors, though anxious, as we have shown, to saddle the public with their office expenses, were just and able lawyers, who weighed and sifted evidence as though it were dust of golden ore, and would touch no 'shaky case.' It would be hard to find men more merciful than the Commissioners. The most daunting thing, after all, about the old revenue laws is the display they furnish of their framers' knowledge of human villainy. Those dreadful plots against comradeship, that incessant prompting to mean betrayals! Small wonder that a humorist of the period said: 'There should be no such thing as King's Evidence. The villain who tenders it should be hanged head downward!'

Once more to the practice of the outports, and the doings of the hardy contrabandists. It is a pity that direct literary touch cannot be established with the latter. Unfortunately they kept no letter-books; the only official documents to which smugglers put their mark were petitions for mercy, offers of composition, professions (usually false) of poverty and penitence, and occasional epistles of treachery. Referring to the Letter

Books of Poole, it is apparent that the ex-collector Milner was still inclined to do his best to get the officers into trouble.

The collector reported that Milner's son-in-law borrowed £500 from Captain Pinney of Poole, and gave as security a bill upon effects. Payment was required and refused, so Pinney took possession, and called a sale. Milner thereupon put in a claim to part of the effects, stating that they were the property of his own son, 'who,' blithely interjected the collector, 'recently broke out of Jayl in this town.' Pinney met the claim with derision.

Now, part of the pledged effects consisted of twenty-eight casks of wine, bought at a sale of condemned goods during Milner's term of office, and these were stored in Milner's garden. Pinney called the two customs surveyors of the port to his assistance, and proceeded to take possession of the wine, but Milner sent for a cooper, and ordered the said cooper to stave the casks. This was done, and

> 'Down ran the wine into the road,
> Most piteous to be seen.'

Then, and not till then, the two surveyors thought they had better have refrained from accompanying Pinney, whence the collector's report. The collector tried his best to gloss over matters. He stated that he made the report simply to justify the officers, who had acted 'inadvertently out of Compassion to the Distress'd [Pinney] and not with any presumptuous Design. Mr. Milner's Conduct,' he wrote, 'is very extraordinary, and full of Cruelty and Revenge.' But the Board neither interfered with Milner nor openly blamed the officers.

In 1761 three riding-officers made an important seizure on information. They also made a private arrangement with the informer that he was to receive out of the proceeds a guinea for each hundredweight of tea, and three shillings for each keg of spirits. After making the seizure they tried to beat him down, but he put his case in the hands of a local attorney. Then the officers offered him 25 guineas. The informer referred them to his lawyer. They appealed to the collector, who reported the case to the Board, and the Board compelled the officers to fulfil their promise.

A riding-officer and two excisemen came upon a gang of smugglers and train of horses, carrying tea. The officers charged boldly, and succeeded in cutting a number of packages adrift. Then the smugglers attacked them, and mauled them badly, finally riding off and escaping with about two tons of tea. 'Mr. Glynn the exciseman,' said the collector in his report, 'was beat in the most Cruel manner about the Head with his own Pistol, which the Smuglers took from him by force. It is doubtful whether he will live or dye. The Riding-officer has been ill ever since.' A country gentleman living near assisted the wounded officers, and the collector, in his report, praised the gentleman most effusively, especially commenting upon the fact that he took Glynn into his house, 'and washed his wounds with rum.' All which was beyond doubt praiseworthy, yet the plain duty of any law-abiding man; and still it seems that the collector was immensely surprised that the like should be done—indeed, he kept on lauding the good Samaritan in an extraordinary fashion.

An anonymous letter reached the Board, accusing the collector of granting certificates to sailors that they were men of the Customs, thus enabling them to escape the press. The Board queried the collector, and the latter referred to Captain Milligan, an undeniable Irishman, who had charge of the press-gangs. Milligan stated that he had never found any such certificate on any seaman whom he had stopped, and concluded his statement thus:

'The information in my Oppinion is False and Scandalous, and the Villain that Sett it on Foot ought to Lose his Ears.'

The officers, in their eagerness to make profitable seizures, sometimes ran astray. The tide-surveyor and his crew went aboard a Guernsey trader in Swanage Bay, and seized several casks of brandy. It is probable that the casks were not legally liable to seizure, for the surveyor made no attempt to detain the master, and did not report the seizure till after the vessel had left. Then he stated that he found the casks ' in a boat.' The collector discovered the facts to the Board, intimating that the officers ' humbly prayed to be forgiven their indiscretion.' The Board cautioned them.

Three customs boatmen, named Barns, Phippard, and Harvey, seized sixty-five kegs of spirits at Swanage. The goods were found by ' creeping '—viz., searching in holes and gullies along the coast, where the smugglers often stored their ' truck ' till it could be carried inland. On the same night two riding-officers found four kegs, and left them with the boatmen, so that the latter might take the whole to Poole on the following morning. The boatmen stored the kegs for the night in their watch-house at Swanage, and during the process of housing two kegs mysteriously vanished. The boatmen seem to have concluded that it was best to keep their own counsel about this, and in the morning they set out for Poole, conveying sixty-three kegs of their own, and four kegs of the riding-officers' seizing. Carriages were not plentiful at Swanage, so they hired a wagon and a dung-cart.

Vehicles more suitable were procured when they arrived at Southhaven, and the wagon and dung-cart proceeded back to Swanage. But when the boatmen arrived at Poole, only sixty kegs could be tallied into the warehouse. The collector gave them ' a reference,' and their reply deserves clear reproduction.

' The Sixty Three Casks of Brandy and Rum that were taken up by us in Swanidge Bay we deposited that night in the watch house. Next day we loaded the same in a Waggon & Dung Plow & do believe the same Number of Casks were put in that Carriage but when we delivered them Three Casks were a-missing & what became of them We can give no Account. We have been to severall Places enquiring about them especially to those People who owns the Plows that brought them. They say they know nothing about Them and never meddled with Them. We assure you we kept by the Plows & never left them till deliver'd. How they should be gone we can't think if t'was not when they were taken from the Carts at Southhaven. As to the 2 kegs we know not anything about or what became of Them To the Truth whereof we are ready to make Oath Witness our Hands this 8th Day of Decr 1761.

'JOSEPH BARNS.
PETER PHIPPARD His X Mark.
RICHARD HARVEY His X Mark.'

The statement, viewed along with the collector's report, is rather misleading, with its complications of carts, plows, and wagons, its inaccuracies as to the real number of casks found, put in charge, and beyond ken. The collector reported on the statement with considerable sardonic force.

'Why they should conceive the Casks were lost at Southhaven sooner than at any other place we can no otherwise account for than by informing your Honours that at Southhaven there is a Publick House.'

Further inquiries were made. The collector interrogated the driver of the wagon, who stated that when the casks were transferred at Southhaven he asked Joseph Barns if they were right as to number, and Joseph answered, 'All is well.' The driver of the dung-cart was questioned, and stated that he asked Peter Phippard if his lot were right as to number, and Peter answered, 'All is well.'

The collector sent another report, stating his belief that after thus ejaculating impressively 'All is well' the boatmen went into the public-house and fell to drinking, and while they were thus engaged seven casks were stolen. No doubt his surmise was correct.

The collector and controller got into trouble through illegally selling damaged tea to a grocer, and afterwards reconsidering matters and refusing delivery. The grocer became litigious, and the dismayed officials reported themselves to the Board, stating that though the tea was only worth half the price they had charged for it, the grocer refused to receive back his money, or to consider a tardy hint that they would give him a few guineas to boot. There was something in this business that is hard to understand. The Board, to save the officers from the exposure of a lawsuit, allowed them to deliver the tea.

In 1762 several ships which had been to Newfoundland arrived at Poole, with news that the French had taken St. John's. They had landed part of their goods, which consisted of drawback and bountied articles, and consequently their cargoes and manifests did not agree. The officers asked the Board for special instructions 'on this melancholy occasion.'

A tidesman charged with being drunk and assaulting a shipmaster named Linthorne made a singularly fluent defence, which ended thus :

'I humbly hope that the blameable part of my Conduct in this affair will be imputed to a sudden absence of Reason and impulse of Passion which all Mankind are or may be subject to. I have neither malice, envy, or Ill design against Mr. Linthorne, and I hope that his heart is as free from those detestable qualities with regard to me.'

A Newfoundland ship, liable to the provisions of the Plantation Acts, landed and reshipped at Poole a cargo of salt fish for Oporto. After she was discharged at Oporto her certificate of landing was sent to Poole in the usual manner. The quantity landed and reshipped at Poole had been 3,228 quintals ; the account of landing at Oporto showed 2,710 quintals. The collector reported to the Board, suggesting that the certificate should be accepted and the bond cancelled, as the Portuguese quintal was larger than the English, and the Portuguese officers had appropriated a number of the largest fish, the customs fees there being paid *in kind.*

The following have been extracted from the Southampton Letter Books of a few years later :

In 1768 the Board sent to Southampton copies of three depositions, made in France by masters of foreign vessels, and transmitted by the French Minister to the British Secretary of State. They were to the following effect :

1. The captain of a Danish vessel reported that while passing through the Channel he fell in with two English shallops, each carrying eight men, who came alongside, and boarded him on either quarter, pistol in hand. They drove the crew below, and by menaces compelled him to give up all the money he had, amounting to 200 livres.

2. The captain of a Dutch vessel reported an encounter with the same pirates. They boarded him, brandishing axes and pistols, beat his crew, searched him by force, and stripped him nearly naked. They took all the money they could find, besides fourteen bottles of wine and two half-ankers of brandy.

3. Another Dutch captain recounted his experience. The same pirates boarded him, took all his money and provisions, and maltreated his crew.

Soon the Board sent copies of three other depositions made by Dutch skippers. The same methods had obtained, the sailors being beaten and driven below, and the captains compelled to surrender all their effects. One Dutch skipper had the temerity to object, and to hint of an imaginary Dutch man-of-war not far away, that would make things hot for the pirates, but one of the Englishmen 'gave him a back-handed blow in the face,' drove him into the cabin, and stole his pipe and tobacco-box, while the rest helped themselves to his wine and geneva.

Directions were given by the collector that the revenue cruisers should look out for, and if possible apprehend, these imitators of John Wilcock of old, but there is no word of success.

The seizures at Southampton were numerous and important. One parcel returned for condemnation included 5,956 pounds tea and 1,603 gallons spirits. The tea was burned ; the spirits were sold. The appraised value of the tea was 2s. 6d. a pound ; of the spirits, 6s. a gallon.

In 1769 a sloop called *The Harvest* loaded in London for British possessions in Africa, and afterwards ran part of her cargo near Southampton. The goods were seized, and the ship was detained. The owner applied to the Board to have his ship released so that she might continue her voyage. The Board declared her forfeited, but allowed her to complete her voyage, the owner to give security that he would then return her for condemnation. Later the vessel was reported as wrecked. The owner absconded, and the surety became bankrupt.

Information was received that six Irish wherries had left Dunkirk laden with goods for running on the south coast of England. The revenue cruisers were instructed to keep a sharp look out.

A seizure of '12,000 Chip Hats' and a quantity of annatto was made on information. The Board instructed their solicitor to prosecute the chip hats to condemnation in the Exchequer. The annatto was declared not dutiable, yet forfeited by being imported in contravention of the Navigation Act.

Captain Collingwood, of the revenue cruiser *Tweed*, inquired of the Board as to the amount due to him and his company on account of a large seizure of brandy. The Board replied that one-third only of the net proceeds would be awarded, unless he succeeded in capturing the smugglers concerned.

An officer stationed at Jersey seized two sloops, apparently without sufficient cause ; for an action was entered against him by the owners, and he was made liable to pay £65 as damages. The collector at Southampton, who had control of the revenue officers in the Channel Islands, reported the matter to the Board, and stated that the officer's household goods had been seized in satisfaction of the award. He was directed to pay the £65 out of the port moneys in hand.

The collector was instructed to caution all officers who might seize vessels that when the vessels were condemned they were not to appropriate them and substitute others. It appeared that ships appraised at a high price had been privately disposed of, and old and worthless craft sent to the burning-ground in their stead.

On account of great frauds committed in the trade between Southampton and the Channel Islands, a Mr. John Major was allowed to fit out a vessel of 100 tons and a 'tender' of 50 tons, to cruise in the neighbourhood of Jersey and Guernsey, and along the English coast as far as the Rame Head at Plymouth. This venture, as will be seen, turned out disastrous for Mr. Major.

There appear to have been many mistakes and informalities in sufferances granted for coastwise goods, and these were usually attributed by the traders to oversight on the part of their clerks when entering the goods for shipment. In all cases the goods were detained till the Board's decision was made known, which usually followed the old lines, directing release 'on a reasonable satisfaction being made to the detaining officers.'

A small vessel left London for Southampton with 15 hogsheads of bonded tobacco, covered by the usual coast dispatch. The surveyor of the London coast-waiters, evidently a person prone to subtle imaginings, got to thinking that these goods might be run during the voyage, and that the vessel might then proceed oversea, take in similar packages, and land and warehouse the new packages at Southampton under cover of the coast dispatch. It is not clear how anything could be gained by such a complicated move, or how it would be easier to run goods removed for warehousing than to go oversea in ballast, procure a cargo, and run it offhand. For it is clear that the run would occur at some unfrequented place, and its success depend upon the absence of the riding-officers. If the riding-officers found the vessel landing her bonded cargo they would seize it, just the same as if it had been brought direct from oversea. Perhaps the surveyor had remoter contingencies under contemplation, for he put a private mark on each package, and apprised the Board, who thought it worth while to transmit the information to Southampton. When the vessel arrived the casks were inspected, and the private marks could only be found on one or two, and in those cases they were incomplete. The Board directed the collector to send the tobacco back to London in charge of an officer, in order that the packages might be examined by the ingenious person who had marked them. The affair seems to have ended in nought.

The surveyor-general of Hants and Dorset, one Fiennes Eddowes, overhauled the port of Southampton, its 'members,' and its 'creeks,' and found fault with many things. He was especially severe upon the collector and the controller of Cowes, who had made it a practice to keep back large sums 'to pay salaries and meet exigencies,' and had failed to record the nature of the said claims and exigencies. He found that since his last survey there had been three occasions upon which over £2,000 at a time had been thus retained, eight retentions of over £1,000, and seventeen of over £500. Thus it appears that the officers exceeded their prerogative upon twenty-eight quarterly occasions, and that the surveyor-general's visits were at intervals of seven years at the very least (most likely ten). Fiennes Eddowes also observed that too many extra tidesmen were employed, some of whom had been placed by the collector on board a sloop owned by him, to cruise in pursuit of smugglers for the collector's private advantage in the way of seizure awards. Thus the public had been paying men in order that the collector might benefit.

Goods which had been improperly entered had been put right as to entry, and the extra duties taken, without the Board's cognizance. Improper bonds had been used to cover the exportation of corn to Jersey. Seized *prohibited* goods had been sold for home consumption, instead of for exportation. Mr. Eddowes also intimated that he suspected the coal-meters of fraud, as coals shipped at Cowes frequently turned out unsatisfactorily on discharge. Casks of exported tar had been granted bounty without being gauged.

He severely censured both collector and controller, and then went through the district, awarding censures at most of the stations.

In March, 1770, a warehouse hired by the collector of Southampton to accommodate a seizure made by one of the revenue cruisers was broken into during the night, and three casks of brandy were carried away.

Two London officers visited the port in consequence of private information, and made a large seizure of smuggled hops.

The Board transmitted the Attorney-General's opinion upon the matter of imported train-oil of Newfoundland. In spite of the numerous provisions of the various revenue Acts, or perhaps in consequence of their extreme elaboration, the regulations do not appear to have been systematically administered, and the Crown lawyers were frequently called upon to clarify the faculties of the officers at various ports. Below is a decision upon the vexed subject of exemption of oil from duty.

'I think the only Oil which is exempted from Duty is Oil taken and imported in British ships which do but in part belong to British owners, not such Oil when the rest of the property of the Ships belongs to Americans or Dutchmen. It is not a British ship unless it is entirely a British ship. I am therefore of opinion that Oil taken and imported in Ships belonging in part to Americans and in part to English, on whichever side the Majority of Owners is, cannot be imported duty-free,' etc.

This may have conveyed illumination to the collector of Southampton, yet ordinary minds will make neither head nor tail of it. It is scarcely probable that the Southampton clerk transcribed it incorrectly, for it was intended to remain in the records as a reference in case of doubt. No doubt it was rarely referred to, and the collector and his successors jogged along as best they could, hoping that all would be well, and that Mr. Fiennes Eddowes would refrain from prying too deeply into their accounts of 'Oil and Blubber.' Evidently the Attorney-General desired that they should, for he added a note thus: 'But if the Merchant has been led to Trade upon the faith of such practice it is fit such faith should be kept.'

One hundred bales of chip hats were seized on a vessel from Dunkirk, condemned, and sold for £517 15s. Thereupon arose a squabble about the shares due to the various seizing-officers.

An inhabitant of the district sent an extraordinary letter to the Lords of the Treasury. It commenced thus:

'My Lords,

'I beg leave to inform you that there are two Bays or Arms of the Sea on each side Christchurch Haven in Hampshire that are constantly frequented by a most daring crew of Smuglers who appear to hold all the Revenue Laws in Open Defiance.'

It went on to recommend that a troop of dragoons should be sent to Christchurch, and stated that at the time of writing the smuggling cutter was lying in Christchurch Bay, *flying his Majesty's colours!* This amazing epistle was signed 'Richard Hughes of Wick near Christchurch.'

News came to Southampton of a Dutch ship cruising from port to port in the Mediterranean. She had put into Malta with her master and fourteen sailors dead of plague, and only twenty-three survivors. The Grand Master of the island had her towed out to sea. She tried to enter Tunis, but the Bey refused to admit her. She entered Naples, and was driven to sea again, and the Italian officers of health placed sentries along the coast to prevent the survivors landing. The various British sloops and men-of-war were apprised, and directed to keep her out if she appeared on the British coast. What became of this plague-smitten craft in the end? Was she found derelict at sea, her deck strewn with rotting corpses? The story of Vanderdecken seems a pleasant tale, when the possibilities of this ghastly cruise are considered.

Southampton's record of seizures is imposing. Below is a list of seized goods and appraised values for the quarter ending June, 1770:

	£	s.	d.
239 gallons brandy	71	14	0
166 ,, rum	49	16	0
54 ,, geneva	16	4	0
256 pounds tea	28	16	0
	£166	10	0

Another parcel during the same period:

	£	s.	d.
230 gallons brandy 207 ,, rum 43 ,, geneva 2,386 pounds tea	390	11	0

Another during same period:

388 gallons brandy 343 ,, rum	219	6	0

Another during same period:

518 gallons brandy 316 ,, rum .. 34 ,, geneva	260	8	0

In addition to these, there were parcels of dimity, muslin, linen, and flowered lawns, and a host of petty seizures of various kinds of goods. The total appraised value was £1,343 12s. 2½d., and the Exchequer and solicitor's charges on proceeds amounted to £27 17s. 1d.

Tidings were sent to the Board that Mr. John Major, who during the previous year had been appointed to cruise on the coasts of Guernsey and Jersey, and to sweep the

Channel free of smugglers as far as Plymouth, was a prisoner in Guernsey Castle, on account of two risky seizures which he had made. Mr. Stiles, a customs officer of Portsmouth, was sent to Guernsey by the Commissioners, to inquire into the case and to desire Major's 'enlargement,' in order that he might appear before them. Stiles was to draw upon the Southampton collector for expenses.

Later news came that both of Major's ships were ashore, and in a state of wreck. The Board desired the collector to send 'a trusty tidesman' to Guernsey with a letter, instructing Stiles to dismiss the mates and mariners. From a reference in a subsequent memorandum it appears that Major was also dismissed.*

Irregularities having occurred in compositions effected between officers and informers, the Board issued orders that no officer should compound an information till the full particulars were made known to them. The licence issued by the Exchequer Court authorizing a composition was to be attested on oath, sent to the Inspector of Prosecutions, and by him transmitted to the Attorney-General. From this it would seem that the Exchequer officials had been in the habit of granting such licences at the private request of the officers concerned.

Instances had occurred of commanders of revenue sloops appropriating part of the seizure awards due to mariners. The Board recited the legal rates of award, and enjoined that the captains were not to stimulate their men by promises of money. Said the wary Commissioners, being no doubt fully aware of the dangerous influence of blood-money: 'It may invalidate their testimony in case there should be occasion to make use of them upon a Tryal.'

The Irish smugglers appear to have been very daring. An advertisement by the Irish Commissioners of Customs

* In April, 1775, a Mr. 'James' Major was appointed commander of a revenue sloop at Stockton. It is possible this was the same man. In 1779 he was convicted of threatening to kill Sir William Musgrave, one of the Commissioners.

reached Southampton, offering a reward for the capture of certain ' fellows ' who had murdered a revenue officer, attacked ' the King's Barge ' in the Bay of Dundrum, and captured and plundered the *Pelham* cutter at Beaumaris. Further news came of their doings. They were stated to be in the habit of making four voyages yearly to Dunkirk. They had four ships, well manned and armed, and the little squadron was commanded by one John Connor (called ' Jack the Bachelor '). The ships were classed thus :

A small cutter carrying six carriage-guns, besides swivels and small-arms. Two large cutters with eight carriage-guns each, besides swivels, etc. A large schooner-rigged wherry with six carriage-guns, etc. The captains were Thomas Field, Thomas Knight, John Creenan, and the redoubtable Connor. Several of the smugglers were described in picturesque fashion :

' Jack the Batchelor. A low-set fellow with a small stoppage in his speech. About 35, etc.

' Patrick Bawn, one of his crew, a middle-size well-made fellow, a Flatt nose, about the age of 36.

' Patrick Farren, a middle-size fellow, a little mark'd with the Smallpox, about the age of 30.

' Nicholas Kean, a middle-size well-made fellow, a Fresh complexion, about the age of 48.

' Thomas Field. He is a set well-made fellow about the age of 44.'

A series of quarrels took place at Southampton over seizure-money, always a fruitful source of dispute among revenue officers. An officer accused the collector of apportioning awards unfairly. The Board investigated the circumstances, rectified matters, and rebuked the collector.

About this time there were many large seizures on the coast. In most cases the smugglers escaped, sometimes after severely beating and wounding the riding-officers.

An advertisement of a gang of famous housebreakers,

who were attempting to escape from the country, was sent to Southampton, and the officers were directed to scrutinize all passengers outward.

The peculiar hostility between customs and excise officers was exemplified twice at Southampton in 1773. A customs officer complained that an exciseman had boarded an incoming vessel and commenced to examine the passengers' baggage prior to the arrival of the customs men. Soon after there was another dispute as to priority of claim to search. The Customs Board recited the ancient regulation on the matter: 'He who gets there first has first rummage.' There can be no doubt that the excisemen were fond of encroaching.

The captain of the *Anson* revenue cutter, foreboding a run at a certain spot, landed his crew, and placed them in ambush. They remained there through the night, hearing nothing and seeing nothing, and at daybreak he directed them to go on board the vessel. Just as he was abandoning his post, down came several riding-officers at full gallop. (It appears that while the *Anson's* crew were watching for a run, the riding-officers had been watching them.) The officers entered a stable hard by, pulled down a panel or two, and hauled forth 250 bags of tea. Upon which the *Anson's* men vociferously asserted their claim to participate in the seizure, and the claim was met with equally vociferous derision. So the riding-officers went off with their booty, and the captain of the *Anson* took his crew before the nearest justice, and piled affidavit upon affidavit, claiming that had he not watched all night the tea would have been carried off by smugglers. His claim, backed by a sheaf of depositions, went up to the Board, and met with the ill success it deserved.

A document was transmitted from London to Southampton, furnishing details of a concealment discovered on board a small vessel.

'He therefore renewed his search, and the better to enable him to discover any concealment, he admeasured the Distances of the Bulkhead above and below the Deck.

In comparing this Distance from the forepart of the Mast to the inside of the Stem upon Deck with that below the Deck, he found a difference of 3 feet. On pursuing this Discovery it at Last appeared that a false Bow, in every respect imitating the real Bow, had been built up within Board 3 Feet from the Inside of the Stem. This consequently left a vacancy between the false and real Bow which in this little Vessel was so considerable as to contain 750 lbs. of tea, and sufficient for 3 cwt. more,' etc.*

In 1775, the Mother Country being at war with the American colonies, a sharp look out was kept for vessels bringing intelligence to sympathizers with the Rebellion. A letter from the Treasury was sent to Southampton by the Board, stating that information had been received that a vessel, supposed to be an 'advice boat' from America, had passed Cowes during the night, and landed a person who at once set out for London, and that the vessel, after cruising off and on for a space, departed and was seen no more. The commanders of the revenue sloops were urged to vigilance in searching all vessels suspected of the like, and directed, did they find American letters on board, to seize them and detain the ships concerned.

A riding-officer and two boatmen, in attempting to make a seizure on the coast, were terribly beaten by smug-

* The document went on to describe in stately periods the various devices incidental—a false 'apron,' a false ceiling, false breastworks, delusive planks, entrance between bitts and stem, and the iron ring of the admitting trap 'tarred over and let in.' All which may have at the time seemed very wonderful; but he would be a poor customs rummager who failed to discover such a device on board a vessel little larger than a modern dingy. Anyone who has seen a skilled rummager at work in one of the vast engine-rooms of a modern liner, crawling through the maze of bilges, exploring the 'columns,' threading all the manholes of the screw alley, groping in the oil-tanks, smelling his way beneath the enormous boilers, winding in and out amid the complicated machinery, and ending by stripping to the waist, and burrowing amid the coals in the bunkers, to emerge at last with a few pounds of 'hard' sewn up in canvas, will have a better idea of the art of searching than can be gained from the above.

glers. The famous Captain Warren Lisle, most vigilant and determined of seizing-officers, was directed to interview the wounded men, and afterwards do his best to discover the offenders. (Some of this gentleman's exploits have already been narrated, and readers may be assured that he really ' did his best.') There is a peculiar sameness in the accounts of coast seizures, occasionally broken by details which possess a sameness of their own. Either the officers seized the goods and the smugglers escaped, or the officers were beaten within an inch of their lives and the smugglers carried out their run. It would seem that the latter occurred whenever the officers attempted to make arrests.

An honest shipmaster brought into Southampton 28 hogsheads of wine which he had found floating in the Channel, and surrendered them to the collector. It was a risky thing to do, for it is likely that if he had been boarded ' within the limits ' by one of the revenue cruisers protestations of honest intention would not have availed him. The collector sent an account of the goods to the Admiralty.

The following letter reached Thames Street:

CHRISTCHURCH,
' *13th Sept.*

' GENTLEMEN,

' I most Humbly beg Leave to acquaint you that James Noyce, one of the Custom-house officers at Christchurch, does at this time carry on the trade of a Collar-Maker as usual before he was an Officer. Whereby I am greatly injured in my Business as a Collar-Maker, and my Family deprived of Subsistence. Your Humble Petitioner therefore craveth your kind Relief, as he is informed it is not usual or Legal for King's Officers to Carry on any Business.

' Your Honours' most obedient and most humble Servant,

' JOHN WHITE.'

The Board directed instant inquiry, with a view to restraining James Noyce from unfair competition with his neighbour.

A fellow arrested for receiving 600 gallons of smuggled brandy wrote to the Board, stating that he lodged the goods in his outhouse at the request of certain seafarers, who told him they had landed them because their ship was in danger. He pleaded the usual small wife and large family, and expressed a hope that his extreme humaneness might not be counted as a crime. None can with certainty measure the extent to which he may have been thus spiritualized, or decide whether it was the cause of his adding that if proceedings against him were stayed he would at once betray his comrades. Insincerity and inherent treachery were apparent in every line of this epistle, which the writer called his 'ingenious [ingenuous] confession.'

The Board sent a memo. to the collector, lucidly defining the main points of the Plantation Acts, thus :

1. All Plantation goods not specially excepted, intended for foreign ports, were to be brought to Great Britain, landed, examined, taken to account, the duties paid, and the goods reshipped. If British goods were to accompany them, the Plantation cargo was to be thus dealt with before the British goods were shipped.

2. All British goods not specially excepted, shipped in Great Britain for the Plantations, were to be duty-paid before shipment ; and if any excepted British goods were to accompany them, such goods were not to be shipped until the dutiable cargo had been put under hatches.

The Board alluded to a practice prevailing at certain ports of evading the regulations quoted under (1) by making a rough computation on board, and charging a certain sum as duty without insisting upon the goods being landed. They forbade the continuance of this practice. It is astonishing that such a method could ever have been ventured upon in the teeth of the formidable statutes, and evident that in remote ports the collectors did almost as they chose.

In 1781 the Treasury received the following letter from Dunkirk, and sent it to the Board :

'I think it the duty of every Friend of his Country to think seriously of the trade now carried on with our Enemies and at Dunkirk, by several large Cutters belonging to Folkestone and Hastings, authorized by letters of Marque from England, and passes from France.'

The letter went on to particularize ships, owners, masters, and equipment. The goods run were tea. There was Captain Thomas Wood, with his 'deep-waisted' cutter of 200 tons, carrying sixteen carriage-pieces and forty men, and he usually ran his cargo between Dunwich and Orfordness. The vessel's rendezvous was at Folkestone, and her owners were Proveau and Pinfold. Proveau was a Frenchman living at Dunkirk ; Pinfold an Englishman living at Folkestone. There was Captain Robert Tapley, with his 180-ton cutter, carrying fourteen guns and forty men, and he usually ran his cargo in Cornwall. There were Solomon Bevel and Marks Bayley, who jointly navigated a 200-ton cutter carrying fourteen guns, and 'ran' between Beachy Head and Shoreham. There was also Anthony Warman of Folkestone, with his cutter of 90 tons.

The Board transmitted this picturesque information for the enlightenment of the Southampton officers. It will also enlighten readers. They will perceive that often the bold patriot who asked for letters of marque had three strings to his bow. If he fell across a French merchant ship, he towed her into an English port and claimed prize dues. He was also in the confidence of the French authorities, and for a consideration supplied them with tidings of the movements of the British fleet, and the general state of affairs in southern England. And he smuggled whenever a chance offered. Other little tricks were at his command ; he carried criminals, both French and English, clear of the eager claws of Justice. Thus his vocation was both profitable and exciting. It is likely, after all, that he would lean a little to the side of the land of his birth, and that some of the information that he furnished to the French would be profoundly misleading. And during his spells ashore at Folkestone, as he sat carousing with his comrades, no doubt his favourite toast was, 'Here's luck to long wars and high duties!'

The captain of one of the revenue cruisers applied for letters of marque. Allowed, but the revenue not to suffer by the indulgence. No compensation if his ship were damaged in fight, unless the fight were with a smuggling vessel. Not to leave his station on pretence of engaging the enemy. Thus he could do little privateering unless the French ventured within the limits of his station.

The excise officers seized a quantity of wine in a 'warehouse' belonging to a person who horsed the road-wagons travelling between Southampton and London. The Customs Board were of opinion that there were no grounds of prosecution, unless the excisemen could prove that the jobmaster received the wine, knowing it to be contraband.

The following order was communicated as an incentive to heroism: 'On account of great increases in the Size and Force of smugling vessels, accompanied with such violent Outrages that in Defiance of all Law they have the Audacity not only to carry on their illicit Designs in Sight of the Revenue Cruisers, but whenever they have approached within a certain Distance have actually fired into and threatened to sink them, and that in such case the Mariners engaged in our Service have frequently refused to bear down and Repel their Attacks, alledging by way of Excuse that no Provision is made towards their Support in case they should receive an injury therefrom,' etc. The Board promised an annuity of £10 to any revenue mariner who might lose a hand or foot, or receive any serious injury, in such encounters, and to pay surgical expenses if he were only slightly wounded.

Soon after this the widow of a Southampton riding-officer who had been murdered by smugglers received an annuity of £15, and a yearly allowance of £2 10s. for each of her children under the age of fifteen.

The owner of a brick-kiln at Fawley approached the Board, stating that he had been 'continually teased and threatened' by the customs officers of Portsmouth and Southampton, who had told him they would seize any bricks shipped coastwise by him, unless he took out a cocket for every shipment. He pleaded that the vessels employed were very small, that the cocket expenses would, in all, amount to about 40s. on each consignment of about 10,000 bricks, and that he could not carry on his business under such conditions. 'If I have to do this it will ruin the brick-kiln.' 'As to Bricks, no man can say that ever a Cargo was Smugled, as they would not pay the very Freight to carry them abroad.' He stated that the Isle of Wight brickmakers were allowed by the Board to ship bricks coastwise with a 'sufferance' only, costing but 2s. per consignment.

Mr. Charles Clapham, Chairman of the Committee of Yorkshire Woollen Manufacturers, informed the Board that a foreigner had been detected in attempting to export a machine lately invented for spinning wool, and a model of another machine for preparing wool for spinning, and that there was another foreigner residing in Leeds, and engaged in the secret exportation of 'press paper,' an article used in the finishing of woollen cloth. The Board sent a memo. to Southampton, urging the collector to do his best in discovering such exportation.

The Italian silk merchants of London complained to the Treasury that their silks, imported from Italy via Ostend, had been detained as quarantinable. At this time imports from the Mediterranean coast of Italy were liable to quarantine, the plague prevailing in Turkey, etc.; but the silk merchants pleaded that their goods were manufactured in the interior of Italy, and taken overland to Ostend for shipment, and that therefore they had 'no communication' with the Levant. The Treasury thereupon freed such goods from quarantine, and the Board apprised the various collectors to that effect.

A smuggler who had been pressed informed the Board of an old smuggling transaction in which he had been concerned, and asked to be released from his ship in order to give evidence against his comrades. But the customs solicitor stated that the men informed upon could not be found. So the informer had to remain, and unwillingly defend his country.

A communication from the Privy Council reached Southampton, to the effect that the plague raged in Servia, and that 'a new distemper' had broken out in Belgrade. 'It begins with a wen on the throat, and death follows after three or four days.'

The *Rose* revenue cutter, the master of which had been recently granted letters of marque, captured the *Fox*, a well-known smuggling vessel, after a fierce engagement, in which the *Rose* was so badly damaged that, after being temporarily patched at Southampton, she was sent to London to lie up for repairs. The appraised value of the *Fox* on condemnation was £1,450.

The collector received a copy of certain correspondence between Sir William Hamilton at Naples and the Earl of Hillsborough. The former, in a letter dated July 31, 1781, conveyed intelligence of a startling kind. He stated that a vessel from Smyrna, with a foul bill of health, after being driven away from Ancona, had been quarantined at Venice, and her crew taken into the lazarette; that another from Alexandria, with pestilence raging on board, had been conducted to Corfu by a Venetian ship, and that during the voyage her captain and three mariners escaped; also that a Venetian vessel infected with plague had been burned with all her cargo at Malta, and her crew lazaretted. A Swedish vessel with plague on board had been driven away from Venice, and was adrift in the Mediterranean, and many other plague-smitten Levant traders were cruising in those waters. The king of Sicily had given orders that all Levant traders should be kept at a distance, and that the cavalry guard along the coast should be doubled to prevent the landing of infected persons. The British ambassador at Constantinople also wrote, stating that the plague was 'raging with dreadful fury' at Salonica. The collector apprised the captains of cruisers and the preventive staff generally.

A memo. from the Treasury arrived, embodying an extract from a letter sent by Lord Hillsborough. 'Intelligence has been received at my Office that it has become a capital trade on the coast of Kent and Sussex to build and sell to the Enemy cutters which are used as privateers by them, and that a Considerable Quantity of Cannon and Ammunition is carried from that Coast to France.' It went on to repeat information of forty pieces of cannon which were said to be lying concealed on the Kentish shore, and intended for the use of the French. It concluded, 'Will get further information of this.'

The collector issued an advertisement as below, offering a reward of £100 for the apprehension of certain persons who had rescued smuggled goods: 'Whereas, on Friday the second Day of this Instant November, A Large Seizure of Brandy was made by several of the Officers belonging to this Revenue in the Parish of Christchurch, Hants, & whilst the said Officers were endeavouring to convey the same to a Place of Safety a Daring and outrageous Gang of Smuglers on Horseback, to the number of 12 and upwards, some of whom had their faces black'd & were otherwise disguised, Armed with Blunderbusses, Muskets, Pistols, & other Offensive Weapons, forcibly & violently assaulted, beat, and wounded the said Officers, & carried away the said Seizure,' etc.

The Board issued an order as follows:

'CUSTOM HOUSE, LONDON,
'*5th Jan.* 1782.

'The enormous Increase of Smugling, the Outrages with which it is carried on, the Mischiefs it Occasions to the Country, the Discouragement it Creates to all fair Traders, and the prodigious Loss the Revenue Sustains by it,' etc. The Board announced that they were 'Desirous to give a Great Cheque to this National Evil,' yet they were much dismayed at the officers' want of success in making captures, and believed that this 'defect' would not have been 'if the Instructions and Orders given by this Board had been duly Observed.' 'We therefore enjoin you carefully to peruse those Orders, And the fresh Set of enlarged Instructions herewith sent.'

Yet large quantities of goods were occasionally captured. The Southampton record for the second half-yearly term in 1781 was striking. One seizure consisted of 3,305 gallons brandy and 1,620 gallons rum; another of 85 gallons brandy, 70 gallons rum, 251 gallons geneva, 92 pieces muslin, and 7,563 pounds tea. There were also many small seizures, and the total appraised value was £3,854 14s.

The Attorney-General's opinion upon the matter of a husband's responsibility for his wife's contraband ventures was quoted in a Board's letter. It was to the effect that if the wife smuggled without her husband's privity she might be proceeded against summarily before justices. The husband need not be summoned, but in the information and proceedings the woman should be described as 'A.B., the wife of C.D.,' etc., and if she were convicted the justices might distrain on the husband's goods, unless there were a return of *nulla bona*, in which case the wife might be committed.

One of the revenue cruisers attacked the *Kite*, a smuggling cutter of 100 tons, belonging to Folkestone. After a long engagement the *Kite* beat her off, and escaped. A few days later the Portsmouth revenue cutter and the 'Excise cutter of Cowes,' while cruising in company in Sandown Bay, sighted the *Kite*. Being afraid to attack, they signalled for assistance to a Government cruiser that was near, and the latter, in company with the cutters, bore down upon the Folkestone vessel. The smugglers thereupon took to their boats, landed in Shanklin Bay, and escaped. On boarding the *Kite*, the officers found three of her crew in the forecastle, desperately wounded. Her cargo had been run, except a few gallons of spirits. It turned out that during the previous year she had gone under the name of the *Union*, and had been captured, condemned, and afterwards restored to her owners, they paying a heavy fine. She had then been altered and renamed, and her captain had actually succeeded in getting her approved as a privateer. The letters of marque were found on board by the officers.

It may be well to conclude this chapter with a comprehensive review of the general condition of the Customs at this interesting period. Evil indeed had the state of the ancient department become. The bad old systems of specialization of duties and cherishment of sinecures constituted a serious menace to the trade of the kingdom.

London possessed about three-fourths of the import trade, Liverpool one-eleventh, Bristol one-seventeenth, Hull one-forty-sixth, and the balance went to sixty-nine minor ports. About three-fourths of the sum expended in drawbacks and bounties was paid in the port of London. It was not uncommon for about a dozen of the minor ports to show deficits, the expenses of management greatly exceeding the gross receipts. Usually these deficits occurred at ports where not a penny was disbursed as drawback or bounty.

Each outport throughout the kingdom had been certified since the Restoration, under the terms of an Exchequer commission, as a place approved for the transaction of import and export trade. When an investigation was held with regard to this in 1783, the commissions granted to Minehead, Chepstow, Gloucester, Llanelly, and Scilly could not be found.

Forty-four revenue cruisers, carrying in all 1,041 men, and costing between £40,000 and £50,000 annually, guarded the coast from Berwick to Land's End, and occasionally some of these were directed to scout between Ireland and England. Twenty of the cruisers were 'on the Establishment'; the others were run 'on contract,' and often the contractor was a customs official. The contract system, especially when managed by collectors as a private venture, was found to work badly. The largest and best-armed cruisers plied off Colchester, Dover, Sandwich, Deal, Rye, Southampton, Cowes, Poole, and St. Ives. The guard was strongest from Margate to Poole.

The principal 'seizing ports' were London, Yarmouth, Harwich, Dover, Sandwich, Southampton, Cowes, Plymouth, and St. Ives. The value of the seizures made at London was about one-third of the total. In one year (profitable both to smugglers and seizers) the London return of the value of seized goods was over £60,000. In the same year Dover returned £13,000, Cowes £10,000, Plymouth nearly £9,000, Sandwich £6,500, Southampton nearly £7,000, Harwich nearly £7,000, Yarmouth nearly £5,000. The west-countrymen had improved but little on their ancient reputation, for St. Ives returned nearly £11,000—nearly treble the gross revenue produce of the port. Yet certain goods might be bought freely by coast-dwellers, at prices amounting to little more than one-third of the duties to which the goods were liable. So huge and industrious was the force engaged in contraband that the smugglers suffered by competition, and often had to 'undercut' prices.

The systems of account and collection were preposterous. The number of 'branches'—for every duty was kept apart—ranged between ninety and one hundred. Of these, five were Plantation duties, and between twenty and thirty repealed duties, the latter figuring in account because many of the claims under them had not been fully answered. Each branch was a fiscal puzzle. There might be a dozen varying rates of duty on one article, each rate involving a separate computation. The number of branches was increased in every Session, for if Parliament took one duty off it speedily added two or three new ones. The correspondence between the outport collectors and the London Board was voluminous and bewildering, for the officers were continually asking for information upon points of revenue law and practice, and this may account for the scarcity of visits by the Commissioners. The officer who was an accurate computer of duties in one or two branches was esteemed a treasure. Tables of net duties published for the guidance of merchants and officials were often misleading, and the erroneous calculations influenced collection many years before they were detected.* It must be borne in mind that the duties were computed to remote fractions.

The central account was in a hopeless muddle. The various outport collectors sent the net produce of their ports to the Receiver-General in London, using bills and notes as instruments of remittance. The London takings reached the Receiver-General in gross, usually in the form of money or bonds. The Plantation collectors remitted their balances in bills or bullion. (The proceeds of the 4½ per cent. tax were, as previously stated, mostly remitted in kind. But this was a separate branch entirely, and in our accounts of Plantation returns we ignore it. It produced about twice as much as all the other Plantation duties put together.) Certain expenses of home and colonial management were paid by the Receiver-General out of the Plantation receipts.

When remittance was thus made, an account of the same, with a statement of the deductions, if any, made from the gross receipts, was sent to the Controller-General. That official compiled an annual return, in which the Receiver-General was charged with the total of sums advised, and this went to the 'Auditor of Imprest.' The Receiver-General furnished for the same period an account of receipts and disbursements, and sent it to the same office of audit. The accounts were from January 6 in one year to January 5 in the next—

* Note particularly 'Crouch's Survey of the Customs,' considered an infallible mine of reference for many years.

both dates inclusive—and puzzling accounts they were, for it should be stated that not only were the receipts under the various branches kept apart, but an attempt was made to apportion in similar fashion the expenses of collection. The headings of the various columns were venerable formulæ, and would appear to have been contrived with a view towards mystification. When these circumstances, with the brief hours of employ, and the general drowsiness prevailing in ancient Government offices, are taken into consideration, none need wonder that the accounts were usually presented for audit when about two years overdue. Then the Auditor of Imprest got to work, and what did he ? Merely checked the casts ! The two accounts never agreed, but that did not trouble the scrutineer. Even if they had agreed, it would have proved little, for the Auditor, not being a customs official, was quite ignorant of 'the practice.' He knew not the methods of receipt of duty ; he did not understand the system of computation used for any separate rate on any article in any branch ; the amounts stated as incurred for salaries and incidents might be excessive, but he knew not how to detect an overcharge. So he sat quiet, checked the casts, and never called for a single minor voucher. His audit was a solemn farce.

As to collection. There were five collectors in London, seventy-two at the outports, twenty-six in the Plantations.

The London collectors or cashiers paid in the bulk of their takings during the current year, *always reserving a portion.* For instance, the Collector Outwards (the duke of Manchester) instructed his deputy to bank a large sum of public money in the principal's name. Occasionally the deputy drew a portion and paid it into the Receiver-General, but it is observable that after such withdrawal he invariably banked a sum larger than that withdrawn, and thus the patentee's balance throve steadily upon public money, till certain Commissioners of Account interfered. It docs not appear that the moneys thus reserved were actually *appropriated*, but the practice of 'keeping a bit in hand' was general. The Receiver-General had no power of detecting, neither had the Controller-General, except by observing that the receipts as a whole were falling off. When a collector's account was rendered, the casts were checked, and no more. The Board had little power of intervention. The patentees who dominated the various offices of receipt were practically independent of the Commissioners. The latter might stop a patentee's salary if they came to know that he was acting to the prejudice of the Revenue, but it does not appear that they had any power to push investigation. They might not scrutinize his books or check his cash.

At the outports many accounts of dead or dismissed collectors remained unliquidated. The outport books were clogged with records of these ancient liabilities. Many of the duties unaccounted for belonged to branches that had since been repealed, and they had been computed by methods which had passed out of ken. The current accounts were bemuddled. A collector might have paid in every penny of net duty he had handled, and still have undischarged accounts of his own, so mysteriously did receipts, drawbacks, allowances, and bounties, cross and intermingle.

The Plantation business was still worse. It appears that the accounts were never passed in the Exchequer, so hopelessly imperfect was their condition. Balances a century old were still 'depending.' As previously stated, the remittances were in bills and bullion. Often the Receiver-General let the bills lie unrealized for long periods. But one construction can with reason be placed on such conduct—viz., that the person on whom the bills were drawn recompensed him for the delay. One year, though the Board had stopped the salaries of a number of colonial officials for misbehaviour, the colonial and home charges of management swallowed all the gross Customs produce of the Plantations, except £4 7s. 8¼d. Yet the Receiver-General paid into the Exchequer on account of the Plantations for that year over £5,000! It is probable that he realized on his stock of unpresented bills, yet by no means certain; for on another occasion, when the charges exceeded the gross produce, and he was unable to complete payment of the home management, he made up the deficit by appropriating a sum from a British Customs branch. It is apparent that so long as a tolerable amount was paid into the Exchequer yearly no one was troubled as to outstanding matters and cash balances.

It may cause surprise that the collection of Plantation customs was continued when the net proceeds were so insignificant (rarely amounting to £5,000 a year). But it must be remembered that the Plantation collectors administered the Act of Navigation, and the laws regulating Plantation commerce. The takings really formed a 'Commercial Police Fund,' the 'police' acting as guardians of the Imperial interest, collecting maintenance in the form of customs duties, and transmitting to the Imperial Exchequer any trifling balance that might remain. Nor must the extent to which the colonies contributed towards their own embarrassment be measured by the 'gross produce' of the Plantation customs. The officers took fees and extorted 'gratuities,' and these did not appear in the account.

The Scottish Receiver-General made a practice of withholding even larger sums than his fellow-accountants in London, although the Scottish return was in all respects eminently unsatisfactory. During one year the English gross produce was over £3,700,000, and the Scottish barely £250,000. So heavily did salaries and local bounties bleed the Scottish total that the net produce was little over £90,000. Two years later the Scottish Receiver-General transmitted to the Receiver-General in London, to be paid into the Exchequer, a sum for the year amounting only to £60,000. When the returns were so trifling, the Scottish cashier should have known better than to keep back occasionally a sum of £40,000 or £50,000. What would have been thought of the collector of Bristol, where the gross return often approached that of all Scotland, if he had kept back half of the net proceeds ?

The Coinage duty, both in England and Scotland, failed to meet the expenses of the London and Edinburgh Mints, and the deficiency had to be made up out of the Supplies of the year. The Exchequer officials never knew what these yearly grants amounted to.

The 'manning' of the higher customs offices was both costly and defective. Most of the more lucrative posts were held by people of rank, who never performed any of the duties, but entrusted them to deputies. In many of the offices there were no duties to perform. All these 'employments' were secured by patents granted by the Crown. Some of the endowments were 'for life,' some 'during pleasure.'

There were three other methods of appointing officials. The Treasury appointed by Constitution or named by warrant. The Chancellor of the Exchequer might appoint by warrant. The Board of Customs appointed inferior officers by commission or order.

The sinecurists endowed by royal patent named their own deputies, in some cases subject to approbation by the Treasury. We may take the 'patent customer' at the outports as representative of the obsolete type of office, the 'patent searcher' as representative of the radically useless.

It has been stated in a previous chapter that when Customs farming was finally abolished in 1671 a new staff of collectors and searchers appeared at the outports, but the old 'customers and searchers' were allowed to remain. Thus arose the system of having a collector, a controller, and one or more searchers, to do the actual work, and a patent customer with a controller, and a patent searcher as well, to do little or nothing but pocket salaries, fees, and gratuities.

The patent customer did absolutely nothing. His deputy collected the principal's perquisites and his own, and sent the principal's share to Bath, Brighton, London, or wherever the principal might happen to be. Sometimes the patent controller acted as customer's deputy; sometimes the patent controller was non-resident, and had a deputy of his own. Sometimes the *actual* collector acted as deputy to both patent customer and patent controller. The patent controller, when resident, pottered a little with the 'coast bonds' (quite a superfluous exercise, for the actual controller also dealt with those documents, and duplication was unnecessary), and sent certain quarterly accounts to the Controller-General, which were never inspected on receipt, but tied up in bundles and put away. The patent searchers did absolutely nothing. Their deputies collected fees and gratuities.

Some of these sinecurists lived abroad, and whenever an inquiry was held into the matter of emoluments it was found difficult to trace the absentees. Yet it is certain the deputies knew where their patrons resided, or they could not have remitted the emoluments. It would appear that they were instructed to forget addresses, except when forwarding the spoil.

Sometimes a patentee held several sinecures, and sometimes, for cheapness, two or three patentees employed one deputy among them. These arrangements illustrate still more vividly the utter uselessness of both patentees and deputies. About 150 of these officials were quartered upon the outports, and so vigilant were some of the deputies in collecting fees that small trading contracts were frequently abandoned because the Customs exactions would have swallowed all the profits. It was not uncommon to postpone the departure of one of the many coasting 'hoys' because the freight was insufficient to answer these wicked impositions.

In one year the gross Customs produce of the port of Cardiff was but £54, which proves that Cardiff was a quieter port than the Cardiff of to-day. Of course there was a large deficit, for the salaries and incidental expenses of the actual collecting staff amounted to several hundreds. Yet the patent customer's takings were £504, his deputy acknowledged receiving £23, the patent controller took £332, and the patent searcher £162.

The returns from Carlisle were trifling, yet during one year the patent customer's perquisites were £343, the patent controller's £211, and the patent searcher's £185.

(Note that the bulk of the above was collected from coastwise traffic, or from export transactions that yielded no revenue except to the patentees.)

Extremely profitable to patent officers was the ancient port of Chester. In one year the patent customer received £1,593, his deputy acknowledged receiving £103, the patent controller received £766, and the patent searcher £1,323.

Averaged, the fees taken by patent customers at outports were to the customers' salaries as 10 to 1 ; those of the patent controllers and searchers 12 to 1. And none of these officials did a stroke of useful work.

It had been a practice since the days of yore to issue 'port-books' to the various outports. These were forwarded periodically by the Remembrancer of the Exchequer, but for many, many years scarce any use had been made of them. Sometimes certain items, previously recorded elsewhere, were entered, and the books returned to the Exchequer as of old, but in most cases they were thrown aside when received by the outport men, and never handled more. The Remembrancer kept an account of the books sent out and those returned, but though the output was huge and the return diminutive he never queried for the balance. Why should he? He had his allowance for transmission, and the Exchequer Usher (Horace Walpole) made a handsome profit on stationery. So the dreary fraud went on, year after year, though Commissioners of Inquiry raged and protested. It should be mentioned that had the books been regularly used and returned they would have served no practical purpose. The entries would have been mere duplicates or triplicates of entries which in themselves were valueless.

It appears that all the actual collectors of revenue at the outports were nominated by Treasury Warrant. Record has already been made of one appointment of an incompetent person, and of an arrangement between the Lord Treasurer and the Board of Customs that the latter should in future apprise Whitehall of any similar slip that might occur. Yet it is evident that this was but a fleeting reform, for many years later the Board were practically impotent in that respect. They merely inquired, whenever a new collector was named, whether he had been previously dismissed from the Customs! If he had, they returned the warrant. But they could go no further. If he had not been dismissed, they had to appoint him at once, and at his leisure he entered upon the important office, without the slightest official instruction in its duties. It might be found, after he reached his port, that he was quite ignorant of Customs work, and either unable or unwilling to learn. And yet when the Treasury approved a landing-surveyor, a landing-waiter, or a coast-waiter, the Board had power to place the nominee under instruction.

There were many useless officials in the port of London, and some of them were extremely expensive to the public. It must be stated that a Commissioner of Customs, although his office was no sinecure, had no Customs emolument except his salary, and an allowance for the extra work entailed by administering the quarantine regulations. There were nine Commissioners, each of whom received £1,000 a year, and £200 as 'Quarantine allowance.' Judging from the memoranda, they had to perform a deal of intricate and often distasteful work.

In the secretarial department were eighteen clerks, supported by salaries, fees, allowances, and gratuities.

In the legal department there were six solicitors, with salaries, allowances, and law fees (*vide* p. 310).

There was a gentleman named Poyntz, who was 'Inspector of Prosecutions.' He dealt with informations, and the king's share of the proceeds of seizures (*vide*

p. 344). It appears that he had little to do, and much for doing it. ('Heavy has been, and still is, the expense to the public of this useless office'—*Report of Messrs. Anguish, Roe, etc.*) He had held his post by patent since 1741. During the ten years from 1772 to 1781 inclusive, his annual perquisites averaged about £3,700. But when, in 1781, the Board were empowered to amend the application of the king's share, his yearly takings dropped to a little over £1,400. He then petitioned the Treasury, stating that he had made his future arrangements under the impression that his income would remain at the high figure. This, though he admitted that the takings had risen immensely since the date of the patent. And the Treasury granted compensation. The Great Commoner's son signed the Minute of grant, thus establishing another record of what Junius had once called the 'benefit of complaining.'

There was an office called 'The Receipt of Fines and Forfeitures from the Outports.' In 1777 the principal was dismissed. He owed the public over £20,000, about half of which was subsequently recovered from his estate. In 1782 his successor was found to be in arrear to the amount of £7,500. The public lost over £4,000.

There was an officer called 'The Customer of Cloth exported and of Petty Custom outward.' The outward cloth duties had long been abolished except on white woollens, and Petty Custom outward was no more. During ten years, from 1775 to 1784 inclusive, the duties collected on white woollens averaged about £64 a year. The fees and gratuities taken by the 'customer' averaged £76. For, though Petty or Aliens' Custom had lapsed, this patentee still collected fees, etc., from alien exporters.

Nearly all the more profitable offices were sinecures. The patent Collector Inwards received in all over £2,700 a year, and the patent Collector Outwards over £2,100. Neither of them ever attended. The Surveyor of Subsidies and Petty Customs, whose occupation had long ceased, made £1,850 a year. He had nothing to do, and a deputy and a clerk to help him, whose perquisites amounted to £180.

In the three offices mentioned below the work was done by deputies and clerks. The principals did not attend, but their perquisites were collected and transmitted by the underlings, and amounted to the following sums:

	Per Year.
Supervisor of Receiver-General's duties	£660
Registrar-General of British Ships	690
Inspector-General of Imports and Exports ..	780

The two patent searchers at Gravesend, who never went afloat, and rarely even saw the river, divided between them £1,200 a year. The Registrar of Seizures made about £500 a year. He was one of the unemployed.

The established officers who really went on duty and performed useful work also charged fees and received gratuities. Some of the memoranda of receipt are extremely suggestive. For instance, the Receiver-General, in addition to many other fees and gratuities, took during one year over £100 as 'compliments on salaries and debentures.' This meant that officers, when taking their salaries, and merchants, when cashing their drawback certificates, left small sums on the counter as presents to the lordly paymaster. When duties were paid to the various receivers, it was the practice for the payers not to take change for an odd sixpence. No doubt they were equally polite when cashing debentures.

The Receiver-General's chief clerk charged the owners of whalers 10s. 6d. each, whenever he 'marked their papers' for the Greenland Bounty. The chief Teller in the Pay Office had a fee of £250 for paying the London Establishment. His assistant usually received about £25 as 'New Year's gifts from inferior officers.' Another clerk had £10 a year in gifts from patentees, and six guineas in Christmas-boxes from the tradesmen who supplied the Custom-house with coals.

There was an office called 'The Receipt of Great Custom outwards.' There had been no collection since the abolition of the outward wool and lead duties, yet the officers continued to draw their salaries, and levy fees on coastwise traffic.

The Long Room officers were divided into four classes. Class 1 dealt with export and import business. The fees collected in this department were to the salaries received as 5 to 1. Class 2 dealt with imports only, and the fees were as 4 to 1. Class 3 dealt with exports only, and the fees were as 18 to 1. Class 4—the jerquers—merely checked books and warrants. In this branch the salaries exceeded the perquisites, for the latter could only be collected from shipmasters who were paid portages, and 'inferior officers' whose landing-books had been certified.

The Usher of the Long Room rarely attended. His clerk and deputy did the work, which consisted principally in collecting fees on the various oaths made to bonds, manifests, etc. The Usher had 2d. for 'every oath outwards.' The deputy had 6d. for every transaction necessitating one to three oaths, and 1s. on four to six. Then came the clerk, and took fees on the same scale as the deputy. Thus a single oath cost 1s. 2d., of which the Usher had 2d., the deputy 6d., and the clerk 6d.

The landing-waiters made about £220 a year each in fees and gratuities—nearly three times the salary of their office. Their 'gratuities' were for attending at 'sufferance wharves' to supervise work which should have been performed at the 'legal quays,' and for working after or before the legal hours.

The gaugers were appointed by the Treasury. Usually they received 3d. a cask from merchants, and 7s. 6d. for every 100 barrels of tar gauged. Their gratuities were about double the amount of their salaries.

The chief patent searcher's official income, after paying his deputy, etc., was about £500. The five patent under-searchers did better still. Only one of them attended. He paid no deputy, and his takings amounted to about £900 a year. The other four were sinecurists. Each of them employed a deputy at £160, and pocketed about £740.

The officers who attended at the East India Company's warehouses received many gifts of tea and spices, besides 'compliments,' Christmas-boxes, etc.

There were sixteen 'Land Carriage officers,' and a surveyor to direct them. Their work consisted in hanging about inns in London and Westminster, for the purpose of peeping into carriages and stables, to ascertain whether uncustomed articles were conveyed under the seats or concealed amid the straw and hay. So far as can be ascertained, they collected no fees, nor does it appear that they made any seizures.

Besides the officers specified, there was an army of coast-waiters, tide-waiters, boatmen, constables, door-keepers, and messengers. We find from the Board's memoranda that these had often to be rebuked for trying to extort illegal fees and gratuities. The large staff of river inspectors, surveyors, etc., appear to have subsisted principally upon salaries.

The laws were still in existence forbidding officers to take more in fees than the amounts prescribed by Parliament. Yet many of the fees were 'of usage' only. It had been repeatedly directed that tables of fees should be posted at the various ports, and lists of transactions which were exempt. The first direction was occasionally complied with; the last never. The officers, especially at remote ports, charged almost at will. Extra dispatch could in most cases be procured by augmenting gratuities. Occasionally one officer would collect the fees for several transactions, and divide them among the officers concerned, and often there was a squabble over the division.

Another grievance of which the mercantile public complained bitterly was the delay caused by the brief 'clerical hours' and the numerous customs holidays. The Long Room hours at this period were from nine till noon. The jerquers attended from nine till three. The searchers attended from nine till four, and took two and a half hours for lunch. Outside, of course, the working day was much longer. There were forty-five customs holidays in a year, commencing with ' Circumcision ' and ending with ' Holy Innocents.' The ships from foreign usually arrived in fleets, and there was much delay when a couple of holidays occurred during one week (sometimes on successive days).

But there were premonitions of reform. Various committees of inquiry had pried into the dusty corners and mouldy crannies of the Revenue departments, and the maritime branch had not escaped its share of overhauling. The Board of Customs clamoured louder than ever for wider powers of control, reward, and punishment. The official atmosphere was stirred with whispers of consolidation and retrenchment. Consolidation was at hand, though it was not destined to confer lasting benefit. Retrenchment was about to be attempted—attempted cautiously, and not always in the quarters where retrenchment was most desirable.

LIST OF AUTHORITIES.

Wine: 3 Geo. III., c. 12.

Protective measures and prohibitions: 4 Geo. III., c. 9; 4 Geo. III., c. 15; 4 Geo. III., c. 26; 4 Geo. III., c. 27; 5 Geo. III., c. 12; 5 Geo. III., c. 45; 5 Geo. III., c. 48; 6 Geo. III., c. 12; 6 Geo. III., c. 49; 6 Geo. III., c. 52; 7 Geo. III., c. 30; 7 Geo. III., c. 2; 7 Geo. III., c. 41; 7 Geo. III., c. 46; 9 Geo. III., c. 38; 10 Geo. III., c. 17; 11 Geo. III., c. 37; 11 Geo. III., c. 50; 12 Geo. III., c. 50; 13 Geo. III., c. 43; 14 Geo. III., c. 19; 14 Geo. III., c. 5, 11; 14 Geo. III., c. 39; 14 Geo. III., c. 42; 14 Geo. III., c. 45; 14 Geo. III., c. 54; 15 Geo. III., c. 10; 15 Geo. III., c. 18; 'Instructions to Guy Carleton' (Canadian Archives); 15 Geo. III., c. 34, 35, 37; 15 Geo. III., c. 45; 16 Geo. III., c. 5; 17 Geo. III., c. 27; 18 Geo. III., c. 12; 18 Geo. III., c. 13; 18 Geo. III., c. 55, 56; 19 Geo. III., c. 48; 19 Geo. III., c. 53; 20 Geo. III., c. 46; 20 Geo. III., c. 55; 21 Geo. III., c. 16; 21 Geo. III., c. 50; 22 Geo. III., c. 71; 23 Geo. III., c. 79; 24 Geo. III., c. 21; 26 Geo. III., c. 40.

Departmental incidents: Sir William Musgrave's 'Memoranda'; Poole Letter Books; Southampton Letter Books; Fifteenth Report of Sir Guy Carleton's Committee.

Permanent branches of revenue: 5 Geo. III., c. 35; 9 Geo. III., c. 25; 18 Geo. III., c. 27; 19 Geo. III., c. 25; 20 Geo. III., c. 30; 20 Geo. III., c. 52; 21 Geo. III., c. 16; 22 Geo. III., c. 28;

22 Geo. III., c. 39, 61, 66 ; 24 Geo. III., c. 11 ; 24 Geo. III., c. 24 ; 24 Geo. III., c. 36 ; 24 Geo. III., c. 46 ; 24 Geo. III., c. 49, 51, 53 ; 26 Geo. III., c. 42 ; 26 Geo. III., c. 59.

Isle of Man : 7 Geo. III., c. 45.

Excise Duties : 9 Geo. III., c. 6.

Frauds : 12 Geo. III., c. 55 ; 17 Geo. III., c. 41.

Temporary imposts : 13 Geo. III., c. 67 ; 21 Geo. III., c. 32 ; 24 Geo. III., c. 18.

East India Company : 14 Geo. III., c. 34 ; 24 Geo. III., c. 38 ; 25 Geo. III., c. 74.

Hull : 14 Geo. III., c. 56.

Quebec : 14 Geo. III., c. 88.

Privateers : 17 Geo. III., c. 7.

Preventive measures : 17 Geo. III., c. 41 ; 18 Geo. III., c. 40 ; 3 Geo. III., c. 22 ; 19 Geo. III., c. 69 ; 21 Geo. III., c. 39 ; 24 Geo. III., c. 47.

Tobacco : 19 Geo. III., c. 35 ; 22 Geo. III., c. 73 ; 23 Geo. III., c. 75 ; 25 Geo. III., c. 81.

Accounts : 20 Geo. III., c. 54 ; 25 Geo. III., c. 19.

Officers : 22 Geo. III., c. 41 ; 22 Geo. III., c. 75.

Treaties : 22 Geo. III., c. 46.

Exchequer : 23 Geo. III., c. 82.

Repeal of ancient duties : 24 Geo. III., c. 16.

CHAPTER IX

THE GREAT REFORMATION IN METHOD, AND THE SUBSEQUENT LAPSES

1787–1800

THE various branches of Customs revenue were 'consolidated' by the thirteenth statute of the twenty-seventh year of George III.'s reign. The Act opened with a statement that was certainly unchallengeable:

'Whereas the present mode of charging and computing the several duties of Customs and Excise, and other duties under the management of the Commissioners of Excise in England and Scotland respectively, is in many instances intricate and complicated, and productive of much embarrassment to the persons who are to pay the same, as well as of great perplexity in the Accounts of Public Revenue,' etc.

The Act provided that from and after May 10, 1787, the existing customs and excise duties should cease, and be replaced by new duties, and that the said new duties should not be subject to discount. The drawbacks were also to cease, and be renewed in other form.

The separate Boards for England and Scotland were maintained, and enjoined to keep separate accounts of revenue. The methods of prevention and prosecution survived, and all goods previously duty-free continued exempt. The hours of lading and discharge, the officers' fees, and the official hours of attendance, remained unaltered. The bounties on exported goods endured. The restrictions upon French commerce were removed. A slight alteration was made in the method of abating duty on damaged goods, it being provided that the amount of abatement should be settled by 'two indifferent* merchants.' The bounty called 'Portage,' payable to masters who reported their cargoes satisfactorily, was abolished. Nearly all the regulations annexed to the old 'Book of Rates' were repealed.

Under the new method the duties on all goods, except coal, might be bonded—*i.e.*, payment might be postponed until the merchant required his goods for sale, he furnishing security. The East India Company were to pay their customs when due,† instead of, as before, paying them in gross at stated periods. In order that customs moneys might reach the Receiver-General as early as possible, the duties collected in London were to be paid in on day of receipt. Drawbacks and bounties payable in London were to be disbursed by the Receiver-General; at outports the collectors might pay. The Act stated that under the previous system many collectors had applied moneys taken as duty to the wrong 'branches,' and that their accounts remained 'unsettled and unliquidated,' and it directed that all such erroneous accounts should be promptly closed.

By the new system the duties upon most articles, instead of being levied as percentages upon value, were expressed in definite sums. The principal exceptions were the rates on the East India Company's goods (which in most instances were *ad valorem*, duty being computed as a percentage on the gross prices obtained at the periodical sales) and on unenumerated goods. Unenumerated goods were to be assessed as to value according to importer's or exporter's declaration, but the collectors were still empowered to buy them if undervalued.

The new duties, drawbacks, etc., were expressed in six schedules, as below:

Schedule A included the duties inward and outward upon most articles, and the drawbacks payable.

* Disinterested. † As soon as possible after sale.

Schedule B included the duties and drawbacks upon the East India Company's goods.

Schedule C included the duties and drawbacks upon goods distinctively French.

Schedule D included the duties and drawbacks upon 'other unenumerated goods'—*i.e.*, articles that varied much in quality, and therefore could not be safely charged with specific duties.

Schedule E included the duties outward on unenumerated goods.

Schedule F included the excise duties, drawbacks, allowances, and bounties.

All customs, excise, and inland duties were to be carried to one fund, called 'The Consolidated Fund.' The Coinage duty was abolished, and the Treasury were empowered to issue a sum of £15,000 annually out of the customs receipts, towards the maintenance of the Mint. Denizens and aliens paid the same duties, but telling advantages were granted to certain goods brought in British-built ships. As of old, the wine duties were lighter at outports than at London.

The rates on French goods were considerably lessened by the new Act. To give an idea of the enormous burdens that had been gradually piled upon French trade, and the large reduction considered necessary, we quote the tunnage at various stages of the period extending from 1611 to 1787. The rates given are those levied at outports, upon wines imported in British-built ships, for sale, and filled at landing. Up to 1782 the rates are 'denizens' duties.'

French Wine, the Tun of 252 Gallons.

	£	s.	d.		£	s.	d.
1611	2	0	0	1787	25	4	0
1725	48	11	8	Excise duty ..	17	17	0
1774	64	11	8				
1782	90	3	10	Total	43	1	0

We now furnish the duties on a few other familiar articles. When at any period used there was a discount allowed for ready-money, or a preferential rate for goods brought in a British-built ship, or a preferential rate for denizens, we deduct the discount, and select the preferential rate. Thus we quote the *lowest* net duties payable. Fractions rejected.

Candles of Tallow, per Cwt.

Year	£ s. d.	Year	£ s. d.
1600	Not on list		
1611	Not on list	1774	1 4 1
		1782	1 6 2
1660	0 1 4	1787	1 12 8
1725	1 2 8		

Venice Soap, per Cwt.

Year	£ s. d.	Year	£ s. d.
1600	0 1 8	1774	1 19 6
1611	0 3 4	1782	2 2 0
1660	0 2 10	1787	Not on list
1725	1 16 6		

Currants, per Cwt.

Year	£ s. d.	Year	£ s. d.
1600	0 1 6	1774	1 2 1
1611	0 4 10	1782	1 2 2
1660	0 5 8	1787	1 3 4
1725	0 16 1		

White Unrefined Sugar, not of Plantations, per Cwt. (*Plantation Sugar was preferentially treated.*)

Year	£ s. d.	Year	£ s. d.
1600	0 3 4	1774	1 15 6
1611	0 8 4	1782	2 3 4
1660	0 6 11	1787	2 5 6
1725	1 0 10		

Refined Loaf Sugar, per Cwt.

Year	£ s. d.	Year	£ s. d.
1600	Not on list		
1611	Not on list	1774	4 2 1
		1782	4 14 6
1660	0 16 1	1787	4 18 8
1725	2 8 6		

Leaf Tobacco, not of Plantations, per Pound.

	£	s.	d.		£	s.	d.
1600	0	0	4	1774—Spanish	0	2	3
1611	0	1	4	French	0	6	8
1660	0	0	5	1782—Spanish	0	2	11
1725—Spanish	0	1	6	French	0	8	2
French	0	5	10	1787—All leaf tobacco not of Plantations	0	3	6

Leaf Tobacco of Plantations, per Pound. (Irish-grown= Plantation.)

	£	s.	d.		£	s.	d.
1600	0	0	4	1774	0	0	6
1611	0	1	4	1782—From place of growth	0	0	10
1660	0	0	1	1787	0	1	3
1725	0	0	4				

Apples, per Five Bushels. (The duty was levied per one or three bushels. The duty on five bushels is given to effect comparison with the earlier rates, which were so low that the poundage on a single bushel cannot conveniently be quoted.)

	£	s.	d.		£	s.	d.
1600	0	0	1	1774	0	10	4
1611	0	0	1	1782	0	10	10
1660	0	0	1	1787	0	11	8
1725	0	10	4				

White Salt, per 40 Bushels of 84 Pounds each.

	£	s.	d.		£	s.	d.
1600	0	1	4	1774	0	9	10
1611	0	1	4	1782	0	10	10
1660	0	1	3	1787	0	11	5
1725	0	8	6				

Before comparing the duties on wheat, we must recapitulate the conditions governing rates. From 1600 to 1787 there was a specified 'plenty price'—a standard (varying occasionally) which indicated full garners and a plentiful supply of bread. In 1600 and 1611 the 'plenty price' did not affect the import duty, but when the standard was exceeded wheat might not be exported. In 1660 and afterwards, when the 'plenty price' was exceeded, the import duties were lowered. For instance, under the Consolidating Act of 1787, when wheat was at less than 48s. a quarter, the import duty was £1 4s. 3d.; when it was at 48s. or more the duty was but 6d. The rates quoted for comparison are those levied when wheat was at the 'plenty price'; therefore they are the *highest* duties payable.

Wheat, per Quarter of Eight Bushels.

	£	s.	d.		£	s.	d.
1600	0	0	4	1774	1	1	9
1611	0	0	4	1782	1	3	1
1660	0	1	10	1787	1	4	3
1725	0	19	9				

Below is a comparison of the 1782 and 1787 duties on certain other goods:

	1782.			1787.		
	£	s.	d.	£	s.	d.
Wax candles, per pound	0	1	1	0	1	8
Hard soap, per cwt.	2	2	0	2	4	0
Soft soap ,, ...	1	15	8	1	17	5
Hay, per load of 18 cwt.	0	10	6	0	11	0
Hops, per cwt.	5	13	4	5	18	10
Thrown silk, dyed, per pound of 16 ounces	1	1	6	1	4	9

It will be observed that the tendency of the new Act was to increase rates, except on French goods. In comparing the seventeenth century duties with those of the eighteenth, it should be taken into account that the value of money decreased during the 187 years under survey. This should also be borne in mind when the annual proceeds are compared. It will now be useful to state the amounts paid into the Exchequer, from Customs, at certain stages during the period extending from 1600 to 1787.

*The net yearly Customs revenue during the reign of

* This was never intended to be a statistical treatise, yet great pains have been taken in comparing tables furnished by previous writers who dealt largely in figures. It would seem that many of the tables given by them are misleading. They have occasionally misapprehended returns, through confusing the amounts stated as 'Net Produce' with the amounts actually paid into the Exchequer. It is difficult to explain the difference

James I. can rarely have approached £200,000. During Charles I.'s reign revenue matters were immensely confused by the squabbles between king and Parliament, and thus it is unsafe even to guess at returns. Proceeding to Commonwealth times, we find in Thurloe's collection an estimate of a year's proceeds of Customs and Excise, and from this we assume that the average net Customs return under the Protectorate was about £450,000.

In the early part of Charles II.'s reign Sir Philip Warwick held that though the rates and scope of taxation had increased the proceeds were less than under the Commonwealth. Davenant maintained that towards the end of the reign Customs and Excise produced about equal amounts, and he quoted the Excise return as about

---

between 'Net Produce' and 'Payments into Exchequer,' as shown in the old customs tables of proceeds, but an attempt must be made to display an annual account.

The 'Gross Receipts' from each branch were shown and totalled, and the total represented the 'Gross Produce.' From this was deducted the amount of 'Payments,' made up of drawbacks, bounties, salaries, and incidents. The residue was the 'Net Produce,' but the exact amount of this was not paid into the Exchequer. A considerable sum, made up of 'Debts decreased in Money,' 'Debts decreased on Bonds,' and 'Moneys overpaid,' was added to the 'Net Produce,' and another large sum, made up of 'Debts incurred in Money,' 'Debts incurred on Bonds,' and 'Overpayments decreased,' was deducted. Thus in one year the actual 'Payments into Exchequer' might greatly exceed the 'Net Produce,' and in the following year the 'Net Produce' might exceed the 'Payments into Exchequer.' It would be possible to quote instances in which a statist has mixed these varying returns, yet called one series of results a table of actual payments, and another a table of net products.

The sums quoted from 1700 to 1787 in the present treatise are taken from a Parliamentary Return furnished in 1869. This may be approximately correct. Yet one thing is certain: the Parliamentary Return renders no exact information as to the growth of the revenue year by year, for the East India Company were often in arrear to the extent of hundreds of thousands of pounds, and made up the deficiency in a subsequent year. The revenue officials who acted as receivers in London and Edinburgh were also in the habit of withholding large sums, as has already been stated. Therefore it has been deemed best to make comparison at intervals of *ten* years, comparing 1732 with 1742, etc.

£500,000 per annum. It is likely that the average net Customs yield under Charles did not exceed £450,000 a year. (See p. 118 of this treatise, in which the return of 1680 is stated. That return was, of course, much larger than the yearly product at the beginning of the reign.)

After 1688 taxation increased immensely. Population had also increased since the time of the Commonwealth, and the Navigation and Plantation Acts were held to have assisted English commerce. Yet the Customs return for the four years ending in 1692 was only about £2,800,000—say £700,000 a year. From 1692 to the end of William's reign four permanent branches of Customs and one complete Subsidy were added. In 1702 the return was about £1,470,000.

During Anne's reign ten permanent branches and a Subsidy—made up by the combined $\frac{1}{3}$ and $\frac{2}{3}$ Subsidies—were added. In 1712 the return was about £1,481,000.

From 1713 to 1722 two permanent branches were added. Return for 1722, £1,490,000. Return in 1732, £1,690,000. From 1733 to 1742 Sir Robert Walpole was at the head of public affairs. Return in 1742, £1,280,000 only. From 1743 to 1752 the Glass Duty, a Subsidy, and several permanent branches, including the 'Additional Wine Duty,' were added. (This last came out in 1745, and though there was much wine-drinking about that time, the 1746 return was but £1,017,000). In 1752 the return was £1,630,000. A Subsidy was added in 1759, and the return for 1762 was £1,820,000. From 1763 to 1772 several permanent inward and two outward branches were added. Return for 1772, about £2,500,000. From 1773 to 1782 several important branches were added, and two imposts, each of 5 per cent. on proceeds. Return for 1782, about £2,900,000.

During the latter part of the period traversed, export duties had been removed from many kinds of British goods, and the systems of drawback and bounty had been extensively remodelled. It is likely that in 1782 about

£2,000,000 had been taken from the *gross* receipts to meet debentures under the above heads. Still, £2,900,000 appears a paltry return.

It is evident that the fiscal experimenters were slowly learning better doctrine. The Consolidating Act was not a dazzling effort, yet it was a step in the right direction. It was received with acclamation, especially by merchants. Even the increased duties were for the time overlooked by the rejoicing community; for it was a blissful change to be able to ascertain the duty on a parcel of goods by a single computation, instead of struggling through a dozen. The saving effected in stationery alone must have been great, and little may justly be said against any measure that dethrones circumlocution.

Further increases were soon deemed necessary. Additional duties were levied on foreign glass, and placed with the Excise.

It was enacted that foreign goods liable to Excise duty should be entered with the Excise within thirty days after report of ship. A clause of this Act stated that foreign spirits had for many years been tested by 'Clarke's Hydrometer,' that the instrument was not accurate, and that experiments would be made with a view towards securing a more elaborate test. Another clause empowered excise officers to administer the oath necessary on the exportation of goods liable to drawback.

The next Act of the Session provided that any cutter, etc., belonging to the king's subjects, and found within four leagues of the coast, having a bowsprit of a length more than two-thirds that of the vessel, should be forfeited. All seized goods sold at the King's Warehouse were to be stamped before delivery. Every boat plying within four leagues of the coast was to have its name lettered on the stern. The *customs* duty on geneva, which under the Consolidating Act had been 5d. a gallon, was made equal to the customs duty on brandy (9d.).

The Board directed that East Indiamen should not be allowed to come into the channels of the Thames near

London, but should anchor in Long Reach, and that their cargoes should be reported within twenty-four hours of reaching Gravesend. This was intended to prevent smuggling. The directors of the Company arranged to send a fleet of hoys to Long Reach whenever one of their vessels arrived, to bring her cargo to London. The East Indiamen were to be strictly watched while at their new anchorage, and their ports and scuttles secured each night under joint locks of the Crown and Company. The Board found occasion to censure their river inspectors, who had thrown obstacles in the way of this scheme.

The Board requested the Commissioners of Excise to order the excise officers not to gauge imported spirits unless a customs man were present, and not to deliver the goods unless with customs cognizance, and intimated that if the request were not complied with they would direct the tide-waiters to watch and follow all such goods to their destination.

It appears that the regulated quantities of rum and sugar allowed for consumption in the Isle of Man were shipped at Liverpool. Up to a certain date in each year the Liverpool collector received tenders from merchants who were desirous of supplying the goods, and on the date specified the Board apportioned the trade equally among the merchants who had tendered.

The deputies of the late duke of Manchester (Collector Outwards) were permitted to retain office pending the issue of orders from the Treasury. The Board empowered them to continue the allotment of fees collected, 'keeping the same proportion for themselves as of old.'

Much friction was caused by the inquisitorial enforcement of the taxes upon wearing apparel. The Board advised their officers to be tactful, and to discriminate between clothing worn by passengers and clothing imported unaccompanied. The order concluded, 'This will save our time, which may be more usefully employed than in deciding constant applications.'

Hannah Randall was granted a gratuity of £30. It

appears that she had given evidence against several customs officers who had been charged with conniving at fraud on board the *Deptford* East Indiaman.

Customs 'guard-boats,' each with six boatmen and a 'sitter,' were stationed at Sheerness, Whitstable, Sandgate, Eastbourne, and Bridport, to prevent smuggling.

It was proclaimed by the Board that certain errors, which had for many years acted to the prejudice of the revenue, had been discovered in Crouch's 'Survey of the Customs,' a handbook previously much esteemed.

The department became convulsed on the matter of American corn. Sir Joseph Banks, President of the Royal Society, communicated with the Treasury as to the 'flying weevil' and the 'Hessian fly,' insects that had seriously damaged the wheat crop in the United States. The correspondence, in which several American experts took part, is too extensive to quote in full, yet it is extremely interesting.

It appears that the Hessian fly was first observed at Staten Island in 1776. The Hessian auxiliaries landed about the same time, and to this coincidence the insect owed its title. Sir Joseph Banks refused to believe that the fly was taken over in the baggage of the Hessians, but the colonists cherished that idea. A letter to General Washington from Colonel Morgan, of the American army, was quoted, stating that the writer witnessed the first passage of the pest across the Delaware. 'It travelled,' said he, 'like a cloud, neither water nor mountain impeding its progress.'

The fly attacked the young wheat when first sprouting in autumn, and appeared as a caterpillar, which afterwards became fixed in chrysalis between blade and stalk, emerging as a fly about the end of the year. Observers were undecided as to whether this fly survived, or laid eggs which endured the cold of winter; but they were unanimous as to the invisibility of the eggs, if eggs there were. A similar caterpillar appeared in spring, and preyed upon the plant. The ravages committed by this insect were described as dreadful and resistless. It annually devastated the province of New York, part of Connecticut, and the borderland of New Jersey, and threatened the entire corn-land of the United States. Doleful indeed was the tone of the American advices: 'Unless means be found to impede its progress, the whole American continent will be overrun. Were it to reach Great Britain, it would be the greatest scourge that island ever experienced. Were a single straw containing the insect, egg, or aurelia, to be carried and safely deposited in the centre of Norfolk in England, it would multiply in a few years so as to destroy all the wheat and barley crops of the whole kingdom. There cannot be so atrocious a villain as to commit such an act intentionally. To us it appears unlikely that any means within the bounds of human wisdom will be found to destroy the fly.'

Certain methods had been tried, such as rolling the wheat before the first autumn frost, dressing the land with lime and ashes, sheltering the young plant with seaweed or straw, etc. All were unavailing, but it had been found that a particular kind of wheat (the 'yellow-bearded' variety) was impregnable.

Danger to British agriculture from the assaults of the flying weevil was the burden of the next missive from the naturalists. The insect was described as a minute moth, 'much like that infesting woollens.' Its eggs produced a tiny caterpillar, that preyed upon ripe wheat. The moth differed from the European weevil in possessing wings and immense energy, and attacking wheat in the field as well as in the rick. This horrid pest first appeared in Carolina, and then travelled northward, following the extension of wheat-farming, and rapidly becoming acclimatized in the colder regions. Sir Joseph Banks feared that it might be brought to England in American corn cargoes. He had discovered it 'as a worm' in many samples of American corn, but always dead, and he prescribed an experiment by means of which the customs officers might detect it. The experiment was but the ancient method of throwing the corn into water, and scrutinizing such grains as floated. 'In some may be found the worm, or the husk of its chrysalis, or the mere shell with excrement which the insect has left.'

In consequence of these disquieting reports, American corn was forbidden customs entry. There is record of the stoppage of a cargo from the United States. The corn was destroyed, and the rest of the goods were landed and placed under Crown lock. Later an outrageous order was issued, to the effect that wheat infected with flying weevil might be 'applied to the use of the navy.' Subsequently this was countermanded, and instructions were given that the infected wheat should be 'ground down at the ports where the same was imported.'

Edward VI.'s Act, prohibiting the exportation of white ashes, was repealed in 1788.

The laws prohibiting the exportation of wool, except the regulation that wool might not be housed within ten miles of the sea in Kent and Sussex, were repealed, and fresh prohibitive provisions enacted. The exportation of live sheep from Great Britain and the Channel Islands was forbidden. Persons exporting wool were made liable to a penalty of 3s. for every pound of wool. Wool carried coastwise without entry was made forfeitable.

Another Act provided for the regulation of the African slave-trade. Only a certain number of slaves per three tons of the vessel's capacity might be carried, unless they were children or below a certain stature. When a slaver arrived in the West Indies the master was to make a declaration before the Customs that all legal conditions had been complied with, and the customs officers were to inspect the vessel and count the slaves.

All surgeons of slavers were to give bond before clearing outwards for Africa that they would keep an authentic journal of the voyage, which journal was to be produced to the Customs at first port of arrival. No vessel was to be cleared outwards as a slaver unless she carried a duly qualified surgeon. If the master, on arriving at the West

Indies, could satisfy the Customs that not more than 2 per cent. of the slaves had died during the voyage, he was entitled to a reward of £100, and the surgeon to £50.

Two Commissioners of Customs in England and one in Scotland were appointed to inquire on oath into Customs emoluments, and to report to the Treasury.

An Act of 1789 repealed certain clauses of the Consolidating Act relating to tobacco and snuff, and placed new duties on the articles. It enjoined that after a specified day in 1789 customs entry of tobacco should be confined to goods from the American Plantations and the United States, and tobacco grown or produced in Ireland, or in the Plantations belonging to the Spaniards and Portuguese. The legal tonnage for tobacco vessels was fixed at 120 tons, and the legal weight for a package of tobacco at 450 pounds net. American tobacco might only be imported from the United States, or the British-American Plantations, in American and British built ships. The British 'tobacco ports' were re-defined: London, Bristol, Falmouth, Liverpool, Lancaster, Cowes, Whitehaven, Hull, Greenock, Leith, and Port Glasgow.* All tobacco from the United States was to be accompanied by a special manifest, to the correctness of which the master was to make oath. The hatches of all tobacco vessels were to be locked down by the Customs, except during hours of work. The Board were empowered to appoint places for the mooring of tobacco-ships, and to provide warehouses for bonding the goods. The exportation of tobacco to the Channel Islands and the Isle of Man was made subject to special licence by the Board, and limited to a certain quantity per year. All persons employed in tobacco warehouses were to be licensed. Certain articles used in 'imitating' tobacco were quoted: walnut, hop, and sycamore leaves. It was directed that a permit should accompany all removed tobacco.†

* Newcastle-on-Tyne was added to the list in 1791.

† Part of this Act deserves quotation: 'If any tobacco, tobacco stalks, Spanish, Returns of tobacco, Tobacco stalks for Tobacco Stalk Flour, Snuff work, Tobacco stalk Flour, or Snuff,

The Act also provided that all tobacco of four pounds weight or upwards, removed after 5 p.m. or before 7 a.m. in winter, or after 7 p.m. and before 5 a.m. in summer, should be liable to forfeiture, together with all boats, carriages, or horses used to convey it. The Act also prohibited the hawking of tobacco, and rendered forfeitable all roll tobacco produced for exportation, and containing more than 20 per cent. of water or foreign ingredients. It recited the old proviso that no customs officer who made a seizure should be entitled to reward, unless he had given notice of his capture to an excise officer, and it reaffirmed the right of excise officers to board and rummage vessels. This terrific statute contained 173 clauses.

Another Act removed the outward duty from unwrought tin exported to any place beyond the Cape of Good Hope, and hinted that the trifling relaxation might benefit British commerce to a marvellous extent. Exporters of tin were to furnish security at ports of shipment that the goods would be landed according to entry outward. The bonds were to be discharged as follows :

If the goods were to be landed in China, by a certificate from the chief supercargo officiating there for the East India Company.

---

removed under Colour of any permit, shall be seized, or if any Action shall be brought by the Owner or Claimer of any such Tobacco, Tobacco stalks, Spanish, Returns of Tobacco, Tobacco Stalks for Tobacco Stalk Flour, Snuff Work, Tobacco Stalk Flour or Snuff, against any Officer or Officers of Customs or Excise, or any Person acting in his or their Assistance, for such seizure of any such Tobacco, Tobacco Stalks, Spanish, Returns of Tobacco, Tobacco Stalks for Tobacco Stalk Flour, Snuff Work, Tobacco Stalk Flour, or Snuff, the proof that such Tobacco, Tobacco Stalks, Spanish, Returns of Tobacco, Tobacco Stalks for Tobacco Stalk Flour, Snuff Work, Tobacco Stalk Flour, or Snuff, being such Tobacco, Tobacco Stalks, Spanish, Returns of Tobacco, Tobacco Stalks for Tobacco Stalk Flour, Snuff Work, Tobacco Stalk Flour, or Snuff, as is or are mentioned in such permit, although such Tobacco, Tobacco Stalks, Spanish, Returns of Tobacco, Tobacco Stalks for Tobacco Stalk Flour, Snuff Work, Tobacco Stalk Flour, or Snuff, shall appear to have been kept in the Officers' Books or Account of the Stock from which such Tobacco, Tobacco Stalks, Spanish, Returns of Tobacco, Tobacco Stalks for Tobacco Stalk Flour, Snuff Work, Tobacco Stalk Flour, or Snuff, was or were removed,' etc.

If the goods were to be landed in the East Indies, by a certificate from the Governor or Council of the Company.

If the goods were to be landed at a place beyond the Company's jurisdiction, by a certificate from two principal merchants.

In all cases the certificates were to be forthcoming in Great Britain within thirty months from date of bond.

Inquiry had been resumed as to the flying weevil and Hessian fly, and copious information had been furnished to the Privy Council by Phineas Bond, British consul at Philadelphia. All the papers on the matter were laid before Parliament. On November 28, 1789, the Privy Council advised the king to revoke the prohibition of American corn.

It had been usual, whenever duty was overpaid, to adjust the matter by allowing the payer to export goods duty-free up to the amount of excess. The Board abolished this clumsy method, directing that over-entry certificates should be granted, and the overpaid moneys returned.

Comprehensive instructions were issued to the gaugers. Casks of wine and spirits were to be gauged by both Customs and Excise on importation, there being heavy excise duties on both classes of goods. 'Standards of allowance' were prescribed, varying according to the types of cask, but the gaugers were directed, whenever the casks had 'copped bouges, indented bung-staves, squeezed quarters, or dished or buckled heads,' to consult upon such distortions of shape, and then submit their decision for the landing-surveyor's approval. It would seem that the casks in which wines and spirits were imported were of much the same 'standards of content' as those used in recent times—say down to 1880.* For instance, the standard content of a port pipe was shown as 137 gallons.

* Within the last twenty or thirty years the standards have in many cases been departed from. Port pipes may be found to hold 125 gallons, and brandy puncheons 130. Brandy hogsheads may be met with that contain 65 gallons; in fact, standard construction is the exception, not the rule.

The wine gallon contained about 231 cubic inches, and 137 gallons old measure would be about 114 modern. But the prescribed standards of allowance show that the casks were thinner and of better shape than those now used, the sherry butts especially. The method of recording measurements was similar to the modern system, the length, head, bung, wet inches, full content, and liquid content being 'razed' upon the front head; but the spirit ullages were cast out to the gallon, instead of to the tenth part of a gallon. The customs gaugers were enjoined to be courteous and friendly with the excisemen, 'studying on every occasion to preserve that harmony and good understanding between the officers of both departments that is so essential to the Publick Service.'

Other instructions were issued, specifying the conditions under which vessels seized for smuggling might be sold for 'breaking up.' Buyers were to dismantle their purchases under customs supervision, separating planks, unhinging rudders, unshipping windlasses, removing sternposts, and then sawing through the keels in three equidistant places.

Both Customs and Excise Commissioners issued instructions that whenever a ship arrived with a cargo of spirits the first officer going on board should dip all casks stowed above the hatches, and record the wet inches in the 'blue book.' If a customs man were first, the first excise officer visiting the ship was to check the wet inches by redipping, and *vice versa*. It appears that many casks thus carried had been found almost empty when landed on the quays.

All the London jerquers were censured for irregular attendance.

An expert named Betts was appointed to estimate the values of imported violins and violoncellos, and particularly enjoined to report upon previous valuations, the Board being desirous of preventing illegal combination betwixt officers and importers.

One Valentine Green was allowed by Treasury warrant

to import, duty-free, certain copies of pictures, produced at Dusseldorf.

The Board directed that no sufferance for landing foreign goods should be granted to any London wharf 'below Brown's Wharf near Hermitage Bridge on the north side of the Thames, and St. Saviour's Dock on the south side,' and that no foreign goods, except iron, should be landed above London Bridge. Several notable places were exempt from the former restriction—the King's yards at Deptford and Woolwich, the East India Company's wharves at Blackwall, and the Greenland Dock. At certain wharves both coastwise and foreign goods might be landed if kept separate. These were Irongate, Watson's, Hawley's, and Brown's on the north side; Chamberlain's, Cotton's, Hay's, Beal's, Griffin's, Symons's, Stanton's, Davis's, and Eustace's on the south. At Carrington's, Hogarth's, Scott's, Meriton's, and Topping's foreign goods only might be landed, and the packages were to be examined 'on the open quay.' The only two places above-bridge approved for the landing of foreign iron were Dyer's Wharf and the historic Steel Yard.*

The Board apprised the Treasury that the Tobacco Warehouse on Tower Hill was not large enough to accommodate all the tobacco imported into London, and they had therefore been compelled to hire additional accommodation.

The Treasury called for quarterly returns of the fees taken by the London Collector Outwards (the duke of Manchester's heir). The London jerquers were again censured for non-attendance. (Their prescribed hours of employment were from nine to three.) It was discovered that certain returns required from the indoor customs officials in 1788 had not been furnished (1790).

* Later Harrison's and St. Katherine's Wharves were granted sufferances for foreign goods, and the Carron Wharf for iron. Although the Hanse Leaguers had lost nearly all their old trade and political influence, the famous Steel Yard remained in their possession till well on into the nineteenth century. In 1853 the premises were sold for £72,000.

Orders were issued that no officer, except one of the solicitors, should quit his work to attend at the Treasury, without first acquainting the Board.*

The East India Company fell behind with their payments, and were ordered to deposit £15,000 per cargo on the duties in arrear.

The Board decided that too many tide-waiters per ship were allotted as watchmen, and reduced the numbers thus:

On ships with wine cargoes, from three tide-waiters to two.

On ships with tobacco cargoes, from five tide-waiters to four.

On short traders (Continental packets), from four tide-waiters to three.

On ships from Hamburg, from four tide-waiters to three.

On ships from the Levant, from four tide-waiters to three.

This alteration effected a saving of £2,480 per annum.

It is evident that the provisions of the Navigation Act were as charitably administered as of old. A cargo of cotton and mahogany imported from the United States, 'yet not the growth thereof,' was allowed to be entered and landed. Instructions were given that all similar cargoes might be privileged for a period, till the merchants became fully aware that such goods were prohibited.

It was enacted that from and after August 1, 1790, any subject of the United States might settle in Bermuda, Quebec, or Nova Scotia, and carry his effects and negroes thither in British ships free of duty, provided that the value of the effects did not exceed £50 for each white person and £2 for each negro.

Another Act directed that all foreign tobacco for home consumption should be duty-paid on the weight ascer-

* This appears to have been intended to suppress visits by the higher officials, who frequently pestered the Treasury with private schemes.

tained at delivery, and that none should set up a tobacco factory within five miles of the coast, except at 'a tobacco port.'

Additional excise duties were placed on foreign spirits, to be paid before landing, unless secured by bond.

An extra customs duty of 2s. 8d. per cwt. was levied on sugar. A separate appropriation was made of the moneys arising from this impost. The first year's produce was to go to the Consolidated Fund, and afterwards the proceeds were to be applied to paying the interest on a loan of £1,833,000. Thus the bad old system was revived.

Parliament repealed a number of Acts dealing with the duties and restrictions on corn. It also repealed Charles II.'s prohibition of forestalling and engrossing. The second clause of the new Act commenced: 'Whereas it will be for the Benefit of the People of this Kingdom that the Circulation and Trade of Corn should be free from all improper Restraint.'* The Act, by its 'Table A,' provided that wheat, when under 44s. a quarter, might be allowed a bounty of 5s. on exportation. Table B prohibited exportation when the price reached 46s. Table C specified the quantities of British corn that might be shipped from various ports and to various places.

The duty on foreign wheat was fixed at £1 4s. 3d. when the price was under 50s. a quarter. This was called 'the High Duty.' When wheat was at 50s. or under 54s. it was liable to a rate of 2s. 6d., 'the first Low Duty.' When at 54s. or over the rate was 6d., 'the second Low Duty.' But upon wheat from Ireland or the Plantations the High Duty was leviable only when the price was under 48s.; the first Low Duty when at 48s. or under 52s.; the second Low Duty when at 52s. or over. 'Regulating prices' were also specified for barley, oats, etc.

* This may have been brought about by Adam Smith's statement in 'The Wealth of Nations' that the restraint of engrossing was undesirable. Plain people who have read of the 'cornering' that afterwards took place may be disposed to question the accuracy of Adam Smith's judgment in this particular case.

Corn might be bonded on landing, and on delivery from warehouse for home consumption it was liable to the duty payable at time of such delivery, and the first Low Duty as well. A vessel laden with corn, and arriving at a port where the price was low and the High Duty in force, might depart with her cargo to another port where the price was higher and the duty lower. The maritime counties and chief ports were districted with regard to the proclamation of price, as below:

1. Kent, Essex, Sussex, and the City of London.
2. Suffolk and Cambridgeshire.
3. Norfolk.
4. Lincolnshire, and East and North Ridings of Yorkshire, including Hull.
5. Durham and Northumberland, including Berwick.
6. Cumberland and Westmoreland.
7. Lancashire and Cheshire.
8. The counties of Flint, Denbigh, Carnarvon, Merioneth, and Anglesea.
9. The counties of Cardigan, Pembroke, Carmarthen, and Glamorgan.
10. Gloucestershire, Somerset, and Monmouthshire.
11. Cornwall and Devon.
12. Dorset and Hants.
13. The counties of Fife, Kinross, Clackmannan, Stirling, Linlithgow, Haddington, Berwick, Roxburgh Selkirk, and Peebles.
14. The counties of Dumfries, Wigton, Ayr, and the Stewardry of Kircudbright.
15. The counties of Argyle, Dumbarton, Lanark, Renfrew, and Bute.
16. The counties of Caithness, Sutherland, Ross, Inverness, Cromarty, Nairn, Elgin, Banff, Aberdeen, Kincardine, Forfar, and Perth, with the Orkneys and Shetlands.

The prices regulating duty in District 1 were to be those quoted at the London Corn Exchange, Mark Lane. Every corn-factor had to make a weekly return to an appointed inspector, who then apprised the London collectors of customs. In Scotland the prices were to be fixed by juries convened by the sheriffs. Each jury was to consist of two freeholders, two farmers, and other 'reputable men.' No buyer of corn might sit as juryman.

'The Controller of the Great Customs of Wool and Leather,' whose office must have been a sinecure of long standing, was granted three months' leave, 'on account of derangement of his mind.'

Correspondence took place between the Board and the Treasury as to the Receiver-General's bond, and it was decided that the amount of security should at least equal the average weekly sum paid by him into the Exchequer, and that no one of his sureties should engage for more than £10,000. The 'average weekly sum paid into the Exchequer' was stated at £70,000.

The Customs 'Conscience-money' from 1771 to 1791 was £949, which included one sum of £400, one of £300, and one of £210, the balance being made up by petty contributions.

It had been the practice, when a subordinate official was found unworthy of further employment, to 'desire' his principal to dismiss him. The Receiver-General, being 'desired' to dismiss one of his clerks, took no notice of the message, and the Board called upon him for an explanation. He replied laconically that he had not been 'ordered.' The Board then *commanded* him to dismiss his underling, and provided that in future all directions to dismiss should be peremptorily worded.

In 1792 the allowance to 'The Lecturer of Barking Parish' was reinstituted. The Board paid the costs and damages incurred by certain officers of Bristol, who had been proceeded against in the public courts for searching a house without cause or warrant.

Certain moneys, which had been taken as fees in offices where the patents of the original holders had lapsed and not been regranted, were paid into the bank to the account of two of the Commissioners, pending further directions as to disposal.

The lands and effects of the deceased collector of St. Vincent were confiscated, on account of frauds previously committed by him. His widow made 'claim of dower,' and was granted £40 per annum 'as full compensation.'

The Receiver-General's right of fees was abolished, and he was granted a yearly salary of £1,500,* and an allowance of £480 for clerks and messengers. (In 1793 the 'allowance' was cancelled.)

One of the inspectors suggested that duty should be charged upon the calico used as wrappers for the bale goods imported by the East India Company. The Board concurred, and gave him a gratuity of £500.

Certain new wharf privileges were granted. Dundee Wharf, Wapping, received a sufferance to land coastwise goods. Lucas and Spencer's Wharf was made a legal place of discharge for ships employed in the whale fishery. A sufferance was granted to an alien, Mr. Moses Ancona. He was allowed to land marble of his own importing at Pedlar's Acre,† on condition that he paid a customs watchman to guard the goods.

In 1792 Parliament reduced the excise duty on candles by ½*d. a pound.*

It was enacted that the drawback on Plantation sugar, and the bounty payable on sugar refined from Plantation muscovado and exported, should cease when the price of imported raw sugar was over 60s. per cwt., exclusive of duty. This was to endure for a period, then the price annulling drawback was to be 55s. per cwt., again for a period, and then the annulling price was to be 50s. The Clerk of the Grocers' Company of London was to gazette the price of the imported raw article. Sugar and coffee from countries other than British possessions might be

* His fees amounted to about £1,000 a year.

† In Lambeth, near Westminster Bridge. The site was left to the parish of Lambeth in 1504 by a pedlar, on condition that the testator's effigy should be painted upon one of the windows of Lambeth Church.

warehoused for exportation free of duty, if carried in British ships. Thus Parliament undid the work of the simplifiers of tariffs.

An Act was passed relieving the coasting trade of Great Britain from the heavy expenses previously imposed by the regulations as to cockets, bonds, and stamp duties on the same (*vide* p. 363).

It was provided that the exportation of naval stores, such as pig-iron, bar-iron, hemp, pitch, tar, resin, turpentine, cordage, masts, yards, oakum, sheet-copper, etc., might be prohibited by royal proclamation or Order in Council whenever prohibition might seem necessary.

The exportation of wheat, wheat-flour, bread, and biscuit was forbidden for a period, and the king was empowered to prohibit the exportation of potatoes and of all kinds of corn, and to permit the importation of corn at the Low duties. Thus the recent Act regulating duty by price was for a time nullified.

The next Act was levelled against aliens. 'Whereas a great and unusual number of Persons have lately resorted to this Kingdom, and much Danger may arise to the Publick Tranquillity unless due Provision be made in respect thereof,' etc. Shipmasters were to furnish the Customs with particulars of all aliens carried, and the customs officers were to ascertain the aliens' names, occupations, etc., and to grant each alien a certificate if his record were satisfactory. The officers might detain arms, etc., brought by the strangers. The king might, by Order in Council, prevent all aliens other than merchants from landing in Great Britain. Each alien who was allowed to land received a passport signed by a chief magistrate. On reasonable suspicion warrants might be granted for the search of houses occupied by aliens. Ambassadors, and aliens not above fourteen years old, were exempt from this Act. If an undesirable alien were banished, and returned, he was liable to transportation. If, after undergoing his sentence, he made another attempt, he became liable to death without benefit of clergy.

Great Britain had declared war against her old enemy France, and many people believed that one of the chief reasons of quarrel was that the French revolutionists were bent upon the conquest of Europe and the suppression of all taxes. Yet one might assume that the English people, after a century's experience of the inseparableness of war and taxation, should have known better ; that they should have realized that no nation can even attempt to subjugate a continent unless it charges its own resources recklessly to provide the means ; and that if the tremendous effort succeeds, the result will certainly not be a total abolition of imposts.

The spirit of Parliament was soon made manifest. An Act was passed providing that any person who should supply, or assist in supplying, the French with arms, ammunition, naval stores, coal, iron, lead, copper, Bank of England notes, bullion, corn, or victuals, without royal licence for the same, should be 'deemed a traitor,' and suffer death.

Another Act provided that drawback might be allowed on wine shipped for the use of naval officers, up to a specified quantity per year, varying from six tuns in the case of an admiral to half a tun in the case of a lieutenant. (Most of the old admirals were sturdy drinkers, and fond of treating their subordinate officers ; still, 1,512 gallons a year was a liberal allowance.) It was provided that Plantation and American tobacco might be shipped duty-free for the use of naval seamen. After being warehoused at importation, the goods might be removed to Rochester, Portsmouth, or Plymouth, re-warehoused with the Customs, and then issued duty-free as provided.

Parliament still further complicated the Plantation Acts. But one of the numerous alterations need be quoted. It was provided that Plantation goods which had been imported into Ireland might afterwards be brought to Great Britain in British or Irish ships, if accompanied by a certificate.

It was also enacted that vessels condemned for smuggling might be sold for use as privateers.

The Board discovered that a person who had been sworn in as an established tide-waiter had been engaged for many years in 'practices detrimental to the Excise Revenue.' They dismissed him.

The Treasury authorized the Board to grant letters of protection against impressment to lightermen employed in conveying bountied or drawback goods for shipment, the document to be the same as granted to the sailors on board revenue cruisers.

The revenue lawyers withdrew from a prosecution for smuggling, the Crown costs being paid by the defendant. Then they apprised the seizing officers that they might continue the prosecution if they wished. Needless to state, the officers failed to profit by the permission.

The Treasury asked the Board to furnish a list of notorious smugglers who were in confinement or under prosecution, to the end that they might be excluded from the scope of a general pardon that was contemplated.

In 1794 the Collector Outwards was directed to obtain from shipmasters, when they reported their cargoes, an account of the places where their ships were moored, and to placard it for the information of merchants and officers. At this period the Thames near London Bridge was terribly crowded with vessels. The legal quays were overcharged with goods, and the Board were compelled to extend the quay privileges to many 'ordinary wharves.'

An additional excise duty, payable before landing of goods, was levied on foreign spirits. The previous additional duties, and the additional duties on sugar, were made perpetual. An additional duty was placed on foreign bricks.

The duties on foreign paper were repealed, and fresh duties levied *by weight,* instead of by ream as before. The duty on foreign-bound books was increased. It was provided that the Board might reward officers for seizing pirated books. Additional duties were placed upon foreign glass.

Fresh preventive regulations were added to the already formidable roll. It was enacted that any cutter, lugger, etc., belonging to the king's subjects, that was found, provided with arms and ammunition, within the limits of any port or four leagues of the coast, might be seized and made forfeitable, unless licensed by the Admiralty ; and that any rowing boat of a specified length, and having planks not of a specified thickness, should be similarly liable. The limits within which hoverers might be seized were redefined by a series of imaginary straight lines, cutting off sections of the indented coast, thus :

'A straight line from Walney Island to the Great Orme's Head.

'A straight line from Cromer to the Spurn Head.

'A straight line from the Mull of Galloway to the Point of Ayr in the Isle of Man,' etc.

British slate, stone, and marble, carried coastwise, were made liable to coastwise duties, and the duty on Guernsey granite was made *ad valorem*.

Cap. 68 of 1794 strengthened the Navigation Act.

In 1795 additional duties of excise were charged upon foreign wines, at the rate of £30 a tun on French and £20 on all other wines. Wines previously duty-paid, but found upon excise survey to be still in the hands of dealers, were liable to this impost. Additional excise duties were placed on foreign spirits. Soon after this additional excise duties were placed on tea, at the rate of 7½ per cent. of the gross prices obtained at the East India Company's sales, and other imposts upon cocoa and coffee. Additional customs duties were put upon oranges, raisins, waste silk, and various kinds of wood, and the export duties on coal and rock-salt were increased.

During this year and the next there were several applications by customs officers for permission to absent themselves from duty in order to join the various fencible regiments. A tide-surveyor went to the Bedfordshire

Militia. A tide-waiter received six months' leave at the request of the colonel of the West London Militia, the colonel stating that he required the tide-waiter to assist in 'forming the regiment.' A landing-waiter was allowed by Treasury Order twelve months' leave, to act as adjutant of the Lancashire Militia. An acting patent searcher was granted leave, 'to attend his military duty.' An established waterman was allowed six months' leave, in order that he might qualify as a pilot, pilots being urgently required 'for the public service.'

The regulations as to the breaking-up of vessels condemned for smuggling were amplified. Read in their new form, they convey a sensation of ferocious solemnity. The ballast, masts, pumps, and bulk-heads were to be taken out, the decks ripped fore and aft, the beams sawn asunder, the bottom planks ripped off, the keels cut into four pieces, and the stern-posts into three. Boats condemned were to be cut through the thwarts, the hulls sawn into four parts athwartships, and the stems and sterns into two.

The Customs Housekeeper complained to the Treasury of the high price of provisions, and requested an increase in her allowance. The Treasury referred the request to the Board, stating that they were not prepared to admit that the rise in the price of provisions was other than temporary, yet if the Board wished it the allowance might be made. The Board allowed £100 a year extra, to be expended in paying increased wages to the servants.

A customs doorkeeper behaved unbecomingly to one of the Commissioners, and was suspended. The Secretary was told to 'exhort the doorkeepers and messengers, in the most solemn manner, to observe proper behaviour in their several stations.'

Sir Jamieson W. Gordon and a Mr. Charlton had been joint patent collectors of Newcastle-on-Tyne. Mr. Charlton died, and his partner made application to be allowed to receive the emoluments of the two situations. This cool proposal was negatived.

Earl Spencer and Mr. Thomas Grenville, who had been on a mission from the king to the emperor of Germany, were allowed on return to bring a butt of wine each duty-free. The Countess of Mornington was allowed a number of patterns of French dresses duty-free, giving security to return them abroad within three months.

The river inspector was ordered to repair to the Downs, and keep a watch upon the West India fleet, as soon as news reached London that the ships had been sighted. The Board issued fresh orders as to the surveillance of East Indiamen, stating that they were resolved to dismiss any watchman or officer who, 'whilst guarding the gangway, neglected to search any person who might leave the ship.' The watchmen put to guard East Indiamen were furnished with great-coats, lanthorns, and *rattles*.

It appears that the Board had been asked to assist in drawing up a scheme for improving the port of London. The Thames at this time was often dreadfully crowded, especially when any of the merchant fleets arrived. Plunder and smuggling were rampant, and the need of better accommodation for shipping was urged by all classes of the water-side community, except the hardy rogues who profited by the existing confusion.

Extra duties of excise were laid on imported tobacco, being 4d. a pound extra on Irish, Plantation, and American goods, and 1s. a pound on other tobaccos. It was provided that tobacco might be shipped from warehouse duty-free, for use of soldiers on board transports.

The drawbacks and outward bounties on sugar were reduced.

A ludicrous statute appeared in 1796: 'Whereas it is expedient for the more effectual preserving and encouraging of the manufacture of blacklead melting-pots in this country to reduce the duty payable on the importation of foreign blacklead,' etc. The Act reduced the duty in question to 1s. a cwt. It almost seems as though Parliament imagined that from the date of enactment blacklead melting-pots would be turned out as plentifully as horse-nails, and that if afterwards the high rate on blacklead were re-enforced every maker of melting-pots would soon be begging by the wayside.

The clauses of the Consolidating Act of 1787 that dealt with the landing of foreign goods were recited, and the statement that all foreign goods landed otherwise than in the presence of the proper officer of customs were forfeitable was reaffirmed. It appears that the overcrowding of the legal quays was partly due to the slackness of officers, who had neglected to enforce their prerogative of placing in the King's Warehouse all foreign wine not entered within twenty days after report.

The provisions of Charles II.'s Butter Act were recited and strengthened.

Parliament brought out a string of new imposts, levying additional customs duties upon wine, at the rate of £30 a tun on French and £20 on other wines, and additional duties on sugar (2s. 6d. a cwt. extra on Plantation and East India sugars, 5s. on others). The extra duty on Plantation sugar might be drawn back if the goods were exported. Loaf sugar refined from Plantation muscovado and then exported was granted an additional drawback of 4s. per cwt., and other sugar refined from Plantation muscovado an additional drawback of 2s. 6d. An impost of 10 per cent. upon the produce of all customs duties was applied to brimstone, hemp, unwrought iron, and staves, imported from Europe, and a similar impost of 5 per cent. to all other foreign goods.*

Certain provisions towards commercial reciprocity between Great Britain and the United States were expressed in an Act of 1797, being principally as below:

1. American goods in American ships were to be liable only to such British duties as applied to other merchandise imported in British ships.

2. American raw produce imported in American or British ships was liable only to such British duties as

* The excise tax on dogs appeared about this time.

applied to the raw produce of British possessions imported in British ships.

3. American leaf tobacco imported in American or British ships was liable only to the duties on leaf tobacco from the British Plantations, plus 1s. 6d. per 100 pounds.

4. The same British bounties were to be paid on goods exported to the United States as were paid on similar goods exported to the British Plantations.

5. As British ships trading in the United States paid heavier American tonnage dues than American ships did, it was provided that such American ships as traded in Great Britain should pay tonnage dues equal to the excess. If such tonnage dues on an American ship in Great Britain were withheld more than three months after her arrival, the British Customs might seize and sell the ship, deduct from the proceeds the tonnage dues and the expenses of detention, and give the residue to the shipowner.

6. American vessels might trade freely with British possessions in the East Indies, on condition that they carried all goods shipped in the East Indies *direct* to the United States.

After all this toil towards equalization, the Americans continued to impose certain heavy duties on European and Asiatic goods taken to the United States by British ships. Therefore, and notwithstanding the provisions expressed above under 1, 2, and 3, an impost of about 10 per cent. was laid upon American goods brought into Great Britain by American ships. This contradictory provision was intended to endure till the Americans repealed their extra duties upon British-carried goods.

The Act contained an extradition clause, providing that the respective Governments should surrender refugees charged with murder or forgery.

Another Act provided that the captains of privateers should keep journals, and produce them at the request of any collector of customs, or of any master of a ship of war or revenue cruiser. A false entry in a journal was punishable with a fine of £500, and this harsh penalty attended various infractions. The Act was necessary, yet it may have had little restraining effect upon the redoubtable rogues who went a-privateering.

An additional duty of 3d. a pound was placed on warehoused pepper, and made payable when the goods were delivered. A second impost was levied upon the proceeds of customs duties—import, export, and coastwise—not to apply to tea, sugar, wine, tobacco, olive oil, and calico, or to the proceeds of the previous imposts of 10 and 5 per cent.

It will be apparent that the taxes had been largely augmented since the issue of the Consolidating Act, and that the tariff was sliding into the toils of complication. It should be stated that some little attempt had been made towards ease in certain remote branches of revenue ; for instance, lime, limestone, and *manure* had been granted exemption from the coastwise regulations, and Plantation arrowroot, linseed-cake, and rape-cake, imported in British ships, had been made duty-free.

The vessels of all friendly nations were empowered to trade in the British East Indies, subject to the approval of the East India Company's directors.

The customs staff of the port of Liverpool was increased. The Treasury directed the Board to reward the customs staff of Milford and Pembroke, and the masters and mariners of the revenue cruisers stationed there, for vigilance and zeal 'in the defence of their country.' A collector, a controller, and two landing-waiters were appointed at the newly acquired colony of Demerara. The collector received £70 a year as salary, the controller £50, and the landing-waiters £35 each.

Certain privileges with regard to customs examination were extended to manuscript of the late Sir William Jones, Orientalist, on its arrival in England from Bengal. Sir Gilbert Elliott, late viceroy of Corsica, was allowed to import a tun of port and a tun of sherry duty-free.

A tide-surveyor stationed at Portsmouth was desirous

of producing a scheme for preventing the embezzlement of naval stores. The Board gave him permission to employ his spare time in this pursuit, 'under the supervision of the Admiralty.'

In 1798 a wine debenture was laid before the Board, signed by a person *not known to the Commissioners.* The Board censured the Examiner of wine duties.

A collector and controller were appointed at Montreal. The collector's salary was £80 ; the controller's £70.

During this year the port of London was crowded with vessels from the West Indies, loaded principally with rum and coffee. The Board allowed these vessels ten days beyond the usual time allotted for discharge.

It was enacted that vessels liable to quarantine should hoist quarantine signals on meeting other vessels at sea, or on coming within four leagues of a British coast. It was also directed that foreign glass should be forfeited unless imported in packages weighing not less than 5 cwt., and stamped on the outside with the word 'Glass.' Foreign glass was to be specially reported.

An additional duty was levied on foreign salt.

The Aliens Act was amended. No alien might leave the kingdom unless he carried a passport signed by a Secretary of State. The passport was to be produced to the Customs at port of departure. After it had been signed by the collector, the bearer had to produce it to the captain of the ship in which he was about to embark.

Exportation of British spirits to the Isle of Man was prohibited, and the Board of Customs were empowered to grant licences for the importation into Douglas of foreign brandy 'from any place,' at a duty of 3s. per gallon, up to an amount not exceeding 10,000 gallons per year. The quantity of tobacco previously allowed to be imported into the island had been found insufficient, and it was provided that British ships licensed by the Board of Customs might carry tobacco thither, from Great Britain, to the amount of 60,000 pounds per year, at a duty of 6d. per pound, and wine 'from any place' to a yearly quantity of 70 tuns, the wine being liable to the Manx duties and an added £8 a tun. The Board might also license Manxmen to import live sheep from Great Britain to the number of 100 per year. Each importer of sheep was to announce his intention a month beforehand. No cloth or cotton yarn were to pass into the island except from Great Britain. Cotton yarn or cloth produced in the island were to be duty-free in Great Britain. The Treasury might under special circumstances authorize the Board of Customs to license larger quantities of goods than those specified. The conditions of the above Act were to endure until 1801.

That peculiar impost, the Convoy duty, was instituted during 1798. No vessel was to sail from Great Britain without convoy, under penalty of £1,000. If a vessel, sailing under convoy, were wilfully navigated so as to separate, her master's share of insurance was to be void. Coasting vessels, ships trading to Ireland, ships licensed by the Admiralty, ships not registered, and the vessels of the East India and Hudson's Bay Companies, were exempt. To recompense the Government for its unwelcome protection, small duties were levied on certain imports and exports, in some cases by weight, in others by value, and trading ships were made liable to tonnage duties, varying from 6d. per ton on vessels trading with Ireland to 3s. per ton on vessels trading with the East Indies.

Later it was enacted that any of the king's subjects who during the continuance of the war visited France, or any place under French occupation, or corresponded with the French Government or anyone in France, should be liable to death without benefit of clergy, unless they held licence from the king thus to travel or correspond. This made the smuggler's vocation extremely perilous, yet smuggling prevailed the more.

Cap. 86 of 1798 caused commotion in the Customs. It stated that certain offices, usually granted by letters patent, and often executed by deputies appointed by the patentees, had become unnecessary; that such as were vacant should at once be abolished; and that such as were occupied should cease when they became vacant. The officials affected were the Inspector of Prosecutions, the Inspector of the books of the Patent, the Surveyor-General of the Customs and Subsidies of the port of London, the Patent Customers at the outports, and the Keeper of the Books and Entries for the port of London.

Other offices were deemed partly useful, with a stipulation that the Board might by permission of the Treasury provide otherwise for their occupation, or combine two or more of them into one. These were the offices held by the Registrar-General of trading Ships, the Inspector of the outport collectors' accounts and vouchers, the Controller of the Customs in London, the Collector of the Subsidy of Tonnage and Poundage in London, an official rejoicing in the complicated title of Collector of Customs of Tonnage and Poundage outward in London and Keeper of the Cocket Seal, and another known as the Chief Patent Searcher of the Customs in London; together with the controllers at all outports, the patent searchers at outports, two patent searchers at Gravesend, five under-searchers in London, nineteen king's waiters in London, and four king's waiters in Bristol.

It was further provided that certain offices, when vacated, should be granted no more, unless at pleasure of the Board and the Treasury; that if it were decided to refill them the Board might fix the salaries appertaining, but that whenever one was totally abolished the clerks and deputies affected might receive compensation. Whenever one of the abolished offices was revived, the Board were to apprise Parliament, stating reasons for the revival. So far as we have been able to trace, none of them was revived, so that it may be taken that early in the nineteenth century the crowded quays, and the corridors of the Custom-house, were illuminated no longer by the occasional presence of the following stately figures:

The Receiver for Sales of Condemned Goods, the Receiver of the King's share of fines and forfeitures from outports, the Controller of the same, the Accountant of petty receipts, the Customer of Cloth and Petty Custom in London, the Controller of Pretermitted Customs, and the Examiners of outport books. Most melancholy to relate, the three venerable gentlemen mentioned below also disappeared, and the golden links that had connected the department with hoary Eld were shattered for ever.

The Collector of Aliens' Custom in London.

The Collector of Customs of Hides, Woolfells, Lead, and Tin, and Keeper of the Cocket Seal to that office belonging.

The Controller of Customs of Hides, Woolfells, Wool, Lead, and Tin, and of the Subsidy of Three Shillings for every Dolium, and of Twelvepence for every Pound in the Port of London.

(It is likely that for many years no merchant had found it necessary to approach the last-named Illustrious One by letter, which was fortunate, paper being dear.)

The office of Collector Outward in London had been granted in 1782 to the duke of Manchester. The patent had not been perfected, yet the Act continued the emoluments of the office to the duke's sons as though such perfecting had taken place. It was provided that the office should be maintained till the informal lease expired; the Board to appoint persons to execute 'the necessary duties.' When the lease expired, the office was to be abolished. Therefore it appears—

1. That the office was *unnecessary*.

2. That it was granted, as a lucrative sinecure, to wealthy nobles.

3. That the grant was informal.

4. That the expensive grant was continued despite the informality.

5. That, in order to cloak the proceeding, deputies were to be maintained to perform 'the necessary duties.' Who paid the deputies?

The salt duties were repealed, and new duties levied.

The Scottish excise on salt was less than the English, and when Scottish salt came into England the extra English duty had to be paid. Exported home-made salt was allowed a drawback of the excise duty. Bounty at varying rates was allowed on 'exported dried cod, ling, or hake, in length 14 inches from the bone in the fin to the third joint in the tail,' on the same fish 'wet,' on salmon, white herrings, red herrings, 'clean shotten' red herrings, dried sprats, pilchards, and beef or pork cured with duty-paid salt. The importation of salt from Ireland, the Channel Islands, and the Isle of Man, was prohibited.

In 1799 new duties were imposed on the East India Company's goods. These were peculiarly arranged. A slight *ad valorem* duty was levied on the goods at import, payable when they were warehoused, but the Company might postpone payment by entering into bond. Such goods as were afterwards exported had to bear the convoy duties on shipment. Goods sold for home consumption were liable on sale to the convoy duties, and to new duties payable by purchasers, the said new duties vastly exceeding those previously levied. Below are given a few of the alterations :

	Previous Duties. Per Cent.			*The New Duties.* Per Cent.		
	£	*s.*	*d.*	£	*s.*	*d.*
Arrangoes, on sale price ..	31	13	4	53	9	1
Chinaware	47	10	0	109	8	6
Cotton manufactures ..	50	0	0	122	4	5
Cowries	31	13	4	53	9	1
Drugs, manufactured ..	40	0	0	78	11	5
,, unmanufactured ..	31	0	0	51	14	10
Japanned ware	49	10	0	119	10	9

This Act was stated to be in encouragement of East Indian trade.

Imposts were levied on imported sugar, and the drawbacks and bounties on exported sugar reduced. The export duty on coffee was increased.

Another Act increased the bounty on exported pilchards.

American goods brought by the ships of nations in amity with Great Britain were allowed to be warehoused, and afterwards exported free of convoy duty.

It was provided that Matthew Boulton, a Staffordshire engineer, might export machinery for erecting a Mint at St. Petersburg, and send English workmen to erect the same, notwithstanding the previous Acts forbidding the exportation of labour-saving machinery and the foreign employment of British artificers.

It was provided that Levant goods might be admitted, by Order in Council, even if brought in ships without clean bills of health. The convoy duty on British goods exported to the Levant was reduced.

The crowded condition of the river Thames and the legal quays had been alluded to in an Act of 1795. Cap. 69 of 1799 (local) commenced: 'Whereas considerable disadvantages to the trade of the Port of London arise from the circuitous course of the river Thames round the tract of land called the Isle of Dogs,' etc. It provided that a canal might be cut from Blackwall to Limehouse Hole, under control of the Common Council of London. The moorings in the Thames from London Bridge to Bugsby's Hole, previously leased to Lord Gwydyr, were also to pass under control of the Common Council, the holder being compensated. The Council were to supply new moorings, under supervision of the Trinity House.

The second part commenced: 'Whereas the ships in the West India trade frequently arrive in large fleets, and occasion great crowding, Confusion, and damage, and their Cargoes, being carried in lighters to the legal quays, cause upon the said quays great obstruction, and are exposed to pilfering,' etc. It proceeded that certain persons whose names were specified had agreed to form a company, with a capital of £500,000, to be called 'The West India Docks Company,' and to construct docks. After completion of the docks, dividends were not to exceed 10 per cent. The Trinity House were to approve the Dock-Masters, and were also to approve a Harbour-Master for the port of London. For twenty-one years all goods coming direct from the West Indies were to be landed in the new docks. Tobacco might be unshipped at the dock quays, and removed thence, without examination, to the King's Tobacco Warehouse. The Board of Customs, if satisfied at any time that the docks were full of shipping, might allow West Indiamen to discharge at the legal quays on the riverside. Outward-bound West Indiamen were to be loaded either in the docks, or in the river below the Blackwall entrance to the Canal.

All vessels docked were to be expeditiously unloaded, and then, if not intended to be loaded at once, were to be removed to the river. In recompense of the concession to the public convenience, the king was allowed certain tonnage dues on all ships coming to the port. These dues were to be paid in at the Custom-house. It was provided that the Treasury might advance money out of the Consolidated Fund to purchase land as site for the docks, and the residue of the Crown tonnage dues, after the expense of the river moorings and the salary of the Harbour-Master had been defrayed, was to be applied to repaying the moneys thus advanced by the Treasury. The dock rates were specified. The Common Council of London were empowered to charge transit dues for vessels passing through the Canal. The customs officers were empowered not to allow vessels concerned to enter inwards, till such dock or transit dues had been paid.*

* Soon afterwards an Act was passed authorizing the construction of a tunnel, wide enough for the passage of cattle and carriages, under the Thames, from Gravesend to Tilbury. This scheme proved abortive. The estimated cost was only £50,000! The stoppage of the works appears to have been due to an inrush of water and a mysterious fire, which destroyed the steam-engine and woodwork connected with the undertaking. The fire was thought to have been intentionally ignited, the blame being by some cast upon the authors of the undertaking, by others upon the Gravesend watermen.

In 1800 an additional excise duty at the usual rates was placed on foreign spirits. The total excise duties on foreign spirits after the passing of this Act were :

	Per Gallon. £ s. d.		*Per Gallon.* £ s. d.
Single spirits from the Plantations ..	0 6 11	Double spirits from the Plantations ..	0 13 4
All other single spirits ..	0 8 5	All other double spirits ..	0 16 5

The customs duty was payable as well.

At the end of the preceding chapter was furnished an account of the general condition of the Customs department immediately prior to the passing of the Consolidation Act of 1787. As no further information in detail will be submitted with regard to the English Customs in this volume, it may be judicious, at this stage, to furnish another general review.

The benefits conferred by the Consolidation Act were vast, and the commerce of the country increased in consequence. The average annual net produce of the Customs, from 1789 to 1796 inclusive, was about £4,150,000. The cost of collection, compared with the *gross* receipts, was about 6¾ per cent.

The gross produce of 1796, after being decreased by a charge of £1,457,352 for drawbacks, allowances, bounties, etc., and nearly £400,000 for 'charges of management,' yielded a 'net produce' of over £4,500,000, the highest return made up to that date. Out of this 'net' nearly £40,000 was devoted to certain Scottish purposes, over £850,000 to 'bounties for encouraging national objects,' over £26,000 to bounties for naval seamen, and the residue, amounting to £3,612,676, was paid into the Exchequer. It should be mentioned that the return included the Scottish customs, but the Scottish contributions were still remarkably small. For instance, in 1782 the gross produce of English and Scottish customs had been in the proportions of about 15 to 1. In 1796 the proportions were as below:

England and Wales:	gross produce,	£6,118,391.
Scotland:	,, ,,	263,511.

=say 23 to 1.

The value of English imports had increased from £11,650,000 in 1783 to £21,000,000 in 1796. Exports had increased in value from £13,900,000 to over £29,000,000.

There were about 1,200 articles rated for duty—900 by rate, the rest *ad valorem*. The amount raised on 1,040 of the 1,200 articles taxed failed to realize a total of £100,000 a year. Several new special branches had been added since 1787, and experts had already begun to talk of a reconsolidation. Certain reforms had been effected in the practice of the department. The Receiver-General in London had been directed to make up his accounts every Saturday, and to pay the moneys into the Exchequer every Wednesday. Thus he was no longer able to retain large sums of public money, nor were the various London collectors able to bank to their own accounts the outstanding proceeds of customs duties. But it appears that the Receiver-General at Edinburgh still neglected to forward his remittances promptly, and sometimes kept back large sums, amounting to more than a quarter of the gross annual produce of the Scottish Customs.*

Many abuses remained. The Plantation balances had not yet been passed in the Exchequer. Though many of the patent offices had been abolished, the idiotic and expensive practice of issuing port-books was still pursued.

* A Committee of Finance, that sat during the concluding years of the century, made a startling pronouncement upon the tactics of this official. 'The compensation,' said they, 'which the Scottish Receiver-General may be entitled to ought to be by salary, not by profit derived from the use of the public money.' It appears that Mr. John Campbell thought nothing of retaining for long periods sums amounting to £50,000 or more, though he gave security for but £25,000. The Committee recommended that an effective officer should be put to fill the post, at about half Mr. Campbell's emoluments.

It had been recommended by Committees of inquiry that the Prisage, Butlerage, and Duty on Coals should be taken from the grantees and re-vested in the Crown, and the Board of Customs had supported the recommendation, but the reform had not been effected. The Auditors of Imprest still dealt with the Customs Annual Accounts, but it is apparent, from a scrutiny of the documents, that the auditing had become effective.

Selected Commissioners of Customs had visited the outports, and noted the evil influence of the customs charges upon coastwise traffic, the disastrous results of a system that entailed expensive bonds and sufferances upon almost every incident of mercantile intercourse betwixt creek and creek. Reform had been effected, and relief afforded to the quaint and homely coastwise trade.

Forty-six useless and expensive offices had been abolished, and many others would lapse on the death of holders. The ideas that the method of bonding duties should be amplified, that fees and gratuities should be done away with, that the system of appointment by patent should be limited, and that effective officers should be promoted by seniority, were fast coming into favour. But the preposterously brief 'clerical hours' and the huge list of holidays endured.

Many of the revenue cruisers were still run 'on contract.'

Although forty-six offices had 'fallen in,' and many others had been abolished by the Treasury and the Board, the staff had increased in numbers on account of the great increase of commerce.

Some historians seem to have been of opinion, with regard to the tremendous naval, military, and disbursive efforts of the British people at this period, that 'all these things had to be.' Though the framers of statutes erred occasionally, their intentions may have been laudable and patriotic, for every care was taken that British ships were manned by British mariners, and it is certain that agriculture was not despised, as it came to be in mid-Victorian days. The older legislators longed to make Britain supreme in trade, yet strove, as far as their abilities allowed, to enable her to grow sufficient corn to feed her people for a space if her fleet failed to protect her.

Once more across the Border. It appears from the Montrose records that on May 3, 1787, the Commissioners of Customs at Edinburgh had to blame both themselves and the Montrose officers for failing to reward certain soldiers of the 7th Regiment of Foot, who had assisted in making seizures. The Scottish Board rectified matters by allowing the soldiers a sum out of the king's share, and the Montrose officers had to disburse a like sum out of their own receipts.

The Board also blamed the collector for not seeing that the reports of foreign ships were properly made out. Manifests had reached them in which the amounts of goods were stated in figures instead of words, and the cargoes described as consisting of packages, 'contents unknown.'

On May 9, 1787, the Board forwarded copies of the momentous 'Consolidating Act' and the Tables appertaining, and blandly yet curtly threw all responsibilities of administration upon the collector and controller. 'We order you carefully to consider these, to the end that you may in every respect comply with the directions therein contained, as no excuse will be received for your not doing so.'

An excise officer made a seizure of 1,125 pounds tobacco, and 2,446 pounds tobacco stalks. He was awarded 3d. a pound on the tobacco, and 1d. a pound on the stalks, with a sum for expenses—in all £26 11s. 1d.

Later the Board sent certain instructions as to the Consolidating Act. Goods upon which the duties were reduced by the Act, carried in ships arriving before

May 10, 1787, were to be charged with the old duties, and the Board would afterwards return the difference. (This would apply to few except French goods. No instructions were given as to how other goods thus brought were to be dealt with; but no doubt they would be liable to the increased duties.)

The collector of Dumfries had gone astray in dealing with Scottish salt removed to England. The inland duty on Scottish salt was less than on English, and such salt when removed across the Border had to pay the difference between the two duties. He of Dumfries had left it to the English officers to collect the difference on arrival of the goods, whereas he should have taken it before the goods left Scotland. The Board apprised the Montrose officers.

On June 28 the Board sent a copy of a letter received from the Treasury. Scottish officers of customs had been charging their countrymen illegally. They had taken certain coastwise fees which had lapsed of yore; they had charged fees for dealing with parcels of goods of less than £5 value, and doubled the legal fees on shipments of coal. The Board ordered these malpractices to be discontinued on pain of instant dismissal, irrespective of rank of offender. A copy of the order was to be displayed at the Custom-house, and the officers were to sign it, 'that they may not pretend ignorance.'

On July 12 word was sent that the collector of Aberdeen had allowed a ship from Leghorn to discharge her cargo without performing quarantine. The Montrose officers were warned not to transgress thus. 'Only the fidelity and general good behaviour of the collector and controller of Aberdeen saved them from being dismissed. This will avail no officer in future.'

The London Board apprised their Edinburgh colleagues of a recent decision by the Attorney-General as to the conditions under which a British-born person might become an American citizen. 'Very difficult questions,' quoth the lawyer, 'may arise in consequence of the independence of America, but if I understand the present question it is whether a man born in Great Britain, and not resident in America at the time of grant of her independence, can make himself a subject of America. I am of opinion that he cannot. The man is a British subject, and may not legally command an American vessel in a British port.'

A startling exposure of official slackness occurred at Ferryden. To convey an accurate idea of the matter reference must be made to the regulations dealing with the lading and unlading of coastwise coal. All such coal was supposed to be accurately measured at shipment, and the quantity thus ascertained was reported at place of discharge. The duty was paid in a lump sum, and then the coal was measured out. If it proved to be less than the quantity paid on, there was no remission of duty, it being assumed that the master had landed part of the coal during transit, but if it proved to be more, a ' post entry ' had to be passed for the quantity in excess, and the extra duty made good.

There was a brisk trade in coal between Sunderland and Ferryden. At Sunderland the coal was measured in per Newcastle chalder, but at Ferryden it was measured out per Winchester chalder, and it must be borne in mind that the Newcastle chalder was almost twice as large as the Winchester measure. It appears that the Sunderland skippers merely reported so many ' chalders,' without specifying the kind of chalder used. It follows that each cargo should have measured out almost twice the quantity reported and duty-paid, and that in each case a post entry should have been passed for a sum almost equal to the duty originally deposited. Strange to tell, the years had flown by, and colliers a-many had come and gone, yet no post entries had been furnished. The customs tidesmen at Ferryden acted as coal-meters, and the landing-waiters were supposed to supervise them, and to tally the measures in the official books. When a cargo was discharged, the account was made up, and the books went to the collector at Montrose. He checked the records, initialled the duty accounts, and closed each transaction. How came it that the cargoes invariably turned out according to transire, when the great chalder was used at shipment, and the small one at discharge ?

The answer is that at Ferryden the coals were merely measured *on paper*. The landing-waiters winked at the tidesmen's misdeeds, and cooked their own accounts. The Sunderland skippers said nothing, and thus matters had proceeded for years and years, the Sunderland trade thriving, and Ferryden gradually increasing in importance as a place for the landing of English coal. It is scarcely probable that the officers were bribed. Coal-measuring is dirty work, and no doubt it was mere consideration of personal convenience that led to the practice of accepting the reported quantity as correct. The Ferryden officers did not know that the great chalder was in use at Sunderland, and the Sunderland skippers were not the men to enlighten them.

One day a new tidesman, named David Fettie, was appointed to the duty. He insisted on actually measuring the coals, and a huge post entry had to be called for. The same thing occurred with the next cargo measured by him, and the Montrose collector at once communicated with the Sunderland customs officers. Then the entire business was laid bare, and the collector reported matters to the Commissioners at Edinburgh, who sent back a demand for the last few years' coal-books, and it is conceivable that when they arrived the Commissioners scanned them dubiously, noting the extreme symmetry of the tallies, and the absence of grimy finger-marks. The further inquiry went, the worse did matters appear. But it seems that the magnitude of the considerations involved stayed the hand of Authority. The Board censured the tidesmen and landing-waiters, and gave the collector and controller weighty warning. The letters conveying the censure occupied many pages, therefore they may not be reproduced, yet are well worth reading, one bears some evidence of having been composed by the great political economist who was at that time a member of the Scottish Board. They were solemn productions, yet coloured by one humorous passage, levelled at the landing-waiters, who had stated in defence that they were kept too busily occupied with the foreign trade to be able to apply themselves to supervising the discharge of coal cargoes. But the Board had observed that though the landing-waiters had not had time to attend, they had collected the fees incidental. And therefore they adjured them, while the foreign trade remained brisk, to abandon the coal-measuring fees in favour of people like David Fettie.

Information was sent from Edinburgh of a Pittenweem sloop which had gone to Flushing, and been sold there to a smuggling syndicate. The command of the sloop had then been granted to a foreigner, and her original captain had thought it worth while to ship in her as an ordinary seaman. She took in a cargo of brandy, and ran the greater part of it at Tweedmouth, but was driven off by a gale before she could complete discharge. Then she returned to Flushing. During the voyage she was challenged by a revenue cruiser, and made answer that she was from Hull with timber. The cruiser thereupon let her pass. Who sent this information? It must have been some one who took part in the run.

A most extravagantly worded letter reached the Scottish Board, accusing the collector's clerk at Montrose of illegal connivance. It commenced, 'In the course of my nocturnal perambulations I observed a piece of business which I was somewhat surprised at,' and went on to state that the collector's clerk deliberately sent the customs boat on a wild-goose chase, and then with two boatmen assisted certain friends of his to run a large quantity of contraband goods. 'Many such things happen. The officers seldom make seizures, and then but small ones, and from people not in their confidence. More villainy is carried on and contrived by that clerk and his adherents than by all the revenue officers in Scotland.'

The Board appear to have attached little importance to this, thinking it likely that the letter was from some pompous scoundrel desirous of stepping into the clerk's shoes. It was signed 'An Observator.'

During 1788 many seizures of goods concealed on board regular traders were made at various ports, and the Board directed that shipmasters should be warned that in all such cases proceedings would be taken to condemn the ships as well as the goods. 'Hitherto,' said the Board in confidence to their subordinates, 'we have refrained from doing so, thinking that the concealments may have been encouraged by the improper lenity, negligence, or connivance of officers.'

The seizures at Montrose during one quarter reached the following amounts:

1,643 pounds tobacco, and 1,122 pounds tobacco stalks, captured by Customs.

1,605 pounds tobacco, and 1,099 pounds tobacco stalks, captured by Excise.

John Watt, customs boatman at Montrose, attempted to seize certain carts conveying tobacco across 'the Links,' and the smugglers treated him to a pistol-shot at short range. Later the Board granted payment of a doctor's bill, amounting to £8 19s. 6d., for 'extracting a Bullet from the Belly' of the said unlucky John, the doctor protesting that he had made the bill 'as reasonable as possible.'

It was a Scottish revenue practice to pay drawbacks and bounties to agents as well as principals. The Board directed the Scottish collectors to conform to the English practice of paying the allowances to principals only. Later, at the advice of the Lord Advocate, and application of the Glasgow merchants, they allowed the old system to continue, with certain qualifications.

The officers at Montrose made a curious seizure of unreported goods, the parcel consisting of a few dried tongues, a piece of salt beef, a ham, and a pot of pickled eels. The Board allowed the ham and tongues to be delivered on payment of duty. The beef and eels were compounded for by payment of 5s. 6d. per £1 value.

The amount of tobacco seized during the quarter ending April, 1789, was as follows:

Customs: 8,359 pounds tobacco, and 2,187 pounds tobacco-stalks.

Excise: 2,607 pounds tobacco.

The Board issued instructions to amend the oath used by manufacturers who desired to remove tobacco 'from warehouse to mill,' it being thought that the terms of the oath in use were not sufficiently solemn. The words, 'as he shall answer to God,' were therefore interpolated.

It having been discovered that some of the Scottish officers, on exchanging or resigning offices in favour of others, received large sums of money for the concession, the Board directed that all parties to such transactions should make oath, as in England, that no money had passed between them.

In 1790 an order was issued by the Privy Council authorizing the capture of all 'straggling seamen' fit to serve in the navy. Sir George Holme, 'regulator of the Impress,' requested the Scottish Board to order the captains of revenue cruisers to detain the crews of all smuggling vessels fallen in with, and communicate with the head Impress officer at Leith, who would then take steps to secure the culprits for his Majesty's service.

The collector sent to Edinburgh his yearly 'Account of Ages and Capacities' (a return specifying the age, official attainments, and private character of each officer employed under him). In this he gently insinuated that certain tidesmen, including the two who for years had so unsuccessfully checked the output of coal at Ferryden, had a habit of crooking the elbow overmuch. In return he received a sharp rap o' the knuckles. The Board commented upon his statement that he reported principally from hearsay, and told him it was his business to see all the port tidesmen every day, and those at the creeks frequently, 'so as to be able to report their real behaviour.'

He was to caution the tidesmen concerned that unless they refrained in future they would be dismissed, and in his next report to state whether the land-surveyors, landing-waiters, and coast-waiters were 'sober men.'

The captain of a Greenland trader back from the whale fishery claimed the usual voyage bounty, but the Board refused to allow it, as he had not carried the prescribed complement of 'green men.'

Mariners of Greenland ships were exempt from press, and collectors had power to grant them 'certificates of protection.' Tidings reached Edinburgh that the certificates were often granted to others for a pecuniary consideration, and the Board called for a return of all documents of protection previously issued.

Two landing-waiters at Port Glasgow had made it a practice to underweigh sugar. An invoice of two cargoes thus improperly weighed came into the possession of an officer at Greenock, who sent it to the Glasgow collector. The collector reported the matter to the Board, but his report was diffident in tone, and absurdly partial in defence of the offenders. The Board sent a Mr. Osborn to investigate, and so many and remarkable were his discoveries that the Board dismissed the two landing-waiters, and censured the rest of the staff, being particularly severe upon the controller. A full report of the case, with the Commissioners' remarks, was sent to all the Scottish ports.

If a case of the kind occurred in modern days, the port concerned would be provided with a completely new staff. But in 1790 appointments were usually the result of aristocratic recommendation, and it was a risky proceeding to cancel them. This may account for the leniency shown, and for the lengthy report, which filled many pages of the Montrose letter-book, and in elegant language bewailed the condition of affairs. Such gentle yet cutting censure, such stately moralizing, such impressive admonition, had never before appeared in official manuscript, even above the signatures of the Scottish

Commissioners of the period. The report was unsurpassable in detail; the complicated matter was unravelled and displayed with real literary skill.

It was made plainly apparent that the dismissed officers had carried on fraud for a considerable period, with the knowledge and to the great pecuniary benefit of the Glasgow sugar merchants. They had reserved a means of defence by weighing the casks before they were coopered. In most cases the packages were brought to the scale in a damaged condition, as landed from the importing vessel. They were then underweighed, and afterwards coopered; and thus the culprits were enabled to put forward the plea that portions of the sugar might have escaped after weighing and before or during repair, and that the addition of staves and hoops might have increased the gross weight, and have suggested to the merchants the possibility of increasing the net on the invoices, the customs tare being of course inscribed upon the casks. But the plea, though in a way plausible, did not avail. It was evident, too, that the officers underweighed for lucre, and made the underweighing proportionate to the extent of reward given by the respective merchants concerned. In some cases the discrepancies amounted to a few pounds only on each hogshead; in others to hundreds of pounds.

It was curious, too, that whenever the casks were flagrantly underweighed the landing-surveyor, whose duty it was to check the weighing at intervals, and to record the times at which he checked, did not subscribe his initials against the packages selected, although it was afterwards proved that he had gone through the ceremony of reweighing.

It was also strange that when Mr. Osborn visited the port, and called for the incriminating invoice, the collector had to admit that he had restored it to the merchant concerned. And when Mr. Campbell, the said merchant, was asked for the invoice, he stoutly refused to surrender it, and actually convened a meeting of the Glasgow sugar merchants, all of whom as stoutly pledged themselves to furnish no information to the Crown. The collector and controller, too, had never troubled themselves with superintending the outdoor work, and on this matter the Board pointed out to them that it was their duty to see that the practical customs business was properly carried on. The collector was let off lightest, 'being a young man and new to customs work,' which statement, when the growing trade of Port Glasgow is taken into account, should be admirably illustrative of the qualities then considered necessary to fit one for occupation of an important collectorship. It is a pity that want of space forbids full discussion of this remarkable official document, remarkable equally for its majestic literary qualities, the dignity of its official doctrine, the dexterity of its deductions, the mildness of its punitive prescriptions, and the illumination it sheds upon the revenue methods of its day.

Little mention of the Irish Customs has hitherto been made in this treatise, but, as the Union of Great Britain and Ireland will be the subject of the opening pages of the second volume, the first may be profitably concluded with a brief history of Irish revenue, and a few extracts from the Irish records.

It appears that prior to the conquest of Ireland by Henry II. the revenues of the Irish monarchs were allotted at the meetings of the National Council. The Church was free of all taxes, and it is likely that the royal impositions were light and cheerfully rendered. The petty chiefs were empowered to exercise purveyance, and to billet warriors upon their subjects. After conquest by the English most of the Norman feudal impositions were introduced, but there is reason to believe that little revenue was collected in the districts remote from English occupation.

The Irish Exchequer was located at Dublin early in the thirteenth century, and for a considerable length of time the Irish Treasurer accounted to the English Exchequer for his receipts. The Irish revenue officials were appointed by the English king.

There is little worth recounting in the statutes till the time of Edward IV., when it was enacted that if hides or 'other staple merchandise' were carried from Ulster into Scotland without payment of 'the custom of the Cocket' the goods should be forfeited.*

The next statute prescribed that every merchant trading from England to Ireland should bring 100s. worth of bows with every £100 worth of merchandise, Ireland being 'desolated of bows.' (This would appear to imply that poundage was levied on imported goods.†) Later it was enjoined that hawks carried out of Ireland should be liable to a special impost, 'besides poundage.' (Thus it is evident that poundage was levied on exported goods.) The rates of the impost were as follows :

On each goshawk	1 mark.‡
,, tiercel	½ mark.
,, falcon	10 shillings.

The Irish Lord Treasurer was empowered to appoint the customs officials.

A later statute (14 Hen. VII., c. 1) provided that all Acts existing in England for punishment of controllers, collectors, and searchers who misbehaved should apply in Ireland.

* Acts of Ireland.

† Butlerage was levied, as in England, for the patent appointing Slegh and Sologhan as controllers of Cork and Kinsale empowered the grantees to collect the customs Cocket duties, and the custom of 2s. on every cask of wine imported by merchant strangers.

‡ The Patent Rolls of Richard II. furnish evidence that the king occasionally sent an agent into Ireland to pre-empt hawks and falcons. It appears also that there was a law against absentees, for in the patent appointing Richard's yeoman Lowyk gauger and general surveyor in Ireland the grantee was directed, after rendering an account to the Irish Exchequer, to bring his takings to England, the statute against absentees notwithstanding.

Poundage was levied by statute at 12d. on all goods exported or imported; wine and oil, which were subject to Prisage, excepted. (Bulk not to be broken at import till goods entered in the customer's books.) Most writers on Irish revenue seem to have thought that this was the first levy of poundage. The quotations furnished above may perhaps be held sufficient refutation. It is tolerably clear that poundage was introduced into Ireland soon after its appearance in England (and that Prisage and the Ancient Custom existed from the beginning of English occupation). Yet it is unlikely that it was collected regularly in the districts beyond the Pale.*

Henry VIII. prohibited the exportation of Irish wool. The Act was extensively infringed, and it appears to have been imperfect, as no provision was made towards granting the customs officers power of 'entry and search.' It was reaffirmed and amended by a later Act, which provided heavy penalties upon negligence on the part of the searchers. One Edward Abecke, a Manchester merchant, was allowed partial exemption. He was empowered to ship £40 worth of Irish wool per year to England.

The three ports mentioned were farmed by four merchants, who paid £307 a year, made up as below:

For Dublin	£146	13	4
For Drogheda	138	6	8
For Dundalk	22	0	0

During Elizabeth's reign it was found that the prohibition of wool had been frequently evaded, both by 'stealing' (smuggling) and by the obtaining of licences

* During Henry IV.'s reign William Mirson and John Mirson, Englishmen who acted as collectors of Irish customs, were allowed to employ deputies, the country being in so mutinous a condition that the Mirsons found it dangerous to visit remote ports unless formidably guarded. (It is possible that the unfortunate deputies went without escort, and took more chances than duties.) Ireland seems to have suffered in trading with England. The Rolls show that much 'old' (corrupt) wine was shipped to Ireland. In one of the licences it was stipulated that the wine should be of a kind not drinkable in England.

from the higher resident officials. Therefore a prohibitive duty was levied, applying not only to wool, but to several other agricultural products. Below are the rates (outward):

Wool, 5s. per stone (8 pounds).
Flax and yarn, 1s. a pound.
Fells, 4d. each.
Deer-skins, 2s. 6d. each.
Beef (salted), 1d. a pound; 5s. a firkin; 10s. a half-barrel; £1 a barrel; £2 a hogshead; £4 a pipe.
Tallow, 2s. a stone.
Wax, 1s. a pound.
Butter, 6d. a pound.

Heavy port duties were levied on the goods, in addition to the customs.

Another statute restricted the importation of wine to certain ports, and prescribed the following imposts:

Spanish and Levant wines in denizens' ships: 40s. a tun (coin of Ireland).
French and German wines in denizens' ships: 26s. 8d. a tun (coin of Ireland).
Spanish and Levant wines in aliens' ships: 53s. 4d. a tun (coin of Ireland).
French and German wines in aliens' ships: 40s. per tun (coin of Ireland).

The Lord Deputy was allowed 20 tuns a year duty-free for the use of his household, and empowered to prescribe the quantities to be granted duty-free to peers and to members of the Council.

It was enacted that woollen cloth and woollen stuff might only be exported by merchants of the Irish staple towns, or by such English merchants as bought from them.

The next Act rendered smuggling of wool felony, the heavy duty having failed to keep the wool in the country.

On account of depredations committed by French pirates, Messrs. Walsh and Wise, Waterford merchants, were allowed to take certain duties upon the ships and goods of French traders in Irish ports, till they recovered the amount lost by piracy (£1,300). They levied 18d. a ton as tonnage dues, 3s. a tun on wine, 2s. a ton on iron, and 18d. a ton on salt.

The wine impost was reaffirmed.

In 1610 Robert Cogan was made surveyor-general of Irish Customs, his appointment being 'a reward for good and painful services taken in setting of the Customs of Ireland.' He had a salary of £100 a year, and was allowed to nominate officers.

In 1627 Charles increased the duties upon certain Irish goods exported otherwise than to England. The principal commodities surtaxed were fish, butter, salted flesh, hides, candles, iron, wool, cattle, horses, and corn. Wool and hides might only be exported under royal licence. The reason furnished was that Ireland, 'by reason of peace and plenty,' had been enabled to export goods not only to England, but to countries not friendly. Falkland was Chancellor of Ireland, and it is evident that Butlerage was still levied, or that Elizabeth's wine impost survived, for Lord Hay held a lease of the Irish wine duties, granted in 1613, and paid £1,400 a year for his farm. Charles I. issued a close writ, directing Falkland to pay one Cave, a customs officer, a special fee of £107 10s. a year, Cave having been diligent 'in reforming the "Book of Rates" and advancing the Irish Customs.' Later Cave petitioned, stating that his wages were in arrear.

Meanwhile Lord Hay repeatedly complained that the Irish wine importers were destitute of money,* and that he had frequently taken bonds from them for subsequent payment, released their goods, and failed to recover. Charles directed Falkland to exert himself on Hay's behalf. It seems that Falkland was unable to render much assistance, for Charles communicated with him again, stating that it had been stipulated in the patent of grant that the rent should be abated if trade declined; that trade had declined, and Hay had not complained, yet

* Yet the king's Declaration (see above) had stated that Ireland had become a land 'of peace and plenty'!

he should not suffer. Therefore the Irish Exchequer officials were instructed to allow the expenses of Hay's agents 'in a large, ample, and beneficent manner.'

In 1631 Charles laid a heavy impost upon Irish exports and imports.

Irish Commissioners of Revenue were appointed soon after the Restoration. The first was Sir George Blundell. In 1662 five others were appointed—Gorges, Smith, Dodson, Bligh, and Muschamp. They managed the tunnage on wine and oil, and the poundage on imported and exported merchandise, as granted by an Act dating from December 31, 1661. Later they received another commission, empowering them to manage 'the Excise or New Impost,' and the inland excise on beer, ale, etc. Later 'additional duties' were placed upon certain imported goods. The 'New Impost' was paid by the first buyer of foreign merchandise and wine.

An official was appointed, described as 'Taster of Wines and other Liquors, and Surveyor of the Outs and Defects of the same.' By 'outs' were meant such casks of imported wine or spirits as were found almost empty when landed. The servants of this patentee (the work was performed by deputies) surveyed all 'outs,' and if satisfied allowed them to pass duty-free. They had also power to taste all imported wine and spirits, and decide as to quality. It is conceivable that there were many persons in Ireland, and in England too, who would have desired no better occupation than to act as deputies gratis. The patentee took fees, and his office was tolerably lucrative. Sometimes the patent was divided between two.* The fees incidental were as follows: 'For every butt, pipe, puncheon, or large cask tasted or surveyed, 6d.; for every hogshead, tierce, barrel, rundlet, or smaller vessel, 3d.'

The 'king's ports' were Dublin, Wexford, Waterford, Kinsale, Cork, Dingle, Limerick, Galway, Carrickfergus,

* In 1772 it was held by the Hon. John Beresford and Marcus Beresford.

Strangford, and Drogheda. Drogheda included Dundalk and Carlingford, Carrickfergus included Belfast, Dublin included Wicklow and Arklow.

According to Sir William Petty, England exported goods to Ireland to the value of £60,000 a year, and the Irish exports to England reached a yearly value of £150,000, the excess being principally in Irish cattle and sheep. Irish agriculture had prospered since the settlement of the Cromwellians. (It will be remembered that the exportation of Irish live stock to England was forbidden in 1664.) Sir William estimated the average weight of an Irish fleece at two pounds. He commented upon the extensive use of tobacco, and stated that the smoking of that weed in short pipes, together with 'sneezing' (snuff-taking), formed the chief pleasure of the Irishmen's lives.*

The newly appointed Commissioners at once started a survey, there being many arrears. It is stated that up to 1658 the amount overdue had been £6,300; thence to 1660, £35,000; thence to 1662, £29,000. £25,800 was owing in the port of Dublin alone.

The Commissioners had to manage the Crown-rents, composition-rents, and quit-rents. Crown-rents were

* Undoubtedly he regarded the native Irish with unmeasured contempt. His treatise teemed with bitter reflections upon their habits. The spectacle of a well-ordered, well-meaning Englishman, busily applying cold figures to the inner life of a quaint and vagarious race, is by no means rare, yet not one whit the less amusing. Indeed, Sir William's book is well worth reading on this account alone. What can be better than his lugubrious reference to the condition of affairs at an earlier date, when an Englishman was held guiltless for killing an Irishman? His summary of matters relative to Irish shipbuilding is equally quaint. It appears that even in his day the Irish attributed Ireland's deficiency in shipping solely to 'the policy of the English.' He treated the argument in ruthless fashion. Said he: 'I have never perceived any impediment of building or having ships in Ireland but men's own indisposition thereto.' He went on to state that the Irish preferred buying ships from the Dutch to building them, and that most Irishmen were naturally averse to a seafaring life, and would rather 'eat potatoes and milk on dry land than contest with the winds and waves with better food.'

proceeds of patents granted to favourites, enabling them to hold Church lands vacated at the Reformation, and lands forfeited by rebels. Composition-rents were acknowledgments from the holders of certain lands in Clare and Connaught, made in lieu of 'Cess and Press,' and dating from the time of Elizabeth. Quit-rents were dues from lands which had been forfeited in the rebellion of 1641, and then granted to adventurers (mostly Cromwellians). The Commissioners also accounted for 'Hearth-money'—in short, they supervised the entire Irish Revenue. They had not all equal powers; the usual number of their body was seven, of whom only five were competent to deal with the inland duties. The arrangement of the Irish Board down to 1772 furnishes a confusing branch of study; therefore it may be best to give only a rough indication of the history of the staff, ending with as concise a description as possible of the course of revenue practice, and a few pages of narrative.

In 1663 one of the Privy Councillors was appointed to sit with the Commissioners. The king leased the tunnage, poundage, and import excise, the farmers paying £55,000 a year, and being allowed to act as extra Commissioners. Then he leased the inland excise to the Earl of Orrery and Lord Kingston for £36,600 a year. Only three of the original Commissioners remained in office, to audit the farmers' account.

In 1664 the inland excise was let to farm at £39,000 a year. The odious tax of Hearth-money was instituted, and farmed for £30,000 a year.

In 1669 the king let the entire Revenue to eleven persons, mostly citizens of London.

In 1671 the farm was granted to Lord Ranelagh and others. The Lord Lieutenant, the Archbishop of Dublin, the Lord Treasurer, and six others, were made temporary Commissioners, to supervise the farmers' proceedings.

In 1675 the king leased the Revenue to twelve farmers, and appointed the Irish Chancellor of the Exchequer, with ten others, as supervising Commissioners. In the following year he leased it afresh to a number of financiers, mostly London citizens, for £240,000 a year, and appointed Commissioners to supervise and audit.

In 1677 the brothers Bridges, London citizens, advanced the king £36,000 odd for the Irish military establishment, and were put on the Revenue to recoup. They were empowered to recover the money advanced, and other sums which would amount to a surplus of about £11,000. To secure this they levied 1s. in the £1 on the farmers' payments.

Some of the officers' legal perquisites, as stated in the regulation 'Table of Fees,' were taken in the form of petty prisage. The following have a quaint suggestiveness:

'Out of every barque or boat for bringing in apples: To the Searcher, one hundred of the same.

'Out of every barque or boat for bringing in oysters: To the Searcher, one hundred of the same.

'For Gaging every Tun of wine: To the Gager, fourpence: Besides out of every ship bringing in wines, one small bottle of wine for a Gaging bottle.'

Farming ceased in 1682, and thenceforward the Revenue was under sole management of the Commissioners. A Receiver-General was appointed in 1683, to act instead of the Vice-Treasurer. The new official was one Price, a London merchant, who had lent the king £16,000. He received a salary of £1,000 a year, besides fees. In 1688, two persons named Bond and Doe were allowed to pay him out, and divide the appointment between them.

When William III. reconquered Ireland, new Commissioners and a new Receiver-General were appointed. The Commissioners were called upon to manage additional quit-rents upon lands forfeited because their owners had supported James II. (In 1715 the renowned duke of Ormond was expatriated. The Ormond family had furnished a couple of Lord Treasurers, and held the Prisage of Ireland for many years.)

In 1704 the Board were entrusted with the collection

of the tonnage dues on vessels, which dues were appropriated to the upkeep of lighthouses on the Irish coast. The tonnage duties had been imposed soon after the Restoration, and their proceeds granted to Sir Robert Reading and his heirs, on condition that the grantees kept the lighthouses in good working order. This they had failed to do, so the Irish Parliament dispossessed them.

The Prisage was taken from its holder, the Earl of Arran, who had succeeded to the forfeited estates of the Ormonds, but he and his family were granted £3,500 a year as compensation. Later the grant was made £4,000.

Some rather interesting correspondence took place between the Irish Commissioners and the Treasury in 1724 on the subject of 'Wood's halfpence.' On August 29 the Commissioners wrote, acknowledging receipt from the Treasury of a copy of the bond entered into by Wood. Their letter continued :

'We humbly beg leave to assure your Lordships that we never gave any orders or Intimations to prevent or obstruct ye circulation of ye said Halfpence.

'As to your Lordships' commands to order all our officers not to receive in any one Paiment above fivepence-halfpenny in ye said copper coin, we think it our indispensable Duty—from ye Disorder this nation is in at present about these Halfpence, & ye Declarations that have been sign'd by all sorts of People & publish'd that they will not receive or utter them. We are under ye utmost difficulty to execute the same. . . .

'Y^e Acts of Customs & Excise having upon this occasion been inculcated into ye minds of ye People, by repeated Pamphlets and Papers dispers'd over ye Kingdom, informing them that all ye King's Dutys are to be paid in Sterling Money, or current money of England, as ye said Acts express :—And tho' we apprehend that Mr. Wood's Halfpence are not intended by your Lordships to be paid otherwise than by way of change, yet ye Prejudice conceiv'd against them is such that this Argument will have but little force.'

They proceeded at some length, stating their belief that the introduction of the halfpence would disturb and complicate the collection of revenue, and that there were not sufficient safeguards against Mr. Wood issuing and circulating more than the £40,000 worth stipulated in the patents.

The issue of port-books to the collectors was continued up to the middle of the eighteenth century, though the books were obsolete. It appears that this was done for no other purpose than to enrich the Remembrancer and the Pursuivant. These Exchequer officials charged heavy fees, the Remembrancer extorting 10s. for issuing each book, and the Pursuivant 3s. 4d. for delivering the same. The collectors refused to pay the fees, and the issue of the unwelcome documents ceased.

Separate Boards were appointed in 1772, one set of Commissioners managing the tunnage and poundage, the other the remaining branches of revenue.

In 1783, that year of disastrous inquisition into revenue methods both in Great Britain and Ireland, elaborate instructions were sent from Dublin as to the transmission of outport accounts and balances, the Board stating that many collectors had deceived the Accountant-General by means of false returns, and shown considerable sums as 'arrears of duty' which had been collected. About a dozen collectors were dismissed, the total defalcations amounting to a huge sum.

In 1779 the Irish Parliament passed resolutions in favour of free trade. In 1793 an Act was passed empowering Ireland to share in the East India trade.

The business of the port of Dublin had increased so much during the eighties that the 'Old Custom House' was found unsuitable, and a new one was erected. In 1796 docks were opened at Dublin.

A general review of the Irish revenue, from 1662 to the end of the eighteenth century, reveals little of interest, compared with the varied aspects of English revenue during the same period. The customs duties were much lighter than those obtaining in England. The allowances for leakage and damage on wines imported were much the same as the English allowances. The poundage was preferential with regard to British and Plantation goods, which paid about six-sevenths of the amount charged upon foreign merchandise.

The 'import-excise' levies were payable by retailers. Merchant-importers were exempt, provided they entered into bond for securing payment of the duties by the retailers who bought the goods from them. Retailers were not allowed drawback if they exported goods after paying the import-excise, but a merchant-importer might discharge his bond for the excise duties by exporting his goods. Thus there were two distinct classes of importers. The most favoured were the 'merchants,' but they might only sell their goods to be sold again; they might not offer them to the actual consumers. The other class included the retailers, and those who imported for private use. These last were called 'consumptioners.' In practice, the merchants usually found it profitable to pay the import-excise themselves, as they secured an abatement by doing so, and then charged full prices to the retailers, who were not entitled to abatement in any case.

Most of the 'additional duties' were appropriated to various branches of expenditure—'the Loan,' 'the Tillage,' 'Lagan navigation,' etc. One of the later inland duties, the hawkers' and pedlars' licence branch, went to the maintenance of 'Protestant Schools.'

There is not much worth quoting as regards the interior economy of the Irish revenue department. The salaries paid were merely nominal, but the officers reaped an abundant harvest of fees. The duties were loosely collected; even the imposition of fees appears to have been conducted in vagarious fashion, for when in 1762 one of the landing-waiters complained that the merchants refused to give him the usual 'gratuities,' the Board merely directed him to furnish a return upon oath of the total amount withheld, and they would make it good. It seems that some of the officers' relatives had queer notions upon such matters, for in 1781 the Board found it necessary to proclaim that the right of taking fees ceased at death. It must not be inferred from this that the shades of the departed continued to plague merchants; the fact was that certain officers' widows had appealed to be allowed to continue their husbands' depredations.

Some of the instructions to officers were comical. Goods 'infected with the plague' were directed to be sunk 'in 20 fathoms water at 14 leagues from land,' and we presume that the collector who tried to carry out this order literally had some trouble in finding the regulation depth at the regulation distance. Coast-waiters were ordered to go at sunrise and sunset to 'the highest spot in the neighbourhood,' and take a good long look around, to ascertain if any suspicious vessels were in sight. The customs gaugers seem to have been on capital terms with the wine-merchants, for in 1725 these latter were forbidden to continue a practice of giving the officers, *before the casks were gauged*, 'some gallons thereof under the name of the gauger's bottle.'*

Certain prohibitions and restrictions may be quoted:

1. East India goods might only be imported via England.
2. Asiatic, African, and American goods were subject to the Navigation Act.
3. Russian goods might only be imported in British, Irish, or Russian ships.
4. Plantation goods might only be imported via Great Britain.
5. Hops might only be imported via Great Britain.
6. Glass might only be imported when British.

A few articles of merchandise were duty-free inwards, the most important being dyeing drugs, linen cloth *made in Great Britain*, looms, and wool. Irish fustians, Irish

* See p. 431. It appears that the 'small bottle' had grown into a demijohn.

flax seed, Irish flour, Irish linen cloth, and Irish rape oil were duty-free outwards. A premium was granted on Irish corn and flax seed exported in British or Irish shipping, when the price in Ireland did not exceed a certain specified sum. Irish fish and Irish sail-cloth were also bountied.

It must be admitted that the revenue regulations applicable to Irish commerce favoured Great Britain and harassed Ireland. The restriction most baneful was that upon wool and woollen products, which might only be exported to British ports. Thus the Irish woollen manufacture was slowly strangled. Irish agriculture also suffered, both by this and restrictions upon the exportation of Irish cattle to Great Britain. The products of the Plantations and the East Indies might only reach the western island through the ports of her more powerful rival. An utter and appalling selfishness was manifest in all English commercial dealings with Ireland. On certain occasions relaxations were made, noticeably towards the end of the American war, but they were relaxations dictated by selfishness. In the struggle for commercial supremacy, neither nations nor individuals have ever shown tenderness to each other. The strong have always oppressed and defrauded the weak, and, so long as men or nations subsist and prosper by buying and selling, this will be the case.

A remarkable instance of this grim practice with commercial men of thrusting burdens upon the feeble, and setting the able free, is discovered in the continuance in Ireland of that dreadful tax, Hearth-money, a duty of 2s. per annum on every hearth, firing-place, or stove. If a house had no chimney, and there were many such 'houses' in the Ireland of that day, it was charged for two hearths. This practice actually found support amongst certain writers, who urged that it was likely to bring about the building of one-chimneyed houses. But Hearth-money was levied on *the tenant;* therefore the landlord continued to build and let chimneyless hovels. Paupers were exempt under the Act, but in practice none was let off unless '*unable* to labour by reason of age, sickness, or bodily infirmity.' A man might be unemployed half a year at a time, but Hearth-money was still demandable from him. The following quotations give different but interesting views on the Hearth-tax.

The first is from a book published by Nicholas Eaton, Equalizer of Duties at Dublin in 1767. Said Eaton: 'There are Numbers of idle lazy Beggars in this Kingdom who live entirely upon the mistaken Charity of the Publick. . . . Such indolent vagrants were never designed to be favoured by this Act, which ought strictly and literally to be put in Force against them.'

The next is an utterance by Mr. Howard, Attorney to the Exchequer, a gentleman who in 1772 produced a luminous treatise on Irish revenue. He expressed himself thus with regard to Hearth-money: 'I could wish that the Hearth-tax were arranged as the House-tax is in England, under which cottages are exempt, and that the occupiers of the many wretched hovels here had been exempted even as the cottagers there, and the deficiency supplied by enlarging the tax upon those of sufficient ability to pay.'

The returns of Irish revenue are vague, and appear to be full of confusing contradictions. It is rather strange that in 1664 the Revenue should have been *farmed* for £124,000, and in 1676 for £240,000, and that the net return in 1688, when no farmers' profits preyed upon the balance, should have been only £150,000. The land was convulsed by rebellion at the latter date; still, the statements are curious. The Revenue swelled gradually from £150,000 in 1688 to £1,560,000 in 1801—say an average rise of £12,500. Yet the return in 1799 shows an increase of £200,000. Perhaps a deal of revenue had been left uncollected during 1798, and the arrears were made good in 1799.*

* It is evident that trade was suspended for a time at Wicklow in 1798 (*vide* p. 439).

The Wicklow records furnish rather interesting details of the Irish practice towards the end of the century.

In 1795 the Irish Board apprised the Wicklow collector that they had received the Lord Mayor of Dublin's quarterly statement of the prices of corn; that the said prices were on the high scale, except as regarded beans; and that consequently all corn except beans must be prohibited from exportation; also that vessels carrying butter from Ireland to Portugal (about the only export trade to that country) were to bring back salt. Bond was to be insisted on for fulfilment of this condition, the amount of such bond to be £1,000 for a vessel under 200 tons, £2,000 for a larger vessel.

An importer applied to Dublin for leave to land 'a general cargo' at Ballymoney, consisting of salt, tobacco, pipes, scythe-stones, and shot. The Board directed the collector to ascertain the use to which said shot was to be put. The collector replied that it was for the use of sportsmen. 'This,' he stated, 'I have no doubt of.'

There were mines at Arklow, worked by the 'Hibernian Mine Company.' The Company were constantly complaining that their importations of coal, etc., were obstructed by the customs officers. The Board wrote the collector, directing him not to delay the Company's business. Later Sackville Hamilton, Secretary to the Lord Lieutenant, apprised the Board that a gold mine had been discovered near Arklow, and that thousands of people were resorting thither, and gathering the ore.

Evidently great things were expected, for the Secretary complained that whisky booths were becoming plentiful in the vicinity of the mine. The Board told the Wicklow collector to proceed to the locality and protect the ore, 'as the property of His Majesty's Government.'

But the collector was not going to trust himself amongst the mustering peasantry, especially as whisky booths were plentiful thereabout. He sent word back that sufficient force could not be gathered in the neighbourhood to overawe the amateur miners. Besides, he was suffering from rheumatism. Further instructions desired. Directly afterwards he wrote again, asking if his letter had miscarried, as 'he had heard nothing of the soldiers.' Evidently the collector knew how to take care of himself. Soldiers were sent in plenty, and he then carried out his instructions.

In 1796 the Board received a memorial from the Hibernian Mine Company and the inhabitants of Arklow, stating that though they imported annually 5,000 tons of coal, besides large quantities of iron plates and fire-bricks, there was no adequate provision for reporting vessels and paying duty; that each shipmaster had to go to the Custom-house at Wicklow to report, clear, etc., and thus had to travel in all seventy-two miles on customs business. They suggested that the officer stationed at Arklow should be allowed to 'invoice and clear vessels,' and to take duties. This the collector stoutly opposed, no doubt with an eye to his fees. He stated that Arklow was only twelve miles away, and that the masters made but two journeys, thus travelling only forty-eight miles. It seems that the petitioners had exaggerated; still, the Board thought fit to comply, deeming the mines 'of great public utility.' So the collector was ordered to entrust the customs business of Arklow to a 'proper person,' who might take duty on bricks, coal, iron plates, rock-salt, and slate inward, and on copper, ore of copper, and iron outward.

In 1798 the collector reported thus: 'The very wretched and disturbed state of this part of the kingdom has put a total stop to all business, consequently neither duties can be ascertained or obtained, nor vouchers returned.' The Board asked for fuller particulars. The collector then sent word that there was no part of the county of Wicklow but was in a state of disturbance, that the troops had been 'watching the rebels day and night,' and that during the night previous there had been an engagement,* in which

* There is an account of this battle in Sir Jonah Barrington's 'Rise and Fall of the Irish Nation.'

General Needham, at the head of a force of yeomanry and militia, had defeated a body of insurgents 20,000 strong. 'The rebels,' said he, 'burn and destroy the houses of all the protestants they come to, and massacre such as they can find.'

Later the collectors on the east coast of Ireland were told to supply the collectors of the western English ports with specimens of their handwriting, and of the form of passport issued to persons leaving Ireland for England. All collier brigs arriving from England were to be searched for arms and ammunition. During the whole of the year the Irish collectors sent the officers commanding the militia supplies of money, usually in halved bank-notes. Towards the end of 1798 the Board called on the collectors for reports as to how persons licensed to deal in gunpowder had demeaned themselves during the disturbances.

An application being made for a sufferance to land salt at Arklow, the collector advised that permission should be withheld, stating that if the salt were landed and stored at Ballymoney parties friendly to the rebels would make it their business to supply them, and that this would defeat the intentions of the generals commanding the loyalists in the district, they having up to that time been successful in preventing the rebels from obtaining salt to use with their provisions, 'thereby causing the death of numbers of them.' The Board considered this benevolent missive, and directed the collector to see that the salt was landed at Gorey, and placed under customs lock.

In 1799 a large vessel, with a valuable cargo, and bearing letters of marque, went ashore near Arklow, and had to be lightened by delivering part of her goods. The Board ordered the collector to see that the cargo delivered was lightered safely to Dublin, and to obtain soldiers to guard the ship during the transaction.

There was a deal of trouble with the Wicklow lighthouse-keepers, whose wages, together with the upkeep of the lighthouses, were paid out of the customs receipts. It was common for shipmasters to lodge complaints at

Dublin that the lights could not be seen, yet the lighthouse-keepers' affidavits that the lamps had been kept regularly burning came in every quarter as usual. In the end the Wicklow gauger, a Mr. Dudgeon, was ordered to ride the coast at night, to keep an eye upon the lights, and to make occasional surprise visits, to see that the attendants were awake and alive to their duty.

The collector complained that a number of soldiers were billeted in the Custom-house, that they were usually in a condition of drunkenness, and that he was afraid they might set fire to or rob the building. He stated that the soldiers kept the doors open night and day, and came and went as they pleased, and that he was constantly in great apprehension, 'from the character of such people.' The Board told him they were unable to interfere, but that he might apply to the magistrates. (It is probable that the magistrates were equally indisposed.)

In 1800 the Board called for a return of bounty-money paid to Irish fishing vessels. The Wicklow collector reported that nothing of the kind had been paid in his district since 1789. Thus it would seem that the Irish fisheries were in a poor condition—even bounties failed to keep them going; and that the Board did not interest themselves much in the matter, or they would have called for the return earlier.

Indeed, the customs business seems to have been conducted in happy-go-lucky fashion. Letters on important matters sometimes remained unanswered for months, and returns asked for at the beginning of one year were sometimes supplied at the end of the next, and then only after repeated inquiries. For instance, in 1800 the Wicklow collector was drummed up for a return of the values of revenue offices in his district, a return which should have been supplied long before. He sent an account of the values of the excise offices, but not of the customs. Later he supplied the values of all the customs posts except his own, so the Board fined him 10 guineas for the omission. Then he sent an account of his own complete receipts, placing them at £400 per annum—a considerable sum for that period, in a poverty-ridden land too. The Board were appeased, and remitted the fine.

Mr. Dudgeon, the gauger appointed to watch the lights, sent in a statement, vouched by several fishermen, to the effect that since his appointment as watcher the lights at Wicklow Head had been kept going better than at any time within memory. Soon afterwards there were several complaints from shipmasters, and the Board called upon Dudgeon for an explanation. Dudgeon thereupon furnished affidavits from the lighthouse-keepers, corroborating his statement. He was told that his allowance of 30 guineas per year for watching would be continued 'experimentally,' on condition that he did his duty. This put him upon his mettle, and later he furnished a report that, detecting a dulness, he visited, and found that the dulness was due to want of snuffing.

The coasting trade was almost at a standstill. During six months of 1800 only five coasters discharged in Wicklow Bay, the total deliveries being 10 barrels herrings, 26 tons potatoes, 510 barrels oats, 3 tons meal, 50 barrels wheat, and 5 barrels tar.

The Board asked for an account of some wine and fruit seized at Arklow in 1798. The landing-waiter there reported thus: 'The oranges melted away in the cases, and the wine was taken by the soldiers during the rebellion.'

The coast-waiter at Bray applied for permission to take entries and duties at that place. He had succeeded his father in the employment, and the father had been allowed to deal with moneys. But the Wicklow collector reported against the application, stating that the father had rarely returned any duties, and had been altogether an unsatisfactory official. Indeed, 'the late Mr. Brown' had for years succeeded in baffling all attempts at investigation of his very peculiar revenue transactions. Quoth the collector: 'When vessels were found by the Dublin officers to have discharged there, Mr. Brown said the duties had been paid at Wicklow, and when found by the Wicklow officers, Mr. Brown said the duties had been paid at Dublin. At last we made a clean detection,' etc. But what was done to Brown, senior, does not appear, nor any explanation as to why Brown, junior, was allowed to succeed him.

It will be seen from these brief memoranda of practical matters that the Irish Customs, compared with the English, was a quiet and unpicturesque department. There was occasional smuggling, but the contrabandists, with the exception of 'Jack the Bachelor's Gang,' made a poor figure beside the smugglers of Dorset, Hampshire, Sussex, and Kent. The extreme poverty of the land, and the Irish deficiency in maritime enterprise, may have been responsible for this. It needs a numerous class of skilled watermen and a tolerably free circulation of money, as well as a tremendous tariff, to bring smuggling to the perfection it reached in southern England during the eighteenth century. The contingencies must be favourable, and the actors fitted for their parts, ere the drama of lawlessness can be properly played.

It has been thought judicious to end the volume here, in order to begin the next with an account of the amalgamation of British and Irish Customs under the Act of Union. It would be idle to pretend that full justice can have been done, in one book, to the huge possibilities of the older Customs history. We have tried to present a simple and coherent narrative, and, in dealing with the history of smuggling, to display, not the most picturesque incidents, but those which appear to illustrate the spirit of the time, and the practice of a venerable Revenue department. It is impossible that the Customs history of the nineteenth century will be so deeply impregnated with the glamour of contraband, yet it may be found to possess even more potent elements of interest. The records will be more comprehensive, easier of access, perhaps more reliable.

LIST OF AUTHORITIES.

Act of Consolidation: 27 Geo. III., c. 13.

Imposts subsequent to consolidation: 27 Geo. III., c. 28; 31 Geo. III., c. 15; 34 Geo. III., c. 4 and 15; 34 Geo. III., c. 20; 34 Geo. III., c. 27; 35 Geo. III., c. 20; 36 Geo. III., c. 123; 37 Geo. III., c. 15; 37 Geo. III., c. 110; 38 Geo. III., c. 43; 39 Geo. III., c. 63.

Excise duties: 27 Geo. III., c. 31; 31 Geo. III., c. 1; 32 Geo. III., c. 7; 35 Geo. III., c. 10; 35 Geo. III., c. 12, 13; 36 Geo. III., c. 13; 38 Geo. III., c. 89; 40 Geo. III., c. 23; 34 Geo. III., c. 3.

Preventive measures: 27 Geo. III., c. 32; 33 Geo. III., c. 70; 34 Geo. III., c. 50; 36 Geo. III., c. 82; 38 Geo. III., c. 33.

Departmental incidents: Sir William Musgrave's 'Customs Memoranda'; Montrose Letter Books.

Repeal of Ancient Duties: 28 Geo. III., c. 16.

Protective measures and prohibitions: 28 Geo. III., c. 38; 30 Geo. III., c. 4; 30 Geo. III., c. 27; 31 Geo. III., c. 30; 32 Geo. III., c. 43; 33 Geo. III., c. 2; 33 Geo. III., c. 3; 33 Geo. III., c. 27; 33 Geo. III., c. 63; 34 Geo. III., c. 68; 36 Geo. III., c. 79; 36 Geo. III., c. 86; 37 Geo. III., c. 97; 38 Geo. III., c. 79; 39 Geo. III., c. 65; 39 Geo. III., c. 95.

Slave trade: 28 Geo. III., c. 54.

Establishment: 29 Geo. III., c. 64; 38 Geo. III., c. 86; Fourth Report of Select Committee on Finance.

Tobacco: 29 Geo. III., c. 68; 30 Geo. III., c. 40.

Coasting trade: 32 Geo. III., c. 50.

Aliens: 33 Geo. III., c. 4; 38 Geo. III., c. 50.

Drawbacks: 33 Geo. III., c. 48.

Privateers: 37 Geo. III., c. 109.

Isle of Man: 38 Geo. III., c. 63.

Convoy duties: 38 Geo. III., c. 76.

East India Company: 37 Geo. III., c. 117; 39 Geo. III., c. 59.

Exemptions (special): 39 Geo. III., c. 96.

Quarantine: 39 Geo. III., c. 99.

London Dock Charters: 39 Geo. III., c. 69 (Local Act).

Irish Customs: Irish Acts, 12 Edw. IV., c. 1, 2; 20 Edw. IV., s. 2, c. 1; 14 Hen. VII., c. 1; 15 Hen. VII., c. 1; 13 Hen. VIII., c. 2; 28 Hen. VIII., c. 17; 11 Eliz., s. 3, c. 10, and s. 4, c. 1; 13 Eliz., c. 1, 2; 28 Eliz., c. 4; Lodge's 'Patentee Officers'; Patent Rolls, 19 Rich. II., p. 1, m. 19; Patent Rolls, 1 Hen. IV., p. 6, m. 8; Irish Calendars, 1532; Acts of Privy Council, 1579; Irish Calendars, 1625, 1626, 1627; Fœdera ('De Declaratione pro incremento Subsidiorum in Regno Hiberniæ'—'Declaration for the Imposition of divers Subsidies'); Petty's 'Political Anatomy'; Irish Table of Fees; Treasury Papers, vol. 248; Dublin Order Books; Eaton's 'Book of Rates'; Wicklow Letter Books.

CUSTOMS LITERATI

GEOFFREY CHAUCER	JOHN DENNIS
WILLIAM CONGREVE	ADAM SMITH

CHAUCER.

THE Chaucers were originally a family of cordwainers. Geoffrey's grandfather, Robert le Chaucer, became attorney or clerk to the king's Butler during Edward II.'s reign, and was afterwards made collector of the 'Petty Custom on Wine' (Butlerage). It seems that the family abjured connexion with their ancient calling, for they left the Ward of the Cordwainers, and settled in the Vintry. Robert's son John, Geoffrey's father, became deputy to the king's Butler at Southampton, and for a time was collector of customs at that port.

Geoffrey appears first as a servant in the household of the countess of Ulster, and afterwards as an esquire in the French wars. His military experience was brief and disastrous. He returned to England, and stepped into the good graces of John of Gaunt. Another upward step brought him upon the threshold of the king's favour, and he was employed in various confidential foreign missions. There is every reason to believe that he displayed great tact and intelligence while thus occupied, and that the allusions to 'good service done,' which appeared in one or two of the patents subsequently endowing him with office, were no idle formulæ.

In 1374 he was granted a pitcher of wine daily from the London Prisage, and later in the year he was made controller of the Custom and Subsidy of wool, fells, and leather in the port of London, the patent to continue 'during the king's pleasure.' The appointment was reaffirmed in 1377.

At this time Chaucer lived in Aldgate, and must have been in affluent circumstances. Both he and his wife Philippa were in receipt of annuities. Occasionally he was employed oversea, and the advances then made him to cover expenses were extremely liberal. His regular income may be stated thus :

By his wife's pension	25	marks	a year.
By his own (paid by the king)	20	,,	,,
By his own (paid by John of Gaunt) ..	15	,,	,,
By his salary as controller	15	,,	,,
By value of his wine allowance.. ..	12	,,	,,
	87	,,	,,

He must also have saved money out of his allowance when employed abroad on the king's business. None can doubt that as controller of the London wool duties he received many secret gifts from merchants, and there were other perquisites; for instance, in 1376 he gained over 100 marks in one sum, as reward for a seizure of uncustomed wool. His total income may be stated as about 150 marks—say £1,500 in modern money.

In 1382 he was made controller of Petty Custom in London, and permitted to employ a deputy. In 1385 he was allowed a permanent deputy, and that period may be deemed the high-water hour of his prosperity. It is likely that he did little customs work, for he gave up his Aldgate house. Soon after this he was made a justice of the peace in Kent. Few poets have done as well, but be it borne in mind few have so well deserved.

In 1386 misfortune overtook him. He lost both his customs appointments—Adam Yerdley succeeding him as controller of the wool duties, Henry Gisors as controller of Petty Custom. In 1388 he lost his annuity; but in 1389 he was taken into partial favour, and made Clerk of Works, receiving 2s. a day. As he was empowered to pre-empt building materials, it may be assumed there were perquisites appertaining. Perhaps 60 marks a year (£600 in modern money) may represent his annual income. The duties of the new office must have been onerous. At various periods he had to supervise the repair of the Royal Chapel at Windsor, and of the historic Wool Quay. He was employed for a time as Commissioner of Sewers and Drainage on the upper marshes of the Thames, and while thus occupied lived at Greenwich.

In 1390 Chaucer, while employed on his official duties, fell into the clutches of one of the gangs of brigands that infested the highways during Richard's reign, and was robbed of horse, equipment, and a considerable sum of money. The robbery took place 'near the Fowle Oak, Hatcham.' Thus much is certain, but in some of the records two subsequent robberies are mysteriously interwoven with the Hatcham affair. That Chaucer should have allowed himself to be robbed three times within a few months, and on two, if not three, occasions by members of the same gang, is almost incredible, yet the records appear to avouch it. It is possible that the mystery attaching to the thefts may have discredited him, for he ceased to be employed officially.

Later he was granted 30 marks a year, an annuity but imperfectly paid; and later still a cask of wine yearly (in some records quoted as a tun, in others as a butt). He fell into pecuniary difficulties, and at one period was compelled to shun the attentions of the sheriff's officer. In 1399, with the proverbial inconstancy of a poet, he burst into song in welcome of the man by whom his late benefactor had been dethroned and imprisoned. Henry granted him an annuity of 40 marks. Upon this allowance—for his previous grant had lapsed—he subsisted for a brief space, residing in a house that stood in the garden of St. Mary's Chapel, Westminster. His remains ennoble the historic 'Poet's Corner.'

He died poor, and, as 'The Retractation' shows, sincerely penitent. Other poets have died as poor as he.

Few, it is to be feared, have died as penitent, yet many have had more to repent of. The man who regretted having written the 'Canterbury Tales' must have been a vassal of Contrition.

CONGREVE.

William Congreve was born at Bardsey, in Yorkshire. The date of his birth lies somewhere between 1669 and 1672. Shortly after the event his father, who was a younger son of an ancient Staffordshire family, obtained a military appointment in Ireland. Thus it came about that Congreve's boyhood was spent in the Irish Midlands, and that his earliest studies were performed in the famous town of Kilkenny. The elder Congreve obtained a situation as manager of an estate owned by the Burlington family, and vacated his military employment.

Congreve went from Kilkenny to Trinity College. From Dublin he proceeded to London, and studied at the Temple; but he had no liking for the law, and the effects of distaste were soon manifest in the form of fictional literature. He wrote a novel entitled 'Incognita, or Love and Duty Reconciled.' (Dr. Johnson declared that he would rather praise the work than read it, and Leigh Hunt stated that he had read it, and was unable to praise it.)

Congreve's first play, 'The Old Bachelor,' came out in 1693. It gained the enthusiastic approval of John Dryden, and was tolerably successful. Soon after this he produced the 'Double Dealer,' which gained little favour. In 1695 appeared 'Love for Love,' which must have been more fortunate, for the celebrated Betterton, then manager of the New Theatre, made an arrangement with the author, under which Congreve was to supply him with a play a year.

Congreve failed to observe the letter of this agreement, and his next piece, 'The Mourning Bride,' did not appear till 1697. It was eminently successful; why is difficult for plain thinkers to divine. Congreve's previous productions had been brisk, sparkling comedies, and the 'Mourning Bride' was an extremely turgid tragedy.

In 1700 Congreve made his final effort in comedy, and it was unsuccessful with the public. 'The Way of the World' fell flat, and its talented author retired, disgusted and incurably resentful. Its collapse has been attributed to the assaults of the celebrated Jeremy Collier, who had initiated a crusade against the obscenities of the stage. Congreve produced afterwards many pieces of verse, but these were not even of ordinary merit. Some of them, indeed, are utterly ridiculous. It is marvellous that so witty a man could have written them.

It seems that Congreve gained little money by his plays, but he was a keen man of the world, and well able to profit by the impression they had made in certain quarters. He stood high in the esteem of Lord Halifax, and repaid with a deal of bad verse the valuable assistance of his aristocratic patron. Halifax procured him a Commissionership of Hackney Coaches, and other valuable offices. In 1700 he was made patent* customer of Poole, in 1714 one of the five under-searchers in the port of London, and later he was endowed with a colonial secretaryship. The appointments were practically sinecures, and must have brought in considerably over £1,000 per annum. Congreve's remarkable personal gifts, placable manners, and aristocratic bearing, endeared him to many women of quality, and several of the leading ladies of the stage. Thus he was enabled to live in a style suitable to his extremely elegant inclinations. To the end of his life he was a true specimen of the 'fashionable gentleman' of his day. He died in 1729, leaving a considerable sum of money, and was buried in Westminster Abbey.

* The London grant does not appear on the Roll, but there can be no doubt as to the appointment, for there is a transcript of the patent in 'Customs Book, 15,' and another of the Treasury order directing that Congreve should be 'sworn in,' and appointing Joshua White as his deputy.

DENNIS.

John Dennis was born in 1657. He was educated at Harrow, and later went to Cambridge. It has been stated that he was expelled from the latter seat of learning for drawing sword upon a fellow-collegian.

His first attempt upon the public favour was made in 1697, when he produced a play called 'A Plot and no Plot,' which failed utterly. In 1700 he brought out 'Iphigenia,' and this also failed. It was followed by an adaptation of 'The Merry Wives of Windsor,' also unsuccessful.

In 1704 he made another attempt, bringing out 'Liberty Asserted.' This was his only success. In 1705 he produced 'Gibraltar,' another fiasco, and followed with a rather grotesque adaptation of Shakespeare's 'Coriolanus.' During the same year he was appointed queen's waiter in the port of London.* Still he could not refrain from flirting with the Tragic Muse. In 1709 out came 'Appius and Virginia.' He also wrote various pieces of verse, mostly addressed to great men of the day, and as fulsome as such pieces usually are.

The best of Dennis is in his criticisms, which are powerfully written, and impregnated with humour of a peculiarly pungent kind. His analysis of Addison's 'Cato' is masterly, and in all English literature there is nothing more amusing than the paper war between Dennis and Steele. Both antagonists are at their best, but Dennis

* Dennis's appointment appears on the Roll (m. 13) dated June 14, 1705. He succeeded one 'Tutchin Martin, defunct.' On the accession of George I. the appointment was reaffirmed, Dennis, of course, becoming a 'king's waiter.' The Treasury notice was signed by Godolphin, the notice of reaffirmation by 'Halifax,' R. Onslow, William St. Quintin, and Edward Wortley. See Swift's amusing lines :

> 'Why has my Lord Godolphin's special grace
> Invested me with a queens-waiter's place,
> If I, debarred of festival delights,
> Am not allowed to spend the perquisites ?'
>
> *John Dennis the Sheltering Poet's Invitation.*

wins easily. His 'Sir John Edgar' is one of the most telling and ferocious satires ever penned.

In 1715 Dennis sold his post in the Customs, and thenceforward his experience was one of disaster. He lived to the age of seventy-seven, and it is distressing to learn that he died blind and poverty-stricken. His latter days are stated to have been intensely wretched, but this is unlikely, for he was a man of indomitable spirit, and his keen and vigorous wit seems to have been unimpaired to the last. It may reasonably be asserted that the English estimation of Dennis's literary powers is by no means as high as it should be. His plays were undoubtedly bad, but there have been few critics as able and fearless, and as skilled in wielding English, as old 'John Dennis of the Custom House.'

SMITH.

Adam Smith came into the world on June 5, 1723, as the posthumous child of the customs controller of Kirkcaldy. During his infancy he was kidnapped by gipsies, and only recovered after a strenuous search. The dark people have been credited with a deep purpose in stealing the children of house-dwellers. Strong and healthy infants, likely to effect profitable 'crossing' in the Romany blood, were the usual objects of depredation. As little Adam was an extremely delicate child, it is likely they anticipated need of a 'patrico.'

Adam received his early education at the Kirkcaldy Grammar School. His mental gifts were even then conspicuous, for he was a greedy and discerning reader, and his powers of memory were remarkable. As is usual in such cases, he was physically feeble, and unfitted to take part in the tumultuous recreations of boyhood.

At the age of fourteen he went to Glasgow University, and three years later to Balliol College, Oxford, where he remained till he was twenty-four. His immense application to study was not encouraged by the English professors. Oxford furnished him with books and leisure, and little else. He had been intended for the Church, but his extensive studies and philosophical turn of mind frustrated the scheme. So he returned to Kirkcaldy, and till the end of 1748 resided with his mother.

Later he gained the patronage of Lord Kames. He removed to Edinburgh, and became distinguished as a lecturer upon polite literature. In 1751 he was made Professor of Logic and Moral Philosophy at Glasgow University. In 1759 he published his 'Theory of Moral Sentiments,' a work which at once secured popularity. Then he accompanied the young duke of Buccleuch in a tour upon the Continent.

On his return to Scotland, he threw himself with great ardour into the prosecution of a long-cherished literary project. After a severe course of study, he produced his 'Wealth of Nations,' a treatise at once acclaimed, and destined to found an entirely new scheme of economics. His lordly patrons appear to have resolved that the author of a work so creditable to the Lowland Scottish mind should not depend for pecuniary reward solely upon the shillings of a responsive public. In 1778 Adam was made a Scottish Commissioner of Customs. It is our opinion that the stately pronouncement upon the erratic practice of the ports of Montrose and Ferryden was furnished by him. His salary would certainly not be less than £500, and as he appears to have enjoyed an annuity of £300 as well, he was undoubtedly 'in a tolerable position.' He seems to have been fond of a bottle of wine, a game of whist, and the society of well-informed people, and it is likely that auld Edinburgh provided him with many an opportunity towards such eminently rational enjoyments.

One of his biographers has expressed disapprobation of the Customs appointment, asserting that it arrested Smith's literary labours. 'The performance of petty routine duties,' says the uncompromising commentator, 'engrossed the greater part of his time.' No doubt Adam

Smith was an earnest and painstaking Commissioner, but it should be borne in mind that he had several assistants, and the task of supervising the collection of the trifling revenue then furnished by Scotland could scarcely have wearied the mind that had constructed the 'Wealth of Nations.' And though the duties were light, they were not mechanical. They involved *practical* contact with matters of trade and revenue—a form of discipline which a scholarly recluse like Adam Smith stood in urgent need of. The great defects of the 'Theory of Moral Sentiments' and 'Wealth of Nations'—the great and apparent defects—were lack of knowledge of the world and the innumerable complexities of human nature. It is possible that Adam Smith, being an eminently receptive person, learned much while he was a Commissioner of Customs. And perhaps this may explain why he ceased to write books.

Undoubtedly he had given the world his best, and was conscious that a sedate and restful autumn should follow the abundant yield. So he did as Johnson had done. It should be remembered that he had acquired a position much more lucrative than that enjoyed by the Sage of Fleet Street. Yet Johnson had outdone him in literary achievement, though compelled to fight a way through obstacles which Adam Smith would never have been able to overcome.

Smith's society was almost as ardently courted in Edinburgh as Johnson's had been in London, yet modern students of 'the original' in mind and character would have deemed five minutes of Johnson worth a year of the Scottish philosopher. The milder social virtues may have been preferred in Edinburgh, and in these Smith certainly excelled. His benignity and sweetness of character are manifest in all his writings.

In 1787 Smith was made Lord Rector of Glasgow University. His extreme sincerity and loyalty were fully exemplified in his acknowledgment of the distinction. He attributed all his success to the managers of the institution. 'They educated me; they sent me to Oxford.' He might with justice have added: 'And at Oxford I educated myself.'

He died in 1790, of a most painful disorder, the pangs and distresses of which he endured with characteristic firmness and dignity. Many men have possessed more striking gifts, few have been more deserving of the title of 'Scholar.' His works bear every evidence of sustained and laborious though occasionally imperfect thought. And he wrote 'the English' beautifully.

APPENDIX

ILLUSTRATIVE DOCUMENTS

Preamble of C. 4, 3 Edw. IV., prohibiting foreign manufactured goods.

'COME en le dit p'lement, p' lartificers des mestiers mainuelx, homes & femes, en la Cite de Loundres & autres Citeez, Villez, Burghs, & Villages, deins cest roialme & Gales inhabitaunz & reseauntz, piteousment ad estre monstre & compleigne coment toutz ceux en gen'all & chun deux sont g[a]undement empov'ez & grevousment endamagez & p'judicez de leur encrece du mond & vivre cotidian, p' la g[a]und multitude des div's chaffares & wares, a leur mestiers & occupacions app'teign'tez, esteantz pleinement ov'ez & p'st faitz al vende, si bien p' les mains destraungez esteantz enemiez du Roy, come autres en cest roialme & Gales de la le mere amesnez, si bien p' m'chants estranges come deinszeins & autre p'sones,' etc.

The above may be freely rendered thus : ' Whereas piteous complaint has been made in the said parliament, by the artificers of mysteries of handicraft, men and women, inhabiting and resident in the City of London and other cities, towns, boroughs, and villages in this realm and Wales, how that they all, each and in general, are greatly impoverished and grievously injured and prejudiced in their worldly increase and daily living, by the great multitude of various commodities and wares appertaining to their mysteries and occupations, being fully wrought and made ready for sale, as well by the hands of strangers being enemies of the king, as by others of this realm and Wales brought oversea, as well by merchant strangers as by denizens and other persons,' etc.

(The context prohibits a variety of manufactured articles.)

Extract from 'A Remembrance to my Lord Protectours Grace' (Duke of Somerset), 1547. Probably supplied from the Exchequer Memoranda. Embodying suggestions of a new tax upon cloth, and a tax of 1d. on each sheep, etc.

'The p'fetts of Custome and subsidie of wolls, wollfells & clothes* and the Aulnage therof, in the 28th yere of the reigne of Kyng Edward the thirde,

	£	s.	d.
'Shipped over the same yere in wolle, 34,760 sacks, whiche rated at 40s. the sacke for Custome and subsidie amountithe to	69,558	0	0
'Shipped over the same yere in fells, 348,451, whiche was rated at 2d. the fell, amountithe to	2,900	0	0
'Shipped over the same yere in Clothes, 2,483, w[ch] rated after 14d. the cloth amountithe to	144	0	0
'The p'fetts of the Alnage the same yere	344	3	7
	£72,946	3	7'

(Noted on document) 'Memorand.†—that here is no difference made betwene the Custome of the Straungers and Englysshmen, but all rated after one soorte, that y[s], after 40s. the sacke, where the Straunger paieth for ev[y] sacke £3 16s. 8d.'

(Noted in other handwriting) '*And so it maye be gathered that the p'fett of the Custome and subsidies was greater.*'

(Original handwriting) 'Sacke of wolle conteyneth 13 todde. A todd conteyneth 28 li.‡

'Allowed to ev[y] todd 20 sheere shepe, because it is thought that ther was not so many pasture sheepe in the tyme of Kyng Edward the thirde as be nowe, but moste Men kept on the Comons. And after that rate for ev[y] sacke there must be accompted 260 sheepe. Accompted after that rate for 34,760 sacks ..	9,037,600 sheepe.
'Allowed for every clothe 3 todde and to ev[y] todd 20 sheepe, and so for ev[y] clothe 60 sheepe. To make 2,483 clothes ther must be accompted	148,980 sheepe.
'It appeareth also by the Wolfells that were shipped, whereof the bodies were eaten or perisshed in the Realme, that ther were that yere also	348,451 sheepe.
'So that after this rate it may be justly and truly saied that ther were in the Realme in the 28th yere of the reigne of Kyng Edward the thirde	9,535,031 sheepe.'

* Cloths.

† Evidently denizens were not allowed to export wool during that year.

‡ Lbs.

'The p'fetts of Custome and Subsidie of Wolle, Wollfells, and clothes, and the Aulnage thereof, the 38th yere of the reigne of Kinge Henry the eight.

	£	s.	d.
'Shipped over the same year in wolle by Englysshmen 1,136 sackes, and whiche rated at 40s. the sacke Custome and Subsidie amountithe to	2,272	0	0
'Shipped over the same yere by Straungers in Wolle 419 Sacks, which rated at £3 16s. 8d. the sacke amountithe to	1,625	3	4
'Shipped over the same yere in wollfells 363,829, whiche rated at 2d. the fell amountithe to ..	3,031	4	10
'Shipped over the same yere in Clothes 172,017, rated after 14d. the clothe, amountithe to ..	10,056	13	2
'The p'fetts of the alnage of the same yere	758	14	0
	£17,743	15	4
'And so it appereth that Kyng Edward the third had more yerely by his Custome then Kyng Henry the eight had by*..	£55,202	8	3

'And before the said Kyng Edwarde had for two yeres a Subsidie of the 9th sheepe, the 9th fleese,† the 9th Lambe, and the 9th parte of all the goodes of Marchaunts and Denyzyns.

'At the rate of 20 sheepe to the todd, 260 to the sacke and 60 to a clothe it appereth by the woll, wollfells and clothes carried out of the Realme in the 38th yere of the reigne of Kyng Henry the eight that ther were in the realme the same yere .. .. 11,089,149 sheepe.

'In all this accompte no mention is made of the sheepe whose wolle was made into Clothe and cappes spent that yere in the Realme, nor of skynnes tanned, lether, or parchement. And therefore it maye be trulye saied that ther wer more sheepe than is before reherste.'

(This curious document may not be altogether reliable. It will be observed that the amounts of duty, except in one instance, do not agree exactly with the quantities and rates, but there may have been 'remnants.' It is by no means certain that the 40s. rate quoted for wool and fells in Edward III.'s reign includes the Ancient Custom, or that 2d. a fell represents the fell duty even at the 40s. rate, for the duty was then charged on 300 fells, instead of 240 as computed. But the calculations as to sheep are worked out correctly, and the totals are rather surprising. If an estimate

* Henry had tunnage, poundage, and the wine impost. † Fleece.

be made to account for the wool used in the kingdom the results will be almost incredible. It is likely that the estimate of sheep for Henry VIII.'s time is approximately correct as regards its connexion with the wool, fells, and cloth produced for shipment. If we increase it by one-half to account for the wool used in England, the result may be stated as 15,000,000 sheep. If the same proportion per head of population obtained at the present day, what a noble shearing-time! It appears that the old writers were correct when they maintained that English wealth was founded on English wool, and that the true emblems of England's strength were the long bow and the shepherd's crook.)

Order in Council, supporting the Merchant Adventurers in their dispute with one Thomas Clecher. Date, 1570.

'Trustie and welbeloved, we grete you well, and beinge enformed that divers p'sonnes not free of that your Company, nor brought upp in trade of m'chaundize, do not only empeche your trade, as well by unskilfull and disorderly occupyinge, as also by violatinge suche yor pryveleges by great traveile and charge of o^r progenito^{rs} graunt apteyned and graunted: And amongst other, that one Thom^s Clecher dothe without order or Authoritie entermeddell wth trade of m'chaundize in the lowe Countreis of Holland, Zeeland, Brabant, and Flaunders, and non'thelesse dothe stubbornely and obstinatly refuse to abide suche orders as other of yor compeny doo, and also dothe attempte to caull s^d previleges in question by the Lawe there: Wee, myndinge the p'servacon of good orders and the may'tennance of that your compeny, do will and comaund ye that by vertue of theis s^d Letters ye do in o^r name comaund the said Thomas to s^{r}cease* his sewte† there and stande to abide and obey suche yor orders as is amongst ye provyded for suche offenders: And o^r further will and pleasure is that if at anny tyme hereafter anny p'son not free of that compeny do attempte to trafficke into the said lowe Countreis, or to break or violate your privileges and good orders, that ye doe likewise by vertue of these our L^{res} comaund in o^r name all and any suche p'son and p'sonnes to appere before ye, and to stande to abide and obey all suche good orders and ordinaunces as by ye have bynne made and ordeyned. And if either ye said Clecher or anny other disordered p'sonne do refuse to accomplish the contente of theise our L^{res} that then ye do comaund hym or them in o^r name to appere before o^r Pryvie Councell, and that ye do

* Surcease. † Suit.

adv'tise o^r said Councell thereof with the p'ticulars of his or their offence or mysdemeano^r, to th'entent we may take suche order wth hym as may be to the example of anny attempting the like, and the p'servacon of yor previleges and good orders wch we mynde by all meanes to mayneteyne.'

Précis of a Warrant to pay certain customs moneys to Raleigh and Hawkins. Date, 1591.

'Whereas there is paieable unto Sr Walter Raleigh, Knight, at the Ann'ciation of O^r Lady next, the some of £1,000, and at Michael^s then next following £1,000, to be taken out of such Customes as shall growe due for the Custome of ov^r-lengthes* and remnaunts of clothes† to be transported, this to give order unto the Customers of the port of London to paie unto the said Sr Walter Raleigh such somes of money as shall appeare to be in theire hands, arising out of the Customes aforesaid since Michal‡—last past: And in case the same shall not suffice to make up the some of £2,000, then to paie unto him of her M^s treasure in the Receipt such further somes as shall want of the said some of £2,000, and to recale the same againe into the Receipt of th' Exchequer at the hands of the said Customers as it shall growe due upon the said Customes of ov^r-lengthes and remnaunts of clothes: And further to paie unto Sr John Hawkins, knight, Treas^r of her Ma^tys navie, the some of £500 of her M^s treasure in th' Exchequer, for the furnishing and setting in order of her Ma^tys Shipp called the *Crane*, appointed to serve at sea under the charge of the saide Sr Walter Raleigh.'§

A Scheme for remodelling James I.'s 'Book of Rates.' (The document appears to have been submitted to Cranfield, the surveyor-general of Customs, and is a fair specimen of the incoherent propositions occasionally tendered by interested fiscal 'reformers.')

'Comodities not to be altered in Custome or Impost, but to remayne in the book of rates as they nowe are:

'*Outwards.*—Baies.‖ (This may well be put into the rate, and the Imposicon removed). Lead. Tynn.

'*Inwards.* — Sugars (In Farme to the Queenes Matie), Beaver hatts, starche (both forraine manufactures), Whalefynns, cloves, mace, nutmegge, Synnamon,¶ gynger.

* Over-lengths. † Cloths. ‡ Michaelmas.
§ Against the Spanish plate-fleet. ‖ Bays. ¶ Cinnamon.

'Comodities w[ch] are to be Improved* in the rates and Impost:

'Silk of all kynds, wrought and unwrought, one-third in both, except Rawe Silke long and short, w[ch] shalbe improved ⅓ in the rates onlie, w[thout] anie imposicon at all. Pepper ⅓ in both. Lawnes and cambricks to be improved ⅓ both in custome and Impost. Incle,† wrought, to be improved ⅓ in both. Fustians of all kyndes to be improved ⅓ in the rates onlie, and the imposicon to be whollie taken away. Currants, the imposicon of them to be setled at 5s. 6d. p-hundred, as the late Queene left them. Tobacco to be improved to 20s. in the rates onlie, as the king's ma[tie] wth his privie counsell latelie ordered it. French wynes to be improved in the rates onlie to 16£ a tonn. Sweet wynes to be improved in the rates onlie to 8£ p-butt. Rhenish wynes to be improved in the rates onlie to 3£ p-aum. Wyne vinagar to be improved in the rates onlie to 8£ a tonn.

'Comodities uppon w[ch] are Impost, w[ch] shalbe whollie taken off and put into the rates, w[thout] streyning‡ uppon the subject, and must be done out of necessitie, for the tyeng§ strang[rs] to make imployement.

'Holland cloth, callicoes, dyap[er],|| damask, and all other kyndes of forraine lynnin cloth, excepting 8 or tenn sorts. Playing cardes, Estridge fethers, hopps, pynnes, oyle, tap'strie, indico,¶ qucheneile,** druggs, cloth of gold or silver.'

(Here follows a recapitulation. Then the proposer continues his rambling statement.)

'As alsoe all the other 1,200 Comodities conteyned in the book of rates, and here not menconed, to remayne as nowe they are, w[thout] improvement or alteracon, ether in Custome or Impost.

'Memoranda.

'The ports are whollie eased in this alteracon, who, being manye in parliament, make all the claime. The comon wealth in gen'all eased, there being nothing nowe chardged but Dellicacyes and sup'fluityes, w[ch] beggers the state. The kynge looseth as much on the necessarie things by undervaluing as he gaynes by these fewe sup'fluityes, they being manye in number, and these but fewe. So that the chardging the one and undervaluing the other is done by his Ma[tie] wth the advise of his Counsell, for the publique good, and not for gayne as is surmysed. This maie be done, and all the farmes manteyned, w[thout] anie alteracon or difficultie. For the

* Raised. † Inkle (linen tape). ‡ Oppressing.
§ Compelling. || Diaper. ¶ Indigo.
** Cochineal.

kynges Offic^{rs} may receave to his Maties use the difference betweene the Customes and Imposicons, wch are nowe fell, and wch were before. And they maye lykewyse forbeare to demaund these wch his Matie hath remytted. And there is no alloweance to be made to anie farme^{rs}, by cause all the Imposicons wch his Matie hath dischardged are in his owne hands.'

Part of C. 24, 16 *Chas. I.* (*Long Parliament*), 1640.

'Whereas many thousands of your Majestie's good and loving subjects, with their ships and goods, have of late time beene surprised and taken at Sea * * * by Turkish, Moorish, and other Pirats. * * * And whereas as well your Majestie's subjects as Strangers * * * have ever sithence your Majestie's accesse unto this Crowne been charged with the payment of great Sums of money under the name of Custom, and that without consent of Parliament ; which, had they been legally taken, ought to have been cheifly imployed to the safeguard of the Seas * * * but have been exhausted by evil Ministers, and not applied to their proper uses :'

(The Act stipulates that an additional levy of 1 per cent. on all duties—presumably 1 per cent. extra on all goods liable to poundage—shall be made, to provide immediate protection against the aforesaid pirates. The moneys to be received by the Mayor and Chamberlain of London. The Act concludes as below.)

'That your Majesty would in time to come be pleased to intrust such Ministers as may faithfully imploy the moneys raised by Tunnage and Poundage unto the right and proper uses,' etc.

Order to the Remembrancer of the Exchequer to proceed for arrears against the lessees of the Customs farm of 1662-1667. *Date, August* 25, 1671.

'After our hearty commendacones :

'Whereas the late Farmers of his Ma^{ts} Customes for five yeares ending at Michael — 1667, are indebted to his Matie in a greate sume of money upon their Accompt, wch they have long delayed to pay. & doe still detaine in their hands to his Mat^{es} greate p'judice. & whereby the same is in danger to be lost, these are therefore to desire and direct you forthwith to cause pro^{sses} * of immediate payment to issue out against

* Processes.

the bodies, goods, and lands of ye said farmers & their heires, Execut^{rs}, & Adm^{rs}, in order to ye satisfaccon of his Ma$^{ty's}$ debt due from them : And soe now bid you heartily farewell, and remaine, &c.'

Petition of Joshua Wright, referred favourably by the king to the Treasury, in order that the Commissioners of Customs might provide employment as requested. Date of transmission to Treasury, December 6, 1679.

'Humbly setting forth to his Ma^{ty} that his father, Erasmus Wright of ye Citty of Bristoll, Merch^{t}, in ye yeare 1643—his Highness Prince Rupert then besieging ye s^{d} Citty—was by a great shott slayne, whiles he was giveing his Highness an acco^{t} of the Rebells strength in ye sayd Citty, whereby his famely suffered much : Ye Petit^{r} also beeing taken in ye yeare 77 by two Algerine men of warr in sight of Silly,* lost all his goods to his utter ruine : That in July, 1678, upon ye humble Peticon of ye s^{d} Wright for a Landwaiter's place in ye Port of London, his Ma^{ty} granted a Refference thereon to ye then L^{d} high Treas^{r}, but ye Petit^{r} not obteyning ye effects thereof prays that in memory & compassion of his father's death as aforesaid, & his own great losses, a speciall order to enter into ye s^{d} place or imploy, wth ye first vacancy that shall fall.'

Treasury Warrant to the Commissioners of Customs to unite two revenue offices in the American Plantations, and grant the combined salaries to the person remaining in office. Date, April 7, 1679.

'After our hearty Comendacions :

'You haveing presented unto us Nicholas Spencer, Esqr, as a fitt person to be Collector of his Mat^{s} Customes at Potomack River in Virginia, for the whole collection, Mr. John Washington† who was formerly joyned with him being deceased : These are to pray and require you to issue forth your deputacon to the said Nicholas Spencer to be the sole Collector at the said place accordingly, with the allowance of Sallary which both received, and under such instructions to be given him as you shall thinke fitt for his Ma^{ts} service : And for soe doeing this shall be your warrant.'

* Scilly. † George Washington's great-grandfather : died 1677.

Précis of a Return furnished to Admiralty by Customs, January 29, 1702. (*Illustrative of the effect of the Navigation Act.*)

	1695. Total Tonnage of Ships that cleared from London.	1701. Total Tonnage of Ships that cleared from London.
English	65,786	132,634
Foreign	52,138	34,773
	117,924	167,407

Comparative Trade of Ports in 1701. (*English tonnage.*)

London, 132,634; Bristol, 17,338; Ipswich, 11,170; Newcastle, 11,000; Yarmouth, 9,914; Liverpool, 8,619. (Bideford furnished almost as large a return as Liverpool; so did Exeter. Scarborough's tonnage almost equalled that of Hull.)

From 1695 to 1701 inclusive, over 1,000 ships in ballast entered the port of London. Thus it would seem that the export trade preponderated.

Extract from a statement of the Public Revenue of Scotland for five years subsequent to the Union (May 1, 1707, *to May* 1, 1712).

			£	s.	d.
'The Excise from 1st May, 1707, to 1st May, 1712..			259,175	10	6¼
'The Customes in that time	£171,811 16s. 7¼d.	In Money	245,452	11	5
	£55,435 7s. 3d.	Outstanding Bonds			
	£18,205 7s. 6¾d.	Seizures actually paid			
			£504,628	1	11¼

'These two Revenues of Excise & Customes for these five years do make annually the sum of £100,000, and a surplus £4,628 1s. 11¼d. to compensate the drawbacks which may happen to be taken out of the Bonds stated above as a part of the Customes, and is given here by gross, because the Commissioners of ye Customes have not thought fitt that the amount of those drawbacks should appear by the account sent to the Commissioners of Equivalent.'

(By the same return it appears that the Crown rents produced annually about £5,500, the Compositions in Exchequer £1,943, the Land Tax £48,000, and the 'poste office' *about £3,000!* The Coinage duty brought in about £1,500. Thus the total annual Scottish revenue barely reached £160,000.)

English Export Trade in Corn, Malt, and Oatmeal.

'*An Account of Corn exported out of England from Christmas, 1720, to Christmas, 1727, with the value thereof by the medium prices that the several sorts of Corn bore at Bear Key* at Midsummer Day in the several respective years.*

Years.	*Barley.*			*Malt.*				*Oatmeal.*			*Rye.*				*Wheat.*			
	Qrs.	s.	d.	Qrs.	£	s.	d.	Qrs.	s.	d.	Qrs.	£	s.	d.	Qrs.	£	s.	d.
1721	11,608	15	6	338,942	1	3	0	3,538	10	6	69,697	0	14	0	81,632	1	5	0
1722	37,730	12	0	366,526	0	16	6	1,000	11	0	42,579	0	12	6	178,880	1	3	6
1723	45,789	19	6	305,063	1	2	0	541	13	6	12,737	0	16	6	157,719	1	10	6
1724	10,289	15	0	241,895	0	19	0	516	12	0	23,441	0	18	6	245,864	1	5	6
1725	13,782	18	6	294,025	1	2	6	1,447	12	0	20,539	1	4	6	204,413	2	7	6
1726	20,017	13	0	325,925	1	3	6	1,412	11	6	18,835	0	16	0	142,183	1	12	0
1727	8,688	18	0	241,428	1	3	0	2,204	11	0	9,169	1	1	0	30,315	1	10	0

'John Oxenford, A.S.I.G.

'Inspector-General's Office,
'Custom House,
'15*th August*, 1728.'

* Bear Quay stood near the Custom-house, London. It should be observed that the figures are Midsummer prices (just prior to harvest-time, when corn would be at its highest value).

Extract from the collector of Colchester's letter to the Board of Customs, April 16, 1748.

'This morning about two o'clock two persons went to John Bloys (he being then at a granary upon the Town Key) and inquired where the Custom-house was, pretending that a Seizure of Tea had been made, and must be immediately lodged there, or it would be rescued by the Smuglers who were in pursuit of it: Upon which Bloys went to the Custom-house with the said men, and called upon Thomas Coker the collector's servant: Upon which Coker came downstairs and opened the door of the collector's house: Immediately upon the door being opened the two men took hold of Bloys and Coker by the collar, and, presenting pistols to their breasts, swore they'd kill them that moment if they made any noise or resistance: Near Thirty Smuglers armed with Blunderbusses and Pistols came into the courtyard, threat'ning with dreadful Imprecations,' etc.

(The letter proceeded to state that the smugglers broke into the King's Warehouse, and carried off a quantity of tea, previously seized near Woodbridge Haven by Robert Martin, captain of a revenue cruiser. It ended as below.)

'The King's Warehouse is a very secure place, but the greatest security imaginable would not have prevented these desperate villains from effecting their design, they having told Bloys and Coker that had they met with resistance they were resolved to have murdered every person that obstructed them, and came fully determined to have the goods or die in the attempt. Mr. William Lisle, supervisor of the riding-officers, and several other persons, went after the Smuglers, and heard they were got to Hadleigh in Suffolk by 6 o'clock in the morning, and what became of them afterwards they could not hear.'

Specimen of Information laid in the Irish Court of Exchequer relative to East India goods, imported into Ireland without previous unshipment in Great Britain.

'Be it Remembered, that Thomas Foorder, who as well on behalf of our sovereign lord the King as of himself prosecutes in this behalf, came before the barons of his Majesty's Court of Exchequer on the 2nd day of June in this term, in his proper person, and as well on behalf of our sovereign lord the

King as himself gave the said Court to understand that on the 2nd day of July, in the year of our Lord one thousand seven hundred and fifty nine, at Shiphaven in the county of Londonderry, he did seize and arrest to the use of our said lord the King and himself the said Thomas Foorder a certain ship or vessel called the *Swift* sloop, with all her guns, tackle, furniture, ammunition, and apparel, and the following goods and commodities then and there on board the said ship, that is to say, 21 casks of green tea, 102 casks of bohea tea, and one cask of rhubarb, for that the said goods and commodities, being of the growth, produce, and manufacture of the East Indies,' etc.

Extract from a Letter furnished by Mr. Heron, collector of Potomac River in Maryland, January 3, 1765, *giving particulars of an assault committed on him whilst he was trying to sell a ship and certain goods, condemned under the Plantation Acts.*

'The numberless abuses and continual threatnings to shoot me, &c. makes me sensible of the melancholy situation of this office * * * this office is seated, as I can almost say, amongst nothing but a gang of smuglers. * * * No one would bid, most of them being concerned in the illicit trade. * * * On the day appointed for sale of the brig I gave attendance for that purpose, accompany[d] by Mr. Gibbs, Comptroller of the Customs at Annapolis,' etc.

(The letter goes on to state that none would bid for the condemned ship, and that her captain, with a number of supporters, 'all Scotch,' attended. The captain, after making himself furious with drink, attacked Heron with a club, the other Scots holding Heron's arms meanwhile. 'He certainly would have murdered me, had not the man of the house, who is a very strong bold fellow, released [rescued] me.' The letter ends as below.)

'I humbly hope your Honours will contrive ways and means for our better protection from the Insults of such a Villanious set of People. I never go out but am doubly armed with a hanger, a pair of pistols in my Pockets, and another before me.'

Patent appointing Resident Commissioners of Customs in the American Plantations (*September* 8, 1767).

'George the Third by the Grace of God, &c.: To our Trusty and Wellbeloved Henry Hulton, John Temple, William Burch, Charles Paxton, and John Robinson, Esquires, Greeting: Whereas by an Act of Parliament lately passed to Enable us to put the Customs and other Duties in the British Dominions in America, and the Execution of the Laws relating to Trade there, under the management of Comissioners to be appointed for that purpose and to be Resident in the said Dominions, It is Enacted that the Customs and other Duties Imposed by any Act or Acts of Parliament upon any Goods or Merchandises brought or Imported into or Exported or carried from any British Colony or Plantation in America may from time to time be put under the management and direction of such Comissioners, to reside in the said Plantations, as Wee, our heirs and Successors, by our or their commission or commissions under the Great Seal of Great Britain, shall Judge to be most for the advantage of Trade and Security of the Revenue of the said British Colonies,' etc.

(The new Commissioners were given powers similar to those exercised in England by the Commissioners at London. They might appoint, remove, or displace inferior officers, or take security for their good behaviour. They might issue warrants for payment of rewards and 'incidents,' and compound for petty seizures. They might administer oaths, and empower the Cashier to pay salaries out of the customs takings. They might search ships by day or night, and—bearing a writ of assistance—warehouses, etc., by day. Admiralty officers, justices, etc., were enjoined to assist them. They were to obey orders received from the Treasury, and to see that the duties were properly collected and paid in to the Cashier. After salaries, etc., had been paid, the surplus was to be remitted to the Receiver-General of Customs in England, who was to apportion the moneys to the respective Customs branches, and pay them into the Exchequer. An advice of moneys thus remitted was to be sent to the English Commissioners of Customs.

The salary of a resident Commissioner was £500. The Commissioners' powers extended over the whole coast of the American Colonies, from Davis's Straits to the Capes of Florida, as well as Bermuda and the Bahamas.)

Extract from a Petition sent by the collector of Boston, Massachusetts, to the Commissioners of the Treasury, December 16, 1775.

'Humbly Sheweth: That your petitioner was appointed collector in August, 1773.

'That soon after, that spirit of Resistance to the Revenue Laws, which had shewn itself on many occasions, began then to breake out into open Acts of Violence, particularly in the Destruction of the Tea belonging to the East India Company, during which Transaction your Petitioner executed at hazzard of his life the Duties of his office, and although left without any other support than the Comptroller he never quitted his station during all that scene of anarchy and Confusion which then prevailed in the Town of Boston, and when all the other officers of the Crown were obliged to leave the Place, and take Refuge in the Castle and elsewhere.'

(He went on to state that when the port was closed by the Act of 1774 he and the comptroller were removed to Plymouth, Massachusetts, that the ships usually discharging at Boston entered and cleared at Salem, and that he thus received nothing but his salary—£100 a year—and lost the fees he had been accustomed to take from the merchants and shippers of Boston.)

'Your petitioner is the more encouraged to hope as he has been informed that your Lordships had ordered a Minute to be made that the Officers of the Customs should be compensated,' etc.

(He stated he had his account made up accordingly.)

'But your petitioner has received for answer that the People of the Country had stopped all communication between Boston and Plymouth,' etc.

(The books and accounts had been removed to Plymouth.)

'And in all probability would be destroyed by the Populace, as they had seized the Boat belonging to the Customhouse and dragged her up into the middle of the town,' etc.

(He asked for compensation, and furnished an account of the perquisites he gained from August 16, 1773, to June 1, 1774. It appears that the collector's fees in the port of

Boston for ten and a half months amounted to £1,259 9s. 6½d. 'lawful money,' which represented in 'sterling value'—lawful tender of the Colonies = ¾ths sterling—£944 12s. 1⅜d.)

'The above is a true account of the money I received for my Fees of Office during the Time therein specified.

'RICHARD ACKLOM HARRISON.'

Specimen of a customs document, securing to the bearer immunity from impress (vide p. 421).

'These are to certify whom it may concern: That the bearer *Edward Reed* aged *36* years, *5 feet 8 inches high, brown complexion, wears his hair, the middle finger of his right hand crooked*, is a

'*Harpooner*, belonging to the ship *Marianne* in the Greenland Trade, and hath given security to the Commissioners of His Majesty's Customs to proceed in the said Ship to Greenland the next season, and is not to be imprest from or out of the said Service; By virtue of an Act of Parliament passed in the eleventh year of his present Majesty's Reign, intituled, *An Act for the better support and Establishment of the Greenland and Whale Fishery*: Witness our hands and Seals of Office, Custom House, *London*; Dated the *3rd* day of *August*, One thousand Seven Hundred and Eighty *Two*.

'WM. BATES, Dy. Coll[r].
W. FLETCHER, Dy. Comp[tr].
I. FATHWELL.'

Statement made before the collector of Penzance, by an inhabitant of Newlyn, Cornwall.

'Deposeth: That on the 17th day of July, 1783, he, with Anthony Hallah, Francis Hocking, John Tregurtha, John Maddein, Richard Kelynack, Paul Tonkin, Richard Tonkin, William Maddein, Thomas Rowe, John Thomas, James Goodlines, Jacob Thomas, Richard Yeoman, Francis Ruffneck, a man nicknamed "Jolly," and six others, boarded a foreign brigantine, about six leagues from the Lizard, and feloniously and piratically took and carried away about 60 loaves white sugar, a quantity of spices, about 1,000 pounds coffee, &c. &c. * * * And out of another foreign brigantine three casks and one chest silk handkerchiefs, and about three gallons brandy, &c. &c.'

(The collector in his report on this deposition stated as below, for the information of the Board of Customs and the Admiralty.)

'We are now surrounded with a set of the most abandoned fellows in this Nation, and it is almost impossible for any of the officers of this Revenue to make their appearance out of doors without being insulted and ill-used.'

Letter from the Secretary of Customs to the Secretary to the Admiralty, December 17, 1788.

'The Commissioners finding it necessary to apply to Captain Horatio Nelson, Commander of one of His Majesty's Ships of War on the West India Station, in respect to the Seizure of two vessels carried into Nevis in the year 1785: I am commanded to request you will favour me with his address, in order that a Letter may be written to him on that Subject.' (Minute, endorsed by Admiralty: 'Let him know it. Burnham, Norfolk.')

Treasury Warrant empowering the Commissioners of Customs to pay an additional sum to Nelson, on account of the seizure of a vessel in the West Indies.

'Having considered your Secretary's letters of the 20th Decr. 1797, and 9th and 11th January, 1798, with their several enclosures, upon the subject of a Decree made by the High Court of Admiralty, reversing a Decree of the Court of Admiralty at Nevis against a ship called the *Jane and Elizabeth*, which was seized by Sir Horatio Nelson in the year 1786 at Barbadoes, and we being of opinion that Sir H. Nelson should be indemnified at the expense of the Crown: These are, under the particular instances of the case, to authorise and require you to direct payment to be made, out of the King's share of seizures, of the sum of £1,131 6s. 6d. which, with the sum of £175 8s. 7d. received by Sir H. Nelson, will make up the sum awarded to be paid by the Decree of the Court of Admiralty, for which this shall be your warrant.'

Extract from the journal of Pendock Neal, captain of the Lord Hawke, a vessel cruising under letters of marque. Journal forwarded to Admiralty by the collector of Plymouth, 1798, (*vide p.* 402.)

'Aug. 12th, 1798. Took the brig *Argo* with Brandy and dry goods (Chartered by French merchants).

'Aug. 16th, 1798. Retook the *Mary and Elizabeth* of Dartmouth.*

'Aug. 23rd, 1798. Captured the *Nostra Senora del Carmena* (with four others, names unknown) loaded with wheat, and a lugger with coffee and sugar.

'Sept. 6th, 1798. Destroyed a French privateer with 40 men, which had taken our boat.

'Sept. 7th, 1798. Took the Spanish packet *La Edad del Oro*, loaded with cocoa, from Vera Cruz. She threw the mail overboard, which was recovered after it had sunk by John Watson, a seaman of the *Lord Hawke*, who cut the ballast from it after it was a considerable way under the water.'

Extract from declaration made before the collector of Greenock, September 3, 1798, *by John Jamieson, master of the 'Margaret' of Greenock, who shortly after leaving Sligo with a cargo of kelp had been captured by the French squadron that conveyed the troops used in Humbert's invasion.*

Jamieson deposes that his ship was seized by 'Three French vessels full of troops. That he thinks the total number of Troops landed did not exceed Eighteen Hundred men. That his vessel was filled with Military stores, and discharged the same at Killala on the morning of the 23rd August. That the declarant was permitted to remain on board his vessel all the time that the French were at Killala, and was allowed to go on shore to the bishop's house with a guard. That he was in the town of Killala on Wednesday last the 29th ult. about two o'clock in the afternoon, by which time the Enemy were joined by a great number of the country people, who were immediately clothed in uniform, and furnished with arms and ammunition. That he heard that upwards of 3,000 of the country people had joined the enemy at Killala. That he was informed by the Frenchmen that they had landed 60,000 stand of arms. That the French frigates left the Bay early on the morning of the 24th with a contrary wind. That in the afternoon of the 28th a 64-gun ship, three

* This vessel had been captured by the enemy.

frigates, and a King's Cutter* came into the Bay, and burnt the brig and some other vessels lying there, and remained there. Declared that when at Killala on Monday the 27th† he heard that on the day before the enemy had defeated General Lake at Castlebar, and that he saw some of the King's troops brought in as prisoners to Killala.

'JOHN JAMIESON, *Deponent.*
CHAS. OGILVIE, *Collector.*'

* Revenue cruiser. These vessels often performed most valuable work in addition to their ordinary spells of duty, being used as advice boats, transport boats, etc.

† 27th altered to 28th.

INDEX

REPRINTS OF ECONOMIC CLASSICS

THE KING'S CUSTOMS

VOL. II

CHARLES W. PEACH, A.L.S.

Frontispiece.

THE KING'S CUSTOMS

VOL. II

AN ACCOUNT OF MARITIME REVENUE, CONTRABAND TRAFFIC, THE INTRODUCTION OF FREE TRADE, AND THE ABOLITION OF THE NAVIGATION AND CORN LAWS, FROM 1801 TO 1855

BY HENRY ATTON & HENRY HURST HOLLAND

WITH A PREFACE BY F. S. PARRY, C.B.
DEPUTY-CHAIRMAN OF THE BOARD OF CUSTOMS AND EXCISE

REPRINTS OF ECONOMIC CLASSICS

AUGUSTUS M. KELLEY · PUBLISHERS
NEW YORK · 1967

First Edition 1910

(London: John Murray, *Albemarle Street W*, 1910)

Reprinted 1967 by

AUGUSTUS M. KELLEY · PUBLISHERS

LIBRARY OF CONGRESS CATALOGUE CARD NUMBER

67-21884

PRINTED IN THE UNITED STATES OF AMERICA

by SENTRY PRESS, NEW YORK, N. Y. 10019

PREFACE

In the history of the British Customs, as perhaps in the history of civilized Europe, the end of the eighteenth century may be said to mark 'the passing away of old things.' Our authors' first volume described a Britain in which the consumer was in a way at the mercy of the producer, the labourer defenceless against the employer. The consumer's only remedy lay in smuggling, the labourer's in riot. Almost every article of import was dutiable ; the income tax was unknown.

The present volume describes a period during which it might have been truly said, 'Lo, all things are becoming new.' The navigation and corn laws disappeared, the slave trade and slavery were extinguished, the copyright laws were remodelled, the ancient levies of 4½ per cent., prisage, butlerage, and many of the old import prohibitions and restrictions, were abolished. Labour organized its forces ; indeed, the evolutionary methods of trade unionism interwove themselves so closely with those of free trade that their results have been often confounded. The Colonies, with the precedent of the American Revolt to guide them, asserted with success their fiscal independence, the home Government meanwhile gracefully doing its best to disprove Burke's acrid maxim that 'to tax and to please, no more than to love and to be wise, is not given to man.'

Administratively speaking, the period at which this second volume appears is scarcely less important than that described at pp. 88-92, when the separate Customs Boards of the three kingdoms were centralized in Thames

Street, for it is little more than a year ago that the amalgamation of the services of Customs and Excise gave to one Board full control of the indirect taxation of the United Kingdom. Our authors have not hesitated to emphasize the popular objections to Customs and Excise duties ; still, the joint establishment may be allowed to secure comforting assurance against any fears of imminent dissolution, by contemplating the equally obvious objections to direct taxation.

Customs history, properly studied, may be found fruitful of striking lessons. Possibly the most novel of these is the vital importance of discriminating clearly between names and things. To mention an instance that is near to all of us : the terms ' Free Trade ' and ' Protection ' existed a century ago, but whether they meant the same as they mean to-day is a question worth deep individual consideration. It is as a welcome help towards closer thinking on such matters, and not merely as a picturesque account of old days, old commerce, old taxes, old evasions, and the struggles of the old legislative mind, that this work deserves the attention of the reading public, both here and in the Colonies.

F. S. PARRY.

INTRODUCTION

THIS treatise deals with that memorable period during which the British Customs system was gradually moulded into the form suggested by Adam Smith. The sources of authority and quotation have been found in departmental records—accounts of the practical working of the revenue, navigation, slave, corn, fishery, and copyright laws, preserved in a room at the Custom House, London. These are by no means so numerous as they might have been, had half the care in custody which now obtains been practised in the past. It is evident that many documents have become dispersed or been destroyed—documents which might have been of great use to future historical students—students who may be more desirous to understand their ancestors' habits and doings than to study battles, dates, and coronations.

One tolerably good 'find' has been made quite recently. The 'Plantation Papers,' relating to colonial Customs matters from 1814 (the date of the burning of the Custom House) to the termination of the British Customs Board's control of colonial revenue, have been discovered in the cellars of the King's Warehouse. Among these are many documents highly illustrative of Customs and commercial proceedings in the colonies, and we have taken the opportunity of quoting from them at considerable length.

The practice pursued in vol. i. of blending revenue and departmental history in the first part of each chapter, and preventive laws and smuggling incidents in the second, has been followed in this volume. The list of 'Illustrative Documents' has been made retrospective, and much more extensive than the previous one, many readers having expressed a desire in that direction.

Great care has been taken in selection and quotation, yet the documents used have been so numerous and complicated that it is possible we may here and there have committed slight blunders; but we think that these, if they exist at all, will merely take the form of unimportant errors of detail. The labour has been arduous, and the exigencies of duty and locality have compelled us to work separately and confer by correspondence.

We beg to express our sincere thanks to their Honours the Commissioners of Customs and Excise for allowing access during unofficial hours to their recently collected old books and manuscripts, and to the Marquis of Londonderry for the use of his library at Wynyard Park, also to the editors of the *Athenæum*, *Vanity Fair*, the *Annual Register*, and the *Times*, for their kind permission to use certain material.

THE AUTHORS.

CONTENTS

LIST OF ILLUSTRATIONS

ERRATA

Page 68, line 2, *for* 'island' *read* 'colony.'

Page 136, line 28, *for* 'square-rigged' *read* 'fore-and-aft.'

THE KING'S CUSTOMS

CHAPTER I

HUNGER AND CONSOLIDATIONS

1801—1825

BEFORE entering upon the purely fiscal history of the first half of the nineteenth century, it is necessary to deal with a matter of even greater importance. Nothing is so momentous as the question of physical sustenance, and at no period of English history has the question assumed so ugly and daunting an aspect as in the year 1801. To a certain extent this was caused by alterations in the laws affecting the importation of corn. Be it borne in mind that the enforcement of those venerable statutes lay with the Customs.

There is much misconception at the present day as to the structure and tendency of the old Corn Laws. Most people think that protection of English agriculture was a measure adopted during the first forty years of the nineteenth century, and that the dearness of bread then prevailing was due to Protection only. This is a fallacy. The supply of corn had for hundreds of years been an important subject of consideration with English legislators, and many thoughtful people believed that a sliding scale was the best method of insuring cheap bread, and at the same time safeguarding the interests of agriculture and the landed gentry. It is necessary to examine into this. Yet, before displaying cold figures, it must be repeated that at the beginning of the nineteenth century the ogre of starvation was firmly installed in Great Britain. No matter of a famine price for a month or two, as occasionally of old, to fall as soon as the golden bounty of a full harvest glistened in the sunlight. Certainly, for the first time in English history, there was prospect of *permanent* dearness of bread.

A recapitulation of the ancient laws governing the importation and exportation of corn is necessary. By the Old Subsidy of 1660 the poundage *value* for imported wheat was fixed at £2 a quarter when the market price of wheat did not exceed 44s. When it exceeded that price, the poundage value was 6s. 8d. Proportional 'regulating prices' were fixed for barley, rye, oats, etc. The outward poundage value was £1 a quarter, irrespective of price (see below).

MARKET PRICE NOT EXCEEDING 44*s*.

	Poundage Value. £ *s.* *d.*	*Duty.** £ *s.* *d.*
Wheat, imported, per quarter ..	2 0 0	0 2 0

MARKET PRICE EXCEEDING 44*s*.

	Poundage Value. £ *s.* *d.*	*Duty.* £ *s.* *d.*
Wheat, imported, per quarter ..	0 6 8	0 0 4

	Poundage Value. £ *s.* *d.*	*Duty.* £ *s.* *d.*
Wheat, exported, per quarter (irrespective of price) ..	1 0 0	0 1 0

The first important alteration was effected by the Act of 1670, 'for encouragement of Tillage.' The poundage

* The duty was 5 per cent. of the 'value.'

on imported corn was abolished, and the duty made as below:

MARKET PRICE NOT EXCEEDING 53*s.* 4*d.*

	£	*s.*	*d.*
Wheat, imported, per quarter	0	16	0

MARKET PRICE EXCEEDING 53*s.* 4*d.* AND NOT EXCEEDING £4.

	£	*s.*	*d.*
Wheat, imported, per quarter	0	8	0

MARKET PRICE EXCEEDING £4.

	£	*s.*	*d.*
Wheat, imported, per quarter	0	0	4

The Corn Bounty Act of 1689 prescribed an export bounty at the rate of 5s. a quarter whenever the price of wheat did not exceed 48s. All export *duties* on corn were abolished in 1700.

The above scale for regulating duty by prices remained in force till 1773, but it must be understood that as each additional Subsidy was levied on merchandise the *duty* payable on wheat was increased. The *net* duties (fractions rejected and discounts deducted) payable in 1770 were:

PRICE NOT EXCEEDING 44*s.* A QUARTER.

	£	*s.*	*d.*
Wheat, imported, per quarter	1	1	9

PRICE EXCEEDING 44*s.* AND NOT EXCEEDING 53*s.* 4*d.*

	£	*s.*	*d.*
Wheat, imported, per quarter	0	16	11

PRICE EXCEEDING 53*s.* 4*d.* AND NOT EXCEEDING £4.

	£	*s.*	*d.*
Wheat, imported, per quarter	0	8	11

PRICE EXCEEDING £4.

	£	*s.*	*d.*
Wheat, imported, per quarter	0	1	3

During the years extending from 1696 to 1773 statistics of English imports, exports, and prices were compiled in the office of the Inspector-General of Imports and Exports, Custom House, London.* Through those seventy-eight years, *according to the official returns*, wheat was rarely at what would now be deemed a high price. So well accustomed were the lower classes to what we should call cheap bread that during the reign of George II. there were riots to prevent the exportation of corn from England, and to resent the price of foodstuffs, when, according to the statistics, the *average* price of wheat did not exceed £2 a quarter. The average price of wheat during the period from 1696 to 1764 was 33s. 3d. a quarter.

It appears that prices were mounting in 1765, so exportation of corn, etc., was prohibited, and foreign corn admitted duty-free, during a period of several years. It is apparent that from 1696 to 1764, inclusive, low prices had been maintained though the high scale of duty must have been leviable. The prices were not really high even from 1765 to 1773. The average was about 45s.

It should be observed that the inefficiency of the home-grown supply to meet the demand was contemporaneous with the full operation of the Enclosure Acts, the effacement of cottage industries, the expansion of the factory system, and the consequent commencement of the efflux from country to town. An element of obfuscation intrudes here. It may be asked : 'Were not the Enclosure Acts supposed to have increased the acreage of arable ? And was not the system of cultivation steadily improving ? And say you not that the import duties were removed for a space ? Then how can you explain the rise in prices ?' A straight cord runs through all the apparent intricacies of the question. It is a homely fact that when the peasant has a pig, a cow, and a share in common land, he is not confined to a bread diet. When many thousands of such peasants are seduced or driven into the cities, the land becomes less *useful*, despite scientific farming and

* Charles Davenant and Horace Walpole held the patent of this office at various periods.

enclosures of common. When the number of people who can with ease produce ***their own*** food grows less, when the cities become crowded, when, in addition to these circumstances, the importation of fruit, meat, and fish is limited by primitive methods of traffic and repeated wars, most of the poor have to fall back upon bread alone. Up goes the price of corn. As misery increases the poor become more prolific : it has ever been thus. The streets are full of puny, squalid children ; the sweater has his way. Up goes the price of corn.

In 1773, in order that the slow rise in price should not proceed too far, the regulating figures were altered. The duty then stood thus :

PRICE NOT EXCEEDING 44*s*.

	£	*s.*	*d.*
Wheat, imported, per quarter	1	1	9

PRICE EXCEEDING 44*s*. AND NOT EXCEEDING 48*s*.

	£	*s.*	*d.*
Wheat, imported, per quarter	0	16	11

PRICE EXCEEDING 48*s*.

	£	*s.*	*d.*
Wheat, imported, per quarter	0	0	6

But this had no effect. The unfavourable conditions were being slowly intensified. Factories were rising in localities hitherto immune, the urban population was increasing at an ominous rate. Busy people still strove to stave off the evil day when it should depend upon foreign supplies as to whether the poor should starve or be filled. Much waste land was reclaimed in the maritime counties, and in the sylvan parts of England the axe resounded in the woodlands. The rise, though resistless, was gradual. The average price for the twenty years succeeding 1773 was about 44s. a quarter—greatly in excess of 33s. 3d. ; still, not intolerable.

It will now be seen that for nearly one hundred years the *average* price of wheat in England was so low that the high duty on foreign corn must have been leviable during most of the period.* We are confronted with the spectacle of a plenteous supply of cheap bread while a bounty was paid on the exportation of home-grown corn and a high duty levied on foreign.

The 'imposts on proceeds,' and the alterations under the Consolidation Act, left the duties immediately after 1787 as follow:

PRICE UNDER 48s.

	£	s.	d.
Wheat, imported, per quarter	1	4	3

PRICE AT OR ABOVE 48s.

	£	s.	d.
Wheat, imported, per quarter	0	0	6

In 1791 the duties stood thus:

PRICE UNDER 50s.

	£	s.	d.
Wheat, imported, per quarter	1	4	3

PRICE 50s. OR UNDER 54s.

	£	s.	d.
Wheat, imported, per quarter	0	2	6

PRICE 54s. OR ABOVE.

	£	s.	d.
Wheat, imported, per quarter	0	0	6

Soon it became apparent that no sliding scale could prevent dearness, and that the scale last adopted had worked as a factor in raising prices. The imposts of 1796 and 1797 increased the corn duties. In 1800 they stood thus:

	High Duty.			*First Low Duty.*			*Second Low Duty.*		
	£	s.	d.	£	s.	d.	£	s.	d.
Wheat, imported, per quarter	1	6	$8\frac{2}{20}$	0	2	9	0	0	$6\frac{12}{20}$

During the concluding years of the century, despite the danger to commerce by the widespread European wars, the importation of corn into Great Britain had increased

* Not at every port, for the prices occasionally varied much in different counties; but it is evident that, with such low average prices, corn could rarely have been dear, even in the districts most unproductive.

rapidly. Still the price had kept on climbing, climbing. From 1696 to 1773 the exports of corn had always exceeded the imports; the import duties had been high, and the prices extremely low. From 1774 to 1794 the imports slightly exceeded the exports; the import duties were higher than of yore: the prices had increased, yet were reasonable. During the last few years of the century the imports greatly exceeded the exports, the duties mounted, the prices gradually became tremendous. It is therefore clear that dearness of bread is not always a direct result of high corn duties. One may find it necessary to burn all the time-honoured reference-books ere a correct conclusion on this matter may be achieved. When economics fail to enlighten, a judicious blend of ethics and common sense may avail. It would seem to be inevitable that, when the poor are driven from the land, the poor will in the end have to bear the suffering entailed by deprivation.

One undeniable cause of high corn prices must not be overlooked. The old restraints upon engrossing had been swept away in 1791. Their abolition was due to the teachings of that incorrigible doctrinaire, Adam Smith. For forty years subsequent to 1791 the engrossing of corn became a popular branch of speculation.* Rents grew higher as prices went up; even in counties remote as Wilts and Somerset the rent of an ordinary farm rose from 15s. per acre to £3. It was as though a great curse had fallen upon the home territories. The manly sports and exercises, for which rural England in particular had long been famous, began to fall into disuse. The physique of the agricultural labourers deteriorated; child labour and adult slavery were fast removing even the signs of humanity from the toilers of the great industrial towns. There is no part of English history so terrible as that of the years from 1790 to 1830.

Below is a return of the average prices of wheat in

* When corn was at its highest, the ports were often crowded with corn-laden ships, discharge being purposely delayed.

England from 1792 to 1800, and of the quantities imported and exported.

	Average Prices. s. d.	*Quarters Wheat Imported.*	*Quarters Wheat Exported.*
1792	42 11	20,201	250,982
1793	48 11	429,350	44,866
1794	51 8	324,637	116,273
1795	74 2	287,930	677
1796	77 1	820,381	677
1797	53 1	456,903	23,076
1798	50 3	394,407	22,138
1799	67 6	445,047	16,960
1800	113 7	1,174,654	7,866

Below is an account of the average prices of wheat at Dublin market (per barrel of 280 pounds = $\frac{5}{9}$ of an English quarter).

PRICES IN IRISH CURRENCY.

	s. d.		s. d.
1792	23 4	1797	26 7
1793	28 0	1798	28 3
1794	32 4	1799	38 4
1795	38 1	1800	62 0
1796	37 11		

Thus the average price of a quarter of wheat in England during the nine years quoted may be stated roughly as a little over 64s., and the average price per English quarter of wheat in Ireland may be expressed as a little over 58s. in *English* currency. The British shortage raised prices in Ireland. Great Britain became compelled to buy oversea : Ireland, especially in time of war, was the market most convenient to buy in. Ireland *had* to sell. In England the price of corn usually regulated rents ; in Ireland the middleman had fostered sub-letting, especially in the southern counties.* (The

* Extract from evidence given before a Commission of Inquiry held early in the nineteenth century : ' The noblemen and gentlemen in the south of Ireland. in a greater degree than those in the north, let their lands to a class of people called middlemen. These in some instances keep large tracts in their own hands, in other instances they underlet tracts of considerable extent to

cotters in Ireland, be it remembered, had no such privileges as the cottagers and commoners of England, prior to the Enclosure Acts, had enjoyed.)

Readers of our first volume may remember that the concluding portion contained a short review of the condition of the British Customs towards the end of the eighteenth century, and a brief history of Irish revenue. As the fiscal contingencies of the Union of Great Britain and Ireland now present themselves for enumeration, we cannot do better than preface the account with another review of the condition of both the British and Irish departments.

To commence with England. In spite of the Act of 1798, there remained an imposing list of Customs sinecures, the total yearly emoluments amounting to about £25,000. The Customs revenue had increased considerably, partly through the duties being higher, partly through the growth of commerce.

The Scottish contributions to the revenue of Great Britain were still unimportant. The proportions of the Customs returns (gross) in the two countries may be stated as about 20 in England to 1 in Scotland. The Scottish list was packed with sinecurists and pensioners. Among the latter were no fewer than four Cockburns and eleven Hays.

The Irish revenue business was carried on in a very slack way ; the British method, bad as it was, appears in comparison exactness itself. Whenever Commis-

---

other tenants under them. And sometimes that second class of tenants underlet again to others, till at last the property comes to be divided into lots of an acre or half an acre, and sometimes still less than that.'

Here was a numerous class of small holders, deprived by the middleman system of everything that tends to make division of land beneficial. (The witness was no local agitator, but a Scotsman acting as steward and valuer in Ireland.)

sioners of Inquiry were sent across channel to overhaul matters, most amazing anomalies were recorded. Huge defalcations were dragged into publicity, and the system of accounts shown to be especially blamable. The old Revenue Board had been rearranged towards the close of the eighteenth century, the number of Commissioners being reduced to nine—four sitting for Customs, two for Excise, and the other three as Commissioners of both Customs and Excise. The scope of the work to be performed by each set was not exactly definable ; indeed, so jumbled was the control that certain Commissioners of an Inquiry held soon after the Union declared themselves unable to state which set was responsible for any particular branch of the duties.

Fees were charged at an exorbitant rate—as means towards official emolument—and many of these were unsanctioned except 'by usage.' The scale had been fixed by statute shortly after the Restoration, but it had been increased in 1695, and the increase sanctioned by the Irish Parliament. Soon the scale came to be altered 'by usage,' and always in the direction of increase. At the end of the eighteenth century there were no two Irish ports at which similar fees were charged. If a merchant complained to the Board, the latter directed the officer concerned to comply with the 1695 scale, but took no steps to enforce compliance unless the merchant complained again and again.*

* The following letter, sent by the collector of Dundalk in answer to a query as to his emoluments, illustrates the vagariousness of the Irish system of fees :

'I am under the necessity of informing you that I am utterly ignorant of the nature or amount of the fees of the patentee officers, and no trace of them' (no trace of an authorized scale) 'can be discovered in this office, nor any clue which can enable me to comply with the order in question. The employments of the patentee officers have degenerated into sinecures from time immemorial, and, my predecessor having constantly contracted to receive the fees of those officers for a much longer period than I can possibly learn the date of, the patentees' fees have become blended with those of the collector, and from ancient usage no separate charge is ever made. I found things in this state on being appointed, and made no alteration, except having the

Most of the Irish foreign trade was transacted at Dublin. The collector of that port, when accounting for his net receipts, always kept a large sum in hand. The outport collectors were supposed to remit monthly, but this was rarely done, whence many defalcations.*

---

deputation of the patentees made to my first clerk instead of myself, who, however, has no emolument thereby.'

(The explanation of this is that, having no authorized scale to go by, and the patentees being non-resident, the collector had ordered his clerk to levy, as best he could, fees on foreign and coastwise traffic, at the highest rate the merchants would endure. Then the collector divided the spoil into three equal portions—one portion for himself, one for each of the patentees. Each portion amounted in the year under question to £662 16s. The collector's hours of employment were ten till three, and he was a captain in the yeomanry.)

* Below is an extract from the Irish Exchequer Memoranda, showing proceedings taken and pending against various collectors of customs and hearth-money, their sureties, etc., towards the end of the eighteenth century:

'His Majesty against William Doyle, heir of Charles Doyle. Also against the heir and tertenants' (actual occupiers of landed property) 'of Thomas Bunbury. Also against Francis Vernon Wilson. Also against Samuel Wilkinson.' (Charles Doyle, Bunbury, Wilson, and Wilkinson were sureties for George Martin, late collector of Dublin, whose defalcations amounted to over £9,000. The sheriff of Carlow returned Wilson 'not to be found.')

'Same against Meredith Workman, formerly collector of Dundalk, with John Bond and the Rev. James Smith, his sureties.'

'Same against George Parker, late collector of Wexford, with Admiral Parker and Captain Parker, his sureties.' (Defalcation £4,998.)

'Same against James Cavendish, late collector of Dundalk, with Sir Henry Cavendish and Guy Moore Coote, his sureties.' (Defalcation £2,569.)

'Same against Simon Marshall, formerly collector of Galway, with Richard French and John Eyre, his sureties.

'Same against Joseph Matthews, late collector of Kilkenny, with Arthur Webb, senior, and Arthur Webb, junior, his sureties.' (Defalcation £2,768.)

'Same against John Dalton, late collector of Athlone, with the Hon. Peter Brown-Kelly and Sir Patrick Bellew, his sureties.' (Defalcation £1,939.)

'Same against William Ormsby, late collector of Sligo, with George Ormsby and Robert French, his sureties.' (Defalcation £5,155.)

'Same against Sir Edward Newenham, formerly collector of Dublin, with Alicia O'Callaghan and Jane Pierce, his sureties.' (Debt £1,395.)

There was much circumlocution in dealing with ships and goods, and this was enforced solely with a view towards multiplying fees. When a shipmaster reported a cargo inwards, not only the collector, but the patent customer, the controller, the surveyor-general, and the searcher (or their deputies for them), insisted on initialling the report, though they never examined either it or the goods to which it related. This was done so that each might charge a fee. When a ship cleared outward double fees were charged, one scale by the patentee searcher, one by his deputy. The patentee was always absent, so could check nothing. The deputy was always present (in his office, to collect the patentee's fees and his own), but he checked neither clearance nor goods.

Every entry for goods which were duty-paid at landing was quintupled, so as to secure five sets of fees. The documents were supposed to be subjected to a circuitous system of check, yet inaccuracies slipped through by the hundred. Even then, during six years the number of surcharges and rebates in the port of Dublin was over 17,000.

The privilege of landing goods *ad visum* (popularly known as ' by bill of view,' in England called ' on sight ') was scandalously abused. The system had been originally intended to act as an occasional indulgence. For instance, if a merchant's imports were not fully advised on his invoices, he might depose to that effect, and request permission to ' view ' the goods on landing, and then ' perfect

(Thus it appears that two successive collectors of Dublin were being prosecuted at the same time.)

Besides the above, proceedings were taken against the persons and sureties of twenty-six collectors of hearth-money. In three cases the sheriffs concerned reported, ' No bodies, goods, chattels, iands, or tenements '; and in eight cases, ' No goods, chattels, lands, or tenements.' In the case of a collector named Sankey, the sheriff of Tipperary returned, ' No goods, and both sureties dead,' and in the case of one Burrows the sheriff of Wexford returned, ' One surety dead, the other surety and the principal not to be found.'

the entry ' within seven days. The goods were put into the King's Warehouse for safety till the transaction was completed. This reasonable regulation had been extended and relaxed ' by usage ' till at each port the King's Warehouse had been converted into a kind of ' duty-free warehouse,' unsecured, so far as the merchants were concerned, by bond. The King's Warehouse in Dublin being crammed with ' Bill of View ' articles, the authorities hired several private warehouses, which were soon filled with similar goods. Often the articles remained there for months, the entries meanwhile unperfected and the duties unpaid. Then certain merchants were allowed to take ' Bill of View ' goods to their own warehouses, and keep them there as long as they chose, nor were the doors fitted with Customs locks. This loose system was extended gradually so as to apply to the greater part of the foreign goods landed in Dublin. The landing-officers' examination of goods was extremely inaccurate, especially with regard to spirits, the gauging being random, and the hydrometer used in testing quite an imperfect instrument. The most inexperienced reader will perceive that when goods thus erratically examined were at once handed over to the owners, and left in their charge, unsecured by bond, till they thought fit to pay the duties involved, many opportunities must have arisen for collusion between merchants and officers. That collusion of the grossest kind took place is evident from the official statement that in 1800 it had become apparent that goods landed upon Bill of View had passed into consumption without duty being paid on them to an extent representing a loss to the Revenue of £200,000. Yet so muddled were the accounts that proceedings could not be taken.*

* An attempt at stock-taking was made in Dublin, but so little reliance could be placed on the accounts that it was decided not to essay anything in the nature of a complete check, but merely to count the packages ! The original account of goods landed on bill of view (goods that had been duty-paid being, of course, deducted) showed 29,972 packages. The indoor ' jerque ' account

There were great frauds in the exportation of Irish-made spirits, the goods being tampered with while in transit from distillery to export ship. The account of moneys received as proceeds of fines and forfeitures was terribly inexact. And it should be mentioned, as an exemplification of the assiduity with which the average man will persevere in collecting, for his own benefit, trifling sums of public money, that certain high officials and wealthy noblemen were in receipt of a few pounds each per year, as commutations of the old exemptions from wine duty granted during Elizabeth's reign.*

The victualling of the revenue cruisers was in the hands of two Dublin merchants, and the prices charged did by no means correspond with the market rates. These worthy burghers paid the Inspector of Cruisers a handsome commission upon all stores and provisions ordered by him.

The Customs hours (' all round ') were nine to three in summer, and ten to three in winter.

Thus we have made it plain that Revenue matters in Ireland were pervaded by that happy spirit of irresponsibility, and conducted with that utter disregard of routine and precision, so characteristic of Celtic financial procedure. To some this statement may appear unfair, for at the time official departments in England and Scotland were not above suspicion, and, indeed, it is evident from the nomenclature that most of the revenue officials in Ireland were of English descent. But the most Irish person in existence is your Irishman whose ancestry has been typically English, and, when every possible allowance has been made, it remains undeniable that in the record of Irish revenue lapses there is some-

---

showed 31,023. Comparison was then made with another indoor account kept by ' The Clerk of the Check.' This showed 44,859. When the computers went to the warehouses and counted the stock, they found only 8,369. The investigation lapsed.

* See vol. i., p. 426. (The original grant had been broken up into many portions.)

thing racy of the soil, a touch of the utterly and genially picaresque, that does not appertain to the English and Scottish depredations.

By Cap. 67 of 40 Geo. III. the British Parliament enacted that the Union of Great Britain and Ireland should take place on January 1, 1801, and the respective countries be thenceforth called 'The United Kingdom of Great Britain and Ireland.' They were to be represented in one and the same Parliament, and their inhabitants were to be placed on the same footing as regarded trade and navigation. All commercial prohibitions and bounties in force between them, except those referring to corn, flour, etc., were to be repealed, and, with certain exceptions, commerce between them was to be duty-free. Below is a summary of the new fiscal arrangements.

The following goods were liable to *ad valorem* duties of 10 per cent., on importation from either country to the other: Apparel, wrought brass, cabinet ware, carriages, wrought copper, cottons, glass, haberdashery, hats, wrought iron and hardware, gold and silver lace, thread, and bullion, millinery, stained paper, pottery, manufactured leather, silk manufactures, and tin plates. These duties were to exist for twenty years.

Certain goods, being products or manufactures of, and liable to excise duty in, the respective countries, were made liable to countervailing duties on importation from one country to the other. Parliament might rearrange the said countervailing duties, or impose others. Goods thus liable were entitled to a drawback on shipment, equal to the countervailing duty demanded in the country to which they were exported.

The woollen manufactures known from ancient times as 'old draperies' and 'new draperies' were to pay, on importation from either country into the other, the duties previously payable in Ireland. The duty on Irish coal brought into Great Britain was to be the previous British duty, and no more. The duty on salt brought into Ireland from Great Britain was to be the previous Irish duty, and no more.

Calicoes and muslins, imported from either country into the other, were to pay the amount of the previous Irish duty, and no more, till 1808; thenceforth the rate was to be reduced annually so as to reach 10 per cent. on the value in 1816, and to remain at that rate till 1821. Cotton yarn and twist, imported from either country into the other, were to pay the amount of the previous Irish duty, and no more, till 1808; thenceforth the rate was to be reduced annually so as to expire in 1816.

If goods liable to duty on export from Great Britain to foreign parts, but duty-free if exported to Ireland, were shipped in Great Britain for foreign, and passed in transit through an Irish port, that, of course, did not exempt the goods from the British export duty. The same rule applied to Irish goods exported through Great Britain to foreign ports; they paid the Irish export duty when shipped in Ireland.

If foreign or colonial goods paid duty in either country, and were then shipped to the other, the import duties paid were to be drawn back, or they might be placed to the credit of the country to which the goods were exported.

For twenty years subsequent to date of Union the respective contributions towards the united expenditure were to be in the proportions of fifteen from Great Britain and two from Ireland. This arrangement was to be revised at the end of the period by—

Comparison of values of imports and exports during a given period; or

Comparison of values of beer, sugar, wine, spirits, tobacco, tea, and malt consumed; or

Comparison of national incomes.

The scale was to be afterwards revised at periods of not less than seven and not more than twenty years, unless the United Parliament should decide that expenditure should be defrayed by equal taxation on commodities in both countries.

The Irish revenues were to be funded, and charged with the interest on the Irish debt, and with the reduction of the said debt by means of a sinking fund. The residue was to go towards defraying the expenditure of the United Kingdom. If any surplus then remained, it was to be applied to reducing Irish taxes, or to other Irish purposes.

In regulating subsequent taxation, no article imported into Ireland was to be charged with a duty higher than that payable on the said article in England.

Any loan raised after the Union for the United Kingdom was to be a joint debt, and borne in the proportions above mentioned; but this provision might be altered by the United Parliament. The Parliament was also authorized to formulate new devices if at any future period either country's debt were liquidated (quite an unnecessary proviso).

All revenue derived from colonial possessions was to be applied to the benefit of each country in proportion to the country's contribution towards the united expenditure.

Thus each country had its own scale of duties on foreign and colonial goods imported; certain articles carried between the two countries were subject to various duties and restrictions, and the rest of the trade across the Irish Channel was duty-free. Between the date of Union and the operation of Cap. 72, 4 Geo. IV., an immense number of variations were made in the above arrangement. A full account of these would mystify and disgust readers, and serve no useful purpose, so we shall merely mention, as we proceed, certain striking acts of alteration. Only genuinely *historical* statutes, affecting the Customs in either country, will receive full notice.

The Act brought about a considerable reduction in

the Irish Customs establishment. In the list of compensations for offices vacated the following are worth notice :

Office.	*Compensating Grant (Annual).* £	*s.*	*d.*
One Exchequer Baron	2,000	0	0
Auditor of Imprest (office held by Earl of Westmeath for self and Countess) (each)	1,000	0	0
One Customs Solicitor	716	14	4
One Deputy-Paymaster of Corn Premiums ..	670	0	0
Another	286	19	4
Four clerks of port permits (in all)	397	15	5½

Amongst the compensations granted for loss of fees on account of the new arrangements appear :

Office.	*Compensating Grant (Annual).* £	*s.*	*d.*
One Assistant-Examiner of Customs	600	0	0
A collector	305	5	9
Another	168	17	0
A jerquer's clerk	326	5	9
Another	163	2	10
A clerk of debentures	163	1	11
A clerk of minutes	59	4	10

The *British* Quarantine Acts were consolidated by Cap. 80, 40 Geo. III. Certain tonnage duties were placed on vessels that performed quarantine in Great Britain, and these were applied to the erection of a lazaret on Chetney Hill, Kent. It was provided that if a customs officer performing duty as a quarantine official deserted his post, or knowingly permitted goods, ships, or persons to escape from quarantine, he should suffer death. Persons who escaped from quarantine were made liable to the same penalty.*

* Alarmists were never wanting. Some urged the Government to strengthen the smuggling laws in the interests of public health. 'The wisest and severest laws that can possibly be enacted will never sufficiently secure us against the secret and subtile infection of the plague, so long as there is a single smuggler on our

The Thames police force was instituted by Cap. 87, 40 Geo. III., 'for the more effectual prevention of depredations on the cargoes, stores, and materials of vessels.' In the Act of institution appeared this sentence: 'Whereas divers ill-disposed and suspected persons and reported thieves frequent the said river, its quays, warehouses, and the avenues leading thereto.'

Cap. 107, 41 Geo. III., amended the Copyright Act, providing that the authors of all books composed in the United Kingdom, but not printed or published prior to July 2, 1801, and of all books subsequently composed in the United Kingdom, were to have the sole right of printing and reprinting the same for fourteen years from date of first publication. (They might assign this privilege.) Contraveners, including importers of pirated books, were to forfeit to the proprietor of copyright the books dealt with, and he was to have them made into waste. The offenders were to forfeit 3d. a sheet, half to go to the Crown, half to the informer concerned. This Act reaffirmed the existing provisions against the importation of books first produced in the United Kingdom, and printed or reprinted elsewhere. As of old, customs officers were to be rewarded for seizing pirated books.

In December, 1802, the following notice was posted at the London Custom House, and copies were sent to the outport collectors, who were instructed to secure publication thereof in the local papers: 'Whereas advertisements have at different times appeared in the newspapers, offering sums of money for the procuring of places or situations in the Customs, etc.' The notice then referred to the Statute of 5 and 6 Edw. VI., which disabled purchasers of offices, and rendered forfeitable the offices of such as assisted in the sale. A reward of

---

extensive coasts. This is a point of most awful consideration, and calls for the immediate deliberation of the Legislature.'—*Letter from Abbott, of the Levant Company, to Lord Grenville, November* 20, 1800 (*Dropmore Collection*).

£100 was offered for satisfactory evidence of the trading of offices in the Customs.

The provisions of the Act of 1782, disqualifying British customs officers from voting at Parliamentary elections, were extended by Cap. 25, 43 Geo. III., so as to include the Irish Customs.

Cap. 56, 43 Geo. III., regulated the Plantation passenger traffic. Said the preamble : 'Persons have been seduced to leave their native country under false representations, and have suffered great hardships on shipboard for want of water and provisions.' It was enacted that no British vessel might take passengers from the United Kingdom to the Plantations in a greater number than one to each two tons burden. The parts of the ship that were occupied with cargo were not to count in estimating burden, and the crew were to be counted as passengers. Before the vessel sailed, a magistrate and the customs officers of the port were to attend, muster the crew and passengers, and allow any passenger to leave who was desirous of doing so. Passengers were only to be taken on board at places where customs officers were stationed. A certified copy of the muster-roll was to be given to the master. If the vessel carried fifty or more, she was also to carry a certificated surgeon and a proper medicine-chest. Both master and doctor were to keep journals, and on return produce them to the Customs. (Foreign vessels might only carry passengers in the proportion of one to each five tons burden.) Bond was to be given to the Customs as to seaworthiness of ship. Ships of war and revenue cruisers might board and search during voyage, and check the muster-roll. An abstract of the Act was to be displayed in every custom-house in the United Kingdom.* (It is illustrative of the extreme tenderness with which the humanitarians of the day regarded the negro, and of their callousness as to the sufferings of their own countrymen, that similar

* Later the Act was amended, the magistrate's attendance being declared unnecessary.

provisions had been applied to the slave trade *in 1788*. Yet the horrors of Plantation passenger traffic had been exemplified thousands of times during the previous two hundred years.)

The Customs tariff of Great Britain was re-consolidated by Cap. 68, 43 Geo. III. The Act stated that many new duties and separate accounts had been instituted since the Consolidation of 1787, and that the computation of duties had 'again become complicated and intricate.' Many of the duties were increased. The produce of the additional duties was estimated at £250,000. Even foreign wool, which, to stimulate the woollen manufactures, had previously been kept free of all imposts except the convoy duty, was made liable to a slight duty under this Act. The excise duty on tea, which under the Act of 1787 had been £12 10s. per £100 value, was made 50 per cent.

Now appeared those terrible imposts, the so-called 'temporary' war duties, increases upon the consolidated rates, amounting in most cases to 12½ per cent. (Cap. 70, 43 Geo. III.).

What is known as the 'First Warehousing Act,' Cap. 132, 43 Geo. III., was the next important revenue measure. This has been frequently referred to as the first step towards 'bonding' dutiable goods, but the designation is absurd. Postponing payment by entering into bond for the amount of duty involved was an ancient practice ; indeed, it would be difficult to state the precise period at which the system commenced. There can be no doubt that from time immemorial it had been a practice to forbear in certain instances the prompt collection of duty, but in such cases the merchant was liable for the *full* duty as payable on landing, no matter to what extent his goods might diminish by natural waste before he cleared them. This explains the old Customs discounts, granted to merchants who paid duty on their goods *at time of landing*. The East India Company had for a long period enjoyed what amounted to bonding privileges, the duties on their goods being forborne till after sale. In 1714 tobacco had been allowed to be warehoused on the merchants' own premises, they paying a small portion of the inward duty, and completing payment when the goods were sold, or drawing back their partial deposit if the goods were exported. This system continued till 1789 (see the Tobacco Act of that year, in vol. i., p. 385), and many, many cases there were, according to the Receiver-General's books, in which the transaction was never consummated, the merchant selling his goods and then failing, or the sureties levanting, or some outrageous claim being made on the authorities' clemency on account of loss by decay, fire, etc. In 1742 Plantation rum was allowed to be warehoused without payment of the excise duty (see vol. i., pp. 206, 207), and in 1765 it was provided that rice might be warehoused at certain ports on payment of a small portion of the import charge. (In 1797 it was allowed to be warehoused duty-free.) In 1767 coffee and cocoa were allowed warehousing privileges—only part of the import duty to be paid, and the rest at clearance (drawback if exported). All these facilities had been intended to favour *export* trade, to relieve the merchant from paying duty on goods which might ultimately be sold in foreign markets.

But the Act of 1803 went considerably farther. It allowed cotton, ginger, indigo, mahogany, molasses, pimento, and rum from the West Indies, and cocoa, sugar, and coffee from any place, to be bonded at the West India Docks, London ; and rice, tobacco, wine and spirits, other than from the West Indies, to be bonded at the newly-constructed London Docks, Wapping. Many other classes of goods might be bonded at such places as the Treasury might appoint. The Act was in a way experimental, it being provided that the Treasury, by Order in Council, might extend the privileges to other goods and other ports. (In 1805 special authorization was granted to the Treasury in this respect, there being a host of applications from various ports for permission to share in the benefits conferred by the Act.)*

The goods warehoused were to be secured under locks, in most cases the joint locks of Crown and warehouse proprietor. When required for home consumption, they were to be liable to the duties then leviable, upon the quantities ascertained at delivery. They might be exported from warehouse on payment of the temporary war duties only, but a certificate of landing at the place of destination was required. Goods not cleared within fifteen months were to be sold. If they failed to realize a price covering the duty they were to be destroyed. If they realized more than the duty, the Crown was to be satisfied and the overplus to go to the proprietor. Goods liable to excise duties were to be entered with the Excise as well as with the Customs, and the excise officers were to be present on delivery. (The provisions of this statute were extended considerably by Cap. 126, 48 Geo. III.; Cap. 142, 52 Geo. III., etc.)

It appears from Cap. 156, 43 Geo. III., that at this period the Prisage and Butlerage of England were assigned to—

The King, on all liable wines brought into the ports of Lancashire; the Prince of Wales, on all liable wines brought into the ports of Cornwall and Plymouth; the duke of Beaufort, on all liable wines brought into the ports of Swansea and Chepstow; the marquis of Bute,

* It might have been to the public advantage if, prior to making a compact with the London dock companies in 1907, inquiry had been made into the old methods of fostering London trade. From time immemorial up to the beginning of the nineteenth century the great city enjoyed remarkable commercial privileges, the desire of legislators being to centralize trade as far as possible, and thus facilitate the collection of Customs revenue. The official with the inkhorn and tuckstick was the active agent in more than one stupendous change. The independence of the United States, and the present dropsical condition of the British metropolis, are due to him and his mentors. (London's preponderance in trade began to decline directly her privileges were withdrawn.)

on all liable wines brought into the ports of Cardiff; the duke of Grafton, on all liable wines brought into the remaining ports of England.

(Prisage and Butlerage were not leviable in Scotland. See vol. i., pp. 166-167.)

Various committees of inquiry had recommended that these ancient impositions should be re-vested in the Crown. The Treasury were accordingly empowered to treat with the grantees for surrender, on consideration of annuities, to be granted by Parliament out of the Consolidated Fund.

By Cap. 124 (local and personal), 43 Geo. III., the Treasury were authorized to advance £100,000 out of the Consolidated Fund, to repair and extend the moorings in the Thames, and to improve the Thames navigation,* the loan to be repaid out of the proceeds of additional tonnage rates. They were also empowered to buy the London 'legal quays'—viz., the string of landing-places, approved under the Acts of Elizabeth and Charles II., extending from London Bridge to the Tower Dock, at which, previous to the construction of docks in London, all foreign merchandise had been landed, and from which all goods for exportation to foreign parts had been shipped or water-borne for shipment, except certain rough goods and occasional cargoes, allowed special privileges under 'sufferances' or Treasury warrants. (Some of these quays, notably 'Brewers' and the 'Wool Quay,' were extremely ancient. Most of the East India Company's goods were lightered from and to the ships, and discharged at or water-borne from a quay called 'Somers and Lyons' near the Custom House.) Billingsgate Dock, and the piece of ground adjacent, then known as 'Room Land,' were exempted from the provisions of this Act, and it was provided that the Fish Market and its appurtenances should not be interfered with. The purchase was to be completed

* Another instance of the fostering of London's commercial interests.

within three years, but this period was repeatedly extended.*

The building of the East India Docks was authorized by Cap. 126 (local and personal), 43 Geo. III. The preamble ran: 'Whereas the ships in the employ of the East India Company are of a larger size than other vessels employed by merchants in trade, and many of them nearly equal in bulk to ships of the line in the Royal Navy.'

A Treasury warrant, worded thus, reached the Board of Customs: 'Having considered your Secretary's letter aforegoing, these are to authorize you to cause articles, the produce of New South Wales and Norfolk Island, to be admitted to entry on payment of duty, as if the produce of, and imported from, any British Plantation in America; also that articles exported to New South Wales and Norfolk Island should be subject to such duties and drawbacks as on exportation to the British colonies.' This would appear to mark the initiation of important trade with the Antipodes.

A rather curious trial took place in the Exchequer during the year under survey. A ship from Virginia arrived in the tier off Wapping Old Stairs, having on board a quantity of staves and 524 casks of leaf tobacco. By the letter of the law regulating the importation of tobacco the minimum 'legal weight' at which packages of tobacco might be imported was 450 pounds net. (This regulation was a device to prevent smuggling. See vol. i., pp. 143 and 385.) Tide-surveyor Haskings went on board as soon as unlading commenced, and found that

* It is evident that purchase was soon initiated, for we find that in 1805 Mr. Dutton, the occupier of Brewers Quay, was paying £1,500 a year as rent to the Treasury. On January 8, 1806, the Customs Secretary applied to the East India Company as to Somers and Lyons Quay. The directors replied that the Customs Solicitor had offered them, *pro forma*, £100 as a Crown tender for the quay, but they would take £40,000 if the Treasury would grant them legal quays for their goods at Cock Hill and Stone Stairs, Ratcliff. (In 1831 the Treasury, fearing that the quay trade would fall off, proceeded to dispose of their purchases.)

two of the packages were rather badly broken, and on weighing them net he discovered that one was 70 and the other 107 pounds short of the legal weight. The damage had been caused by 'avaricious stowage,' the casks having been 'screw-jacked' at lading, so as to squeeze them into as small a space as possible. Other casks had been cracked by the use of the screw-jack, and these, with the two packages found to be defective, were detained by the officer. It appears there was no suspicion of fraud, but the letter of the law had been violated. The importer of the goods was exchequered, and many packages of tobacco, landed in similar condition from other American ships, were detained pending result of the trial. The case went before a jury, and a verdict was given for the defendant. The Crown sought and obtained a new trial. It is matter of regret that the records do not supply the result, although they consist of many pages, mainly devoted to the most persistent and abominable wrangling and hair-splitting. It is amazing that such a case should be taken up by an Attorney-General, for it is quite evident that it was merely a matter of crowded stowage. The Crown lawyer stuck valiantly to his case, defining the Crown's attitude towards the merchant thus : 'You shall not use such machinery as shall damage the packages, and cause them to arrive in a prohibited condition.' (But why, in the name of equity, should the *importer*, an Englishman resident in London, be prosecuted for the act of a Virginian stevedore ?)

Arbitrary as some of the Customs prosecutions were, they were not so harsh as certain actions entered by the Excise. Baron Macdonald, the Exchequer judge who presided during the above case, quoted an extraordinary suit preferred by the latter department. An immense quantity of coffee, taken as prize from French and Spanish vessels, had been shipped from the West Indies to London. Owing to the vastness of the consignments, proper casks could not in all instances be obtained, and many of the packages, when landed at Custom-house Quay, were found to be under the legal net. The customs officers overlooked this unimportant informality, and the prize agents paid duty on the goods. Then the excise officers intervened, seized every cask which was in the slightest degree under weight, and secured condemnation of the goods in the Exchequer, thus casting upon the Customs the responsibility of refunding the duties on the seized casks, or of contesting the unfortunate agents' claim for rebate. 'I was obliged,' said Baron Macdonald, 'to declare it was a matter of positive regulations. . . . A very distressing case.' (Readers may be inclined to wonder why regulations should not altogether supersede judges, if a judge were justified in thus conniving at an injustice, through allowing himself to be overridden by the bare letter of the law. Law thus used becomes a mere engine of criminality. An irresponsible despot would be a better adjudicator than a devotee of formula like Baron Macdonald. It is certain that if such a case had been brought to the decision of a savage chief, justice would have been done, the prize agents would have got their coffee, and there would have been an instant reduction in the Excise establishment.)

The commanders and mates of the revenue cruisers became dissatisfied with their full-dress uniform, and asked the Board of Customs' permission to enhance its glories at their own expense. The decorations suggested were: commanders, a silver epaulet, buttonholes bound with silver twist, side-arms, and cocked hats with cockades; buttons on coat to be set three and three, the breeches and waistcoat as usual. Mates: lapels, buttons set two and two, cocked hats with cockades. Minute: 'Allowed, except epaulets.'

Certain provisions of the Act of 1791, regulating the Corn duties, were repealed by Cap. 109, 44 Geo. III., and fresh regulations provided, to the effect that wheat might not be exported if the price exceeded 54s. a quarter, and, if exported when the price was at or under 48s., should be bountied at the rate of 5s. a quarter. The 'high duty' on imported wheat was to obtain when the price was under 63s. a quarter, the 'first low duty' when it was at 63s. or under 66s., the 'second low duty' when it was at 66s. or above. Proportionate regulating prices were fixed for other kinds of corn. The North American colonies were treated preferentially. The regulating prices were to be fixed by striking an average of the prices in all the various districts. The return below will indicate that the second low duty of 6d. a quarter on wheat was payable during the greater part of the first twelve years of the century.

AVERAGE PRICE OF WHEAT, PER QUARTER, IN ENGLAND AND WALES.

Year	£	*s.*	*d.*	Year	£	*s.*	*d.*
1801	5	18	3	1807	3	13	3
1802	3	7	5	1808	3	19	0
1803	2	16	6	1809	4	15	7
1804	3	0	1	1810	5	6	2
1805	4	7	10	1811	4	14	6
1806	3	19	0	1812	6	5	5

By indenture dated March 26, 1806, an agreement was entered into between the duke of Grafton and the Treasury, by which the former relinquished his interest in the Prisage and Butlerage of England, in consideration of an annuity of £6,870, payable by quarterly instalments to him during life, and afterwards to the heirs male of his great-grandfather, Henry Fitzroy, a nobleman who had been quartered on the Prisage and Butlerage by letters patent of 24 Chas. II. (Cap. 79, 46 Geo. III.).

The Customs holidays in London were restricted by Cap. 82, 46 Geo. III., to Christmas, Good Friday, Restoration Day, Coronation Day, the king's, queen's, and Prince of Wales's birthdays, and the public fasts. The hours of employment of the outdoor men were stated as nine to four from November 10 to May 9 inclusive, eight to four for the rest of the year; but this did not affect the officers at the West India, East India, and

London Docks. The fees previously charged by surveyors, warehouse-keepers, landing-waiters, gaugers, inspectors, searchers, tide-waiters, clerks, messengers, etc., were abolished, and salaries granted instead. (The only 'patentees' affected by this alteration were two of the patent searchers.) The prescribed hours of employment might be exceeded if the Board thought it necessary for the public service.

Cap. 97 of 46 Geo. III. provided for free trade in corn, without duty or bounty, between Great Britain and Ireland. Cap. 150 dictated the procedure of the English Customs Receiver-General. Moneys received by him were to be paid into the Bank of England on day of receipt, and the Bank was to keep a separate account. He might retain not exceeding £1,000 to meet casual demands, or the Board might authorize him to hold back a larger sum not exceeding £5,000. He might also retain moneys received as tax on salaries, as contributions to the Superannuation Fund, and on account of repairs to Dover Harbour. If at any time the Receiver-General had not sufficient money in hand to discharge drawbacks, etc., he might draw on the Bank.

We find that in 1806 the net proceeds of the sales of goods collected in Barbados and the Leeward Islands as '4½ per cent. duties' (see vol. i., p. 146) amounted to £25,400 0s. 6d. The goods collected were sugar, ginger, and aloes. Thirty-five pensioners were quartered upon the account, and the disposal of proceeds was as below :

	£	s.	d.
To pay salaries of customs collectors and controllers in Barbados, St. Kitts, Nevis, Antigua, and Tortola	2,476	2	4
Retained as balance in hand by the 'Husband' of the 4½ per cent.	33	16	6
Paid to thirty-five pensioners	19,793	16	8
Paid to Customs Receiver-General, to be transmitted to Exchequer	3,096	5	0
	25,400	0	6

It appears that the Irish revenue had risen at a great rate during the latter part of the eighteenth century and the beginning of the nineteenth. Thus :

	£
Irish revenue (of Customs and Import-Excise only) in 1781	548,389
Irish revenue (of Customs and Import-Excise only) in 1786	928,258
Irish revenue (of Customs and Import-Excise only) in 1791	1,006,069
Irish revenue (of Customs and Import-Excise only) in 1796	1,113,680
Irish revenue (of Customs and Import-Excise only) in 1801	1,787,024
Irish revenue (of Customs and Import-Excise only) in 1806	1,989,684

(In 1811 it reached £2,206,301, and in 1816 £2,653,880.)

By Cap. 12 of 47 Geo. III. it was provided that the patent customers' offices at Baltimore, Belfast, Cork, Donaghadee, Drogheda, Dundalk, Galway, Killibeg, Kinsale, Larne, Limerick, Londonderry, Newry, Ross, Tralee, Waterford, Wexford, Wicklow, and Youghal, and the patent searchers' offices at Dublin, Belfast, Cork, Donaghadee, Drogheda, Dundalk, Galway, Kinsale, Larne, Limerick, Londonderry, Newry, Ross, Strangford, Waterford, and Youghal, the office of surveyor-general of Ireland, and the office of Irish Taster of Wines and Surveyor of the Outs (see vol. i., p. 428), should be abolished as they became vacant. The patentees already enjoying the offices and pocketing the unearned fees were not to be compelled to give attendance. The offices of craner and wharfinger of Dublin, customers (actual) of Dublin, clerk of the ships' entries of Dublin, coast clerk of Dublin, Irish Comptroller and Accountant-General, Irish Examiner of customs, Registrar-General of Irish shipping, and the offices of the controllers at all the Irish ports, were not to be granted in future, unless the Board thought such grant necessary, and then each appointment was to be approved by the Treasury, the Lord-Lieutenant, and Parliament.

Cap. 36, 47 Geo. III., abolished the slave trade. Vessels

contravening might be seized by officers of customs and excise, as well as by those of the army or navy.* By Cap. 51 the provisions of the Act of 1806, abolishing most of the Customs fees in London, and regulating Customs hours, were extended to the British outports. From the list of officers it appears that registrars of tide-waiters, 'sitters' (commanders) of preventive galleys, riding officers, preventive officers, quarantine officers, gatekeepers, and customs coopers, had been in the habit of collecting fees. (From whom, under Heaven, could such fees have been extorted ?)

Cap. 26 of 48 Geo. III. increased the duties on most foreign goods exported from Great Britain, and a later Act extended the provisions to Ireland. The preamble of the British Act is worth quoting : 'Whereas measures which have been taken by powers at war with your Majesty, prohibiting in violation of the law of nations all intercourse with this kingdom, and all trade in any articles of its growth or manufacture, have rendered it necessary for your Majesty to issue orders in Council to counteract the disadvantages which were thereby imposed upon the trade of your Majesty's subjects, and to retaliate upon the enemy the evils which he intended to inflict upon this kingdom.'

The Irish Customs fees were abolished by Cap. 56, 48 Geo. III. (from January 1, 1809). Tables were pre-

* Humane laws may sometimes cause inhuman actions. On June 4, 1811, the Portuguese brig *Falcon* was captured off St. Domingo by H.M. brig *Liberty*, and found to have 384 Africans on board. The Vice-Admiralty Court at Tortola decided that she had been wrongfully seized. Her captors appealed against the decision, and, as the captain could not furnish security to answer judgment, the vessel was detained at St. Thomas's. Her provisions ran out, and, as the judge made no order pending trial of appeal for subsisting the slaves, the latter were soon in a pitiable condition. The captors gave no assistance ; they merely 'hung on' to the vessel. Her condemnation 'with tackle' was all that interested them. Between the date of capture and June 23, 1812, 112 of the wretched negroes perished from disease and starvation, in spite of the efforts of the customs collector of St. Thomas's, who did his very best to provide them occasionally with food and water.

pared, showing the amounts received as fees by the various officers during the three years ending January 1, 1804. An average was struck, and the Lord-Lieutenant then prescribed the amounts which should be granted as compensation.* By this Act the Irish Customs holidays and hours of attendance were made much the same as the British.

A curious complication occurred in Jamaica. The controller of Montego Bay seized the *Bella Americana* for contravening the navigation laws. The vessel was afterwards released, and he was cast in damages by the Grand Court of the island, even although his counsel pleaded in defence that Cap. 22 of 7 and 8 Wm. III. provided that Plantation officers, if sued for any error committed in the execution of their duty, might plead the general issue, and thus claim the exemption enjoyed by customs officers in England. A similar case occurred in 1811. The collector of Falmouth, Jamaica, seized the *Two Brothers*, for landing goods without having entered them on the ship's report. Action was taken against him at the Cornwall Assizes, Jamaica. The seizure was declared illegal, and he was cast in damages in a subsequent action for trespass, the judge declaring that the British laws were inefficient when opposed to enactments made by the Legislature of Jamaica. This in spite of there being statutes on the British rolls making void all Plantation revenue laws that were repugnant to imperial Acts. All the collectors and controllers of Jamaica signed

* There were a great many pensioners on the Irish Customs establishment, some of them receiving large benefits. One, Bernard Shaw, ex-collector of Cork, was listed for a pension of £700 and an item of £2,579 19s. 7d. (whether this last was an annual pension or a lump sum is not clear). Jonas Harrison, export-surveyor of Cork, was listed for £2,600 (evidently an annual pension) and a pension of £50 in right of his wife. (It is probable that Mrs. Harrison had been 'female searcher' at the port in question.)

Lord Avonmore was one of the patentees compensated under the above Act. He had been patent searcher of Cork. He died in 1870, having drawn his pension during sixty-one years. The aggregate amount paid him figures out at £41,470 11s. 11d.

a printed memorial, asking the Board to protect them. The English Solicitor-General's opinion was taken, and he advised that the matter should be dropped, but it is clear that he was influenced by the extremely arbitrary nature of the seizure. As will be seen later, the officers, both in the Plantations and the United Kingdom, frequently strained the regulations with a view to profiting by rewards.

From the commencement of the century to the period last reviewed several Acts had been passed repealing the remnants of the old laws against regrating (buying to turn over). It is evident that Adam Smith's teaching was responsible for these doubtful proceedings, as well as for the previous abolition of the laws against engrossing. The newly-sanctioned engrossing and regrating of foodstuffs worked blithely with the tremendous war taxes in raising the prices of commodities.

Another re-consolidation of the Customs was enacted on June 10, 1809, by Cap. 98, 49 Geo. III., to come into operation on July 5. It did not affect the duties on goods passing between Great Britain and Ireland. It continued the temporary war duties, and in many cases increased the other rates upon goods.

The provisions of Edward VI.'s Act against the trading of public offices, which had previously extended to the offices of Administration of Justice; King's rents, treasures, and revenues; Customs; wardenships of fortresses; and clerkships of Record in England, were amplified by Cap. 126 so as to include the departments under the Treasury, Secretary of State, Admiralty, Ordnance, Commander-in-Chief, Secretary for War, Paymaster of Forces, India Commissioners, Excise, and many others in the United Kingdom and Plantations, including the East India Company. Certain appointments in the royal household, and army commissions, were specially excepted. The Chancery officials in Ireland might trade their offices until death or vacation.

Cap. 64, 50 Geo. III., provided that dutiable goods

warehoused under bond might be removed from the port of warehousing (by sea or inland navigation only) to any other port that enjoyed bonding privileges, but only for exportation from the port to which removed. If the owner, after removal, desired to clear his goods for home consumption, he had to pay *the duties as due at landing*, without any allowance for shrinkage while in warehouse.

On July 12, 1810, the Attorney-General proceeded in the Exchequer against Johan Olkhausen, master of a Dutch galliot 'lying off St. Katherine's near the Tower.' Probably this was the last important case in which proceedings were taken under the old Acts that forbade the exportation of coin of the realm. The prosecuting counsel opened thus: 'Against a foreigner, importing that he was detected in the act of endeavouring to export from this country the coin of the country, against the King's licence. You know very well, gentlemen of the jury, how important it is to prevent that practice if possible. The country is already drained of its coin very much by this practice. Our gold coin sells in another country to a great advantage, and it has been the practice to buy up the coin by giving 22s. for a guinea, and carrying it to a foreign country as merchandise. There are repeated Acts upon this subject, and those of a very ancient date, one so long ago as the reign of Richard II. It is easy to apply for the King's licence, which would not be withheld in a proper case, but to attempt to do it without the King's licence is contrary to law, and the coin is forfeited.'

William James, tide-surveyor of customs, then stated that he went on board the defendant's ship on December 13, 1809, and asked him what money he had. Defendant produced several banknotes and ten guineas in gold, which last he stated were 'for his expenses.' 'I suffered him,' said James, 'to return them to his pocket.' James afterwards found in the defendant's berth two sealed bags, one containing 200 guineas, the other 40.

It was urged in defence that the wisest writers on commercial policy had stated that merchandising coin was not prejudicial to the interests of the realm, also that the action was taken under a statute of Henry IV., which provided that if any king's searcher found gold or silver, in coin or in mass, *passing out of the realm* without licence, such gold or silver should be forfeited ; and that no proof had been furnished that this Dutch shipmaster was passing out of the realm. He was the manager of the vessel ; she had no supercargo ; the ship was his domicile. It had been stated that he might have banked the money. True, but there would have been some risk—witness a recent huge failure in Lombard Street ; indeed, so perilous had banking become that the Dutchman's guineas might be safer even in the clutches of the customs officer who seized them, etc., etc.

Here the judge intervened, and declared the defending counsel to be in error. The ship had been cleared outwards by the Customs, and it had always been held that when a ship had been cleared outwards she was on her outward voyage. Verdict for the Crown.

By indenture made between the Irish Treasury and the trustees of the earl of Ormond, the Prisage and Butlerage of Ireland were surrendered to the Crown,* but these duties within the port of Cork were claimed by the Cork Corporation ; therefore it was expressed in the indenture that the claim might be tried in the King's Bench, Common Pleas, or Exchequer (Ireland), so as to be determined prior to January 1, 1812. The amount to be paid to the trustees of the earl (if the Corporation failed to establish claim to a portion of it) was £216,000.†

It was enacted (Cap. 117, 50 Geo. III.) that a statement of the increase or diminution in public salaries, allowances, and superannuations, should be laid before both Houses annually. Compensations and superannuations were to be sanctioned by at least three Treasury Com-

* See Cap. 101, 50 Geo. III.

† The collection of Prisage and Butlerage in Ireland ceased on July 1, 1811.

missioners, and authorized by Treasury warrant or letter. The conditions under which superannuation pay might be granted were set out thus :

	Proportion of Annual Pay and Emoluments.
Claimant under sixty, with ten years' good service, and infirm of mind or body ..	One-third.
Claimant under sixty, with more than ten and not exceeding twenty years' good service, and infirm of mind or body	One-half.
Claimant under sixty, with above twenty years' good service, and infirm of mind or body ..	Two-thirds.
Claimant sixty or more, with fifteen years' good service, and irrespective of mental or bodily condition	Two-thirds.
Claimant sixty-five or more, with forty years' good service, and irrespective of mental or bodily condition	Three-quarters.
Claimant sixty-five or more, with fifty years' good service, and irrespective of mental or bodily condition	All.

By Cap. 207 (local and personal), 50 Geo. III., Parliament authorized the building of the Commercial Docks, London (really an extension of the dock previously used by whalers, and known as the ' Greenland Dock ').

To illustrate the abuses existing in the Plantation Customs, we quote a few extracts from certain evidence forthcoming. It appears that in 1810 the net emoluments (mostly fees) of the three higher customs officials of the port of Halifax, Nova Scotia, were as follow :

Collector, £1,453 ;* controller, £590 ; surveyor, £561. Yet immense smuggling was carried on with impunity between the adjacent colonies and the United States. Nearly all the tea, three-fourths of the wine, nine-tenths of the spirits, seven-eighths of the soap and candles, most of the indigo, starch, mustard, tobacco; East India cottons, and bandanas, and all the nankeens, sail-cloth, cordage, and anchors, imported into New Brunswick, were smuggled thither by Americans. Many of the inhabitants were patriotically inclined, and would have

* These and the emoluments subsequently quoted are stated in sterling, not in currency.

preferred dealing with the mother country, but for fear of being ruined by illicit competition.

The American Government, to discourage smuggling from the United States to Nova Scotia and New Brunswick, allowed no drawback on American goods shipped thither, but the subtle American smugglers and corrupt American officials easily evaded this provision. The American customs officers accepted delusive manifests, setting forth that the cargoes were for other places, and the smugglers produced on return forged certificates of landing, which the American Customs passed as satisfactory, and on the strength of which drawback was claimed and paid. Meanwhile the goods had been run into Nova Scotia or New Brunswick, where the dilatory and inept Plantation officials sat at their desks, charging fees on clearances, entries, etc., fees no doubt gladly paid by the smugglers, and regarded as warrants of impunity.

The collector stationed at New Brunswick was seventy-six years old—old enough to have learned better methods. The net emoluments of his office in 1810 were £871 ; the controller gained £541 ; the surveyor £464. And, while audacious and deliberate smuggling went on all around them, the preventive officers gained respectively £602 and £302, much higher emoluments than fell to the lot of preventive men of similar rank in England.

The port of Bridgetown, Barbados, was still more profitable to officials. See the return for 1810 : Collector, £3,556 (£3,376 of this had been taken in fees) ; controller, £1,473 ; searchers, £722 each ; landing-waiters, £502 each.

Cap. 55, 51 Geo. III., abolished the Customs Superannuation Fund (see vol. i., p. 166), as rendered unnecessary by Cap. 117 of the previous year. No more official contributions to the fund were to be taken, and the moneys in hand, which the Board had invested, were appropriated by the Receiver-General, and paid into the Exchequer to the account of Consolidated Customs, an account from which all subsequent Customs superannuations and allowances were to be met.* (The Scottish Customs Superannuation Fund was dealt with similarly, under Cap. 60, 52 Geo. III.)

Most of the English Customs sinecurists, whose offices were to become vacant at death of holders (see vol. i., pp. 405-407), were still alive, and punctual in attendance at the pay-seat. Cap. 71, 51 Geo. III., provided that their offices should be abolished on January 5, 1812, they to receive compensation, and all Customs fees in London were to be abolished, except as below expressed :

1. The Customs Solicitors might still charge. 2. The Long Room clerks might still make out entries for the merchants, if the latter were willing, and receive the customary fees. 3. The receivers and collectors might continue to pocket 'the odd pence' superfluous on payment of duties, if the merchants were willing (see vol. i., p. 367). 4. Certain Long Room officials might continue to charge fees for delivering warrants at times other than the usual hours of attendance. 5. The cocket-writers might still charge fees, the merchants to have power to choose which cocket-writer they would honour with their custom. All officials who had taken illegal fees were indemnified, and it was provided that the Treasury might extend the Act to outports on giving notice in the *London Gazette.*

We furnish an account of the emoluments, etc., of various Plantation officers during 1811 (shillings and pence rejected). (See pp. 40-41.)

It should be noted that the amounts shown as 'duty

* The stock of the English Superannuation Fund stood as below :

	£	s.	d.
Arising from official contributions :			
Invested in 3 per cent. Consols	178,459	8	10
Invested in reduced annuities	12,500	0	0
Arising from patentees' fees which had been appropriated :			
Invested in 3 per cent. Consols	63,018	0	0
	253,977	8	10

taken ' in Antigua and St. Kitts do not include the comparatively important duties of 4½ per cent., which were realized in London. Nearly all the ' emoluments ' consisted of fees, to a great extent levied on coasting traffic, the victims being the masters and owners of the little ' drogers ' that plied between island and island. The salaries were nominal : the collector's salary at an important station rarely exceeded £100.

The average annual ' ordinary duty ' taken at Christianstadt, St. Croix, was £740 ; ' the special duty,' taken on American produce and tonnage by Order in Council of 1809, was £4,017 : total, £4,757—quite an important sum, and the collector took as emoluments £3,362 ; the controller £1,211 ; and the landing-waiter £613. At Frederikstadt, St. Croix, the ordinary duty amounted to £18, and the special to £1,860, the collector pocketing as emoluments £2,813 ; the controller £935 ; and the landing-waiter £785. At Quebec the Plantation duties amounted to £1,900, against which there was a charge of £598 as ' incidents.' The officers collected certain inland duties as well, which were applied to local purposes, and produced about £50,000 per annum. On this they received a commission. Their total emoluments appear to have been : Collector, £2,760 ; controller, £1,626.

A curious kind of fraud was practised in connection with the ' rum and lumber trade ' between Quebec and the West Indies. If a cargo of lumber, provisions, or cattle were shipped—say from Quebec to Barbados—a certificate obtained from the Barbadian customs officers that the goods were landed, and then a cargo of rum were laden at Barbados (value of said rum not exceeding value of the cargo landed), the rum might be delivered duty-free in Quebec. This was a device to encourage intercolonial trade, but mark how, by the ineptitude of officials, the system had become a vehicle of fraud. The principal articles of lumber shipped at Quebec were hoops and staves. The rate of value fixed per 1,000 feet had for years been applied to every 1,000

Port.	*Emoluments.*	*Hours.*	*Amount taken as Duty.*	*Remarks.*
St. Lucia	Collector, £2,414 Controller, £834 Landing-waiters, £463 (each)	9 to 1	Not shown	
Kingston (St. Vincent)	Collector, £1,896 Controller, £636 Searcher, £493 Landing-waiter, £293	9 to 2	Not shown	—
Roseau (Dominica)	Collector, £1,182 Controller, £424	9 to noon	Not shown	Trade may have dwindled. In the previous year the collector had taken nearly £1,800
Fort Royal and Trinite (Martinique)	Collector, £1,480 Controller, £635	9 to 1	Not shown	—
St. Pierre (Martinique)	Collector, £3,656 Controller, £1,705	9 to 1	Not shown	—
Pointe à Petre (Guadaloupe)	Collector, £3,025 Controller, £1,173	Not shown	About £86	—
Basseterre (Guadaloupe)	Collector, £1,876 Controller, £814	Not shown	About £55	—
St. John's (Antigua)	Collector, £1,320 Controller, £392	Not shown	About £585	—

Basseterre (St. Kitts)	Collector, £1,904 Controller, £545 Searcher, £450 Landing-waiter, £435	Not shown	About £463	A charge of £212 for 'incidents' against the duty. Collector on leave in England. Landing-waiters proceeding to England
Marigot (St. Martin's)	Collector, £613	Not shown	About £23	Charge of £210 for 'incidents' against duty
Phillipsburgh (St. Martin's)*				
St. Thomas's	Collector, £3,685 Controller, £1,140 Landing-waiter, £571	Not shown	£740	A charge of £228 as 'incidents' against duty
Sandy Point (St. Kitts)	Collector, £3,363 Controller, £85	Not shown	Nil	The collector resided on his estate in Antigua. The controller had been absent for a year. The landing-waiter collected their fees for them. (Charge of £293 as 'incidents.')
Tortola	Collector, £717	Not shown	Not shown	Collector so infirm as to be able to do nothing except collect his fees. Controller on leave in England. Landing-waiter appointed to the port in 1807, but had not arrived. A 'resident,' who acted in his stead, was the only official who did any work

* No accounts forthcoming, but there is a statement that the collector had only visited the office once during three months.

hoops, and thus the total value of every cargo of lumber had been hugely overstated. On the other hand, the value of the rum shipped in the West Indies had been understated, and thus nearly all the rum that reached Quebec passed duty-free. This was good for West Indian distillers, and pleased the thirsty Canadian lumbermen, but it was decidedly against the Plantation revenue.

The nature of Canadian outward traffic may be judged from the following annual list of exports from New Carlisle :

17,000 quintals dry codfish.
1,000 quintals wet codfish.
1,050 barrels pickled herrings.
300 barrels pickled salmon.
20 tuns cod-oil.
100 hogsheads cod-oil.
80 barrels cod-oil.
1,650 tons white pine.
160 tons black birch.
16,839 feet pine plank and boards.
70 cords lathwood.
39 spars.
240 handspikes.

The trade from this port was principally to Portugal. The goods were exchanged at Lisbon and Oporto for wine and fruit. The wine and fruit were taken to England, where the vessels loaded woollens, linen, hardware, tobacco, and salt, which they took to New Carlisle.

The London Custom House was in a dilapidated condition, and Parliament, by Cap. 49, 52 Geo. III., issued directions to the Treasury to purchase land in the vicinity of Lower Thames Street, so that a new custom-house might be erected.

The Revenue claims on flotsam, jetsam, lagan, and wreck were recited by Parliament.* When the goods consisted of spirits or tobacco, the finder was enjoined to

* By an order of December 24, 1803, the Customs Board, on the strength of a decision given by high legal officers, had directed that in future no duty should be charged on derelict goods, thus reversing their decision of 1729 (see vol. i., p. 205). In an order of August 15, 1811, they had quoted the Attorney-General's opinion as to manorial rights. If the officers found the goods, the lord of the manor could not recover them until after a year and a day, except by process under Cap. 4, 3 Edward I.; if the lord of the manor found the goods, the officers could not claim them until a similar period had elapsed.

apprise the Customs or Excise within twenty-four hours. The officers apprised were to demand the duty payable, and put the goods under lock if payment were refused. The manorial rights over wreck, etc., were reaffirmed, the lord of the manor being allowed to keep the goods if he gave bond for the duties payable. Duties to be paid within a year and a day, otherwise the goods were to be taken by the Revenue department concerned (Cap. 159, 52 Geo. III.).

It may be instructive to quote the British duties payable in 1812 upon wine.

Wine per gallon (fractions of a penny disregarded in totals). The gallon used was a little over seven-eighths of the modern measure.

	Imported in a British Ship.			*Imported in a Foreign Ship.*		
	£	*s.*	*d.*	£	*s.*	*d.*
French wine :						
Customs duty	0	5	2½	0	5	6½
Excise duty	0	6	2½	0	6	2½
	0	11	5	0	11	9
Rhenish, German, and Hungarian wine :						
Customs duty	0	5	2	0	5	6
Excise duty	0	4	2	0	4	2
	0	9	4	0	9	8
Madeira wine :						
Customs duty	0	3	6	0	3	9
Excise duty	0	4	2	0	4	2
	0	7	8	0	7	11
Spanish red wine :						
Customs duty	0	4	4	0	4	7
Excise duty	0	4	2	0	4	2
	0	8	6	0	8	9
All other wine :						
Customs duty	0	3	5	0	3	8
Excise duty	0	4	2	0	4	2
	0	7	7	0	7	10

It was provided by Cap. 21, 53 Geo. III., that the Board might grant money towards the subsistence in prison of needy persons who were confined for offences against the Revenue.

Vengeful duties were levied by Cap. 33, 53 Geo. III., on many kinds of French goods, as below :

On French or French territorial products, except wine and silk : An additional temporary Customs duty, amounting to two-thirds of the previous *permanent* duties.

On all French or French territorial silk, except raw silk : An additional Customs duty, described as 'permanent,' amounting to 25 per cent. of the previous permanent duties.

On all French or French territorial goods, except wine, raw silk, sugar, tea, and raw cotton : An additional permanent Customs duty, amounting to 25 per cent. of the previous permanent duties.

The first and second of these duties were repealed by Cap. 65, 54 Geo. III. (Napoleon abdicated in April, 1814).

This Act also laid an additional 50 per cent. on the temporary duties previously levied on exported goods, and a temporary duty of 9s. 4d. a cwt. on all foreign 'hides in the hair' exported to France or French territories.

Additional excises were put on foreign tobacco by Cap. 34, 53 Geo. III., and an additional excise of £63 a tun on French wine, imported or exported. This made the total duty payable on a gallon of French wine—

	In a British Ship. £ *s.* *d.*	*In a Foreign Ship.* £ *s.* *d.*
Customs duty	0 5 2½	0 5 6½
Excise duty	0 11 2½	0 11 2½
	0 16 5	0 16 9

An Order in Council dated May 20, 1813, provided that British ships clearing out for Africa might take arms and ammunition, to traffic with on the coast, to the extent of 10 guns, 10 brace of pistols, and 1 barrel of gunpowder, to every 10 tons of measurement.

On December 10, 1813, the Scottish Board issued

a schedule of missing certificates of ships' registry, from which it appeared that within a limited period ninety-three Scottish vessels had been captured by the French.

On December 23, the Secretary to the Treasury sent the following letter to the Board : 'Gentlemen, I am commanded by the Lords, etc., to desire you will issue the necessary orders for the delivery to Lord Valentia, duty-free, of certain masses of the Rock of Gibraltar, which have been brought home for his Lordship by Captain Turner, of H.M. store-ship *Weymouth*.'

About 6 a.m., February 12, 1814, Mr. Lingham of Thames Street, owner of the vaults which still bear his name, observed a strong light near the river, and found that the Custom House was on fire. This, of course, was long before business hours, and the place was occupied only by the customs watchmen ; a lady named Kelly, who acted as housekeeper ; her brother, General Kelly ; several other relatives ; and the domestic servants who looked after the establishment. On the quay, close to the building, were many casks of oil and turpentine. Mr. Lingham gave the alarm, and a number of people assembled, some of whom exerted themselves manfully in the saving of life and property. Captain Richbell, of the Impress service, with the crew of H.M.S. *Enterprise*, worked wonders in this direction, being ably helped by the Aberdeenshire militia and a company of artillerymen, who came from their quarters in the Tower to render assistance. The East India Company also sent a body of their soldiers to help, but in spite of these laudable efforts the building was reduced to ashes, together with several adjacent warehouses and dwellings.*

(The fire broke out in the bedroom occupied by General Kelly, but the cause is not clear. It appears that Miss

* The landlord of the 'Yorkshire Grey' (a sign still displayed in Thames Street) stated in evidence at the subsequent inquiry that he broke into the Solicitors' room, and rescued an iron chest and a number of books. Then he found that his own house was on fire, and 'went to attend to it.'

Kelly, the housekeeper, spent the previous evening in Aldermanbury. She returned early on the morning of the fire, and interviewed her brother before he retired. He was in failing health, and had to keep a light in his room, but this can scarcely have caused the fire, as she stated it was merely a rushlight, 'kept in an earthenware pan.' The General's deposition was to the effect that the fire broke out in a closet near his bed.)

Some of the spectators and employés behaved with conspicuous heroism. A young lighterman named Drinkald got the casks of oil and turpentine on board a vessel moored at the quay, then broke into the searcher's office and saved many valuable documents, then attempted to break into the armoury and magazine, where a quantity of gunpowder was stored, and, failing in this, headed a sally into the Long Room, and cleared it of most of its contents. While this last work was proceeding the magazine exploded, wounding several of his assistants, but he escaped without a scratch.

A labourer named Carlisle, who was going to his work when the fire was discovered, distinguished himself greatly. General Kelly, who had been badly burned, had got partly out of a window, and hung there in a hopeless condition. A ladder was procured, but it was much too short. Carlisle managed to place a van alongside the building, put the ladder on top of the van, mounted through the flames and smoke, took the General in his arms, and brought him safely down. He also procured the keys of the engine-house from one of the watchmen, broke in—the room being in flames—and brought out the engine. He found the man who looked after the magazine, and asked him to show him the place, so that he might enter and remove the gunpowder, but the man refused to go with him, and this no doubt was wise, for the place blew up immediately afterwards. Carlisle was badly hurt, and had to go into hospital.*

* Miss Kelly gave Carlisle £20 for saving her brother, and the Board made him a 'customs weigher.'

The son of the customs blacksmith made desperate attempts to save the building, and sustained severe burns and bruises. Two maidservants who slept in an upper room perished in the flames. General Kelly died a few days after the event. The newspaper accounts of the fire state that an elderly official displayed great temerity in attempting to reach his offices in the centre of the burning structure, and that after the fire he was observed searching amid the smoking ruins. The bystanders attributed this exhibition of official heroism to a desire to rescue the documents in his charge. They went to his assistance, and succeeded in finding an iron safe. The old gentleman unlocked the safe, took out a bag full of guineas, counted his treasure, and retired precipitately, without uttering a word of thanks.

On March 18, 1814, the Board made a provisional report to the Treasury. They blamed none for the fire, admitting that it was impossible to state with certainty the cause of the disaster.

Immense stores of official records, many of which might now be of great historical value, were destroyed. Yet many volumes survived. Some of these are not connected with Customs matters, yet they are of value, and indicate that at the beginning of the century the Commissioners possessed an extensive *private* library, and that many of the volumes therein were bound and furbished in sumptuous style. At this time the Board kept a private stock of wine in vaults beneath the Custom House. Shortly after the fire an official salvor furnished an account of the wines 'gott out of the ruins of the Comishiners Sellers,' stating them as 1 full butt, 2 full hogsheads, 1 ullaged hogshead, 437 full bottles, 56 ullaged bottles, and 1,134 empty bottles. He also rendered account of 'a quantity of copper coyne, two peecis of silver, and a sixpence,' found in the same shadowed receptacles. The salvors, or some of them, must have been honest folk, for on the day of the fire certain persons who had busied themselves in saving property handed over to the Customs Secretary five bags containing gold and silver coin.

The Board tried to hire Bakers' Hall, but, there being some delay, an attempt was made to secure Ironmongers' Hall instead. The Ironmongers' Company held a meeting on the matter, and their master Warden curtly informed the Customs that his fellow-guildsmen were not disposed to acquiesce. So the Customs business was transacted temporarily at the Commercial Chambers, Mincing Lane.* On April 14, 1814, the Privy Council

* The designing and rebuilding of the new Custom House were entrusted to Mr. David Laing, the Customs 'Surveyor of Buildings.' Competition was not invited; the matter was a close job. Mr. Laing's estimate was £228,000, and the actual cost was £255,000. It can scarcely be claimed that his efforts were praiseworthy, although he afterwards published a rather pompous tome in commemoration of his performance. He produced a formal and intensely sombre structure, which owes whatever picturesqueness it may possess to its outlook upon the crowded river. That there were people, even in Mr. Laing's time, who thought little of his architectural abilities, is evident from a report made in 1819 by several able officials, who stated that better results might have been obtained had the authorities invited competition, and selected such plans as combined 'beauty of design with fitness.' The report contained this telling remark: 'To trust to the person who happens to be Surveyor of the Establishment is not to take the best means of procuring magnificence of elevation or utility of arrangement.'

Though Mr. Laing was not exactly an architectural genius, he was a good business man. His salary as Surveyor of Customs Buildings (£400 a year, with travelling expenses at the rate of £1 a day and 1s. 8d. a mile when visiting the outports) ran on while he was engaged in his new work, so he charged the new work as 'extra service.' Below is his bill:

	£
For making surveys of premises in Lower Thames Street belonging to the Crown ..	100
Plans and drawings for the new Custom House	100
Two sets of working drawings and specifications	150
Commission at 5s. per cent. on estimate (£228, 000)	570
Commission at £5 per cent. on actual cost (£255,000)	12,750
	£13,670

The last item seems a monstrous imposition. The Treasury referred Mr. Laing to the Board of Works, who disallowed the third item. Thus he received, beside his salary and allowances,

directed that British vessels and vessels of friendly powers might be allowed by the Customs to clear for such French ports as had hoisted the white flag and declared for Louis XVIII. The Customs Board thereupon asked at which ports this had been done. The Council were unable to enlighten them, and rescinded the order, except as regarded Bordeaux.

On May 19, 1814, the Treasury gave instructions that foreign persons of distinction arriving in the United Kingdom, and bringing pictures or images 'for purposes of devotion,' might have the articles duty-free.

During the latter part of 1813 Mr. Pellew, the customs collector of Falmouth, had contrived to bring about the seizure of four Prussian ships—the *Teutrauwen, Vrow Maria, Hendrik,* and *Theophilus*—which had each brought French cargoes under licence. The pretext for seizure was that these vessels had arrived at periods much later than those on which their licences expired, and that the vessels themselves did not fully correspond in build, tonnage, ownership, etc., with the particulars furnished in the licences. The collector sent the seized ships to London, and they were moored in the London Docks, pending the usual formalities attending forfeiture.

£13,520 for three years' work, and a year or two later the Treasury were apprised that in future he intended to charge commission upon the actual cost of any Customs building that might be repaired or erected under his supervision, if said cost exceeded £5,000. The officials who referred this astounding announcement to the Treasury intimated that if Mr. Laing were allowed to do the like he should at least be prevented from basing the rate of commission upon the precedent created in the case of the new Custom House.

Later the building was found to be insecure, and the Crown took proceedings in the Exchequer against the contractor (Mr. Peto), it being alleged that he had not performed the piling properly, and that the spandrels of the arches had been filled with rubbish. The contractor threw the blame on Mr. Laing, and the contractor's counsel, in referring to a recent Parliamentary debate on the matter, declared that the Government had prosecuted the wrong man. The Attorney-General stated that Laing would probably be prosecuted afterwards, the Custom House being scarcely reared before it fell to the ground. Verdict for defendant.

On February 16, 1814, another Prussian vessel—the *Lucia Margarita*—arrived with a French cargo at Falmouth, and the captain produced his licence to Mr. Pellew. The period covered by the document and an additional period prescribed by the Treasury as a concession had expired—in short, the vessel was over two months in excess of her grants. Mr. Pellew seized her. The ship's agent then approached the Treasury, pleading that the original licence had been issued on September 26, 1812, for four months; that the vessel had gone to France and taken in a cargo, completing her lading on January 14, 1813; that while coming down the Gironde she was damaged and had to be unladen and repaired; that she reloaded; and then her master had news of several seizures made in England of ships with overdue licences, and that this caused him to remain in port till news reached him of the Treasury's above-mentioned concession; that contrary winds prevented him from sailing; and then he was taken ill, and another master had to be procured. The vessel sailed, and reached Falmouth too late to profit by the extension. Then, continued the agent, the collector seized the ship, and at once started to land her cargo under a writ of appraisement. The agent prayed the Treasury to put a stop to Mr. Pellew's high-handed proceedings, and allow the *Lucia Margarita*, with her valuable cargo (rendered doubly valuable by the immense duties then leviable on French goods), to proceed under British convoy to Bremen or some other port 'not in the enemy's possession.'

The Treasury Commissioners at once took a reasonable view of matters, and desired the Board of Customs to direct the collector to release the vessel at once; warrant to follow. The Board complied. Meanwhile the Treasury had enjoined that the cargoes of the four ships seized and sent to London should be admitted to entry. But neither Board nor Treasury were as yet thoroughly acquainted with Mr. Pellew, collector of Falmouth; his infernal ingenuity in interpreting in his own favour passages of the complicated laws of navigation and revenue ; his mulish stubbornness ; his superhuman self-confidence ; and his bandit-like determination in prey. (Readers must bear in mind that the condemnation of the five vessels and their highly taxed cargoes would have meant a huge pecuniary award to him.) There began one of the most extraordinary official conflicts in history : one subtle, determined customs officer pitted against the legal advisers of two powerful departments—against reason, common sense, and the *spirit* of the law as well.

On March 8, 1814, Mr. Pellew apprised the Board that, in his humble opinion, the four ships in the London Docks were liable to forfeiture, and that he was about to take steps to secure their condemnation. His attorney would be pleased to wait upon the Secretary of Customs, and meantime Mr. Pellew delicately reminded the Board that he had previously asked to be allowed to prosecute at his own risk and expense.

On March 19 the Treasury referred to their previous order, and desired the Board to authorize the Customs Solicitor to call for the issue of writs of delivery out of the Court of Exchequer, on payment by the ship's agent of the usual law costs. On the top of this arrived another letter from Mr. Pellew, referring to previous reports of his, which he feared might have perished in the fire that consumed the Custom House. The five vessels, Mr. Pellew opined, were justly liable to condemnation. He had already on his own responsibility directed legal proceedings. Here he interjected a startling item, which seems to have been news to both Board and Treasury. *He had already succeeded in getting the 'Lucia Margarita' condemned in the Exchequer!* (This was confirmed soon after by a piteous letter from the ship's agent, stating : 'Very hasty proceedings have been taken by Mr. Pellew in the Court of Exchequer, unknown to me.')

The Treasury sought the aid of the King's Proctor, they having meanwhile received an expression of opinion from the Privy Council that the cargoes of the four ships in the London Docks were available for entry. Thus a third great department had declared against Pellew, yet he was not at all dismayed.

The King's Proctor suggested tripping Pellew by means of formalities. The learned gentleman had conferred with the Advocate-General, and they were of opinion that Pellew would not be able to proceed in the High Court of Admiralty as on a 'prize seizure.' As to the contemplated proceedings in Exchequer, they thought that sections 13 and 14 of Cap. 77, 26 Geo. III., would enable the Attorney-General to enter a *nolle prosequi*. Yet there might be other circumstances worth considering, and they submitted that a reference be made to the Attorney-General.

On March 26 the Customs Surveyors at the London Docks asked the Board for instructions as to the four vessels, as they had been informed that, though the Board had directed release, the seizing officer still held on. About this time Mr. Pellew wrote the Customs Secretary from an inn in London. He had left his port in charge of his clerk, for whose good conduct he was prepared to be responsible. The journey had made Mr. Pellew ill, but he hoped that in a few days he would be well enough to wait upon Mr. Delavaud (the Secretary). He wished the Board to be apprised that he had served the Exchequer writs of appraisement for the seized vessels and their cargoes, and he expected their Honours to assist him in carrying the law into effect. Three days later he informed the Board that the officers at the docks had made several seizures on board the vessels—seizures which tended to confirm his action—and he urged the Board to have the cargoes landed and put in a secure place. The Board did not comply with this audacious invitation, but called on him to furnish full particulars of the cargoes seized by him. This was a dexterous move, for how could he furnish full particulars of mixed cargoes, only part of which had been landed ? But there lay the request, suggested by a cunning official connected with the King's Warehouse, who had made a report on the matter, and intimated that the seizing officer was 'the party most competent to render an account of what he himself has done.' But it needed a more subtle sleight than that, to trip Mr. Pellew. He coolly replied that, being an outport officer, he was ignorant of the London method of taking goods to account, and requested instruction from the Board on that point. Had the Board given him instruction they would have assisted towards confirming his seizure, so the matter was dropped.

The Commissioners of Appraisement approached the Board, asking instructions. The writs had reached them in an unusual course, being served by Pellew's lawyer instead of by the Customs Solicitor. They had no account of the goods, so could not proceed. *That* matter was allowed to stand over.

On March 31 the Treasury directed the Board to carry out the previous order and release the ships, and if they received any more letters from Pellew they were to forward them to Whitehall at once. The message stated that Pellew had not only been guilty of insubordination, but had violated the law. He was warned accordingly, but the warning had no effect. He wrote the Board, informing them that 130 barrels of wine, part of the cargo of one of the vessels, had been delivered for exportation, and he requested that the officers might be ordered to see that these goods were at once relanded and secured. The Board, probably fearing that the wine might leave the country before the matter was finally settled, felt themselves bound to comply, meanwhile appealing to the Treasury. The Treasury directed that the wine should be released, and the vessels at once freed from detention.

But Pellew had another card up his sleeve. On board one of the ships—the *Vrow Maria*—were certain packages of brandy, as to which he had entered proceedings at Falmouth, charging the crew with having conspired with a resident of that town to run the goods ashore. (These proceedings had been based on the evidence of an informer, a person described by several responsible inhabitants of Falmouth as a disreputable character.) This, of course, delayed release of the *Vrow Maria.* Then Pellew played his last card. He informed the Board that he had discovered that the *Lucia Margarita* was not a Prussian, but a French vessel, manned and owned by 'the king's enemies,' and travelling with mere imitations of Prussian documents. In support of this he produced the ship's papers, and a written opinion upon them, furnished by an expert. Though there is every evidence that Pellew in all his previous proceedings had acted in the manner of a brigand, and that the charge of smuggling made against the crew of the *Vrow Maria* was a rascally fabrication, assisted in by one of the greatest rogues in Falmouth, there is little reason to doubt that the charge of forgery was justifiable. But the Board and the Treasury had gone too far to withdraw. They could not allow the *Lucia Margarita* to be condemned on a side issue, foster a glaring precedent in encouragement of insubordination, and cause serious international complications, merely because Mr. Pellew's grimy fingers had unearthed one legitimate reason for seizure. The Customs Solicitor was accordingly instructed to apprise all concerned that there could be no condemnation. Pellew then warned him by letter that if he persisted he would be sued for the seizing officer's share of the *Lucia Margarita* and her cargo. It appears that the letter alarmed the lawyer, and the Treasury were asked to state how this contumacious rogue should be dealt with.

The writ of delivery so precipitately granted in the Exchequer against the *Lucia Margarita* was withdrawn by special order of one of the Exchequer judges, and it might appear that the ships were free. But the case was down for trial, so they could not be released, and, just to show his mettle, Pellew formally reseized the *Vrow Maria* on the Falmouth smuggling charge.

The case was tried on May 14, 1814, and it was decided that the Board of Customs had power to restore seizures, when convinced that there had been no real intention of fraud. Pellew contended that in such cases the Board were compelled to cause the owner of the goods to compensate the seizing officer. This contention the Exchequer barons recommended to the consideration of the Board, stating that it was not binding. The writs of appraisement might not be quashed, but the Court stayed all proceedings under them. Thus the ships, with their cargoes, might be delivered, except the *Vrow Maria*. She was to be detained under the charge of smuggling.

This charge was heard soon after, and the Court reaffirmed the opinion that the Board had power to restore seizures, and stated that Pellew had violated the law. Thus the *Vrow Maria* was at last freed.

It appears that Pellew got his costs.* The whole proceeding forms a remarkable illustration of the ferocity with which some of the revenue officers attempted to enforce seizures. Such men were really revenue lawyers rather than officers, and the revenue Acts, badly drafted and unutterably complicated, afforded every facility for enterprises of the kind.†

* It does not appear that he was punished. We find his signature years later as collector of Falmouth.

† The expert's opinion upon the *Lucia Margarita's* papers is worth reproduction. No doubt the statements are correct. Many curious devices were practised at the time to evade the navigation laws :

No. 1. A bill brief, or builder's certificate, purporting to be granted at Stettin May 27, 1806.

Remark : 'The originals are never made out on parchment, but on particular hot-pressed card-paper. The above, therefore, is evidently simulated.'

No. 2. A certificate of property, purporting that the *Lucia Margarita* belongs to Captain Jacob Daene and co-partners.

Remark : 'The paper and stamps do not appear to be genuine. The usual form of such certificates is a printed one in German type, and the particulars filled in in writing. This certificate is made like those they grant for cargoes, and not for ships.'

No. 3. A certificate of the ship's measurement, purporting to be granted at Stettin May 19, 1806.

On August 11, 1814, the Treasury sent a letter to the Board of Customs, referring to many unjust detentions of ships and goods. 'In some of these cases,' said my Lords, 'the precise letter of Acts of Parliament, framed

---

Remark: 'The stamps, type, and paper are so different from any originals as to admit of no doubt of their being very awkwardly simulated.'

No. 4. A certificate from the Prussian consul at Bordeaux, stating that Captain Daene has left his ship on account of ill-health (the gout), and appointed P. Lett in his stead. Dated Bordeaux, November 13, 1813.

Remark: 'This document may be genuine, but does not prove the fact it pretends, being made in France.'

No. 5. A bill of sale for one-third and one-fourth of the ship, from William Stark to Peter Daene.

Remark: 'This paper bears evident marks of simulation. The legend on the wafer seal is badly imitated. The inscription under the notarial seal (in red wax), so far as it is legible, is, strange to tell, composed of French words instead of German and Latin. The witness who has attested it, although he has altered the handwriting from that in the body of the document, was not able to make a German capital *G* of a different shape.'

The expert deals in the same manner with the muster-roll, the 'Protest against the Sea,' the manifest, etc. He displays great powers of research and combination, and winds up as below:

'From these papers it appears that a fallacious attempt has been made to account for the delay of nearly a whole twelve-month by pretended damages at sea, and the captain's ridiculous story of the gout, while in reality, from the casks being perfectly new, it is quite incredible that they should have remained (as the story goes) confined in the ship's hold for nearly twelve months in a hot climate, without fermenting and bursting the casks. From which I conclude, considering all circumstances combined, that the intention must have been to make use of an expired licence, granted to another captain, and probably to another ship (as the tonnage does not agree with that stated on the licence), and this for the nefarious purpose of imposing upon Government, in return for its indulgence of two months' extension of licences.

'There is no burger-brief belonging to the captain, whereas at Stettin captains ought to carry along with them, and produce when required, a German printed burger-brief accompanied by a printed affidavit in German.

'The foregoing is what I have extracted from and remarked upon the papers produced to me of the *Lucia Margarita*.

'FREDK. JAS. ALBERS,
'Commercial Agent, and translator of Languages.

'LONDON,
'*May* 10, 1814.'

many years ago, in time of peace and circumscribed commerce, has been rigorously applied amid all the difficulties incidental to war, and against the manifest spirit of the Acts themselves.' Special mention was made of a case at Bristol, where the officers had detained a consignment of sugar, the marks on the goods being ' R. S.,' and shown on the entry as ' RS ' (merely minus the dots). For this informality in miniature the goods were put under stop, and the official vultures concerned refused to release them except on payment of ' a satisfaction ' at the rate of a guinea per cask. In another case an officer had detained certain hogsheads of sugar for being ' in excess of ship's report,' and it was found on investigation that the goods were reported correctly, but he had made a mistake in counting the packages. In another case part of a cargo had been seized because the marks on the goods did not exactly agree with those furnished on the report. These were Bristol cases, but a worse case had occurred in London. A vessel arrived with a cargo which by the letter of the law might not be landed. The importers applied for special permission to land these goods and warehouse them for exportation. The officers construed this action into ' evidence of intent to land goods illegally,' and actually seized both ship and cargo while the Board were considering the request. Said my Lords to the Board, in conclusion : ' You may confidently rely, without reference to us, upon our full support in whatever measures may be necessary for the punishment of oppressive and contumacious officers.'

During 1814 the Board issued orders to the Plantation Customs to the effect that the officers were to obey the various colonial governors, make public all the revenue Acts applying to the Plantations, refrain from making out manifests of cargoes under compact with the shipmasters, etc., etc. Another order may be regarded as a notable pronouncement on Plantation Customs tactics. It directed that the waterside officers, instead of, as before, confining their attention to dutiable goods, were also to examine goods entered as duty-free. It is evident that this had not been done previously, which may account for a portion of the smuggling that prevailed.

The old wool Acts, which had been eased by Cap. 55 of 20 Geo. III., were relaxed to a still greater extent by Cap. 78, 54 Geo. III. Cap. 156 extended the duration of copyright to twenty-eight years (or as long as the author's life endured). Cap. 171 extended to the Treasury the powers previously possessed by the Board of Customs of restoring seized vessels and goods. (It followed, therefore, that though the Customs Commissioners retained their powers, the Treasury might intervene, and remit, restore, or mitigate, in cases where seizures were made or penalties inflicted, whether under the laws of Customs, Excise, Navigation, or Trade. Undoubtedly this Act was passed because it had been made apparent during the trial of Pellew's case that the Board held powers superior to those possessed by the Treasury.)

During 1814 the Treasury apprised the Board that Liverpool might be admitted to the full privileges of the East India trade, as soon as proper accommodation could be provided for the East India goods likely to be imported there.

The proprietors of the theatres at Drury Lane and Covent Garden applied to the Treasury for exemption from the 'painted and stained linen' duties (Excise) on their stage scenes and decorations. My Lords refused.

On October 26, 1814, the Secretary to the Treasury wrote the Customs Board:

'Gentlemen,

'It being represented to the Lords, etc., that your officers are in the constant habit of opening a bottle of the cases of wine, etc., brought to this country for H.R.H. the Prince Regent, I am commanded to desire that this practice may immediately cease, and that such packages be invariably delivered without such examination. I am also commanded to enclose a memo. of five chests cordials, landed from the *Hibernia* from Bordeaux for H.R.H., and to desire that they may be delivered without examination and without delay.'

By Cap. 26, 55 Geo. III., the corn duties and corn laws were again 'amended.' When the average price of British wheat was 80s. a quarter or more, foreign wheat might be imported duty-free. The rule was applied to the other kinds of corn, thus: rye, beans, and peas, 53s.; barley, 40s.; oats, 27s. If the average price of any particular kind were less, the article might not be imported for home consumption, nor might it, if previously landed and warehoused, be taken out of warehouse for home consumption. Preferential terms were extended to the North American colonies, the prohibitive prices for their corn being: wheat, less than 67s.; rye, etc., less than 44s.; barley, less than 33s.; oats, less than 22s. This arrangement, and the increase (subsequently quoted) in the duties on foreign butter and cheese, resulted from the deliberations of a Commission which sat during 1804-1812, to investigate 'Agricultural Distress.'

The duke of Manchester, governor of Jamaica, applied to the Treasury for his portion of the proceeds of seizures in that island from 1810 to date. The application was referred to the Board, and they reminded the Treasury of a deficiency in Customs moneys at Jamaica in 1810—a deficiency as yet unexplained—in consequence of which all payments of the kind referred to by the duke had been suspended. 'We submit that no further payment can be made to the governor of Jamaica at present.' (The amount due to the duke was stated as £2,051 18s. 3¼d.)

On the return of the duke of Wellington from France, Mr. Eales, assistant-surveyor at the King's Warehouse, attended at the duke's residence, to examine 'upwards of 200 packages of baggage,' and the duchess gave him 'a remuneration' for his trouble. The Customs Secretary came to know, and apprised the Treasury. The Treasury's reply ran as follows: 'The acceptance by your officers of any remuneration of the nature alluded to is illegal and improper. Instruct Mr. Eales to return in the most respectful manner the money received from the duchess of Wellington, informing her Grace that the acceptance of it would be contrary to law and his official duty.'

Many Plantation collectors were superannuated in 1815, probably in consequence of an inquiry previously held. Among these was Sir John Bontein, collector of St. Thomas's. That gentleman wrote an effusive letter to the Board, thanking them for their services in securing him an ample retiring allowance. His letter commenced: 'Having been nominated to a pension of a thousand a year . . . owing to the very handsome recommendation [of me] you have been kind enough to make, permit me to offer your Honours my warmest thanks for your kindness, which I shall ever remember with the deepest sense of gratitude, etc.' (Sir John's baptismal certificate is appended to the letter. It appears that he was 'retired' at the age of sixty-two, and had served twenty-five years in the colonial Customs.)

In 1815 appeared Mr. Jickling's celebrated 'Digest,' a recapitulation of the provisions of all the Customs laws actually in force. It appears that in 1786 one Mr. Frewin (afterwards made a Commissioner of Customs) had submitted to Mr. Pitt a scheme for repealing the obsolete Customs Acts then on the Statute Book. The scheme was frustrated by the breaking out of war with France. Meanwhile Mr. Jickling compiled his treatise, a tome of 1,375 pages in large quarto. On May 15, 1814, the Treasury directed Frewin to proceed with his measure, and named Jickling as his assistant. (Both these gentlemen were rewarded on a munificent scale.* Mr. Frewin's literary exertions secured him a Commissionership, a grant of £2,000 on May 11, 1813, and five subsequent

* See 'Gatley's Memoranda.'

grants, making in all £6,500. Mr. Jickling received £3,000 for his 'Digest' in 1816, and £1,000 in 1818. In 1820 he received £2,000 for acting as Mr. Frewin's assistant—in all, £6,000. It is not too much to state that any zealous worker with a gift towards literary condensation could do all in two years that was performed by these well-paid and highly-rewarded gentlemen.)

In October, 1815, the collector of Antigua forwarded a list of 512 negroes, captured in the French slaver *La Belle* by H.M.S. *Barbados* and *Columbia*. The list makes curious reading, especially as regards the names of the negroes—names probably bestowed by the officers of the vessels that captured the slaver. In the list of males appear 'Marquis Drogheda,' 'Earl Carhampton,' 'Earl Harcourt,' 'Nesbit Balfour,' 'Earl Cathcart,' 'Lord Harris,' 'Eyre Coote,' 'Earl Elgin,' 'Baron Alten,' 'Viscount Lake,' 'Lord Probyn,' 'Patrick St. Clair,' and 'Edward O'Toole.' Amongst the older females are 'Dulcinea Grenville,' 'Lucy Manners,' 'Prudence Darling,' 'Dolly Fuller,' 'Lovely Tarrant,' 'Nelly Brown,' and 'Bab Bland.' Among the girls are 'Virgin,' 'Vestal,' 'Venus,' 'Niobe,' 'Melpomene,' 'Dido,' 'Cleopatra,' 'Charmian,' 'Amoret,' 'Celia,' 'Sukey,' 'Sal,' 'Fatty,' and 'Wowsky.' Ages: males, twenty-six to seven; females, twenty-three to thirteen. The return shows that they were of rather short stature, only eight males being above 5 feet 7 inches. Against each there appears in the 'column of description' the words, 'very fine negro.'

It was provided by Cap. 23, 56 Geo. III., that during Napoleon's stay at St. Helena there should be no trade to that colony except by the East India Company's ships, or other vessels licensed by the king or the governor of the island. (St. Helena belonged to the East India Company; it was not made a Crown colony until 1833.)

By Caps. 25 and 26, 56 Geo. III., new duties were laid

upon foreign butter and cheese imported into Great Britain. Below is a comparison:

Previous Duties.	£	s.	d.	Duties as under the New Act.	£	s.	d.
Butter, per cwt. ..	0	3	3	In a British ship ..	1	0	0
Temporary war duty	0	1	1	In a foreign ship ..	1	5	0
	0	4	4				
Cheese, per cwt. ..	0	2	9	In a British ship ..	0	10	6
Temporary war duty	0	0	11	In a foreign ship ..	0	13	0
	0	3	8				

On May 28, 1816, a complaint from the collector of Shelburne, Nova Scotia, reached the Board, that American fishermen had been in the habit of coming within the limits prescribed by the Treaty of Paris, and taking fish and bait in defiance of the authorities, and that when they wanted food or stores they took them by force from the Nova Scotian settlers. He had written to Captain Wilson, commander of H.M.S. *Portia*, acquainting him that the Americans, to the number of '160 stout men,' were 'parading about' at Cape Negro, 'bidding defiance to the revenue officers.' Captain Wilson captured eight of the encroaching vessels, took them to Halifax, and consulted the Nova Scotian Attorney-General, who was of opinion that the fishermen should be at once released. Released they were, but the collector had not done with them. 'We,' he wrote, 'having observed their thankless and insolent demeanour, exacted from them the usual fees of report (17s. 6d. each), and the provincial officers charged them fees of light dues.'

On September 2, 1816, a person named Kershaw wrote from Boston, Mass., to Mr. Croker, Secretary to the Admiralty, furnishing a statement as to immense smuggling from the U.S.A. into the British North American Plantations. He also stated that many vessels owned by Americans were trading under British licences. 'The law,' said he, 'is evaded through the depravity of some

English subjects, who for a small remuneration procure the official documents, and then sign demonstrations of trust in favour of the real owners.' He then offered his services as a spy. 'I will serve you with integrity and at a reasonable rate. I should think with travelling charges never exceeding three dollars per diem . . . I am young, active, bred to the law, and possessed of some little penetration, besides a great desire to see the vauntings of these people [the Americans] effectually checked.'

A quotation from the opening part of the letter may exemplify this cheap rogue's character: 'Born and brought up in London, and cheered by prospects highly advantageous, that accursed failing which has ruined many proved too fatal to me, and an unfortunate acquaintance with one of the other sex having exposed me to very serious charges, I adopted the resolution to visit this part of the world, until, by my exertions in favour of my own country, I should in some degree merit the royal clemency.' Whether he got his three dollars per diem does not appear, but his statements as to smuggling were communicated to the various collectors.

Although peace had been secured, the ghastly effects of years of war were but the more apparent. Bread was dear, the rent of land had risen enormously, the fiscal experts were still busy—riveting upon commerce the ancient imposts, and devising new ones. Public lotteries were still being run. The nation had entered upon the second and worst phase of the worst period ever endured in England. The factory system was at its very vilest. The industrial eminence of Great Britain was sustained by the wholesale sacrifice of the children of the poor. Yet a few slight concessions had been made to humanity and common sense. The punishment of the pillory, and the disembowelling and quartering of criminals convicted of high treason, had been recently abolished. Tenderness to the negro was preached everywhere, and in many instances by people who had grown rich out of the proceeds of white slavery. There appeared no likelihood of lighter taxation, yet high officials were not wanting to recommend cleaner, cheaper, and more sensible methods of collection. Some of these, as before observed, had cast impatient glances upon the crowded Statute Book, and desired to sweep away hundreds of the stuttering, bewildering revenue enactments.

The various 'temporary' war duties, granted since 1803 upon goods imported into and exported from Great Britain, were made 'perpetual' by Cap. 29, 56 Geo. III. Loans amounting to over £38,000,000 had been charged upon these and the temporary excise war duties. It is evident this had been a futile appropriation, for the Act provided that the duties by it made perpetual should pass into the Consolidated Fund, and *go towards* defraying the *interest* on the said loans.

Several Acts had been passed since 1800, authorizing the exportation of machinery to erect mints in various foreign countries, and relaxing incidentally the laws forbidding emigration of artificers. By Cap. 92, 56 Geo. III., similar provision was made as to machinery and artificers for erecting a mint in the United States (to take effect on January 5, 1817).

It was provided by Cap. 98 that the revenues of Great Britain and Ireland should be brought into one fund, called 'The Consolidated Fund of the United Kingdom,' and that this should be charged with the interest of the national debts of the two countries, the whole of their Civil List charges, and all other charges payable out of the previous funds. The separate Exchequers were maintained, but there was to be only one High Treasurer, with Treasury Commissioners for the United Kingdom, though a Vice-Treasurer *might* be appointed for Ireland. Issues by the Irish Exchequer were to be authorized by the Lord-Lieutenant, and recorded by the Auditor-General of the British Exchequer. Annual accounts of income, expenditure, produce of taxes, arrears, debts, exports, imports, shipping, and application of moneys issued for the national service, were to be laid before Parliament.

The instrument* used by the revenue officers in trying the strength of spirits (Clarke's Hydrometer) had long been deemed unsatisfactory. Cap. 140, 56 Geo. III., provided that an instrument called 'Sikes' Hydrometer' should be introduced on January 5, 1817, an instrument which, said the Act, 'hath with great care been completed, and hath by proper experiment, made for that purpose, been ascertained to denote as proof spirit that which at the temperature of 51 degrees by Fahrenheit's thermometer weighs exactly $\frac{12}{13}$ths of an equal measure of distilled water, and also to determine the strengths of all other spirits in proportion to the quantity of such proof spirit which is contained in them, or which can be made from them, with a degree of accuracy never before obtained.' A 'Table of Strengths' accompanied the instrument, and sliding-rules for casting proof quantities. (The instrument and tables are still in use.)

Cap. 73 (local and personal), 56 Geo. III., authorized the establishment of a 'Benevolent Fund' for the widows, children, and relatives of officers or persons belonging to the *English* Customs. Such officers and clerks of the Port of London as were willing to contribute

* The ancient methods of testing spirits were by oil and deflagration. The oil test was simply to mix spirit with oil. If of a tolerable strength, the spirit floated. The other system was burning the spirit in a brass jar. After the alcohol had been consumed, the residue was measured. 'If it measured more than half, the spirit needed further rectification; if less than half, it was strong; if no residue appeared, the spirit was deemed pure' (Basil Valentine, 1420, quoted in Scarisbrick's 'Spirit Assaying'). Then came the 'proof' test (mixing with gunpowder and burning). 'Clarke's Hydrometer' came into use early in the eighteenth century. Although an imperfect instrument, principally through not being adjusted to fit definite thermometrical indications, it displays evidence of considerable ingenuity. The invention of the instrument now in use is attributed to Bartholomew Sikes, Secretary of Excise.

This Act was confirmed by Cap. 28 of 1818, and it was provided that spirits sweetened so as to defeat the action of the hydrometer should be forfeitable, foreign cordials, British brandy, and British compounds excepted.

were to appoint twelve of the principal officials to act as a committee of formation, and to issue rules. The rules, being ratified by a judge of King's Bench or Common Pleas, or a baron of the Exchequer, were to apply as though specified in the Act. Contributions to the Fund were to be deducted from the salaries of the contributors (2d. in the £ quarterly for eight quarters, then 1d.). Membership not compulsory. Nominees might benefit, though not related. Directors might be sued in the name of their secretary. Profits to go to the benefit of the Fund only. Subscribers to be furnished with a report of the accounts on September 1 in each year.*

The Fund benefited otherwise. There was a patent in existence entitling its holder to the profits of the 'Bill of Entry' (an official return of commercial transactions connected with shipping, issued in the Custom House, London). Half the proceeds of the patent were to go to the Benevolent Fund, the patentee to retain the balance.

The Board of Customs consulted the Crown lawyers on the matter of oysters, and the decision was made public on October 29, 1816. It was to the effect that British-taken oysters brought in British ships were duty-free, and that foreign-taken oysters were dutiable but not prohibited. It seems that there had been some error in the Customs measurement of oysters for duty. At certain ports the officers had measured by the Billingsgate bushel instead of the Winchester bushel. (The Billingsgate measure was twice as large as the Winchester.)

The staff employed at the Custom House in the collection of statistics consisted of an inspector-general, one assistant-inspector, one chief clerk, and fifteen ordinary clerks. Total annual cost, £3,895. (In 1908 there were in the same department 1 principal, 1 deputy, 7 senior clerks, 20 junior clerks, 8 minor clerks, 187 assistant-clerks, 34 boy clerks, 2 typists, and a lithographer. Total cost, exclusive of overtime pay, about £30,321.)

* The Fund is still flourishing.

There had been considerable ill-feeling between the good people of Newcastle and of North Shields, the latter having tried to induce the Treasury to sanction the establishment of a custom-house at their port, and the Newcastle folk being averse to any diminution of their own exceptional privileges. It appeared at first that the Shields men would gain their end, but the influence of the Novocastrians predominated, and the application was refused. The contest gave to the world a Newcastle dialect poet, author of the 'Quayside Ditty,' quoted below :

'Ah, what's yor news th' day, Mr. Mayor ?
Ah, what's yor news th' day, Mr. Mayor ?
The folk o' Sheels, they say,
Want wor Custom-house away,
An' ye canna say them nay, Mr. Mayor.

'But dinna let it gan, Mr. Mayor,
Or ye'll ruin us tiv a man, Mr. Mayor :
They say *a Branch* 'll dee,
But next they'll tak the Tree,
An' smash wor bonny Kee,* Mr. Mayor.'

On February 13, 1817, the collector of Montserrat reported that he had seized twelve mules, value £540 currency, for being imported in a foreign ship, contrary to the Navigation laws. The importing vessel escaped, the adjacent fort being so defective that fire could not be opened on her. 'The batteries at the out-bays,' stated the collector, 'being totally dismantled, affords a perfect freedom for the ingress and egress of all vessels disposed to the violation of the laws.' (Report referred to the Secretary of State for the Colonies, March 15, 1817.)

On May 1, 1817, the collector of St. John, New Brunswick, reported to the Board that the legal importations of tobacco into the island during the past seventeen years were 65,203 pounds, and that of this quantity 59,988 pounds had been exported since, leaving only 5,215 pounds duty-paid. He estimated the *annual*

* 'Kee'=quay.

consumption as 100,000 pounds. Thus 100,000 × 17 — 5,215 = say, 1,694,000 pounds, smuggled into the island from the U.S.A. in seventeen years. He also stated that a number of British and colonial vessels, captured during the American War, were being used as American traders. He quoted a return furnished by Lloyd's, from which it appeared that from June 12, 1812, to December 24, 1814, the Americans captured 1,172 British and colonial ships, and that only 383 of these were re-taken or given up.

Early in 1817 the *Montague* postal packet arrived from the West Indies. Five of her crew had died of yellow fever during the voyage, and eighteen others were down with the same complaint. The captain did not hoist the quarantine flag at Dartmouth, as he should have done, and, strange to tell, the Customs did not visit the vessel there, as they were supposed to do. But quite a number of Dartmouth people went aboard, and some of the ship's company, including the doctor and one of the sick men, went ashore. When the vessel reached Falmouth the master, on being questioned in the usual way by the Customs as to health of company during voyage, made many misleading statements. The ship's papers were forwarded to the Privy Council by the officers, there being doubt as to the master's *bona-fides*, and when it was discovered later that there was yellow fever on board it was too late to recall the papers for fumigation. This raised ugly considerations, for by the law both transmitters and recipients were liable to quarantine. But it seems that the authorities decided to relax the regulations with a view to their own convenience, and this may have been the reason why the master, doctor, and customs men concerned escaped with a caution.

Cap. 10, 57 Geo. III. provided that no passenger ship should sail from the United Kingdom to Canada, Nova Scotia, New Brunswick, Cape Breton, or Prince Edward's Island, unless the master entered into bond not to take more than one adult passenger, or three children under fourteen, for every 1½ tons burden of ship (cargo space excluded). The diet and water supplies were specified, and the administration of the Act left, as usual, with the Customs. (There had been many villainous transactions in connection with the passenger traffic. One method of evading the regulations had been to ship the regulated number of passengers at an English port, and then hover on the coast of Ireland, picking up at a cheap rate numbers of unfortunate people, who joined the vessel by stealing off in boats during the night.)

The Navigation laws were relaxed by Cap. 36, so as to grant to all the king's subjects more extensive powers of trade in the parts (except China) within the scope of the East India Company's charter, but the carrying of tea was still left an exclusive privilege of the Company. Asiatic seamen might be employed in ships trading in the latitudes affected, under licences granted by the governors of ports, but only when British seamen could not be obtained.

Many reforms were effected in public offices.* It was provided that, 'on termination of existing interests,' the offices in the English Exchequer of King's Remembrancer, Clerk of Pleas, Clerk of Pipe, Comptroller of Pipe, Marshal, Foreign Apposer, Surveyor and Receiver-General of Greenwax, Lord Treasurer's Remembrancer, Clerk of Foreign Estreats, Clerk of Nichells, and Comptroller of Firstfruits, should be executed in person, instead of by deputy. The same rule was applied to the three Commissioners' offices, the two entering clerks', and the Receiver-Generals' in the Alienation Office, and to the offices of Master in Chancery and Exchequer Solicitor. The fees in vogue were to continue, and their proceeds to be applied to the furnishing of salaries, residue to go to the Consolidated Fund. A number of useless offices in Ireland were abolished, and others deprived of much profit. Among these were the Customs offices of Pratique Master of the port of Dublin, and Customs storekeepers of Dublin. The salaries of certain Scottish

* Cap. 60, 62, 64, 84, 57 Geo. III.

officials were to be pruned 'on termination,' and other offices were ordered to be performed in person. Among the latter were those of Auditor of Exchequer, King's and Lord Treasurer's Remembrancers, and Presenter of Signatures. Others were to be abolished. These included the offices of the Clerk of the Pipe and Controller-General of Customs. The offices of Auditors, Tellers, and Clerks of Pells in England and Ireland were to be performed in person.

The old Irish aulnage laws (Acts relating to the measurement of cloth) were abolished by Cap. 109. The patent office of Aulnager of Ireland was held by Lord Blaquiere, under a grant of 1797. He was compensated by a pension of £500 per annum, payable to him or his heirs till expiration of patent.

The 'winter' hours for shipping goods in the port of London had been defined by Elizabeth's Act as 7 a.m. to 4 p.m., from September to February inclusive. These were in a way extended by Cap. 116, 57 Geo. III., it being provided that goods which had been sent from the quays during the 'legal hours,' to be shipped in the river, might be taken on board up to the time of sunset.

On January 31, 1818, the collector of Deal informed the Board that on the previous night the officers had stopped a postchaise which was entering the town, and found in it several cases containing gold coin of the realm, but that under the circumstances they did not feel justified in seizing the goods. In reply the Board quoted the opinion of the Attorney-General that coin merely found in transit for exportation was not seizable, and advised the collector to release the goods and keep an eye upon them, so that they might be seized when actually 'passing out of the realm.' The Board's letter ended thus: 'We inform you that a person of the name of John Atkins of Deal is now in the practice of exporting the coin of this country to France, and has very lately been in town for the purpose of purchasing coin to a considerable amount.'

By a patent of June 20, 18 Edw. IV., the power of

appointing the City gauger had been vested in the Mayor and Commonalty of London, in discharge of a debt of £7,000 contracted by the king. The City worthies made a practice of granting this office to some esteemed acquaintance. It seems that in olden times it had been lucrative, but since the establishment of the West India and London Docks the profits of the office had fallen off, most of the gaugeable goods being landed in the docks, instead of at the legal quays within the City. The grantee made claim in the Court of King's Bench in 1807 to levy on goods gauged within the docks. The dock companies disputed his claim, but he succeeded in establishing it, only to find the decision upset on a new trial. In 1817 Parliament allowed him to be compensated, the moneys to be obtained by means of extra charges on fees levied by City brokers.

About the middle of the year a strange circumstance occurred. Captain Stirling, of H.M.S. *Brazen*, captured a foreign vessel called the *Tigress* within three miles of the coast of Trinidad, took her into Port of Spain, and 'libelled' her in the Vice-Admiralty Court for contravening the Navigation laws. He did not hand her over to the collector of customs, as required by law, but held her in charge until she was condemned. Then, under the advice of the Attorney-General for the island,* and with the concurrence of the Judge of Vice-Admiralty, he effected a compromise with the owners of the vessel. They paid him £738 17s. 8d. sterling, and also paid the costs (of course, as monstrous as usual). Captain Stirling then restored the vessel, and divided the proceeds of compromise, taking £128 as his own share, and distributing the balance among his officers and crew.

The proceedings were in two points illegal. The gallant captain should have placed the vessel in charge of the Customs, and when the compromise was effected he

* Henry Fuller, Esq. This learned gentleman's name figures in connection with many strange legal transactions. See Illustrative Documents, No. 35.

should have handed half the proceeds to the Customs, to be placed in the king's chest for subsequent remittance to the Receiver-General, as the 'Crown's share.' It is certain that the Trinidad Customs men were cognizant of the transaction, for a seizure and trial of the kind could not escape their notice, yet they made no report of these illegal proceedings.

(It will be well to trace the matter through all its subsequent ramifications. The London Customs lawyers were informed—by whom does not appear—in 1820, and a letter was sent to Captain Stirling—then resident in England—calling on him to pay promptly to the Receiver-General £64 out of his own share, and then to make arrangements for refunding half the sum he had paid to his officers and crew. He wrote back, admitting his liability, promising to pay the £64 at once, and asking relief in respect of the rest. He urged that he had acted under presumably competent advice, tendered by the Attorney-General of Trinidad. 'I beg the Board will consider an officer of the navy has in such cases no guides but the Crown lawyers, and that his situation is indeed deplorable if, after having been employed, there is no time of his life in which he may hope to consider himself safe from the responsibility of errors in law.' The Board replied that they could grant no relief. Meanwhile they censured the Trinidad collector for not reporting the matter, and hinted that they had at first been inclined to surcharge him with the amount of the Crown's share.

It seems that somehow the matter passed temporarily out of ken. In 1823 the Board found that Stirling had not paid the money, so he was written to a second time. He replied, blandly admitting liability. 'I ought not in justice to keep the £64, nor do I intend to do so.' But he pleaded that it would be too bad to make him pay the other £305 odd. The Board ordered prompt payment of the £64, and told him they would ask the Treasury's directions as to the rest.

No reply was received till about a year later, when

Stirling wrote, stating that he had just returned from abroad, and had found the Board's letter awaiting him. He would be happy to pay the £64 at once, and hoped he might be relieved from the other burden.

Again the matter dropped out of official ken, and, candid and ready in acknowledgment as Stirling had been, he took no steps to revive cognizance. It is evident that he had altered his mind, since that far time when he wrote, 'I ought not in justice,' etc., for not a penny did he tender, and the papers remained pigeonholed *till 1833*, when some inquisitive person dusted and inspected them, and the Board received a memo. from the same, to the effect that Captain Stirling had not up to the present paid in His Majesty's share. Again he was written to. Then he began to show his hand. He answered that he was willing, and extremely desirous, to pay the £64, but feared that such payment might be held to render him fully liable for the remainder.

The Board were in a quandary. If they brought the matter to the notice of the Treasury they would in a way impeach the efficiency of their own department. In the first place, a vessel had been seized, condemned, and released on payment of a sum of money, the Crown had been hindered of its share of proceeds, and the Board had heard nothing of this from the responsible officers. Then the Board had allowed themselves to be trifled with by Stirling, and the papers had been overlooked on one occasion for a year, and again for nine years. The lawyer's opinion was taken. He stated that there was little likelihood of success if legal proceedings were taken against Stirling for either sum. Thereupon a very bland and polite note was sent to the rollicking sea-dog, telling him that if he paid the £64 the Board would waive claim of the rest.

After conducting his own defence during fourteen years with such marked ability, Stirling broke down in the end. Had he but declared that on further consideration he had come to the conclusion that he was not liable even for the £64, it is likely he would have heard no more of the matter. But he failed thus to crown his edifice of evasion. Still, he was not precipitate. He wrote, stating that he had instructed his agent, Sir F. Ommaney, to pay the £64 to the Receiver-General, but the old year went and the new year came, and Sir F. Ommaney did not darken the doors of the office in Thames Street. Then a letter was sent to the agent, and in March, 1834, nearly seventeen years after the seizure of the *Tigress*, and nearly fourteen years after Captain Stirling first promised to refund His Majesty's share informally appropriated, the smaller portion of the debt was discharged. Then fresh trouble arose. The Receiver-General, no doubt alive to the peculiar nature of the whole transaction, took the £64, but declined to give a receipt. Sir F. Ommaney wrote the Board a letter of complaint, *the Board* sent a receipt, and thus this extremely remarkable transaction was adjusted.)

On August 13, 1818, the Secretary to the Postmaster-General requested the Board of Customs to direct their officers to be vigilant in preventing the smuggling of letters outward, the Post-office authorities having come to know that a vast number of letters were carried to Rotterdam and other Dutch ports, to the great detriment of the postal revenue.

On November 20, 1818, the Treasury apprised the Board that a fraudulent scheme had been set afoot by certain speculators. It appears these gentlemen had imported a large quantity of foreign hops, and obtained remission of most of the duty on the plea that the goods were 'sea-damaged.' Then they formed a design to export them and claim the full drawback, as though all the duty had been paid on landing.

The British Customs duties were again consolidated by Cap. 52, 59 Geo. III., it being provided that they should cease on July 5, and be replaced by a new scale. (The Act announced that foreign goods, imported into and then exported from Great Britain, were liable to duty if re-imported.) The duties were in many instances increased. The corn regulations were not affected by the Act. Some of the more important duties, and one or two of the quainter kind, are quoted below :

Anchovies and botargo, 1s. per pound ; caviare, 12s. per cwt. ; eels, £13 1s. 3d. the ship-load. (The importation of eels was exclusively in the hands of the Worcum traders, even as now. The vessels used were all of one type, and of about the same tonnage.) Oysters, 1s. 6d. per Winchester bushel ; stock-fish, 5s. per 120 ; sturgeon, 7s. 6d. the keg. Lobsters and turbots were duty-free. Fresh fish, British-taken and brought in British ships, were duty-free ; so were British-taken-and-cured fish.

Glass manufactures, not being bottles, window, flint, or plate glass, paid 80 per cent. on the value, and an excise duty of six guineas per cwt. Wrought iron paid 50 per cent. on the value ; leather manufactures, 75 per cent. ; foreign-made sails, whether in use or as merchandise, paid at the rate of £104 9s. 2d. for every £100 value. Lemons in a British-built ship paid £1 5s. per 1,000 ; in a foreign-built ship, £1 7s. 6d. per 1,000 ; eggs paid 10d. per 120 ; truffles, 5s. 6d. per pound.

The difficulties attendant on assessment and calculation are evinced by the number of 'divisions of articles,' each chargeable with a specific duty. There were 24 different rates of duty on the various kinds of stone, 53 on oils, 81 on skins, 104 on linen, and 183 on wood.

Tea, coffee, and cocoa were duty-free as regarded customs, but they were subjected to crushing excise duties on delivery from warehouse.

The duties outward stood thus : Coals were liable to a special export duty (besides the duty of 10s. in the £100 value, which was levied on all exported British goods, except corn, flour, linen, and cotton manufactures, woollen manufactures exported to places within the East India Company's charter, refined sugar, molasses, and articles intended for use in the Plantation fisheries, all which excepted goods were free from export duties).

The tonnage rates on ships endured. The only coastwise duties leviable were upon coal, slate, and stone.

During 1818 the controller at Falmouth, Jamaica, had died, and appointed Robert Gilpin, the collector, as his executor. The governor of the island appointed one Joseph Wood, a resident, as controller, pending the Board's dealing with the vacancy. Wood entered into bond in the usual way, but Gilpin, by various excuses, evaded handing over to him the controller's key of the money-chest. After a time a new controller arrived from England, and had scarcely taken up his duties ere Wood died. Gilpin evaded the new controller's request for the key for some time, and then was taken ill, and his spirit went to join those of the two departed controllers. The new controller, after Gilpin's death, succeeded in obtaining possession of both the collector's and controller's keys, and opened the chest, which, according to the books, should have contained about £5,000 in currency. States the report on the matter: 'Only one piece of money, of very small amount, was found therein.' Action was taken against Gilpin's executor, Wood's surety, and the new controller and his surety, at the assizes at Cornwall, Jamaica, in November, 1822, and judgment was obtained against all the defendants. Afterwards the Board released all the defendants, except Gilpin's executor, from the penalties, on condition of their paying the costs incidental.

On March 26, 1819, the Board reported on a letter which had been sent, through Rear-Admiral Harvey, to the Treasury, by Captain Elliott of H.M.S. *Scamander*, stationed at Barbados. The gallant captain stated that smuggling was carried on extensively between Martinique and St. Vincent; that French goods were publicly exposed for sale in the latter island; that he seized an English schooner laden with contraband goods from Martinique, another vessel which had loaded without a permit, and a vessel called the *Bellona;* that the last-mentioned vessel was restored by the Vice-Admiralty Court of

Trinidad; that he seized a brig called the *Problem*, and she was also restored to her owners; and that he received for his trouble, in the last two instances, merely trifling sums as 'satisfactions.' He seized two other vessels, which were condemned, but he had not as yet been paid even the expenses of seizure. He then seized the *Harmony*, and secured her condemnation, which cost him £400 currency in law expenses, and he had not as yet received his share of the proceeds. This letter was sent to the Board, and they stated that, with a view to prevent improper and vexatious detentions, it had been their practice to insist that the responsibility for all seizures should rest upon the officers who made them, and that seized vessels were never released unless with a provision that the owners paid all reasonable expenses incurred.

On August 3, 1819, the Privy Council for Trade reminded the Customs Board that though, under the Act of 1815, the importation of foreign corn had been prohibited except when the British price reached a certain figure, the said Act did not apply to the Isle of Man, and that the Manx legislators had refused to alter their code in the way of assimilation; therefore it was possible for foreign corn to be imported free into the island when the price was low, and then carried to Great Britain as Manx corn. It is curious to fall across such an instance of obstinacy on the part of local legislators, and still more curious that the Council should have thought it necessary to apprise the Board of a contingency of which the Board must have been aware.

On October 8, 1819, proclamations were issued by the Governor of the Leeward Islands that, on account of destruction wrought by the late dreadful hurricane, the Navigation laws might be relaxed for six months, to permit provisions and lumber to be imported into Tortola, Nevis, and St. Kitt's, in vessels of any nationality, and sugar, rum, and molasses to be exported in said vessels up to the value of the import cargo. The Privy Council for Trade desired the Board of Customs to direct their solicitor to draft a bill of indemnity to cover the governor's action—said bill to be laid before Parliament (the usual proceeding in such cases).

A letter dated December 30, 1819, reached the London Board from St. Kitt's, stating that extensive smuggling was carried on from Antigua into St. Eustatia. The Board referred this to the collector of Antigua, and that official made answer that he knew nothing of the traffic referred to. He also stated that by his great zeal in protecting the revenue he had incurred the animosity of the members of the Antigua House of Assembly, and hinted that the information might have been prompted by them. It appears they had attacked him on the matter of fees, alleging that the Customs and naval charges 'had given a formidable and repulsive aspect to the trade of the town of St. John's' (Antigua), 'and acted as a terror to all his Majesty's liege subjects engaged in lawful traffic.'

In a report sent by the collector of Halifax, Nova Scotia, it was stated that the coal-mines at Sydney, Cape Breton, were leased to one Leaver, who paid the Crown 6s. 4d. a chaldron on all coals shipped, and that the lease would expire on December 31, 1820; also that the mines were still being worked by horse-power, as none would erect a steam-engine unless a longer lease were granted.

A review of the condition of the Customs at the end of George III.'s reign becomes necessary. The revenue had swollen since the Act of Union, partly through augmentation of trade—especially export trade—partly through increase in the rates of duty. The values of imports and exports were stated as below:

	Imports (Foreign and Colonial).	*Exports to Foreign Countries and the Colonies.*
	£	£
1817	30,805,655	50,379,629
1818	36,900,681	53,559,710

The net produce of the Customs in England, Scotland, and Ireland, for the year ending January 5, 1819, appears to have been:

	£
England	10,176,794
Scotland	760,926
Ireland	1,860,089
Total	12,797,809

(By 'net produce' is signified the sum remaining after drawbacks and expenses of management had been paid. The expenses of management amounted to over 9 per cent. of the *gross* proceeds in England, and over 16 per cent. of the gross in Scotland and Ireland.)

The whole of the net was not paid into the Exchequer. Large sums were deducted, and applied as bounties towards certain public undertakings. These amounted to:

	£
In England	189,924
In Scotland	85,149
In Ireland	147,556

The balances kept back by the various collectors amounted to:

	£
In England	38,380
In Scotland	47,393
In Ireland	17,104

Out of the English moneys £62,512 went towards building the new Custom House at London. Out of the Scottish £71,332 went towards the support of the Scottish Civil Government. In each of the three countries a sum was withheld because, though collected during the years under survey, it was not due till the following year. Thus the actual payments into the Exchequer were:

	£
From England	9,601,903
From Scotland	432,845
From Ireland	1,635,470
Total	11,670,218

(The Irish returns are expressed in British currency.)

The annual accounts of seizures show that the preventive men were kept busy. From 1816 to 1818 the records of total values on condemnation (in England alone) stood thus:

	£
1816	182,774
1817	76,116
1818	117,776

Yet the amounts recovered in fines and penalties were only—

	£
1816	24,989
1817	28,808
1818	21,360

The gradual extension of the bonding system had proved a great boon to merchants, but they still complained of the restrictions placed upon trade by the system of calling for unnecessary bonds on many trifling transactions. (Great relief had been afforded to the coastwise trade in this respect, but foreign traffic was still hampered.) The annual stamp duty realized on Customs bonds reached the huge sum of £40,000.

The building of the West India, East India, London, and Commercial Docks, had effected great improvement in the trade of the Port of London, but the lessees of the various legal quays and uptown warehouses complained that their business suffered through the system of granting special warehousing privileges to the dock companies.* A commission of 1819 reported in favour of the complainers, urging that 'care should be taken not to grant such exclusive privileges to any one of the dock companies as might operate to prevent that spirit of competition which secures to the merchant a moderate charge for the warehouse rent of his merchandise.'

* It is curious to note that, in spite of special privileges of this kind, the London dock companies have recently been compelled in a way to solicit the public to relieve them of their responsibilities, while the legal quays are able to hold their own. Much coddling, though it may foster for a time, destroys efficiency in the end.

Circumlocution was still rampant in the Revenue departments. Trifling Customs transactions were made subjects of petitions to the Board, the result being much waste of time and paper, for the method of dealing with such applications was horribly imperfect. (It may be mentioned, as an illustration of this, that when cattle, sheep, etc., intended as food for passengers, arrived in or were shipped by the East India Company's vessels, fodder might not be taken on board for their support until special written application had been made to the Customs. The document was referred for the reports of certain officials—men by no means inclined to hurry—and considerable time elapsed before the transaction was *formally* 'allowed.' Meantime the animals were on short commons, unless the landing-officers of customs thought fit to wink at an evasion of formality.) On March 1, 1817, a number of important shipowners had memorialized the Treasury, complaining bitterly of the delay experienced in obtaining answers to applications—applications which the high customs officials persisted in demanding, in many instances without any apparent reason.

The Port of London was overstaffed, but a reduction had been recommended. Abolition of the following offices was suggested: 1 surveyor of searchers, 5 searchers, 13 landing-waiters, 4 'extra' landing-waiters, 35 'occasional' landing-waiters, 1 gauger, and 2 'occasional' gaugers, and the reduction of the jerquers from 5 to 2, and of the jerquer's clerks from 7 to 2 (certainly an instructive suggestion). The 'piazza-men'—preferential tide-waiters, fifty in number, who were employed on the Customs quay or in guarding during transit from warehouse to exporting ship the goods which had been sold by the East India Company to various merchants for exportation—were quite unworthy. Wholesale fraud took place during the conveyance of the above-mentioned goods, and it was recommended that the services of the fifty 'preferentials' should be dispensed with, and the goods sent in charge of licensed lightermen.* It was a common practice with dishonest traders to buy high-duty goods which had been warehoused by the Company for exportation, enter them for shipment (exportation being, of course, allowed without payment of duty), and then convey them inland, producing for shipment a consignment of non-dutiable goods in packages similar to those entered. The Customs examination at shipment was imperfect, and the profitable game went merrily on till discovered (probably by accident). A favourite trick was to buy pepper, a commodity highly rated, and ship oats instead of the odorous berries. As the piazza-men were put in charge of the pepper at the door of the Company's warehouse, and were supposed not to leave their charge till the goods were shipped, it seems that they must have been bribed, or else that they did some tolerably sound sleeping on the way from the legal quays to the East Indiamen's mooring-place.

The emoluments of the Customs Solicitors were still on an extravagant scale. The solicitor for the London district received during the year ending January 5, 1819, as salary £500; other emoluments, £4,163. The solicitor for the northern ports of England took as salary £300; other emoluments, £1,232. The solicitor for bonds and criminal prosecutions took as salary £500; other emoluments, £1,277. The unlucky solicitor for coast bonds took as salary £150. He had no other emoluments, and, needless to state, he had little to do.

Liverpool had become an important trading centre, especially as regarded exports. No fewer than 164 bonded warehouses had been established at this port. The Liverpool Customs business was conducted in an unsatisfactory way. The guard of ships was eminently defective, the tide-waiters who performed that duty being beyond control. Many of them were in collusion with smugglers and waterside thieves. The following statement appears in an official report: 'There is scarcely a robbery com-

* See vol. i., p. 167.

mitted about the docks without a tide-waiter being implicated in it, either as principal or receiver.' Once a system of nightly visits of ships on which tide-waiters were boarded was instituted suddenly. Three visits were paid, and 226 tide-waiters found to be absent.

Below is an account of the chief Scottish trading ports, and their yield of Customs (gross) revenue :

	£		£
Greenock	338,599	Dundee	22,799
Leith	230,987	Glasgow	8,384
Port Glasgow ..	202,210	Perth	6,314
Grangemouth ..	39,684	Montrose	6,213
Aberdeen	23,747		

The yield of the remaining Scottish ports averaged just over £1,000 a port, and the charges of management nearly £1,400.

So unsatisfactory were Scottish revenue matters that certain Commissioners of Inquiry actually interjected in their report a sly censure of the Scottish Board, which evoked a passionate protest from the high officials affected. The Board, in their appeal to the Treasury, claimed reference to the opinion of the mercantile community in Scotland, 'to the numerous persons who have occasion to communicate with us on subjects connected with the revenue of Customs, to the members of the other departments of the public service, and to the different public bodies of this city' (Edinburgh), 'and to your Lordships,' etc., etc.

At many of the Irish outports the expenses of management were much in excess of the takings. It should be observed that one inevitable evil of a high tariff is the necessity of maintaining preventive officers at remote places where little or no legitimate trade is done. Still, the pay of Baltimore's preventive guard could scarcely have been responsible for the condition of affairs at that port, where the average annual amount of duty collected was £420, and the expenses of management were £8,365.

One cause of the apparent smallness of the Irish net

return was the system of defraying the cost of building and maintaining public docks and warehouses out of the Customs moneys. It appears that private capital was not forthcoming. The system might have furnished an encouraging precedent, but for the easy methods pursued by the directing officials, under which merchants were charged such absurdly small dues that there was next to no recompense for the outlay.

'Retrenchment all round' was the cry, but this was not so much an outcome of logical thought as an explosion of dismay at the state of affairs. The country had been at peace for nearly five years, yet most of the taxes were higher than at any previous period. The condition of the poor was appalling. Social anomalies and political disabilities had existed in olden days, but then they had not been found so grievous. There had been many avenues of escape, since blocked; many havens of immunity, since closed.

The accession of George IV. was contemporaneous with the commencement of a series of official reforms. The first Act in this direction (Cap. 7, 1 Geo. IV.) abolished a number of useless bonds and oaths previously required by the Customs in connection with bounties, export transactions, etc. It announced that 'many evil-disposed' officers continued to collect fees, although by law forbidden. It enjoined that persons *tendering* such fees should be liable to a fine of £500. The duties on wood were rearranged by Cap. 37, 1 and 2 Geo. IV., many alterations being made in the system of measurement for duty, and many substantial reductions of duty. The Navigation laws were again amended by Cap. 65, further privileges being granted as regarded trade by the king's subjects with the places within the East India Company's charter. (The Company still retained the exclusive right of carrying tea and trading with China.) The registration of wool carried coastwise in the United Kingdom was abolished.

In 1820 the governor of Trinidad suggested to the Privy Council for Trade that the bonds taken of shipmasters in the Plantation trade to land their cargoes at the ports for which they cleared should be dispensed with. 'It must,' he stated, 'be for the common interest that the cargo should be disposed of at the place which will give the best price for it.' He adverted to the injustice of compelling masters, when carrying colonial goods to Europe, to land and reship them in the United Kingdom, a process 'attended with delay and expense, and in the article of cocoa' (a product of Trinidad) 'very often with damage.' It is instructive to find that, though the Customs Solicitors and high officials who reported on this proposal were against any alteration of the Navigation laws, one or two of them hinted that the said laws were in some cases oppressive; indeed, the Customs controller-general stated boldly that they were 'generally allowed to be a clog on commerce.' The Board, in a report which contained a fine précis of the Navigation laws, declined to recommend conformity with the suggestion. (If the governor's scheme had been adopted, the Navigation Act would have become practically a dead-letter.)

On July 31, 1821, the Board dealt with a complaint made by the House of Assembly, Nova Scotia, in 1820, as to excessive fees taken by the colonial customs officers. The Board were of opinion that in most instances the fees charged were legal, and stated that at some of the Plantations the colonial Houses of Assembly had established scales of fees, which the officers had accepted. It was suggested that the whole system of colonial Customs fees should be revised. 'This,' stated the Board, 'might put an end to the complaints and dissensions which have so long and generally prevailed.'

On August 16, 1821, the following case was tried at the Maidstone Assizes: A vessel called the *Limerick Trader* had been quarantined at Standgate Creek, and her cargo removed to the *Courageux* lazaret hulk for disinfection.

It was found that the goods had been tampered with, and a search of the quarantine officers' berths was directed, a man being also stationed to watch the outside of the vessel. Soon the sentinel saw a number of pieces of silk passing into the creek through one of the ports. This resulted in a charge against one Plucknell, tide-waiter. The defendant's counsel, Mr. Adolphus, raised many quibbles, one being that the indictment was informal, the *Limerick Trader* being named therein as a ship bound to 'the Port of London.' Mr. Adolphus held that no proof of this had been furnished, and that at the time of the alleged offence she was beyond the limits of the port; but it was decided that in getting into Standgate Creek she had passed across the extreme eastern limit. Verdict for the Crown against Plucknell, but judgment stayed, and a new trial ordered (with what result does not appear).

On August 18, 1821, a rather remarkable case was tried at the Dorchester Assizes. A customs officer named Power, stationed at Weymouth, had become unpopular, and one morning, as he was proceeding homeward, a fellow named Brinsley followed him along the street, repeatedly challenging him to fight. It should be mentioned that Power had been made town constable, and his appointment in that capacity seems to have been unwise, for it is evident that he was an excitable person. He lost his temper, entered his house, took down his staff of office, and then went out and menaced Brinsley with it. Brinsley, who had only one arm, thereupon struck him with his fist. Power knocked him down with the truncheon, and then beat him over the head till the weapon broke in two. A young fellow named Davis intervened, and challenged Power to fistic combat, which the latter declined. Both Brinsley and Davis were charged with threatening and assaulting Power in the discharge of his duty, and the former was also charged with a common assault. The case against Davis was abandoned, the principal count against Brinsley withdrawn, and he was found guilty of a common assault only. The minutes of the trial certainly *read* against Power, and it seems strange that both cases were not dismissed. It appeared in cross-examination that he had been deprived of his office as constable since the date of the assault, for 'firing at some boys, and wounding one of them.'

Cap. 41, 3 Geo. IV. commenced: 'Whereas several statutes and Acts of Parliament or certain parts thereof, respectively relating to the importation of goods . . . made and passed at various times before the twelfth year of the reign of King Charles the Second, remain unrepealed, although the same are inconsistent with or rendered unnecessary by the Acts made since that time.' It proceeded in repeal of an immense number of hoary edicts relating to wool, cloth, gauging, places for landing and shipping goods, alien and denizen traders, prohibitions, customs officers, and exportation of coin, and between seventy and eighty Acts relating to the Staple. (The Stapling Acts had been obsolete for over 200 years.) The period affected extended from the commencement of the reign of Edward III. to the date of the Old Subsidy (1660).* The next Act of the Session swept away numerous sections and several complete Acts of the old Navigation laws, and the next consolidated the remainder.

On March 16, 1822, the Board informed all the Cornish collectors that a person named Jones had entered Cornwall from France, for the purpose of enticing workers in iron and tin to leave their native country and settle in France. The news was also sent to Rochester, Faversham, Sandwich, and Deal, so it appears that the artificers were to embark at one of the Kentish ports.

About this time the Treasury and Board were pestered by letters from various amateur fiscalists, propounding schemes of taxation, reform, etc., and usually containing explicit avowals of the authors' mercenary motives.

* See reference to Jickling's 'Digest' at p. 60.

Below is a copy of a letter from the Customs Secretary, addressed to one of these unwelcome correspondents :

'*To Mr. Thomas Ivey, No. 1, Lisbon Place, Halloway, Bath, Somerset.*

'SIR,

'The Commissioners having read your letter of the 10th instant, in which you state that you can suggest a plan whereby the revenue would be greatly augmented, I have it in command to acquaint you that you are at liberty to submit the plan alluded to for the Board's consideration, that they cannot enter into any stipulation with you, but that, should the revenue be benefited in consequence of any communication which you may make, you will be paid such reward as your services may appear to entitle you to.

'G. DELAVAUD.

'*September* 21, 1822.'

On the night of July 24, 1822, the custom-house at Castries, St. Lucia, was robbed of 3,564 dollars. The collector reported : 'We can entertain no doubt but that this outrage has been in a great measure instigated by the futility of the late proceedings against certain inhabitants for smuggling, and the hatred consequently excited against us.' (The papers dealing with the case refer to similar robberies at Harwich and Portsmouth.)

Cap. 23, 4 Geo. IV., provided that the king might appoint one Board of Customs and one Board of Excise for the United Kingdom ; neither Board to have more than thirteen members, and that he might also appoint Assistant Commissioners of Customs and Assistant Commissioners of Excise (not exceeding four of each) to transact current business in Scotland and Ireland, under the control of the central Boards at London. Both Customs and Excise Commissioners were to be under the control of the Treasury. Previously there had been nine Commissioners of Customs in England, five in Scotland, and four in Ireland. Under the new arrangement there were thirteen Commissioners for the United Kingdom. Eleven of these sat in London, one at Dublin, and one at Edinburgh, and each of the two last-mentioned had two resident Assistant or Local Commissioners under him. Any of the Local Commissioners might be directed to remove from Scotland to Ireland, or from Ireland to Scotland, if necessary. The Commissioners who retired under this new arrangement were compensated according to the following scale :

Having served less than twenty years, two-thirds of salary per annum.

Having served a longer period, three-quarters of salary per annum.

(One of the retiring Commissioners was granted compensation at his full rate of salary, on account of length of service.)

The Commissioners who had acted as Chairmen of the previous Scottish and Irish Boards had received salaries larger than they became entitled to as members of the new Consolidated Board. The excess of salary was continued to them.

The Irish Customs takings were still to be remitted to Dublin, and paid into the Irish Exchequer, but the Scottish collectors were to remit direct to London. As soon as the patent for the Consolidated Board was issued, a General Order was sent from the Custom House, London, dated October 16, 1823, apprising all the customs officers of the United Kingdom as to the new Board's jurisdiction, and the liability of officers to be called upon to serve in any part of the United Kingdom. The Treasury enjoined periodical inspection of ports by members of the new Board, and half-yearly reports of the condition, receipts, and expenditure of the Customs establishment. The duties of the Commissioners were allotted as below :

One Commissioner to act as Chairman.

One Commissioner to deal with matters connected with

the King's Warehouse, up-town warehouses, and London Docks.

One Commissioner to deal with matters connected with the other docks in London.

One Commissioner to deal with matters connected with the sufferance wharves.

One Commissioner to deal with matters connected with the coasting business.

One Commissioner to deal with matters connected with the waterside work, except at the docks.

One Commissioner to deal with matters connected with the waterguard.

One Commissioner to deal with matters connected with East India goods.

One Commissioner to deal with the solicitors, Accountant of Petty Receipts, and Receiver of Fines and Forfeitures.

One Commissioner to deal with all other indoor work, including the Long Room.

One Commissioner to deal with tradesmen's bills, and the repair and alteration of Customs buildings.

(All the above sat in London.)

One Commissioner to sit at Edinburgh (with two Assistant or Local Commissioners for Scotland under him).

One Commissioner to sit at Dublin (with two Assistant or Local Commissioners for Ireland under him).

The previous Acts relating to the warehousing of bonded goods were repealed, except as regarded the approval of ports and warehouses, and a new Act was issued (Cap. 24, 4 Geo. IV.).

Cap. 69, passed on July 11, 1823, repealed the duties on certain imported goods, and provided new duties—some higher, some lower. It contained the first specimen of a special duty on cigars, which were rated at 12s. a pound. (There was an excise duty as well.) It repealed the prohibition of manufactured cocoa, which had endured since 1722, and of cocoa shells and husks, which had endured since 1731, but the repeal only affected manufactured cocoa, etc., from the Plantations.* The duties on oil and blubber were still highly preferential with regard to British takers and importers. See below :

	The Tun of 252 Gallons.		
	£	s.	d.
Blubber, caught by the king's subjects, and brought from British colonies	0	13	4
Blubber, of foreign fishing	22	3	4
Train oil, spermaceti, etc., caught by the king's subjects, and brought direct from British colonies ..	1	0	0
Train oil, spermaceti, etc., of foreign fishing ..	33	5	0
Whale-fins, caught by the king's subjects, and brought direct from British colonies	3	3	4
Whale-fins, of foreign fishing	95	0	0

The above alterations of duties did not affect Ireland.

A most important alteration was effected by the Act, it being provided that in future certain duties should not be managed partly by the Customs and partly by the Excise, but should be apportioned by Order in Council, it being advisable that all import duties should be under the Customs Board.†

* During the period of prohibition all cocoa legally imported had been in the 'nib,' and this was called for revenue purposes 'cocoa-nuts.' Students of the old rate-books will do well to bear this in mind.

† The Order in Council was issued on February 2, 1825. It transferred to the Customs the management of the duties previously collected by the Excise on imported coffee, cocoa, tobacco, snuff, pepper, spirits, wine, and all high-duty goods except tea. The change took place on April 5, 1825, and caused a considerable increase in the Customs staff, many officers being transferred thither from the Excise. The instructions issued by the Customs Board in consequence of the change directed that the customs officers were to take an acocunt, in presence of the excise officers, of all the goods, previously under Excise bond, which were brought under Customs management, and to give a receipt for them. The Excise locks were to be removed, and all Excise offices vacated were to be surrendered to the Customs. All bonds entered into for exportation of wine and manufactured tobacco from merchants' stock for drawback were to become Customs bonds, but bonds for the exportation of British-made excisable commodities for drawback were to remain Excise. When tea was landed, the customs men were to deliver it into Excise custody.

This transfer was due to the reports made by a Commission of

The duties on nearly all foreign goods imported into or exported from Ireland were made similar to the British rates by Cap. 72, 4 Geo. IV., and the 'countervailing duties' were abolished. It was provided that the Treasury might fix a date on which all traffic between Great Britain and Ireland was to be deemed coastwise traffic. All Irish duties were to be paid in British currency, and assessed according to British weights and measures.

Cap. 77 provided that the king might by Order in Council assimilate the duties upon goods brought in British and foreign ships, but that this should not apply

---

Inquiry (1818). There had been many complaints by merchants, who had to pay separate duties on the one article. Cases had even occurred in which seizures were apportioned to two departments, the Customs seizing the ship and the Excise the goods.

On June 7, 1819, Mr. Brougham had stated in Parliament that the charge for collecting the Customs was 13 per cent., and for collecting the Excise only just over 5 per cent., and that a saving of half a million might be effected by abolishing the Customs Boards, and empowering the Excise to collect all the revenue on imports and exports. It appears that this statement was made without balancing the facts. The whole charge of the preventive *boat* service, of the administration of quarantine, of the riding officers, and of the Plantation revenue staff, was paid out of the Customs. There was no such 'pull' on the Excise, and the latter department's great return was due to the fact that it collected duty at much higher rates than the Customs did, on the articles most extensively consumed. See below :

	Customs Duty.			*Excise Duty.*		
Tea (British ship)	6 per cent. on value.			90 per cent. on value.		
	£	*s.*	*d.*	*£*	*s.*	*d.*
Tobacco (British ship), per pound..	0	1	0	0	2	2
French wine, Rhenish, etc. (British ship), per tun	65	13	0	78	4	0
Madeira wine (British ship), per tun	44	3	0	52	10	0
Port, etc. (British ship), per tun ..	43	1	0	52	10	0
Plantation rum (British ship), per gallon	0	1	2¼	0	10	4½
Cordials, double (British ship), per gallon	0	5	6½	1	13	3¾
Cordials, single (British ship), per gallon	0	5	6½	0	17	0
Brandy, geneva, etc. (British ship), per gallon	0	1	9	0	17	0

to goods carried by vessels belonging to countries in which British traders were not granted 'equal' privileges. The pilotage regulations for British and foreign vessels were made similar.

From 1817 to 1824 repeated complaints were made by the Council of New Brunswick that the collector of customs was in the habit of levying extortionate fees. An investigation was held, and the collector was censured by the Treasury, and ordered to pay the costs of the inquiry (£250). Even after this arrangement the Council continued to protest against this enterprising official's extortions, accusing him of authorizing the preventive officers at the Bay of Fundy and the Gulf of St. Lawrence to collect outrageous fees, and then appropriating half of the sums collected, and dividing that portion with the naval officer and the controller. It was stated that in one year he had by this method succeeded in pocketing £2,900.*

Cap. 65, 5 Geo. IV., provided that the abominable salt duties should be abolished after January 5, 1825, and Cap. 79 exempted public officials from taking the oath of supremacy.

Cap. 97 repealed the laws forbidding the emigration, without special licence, of British artificers. It will be seen that the legislators were knocking off the old shackles at an alarming rate.

A uniform system of weights and measures for England had been prescribed by Magna Charta, yet many varying systems prevailed. The injunction had been reaffirmed by the Act of Union between Great Britain and Scotland, apparently with little effect. By Cap. 74, 5 Geo. IV., Parliament dictated a standard of lineal measure, a standard of troy weight, and standards of capacity—liquid

* The documents connected with the Plantation Customs contain many similar statements. The colonial administrators were continually complaining of the extortion practised by the customs officers, and the officers retaliating by charging their detractors with favouring contraband dealing. No doubt much that was true was uttered by both sides, much also that was outrageously false or partial.

and dry. The yard was defined as the measure of the straight line between the centres of the two points in the gold studs in the straight brass rod (then in the custody of the Clerk of the House of Commons, and marked 'Standard yard, 1760'), when the temperature of the rod was 62° F. If the standard rod were lost or defaced, it might be reconstructed by comparison with 'a pendulum vibrating seconds of mean time, London latitude, in a vacuum at the level of the sea.'

The standard troy weight was declared to be the standard measure of all weight, and defined as the brass weight held in same custody; date of construction, 1758. This might at any time be reconstructed by comparison with a cubic inch of distilled water, weighed in air by brass weights at 62° F., barometer at 30 inches.

A new gallon measure, much larger than the old wine measure, was prescribed, the standard to contain 10 pounds avoirdupois of distilled water at 62° F., barometer at 30 inches. The gallon for dry measure was the same. The bushel for dry goods which were sold by *heaped* measure was to contain 8 such liquid gallons.

The customs and excise officers were to be supplied with accurate tables, based upon the measures prescribed. (The Act came into force on January 1, 1826.) This statute repealed a great number of laws and parts of laws, extending from the date of the ancient 'Assisa Panis et Cervisiæ' to 1803.

Prior to 1765 the Manx revenue had been a perquisite of the Athol family, and when the Treasury bought the island the family were compensated by an annuity (amounting to one-fourth of the gross Customs proceeds). In 1825 it was directed that the family should be bought out (Cap. 34, 6 Geo. IV.).

Several ports in the Plantations, previously exempted from the ordinary Plantation restrictions as regarded

* On November 25, 1825, the Customs Board directed that all the 'Exchequer weights,' by which the Customs weights at the various ports were adjusted, should be sent to London, so that they might be readjusted and restamped.

certain kinds of Plantation trade, were granted warehousing privileges. The ports affected were Kingston, Halifax, Quebec, St. John in New Brunswick, and Bridge Town in Barbados (Cap. 73, 6 Geo. IV.).

Although a consolidation of the Customs laws and a consequent revision and alteration of duties had been arranged to come into effect on July 5, 1826, certain Customs duties were repealed by Cap. 104, 6 Geo. IV. (July 5, 1825), and other temporary duties granted. A table was included in the statute, expressing the duties which would be payable on goods affected by the new measures of capacity. In this, for the first time, the duties on wine were specified per gallon instead of per tun.

An account of the more important preventive laws, and of certain incidents connected with smuggling, during the period extending from 1801 to 1825, will be informative at this juncture. Choice of the latter is difficult, simply on account of the enormous amount of second-hand material available.

The character of contraband traffic underwent some alteration. The extensive employment of the military and navy in prevention checked the old gallant system under which the smuggling craft 'carried guns and fought their way.' Smugglers, in choosing and preparing their vessels, came to rely more upon speed and less upon armament. Swift-sailing craft, laden with kegs, ready slung, and having 'sinkers' handy, so that the goods could be thrown overboard and submerged if the chase became hot, were much used between the Continent and the southern and eastern coasts of England. The running inland was not to the same extent conducted in the old daring fashion, when troops of horsemen, armed to the teeth, went clanking along the Kentish and Sussex by-roads, their hardy little nags loaded with contraband, debouched at night into the main roads near London, and carried their 'truck' into the suburbs, often past the very noses of the cowering 'land-carriage-men' who were deputed to watch the turnpikes. The goods were more frequently sent inland in fish-baskets, in packs of wool, in bales of hops, and by many other methods of secret stowage. Caves were dug along the coast, in which large quantities of goods were placed, and left till suitable sale could be effected. Concealments on board trading vessels became common, and some of the devices used were extremely ingenious.

Frequent allusions may be found in the records as to immense smuggling on the southern and western coasts of Ireland during the period from 1810 to 1819. Little definite information is forthcoming; still, it is evident that the Irish revenue was extensively defrauded, principally by Americans, huge runs being made, and the goods conveyed inland, with the full cognizance of thousands of people. The Irish Customs men were either powerless or hopelessly corrupt. The chief article smuggled was tobacco. When the coastguard was established vast seizures were made, the Irish record of seized tobacco for 1820 amounting to nearly 400 tons!

Stringent as the laws had been, they were gradually strengthened. In 1802 the limit within which 'hovering' entailed forfeiture of vessel was made eight leagues from the coast, except between Beachy Head and the North Foreland. If at trial of case the distance were not clearly established, a verdict might still be given for the Crown if it could be proved that the ship had *prohibited* goods on board. Persons found signalling from the shore to smugglers were made liable to a fine of £100. Rewards on a most consoling scale were promised to informers. This Act (Cap. 82, 42 Geo. III.) applied to Great Britain only.

On March 4, 1804, the customs officers seized at a house in South Molton Street, London, a quantity of lace, which they held to be smuggled French goods, the pieces not being stamped by the Customs as duty-paid. When the case came on in the Exchequer it was contended in defence that the goods were English-made, and that the English manufacturers of lace had become so expert that it was next to impossible to tell English lace from French. The matter of the goods not being stamped did not affect the case much, for it was shown in evidence that the retailers usually removed the stamps. (The judge, Baron Macdonald, delivered himself solemnly upon this proven infringement of the statute, stating that the stamps should remain, and adding : ‘ The bread of thousands of women and children in this country, who manufacture the article, depends upon it.’) A deadly wrangle took place over the question of opinion as to country of manufacture. Several dealers were called as witnesses for the defence, and they declared that none could tell. Yet the Crown secured a verdict.

On February 25, 1805, the *Tartar* cutter (Customs) and the *Lively* cutter (Excise) chased a lugger into Dungeness Bay. The smugglers ran their vessel aground, and escaped. The revenue men boarded her, and found in her hold 665 casks brandy, 237 casks geneva, 118 casks rum, 119 bags tobacco, 6 packages wine, and 43 pounds tea. The people of Lydd and Dungeness mustered, and attempted a rescue. A company of the Lancashire militia, quartered hard by, advanced upon the rioters, cleared the beach, and enabled the revenue men to carry the goods to a safe place. *Nine years later* two men, named Jeremiah Maxtell and Thomas Gilbert, were arrested, removed to London, and charged at the Old Bailey, as participators in the attempted rescue. The case against them was remarkably defective, and it is a matter of wonder that they were arrested at all on such flimsy evidence. Verdict for defendants.

Cap. 121, 45 Geo. III. opened thus : ‘ Whereas in defiance of the several laws of Customs and Excise great quantities of goods are illegally imported into and landed in the United Kingdom, as well by clandestine means as by open force,’ and proceeded to extend the provisions rendering forfeitable any vessel that had on board spirits, obacco, or tea in illegal packages. The extension applied to vessels not square-rigged, and a startling extension it was, for any such vessel owned or part owned by the king's subjects, or having on board a crew more than half of whom were the king's subjects, was made forfeitable if found with the above-named illegal goods within *100 leagues* of the British or Irish coasts. No vessel of less than 100 tons might bring spirits or tobacco as cargo. The preventive powers previously vested in officers of customs and excise were granted also to all commissioned officers in the army, navy, or marines. Convicted smugglers might escape the ordinary penalties by volunteering to serve five years in the army, navy, or marines.

It appears that in certain localities the collection of inland revenue was an occupation almost as dangerous as the prevention of smuggling. On the night of February 6, 1806, the excise collector of Carmarthen, accompanied by twenty-two other excise officers, went (all mounted and armed) to the village of Llansantfroid, to search for illicit malt. A quantity of malt was found, but a crowd of people assembled and effected rescue of the goods. The officers were driven into the village of Llanor, and they took refuge in a public-house. Soon the place became too hot to hold them, and they retired with their horses to an adjacent field. It appears this was not exactly with good judgment, for the collector, in his report of the affair, described the field as 'the most stony ground I ever knew.' The mob surrounded the officers, and stoned them in barbarous fashion, injuring several of them severely, and maiming some of the horses. In the end the officers drew their pistols, and fired upon their persecutors, dispersing them at once. 'Some of the rioters,' reported the collector, 'are privates in the volunteers. I look upon the greater part of the regiment to be either smugglers or the friends of smugglers. The captain of one company, Mr. Strike, is well known to be the greatest smuggler in Wales.'

On May 24, 1806, the Board of Customs received a

letter from the Treasury on the suppression of smuggling. One paragraph was truly remarkable : 'Their Lordships being aware that, if the measures pursued by Government for the effectual suppression of smuggling should meet with the success which the Legislature had in view, the emoluments of several of the officers of this Revenue will be materially diminished, and in many cases nearly annihilated, are pleased to desire that the Commissioners will report to their Lordships what steps it may be proper to take for rewarding such officers in a manner suited to the importance of their zealous and successful efforts, and the beneficial effects which they will in that case produce on the revenue, the fair and legitimate commerce, and the morals, of this nation.' (Thus it would seem that the extension of legitimate trade, the prosperity of the revenue, and the moral condition of the British people, depended in a great measure upon the efforts of officials, some of whom obtained remuneration in its most ample and assured form by making occasional large seizures and winking at general smuggling.)

On May 25, 1806, Captain Haddock, of the *Stag* cutter, stationed in the Downs, reported that on the night of the 23rd he sent two six-oared boats to intercept several luggers which were standing in towards Deal. One boat succeeded in getting alongside a lugger, and was at once saluted with a volley of small-arms. Several of the boat's crew were badly wounded. All the luggers ran ashore, and about 300 natives of Deal at once assembled and conveyed the cargoes into that ancient and eminently law-abiding town. The weather being very rough, the wounded men were unable to get their boat back to the cutter, and she drifted ashore. The smugglers surrounded and disarmed the sailors, and, stated Captain Haddock, 'kicked and beat them in a most shameful manner.' The hardened wretches then stove in the boat, and stole the oars and rigging. (One of the wounded men died shortly afterwards.)

Cap. 66, 47 Geo. III., provided that any lugger exceeding 50 tons, built in the United Kingdom, should be forfeitable. All vessels not exceeding 50 tons were to carry licences. Boats of the United Kingdom rowed with more than six oars were made forfeitable if found without licence within 100 leagues of the coast (whale-boats, ship's boats, lifeboats, revenue boats, excepted). Vessels of the United Kingdom found with contrivances for sinking, slinging, or smuggling goods within 100 leagues of the coast, were made forfeitable, and foreign vessels were made similarly liable if within the smaller limit (8 leagues, or 4 leagues between Beachy Head and the North Foreland). No vessel of the United Kingdom was to load spirits, tobacco, or snuff, in a foreign port, without licence from the Privy Council, Admiralty, or Secretary of State. It was also provided that the Board of Customs might grant special rewards to officers who detained persons found on forfeitable vessels, and secured their impressment for the army or navy. The power of granting licences to ships, boats, etc., which by an Act of 1784 had been vested in the Admiralty, was transferred to the Customs.

A Treasury order was issued, granting the following scale of awards :*

	£
To the commander of the revenue cruiser by which, in the year ending October 1, 1808, the greatest number of smugglers should be captured, and delivered for service in the navy	500
To the commander, etc., capturing and delivering the second greatest number	300
To the commander, etc., capturing and delivering the third greatest number	200

In 1808 the pensions allowed to the widows of certain higher preventive officers who had been killed by

* This was continued through several succeeding years. The results were not remarkable. In 1810 the first prize was taken with a record of only thirteen smugglers. Then it was directed that only two prizes should be given, and they only when the first winning captain could quote a bag of at least twenty smugglers, and the second of at least fifteen. In 1813 it was decided that the rewards, when payable, should be divided amongst the ships' companies.

smugglers were increased, the widows of ordinary mariners thus killed being left on the old scale. Only six widows benefited by this increase, the relicts of the commander of the cutter stationed at Cowes, of the mates of the cutters stationed at Dover and St. Ives, of the commander and mate of the cutter at Yarmouth, and of a Southampton riding-officer.

In 1809 it was enacted that any person, not a passenger, found on a British vessel from which goods had been thrown overboard to prevent seizure, should forfeit £100. Persons detecting spirits which had been sunk for smuggling purposes were made entitled to one-half the value of the goods (Cap. 52, 49 Geo. III.).

In 1810 most of the provisions of the British preventive Acts were extended to the Isle of Man. The governor of the island, the deputy governor, or any one of the 'deemsters,' might enforce the penalties incidental (Cap. 62, 50 Geo. III.).

On July 7, 1810, the case of Williams *v.* Burgess was tried in the Court of Common Pleas. The defendant, an officer of customs, had searched the premises occupied by the plaintiff, a Wapping pawnbroker. No smuggled goods were found, and Williams claimed redress for the unnecessary invasion. The jury granted him damages at the rate of £1 a minute for the period occupied in searching, but the Court held that his case had failed owing to an informality in the wording of the plea.

A new system of landguard for England was devised. The coast was divided into three districts, one extending from London to Penzance, another from Penzance to Carlisle, another from Berwick to London. There were 120 riding-officers in all, and it is evident that some of them had other means of employment, for the order setting out the districts warned the officers to confine themselves to the performance of their preventive duties.

A case curiously illustrative of the complexities of revenue proceedings was tried in the Exchequer on

December 2, 1811. It appeared that on November 8, 1810, two officers of customs and one exciseman searched a coachmaker's premises in Worship Street, City. They found a large quantity of foreign silks, bandanas, gloves, and silk stockings, and 485 'pieces' of foreign cambrics. A firm of linen-drapers in Cannon Street claimed the cambrics, stating they had taken them in satisfaction of a debt due from a certain Hebrew merchant. This gentleman appeared in court, and swore that he had bought the goods from a firm of importers of cambrics, which firm had paid duty on them. It was found from the Customs books that the last-mentioned firm had paid duty, in 1809, upon several thousand pieces, and though the Israelite could not produce one scrap of paper in support of his statement, a stubborn defence was based upon it. There was not the slightest proof that the Jew had bought goods from the firm that paid the duty; the goods had not been found on his premises, or on the premises of the firm quoted as sellers, but in the possession of a coachmaker who had long been suspected of dealing with the Kentish smugglers. They were found along with silks, etc., that were admitted to be prohibited goods, and they were actually in what was known as 'smuggling packages'—viz., small bales packed between boards, so as to be carried in panniers on the horses ridden by the contrabandists. It is likely that several startling feats of perjury were performed during this trial. Verdict for the Crown.

On June 19, 1812, one Mrs. Selth, of Deal, was charged in the Exchequer with harbouring smuggled or prohibited goods, and with being a wholesale smuggler who employed others to go about and sell her wares. A witness named Sturt stated that in 1810 she was asked by Mrs. Selth to sell smuggled silks, shawls, etc. Sturt declined, but introduced one Mrs. Bishop, who accepted the offer. A reserve price was put upon the goods, and the hawker might keep all obtained in excess. Mrs. Bishop commenced a trade with silks, shawls, cornelian beads, and gloves. The customs officers seized a large quantity of these goods in her house at Dover, and her husband was sentenced to six months' imprisonment. Both she and Sturt went frequently to Mrs. Selth and asked her for money, as Bishop's family were starving. Mrs. Selth refused—whence the information.

It was pleaded in defence that the charge was the result of conspiracy, also that the defendant had a husband alive, though not living with her, and that if anyone was responsible it was he.* The judge held that even if Mrs. Selth's husband were living with her he might not be responsible. Verdict for the Crown.

Certain customs officers charged the Marchioness of Wellesley with attempting to smuggle silks. We quote the letter written to the Board on the matter by the Secretary to the Treasury:

'GENTLEMEN,

'Having laid before the Lords of the Treasury your report of the 5th inst., on the application of the Marchioness of Wellesley, requesting to be relieved from a prosecution, I am commanded by my Lords to acquaint you that, the information upon which your officers proceeded in the case in question appearing to be groundless as to the silks charged to be in Lady Wellesley's possession, and the allegations that her Ladyship is in the habit of dealing with smugglers being unsupported by any sort of proof, their Lordships do not think this a case proper to be vigorously insisted on, and are disposed to wish such a compromise to be made as may mitigate the loss of the party, without at the same time affecting the interest of the seizing officers.

'R. WHARTON.

'*12th May*, 1813.'

A letter was sent on the same day, relative to certain pictures seized by the officers at Penzance in the baggage

* See vol. i., p. 355.

brought by Lord Fife on his arrival from Cadiz, directing that the pictures should be given up to his Lordship on payment of the proper duties.

During the same year the officers seized at the Ship Inn Waggon Office, Borough, a case containing apparel, sent from India by Lady Hood to Countess Spencer. The Treasury directed that such of the seized articles as were prohibited should be warehoused for exportation, and the rest admitted to duty. The Countess was to compensate the seizing officers (amount of 'satisfaction,' ten guineas).

During May and June, 1814, information reached the English Board that several notorious 'smuggling merchants' had left Alderney for Cherbourg, an establishment for smuggling having been formed at the latter place since the declaration of peace, and that a number of smuggling vessels from Lyme, Portland, and the Isle of Wight had gone to Cherbourg, also that vast numbers of 'tubs' were stored on the Cherbourg quays, and many coopers were busily occupied in making others. It was stated that a 'smuggling concern' had been established at Treguier, the members being certain renowned smugglers who had previously been in the habit of running goods into Cornwall, and that a company was being formed in Guernsey for the purpose of smuggling from France into various places on the Cornish coast.

On May 24 and 27, 1814, no fewer than fifteen revenue cases were dealt with in the Exchequer, the defendant in each case submitting to a verdict for the Crown. On June 30, 1814, fifteen other cases were disposed of, all undefended.

No doubt the many inducements held out to revenue informers tended to encourage vindictive and truthless information, and there is good ground for suspicion that occasionally the informer was a mere *agent provocateur*. The case of the Attorney-General *v.* Mary Gamwell appears to reveal black business.

It was tried in the Exchequer on July 1, 1814. The defendant, a haberdasher of Aldersgate Street, was charged with having harboured French gloves, being therefore liable to a penalty of £200, and treble the value of the goods. The informer—one Brown, a hawker—stated that he became acquainted with the defendant in 1812, and that in 1813, at her request, he sold a number of pairs of French gloves, she charging him 3s. a pair—he, of course, charging as much as he could get—that he began to owe her money, that she sued him, that he was imprisoned for debt, and while in the spunging-house laid information against her. This scoundrel had to admit threatening to inform upon Mrs. Gamwell if she did not take him out of the clutches of the sheriff's officer, and the sheriff's officer swore that Brown told him he would ruin the widow if she did not agree to his request. (' Revenge,' said Brown, ' will be sweet.') Verdict for defendant.

On April 18, 1815, the Treasury desired the Board to direct the officers to be vigilant in preventing the clandestine exportation of arms to France. (Lord Sidmouth had received information that this traffic was persistently encouraged by the French Government.)

On July 25, 1815, the Board issued to the officers of revenue cruisers a set of instructions in the method of using the tourniquet, and a list of medicines which were to be supplied for use on board. The medicines were of the good old searching type : vomiting-powders, purging-powders, sweating-powders, calomel pills, laudanum, cough-drops, stomach tincture, scurvy-drops, friars' balsam, mercurial ointment, blistering ointment, etc., etc.

Cap. 104, 56 Geo. III., provided that customs officers should have full powers of search, seizure, prosecution, etc., under the Excise laws, and excise officers full powers under the Customs laws. The powers, previously vested in justices of the peace, to determine Customs cases where the penalty was not more than £50, were extended, and justices were made competent to determine any Customs case, irrespective of amount of penalty. Proceedings were only to be taken on the Board's special order, unless they were in the name of the Attorney-General. This Act reaffirmed many of the old restrictions.

During the latter part of the year much information as to smuggling from France reached the authorities. It was stated that cambrics had been cut into handkerchiefs, and in that form smuggled extensively into Great Britain, and that concealed contraband goods came over in the French egg and fruit smacks, and were run into the southern ports. One of these vessels was found to have double bulk-heads between her cabin and hold, the space within being filled with spirits, wines, and plums. Another was found to have a similar contrivance, stuffed with silk handkerchiefs, between hold and forepeak. Another brought a consignment of cases containing plaster figures. The figures were found to be hollow, and filled with clock movements, bronzes, porcelain articles, and small pictures.

It is apparent that there was much smuggling into the Plantations, for some of the seizure records are quite remarkable, and it is certain that at most not more than one-twentieth of the contraband goods were captured. We submit a few quotations from the Jamaica list :

'*July* 12, 1816.—Spanish schooner *El Carmen*, with wine and oil, seized by Captain Roberts, of H.M.S. *Jay*.

'*July* 16, 1816.—Spanish schooner *Fortuna*, with wine and gin, seized by Captain McKellar, of H.M.S. *Salisbury*.

'*July* 22, 1816.—Spanish schooner *Eugenie*, with wine, brandy, and vinegar, seized by the customs officers of Kingston.

'*July* 27, 1816.—British schooner *Fickle*, with tobacco, seized by Captain Tait, of H.M.S. *La Pique*, and a seizure of 300 bushels of corn by the land officers.

'*October* 2, 1816.—Spanish sloop *Hoppa*, with brandy, gin, wine, and pickles, seized by the customs officers of Kingston.'

In 1817 the penalties and restrictions as to boats with more than the legal number of rowlocks, and vessels fitted for swift sailing and for smuggling, were made still more comprehensive and severe (Cap. 87, 57 Geo. III.).

An officer at one of the outports was about to weigh some cases of bound books from France, so as to assess the duty. (The duty on books was assessed according to weight; those on prints, maps, and drawings, unaccompanied by descriptive letterpress, were special duties.)* He examined some of the volumes, and found that each contained 'a vast number' of valuable coloured prints, with a little letterpress which did not appertain. A further examination revealed that the covers were hollow, and that these contained many valuable prints and drawings.

On March 27, 1817, Messrs. Peate and Newton, midshipmen of H.M.S. *Ganymede,* discovered five 'smuggling caves' in the Sandhills between Deal and Sandwich. These were simply large square holes dug in the ground, surrounded and roofed with two-inch planking, the roofs being covered with deep beds of shingle. Entrance was obtained through traps in the roofs, the traps being covered with iron troughs hidden by shingle.

On June 28, 1817, tidings were sent to the western English ports that six vessels belonging to Cardigan were about to leave for Ireland, where it was intended they should ship salt for running on the western coast of England.

On August 30, 1817, the Board sent information to all the western ports as follows: 'The sloop *British Fair,* of Folkestone, Mark Watt master, about 70 tons, running bowsprit, a quarter-deck, bound from Holland to Ireland with a cargo of tobacco, principally concealed, the vessel having a false bottom'; and on September 4 to all the eastern ports relative to the *Dart,* 110 tons, clench built,

* Books, bound, per cwt., £5 9s. 4d.; unbound, £4 2s. Coloured prints, 50 per cent. of the value; maps and charts, the piece, 1s.

under foreign papers, with an English captain named Marsh, from Holland, with a full cargo of spirits and tobacco, to run at Robin Hood's Bay ; and on September 19 to all western ports as to the cutter *Jane*, 200 tons (foreign papers), with an English commander named Matthews, having a cargo of tobacco and spirits for Ireland.

On October 16, 1817, they sent word to Dublin of the cutter *Earl Spencer*, 140 tons (foreign papers), with an English captain named Whittingham, and carrying a full cargo, also for Ireland.

On October 21, 1817, the Customs Secretary sent the following confidential note to a person named G. Mackay, residing at 24, Princes Street, Westminster :

'In reply to your letter of the 27th ultimo, stating that two persons of the names of the Count de Beaumont and Monsieur Cariat are in the practice of smuggling, I have it in command to acquaint you that officers have been directed to keep a strict watch on the houses of the abovementioned persons.

'G. DELAVAUD.'

On December 12, 1817, the Secretary penned the following significant missive :

'*To Mr. Pelham, Controller at Brighton.*

'SIR,

'The Commissioners having had before them certain examinations of Louis Anthony Losser, a prisoner in the Fleet, as to sundry smuggling transactions at Brighton, in which it appears you are implicated, I have it in command to transmit you extracts thereof, and to direct you to answer the same for the Board's further consideration, and to return your report confidentially under cover to me, marked "Private."

'G. DELAVAUD.'

Early in 1818 the following information was sent to various stations :

Dates when Sent.	*Particulars.*
Jan, 6, 1818.	To Inspector of River, Gravesend, to look out for *Marquis of Anglesey*, which left Ostend on January 4 with a quantity of goods. To search the crew, they having playing-cards concealed on their persons.
Jan. 6, 1818.	To certain southern ports, that a look-out be kept for the *Ox*, of Folkestone—a long and narrow vessel with a running bowsprit, about to smuggle from Boulogne to Rye.
Jan. 7, 1818.	To collector at Lyme, to prosecute eleven persons detected in carrying smuggled goods, and four others known as receivers.
Feb. 6 and 7, 1818.	To the Admiralty and seventy-five outports. To look out for the *Jane*, 200 tons, forty-four men, sixteen guns, which left Flushing January 24 with tobacco, tea, and 5,000 bandanas ; also the *Idas*, 135 tons, thirty men, not armed, which left Bremershaven with tobacco and tea. (Both the above expected to run in the north of Ireland.) Also the *Unicorn*, ready to sail, with tobacco stowed in her false bottom and false sides. (' May run in the north of Ireland, or at any intermediate port.') Also the *Dart*, 120 tons, which left Flushing February 2, with 500 ankers of spirits for Redhead, Scotland. Also a long and narrow cutter called the *Renard*, 70 tons, under foreign colours, which sailed from Flushing February 4, laden with rum, geneva, and tobacco.
Feb. 16, 1818.	To the Admiralty and outports. To look out for a cutter (crew mostly foreigners) which went ashore in a fog near Calais on 12th. (She was got off, and proceeded down Channel.) She had previously left Flushing laden with small kegs of spirits, nominally for Rio de Janeiro, ' but was bound, it is conjectured, for the coast of Ireland.'

(At this time there was much information as to clandestine shipment of arms and volunteers at Deal* for the use and assistance of ' the insurgents in Spanish South America.')

* See footnote, p. 110.

In 1818 the penalties applicable to such of the king's subjects (not being passengers) as were found aboard smuggling or 'hovering' vessels were made to apply to foreigners when the vessels carried spirits as cargo. The penalties on illegal unshipment of tea were made frightfully severe (£10 for each pound of tea unshipped or £100 on the total quantity, at the choice of the prosecuting officer.)

In February, 1818, a large quantity of China crape and silk was seized at Deal, concealed among shingle in the ballast-bags of the *Fame* lugger.*

At this period many small parties of cavalry were stationed along the coast to assist the preventive officers. It is doubtful whether these were reliable unless under strict supervision. The 7th Hussars landed at Calais from Dover on April 12, 1818, and, by arrangement with their commander, were searched by the French douaniers. Many of the troopers were discovered to have English lace concealed upon their persons. It appears that a sutler of the 52nd Regiment had paid them to smuggle these goods into France for his profit. The *Benevolent* transport arrived at Calais, with British troops on board, on the 13th. That very night her captain was caught conveying a quantity of smuggled goods into the town. The ship was searched. More smuggled goods were discovered, and many packages were found sunk in the harbour near her. On the return of the transports to Dover several of the masters were caught smuggling by the English Customs officers.

* From the earliest records down to those of the end of the nineteenth century there are mountains of evidence as to the smuggling propensities of the inhabitants of Deal. The peculiar position of the town, and the skill and nefarious energy of its seafaring population, made it a place of resort for shippers of wool and coin, criminals eager to escape the law, and importers of contraband. If we were asked to state which, in our opinion, were the two seaside towns of the United Kingdom that in olden times contained the greatest proportion of daring and violent smugglers, we should without hesitation name Deal and Chichester.

In May, 1818, a boat was seized at Plymouth containing a number of large 'boxes' filled with spirits. The boxes were of hard wood, tapering slightly from the middle, hooped strongly at the ends, and fitted with bungholes and with lines and gear for sinking.

In December, 1818, a vessel was seized at Weymouth. She had reported 'in ballast,' but on removing the ballast the officers found a platform fitted on either side the keelson, extending nearly the length of the vessel. Underneath this were kegs of spirits.

On April 7, 1819, a customs officer stationed at Erith boarded a lugger that was sailing up the Thames, and proceeded to search her. There were but two men on board, and one of these, named Henry Hart, protested against the search. Finding protest of no avail, he caught the officer up in his arms, dashed him violently upon the deck, and then beat him with a stick, winding up by throwing him into the Customs boat and sailing off in triumph. The lugger, which belonged to Rye, was afterwards captured, and found to have a large quantity of contraband goods on board intended for London. Hart was tried at the Maidstone Assizes in August, 1819, and sentenced to nine months' imprisonment.

A number of barrels, entered as containing pitch, were examined at one of the outports, and found to contain plate-glass and East India goods, pitch having been run in at the bungholes so as to conceal the contents.

On July 15, 1819, proceedings were taken in the King's Bench against one Scurrah. This person had become indebted to a London merchant named Laing (amount £200) and, failing to pay, had been imprisoned in the Fleet. His fellow-lodger there was one Hickman, imprisoned at the suit of a Mr. Whalley of Gloucester. Scurrah succeeded in inducing a customs officer named Steel to accept information against Mr. Whalley, to the effect that the latter had sold smuggled goods to Scurrah in 1815, and against Mr. Laing as a subsequent dealer in the goods (amount of duty involved stated as £2,000).

This information had been trumped up by the two debtors. Scurrah was convicted of perjury.

Information was received in August, 1819, that large quantities of French jewellery were smuggled in raised pies, loaves of bread, etc., and in November, 1819, that many tubs of smuggled spirits had been carried inland packed in bags of wool.

The rewards to seizing officers were increased,* and it was provided that land might be acquired on the coasts for the erection of Customs watch-houses. Preventive officers were empowered to haul their vessels ashore anywhere below high-water mark, provided that any part of the crew resided on board (gardens, pleasure-grounds, and bathing-places exempted). The power, previously vested in magistrates, of mitigating the penalty of £100 for being found on board a smuggling-vessel, was taken away. The Treasury still had power to mitigate. It was provided that masters of ships should be compelled to furnish the customs officers boarded on their vessels with sleeping-places under the deck.

During 1820 a seizure was made of casks of spirits fastened to the bottom of a ship by a rope passed through the keel, both ends being rove through holes in the ship's bottom on either side the keel. The casks were fixed head to head in rows, and made fast to the rope. They were carried on deck till danger appeared, then thrown overboard, and drawn by means of the rope under the ship's bottom. Tobacco was seized, rolled up in balls, each ball covered with a skin and 'clayed,' so as to resemble a potato. Three boats were seized having hollow spare foremasts and outriggers, stuffed with contraband. A large seizure was made at Shoreham of contraband goods, concealed in hollow pieces of iron which were used as ballast. A hawser was seized, the inner strands of which were made of tobacco.

From a report made in 1820 it appears that the preventive work in England was arranged thus: Part was

* Cap. 43, 1 Geo. IV.

performed by naval cruisers, under command of the admirals at Plymouth, Portsmouth, and Sheerness ; part by the 'Coast Blockade,' a force under Admiralty control, with Captain McCullock (at Deal) as immediate commander, and stationed from the North Foreland to Newhaven ; part by the 'revenue cruisers,' originally under the Boards of Customs and Excise, but lately placed under the Admiralty ; part by 'preventive boats,' formerly under Customs, lately placed under Treasury (immediate commander, the 'Preventive Controller-General ') ; part by riding-officers, still under the Customs, and assisted by small bodies of soldiers ; and part by a few of the old preventive 'smacks,' which still did duty at the mouth of the Thames and at several outports. The three branches last mentioned were paid out of the Customs. States the author of the report : 'Various seizures have been made since the rewards were augmented, collusively, or under circumstances of strong suspicion of collusion. Several instances of glaring collusion have been proved, and the officers dismissed. Whenever a seizure of considerable quantities of spirits is made near the shore, and no men are taken, that of itself is, to my mind, a presumptive case of suspicion.'

Mr. Lundy Dickenson, a midshipman holding a Customs commission, had made himself unpopular with those incorrigible smugglers, the good people of Radnor Street, Folkestone. In November, 1821, he, with his crew, conveyed three smugglers to the Town Hall, Folkestone, for trial. The sailors composing the escort were then sent back, Dickenson remaining to protect the Crown witnesses. When the case was over he left the court, and was at once surrounded by furious longshoremen. A fellow named Wigden challenged Dickenson to fight, and followed him along the street, the mob howling approval. Dickenson drew his sword and turned upon his tormentors, who at once bespattered him from head to foot with the scourings of the Folkestone gutters. Brandishing a sword in one hand and a cocked pistol in the other, he managed to work his way back to the Town Hall. The constable on duty, one Burton, was drunk. He prevented Dickenson from taking shelter in the building, and even pushed him back among the rioters. Other constables arrived, and actually threatened to take Dickenson into custody for 'breaking the peace'! He then made a dash for 'The Battery,' the mob pursuing him, and stoning him right into his quarters.

Burton was charged at Maidstone with 'obstructing,' etc., and convicted. (During proceedings reference was made to a previous riot at Deal, in which several smugglers were rescued by the mob.)

In the journal kept by Lieutenant Lilley of the Coast Blockade appear the following laconic memoranda, curiously mixed up with the ordinary records as to visiting, creeping for tubs, etc.:

'*Tuesday, April 24th*, 1821.—Rode to the village of Herne Bay, in consequence of firing observed in that direction. Found that Mr. Snow had been dangerously wounded by an arm'd gang of smugglers.

'*Thursday, April 26th.*—Visited Herne Bay, and went into the interior of the country to endeavour at discovering the people concerned. Repeated and vivid flashes of lightning round the horizon.

'*Friday, 27th.*—At 10.20 departed this life Sydenham Snow, who had received 1 musquet-ball thro' the thigh and another thro' the body. Went to Canterbury, and arranged with the coroner.

'*Monday, 30th.*—Conveying the body in military procession to the churchyard at the village of Herne Street. The funeral service perform'd and the corpse interr'd. At the funeral were Capt. McCulloch, Lieuts. Elphick, Dove, Grandy, Barton, Graham, Fayreman, and Byne, 8 midshipmen, and 47 men.'

As a specimen of the work thrown upon judges and juries by the Customs laws, we quote the list of revenue cases at Lewes Assizes, August, 1821:

Collusion.—Several customs officers stationed at Rye arranged a collusive seizure. A smuggler named Heath went to Boulogne, and brought back in his lugger 250 tubs spirits, a quantity of tea and tobacco, and a parcel of bandanas. The lugger 'hovered,' and the goods were put into boats and landed by night at a place called 'The Mullet Pound,' in Rye Harbour, *directly opposite the Customs watch-house.* It appears that a division was contemplated, the smugglers to take part of the goods, and the officers to seize the rest; but a few man-of-war's-men who happened to be in the neighbourhood intruded, and gave unwelcome assistance. Thus the officers were compelled to seize the whole cargo. This enraged the smugglers, and information of collusion was tendered. Several officers were prosecuted, and two of them convicted.

Conspiracy to Corrupt.—Several smugglers were charged with attempting to bribe a preventive man. They arranged with him that a cargo was to be run while he was on watch, and that he was to afford every facility. The goods were run, and the officer was presented with four bank-notes. But he had informed his superior, who arrived with a strong force just as the carriers were about to travel inland. Away went the horsemen, leaving a few tubs, which the officers seized. The watchman handed the rustling 'flimsies' to his chief, and it was found that they were only £1 notes, instead of £5 notes as agreed on. Defendants convicted.

Again.—Two men were charged with trying to corrupt an officer at Bexhill. Convicted.

Warning Smugglers.—Twelve defendants were charged with 'using a device to warn smugglers.' The offence was stated to have taken place in 'The Haddocks,' near Fairlight. Certain officers deposed that, seeing a boat put in at night, and a crowd go down to the beach to meet her, they signalled for assistance by firing their pistols, on which the crowd dispersed, crying, 'Keep off! keep off!' and the boat went out to sea, its occupants shouting derisively, 'You haven't got us yet!' Defendants discharged on their own recognizances.

Rescue of Goods.—A riding officer, stationed at Chichester, while going his rounds, met between Selsey and Sidlesham two men carrying a tub slung on a pole. He stopped them, and announced seizure. They dropped their burden, pulled him from his horse, and clubbed him savagely; then they took up the keg and went away. Both charged and convicted.

In 1821 a boat was seized at Folkestone for having on board six large hollow stones containing tin cases full of spirits. A quantity of silk was seized at Newhaven concealed in hams from Dieppe. The meat and bones had been scooped out, except at the ends, the silk had been wrapped in oiled silk, and then in paper, and fixed inside, the orifices neatly closed, and the whole covered with dirt and sawdust.

By Treasury Minute of February 15, 1822, the whole of the preventive forces, except the Coast Blockade and the naval ships employed (see p. 113), were consolidated, and placed under control of the Customs Board.

In November, 1821, the English Board made their final pronouncement upon a squabble between Customs and Administration in the colony of Demerara. The officers had seized two sloops and a quantity of contraband goods, and placed the vessels in charge of a negro guard. The owner, a notorious smuggler named West, boarded one of the vessels in the night, accompanied by several armed men, and carried her to sea, taking the informer, who was on board, as well. The officers, in their report, blamed the governor and the military for being slack in pursuit of the culprits. This produced a long letter from Major-General Murray, the governor, in which it was made to appear that the officers had not taken proper precautions with regard to the custody of their prize. The Board took sides with the governor, and censured the seizing officer.

Early in 1822 a vessel called the *Fame,* bound to Cork, was wrecked near Bristol. Amongst her cargo was found a cask containing 106 'instruments of iron, apparently well fitted to be fixed at the top of poles, sufficiently long to be managed with effect at a greater distance than a bayonet at the end of a musket.' The Board directed the collector of Bristol to keep a watch upon anyone who might apply for the goods.

On January 26, 1822, the collector of St. John, New Brunswick, reported to the Board that two notorious smugglers named Dunham and Johnston went to the residence of a tide-waiter who had made himself obnoxious to them, and produced a chest, stating that it contained tea. The tide-waiter found it to be empty. He expressed annoyance at this, upon which Dunham took him by the throat, and drove his head through the window. The tide-waiter gasped: 'Do you mean to murder me?' 'Yes!' thundered Dunham, 'we'll have your life before we go!' They then maltreated him further. They were charged in the Supreme Court of the island. Johnston was acquitted, Dunham convicted, but for some reason difficult to divine he was allowed to remain at large.

This showed that New Brunswick was not a pleasant place for strict officials, as was proved further on Valentine's night during the following year. Four officers who were on watch near Carlton Ferry, St. John, stopped a sled loaded with tea. In charge of the sled were 'five stout smugglers,' one of them being the redoubtable Dunham. They overpowered the officers, and drove off with the tea.

On the following night the officers took up position at the same place, accompanied by a squad of the 74th Regiment. Along came two sleds containing, not tea, but smugglers armed with boathooks and bludgeons, and accompanied by some of 'the peace officers' of the town

These attacked the customs men, but the military kept them off. Dunham was present, and extremely busy both with tongue and bludgeon. Among the 'peace officers' who assisted him were 'Nolan, calling himself deputy sheriff, though only a head constable and keeper of the gaol; Featherly, also a high constable; and Lawrence Strivers, a constable.' 'Nolan and Featherly,' said Mr. Kelly, the customs surveyor, in his report, 'were particularly violent, threatening to drive my teeth down my throat.'

It appears that by this time Dunham had paid a £20 fine for his first offence. He was not captured on account of the last till 1825, when he was brought up for trial with two of his accomplices. The judge of the Vice-Admiralty Court, who was a practising lawyer, obtained leave from the governor to defend the smugglers. He urged that the officers had no right to be patrolling in search of seizures, as they were officials who had been appointed locally, and had not as yet been commissioned by the Board of Customs. This plea secured acquittal.

On February 16, 1822, the American schooner *Peru*, from New York with a cargo of tobacco, was seized in the harbour of Kinsale. (It appears she ran aground at Cove.) She had a crew of thirty-one men, and the Customs had to obtain assistance from the garrison at Charles Fort. When the crew were charged, the plea was put forward in defence that the vessel was 'driven in by necessity,' and the case against them was dismissed. Afterwards the master admitted that he had attempted to run his cargo at Glandore, in the Baltimore district. One of the preventive water-guard officers* had given

* The following additional particulars are furnished merely to illustrate the pertinacity with which claims for seizure awards were pursued:

One Dillon (evidently the preventive officer referred to above) put in a claim for special participation in the proceeds of the *Peru* and her cargo. It appears that he was granted £150, but this did not satisfy him, and he seems to have devoted a considerable portion of the following twenty-seven years to attempting to secure a larger grant. Allusion to his case appears among

notice of this attempted run, stating that the vessel carried guns. The Kinsale collector stated in his report that she had no guns, while admitting that she was fitted with gun-ports, and that she might have thrown her guns overboard when she was driven in. He also stated that gun-matches were found on board, and a bag of bullets. The Customs then entered proceedings against ship and cargo. Meanwhile, the vessel's agent served the collector with notices of action on behalf of the master and the owners.

Later two of the crew came forward to prove that the *Peru* was a smuggling vessel, and that it had been intended to run her cargo on the Irish coast. (Various attempts were made to tamper with the informers, and

---

the records of 1849. Annexed to the papers is a copy of a petition intended to be presented to the House of Commons by Feargus O'Connor. This document states that the armed American brig *Peru*, manned by forty-three determined smugglers, and freighted with 2,053 bales of leaf and 1,090 pounds of manufactured tobacco, appeared off the Irish coast in 1822 ; that Dillon, with eleven men in two open boats, prevented her from landing her cargo at Tralong Cove, County Cork, where 400 smugglers were waiting to receive it ; and that he chased her into Kinsale river, expending during the action 187 shot, four rockets, and two blue lights, and leaving his boat-hook in her fore rigging ; and that she was then captured by Mr. Martin, the Kinsale surveyor. It goes on to state that Dillon received a letter of thanks from the Treasury, that £53,252 accrued to the public by the vessel's condemnation, and that afterwards the Treasury, influenced by 'most unfounded reports,' refused to allow him to participate to the extent warranted by his exertions, and accused him of cowardice because he did not board the vessel at sea ; that he then laid his case before Admiral Codrington, who brought it to the notice of Parliament, but the Chancellor of the Exchequer overruled the Admiral's representations. Attached to this remarkable statement are an affidavit made by Dillon's chief boatman, a reference to certain papers relative to the departure of the *Peru* from New York, and a request that the Board of Customs may recommend Dillon's case, so that he may obtain fitting compensation for the great expense he has been put to in prosecuting his claims.

It appears that the authorities had much difficulty in shaking him off. There is a letter from him to the Customs Secretary, accusing the Board of acting unjustly, and incidentally begging the Secretary to befriend him in the matter, and another in which he refers the Board to 'Robinson's Admiralty Reports and Pope's

one of them was maltreated.) The vessel and her cargo were condemned in April, 1822. The only official account of the cargo that can be gathered from the papers to hand states that it consisted of '2,500 to 3,000 bales tobacco of 50 to 60 pounds each.' Some of the tobacco was found to be damaged, and was destroyed. (Dillon's correspondence, see p. 119, puts the amount of cargo at 2,053 bales leaf and 1,090 pounds manufactured, but it is likely he means the sound part, which would be the chief factor in assessing his claim of award.) So it seems that the cargo, as originally shipped, amounted to nearly 70 tons—quite an enterprising venture in contraband.

On March 15, 1822, an officer of the Coast Blockade

Revenue Laws.' The reply is: 'The Board have not the power to allow any expenses of the nature alluded to. They cannot recommend the same to their Lordships.' Dillon returns to the charge, referring to tidings, transmitted to him in the thirties, that Mr. Spring Rice 'malignantly invented and represented to William IV.' that objection lay against Dillon's claim because the latter had displayed cowardice, and stating that Dillon has since received letters from Mr. Spring Rice of different purport, which leave him in bewilderment as to how that gentleman can have previously misrepresented him. He reminds the Board that he has lately been to New York, and hunted out, at great expense, fresh information about the *Peru*, which information he has submitted. He opines the Board cannot be so destitute of honour as not to be aware that a charge of cowardice is the most deadly aspersion that can be cast upon the character of an officer. The Board, he declares, have ruined his reputation, his professional prospects, and his private fortune, and prejudiced all his friends against him. He has expended £5,000 in prosecuting his claim, and received only £150. Minute: 'The Board can only repeat that they have not the power to comply.'

Then appears a letter from Dillon to Sir Thomas Fremantle, the Chairman, and an address to the Commissioners, in which it is asked if anything more could in reason be required by 'an honest Board, governed by truth and justice,' than the proofs already furnished. Minute: 'The Board do not consider any further order necessary.'

In another letter, bearing date 1850, he approaches the Customs Secretary, announcing that he will present another petition to the House of Commons, and declaring that the Treasury and the Board have been misled by the statements of an officer who, on the night of the action, was five miles away, and who, on hearing Dillon's 'heavy firing,' was afraid to venture out to his assistance. (Nothing more concerning the matter has been found.)

stationed at Folkestone seized a boat called the *Wig Box.* Her oars, masts, bowsprit, and 'bumpkin' contained tin tubes full of spirits. The tide-surveyor at Rye seized a lugger called the *Fox.* Her bed cabins had double bottoms, and in the spaces thus created were bales of bandanas. The same officer found on the smack *Isis,* also of Rye, a concealment under the ballast, entrance to which was obtained by removing a panel in the bulkhead of the forehold. The tide-surveyor at Sandwich seized the smack *Albion,* of London, for not being licensed. On rummaging her afterwards at his leisure, he found her to be fitted with most elaborate smuggling contrivances (false bows and a complete false stern).

During May, 1822, the *Badajos,* of London, was rummaged at Kilrush, Ireland, and found to be fitted up for concealments in an extraordinary fashion. The seizing officer stated in his report : 'I cannot more fully describe the vessel than by stating she is two vessels, completely one within the other. The contrivance to admit into the concealment is the most ingenious possible. The crew of this vessel managed their concerns so completely that they had not a boy belonging to the vessel, for fear his youth may lead him to disclose the secret ; all hands were stout, trusty fellows. From a memorandum-book found in the master's cabin, it appears this vessel had one or two similar cargoes in her before the present,' etc. (The goods found were tobacco.) The seizing officer's report was flamboyant as well as ungrammatical. He seems to have been inclined to leave nothing unsaid that could redound to his credit as a searcher, therefore it may be as well to state that the seizure was made solely by information supplied through the collector and controller of Dover.

During this year the Board made a tour of inspection, and it appears from their report that they considered the most likely part of the coast for smuggling was from Seaford west to Plymouth. (It will be remembered that eastward to the Medway the shores were protected by the Coast Blockade.) They had reason to think that the smuggling of spirits was carried on with great success. They found that the preventive men, the riding officers, the dragoons, and the officers of the cruisers, did not work together amicably. The boatmen were 'very fine men.' Some parts were difficult to guard, notably the Wight, where, from the indented nature of the coast, the patrol had to travel 100 miles in guarding 20 miles of sea. The riding-officers were of little use, many of them being old and 'locally connected.' There was a tendency to make collusive seizures. In the Brighton district collusion was apparent, there being many suspicious seizures and few men captured; while in the Chichester district many smugglers were taken, the inspecting commander, Captain Boxer, being very daring and energetic. The smugglers had lately begun to build fast rowing-boats, which they used to run goods from 'hoverers.' The system of selling seized boats locally was bad, for there was no competition, and the smugglers could buy them for next to nothing. The pilots of Portsmouth and the Wight were noted smugglers, and if found 'towing' goods they at once declared them to the officers as wrecked goods salved. The following extracts from reports made to the Board by confidential experts are strikingly illustrative:

'At present the sums expended in defence are very great, yet smuggling is carried on to such an extent that spirits of good quality are sold at 12s. and 14s. a gallon.' The writer goes on to state that there are three favoured methods of smuggling: first, by rafting tubs under water; second, by running from hoverers; third, by transhipping goods into coasters at sea. He knows that recently a hoverer manœuvred off Hastings with impunity, the blockade men 'having neither spy-glasses to see nor sails to pursue.' 'When such things take place as the run at St. Leonard's on Tuesday last at eight in the morning, it is a pretty good proof all is not right.' 'Smuggling has long been carried on, and it requires

Sir Francis Hastings Doyle.

To face p. 122.

('*Vanity Fair*' *Cartoon.*)

people of the country, who know all its bearings—men, too, not overpaid, of the working class—to counteract it.'

The other expert states : 'At Portsmouth much is doing by the Isle of Wight people. At Cowes the trade increases so much that spirits are sold at Newport from 10s. 6d. to 12s. a gallon. There appear to be about thirty-six cutters and boats employed in smuggling to the Wight and Portsmouth. Goods are often run in Southampton Water, and offered at 10s. 6d. a gallon. Much must be doing on the Dorset coast. Brandy is offered at Yeovil at 8s. a gallon. In Sussex the larger cargoes are run by French luggers, some by the Pagham and Brighton boats. Tubs fell lately at Hastings to 7s.' (a gallon). He proceeds that at Rye as much was run as the smugglers could find sale for, and that many people wished to sell their vessels and buy foreign-built craft, thinking the latter would not be liable to seizure unless found within a league of the coast. Tubs were selling at 7s. a gallon at Dover, and at Rochester, though so far up river, the goods were even cheaper.

The Scottish Board announced a seizure at Greenock of twelve kegs Irish whisky concealed in barrels of salt meat (May 2, 1822). The Irish Board announced information that tobacco, lace, and silk were extensively smuggled into Ireland, concealed in hollowed planks and pieces of lumber.

On August 30, 1822, the revenue cutter *Melville* seized in the roadstead at Burntisland the brig *Fortune*, with a cargo of wood and a 'false bottom.' Access to the false bottom was obtained by way of the stern, the panels giving access being secured by screws made to appear like common bolts. She was rigged with a false sternpost, which had to be cut away before the place of concealment could be entered. Below is an account of the contraband goods found therein :

199 bales, containing 4,830 pounds roll tobacco.
3 bags and 2 parcels, containing 323 pounds roll tobacco.
1 keg, containing 10 pounds snuff.
303 kegs, containing 1,096 gallons Geneva.
33 boxes and 213 bags, containing 1,512 pounds tea.
1 box, containing 72 packs playing-cards.

A letter sent by the British Consul at Boulogne reached the Scottish Board, stating that a fine lugger had left Boulogne with a cargo of spirits. Her crew, principally English, numbered about twenty. They had been sent over to man the lugger by merchants interested in the venture, and on the previous day had been seen about Boulogne, *accompanied by Englishwomen.* The letter stated that other luggers were being built, and that a steady contraband trade was carried on by means of galleys.

A letter from Governor Ainslie, Cape Breton, Newfoundland, reached the Board, complaining that large quantities of coal were stolen from H.M. coal-mines in that colony, smuggled into Halifax, and sold there at a price ruinous to the fair trader. The governor stated that the traffic was prejudicial even to the smugglers, as they neglected their farms and fisheries to follow it, and spent the proceeds of their trade in debauchery at Halifax. He desired that a permit might be called for whenever coals were discharged at Halifax. (Orders to the collector accordingly.)

Early in 1823 a tub of spirits was found on the beach at Newhaven, made in the shape of a salmon-kit, and 'cemented over.' A boat was seized at Dover. Her keel, made of tin painted to resemble wood, contained spirits; so did her 'hollow yards.'

Three casks were found floating in a sack off Sandwich. A bag of shingle was attached as 'sinker,' and an inflated bladder with a small tuft of feathers as a 'mark.' 'Such,' states the report, 'was the exact nature of the experiment, that the bladder kept the sack floating one foot under the surface. Had an accident happened to the bladder, and the sack sunk, the feathers were so fixed as to mark the place. On the spring tides the rush of water over the flats causes a quantity of froth. The bladder had the appearance of a body of froth.'

Twelve tubs of spirits were found floating off Rye. A circular piece of sheet-lead, weighing about 9 pounds, had been affixed to each, and the tubs lashed together longitudinally. Thus weighted, 'they rolled unfettered in the tideway,' the lead sinking the casks to a depth of $2\frac{1}{2}$ fathoms. Thus, if the officers were 'creeping,'* they would scarcely feel the casks.

The brigantine *John* was seized in Loch Mahon. She had a cargo of timber, and artfully concealed under the cargo and in a place between the cabin floor and sternpost were 773 bales of tobacco.

The following almost incredible information reached the authorities: 'A clinker-built boat of 26 tons, named the *St. Francois*, Jean Baptiste de la Motte master, from Gravelines, lately passed through the Forth and Clyde Canal to Glasgow. The crew brought over a quantity of lace, concealed in boxes made in the shape of apples, and painted so as not to be easily distinguished from real apples. She landed part of her cargo at Whitby, and, after discharging the remainder at Glasgow, cleared on the 27th May, 1823, for Gravelines.'

The Secretary to the Commissioners of Inquiry into the condition of the Customs and Excise departments called upon the Admiralty for a return of H.M. ships employed in the prevention of smuggling in Great Britain. The following is an extract from the official Minute upon this request: 'Acquaint him that all his Majesty's ships and vessels on the home stations are principally employed in the suppression of smuggling. It is, therefore, absolutely impossible to give any other list than a general list of all the ships in commission within the British seas.'

The English Customs reported to the Admiralty that certain members of the Board had surveyed the coasts of England. With this report went an informative return of the quantities of brandy, tea, and tobacco duty-paid during the past five years, from which it appeared that

* 'Creeping,' dragging or sounding for sunken goods, or prying into holes and gullies along the shore.

either the demand for tobacco had fallen off, or the illicit introduction of it had increased :

Brandy (Gallons).

1818.	1819.	1820.	1821.	1822.
731,277	964,814	1,021,576	1,140,304	1,221,140

Tea (Pounds).

1818.	1819.	1820.	1821.	1822.
22,468,170	22,754,341	22,359,539	22,616,167	24,106,722

Tobacco (Pounds).

1818.	1819.	1820.	1821.	1822.
12,475,432	11,754,834	11,249,342	11,619,505	11,576,063

In the report made on the revenue of Scotland by the Parliamentary Committee of 1823, unfavourable comments had been made upon the Scottish system of prevention. In answer to these reflections, Mr. Arrow, the inspecting commander of Coastguard in the Aberdeen district, furnished a long and interesting statement, in which the system as conducted by Mr. Arrow since the establishment of the Scottish Coastguard in 1819 was lauded to the skies. While admitting that the Scottish fisherfolk and coast peasantry were inclined to assist smugglers, he pointed out that there were certain traits in their character which rendered the establishment of stronger coast patrols unnecessary. 'If the Scotch fishers and coast peasantry had the daring, or, more properly speaking, the want of feeling, that the smugglers on most parts of the English coasts have, the weak patrols of the present force would not be effective. So long as the above orders of society continue their present habits, and the wish to appear at kirk with a clean character, so long will the present force of the Coastguard be effective.' He then furnished certain details as to the smuggling practised on the east coast of Scotland previous to 1819, details which to some extent contradicted his own argument, for, while they did not exactly disprove his statement that the Scottish 'runners' were not violent folk, they proved that, at any rate before 1819, they had not been particularly anxious to preserve the purity of their characters, unless it were that smuggling, unaccompanied by violence, required but an occasional lustration.

He stated that before the establishment of the Coastguard, the coast being left under the protection of the Customs and Excise cruisers and the riding-officers, there was a regular passage of smuggled spirits, tea, and tobacco from Flushing into Aberdeen. Two smuggling syndicates were established at Collieston. Each syndicate owned two vessels, which were kept constantly employed. One syndicate failed in 1802, but the other (directed by two notorious fellows named Mitchell and Christie) held on till 1817, and then 'broke.' But business began afresh in 1818 under the directorship of one James Dickie, who received from five to seven cargoes each 'season.' Arrow furnished a most interesting account of the doings of the old smuggling receivers, who, 'assisted by a Folkestone man named Dangerfield,'* supplied the coast from Aberdeen to Montrose most plentifully with contraband. He stated that in 1809 some fair traders of Aberdeen 'got up a movement' against the Mitchell and Christie firm, and that Christie actually had the impudence to publish an advertisement of challenge in a local newspaper.†

Mr. Arrow insisted that he and his men had broken the back of the old contraband system in that locality. To prove the excellence of his methods, he stated that a person called at his house one night, and made the following statement :

* This desperado is named many times in the 'information lists' as running goods in various parts of the United Kingdom. Many of the old smuggling skippers were Folkestone men, and quite a number of smuggling ventures, some into remote places, were financed by natives or inhabitants of Folkestone.

† This Mr. Arrow quoted as below :

'NOTICE.—Alexander Christie : Notwithstanding—has still on hand for his favourite customers a considerable quantity of anker gin, which cannot in point of quality and flavour be excelled, and a fresh supply daily expected : Also Highland whisky of best quality, and other spirits equal to his neighbours.

'In these pinched times, a discerning public will find this worth their attention.' (From the *Aberdeen Journal*, January 11, 1809.)

'I am employed by the smugglers. You know we have had a vessel on the coast the last thirteen nights, and that we want to land near Aberdeen. For the love of God, let her come in, and give us fair play. You take what you can; let us get off with what we can, or she will go away altogether, as she cannot keep on this coast any longer.'

(This vessel, Mr. Arrow stated, had to run to sea in the end, and was wrecked on one of the eastern islands.)

The testimonials to Mr. Arrow's vigilance and the effectiveness of the force under his control were many and influential. We furnish extracts from a few of them:

Signatories.	*Extracts (condensed).*
A J.P. living near Rattray Head.	'Cargoes were landed in open day between Fraserburgh and Peterhead in 1818 and 1819.'
The Baron-Bailie of Peterhead.	'Many cargoes were run on various parts of the coast between Girdleness and Rattray Head, before the Coastguard was established.'
The Secretary to the Commissioners of General Assembly.	'For thirty years smuggling was carried on to a very considerable extent at Slains and Cruden.'
A Lieutenant-General and J.P.	'Until lately about two miles from Collieston was the emporium of smuggling. I have often seen one—nay, two—luggers at a time unloaded by twenty or thirty fishboats as regularly and systematically as the disembarkation of an army.'
The Minister of Slains.	'Collieston has been a well-known station for smuggling from time immemorial till within three or four years past. There never has been a year from 1794 to 1819 that there were not three or four cargoes of foreign spirits landed, and some years more than double that quantity.'

Signatories.	*Extracts* (*condensed*).
The Procurator-Fiscal.	(This gentleman stated that Mitchell at one time carried on a huge business, being financed by one James of Folkestone. When Mitchell failed, he owed James £5,000.* Before the establishment of the Coastguard, smuggled spirits were sold at every tavern between Peterhead and Aberdeen. 'Gin and brandy were presented to visitors in every farm-house—nay, every cottar's house—in Buchan.')

(All these, and others, testified to a falling off in smuggling since the Coastguard 'arrived.' From a general study of statement and testimonials, it appears that prior to that period Scottish smuggling was carried on by vessels of from 100 to 200 tons, each bringing from 800 to 1,500 tubs spirits, and occasional cargoes of tobacco and tea. A run usually occupied about two hours. The fishermen and country folk, with their wives and daughters, assisted in getting the goods ashore, and stowing or distributing them.)

Early in 1824 the controller-general of Coastguard sent a statement to the London Board (whence it was transmitted to the Assistant Commissioners of Edinburgh) to the effect that he had received reliable information that a cutter called the *Eliza* had landed 700 bales tobacco at Luce Bay, Mull of Galloway; that the tobacco had been stored in 'pits,' and was to be made up into small packages and smuggled into Ireland.

On February 19, 1824, the *Asp* was seized at Rye. She had a false bottom, extending aft as far as the ballast bulkhead, and in this space a quantity of silks and tobacco had been concealed.

Information reached the Assistant Commissioners at Dublin that a cutter of 160 tons, laden with brandy, hollands, and tea, would sail shortly from Flushing; that

* See p. 127.

she carried forty men, was pierced for fourteen guns, was consigned to Ormsby of Sligo and Burke of Connemara, and might run at Clogher Head or on the coasts of Kerry and Cork. She had on board two 'spotsmen' (pilots). A smuggling lugger of 90 tons had left Flushing for Wexford.

On March 20, 1824, a piece of wood made to resemble an ordinary ship's 'fender'* was examined on board a vessel that arrived at Greenock, and found to have been neatly hollowed out and packed with 'crown glass' (eighty-eight panes). About the same time several pieces of timber which had been landed at an outport in Ireland were found to be hollow and to be stuffed with tobacco.

Information reached London that the *Aldborough* yacht had loaded with silks at Nieuport, run the goods in the Humber, and was back in Nieuport shipping another cargo.

On April 15, 1824, the *William and Mary* left London with a cargo of wooden hoops for Waterford. She arrived at Passage on May 7, and the suspicions of the customs men stationed there were aroused. A search was made, and soon it became evident that, after leaving London, she had made a trip to the Dutch or French coasts, taken in contraband, and stowed it beneath her original cargo. The officers found 291 bales of tobacco (weighing in all between 6 and 7 tons).

A clever fraud (repeatedly imitated in modern times) was discovered at one of the English outports. A number of copper cans had been imported, entered as containing orange-flower water. A tube led from the mouth to the bottom of each can. This tube was filled with the scented liquid, but the space between tube and sides was filled with essential oils, liable to a very high rate of duty.

* 'Fender,' a large cylindrical piece of timber with a rope rove through the end, suspended over the vessel's side when she approaches her moorings, to prevent injury to her timbers by contact with other ships or with the pier-head. (Sometimes a 'cork fender' is used—viz., a bag composed of closely interwoven cordage, and filled with pieces of cork.)

The Board advised the outports that information had been received of extensive smuggling by collier vessels, the goods being transhipped into them at sea.

Information was received of smuggling in Kent and Sussex by means of shrimping-nets fitted with hollow poles. In each pole was a tin tube containing about 2½ gallons spirits.

On June 10, 1824, Captain Brace, of H.M.S. *Ganges*, captured two smugglers and a quantity of contraband at Barbados. Under the Plantation laws he had no power to detain *the men* in custody, but, being unaware of this, he kept them in hand till apprised of his error by the collector. After the goods had been condemned the smugglers entered an action against him for illegal detention, which he was glad to compromise by paying them £35 each. The Treasury refunded the money paid by him, otherwise it would have been a disastrous business for Captain Brace, for, though the condemned goods realized £121, the expenses attending condemnation were over £90, made up as below:

	£	s.	d.	
Collector's poundage	2	0	0	odd.
Controller's poundage	1	10	0	,,
Advocate's and Proctor's fees	47	0	0	,,
Judge's, Registrar's, and Marshal's fees ..	37	0	0	,,
Watchman's pay	1	5	0	
Advertising goods	0	16	5	
Paid to drummers*	0	5	6	

We cannot close this chapter more suitably than by reproducing two letters written by the Customs Secretary to informers. It will be seen that the informers were women. Many letters might be quoted from the revenue records which re-exemplify the old case of Samson and Delilah. (We suppress the names, but not the addresses.)

'*To Miss ——, Musical Museum, Spring Gardens.*

'MADAM,

'With reference to your letter of the 23rd ultimo, I have it in command to acquaint you that the coll^{r}. and

* Probably for tattoo at proclamation of sale.

cont[r]. at Shoreham have remitted a bill for £8 12s. 7d., dated 11th instant, and payable at 20 days after date, being your share of the fine recovered from John Boxall for smuggling, and that upon your application at my office you may receive the same on producing a proper receipt.

'G. DELAVAUD.

'*September* 13*th*, 1822.'

'*To Miss ——, Lee Cottage, Lee, Kent.*

'MADAM,

'The Commiss[rs] having considered your application of the 9th ultimo, requesting to be allowed a maintenance on account of the evidence given by you on the trial of the smugglers captured by the *Badger* revenue cruiser, I have it in command to acquaint you that the Board do not see fit to comply with your request.

'*March* 15*th*, 1824.'

The reports of seizures in the Plantations at this period furnished ample evidence of immense colonial smuggling. One seizure note from Jamaica, bearing date October 5, 1824, showed that the contrabandists not only went in for 'running' goods, but occasionally tried to smuggle high-rated goods amongst low-rated. Seventy barrels by the American schooner *Resolution*, and reported as corn, were found to contain amid the corn seventy kegs of brandy. Ten tierces, reported as rice, were found to contain amid the rice twenty-two cases spermaceti candles and three cases China crapes.

The perils of a revenue officer's existence were not confined to encounters with truculent smugglers. Occasionally he came into collision with passengers or travellers who were as truculent, mentally, as the most desperate contrabandist, and if the revenue man happened to be resentful he might be easily betrayed into expressions or actions which would cost him dear. An instance of the kind occurred in 1825. Lord Harborough arrived with his yacht from foreign shores, and landed on the lower coast of the Thames. His vessel was visited by the men of the Coast Blockade, who afterwards admitted that the noble lord's dress and general appearance led them to believe that he was a smuggler. Perhaps Lord Harborough himself was conscious of this, for it appears that he said to Lieutenant Graham, who was in charge of the blockade men: 'Do you take me for a smuggler?' 'Certainly not,' replied Graham, 'but you can't be answerable for what your men might do.' Lord Harborough thereupon applied several racy epithets to revenue men in general, and called Graham 'a highwayman and a robber.' This, Graham afterwards stated, occurred in the presence of many notorious smugglers, who had strolled up to witness the dispute. Graham replied: 'I don't care if this boat is Lord Harborough's or a common man's. Here is my card. I must get the satisfaction of a gentleman. If you don't give it to me, I will kick you and post you.' For this display of manliness the revenue officer was sentenced by the Court of King's Bench, on May 13, 1825, to four months' imprisonment in the Marshalsea.

The chief characteristics of British Customs administration during the first twenty-five years of the nineteenth century may be indicated with profit at the close of this chapter. They took the shape of slow but effective reform of departmental abuses, vigorous but unsuccessful action against smuggling, occasional relaxations of the navigation laws, and repeated consolidations of the Customs statutes. With respect to the first, it may be conceded that the scope of patronage became considerably narrowed, and the burden of Customs emolument was gradually removed from the back of the mercantile community and placed upon that of the public. The second feature has already been made conspicuously apparent to readers. With respect to the third, only a few countries had been favoured, notably the U.S.A. under the Convention of 1819. Wholesale repeal of hundreds of obsolete laws, and novel and effective consolidation of those allowed to survive, were in contemplation, and will form matter for the opening of our next chapter.

LIST OF AUTHORITIES.

Incidence of duties, etc. : The various Books of Rates.

Corn laws : Books of Rates ; Customs corn returns, reports, and statistics.

Colonial revenue and smuggling : Jamaica, 'Treasury,' Antigua, Nova Scotia, Montserrat, Trinidad, 'Treasury Warrant,' 'Council,' Quebec, 'Reports,' Newfoundland and New Brunswick, and 'Promiscuous' Files ; Plantation General Orders, 1814-1815.

British smuggling : 'Exchequer Trials' (Solicitor's Department, Customs) ; Letters to Outports ; Minutes of the English Board, 1806, pp. 314, etc. ; Treasury Board Papers, 1806 ; General Letters, 1780-1813, 1814-1823 ; General Letters, Scotland, 1821-1823 ; General Letters, 1824 ; General Letters, Dublin, 1824 ; General Letters, 1825 ; Treasury Customs and Excise Book 52, Letter 6,207 ; Treasury Customs and Excise Book 54 ; Assize and Promiscuous Trials (Solicitor's Department, Customs) ; Customs Chairman's 'Private and Official Correspondence'; Admiralty Papers (Coast Blockade), 1821 ; 'Illustrative Documents' File (Customs Library) ; Thurso Letter Book, 1822 ; Admiralty Papers, March 6, 1823, March 7, 1823.

Revenue legislation : The various statutes as quoted in text ; Customs Chairman's 'Private and Official Correspondence.'

Statistics of revenue, etc. : 'Finance Accounts of United Kingdom': 'Income and Expenditure,' and various departmental reports and returns.

Reimbursement of Messrs. Frewen and Jickling : 'Gatley's Memoranda' (Customs Library).

CHAPTER II

THE PERIOD OF GRADUAL RELAXATIONS

1826—1844

On July 5, 1826, eleven voluminous Customs Acts, which had been passed during the previous year, came into operation. The first of these, Cap. 105, 6 Geo. IV., revoked all other enactments relating to the Customs. Its preamble echoed the opening clause of the Act which announced the consolidation of 1787. It stated that the laws of the Customs had become intricate, and that it was highly expedient for the interests of commerce and the ends of justice that all the statutes in force relating to the Customs should be repealed, and replaced by new enactments exhibiting more perspicuously and compendiously the various provisions contained therein. Three hundred and eighty-six Customs Acts relating to Great Britain, and fifty-six relating to Ireland, were repealed wholly or in part. Amongst the statutes affected were those historic productions, the Act of Frauds and the various Navigation Acts.

Cap. 106 provided for the management of the department, prescribing thirteen Commissioners for the United Kingdom and the British possessions abroad. One of these was to manage the Scottish Customs, and one the Irish, and each of these last mentioned had two 'Assistant Commissioners' to aid him. The power of the Treasury to prescribe the official hours of attendance was reaffirmed, and the 'Customs holidays' were specified as Christmas Day, Good Friday, and the King's birthday.

Cap. 107 contained the bulk of the departmental regulations of commerce. The law as to 'reporting ships' and 'entering goods' was clearly recited, and the usual meticulous ingenuity displayed in providing against evasion. All goods laden in British ships in foreign ports were to be certified officially at port of shipment, and the certificates produced when demanded officially in the United Kingdom. Goods shipped in the Plantations were to be attested, even as of old. Goods which, after paying customs, were liable to excise duties, were not to be delivered by the Customs except into the custody of an excise officer. The most important classes of foreign goods prohibited from importation were cattle, sheep, swine, and malt (in protection of the native agriculturist), tobacco-stalks (to protect the native tobacco manufacturer), and packages of tobacco and spirits which might be under the legal weight or size. Sworn declarations were required from exporters of drawback or bountied goods. Machines and parts of machinery, for use in manufactures in which the United Kingdom was eminent, were prohibited from exportation.

Cap. 108 dealt with the prevention of smuggling. The following offences entailed forfeiture of ship and cargo: (1) The bringing of prohibited goods by sea within four leagues of the coast between the North Foreland and Beachy Head, and within eight leagues of any other part of the coasts of the United Kingdom. (2) The navigating of square-rigged vessels within 100 leagues of the coast with illegal-sized packages of tobacco or spirits on board. (3) The throwing overboard of goods during chase. (4) The presence within the limits of a port of a vessel found to be 'unaccountably light,' said vessel having had previously cargo or part cargo on board. Gangs of smugglers, numbering three or more, carrying firearms, were made liable to the punishment for felony, persons who assaulted revenue officers to transportation for three years. The making of collusive seizures was rendered punishable by a fine of £500. Spirits found floating at sea were only to be taken up by revenue officers. One merciful provision reappeared, empowering the Commissioners of Customs to contribute, at a rate not exceeding 7½d. per day, towards the maintenance of poor persons imprisoned for smuggling.* (Most of the above were mere reaffirmations of old preventive measures.)

Cap. 109 was a new Navigation Act, on much the same lines as the older Acts. General trade *into* the Plantations was limited to 'British ships.' So was all inter-Plantation trade. Foreign ships might only carry to the Plantations goods which were the produce of, and direct from, the countries to which such ships belonged, but they might take in goods at the Plantations, and carry them to any *foreign* port. The usual 'enumerated' *European* goods (wine, timber, corn, brandy, tobacco, oil, dried fruit, salt, timber, flax, hemp, etc.) might only come from Europe to the United Kingdom, for use therein, in British ships, or in ships of the country in which such goods were produced or from which they were imported. Most of the goods of Asia and Africa, and all goods of America, might only come to the United Kingdom, to be used therein, in British ships, except they were brought in the ships of the country in which the goods were produced, and direct from that country; nor might such goods be brought at all if first landed in Europe. Trade between the United Kingdom and the Channel Islands was to be in British ships. So was all trade between the United Kingdom and the Plantations, and all coasting trade. (It will be noted that a few privileges were thus granted to foreign ships, notably that of trading to the Plantations direct from the ports of their own countries, and exporting foreign goods from the Plantations to any foreign country whatever.)

Cap. 110 reaffirmed most of the old provisions for registration of British ships. Registry was restricted to vessels built in the United Kingdom or the Plantations, and the register was forfeitable if more than 20s. per ton

* Originally enacted by Cap. 21, 53 Geo. III.

were spent at any one time on repairs in a foreign port. Foreigners might not hold property in British ships.

Cap. 111 provided a new tariff. The following extracts illustrate its tendency :

	£	s.	d.
Bacon, per cwt.	1	8	0
Beer, per 32 gallons	2	13	0
German sheet glass, per cwt.	10	0	0
Gloves, men's, per dozen pairs	0	5	0
Iron ore, per ton	0	5	0
Pig-lead, per ton	2	0	0
Linens (damask), per square yard..	0	3	0
Unrefined sugar, East India Possessions, per cwt. ..	1	17	0
Unrefined sugar, British Plantations, per cwt. ..	1	7	0
Unrefined sugar, foreign, per cwt...	3	3	0
Refined sugar, per cwt.	8	8	0

There were many *ad valorem* duties, the percentages ranging from 10 to 60. Whalebone of the British fisheries paid £1 a ton if of British taking, £95 if of foreign. Oil from the fisheries paid 1s. a tun if of British taking, £26 12s. if of foreign. 'Retaliation' was provided for by a clause which empowered the King by Order in Council to levy an additional duty, not exceeding one-fifth of the original, on the goods of any country which surtaxed British goods, or imposed unfavourable tonnage duties on British shipping. He might also prohibit the importation of manufactured articles from any country if the said country prohibited exportation of the raw material to the British dominions. Only four articles of export were specifically taxed—coal, skins, wool, and woollen manufactures.

Cap. 112 provided for the warehousing of goods, or, rather, amended and extended the previous arrangements towards that end (see p. 21, etc.).

Cap. 113 granted export bounties on cordage, linens, sail-cloth, and Plantation sugar refined.

Cap. 114, which was passed 'to regulate the trade of the British Possessions abroad,' specified thirty-two 'free ports' in the British American and West Indian colonies, of which no fewer than ten were in Jamaica. Foreign trade into the Plantations was confined to these ports. Foreign countries which had colonies might only enjoy the privilege, granted generally to all foreign ships, of trading into the British possessions goods the produce of the countries to which the importing ships belonged, and of carrying Plantation goods to any country whatever, when British ships were treated under the 'most favoured' method in the colony-owning countries in question. Certain light duties were levied on British and Plantation spirits imported into the North American possessions, and all other goods (not British or colonial) into those colonies, or into the West Indies or Mauritius, paid *ad valorem* duties. All duties collected in the Plantations (or colonies as it will be best to call them in future), except certain trifling duties still existing under Acts made in 1778 and 1791, were to be paid in by the collectors to the various colonial treasuries, and applied to the use of the colonies. The duties under the two Acts above mentioned remained imperial, and it is possible they were preserved in order to form a pretext for continuing the imperial staff of collectors and officers, the Treasury's power of making appointments, and the Treasury's and British Customs Board's powers of control. Thus still, and indeed for some twenty-five years longer, the colonial Customs were staffed and managed from Treasury Chambers and Thames Street, and there is no more interesting phase of Customs history than that exemplifying the futility of this continuation.

Cap. 115 regularized the previous Customs procedure with regard to the Isle of Man, specifying the goods (wine, brandy, geneva, from foreign countries; and rum, tea, tobacco, coffee, sugar, and playing-cards from or *via* England) which might only be imported in stated quantities under licences granted by the Board of Customs. The expenses of government and administration were to be deducted from the Manx duties, and the balance paid into the imperial Exchequer.

Cap. 116 embodied in its provisions the greater part of

the original Acts governing the carrying of passengers from the United Kingdom to foreign parts.

Before the new Acts came into operation, it was found necessary to pass another (Cap. 48, 7 Geo. IV.) to amend them by rectifying certain errors, supplying certain items previously deficient, and even altering some of the duties. A few Acts repealed were reinstated, and a number of other Acts repealed.

It will be seen that these eleven statutes consolidated the regulations neatly. A mass of puzzling matter was removed from the body of revenue law, yet it cannot be said that even in its new shape that fabric was quite free from complication. As regarded departmental work, a fruitful source of trouble had been retained by continuing the home control of the colonial Customs. The collectors in the colonies, smarting under the loss inflicted on them by the abolition of fees,* were inclined to throw every possible obstacle in the way of the colonial treasurers. The governors found it extremely difficult to obtain from their new subordinates, the collectors, such returns as were required for the information of the various colonial legislatures. Nor were the colonial legislatures or Houses of Assembly free from malicious intent. Cases occurred in which they refused to sanction payment, out of the colonial revenues, of the salaries which had been granted in lieu of fees to the Customs officers. Many disputes arose, but it is likely that in most instances the collectors were in fault.

On February 7, 1826, the collector of Montserrat reported to the Board that the revenue collected in that island was insufficient to furnish his salary. 'Not a shilling,' he wrote, 'has been taken since the commencement of the year.'

On April 2, 1826, the collector of Antigua wrote a passionate and erratically-punctuated letter to the Board, and sent with it a copy of an Antigua newspaper, containing an anonymous letter that cast reflections upon

* On January 1, 1826.

the collector's conduct. It appears that he had made a practice, when selling rum which he had collected under the 4½ per cent. tax in kind, of making a charge for the casks after the rum had been purchased, and that his right to do this, and pocket the proceeds, had been challenged in the local press. Part of the collector's report ran thus :

'The Writer, whoever he may be, is too insignificant, and dastardly, to be sought out by me as a gentleman ; but when my Official Character is attacked and my Integrity challenged ; it becomes me to give to the Board under which I have the honour to serve ; such an explanation of my conduct, in the discharge of my public duty ; as to refute the calumny, of any one of the Inveterate Enemies, I have in this Island, who have been raised up against me, from the Zealous and conscientious discharge of my arduous duties, in it.'

The collector of Dominica had made himself obnoxious to a certain section of the inhabitants of that island by his persistent enforcement of the Acts relating to the abolition of the slave trade. This had produced an extraordinary mass of correspondence, extending from 1819 to 1823, principally on the question as to whether slaves who had escaped from the neighbouring French colonies, and taken refuge in Dominica, should be 'condemned' under the Acts (by which they became the property of the British Crown, and virtually free), or whether they should be restored to their masters if the latter claimed them. The Judge of the Vice-Admiralty Court in Dominica decided against the collector's plea for 'condemnation,' and this evoked a violent protest to the Board, in which the collector declared that, having been attacked in a Dominican newspaper, he had taken proceedings for libel, and cast the paper in £639 damages, and that the Judge, being editor of the paper in question, had given the recent unfavourable legal decision as an act of retaliation. Another huge mass of correspondence grew out of this charge. In the end the collector was censured by the Board, and the matter dropped.

Another skirmish occurred at Grenada. The governor directed the collector to prepare certain returns. After some delay the returns were sent, with a bill for £19 16s. (currency) for trouble attendant upon extracting the necessary information from the official records, the collector stating that there was a precedent for the charge, the Customs Board having allowed similar compensation in 1774. The governor replied that he had neither the means nor the inclination to pay the bill, and referred the collector to the Board. The Board declined to pay. Later another return was called for, and the collector suggested that the governor should send a clerk to compile it. The irritated governor wrote back demanding an answer—yes or no—as to whether the collector would prepare the report. The collector, in reply, stated that he was in a quandary, for if he drew up this report for the governor he would have to delay his periodical returns to the Custom House, London. The dispute was referred to the Treasury, and the collector was censured.

Much of the voluminous correspondence between the West Indian colonies and the London Board of Customs was due to colonial misconception of the complicated laws against the slave trade. During 1825 several slaves were detained by the Customs at St. Kitt's—one for being imported from the Dutch colony of Curaçao ; one woman and her child because they had been brought from Anguilla, and the woman had not been registered according to law ; and two others because they had been imported without being mentioned on the ship's report. The Board found that the slave from Curaçao did not come under the Act, he having been imported previous to the limit period therein stated, and they directed that he should be restored to his owner. But previous to this decision reaching St. Kitt's the governor had directed proceedings in the Vice-Admiralty Court of the island, and the slave had been 'condemned to the Crown,' thus gaining freedom. More reports, and then the Customs Lawyer in London opined that the Court's decision must stand, it having been arrived at by 'competent jurisdiction.' Many such cases occurred at various periods ; the colonial records teem with them.

More trouble occurred in Antigua, where the collector had taken it upon himself to cease paying the produce of the colonial duties into the island treasury, and in this case it is manifest that the sole reason was pique on account of loss of fees. (It should be stated that in most of the colonies local duties were collected long prior to 1826, under Acts passed by the various colonial legislatures. The Act Cap. 114, 6 Geo. IV., was in a way, though not professedly, a measure consolidating previous colonial revenue enactments.) Evidently the Commander-in-Chief of the Leeward Islands was in doubt as to the proper course of procedure, for, after issuing a peremptory injunction that the duties should be at once paid in, he weakened, and allowed the collector to retain them pending further orders. In the end the duties were paid over to the treasurer ; but it is amazing to observe the self-importance of these colonial collectors of old, and the lengths to which it carried them.

It seems as though there was a general conspiracy among the colonial customs men at this period to assert their independence of local legislative control. The collector of Jamaica complained to the Board that the provincial House of Assembly had issued *direct* orders to him to furnish certain returns, and he quoted a Board's Order of 1807, which enjoined that such directions should only be complied with when sent through the governor. He stated that he had been called before the Assembly to receive the command, and that he was liable to be arrested for contempt. The Board directed him to comply, and stated that if any further difficulty arose they would submit it to the proper legal authorities.

It was in Jamaica that the great battle between Customs and colonial control was most stubbornly contested.

Besides the duties levied under the new Act (Cap. 114, 6 Geo. IV., recently quoted), the House of Assembly levied other colonial duties, and insisted upon their collection by certain locally-appointed officials. The island treasurer and the collector disagreed on the point as to whether the salaries of the customs officers were to be provided, as directed by the imperial Act, out of a fixed proportion of the receipts under Cap. 114, 6 Geo. IV., or the same proportion of the receipts under that statute and under the 'permanent' island Act as well, the collector insisting upon the latter course. The island treasurer refused to give the collector an account of the proceeds of the island duties, so the collector put into the king's chest the moneys received under the Act, locked the chest, and bided his time. The governor was drawn into the dispute. He failed to see why two sets of duties should be levied, and directed the collector to discontinue taking money under Cap. 114, 6 Geo. IV. The collector protested that this was illegal, and in his report to the Board stated: 'We earnestly entreat your Honours will prevent as far as possible the interference of the Colonial Assembly with your officers in this island, as their policy in commercial matters is opposite to that of Britain, and thus the carrying into full effect British enactments is not a popular duty.'

Downing Street, Whitehall, Thames Street, and the sun-scorched House at Kingston, were soon at it hammer and tongs. The island assembly forbade for a period the payment out of the colonial treasury for rations for the white troops quartered in Jamaica, and only rescinded this action after receiving an eloquent and serious letter from the Secretary of State for the Colonies. The difficulty was not adjusted till 1832. A Treasury Minute on the matter, issued on August 13, 1830, is worth quoting:

'My Lords do not wish to prolong any controversial discussion by entering into the several arguments which the Committee of the House of Assembly have thought it advisable to adduce, and of which my Lords can in no degree admit the justice or utility.' The Minute proceeded to state that certain tonnage duties recently levied by the Assembly to provide Customs salaries produced more than was necessary for that purpose, and expressed a hope that these new duties would be reduced, so that what appeared to be a provision for salaries might not become a source of island revenue. It also desired that there should be no future lapse of the island grant for victualling troops, and that, as the forthcoming arrangement for Customs salaries was to be retrospective, the amount held back from the victualling grant should also be made up promptly.

Cap. 56 of 7 and 8 Geo. IV. still further amended the recently consolidated British Customs laws, and a few of the duties. One rather interesting clause provided that when goods were imported in packages, and the packages had hollow sides or bottoms in which dutiable goods were concealed, all the goods in the packages should be forfeited. Another stated that all trade with the British possessions in America and the Cape of Good Hope should be deemed to be trade within the limits of the East India Company's Charter. The Navigation laws were slightly eased.

During this year the collector of St. Mary's, River Gambia, got into serious trouble, being suspended by the governor of Sierra Leone (Sir Neil Campbell) on a charge of misappropriation. The governor, in his report to the Board, stated that the collector had furnished no account of 'extra duty' paid on 1,781 gallons of wine, and had allowed 2,385 gallons of spirits to pass duty-free. There was a further charge against him of allowing several consignments to pass, some duty-free, some free of the 'extra duty,' the quantities being as follow: 944 gallons, '3 puncheons,' 481 gallons, 694 gallons, 718 gallons, 710 gallons, 244 gallons, all 'spirits,' with 577 gallons whisky and 93 gallons gin. He had issued 'auction licences' to three persons, and only returned the duty paid by one, and had seized vessels and released them without attempting to secure condemnation. The governor recommended that another man be at once put in his place. The Board replied with considerable hauteur, stating they were not in the habit of dealing with such cases summarily, but always gave an accused official a fair chance of defence. They suggested that Sir Neil Campbell should send them a full account of any investigation which he might have held, with the collector's answers to the charges. The final result does not appear in the records, but it is possible that 'spirits' may have had much to do with the whole matter, and have closed the case before Sir Neil Campbell could reply.

Certain correspondence with the Mauritius at this period throws light upon the complications of colonial revenue. Several English merchants applied to Lord Bathurst, asking that all moneys charged as duties upon their goods at Port Louis under Acts passed in the colonies, such moneys being paid since the issue of Cap. 114, 6 Geo. IV., might be refunded. This being referred to Thames Street, the Board reported against the application, and it appears from the papers that the design of the Act was to establish a *minimum* tariff, that the colonies still had the power of taxing themselves, and that the Act did not abrogate any duties previously levied under any colonial Act. The imperial laws were absolute as regarded trading privileges, not as regarded revenue. (A Treasury Minute confirming this view was issued on April 10, 1827.)

Among the records of this period appears the journal of John Fife, tide-surveyor, Quebec, a perfect example of the art of 'cooking.' Below are certain items :

'*May 1st*, 1827.—Employed boarding vessels arrived from sea, making the necessary reports to the collector and controller, boarding tide-waiters and visiting them, cautioning them to be diligent and strict upon duty, and injoining them at all times to be on the alert for the protection of His Majesty's revenue. 5 a.m. to 6 p.m.'

This record is repeated on most days, but the startling item, 'mustering passengers from 5 a.m. till 7 p.m.,' occurs once. (This would be in connection with the Passenger Acts, and indicates an immense influx of emigrants.) He is shown as on duty *every* day, Sunday included, never for less than twelve hours, usually for thirteen. Sometimes he appears as working from 6 a.m. till 7 p.m., then 'making a visit' at two on the following morning, then going on duty at 7 a.m. and remaining till 9 p.m.! There are no records of seizures. Men who 'fake up' flamboyant journals have no time to keep a lookout.

A petition reached the Council of Trade from the lessees of the coalmines at Sydney, Cape Breton. It stated that in 1826 the king granted to the duke of York all the unreserved mines and mineral rights in Nova Scotia (Cape Breton was an appanage of Nova Scotia at this time), and that the duke leased them to the petitioners for sixty years. They had works at Sydney, at a place near Pictou, and in Lingan Bay, and they asked that 'free ports' might be established at those three places. (Much correspondence occurred on this subject up to 1829. Sydney, Cape Breton, was made 'free' about this period.)

On July 16, 1827, the American trading schooner *Potomac* arrived at St. John, New Brunswick. Two merchants of St. John paid duty on sixteen bales cotton-sheeting which formed part of the cargo. The master landed the goods, and was about to deliver them without waiting for their examination by the Customs. On being called to account for this, he gave vent to his feelings in the turbulent fashion common amongst American mariners of that day, by, as the report put it, 'damning the Customs and the laws.' This may have caused the officers to be dilatory in examination, for one of the importers, who was in attendance, forcibly took the goods away before the examination was completed, and when this was opposed he struck one of the officers a violent blow in the chest. He was proceeded against, and fined £200. An official squabble arose over the legal expenses of the trial, and endured till 1833.

Up to 1826 there had been no collection of customs duties at Labrador, though there were several large fishing establishments on that bleak and barren coast—at Esquimaux Bay, Dumpling Harbour, Sandwich Bay, Domino Harbour, Francis Harbour, Battle Harbour, Cape Charles, Red Bay, and Green Bay. These, except the one at Red Bay, which was owned by a Canadian firm, belonged to various merchants of London, Poole, and the Channel Islands. It should be explained that all stores sent from the United Kingdom to the fisheries in British North America were free of export duties, and duty-free on arrival, but the customs collectors in those colonies had to certify on the cockets that the stores were used by the fishermen only. Therefore all such goods sent from the United Kingdom to Labrador had to be taken to Newfoundland, and inspected there by the Customs before being carried to their final destination. Such respectable British captains as brought goods from foreign parts to Labrador also called at Newfoundland, and paid duty there on their cargoes. Such as were not scrupulous took their foreign goods straight to Labrador, and landed them duty-free. Many American vessels fished in the Labrador waters, and of course the shrewd Yankees did not call at Newfoundland on the way, but carried large quantities of tobacco, spirits, etc., straight to the fishing establishments. Thus commercial honour was heavily penalized.

In 1826 the collector of St. John's, Newfoundland, observing that he received next to no duty on goods for Labrador, made an arrangement with William Langley, agent for one of the Labrador fishing firms, that Langley should survey the coast and collect such duties as were payable. He was to receive no salary, but it was hinted that if results were favourable he might be appointed as collector of Labrador. Langley made an elaborate and admirable report of his work. He appears to have gone to considerable expense, and no doubt he sacrificed much personal popularity, for the fishermen were naturally averse to paying duties. In the sturdy old English way, they pointed out that the new system would harass British and favour American interests, for the turbulent Yankees despised all British revenue enactments. The fishers urged that if duties were collected a permanent customs official should be stationed on the coast, with power to protect the British fishermen from the arrogant and persistent encroachments upon the provisions of the Fishery Convention that were practised with impunity by the Yankees. Still, Langley managed to collect a few hundred pounds, and sent the money to Newfoundland. Whether he kept anything for his trouble does not appear. If he did not (the Newfoundland collector expressed full confidence in him), he had reason to repent him afterwards, as others may have done who have put faith in official generosity. He offered to provide a vessel, to visit the coast three times during each season, and collect as much duty as possible, at a salary of £400. No doubt he would have made an excellent officer, and have worked well in the suppression of smuggling and the prevention of encroachment. After doing his best for three years without pay, he had occasion to return to his native land of Devon, and from thence requested compensation for his services. After a deal of correspondence, in the course of which most ungenerous and unwarrantable suggestions were made as to his integrity, he was granted £150! He was a man of great intelligence, and well acquainted with the hard and dangerous life of the seafarer of that time, and it certainly appears that he was treated most scurvily. It is curious to note the departmental methods. In some instances men who did nothing wonderful were surfeited with grants of money and pelted with offers of promotion; in others far superior men *voluntarily* performed the most difficult, distasteful, and dangerous services, and the very fact that they had performed them *voluntarily* was made an excuse for snubbing and starving them.

The Board in 1829 offered Langley the post of collector at Labrador, with an allowance of 25 per cent. on the takings. Considering that at some comfortable ports collectors were maintained at salaries which exceeded their gross duty receipts, the offer was preposterous, and he refused it. He would have had to give up his mercantile connections, to maintain an expensive vessel and crew, and in a way to collect the duties at the point of the cutlass, besides enduring the hardships of constant cruising on that terrible coast. Indeed, the offer was an insult. In no other part of the Empire was a customs man paid by results. No doubt it was not a studied insult, and this puts the tenderers under still worse reflections. It seems that they were unable to understand the extreme meanness of their own proceedings. So, for some years longer, there was no duty collected at Labrador, the Fishery Convention regulations remained a dead letter, and the merchants of Jersey, Poole, and London craved in vain the protection that had been promised by strings of pompous legal clauses. There are people who hold that laws *cannot* benefit commerce, that the trader must work out his own salvation. Whether this be true or no is hard to tell, but it has been made painfully apparent in many a page of history that laws may *hamper and injure* trade, and that, as our plain-spoken fathers would put it, 'most damnably.'

The Corn Laws were amended by Cap. 60 of 9 Geo. IV. The duties under this Act stood thus :

WHEAT (AND IN PROPORTION FOR OTHER KINDS OF CORN).

Price per Quarter.	*Duty per Quarter.* £	s.	d.
62s., and under 63s.	1	4	8
63s., and under 64s.	1	3	8
64s., and under 65s.	1	2	8
65s., and under 66s.	1	1	8
66s., and under 67s.	1	0	8
67s., and under 68s.	0	18	8
68s., and under 69s.	0	16	8
69s., and under 70s.	0	13	8
70s., and under 71s.	0	10	8
71s., and under 72s.	0	6	8
72s., and under 73s.	0	2	8
73s., and above	0	1	0

(If the price were *under* 62s., the duty was to be raised in the proportion of 1s. duty to 1s. price. If the price were 73s. or above, the duty was to be 1s. only. It is evident that the legislators considered 62s. a fair price—a duty exceeding £1 4s. 8d. would at the time be almost prohibitive—and 73s. unreasonably high.)

By Cap. 76 of 9 Geo. IV. several alterations were made in the Consolidated Acts, principally in the form of installing certain provisions which had existed prior to the Consolidation of 1826, and had been overlooked by the compilers. There was a new proviso that manufacturers who claimed bounty on the exportation of double refined sugar should provide the Customs with samples of the goods they intended to export, which samples were to be retained as 'standards' (of quality), and the bounty, previously granted only to sugars refined from goods of the British possessions, was extended to sugars refined from foreign goods. A few of the duties were altered.

In 1828, on account of abuse of the privilege granted to ecclesiastics of importing religious vestments duty-free, and of the same privilege granted occasionally to professional musicians and to surgeons or hospitals with regard to musical and surgical instruments, the Board announced that in future they would disallow all applications to that end, except when 'a flute or a violin or a professional instrument in ordinary use' was imported. (This reads as though an end were put to duty-free importations of ecclesiastical raiment, but the regulation was not enforced strictly, as later we shall take opportunity of showing.)

In 1828 the first regular collector was appointed for Sydney, New South Wales, and the Board provided him with a roll of instructions. (Previous to this the governor had levied such duties as obtained in the colony,* under Cap. 114, 59 Geo. III.; Cap. 8, 1 and 2 Geo. IV.; and

* New South Wales and Tasmania were under one governor till 1825.

Cap. 96, 3 Geo. IV.) The collector was specially bidden to pay the money collected as duties (having first accounted for 'incidents' and officers' salaries) into the hands of the colonial treasurer.

A complaint reached the Board from the governor of Nova Scotia that, although the Secretary of State had fixed the Customs expenditure of the colony at £6,422, the collector had kept back from the year's duties no less than £9,000. The Board inquired into this, and reported to the Treasury that of this amount £1,788 had been retained to meet the expenses of the first quarter of the following year. The Treasury stated their opinion that £1,788 was too much to keep in hand. Below is an extract from the Secretary of State's letter on the subject:

'Under the excitement which has for a considerable time prevailed, not only at the deduction of the salaries from the gross produce of the revenue, but at the large amount and extent of the Customs establishment, Mr. Huskisson considers the retention a proceeding which it would have been much better to avoid.' (The collector of Halifax had £2,000 a year as salary, the controller £1,000.)

The case of the *Adelaide* became very troublesome. She had been seized by Captain Jones, of H.M.S. *Orestes*, early in 1827, and taken to Bermuda. The Vice-Admiralty Court restored her, with costs and damages against Captain Jones. The reasons of seizure and restoration were as follow: Mr. M'Alister, a merchant living at Trinidad, went to Bermuda for his health, taking with him his family and a free coloured woman. At Bermuda he purchased a girl of twelve and a boy of ten to assist the woman, and, as the mother was loath to be separated from her children, he bought her and the rest of her family as well, making five in all. Before doing this he asked the collector of Bermuda if he would be acting legally in taking these people to Trinidad. The collector held that the laws did not define any particular number that might be reckoned as 'domestics,' and that M'Alister's position entitled him to at least the number bought. All that he required the planter to do was to see that the slaves were entered on the ship's clearance according to law, and to carry with him a certificate of the registry of the mother as an adult slave. This was done, but Captain Jones seized the vessel, alleging that M'Alister was *trading* in slaves.

When the Vice-Admiralty Court restored the *Adelaide,* Captain Jones gave notice of appeal. The collector surrendered the *Adelaide* to her owners, but took bond in a large sum to cover result of future proceedings. Then he referred to the Board for advice, and the Board expressed full acquiescence in the decision of the Vice-Admiralty Court. But Captain Jones prosecuted his appeal in the High Court of Admiralty, England, where the decision was reversed, and the penalty of forfeiture affirmed.

The Board, in their subsequent reports to the Treasury, tried to justify their action and that of the collector of Bermuda, maintaining their ground with a stubbornness almost heroic. Yet it is certain they were wrong. Three of M'Alister's slaves were mere children, one being only three years old. How could these be shown to be 'domestics'? By the letter of the law it was a clear case of trading in slaves, even although M'Alister bought most of the slaves from humane motives.

The costs and penalties, as in all such proceedings, were terrific. The owner of the vessel had to pay £748 (her appraised value under the bond) and a fine of £200. Mr. M'Alister lost his slaves (they being condemned to the Crown, and thus emancipated). He had also to pay a fine of £500. The captain of the *Adelaide* was fined £700. But the bill of costs! So huge was it that the seizing officer actually suggested that the penalties might be waived provided the costs were paid (and £100 to the Treasurer of Bermuda, to be used in the education of negroes). We do not find that this was allowed, but the Treasury blamed both Board and collector most severely for giving unsound advice.

There was trouble in St. Kitts over the officers' salaries. In the quarter ending October, 1827, but £1,305 was collected, and only £565 of this went to the colonial treasury, the rest going as salaries and incidents. The island Legislature passed an Act authorizing the treasurer to proceed against the collector for the amount held back as 'salaries,' but the king disallowed the Act. A verdict had been obtained in the island prior to notice of disallowance, so a case went before the superior Court in England as to the costs incurred, the colony claiming that the costs up to date should be paid by the collector. We find no trace of the decision, but the Board, on February 25, 1828, instructed the collector to take credit for his own costs out of the moneys in his hands, so it seems the other costs went against the colony.

Cap. 43 of 10 Geo. IV. amended the Customs laws, and altered a few of the duties. The clauses most important were those limiting to six years the time during which goods which had been exported could be imported duty-free under 'Bill of Store,' and vesting the power of registering ships in the colonies (other than the East India possessions) solely in the collectors and controllers of customs. (Previously the colonial governors had part in the matter.) The Board directed their officers, when dealing with ether imported from the Channel Islands, to charge a countervailing duty of 17s. 6d. a gallon, as it had been found that to manufacture 1 gallon of ether in the United Kingdom 2½ gallons of British proof spirits were required, which paid excise duty at the rate of 7s. per proof gallon. Another order directed the officers to scrutinize all passengers, and be vigilant in the examination of their baggage, as it was expected that a large quantity of jewellery stolen from the Princess of Orange was about to be brought to the United Kingdom. Another directed that an extract from one of the revenue Acts, fixing upon passengers the responsibility of declaring their dutiable goods, should be printed in French and English, and exhibited on board all passenger-ships arriving in the United Kingdom.

Disputes were still raging in the colonies. The collector of Savannah-la-Mar, Jamaica, complained to the Board that the House of Assembly called him up to Kingston on a frivolous pretext, that the journey cost him £30, and would have cost him £100 (currency) if he had not had horses of his own, and many friends who entertained him by the way. The Assembly refused to pay his expenses. It appears that the collector of Falmouth, in the same island, was also called up, and replied that he could not afford the expense, upon which the Assembly sent the sergeant-at-arms to bring him up to Kingston in a chaise. The chaise went over a precipice, and the collector was injured badly, yet the Assembly refused to compensate him, and even tried (unsuccessfully) to make him pay the expenses of their sergeant-at-arms. The Board declined to intervene.

On July 22, 1829, the Board reported upon an application from the Lieutenant-Governor of Malta as to proposed consolidation of Customs and Excise in that island. It appears that the cost of the Maltese Excise was £308, of the Customs £1,317. The Board drew up a scheme, and offered to propose a new tariff (the original duties had been low). They negatived a suggestion that the trifling manufactures of Malta should be allowed into the United Kingdom duty-free.

Some idea of the lucrative nature of a Resident Naval Officer's duties in the colonies may be gathered from the following. The office of Resident Naval Officer at Jamaica was held by patent up to November 22, 1827, the patentee being one King, of Marston House, Frome, England. Mr. King leased the office to one Atkinson, a Jamaican resident, who paid him £1,500 a year. When the patent was revoked, King received from the Treasury an annuity of £1,500 as compensation. Atkinson continued to collect the fees of the office up to 1829, and, when queried by the

Treasury, declared that the colonial Legislature had allowed him to do this up to the time when *they* abolished the office. This seems strange. Probably few in England knew till then whether the office had been abolished or not.

The first regular Australian Customs collector arrived at Sydney, New South Wales, early in 1829, and reported to the Board that on February 2, 1829, he, the controller, the landing-waiter, the collector's clerk, and the controller's clerk, waited on the governor and took the oaths of office. The late acting collector (an official employed by the governor—see p. 151) had rendered his account up to January 31, and paid the money into the provincial treasury. Later the collector reported that convicts were employed in minor public offices. The tide-surveyor's boat was manned by convicts, who received an allowance—the coxswain 10d. a day, the rest 5d. each. On August 17 another report was sent, stating that Newcastle was the only outport, that its import trade consisted of goods (principally British) previously duty-paid at Sydney, and carried to Newcastle by small craft. The exports were coals, and farm produce for the Sydney market. The landing-waiter had been appointed by the governor in 1828, and acted as pilot as well, the river Hunter being navigable forty miles above Newcastle. Along with this report the collector sent an account of the expenses of his survey of Newcastle, including his hotel bill. The items may be interesting. The packet-fare from Sydney was £3 return, the steward's fee 10s. Below is a copy of the hotel bill at Newcastle :

'Breakfast, 2s. 6d. ; lunch, 1s. ; wine, 1s. 6d. ; dinner, 4s. ; porter, 2s. 3d. ; tea, 1s. 6d. ; bed, 2s.

'Breakfast, 2s. 6d. ; bottle of porter, 3s. ; dinner for two, 8s. ; bottle of sherry, 6s. ; port, 3s. 6d. ; tea for two, 3s. ; bed, 2s.

'Settled, N. McClymont, 12th August, 1829.'

(Thus it seems that prices were reasonable at Newcastle in 1829, except the price of bottled porter.)

Later the collector stated that application had been made to load coals at Newcastle, to be used in manufactures and steam navigation in India, and he asked whether such trade was sanctioned by the laws of Navigation, Newcastle not being a free port. The governor had granted shipment provisionally. The Board sanctioned the privilege, extending it to cattle as well.

On October 29, 1829, a person named Lucas wrote the duke of Wellington, accusing the colonial customs officers of conniving at fraud. The duke referred him to the Board, and he communicated with Thames Street. After repeating his previous accusations, he proceeded :

'If you give me encouragement it shall never go higher, which is much to be wished, as if it is made more public blame may be attached to your Honourable Board. If you will, therefore, give me a promise to employ me, you shall know all before it goes to Earl Grey or into the House of Commons. I trust you will, therefore, have the kindness to answer this free of expense, re-enclosing the enclosed. I need only add that the Custom-house officers I mean are men that can hardly write their names, and the lowest in the world, yet have most handsome salaries.'

Minute : '*Read.*' (Strange to tell, this person had been a captain in the army.)

The Assembly of New Brunswick passed a resolution, worded as follows, to the effect that the colony refused to sanction payment of the Customs salaries out of the colonial funds :

'On motion of Mr. Partelow : Resolved unanimously that the House deeply lament that the proposal of H.M. Government on the settlement of the Custom-house question cannot be complied with. The House, in unanimously coming to this determination, do it upon the principle that the House of Assembly are the sole constitutional judges of the proper compensation to be afforded public officers when their salaries are to arise from taxation within the province, and although the House are well satisfied of the necessity of making proper provision for the officers of the Customs, . . . yet they feel bound to say that the scale now proposed is far beyond what the circumstances of the country will admit,' etc.

This resolution reached Sir George Murray, who sent it to the Board *via* the Treasury. Nothing appears as to the result, except an expression of opinion by the governor of New Brunswick that the Assembly were likely to reconsider matters.

During 1829 Mr. G. A. Thompson wrote the Board from ' Woodland Vale Cottage, Woolwich Common,' furnishing a list of subscribers to a supplement to his ' Alcedo ' (a dictionary of America and the West Indies, translated from the work of Colonel Don Antonio de Alcedo). The Board had subscribed to the original work, but they declined to patronize the supplement.

On January 21, 1830, Sir George Murray wrote the Board from Downing Street, asking whether the customs collector at Bathurst, River Gambia, was within his rights in levying fees on the following scale : For a ship's clearance, £1 1s. ; a manifest, 10s. ; a bill of health, £1 1s. ; '*rol d'equipage,*' £1 5s. ; harbour fees, £1 10s. ; bond on appointment of a new captain, £1 10s. ; quarantine fees, £1 1s. The Board replied that he was, the place not being a Crown colony, and the fees being those leviable in Sierra Leone before that place became a Crown colony.

The Nova Scotian House of Assembly had for some time been behaving obstreperously, and it appears that matters had come to such a pass that communication between them and the officials of His Majesty's Council had been temporarily suspended, and the renewal by the Assembly of certain revenue Acts had not received royal sanction. The customs officers, who, of course, were pleased to get a chance of harassing the Assembly, continued to deliver goods from bond, but charged only the duties under Cap. 114, 6 Geo. IV., and let them go free of a certain impost previously charged under the colonial laws, the Act renewing that impost being unsanctioned. A less warrantable feature of their conduct lay in throwing obstacles in the way of furnishing returns which were required by the Assembly. For instance, when the customs warehousekeeper was called to the bar of the

House to give details as to the persons who had cleared goods without being charged impost, he declined to attend till ordered by his superior officers. In the end the collector furnished the returns required, and reported matters to the Board, commencing thus : ' As much temper has been exercised by the popular branch of the Legislature upon revenue matters, it was to be expected that this department would not fail to be visited with the usual share of narrow-minded jealousy from them.' The Attorney-General for the colony upheld the Assembly, and furnished what he considered to be statements of revenue law in support of their action. This brought him into grips with the Customs lawyer at London, who shattered his sophistries in masterly fashion. Below is a summary of the Nova Scotian lawyer's statements and the London lawyer's comments :

Nova Scotian Attorney-General.	Mr. Woodhouse, Inspector and Examiner of Plantation Accounts, Custom House, London.
1. Warehoused goods are liable to the duties which were payable when they were first imported. Time of importation is time of entrance into port.	No. They are not held to be goods ' for duty ' till they are taken out of warehouse for home use.
2. The bond given as security on warehoused goods is treble the duty that was payable at time of importation. This proves proposition No. 1.	No. The bond is but a collateral security, and furnishes no evidence as to the rate of duty which will be charged at delivery.
3. It is the practice to base the *quantity* for duty at delivery upon the account taken at importation.	This is quite sophistical. The quantity has nothing to do with the rate of duty.
4. If the duties were increased between periods of importation and delivery, warehoused goods could not be charged with the extra duty unless a special clause were provided in the Act. Witness certain revenue Acts of the time.	Warehoused goods would be liable to the higher duty at any rate. The introduction of a clause is a mere explanatory device, not absolutely necessary.

(The Board agreed with their lawyer. The file ends April 25, 1832.)

The collector of Sydney, New South Wales, reported that Mr. Rame, of Sydney, had started a shipbuilding establishment at Hokianga, New Zealand, and desired a British register for a schooner which he had built there. The collector asked the Board's advice, as Sydney merchants were forming settlements at several places in New Zealand, intending to grow flax and export spars. A barter trade was already in evidence, muskets, gunpowder, coarse cottons, and spirits being exchanged for flax and spars. The natives, being under missionary influence, refrained from molesting the settlers. The Board replied that as New Zealand was not a British possession Rame's ship was not entitled to a register.

Later the collector announced the arrival of another ship, built at New Zealand by Rame. Her tonnage was 392, and she carried twenty-seven sailors, of whom fifteen were Maoris. Her cargo consisted of seven bales flax, value £15 ; 100 loads timber, value £700 ; and 130,000 feet plank, value £700.

It appears that Rame had memorialized without avail the Secretary of State for the Colonies, and then gone bankrupt. The trustees of his estate had brought the vessel to Sydney, and there, of course, she was detained—(1) for not being properly manned ; (2) for having no register. The trustees entered into bond with the Customs for £10,000, and the vessel and cargo were delivered up, the bond to await the Board's decision.

Soon a Sydney firm of merchants applied for a register for the *Olive Branch.* This vessel belonged to the Rev. William Williams, a missionary located at the Society Islands, and had been built there under his directions. The Naval Officer at the Bay of Islands granted her a pass, and she took a cargo to Sydney. The merchants urged that if she were not allowed to trade the natives, who at present were much attached to the British, and had helped to build the vessel, might admit the Americans. They stated also that a brig built by missionaries at Tahiti many years before had been allowed a register.

The matter was adjusted by the granting of *licences* to the three vessels in question—the *New Zealander*, the *Sir George Murray*, and the *Olive Branch*—to trade between Sydney and New Zealand, and the last-mentioned might also trade to the Society Islands.

Cap. 4 of 1 and 2 Wm. IV. abolished the system of oath-taking in connection with commercial declarations made to the Customs, and substituted written declaration. 'From the frequent occasions,' said the preamble, 'on which such oaths are required, the reverence and respect which should attach to such solemn obligations have been weakened.' A notable release was effected by Cap. 16, which abolished the coastwise duties on coal and slate, and the export duties on coal carried to the British Colonies. Cap. 30 substituted for the varying duties on wine a simple scale, Cape wine brought direct being allowed the easy rate of 2s. 9d. a gallon, and all other wines charged 5s. 6d. The few remaining Customs fees taken by certain clerks in the Long Room were abolished by Cap. 40.

During 1831 instructions were repeatedly issued as to the quarantining of vessels from the Elbe and Weser. Cholera was rampant in the northern parts of Europe. In October of the previous year the British ambassador at St. Petersburg had announced an outbreak of cholera morbus in the interior of Russia, and its resistless advance upon Moscow, and that at Astrachan the governor and nearly all the police had died of this terrible disease.

A Treasury letter of June 3, 1831, directed the admission of religious vestments duty-free, if proved to be *bona fide* effects, imported by a clerical functionary. Still, all such admissions were subject to the Board's permission, and we find it was sometimes withheld. Sacramental plate might only be admitted duty-free by special permission of the Treasury.

Another Treasury letter, dated June 21, 1831, announced that in future superannuation pay at the highest rate would only be granted to officers who had performed specially meritorious services. Another referred to the application made by a Mr. Hudson, of Hull, that leeches, imported in ships which were liable to quarantine, might be freed from the usual detention. 'Allowed, the bags containing the leeches being first immersed in water.'

In the Husband of the 4½ per cent. duties' account for the quarter ending January 5, 1831, appears a list of certain pensioners quartered on that branch of Customs who had not applied for their pensions. The sums thus outstanding were :

	£	s.	d.
Mrs. Batson	28	8	8
Lady Blackwood	56	11	10
Lady de Ameland	208	4	8
The five Misses Fitzclarence	686	16	3
Lord Farnborough	1,500	0	0
Duchess of Gloucester	250	0	0
Mrs. Gordon..	50	0	0
James Grange	62	10	0
Mrs. Hamilton	54	18	11
Miss Hamilton	27	9	5
The Princess Hesse-Hamburg	274	14	6
Messrs. Hosier and Bernard	150	0	0
Messrs. Hobart and Sullivan	400	0	0
Mrs. Huskisson	41	4	2
Sir Sidney Smith	500	0	0

(£5,200 had been paid into the Exchequer—it is to be presumed as the net quarterly proceeds.)

A gentleman prone to research apprised the Board that the Vice-Admiralty Court at New Brunswick was not legally constituted, as no patent or Admiralty warrant had ever been issued to that end. The Board at once communicated with the Admiralty through the Treasury.

Cases of illegal seizure of vessels, through misinterpretation of the Navigation laws, were frequent in colonial waters. The *Bristol*, a colonial ship registered at Kingston, Jamaica, was seized on March 26, 1831, it being discovered that, though registered as a British-colonial vessel, she was in reality owned by foreigners. Such seizure was, of course, perfectly legal. She was condemned in the Vice-Admiralty Court, and sold, the purchasers being her previous owners. She shipped a cargo for a foreign port, and the collector granted her a clearance, but when she reached Port Royal on her outward voyage Captain Gabriel, of H.M.S. *Magnificent*, seized her. When the report reached London, the Board stated that this second seizure was utterly illegal, as there was nothing to prevent foreign ships carrying goods from the colonies to any foreign country, although they might not *bring* foreign goods except direct from the country to which the ships belonged. The Attorney-General for Jamaica opined that the goods were liable to forfeiture, even if the ship were exempt, the captain being an Englishman, but the Board declared otherwise. Indeed, it is hard to discover on what the Jamaica lawyer rested this latter plea, for nothing appears in the Navigation Acts of the time to prohibit an Englishman from commanding a foreign ship owned by a friendly power. The Treasury decided that there was no legal reason for seizure of either ship or goods. Still the seizers carried the case into the higher Court, trying to secure a verdict of 'probable cause of seizure,' and thus escape the costs, even if the seizure were quashed. But the judge declined to certify to that effect, and the huge expenses fell upon the seizers.

Cap. 51, 2 Wm. IV., imposed a salutary check upon the extortion practised in the Vice-Admiralty Courts. It provided that the king might, by Order in Council, amend the practice and fees, and that tables of fees should be exposed in the various courts. Persons aggrieved might claim that the costs charged should be taxed in the High Court of Admiralty. Cap. 48, 2 and 3 Wm. IV., amended the Customs laws. It prescribed an allowance for waste on bonded spirits (much less liberal than the one at present existing). It remodelled the 'stores' regulations. In the old days stores duty-free from bond had been allowed but to naval ships, and in course of time the privilege had been extended to merchantmen, but only as regarded the shipment of Plantation rum for use of crew. By the new Act, all vessels of not less than 70 tons proceeding on voyages likely to last forty days were allowed stores duty-free. The Prisage and Butlerage of the County Palatine were commuted for an annuity of £803, to be paid to the lessee, and after expiration of lease to the Receiver-General of the Duchy, for the king's use. (The statute empowering purchase was passed in 1803; see p. 24.) A few duties were altered and a few drawbacks abolished, and certain treaties of reciprocity existing between the United Kingdom and various foreign powers were reaffirmed.

Cholera had for some time been prevalent on the Continent. On January 27, 1832, the Customs were apprised by the Privy Council that the disease had appeared at Musselburgh, Fisherrow, Morrison's Haven, and Prestonpans. Orders were issued that coasters from infected British ports should be quarantined on arrival. On February 11, 1832, Stockton was scheduled as an infected port, and London was added to the list three days later. Generally speaking, the parts affected were Scotland, the North of England, and London. Canal-boats arriving from infected towns were quarantined. But it was soon found that these drastic regulations were insupportable.

The Board issued a list of articles allowed to be shipped duty-free from bond for use of crew and passengers, and a comprehensive table of 'probable duration of voyages,' by which the quantities issued were to be regulated. Articles allowed: Tea, coffee, cocoa, spirits, raw sugar, molasses, dried fruit, rice, vinegar, soap, and British-manufactured tobacco, for all persons on board; wine, cigars, refined sugar, and beer, for officers and passengers.

Riots occurred in the Mauritius over the appointment of an unpopular Procurator-General, and Mr. D'Epinay, a member of the Council of Government, convened a public meeting in the interests of tranquillity. Colonel Draper, the collector of customs, who was also a member of the Council, seconded a motion that Mr. Jeremie, the unpopular official in question, should be induced to quit the island. The motion was carried with acclamation, and it appears that the Procurator-General was temporarily removed by means which may almost be pronounced forcible. For initiating this action, Messrs. D'Epinay and Draper were ousted from their offices as members of the Council, and the latter was deprived of his collectorship. The despatch sent for this purpose by Viscount Goderich, Secretary of State, may with justice be described as extravagantly worded. Extracts are appended :

'Mr. Jeremie had been the object of the falsest and the basest calumnies. His life had been openly threatened. Sir Charles Colville appealed, with the utmost earnestness and solemnity, to all the better feelings of the community.' Mr. D'Epinay's action was described as 'proposing to calm ungovernable passions, and stifle the clamours of sedition, if not of treason, by defying the king's authority, and trampling upon his Majesty's rightful prerogatives.' Mr. Jeremie was described as replying 'with a degree of promptitude, courage, and ability which do him the highest honour.' 'It may reasonably be supposed that such a manifestation of spirit and talent in a man of unblemished character and spotless integrity, the victim of unjust prejudices and scandalous calumnies, would have had due effect upon his audience.' The despatch ended with a clang, thus : 'All confidence, therefore, between his Majesty's representative and Colonel Draper being thus destroyed, there is but one course to take : His Majesty can have no further occasion for Colonel Draper's services, and you will remove him at once from his office as collector of Customs, and from his seat in the Legislative Council.'

This thunderbolt reached Port Louis, and the governor launched it at Colonel Draper on February 1, 1833. The colonel wrote the Board at once, requesting their good offices. He stated that he had acted with a view to the salvation of the Mauritius and Mr. Jeremie, 'the colony being on the verge of interminable ruin.' 'In early life,' he continued, 'I was page-of-honour to George III., passed eighteen years in the Third Regiment of Guards, and was selected as aide-de-camp to his Majesty George IV. I can with a safe conscience lay my hand to my heart and say, " I have ever served his Majesty with fidelity, sincerity, and ever attached to his Royal Person, his Crown and Dignity." '

The Board referred this halting yet affecting memorial to the Treasury, and the Treasury merely apprised the colonel that the cause of dismissal was not anything he might have done as a member of the Legislative Council. Considerable ill-feeling was excited at Port Louis over Mr. Draper's case, and several members of the Mauritius Legislature temporarily refused to serve on that body, alleging that Lord Goderich's action was an infringement of colonial rights. This contention was undoubtedly just, but it failed to secure Mr. Draper's restoration.

Another case of Customs partisanship occurred in Jamaica. On January 3, 1832, the collector of Kingston had written thus to the Board : ' In consequence of the rebellion of the negro slaves in various parts of the island, and their firing many of the sugar estates, His Excellency the Governor, with the advice of his Council, has proclaimed the island under martial law, so that all business has been suspended during ten days past.' On January 13 the collector at Montego Bay, Mr. Roby, had sent the Board an account of the insurrection (*vide* Illustrative Document, No. 45). It appears that one Burchell, a Baptist missionary living at Montego Bay, had to some extent sympathized with the insurgents (probably but so far as to protest against the severities incidental to martial law). He was indicted on a charge of treason, but the grand jury threw out the bill. On March 13, 1832, a number of whites assembled at Montego Bay with the avowed intention of treating Burchell to a bucket of tar and a roll in feathers, but he succeeded in getting on board H.M.S. *Ariadne*. The authorities at once made arrangements for his removal from the island. This step was opposed by a number of his personal friends, who had assembled in his defence, well equipped to ' repel force by force.' Among these was Mr. Roby, who had armed himself with loaded pistols. Finding that the authorities were resolved upon Burchell's removal, and had actually allowed an American vessel, which had just arrived, to tranship her import cargo to the *Ariadne,* so as to be able to depart promptly to New York with Burchell on board, Mr. Roby seized the transhipped goods, which were technically liable to forfeiture, the vessel that brought them not having reported inwards. The governor freed the goods, and when Roby reported the matter the Board replied with what was practically a severe censure upon the officer, and threw all the expenses of detention upon him as well. But this did not daunt the heroic partisan. He persisted in attempting to justify his conduct, and came out of the trouble, not only much more easily, but to an immeasurable extent more creditably, than Colonel Draper, ex-page-of-honour, guardsman, and aide-de-camp to George III., had come out of his.

Yet another case occurred. On December 5, 1832, the Treasury ratified the suspension of Mr. Fawcett, controller at Savannah-la-Mar, for participation in 'the riots which led to the formation of the political association called the Colonial Church Union in Jamaica.' The Board sent a circular letter to all 'the slave colonies,'* warning their officers against partisanship.

Trouble occurred in Barbados, where the collector, previous to his retirement from the service on superannuation allowance, had kept back £6,037 10s. out of the last year and a half's collection of colonial duties, to pay the customs salaries. Disputes had been frequent in the island on the subject of salaries ever since January 1, 1826 (the date of abolition of the old system of small salaries and huge fees). The new collector had also kept back £1,006 5s. out of a quarter's duties, and the treasurer of Barbados had entered action against him and his pre-

* Antigua, Barbados, St. Kitt's, Nevis, Montserrat, Grenada, St. Vincent, Jamaica, Tortola, Dominica, Trinidad, Tobago, St. Lucia, Demerara, Nassau, Bermuda, and Mauritius.

decessor. The situation was rendered still more interesting by the professed incapacity of the officers to produce the account of duties taken, they alleging that the Customs documents had been destroyed by a recent hurricane. It certainly appears that colonial opinion was rather unreasonable on the point in debate. Under the old system, in all the colonies, there had been continual protestation against the extortion of fees from merchants. So soon as the expense of maintaining the officers was thrown upon the colonies at large, dissatisfaction of a more general kind obtained. No doubt the real reason for complaint was that the officers were not appointed locally, and made responsible solely to the various colonial Legislatures.

The Customs laws were reconsolidated in 1833, the new system coming in force on September 1. All previous Customs and Navigation Acts were repealed by Cap. 50, 3 and 4 Wm. IV., except a few which related to trade conventions existing between the United Kingdom and foreign powers, registration of aliens, British and Irish fisheries, importation of munitions of war, quarantine, and the East India Company's privileges. The management of the Customs department was reconstituted on much the same lines as before, by Cap. 51. The new Act 'for regulation of the Customs' (Cap. 52) reaffirmed in concise form most of the old enactments. The usual prohibitions of tobacco-stalks, tobacco-flour, counterfeit coin, pirated books, certain agricultural products, etc., appeared, and a list of restricted articles. The export prohibitions showed that it was still held desirable to protect British inventions, for they applied to many engines and machines, production of which at the time was almost exclusively British—viz., machines used in woollen, cotton, linen, and silk manufactures, various engines used in the iron trade and in the manufacture of artillery, various presses and dies, all die-sinking tools, machines used in the manufacture of paper and blowing of glass, potters' and saddlers' wheels, and frames for making clothing. The regulations applying to coasters were drastic, probably on account of the prevailing transhipment of contraband goods into coasters at sea.* The 'times of importation and exportation,' which had previously been on many occasions wrangled over in revenue and navigation cases, were clearly defined. 'Time of importation' meant the time when goods were brought within the limits of the port at which they were afterwards discharged; 'time of exportation' meant the time when goods were shipped on the vessel in which they were afterwards carried abroad. These definitions were to apply in cases of dispute as to when duties were imposed, altered, repealed, or when made or repealed, etc. 'Times of arrival and departure' were also defined strictly. 'Time of arrival' was the time at which report of ship was made or should be made; 'time of departure' was the time at which the proper officer of Customs granted final clearance. These latter definitions were for use when questions arose as to charges or allowances upon *ships*, irrespective of cargoes.

A new preventive Act (Cap. 53) appeared, with the usual comprehensive restrictions and appalling penalties as regarded running, signalling, assembling, aiding smugglers, obstructing and assaulting officers, etc., and the usual alluring hints to intending informers. The ancient and damnable proviso (see vol. i., p. 215) reappeared—a proviso that had instigated thousands of oppressive and illegal detentions—that when vessels or goods were seized, and on trial released, and the officers were able to induce the judge who tried the case to put a certificate on the record that there had been 'probable cause of seizure,' the person aggrieved should not be able, in any subsequent action taken by him for damages, to recover more than twopence, nor might the seizer be fined more than one shilling. The Act furnished specimens of the various forms of information, conviction, and commitment.

* Many of these regulations survive.

The new Navigation Act (Cap. 54) was much the same as that of 1826, except that it was more concisely worded. Cap. 55 reproduced most of the old laws of ship's registry under slightly different wording, and Cap. 56 instituted a new table of duties. Compared with the tariff as consolidated in 1826, it showed a few slight increases and a good many slight deductions. Below is a comparison of the two lists, as regards spirits, tea, and tobacco :

	Consolidated Tariff, 1826.	*Consolidated Tariff*, 1833.
	£ *s.* *d.*	£ *s.* *d.*
Spirits of British possessions in America, the proof gallon	0 8 6	0 9 0
Spirits of East India Company's possessions ..	1 0 0	0 15 0
Spirits of British possessions, sweetened ..	1 0 0	1 0 0
Other sweetened spirits ..	1 10 0	1 10 0
All plain spirits, except as above	1 2 6	1 2 6
Tea, per pound (excise duty only)	96 per cent. on gross sale price if 2s. a pound or less ; 100 per cent. if over 2s.	(Excise duty only, but later in the same year made a customs duty varying from 1s. 6d. a pound on common teas to 3s. a pound on the best.)
Tobacco of U.S.A., Russia, Turkey, or East India Company's possessions, leaf, per pound.. ..	0 4 0	(See all other tobacco, below.)
Tobacco of British American Plantations, leaf, per pound	0 3 9	0 2 9
All other tobacco, leaf, per pound	0 6 0	0 3 0
Cigars or manufactured tobacco, per pound ..	0 18 0	0 9 0

A new warehousing Act (Cap. 57) appeared in the Consolidation, and a new Act for bounties and allowances

(Cap. 58). British refined sugar was the only article entitled to *Customs* bounty. Drawback was allowed on silk goods manufactured in the United Kingdom, on foreign barilla used in bleaching linen, on Norwegian deals and timber used in the Irish, Devon, and Cornish mines, on wrought gold and silver, on rice cleaned in the United Kingdom, on tobacco manufactured in the United Kingdom, and on foreign wine exported. The excise drawbacks were on British beer, bottles, bricks, glass, hops, paper, and soap. Many of these allowances had existed prior to re-consolidation.

The new Act (Cap. 59) regulating the trade of the colonies gave warehousing privileges to nineteen already 'free' ports, and permitted private individuals, subject to licence by the East India Company, to trade with China. Another Act (Cap. 60) regulated Manx commerce, altering in some cases the quantities of tea and sugar allowed to be imported there from Great Britain under licence.

These repeated consolidations show that the aversion of the mercantile community to dubiety and complication had its effect upon the legislative mind. This may appear to prove that the legislative mind is not eminently gifted with foresight. Most revenue legislation is opportunistic, for its evolution is really due to officials, and there is no person less interested, as regards the future, than your typical official.

Cap. 73, 3 and 4 Wm. IV., abolished slavery throughout the British colonies. Cap. 85 limited the duration of the East India Company's privileges of government till April 30, 1854, and removed St. Helena from their list of possessions upon April 22, 1834. From the latter date, also, the Company's exclusive right of trading or licensing others to trade in tea, or with China, was to cease. The Company were to close their commercial business as promptly as possible. Cap. 93 prescribed regulations for the new 'open trade.' All British subjects might engage in commerce with the territories 'beyond the Cape of Good Hope as far as the Straits of Magellan.' Three officers were employed to supervise the trade with China, the expense of such establishment to be defrayed by slight tonnage duties levied in China on import vessels and on import goods. Cap. 101 regulated the tea trade. This Act was to come into force simultaneously with the cessation of the East India Company's trade privileges. The collection of the tea duties was to be transferred from the Excise to the Customs (see the new rate of duties quoted in parenthesis at p. 170). Under this Act tea might still only be imported into the United Kingdom from the territories between the Cape of Good Hope and the Straits of Magellan, and into the Channel Islands, the British American possessions, and the West Indies, from the said territories and from the United Kingdom.

Thus the mighty Company's trading privileges ceased, after continuing 233 years, but the directors retained the power (considerably cramped) of 'governing' for a period the districts from which they had derived their revenues, except their victualling port of call, St. Helena. As a matter of course, the St. Helena Customs came under the London Board's control.

The waterguard, and some of the inferior landing officers, at Liverpool had for more than a year been in a state approaching mutiny. Southgate, a surveyor, and Ross, an inspector-general, were extremely unpopular with their subordinates. On October 28, 1834, the collector of Liverpool forwarded to the Board several anonymous threatening letters which had been sent to the two superior officers in question, and specimens of vilifying correspondence which had appeared in the local papers. He asked if any proceedings could be taken. The Customs lawyers stated that nothing could be done, *even if the writers of the letters were discovered.*

One of the letters to Southgate purported to be in the nature of a warning: 'I would have you to take care of yourself as there is a plot laid to take away your life and likewise the inspector-general's by a set of men that is prepared with Pistols and is determined to sell their lives dear. Take this as a warning for as God is my judge they are fixed upon your destruction,' etc. This was signed 'A Warehouseman.' One written to Ross commenced thus :

'Mr. General,

'You are a great man to be sure and receive a great salary but could not your services be dispensed with and the salary you receive be bestowed on the poor men you think so little of. . . . What says the Author of your being if ye oppress the poor and they cry unto me I will hear and avenge them.'

Matters reached such a pitch that the Board resolved upon an investigation, but ere it commenced an officer named Walsh shot Southgate, who died soon afterwards. It appears that there was general exultation amongst the inferior officers over this event, and Mr. Ross received the following *billet-doux* :

'Hell yawns for another Tyrant. Justice calls aloud for a better sacrifice. The greatest wretch still survives. Heaven has decreed his fall and has numbered his days. Don't wrap yourself with the idea that all is over. Thy days are numbered.'

The investigation was held, and the minutes are rather interesting. Many Liverpool merchants gave evidence, and most of them suggested better pay and conditions for the lower outdoor Customs staff. During the year Mr. Walker, an ex-lieutenant of marines, was made inspector of the Liverpool waterguard. He retained that position till 1844, and it seems that the force during that period was but nominally under the control of the Board.

A curious illustration of the amenities of official life is

furnished by certain correspondence which passed between Quebec and Thames Street in 1834. A document signed 'Scrutator' was sent to the editor of *The Settler*, a Montreal paper, accusing the collector of Quebec and the acting collector of Montreal of having obtained promotion by arranging for the undermanning of the Canadian Customs. The editor incautiously published this. About the same time the Board of Customs received an anonymous letter, accusing the collector of Quebec of soliciting influence in his own interest. Mr. Charles Secretan, who had been dismissed from the post of customs clerk at Quebec, was suspected of being the author of these communications. On being accused to that effect, he admitted writing to *The Settler*, but denied the authorship of the letter sent to the Board. For nearly two years longer this pestilent young fellow continued to bombard Board and Treasury with frothy charges against the Canadian Customs. (The volume of incidental correspondence is quite amazing, and productive of wonder that the Board postponed so long their final recommendation to the Treasury to take no further notice of Mr. Secretan or his charges.)

A striking instance of the villainies practised occasionally by colonial collectors occurred at the Mauritius. The American brig *Hindoo*, with a general cargo from Batavia to Amsterdam, put into Port Louis in distress. It was necessary to sell part of her damaged cargo, but this was opposed by the collector, as contrary to the letter of the Navigation laws. The matter was tried in the Vice-Admiralty Court. The Court allowed sale. The collector appealed. The Court upheld its decision, but declined to grant costs against the Crown. Thus the shipmaster, a distressed mariner, was saddled with his own costs, although the collector was merely insisting upon formalities. The collector, still craving power to seize the goods, submitted the case to the Board. The Customs Lawyer's report threw more light on the rascality of the proceedings than any comment of ours could do.

'A ship in distress is not strictly under the Navigation Acts.' It went on to state that, though not expressly exempted by the letter of the law, a distressed ship should be 'by that equity which is used in construing statutes.' But what of the poor shipmaster, who had been forced into enormous outlay?

An extraordinary robbery was committed at the Custom House, London. There was an official there called the Accountant of Petty Receipts, and part of his duty lay in the receiving of moneys paid as fines and forfeitures, including, as a matter of course, the moneys realized at the Customs sales of seized goods. On the evening of November 27, 1834, he locked the 'King's Chest' in his office as usual. It contained £4,000 in Bank of England notes, and £477 in gold. Another official locked it with a master key, then locked the cupboard containing the chest, delivered the key of the cupboard to the person appointed to receive it, and deposited his own key in the proper place in the office of the Accountant of Petty Receipts.

In the King's Warehouse, hard by, was employed one Mott, a customs officer, and he was very friendly with Mr. Huey and Mr. Seale, landing-waiters at the London Docks. These three gentlemen were, in unofficial hours, 'Corinthians' of the deepest dye. Their little ventures with wine, lovely woman, the racecourse, and the prize-ring, had curtailed their resources, and they had laid a plan to rob the King's Chest on the eve following the next Customs sale. They had employed three eminent 'cracksmen,' May, Jordan, and Sullivan. Mott arranged that a friend of his should buy a cask of rum at the sale, and gave Jordan a £50 note with which to pay for it. Jordan went into the Accountant of Petty Receipts' office on the morning of November 27, tendered the note, observed the business of unlocking the chest, and noted also that there was a large sum of money in it. May managed to get himself locked into the Custom House that evening, found the keys, opened the safe, and carried off the contents, which the gang divided with scrupulous fairness the next morning. The consternation of the Accountant of Petty Receipts, when he opened the chest, must be left to the imagination of readers.

The criminals were not discovered till over a year had elapsed. Huey turned king's evidence. Mott, Seale, Jordan, and Sullivan were transported for life. It does not appear that May was captured. A curious circumstance was disclosed during Huey's statement of evidence —viz., that after the robbery he buried his portion of the plunder in Camberwell churchyard, and left it there for a considerable time.

The official papers connected with the robbery contain several documents illustrative of the morbid excitement generated by events of the kind. One is from a Jew, accusing another Jew, and implicating a young fellow who was a clerk in the office of Petty Receipts. (In consequence of this letter the young man was subjected to close surveillance and exceedingly unjust treatment.) Another letter is from 'Jane Wilson,' and conveys in execrable English the writer's suspicions of 'a person acquintit with the party as gout the notes.' A paper-hanger of South Lambeth also wrote of the suspicious conduct of his next-door neighbour, 'a young woman often visited by a round-faced young man.' And now and then came bewildering missives, addressed to the Custom House, from Miss Casey, an insane female who persisted in signing herself as 'Lady St. John.'

The Nottingham manufacturers had memorialized the Treasury in 1833, praying that stricter measures might be taken to prevent the exportation of bobbin-net machinery. The Board of Customs issued a minute inciting officers to vigilance, and instructing them to allow no machinery to be shipped until it had been inspected by the landing-surveyors. Meantime the Committee representing the manufacturers published a circular, dated from the Star Inn, Nottingham, offering rewards for information which might lead to seizure of the articles of machinery specified, or to the detection of foreigners engaged in pirating them, or in seducing artificers to go abroad. The Manchester Chamber of Commerce approached the Treasury in 1834. The petition commenced: 'Your memorialists have been informed and believe that machinery has of late been illegally exported to a great extent, and that doubts exist as to the powers of making seizures among the officers of Customs, some of whom have disputed the opinion of the law officers of the Crown.' It continued that there was a practice in vogue of obtaining licences for the shipment of 'unrestricted' machinery, and under cover of the said licences exporting goods the shipment of which was prohibited. The memorialists asked that a bill making prohibition comprehensive and licence exceptional might be submitted to Parliament. 'The whole value of the machinery in our cotton mills, which we have been so many years in accumulating, falls greatly short of the value of one year's exportation of the produce of our cotton factories.' (From this they argued that the nation would lose comparatively little if the exportation of machinery were restricted more closely.)

By Treasury Minute of July 1, 1834, the following ports were approved for importation and warehousing of goods from China and the East Indies: London, Liverpool, Bristol, Hull, Leith, Glasgow, Greenock, Port Glasgow, Dublin, Cork, and Belfast. Newcastle was added later. This proceeding had been made necessary by the abolition of the East India Company's charter of trade, under which most articles imported from the Company's dominions had been landed at London, and warehoused under the Company's custody (see footnote, p. 23).

Cap. 15 of 4 and 5 Wm. IV. abolished the Exchequer offices of Auditor, Tellers, Clerk of Pells, and the 'offices subordinate thereto,' and established instead of these a Comptroller-General, with a salary of £2,000 only. This official and his subordinates were to execute their duties in person. The books, records, and standard weights, measures, coins, etc., were to be handed over to him on

October 11, 1834, and on that day the tellers were to pay into the Bank of England all the money in their hands that belonged to the Crown. All such public moneys as had, during at least 700 years, been payable into the ancient Court at Westminster, were in future to be paid into the Bank of England by the various collecting departments, to the credit of the national Exchequer, and were to form a special fund in the Bank's books. Issues were to be paid by the Bank under sign-manual or Treasury warrant. The Treasury might authorize payment without royal order, whenever money granted by Parliament was to be paid out of the Consolidated Fund, or any other fund specially appropriated to any particular service. In all payments fractions of a penny were to be disregarded. The Exchequer fees were abolished.

Cap. 34 abolished the system, enforced under Cap. 21 of 7 and 8 Wm. III., of deducting 6d. per month from the wages of seamen as a contribution towards the revenues of Greenwich Hospital. The average sum thus obtained had amounted to £22,000 per annum. Under the new Act an annual grant of £20,000 was made to the funds of the hospital.

Cap. 49* announced that, in spite of the provisions of Cap. 74, 5 Geo. IV. (see p. 46), many sets of weights and measures of the old types had been stamped and passed in the Exchequer as models of the standards prescribed by the said Act, although in some cases they were highly incorrect as regarded shape ; therefore so much of Cap. 74, 5 Geo. IV., as laid down that all weights and measures should be according to certain Exchequer standards was repealed, and the erratically-shaped articles were declared legal. But copies of the imperial standards were to be sent to the various counties and burghs, and the magistrates were to decide where these were to be located, and to appoint local inspectors of weights and measures. The 'stone' was to be 14 pounds in all cases (previously the London 'stone' had been 8). All weighed articles were

* Amended by Cap. 63, 5 and 6 Wm. IV.

to be sold by avoirdupois, except gold, silver, platina, precious stones, and retailed drugs. It is curious that most of the old Acts relating to weights and measures had to be amended owing to blunders made by the Exchequer officials.

Cap. 89 amended the Customs laws, providing that in future duty should be charged on salved goods sold to meet expenses in cases of wreck, that the provisions relating to spirits imported in casks should apply to goods of that kind when imported in vessels not strictly casks, but answering the same purpose, and altering the duties on a few articles. It provided that the East India Company, though their charter had expired, might still import and warehouse goods.

No Customs Acts of any importance appear on the statute-book during 5 and 6 Wm. IV.

Proclamations were made by the presidents of St. Kitt's, Nevis, and Montserrat, allowing temporary importation of articles, contrary to the laws of Navigation, and duty-free, on account of the great distress caused by the hurricane of August 12, 1835. The necessary bills were directed to be prepared, by which the imperial Parliament might indemnify the governors.

On February 23, 1835, the House of Assembly, Lower Canada, directed Mr. Jessopp, collector of Quebec, to furnish a return of passenger vessels entered at Quebec during 1834. He suggested that the order should come through the governor. On February 28 the Assembly passed a resolution, directing the sergeant-at-arms to arrest Mr. Jessopp for contempt. Mr. Jessopp apprised the governor, who supported his contention. But Mr. Papineau, Speaker of the Assembly (a representative of 'the extreme French party' in the province), issued a warrant to the sergeant-at-arms, and on March 2 Mr. Jessopp wrote from Quebec gaol to the governor, stating that he was about to apprise the Board of Customs that he had been incarcerated. He wrote accordingly on March 6, informing the Board that the colony was in a state of great excitement. (Annexed to the file is a copy of *The Vindicator and Canadian Advertiser,* which bears out Mr. Jessopp's statement.) Many of the British-descended colonials formed themselves into a 'Constitutional Association,' and sent an address to the imperial Parliament, stating that their liberties were endangered by the preponderance of 'the French vote,' and lamenting the partial handing over of revenue administration to the House of Assembly. On March 19 the controller wrote the Board that the governor had prorogued the Assembly and released Mr. Jessopp. On June 13, 1835, Lord Glenelg sent a despatch to the governor, stating that the customs officers' duties were ministerial, and that there was no just reason for the officers objecting to answer questions put by the Assembly, or to furnish any documents required. The officers were to be directed to obey the Assembly's injunctions in future.

The encroachments made by American fishermen still formed ground of complaint by the British North American customs officers. The preventive officer at Gaspé informed the collector of Quebec that theAmericans came close to the shore, and caught bait in defiance of the terms of Treaty and Convention, that they refused to obey his orders to quit, and that one of them—master of the *Bethel*—treated him 'with scurrilous contempt.' The collector apprised the Board, who referred the matter to the Treasury. The governor of Canada wrote to Washington, and the American Government directed the American collectors of customs to warn the fishermen against encroaching. Meanwhile the preventive man at Gaspé asked that an armed vessel might be sent to cruise between Anticosti and Point Miscou, and later the Quebec collector apprised the Board that H.M.S. *Champion* had been put to this employment.

The people of Carbonear, Newfoundland, sent a memorial, with 490 signatures, to the king, furnishing statistics of local shipping and trade, and praying that

Carbonear might be made a free port. The people of Harbour Grace, and the adjacent ports of Bay Roberts, Port de Grave, and Brigus, sent a similar memorial, with 1,074 signatures. (By Treasury Order of October 28, 1835, Harbour Grace was declared a free port.)

The newly-created Legislature of Newfoundland had framed certain laws of revenue, and directed the collector to gather the duties appertaining. It appears that he performed this with an ill grace, and during 1835 he complained to the governor, stating : 'I must observe that I consider this attempt to impose the collection of these duties on the officers of this department is illegal.' He asked the Board to secure him compensation for the additional work, but they directed him to comply with the Legislature's wishes as expressed through the governor, and to ask the governor to provide such assistance as was necessary. They also told him to bear in mind that his salary had been increased from £600 to £800, and that all the Customs expenses in Newfoundland were paid out of the proceeds of Newfoundland taxes.

On May 8, 1835, the Treasury apprised the Board that they had authorized the coinage of silver pieces of the value of 1½d. and 3d. for circulation in the West Indies, and that the customs officers there might receive such coins at the nominal rate. (This was done at the request of the employers of apprenticed coloured labourers.)

The correspondence between the Antipodes and Thames Street during 1835 was rather interesting. First appeared a statement from the collector of Sydney that an establishment of British subjects, provisioned from Sydney, had been formed at Otago, New Zealand, for whaling purposes, by Mr. Joseph Weller, a Sydney merchant. The collector stated that this was but one of several establishments formed during the last ten years, and that the whalers had been in the habit of sending their oil to Sydney, where he had admitted it duty-free, as was the method with all New Zealand products, and then he had allowed it to be shipped to the United

Kingdom as of colonial taking. Mr. Weller was desirous of sending the oil *direct* from New Zealand to the United Kingdom, and wished to know if it would be admitted there at the low rate as colonial-taken. The Customs lawyers objected to this, stating that New Zealand was not a British colony, and the goods would be liable to the duty on foreign-taken oil (£26 12s. a tun, instead of 1s.). The oil must first be shipped to Sydney, and its method of taking certified there; then it might be admitted in the United Kingdom at the low rate as before.

An Order in Council of November 20 constituted Sydney (New South Wales) and Hobart Town and Launceston (Tasmania) free warehousing ports.

On account of repeated reports made since 1831, an officer had been stationed at Botany Bay, to check the extensive smuggling of spirits and tobacco that prevailed in that district. His quarters were in 'The Round Tower.' The collector of Sydney desired that an officer should also be stationed at Broken Bay, 'one of the most populous districts in the colony,' but it does not appear that this was complied with. It is hard to conceive that a solitary officer could be any check upon smuggling in a place like Botany Bay, the abode at that time of many desperadoes. The collector reported cheerily on the matter in 1834-1835, stating that the contraband trade had been subdued to a considerable extent, that the population of Botany Bay was increasing, and that the local Government had commenced to dispose of land in small lots to private individuals 'of the humbler grade of life.'

An application reached the Board from one Egan, a bookseller living at Kingston, Jamaica. In 1834 he had purchased at the Jamaica Customs sales a number of pirated books, seized on landing from New York, and condemned to be sold for exportation. He shipped the books for the United States of America, and then had them re-landed, and the customs officers, being told of this, re-seized them at his shop in Harbour Street, Kingston.

He was fined £100 and £98 costs, and petitioned the Board for relief, but no relief was granted. We furnish a list of the titles, which may supply a hint as to the literature in demand at Jamaica :

Eugene Aram.	Moore's Melodies.
Devereux.	The Vicar of Wakefield.
Paul Clifford.	The Disowned.
The Water-Witch.	Love and Pride.
Lionel Lincoln.	Pelham.
The Bravo.	Mothers and Daughters.
Zohrab.	The Scottish Chiefs.
The Children of the Abbey.	Scott's Poetical Works.
The Arabian Nights.	Moore's Works.
The Pilot.	Byron's Works.
The Abduction.	History of England.
The Red Rover.	The Saracen.
Almack's Revisited.	

The collector of Port Louis, Mauritius, appealed to the Board of Customs. He had refused to pay the 'Caisse de Bienfaisance,' a graduated communal tax, or poor-rate, levied in the island on all persons 'not destitute of means.' He pleaded that the commissariat officials in the Mauritius were exempt, that the customs men had a claim to similar immunity, and that a committee of appeal which formerly officiated, and to which claims were formerly submitted, was no longer in existence, so that the tax was levied at the discretion of the Mauritius officer of Inland Revenue (between whom and the customs men it is likely no great love existed, if the ancient histories of the rival departments, both in the United Kingdom and the colonies, may be relied upon). He also hinted that his salary was inadequate, but the London Customs Lawyer, Mr. Thackeray, informed him that he was liable as a resident. (It may be interjected here that there was still considerable tension of public feeling in the colony, and that in 1833 a gentleman of French extraction, named Malvery, had drubbed and kicked the customs controller in the public street of St. Louis, and escaped with a light sentence, to the unbounded and piteously-expressed disgust of Mr. Jeremie, the unpopular Procurator - General. And when the matter was reported to the Customs Board the lawyers found fault with the collector's method of prosecuting Malvery, and the Board merely marked the paper 'Read.')

The practice of granting 'merchants' samples' of spirits was regularized in 1836. One free sample was granted at importation. If the goods were bonded and required for sale a second free sample was granted. If they were afterwards exported a sample was allowed on delivery for shipment. Thus, if a merchant imported 100 casks, warehoused them for a few days, and then exported them, he could have 300 samples duty-free, though not a penny of duty would be paid except the 10s. per cent. on all exported goods.

During 1836 the Treasury directed the Irish Coastguard to cooperate with the 'revenue police,' a body under the control of the Board of Excise (with a view to the preventing of illicit distillation). The Excise Board issued over 100 excise commissions to officers of the Irish Coastguard.

The Treasury apprised the Board that the French ambassador in London had complained as to the seizure of certain goods at Berbice and Demerara in 1835. From an inspection of the files it appears that the collector of Berbice in 1835 was a thorough dipsomaniac, and that he was on terms of friendship with a notorious smuggler named Graimo, captain of the French schooner *L'Aurore*. Graimo had a smuggling connection in Demerara, and had managed to keep it going by the following ingenious method. He went to Surinam and loaded with Dutch gin. Of course he could not legally carry the goods into a British possession. They could only be taken thither in a Dutch ship, and direct from Holland. But Graimo carried them to Berbice, and the drunken collector allowed him to land them as though brought legally under the Navigation laws, and charged the duty (1s. a gallon). Then the goods were carried to Demerara by a colonial vessel, and landed there as from a British possession.

This breach of the Navigation laws endured until the governor of Berbice suspended the collector for being chronically intoxicated, and appointed an inquisitive deputy, who discovered the frauds. Only fifty cases of gin could be seized ; the rest had disappeared. The seized goods were forfeited, and Graimo was fined £100. In consequence of the interposition of the ambassador, the Treasury allowed the duty paid on the fifty cases of gin at Berbice to be returned, and waived the penalty of £100, apprising Lord Palmerston of their decision.

The collector of St. John's, Newfoundland, submitted a peculiar case for the Board's consideration. A British vessel from Lisbon had arrived at Newfoundland, and the captain in his report declared his crew as 'all British.' The collector found that three of the crew were foreigners, and took the Solicitor-General of Newfoundland's opinion on the matter, which was to the effect that the master was liable to a penalty of £10 for each foreigner reported as a Briton. The Customs Lawyers at London concurred, and stated that the master was also liable to a penalty of £100 for making a false report. But the Board declined to recommend proceedings.

The collector of Launceston, Tasmania, reported that part of the *Haines*, a hulk used as a place for convicts at that port, had been turned into a bonded warehouse, and that large quantities of the spirits stored there had been missed. On a search being made among the soldiers employed in guarding the hulk, many bottles of spirits were discovered, and others were found in the adjacent barracks.

The *Tres Milhas*, a Portuguese schooner with 282 slaves on board, was brought into Port Antonio, Jamaica, by H.M.S. *Racer* on June 14, 1837. Ten of the slaves had smallpox, and the whole consignment was quarantined at Navy Island. The Portuguese crew were released, and sent to Cuba. It appears from the report that the schooner was in a very leaky condition, and the slaves were packed so closely on board that they had barely room to stretch their limbs. 'The poor creatures,' wrote the collector, 'are in high spirits. It has been asserted that they were all inoculated for the smallpox previous to leaving Africa.' The Africans were released from quarantine and apprenticed on December 26, 1837, and the expense of their detention, being £1,837, was defrayed by the colony.

A meddlesome person wrote from Hobart Town to the Board, reminding them that some years back he had apprised them of extensive smuggling from Dieppe into Brighton, and stating that he had since discovered another fraud. He accused the Hobart Town merchants of buying American-taken oil, and shipping it to the United Kingdom as British-taken. He announced himself as an ex-shipowner, and forwarded the message through his son, a solicitor in Cheapside. It appeared on inquiry that the information was quite inaccurate.

On May 25, 1837, the collector of Grenada reported that H.M. brig *Harpy* had captured, off the coast of Martinique, the Portuguese schooner *Florida*, with 280 slaves. 112 of the slaves had volunteered for the 1st West India Regiment, and been sent to join that corps at Trinidad. The rest had been indentured to planters in Grenada. All the negroes had been vaccinated before landing, smallpox being rife at Grenada.

On May 24, 1837, the collector of Dominica reported the capture, by H.M.S. *Griffin*, of the Portuguese brig *Don Francisco*, with 433 slaves, all of whom were landed in good health and spirits, and apprenticed within seven days. The collector ignored the terms of the old indenture form enjoined by the Order in Council of March 16, 1808, which provided that in such cases the female slaves should not be put to field labour. That form, he pointed out, had been framed when slavery existed in the British colonies. (Why the fact that slavery had been abolished should warrant such disregard of an order which subscribed to the dignity of woman may not be evident to the reader, certainly it is not to the writers of these pages.) The *Don*

Francisco was condemned, sold to a Britisher, and granted a British register.

Cap. 92 of 1 and 2 Vict. repealed the 4½ per cent. duties. The Board communicated with the collectors of the Leeward Islands, asking what reductions might be made in the various colonial establishments on account of the discontinuance of the duties.

Cap. 113 of 1 and 2 Vict. abolished the Customs Receivers' privilege of appropriating the 'odd pence' out of the final sixpence when duties were paid, and made droits of Admiralty liable to duty when sold. It contained a clause dealing with British marks on foreign goods, but applying only to cutlery and hardware. It freed officers of the Coastguard and Mounted Guard from turnpike tolls when on duty, and empowered the Board to render traffic between neighbouring colonies coastwise trade. The provisions of the Conventions of Commerce made in 1818 with the United States of America and Portugal were extended to all foreign countries with which treaties of commerce had been subsequently made, or might be made in times to come.

A firm of Liverpool bacon importers approached the Treasury, stating that the allowance for waste on foreign hams while warehoused under bond was insufficient. (The hams were weighed at importation, and on delivery from bond a certain deduction was made from the import weight for duty, to account for the 'waste' that took place by drying.) The Treasury increased the allowance to 5 per cent. for the first twelve months, and 6 per cent. for any longer period.

A curious official dispute was reported to the Board from St. Kitt's. The controller charged his clerk, Mr. Charles Augustus Berkeley, with disobedience, disrespect, and an attempt to provoke a breach of the peace. Berkeley denied the charge 'totally and unequivocally.' (The customs men of the period were fond of 'fine writing.') He stated that the controller insulted him while he was 'anxiously and intently engaged in making up the complicated quarterly accounts.' The statement of exculpation continued: 'Casting upon me a look of vengeance, he' (the controller) 'said, "You are a d—d impertinent fellow, and if you were not in a public office I'd break your head." What reply did I make to this abuse, this insult? Not a word! I felt, God knows I felt keenly, but I governed my temper. I uttered not a reply, but calmly continued to do the public business.' The Board directed Berkeley to obey his superior officers, and the controller to refrain from using intemperate language.

On November 6, 1838, four casks were landed at St. John's, New Brunswick, the contents being entered as 'copper spikes' (duty-free). On being opened they were found to contain copper tokens. (A specimen of the tokens is annexed to the file. It is a fine copper coin, almost the size of a penny. On one side is a head—certainly not the queen's—and the wording, 'Pure Copper, preferable to paper.' On the reverse side is an allegorical figure, the date 1838, and the wording, 'Trade and Navigation.') Inquiry elicited that the coins had been made in Birmingham, to the order of a person living at Strabane, Ireland, and this person had just been bailed on a charge of uttering base coin.

The London Customs Surveyor-General and the Customs Solicitor differed as to the legality of the importation, the former holding that the goods were not liable to seizure, as they did not purport to represent with any great similarity coins then in use, but were merely intended to be used as convenient articles of circulation. The Solicitor held that the coins were base, though not counterfeit, and insisted that the laws were intended to prohibit all but legal tenders. The Bench officers in the Long Room were consulted, and they sided with the Surveyor General, holding that the goods were 'not coins.' The Board directed release, and when in the following year 25 hundredweight of tokens were seized at St. John's, Newfoundland, they made a similar order.

Lieutenant Robinson, of H.M.S. *Skipjack*, seized the

American schooner *Concord* for encroaching on the fishing limits. The seizure note read as follows :

Cause of Forfeiture.	*Goods.*	*Value.*
At anchor off the S.W. Point of Grand Manan. For breach of treaty with H.B. Majesty and the U.S.A., having set nets to catch fish within the limits of the British territory—say, within three miles from the shore.	Quantity said to be about 30 quintals of cod, hake, and haddock (green),* caught by citizens of the U.S.A. in a vessel of that country called the *Concord*, of East Machias, burthen about 26 tons.	Fish, £25 (currency). Schooner, about £30 (currency).

(The master's name given as J. Adams ; the owners' names as J. Foster and Jabez Norton, all of Great Machias.)

After a month had elapsed from date of seizure (no word being received of appeal) the collector condemned and sold the vessel as though seized under the revenue laws (sect. 25, Cap. 89, 4 and 5 Wm. IV.). He then submitted his proceedings for the Board's approval, stating : 'As this is the first case of the sort which has occurred at this port, we trust we have acted legally.' The Customs Lawyers reported that the vessel was justly liable to forfeiture, and that the collector had dealt with her in the proper way.

Certain Liverpool shipping agents inquired of the Board whether a Sicilian or Neapolitan vessel, loaded or in ballast, might go from Liverpool to Newfoundland, take in a cargo of fish, and carry it to Italy or the Sicilies, also whether such a ship might go, loaded or in ballast, from England to Newfoundland, or whether she lay under any disability compared with British vessels. The Customs Lawyer reported that she might not carry goods from England to Newfoundland, nor was he aware of any Order in Council permitting her to load there. The Bench officers reported that no foreign ship might carry

* Uncured.

goods laden in the United Kingdom to Newfoundland, and that no Sicilian or Neapolitan ship might load there. (The prohibition of loading must have obtained because the King of the Sicilies did not grant reciprocal rights to British commerce. Otherwise the vessel might have gone from England in ballast, and loaded fish for any foreign port whatever.)

A British-American syndicate submitted a case to the collector of Jamaica, who referred it to the Board. They desired to establish a line of steamboats between New York and Kingston, and wished to know if they could obtain British registers for the ships. The collector opined that if the company were composed of Americans only the ships could only bring American produce. For instance, they could not bring goods from St. Thomas's. But part were Britishers. Could *these* have British registers for such of the ships as they owned? No, because the profits were to be pooled with the Americans. But the Bench officers in London held that the pooling of profits would not affect the privileges of such of the ships as were *exclusively* owned by Britishers. The Board concurred.

Cap. 44 of 2 and 3 Vict. prohibited temporarily the carrying of cargo on deck by timber ships from British North America during the period from September 1 to May 1. This was on account of 'great loss of life and severe sufferings' occasioned by reckless deck-loading. (The regulation was continued by subsequent enactments, and extended to ships from Honduras, and is still in existence.) Each captain on arrival in the United Kingdom was to produce a certificate from the British North American collectors of customs, to the effect that all the cargo was under hatches when the vessel left North America.

A Treasury letter of January 22, 1839, called for a report from all the collectors of the United Kingdom as to their method of enforcing the Emigration Acts. It appears that Dr. Poole, the 'inspecting physician of emigrants' at Grosse Isle, Lower Canada, had reported that the medical superintendence on emigrant vessels was extremely defective. He stated that most of the persons calling themselves surgeons of emigrant ships were unlicensed students, or apothecaries' apprentices and shopmen, with little professional knowledge, and that the lists of passengers certified to by the British customs collectors were seldom correct, which rendered it difficult to find out the number of deaths during voyage. The passenger accounts were falsified from two motives, the ages being often understated so as to evade the colonial emigrant tax, and the passenger space encroached upon by counting adults as children.

A Liverpool merchant named Holt had entered at various times large quantities of glass for exportation on excise drawback, and the customs searchers of the port, whose duty it was to examine the goods at shipment, and ascertain whether they corresponded in quantity and value with the statements on the specifications, had been in the habit of passing them without examination, and in some cases even allowing shipment before the specifications were produced. Holt had taken advantage of this to ship ordinary rough goods not entitled to drawback, and had thus defrauded the Excise to the extent of £70,000. The fraud was discovered in 1839, and the officers appear to have got off rather easily. The senior searcher was dismissed, the others were reprimanded, and the inspector-general and landing-surveyors of the port were censured.

New instructions were issued as to dealing with packages brought for foreign ministers. Any package produced by a messenger, and declared to be a despatch-box, was to be passed at once without search, unless the officers had suspicion, in which case they were to apprise the Board. Packages declared to contain goods for foreign ministers were to be put in the Queen's Warehouse, to await a Treasury Order.

In paying to the island treasury the duties collected

under Cap. 59, 3 and 4 Wm. IV., the collector of Dominica tendered no less than £98 0s. 4d. worth of 2d. and 4d. silver pieces, which the treasurer refused to accept, but in the end the governor directed him to take the money.

The House of Assembly, Upper Canada, sent a petition to the queen, praying that the prohibition of the importation of tea from the United States of America to Canada might be removed, and that such tea might be allowed to come in on payment of a certain duty. The Customs Lawyers were accordingly directed to draft a bill to that end, the amount of duty leviable to be settled by colonial Statute. The file contains statistics of tea exported from the United Kingdom to British North America and the West Indies :

	To British North America.	*To British West Indies.*
	Lbs.	Lbs.
1837	1,193,987	64,330
1838	1,397,837	73,435
1839	1,722,622	59,795

The Board had directed inquiry to be made as to revenue matters at Broken Bay, New South Wales. The commander of the *Prince George* revenue cutter, stationed at Sydney, furnished a report, stating that about twenty vessels traded to the Hawkesbury, and that the population of Port Stephen was fast increasing. 'The Australian Agricultural Company hold all the land there.' He proceeded that Twofold Bay was used by vessels in the cattle trade, that Jervis Bay was used but as a place of shelter, and that there was a coasting trade between Port Macquarie and Wollongong. He had visited Western Port, but found no vessels there ; and he had not heard of any smuggling. In 1839 the collector of Sydney reported to the Board that Botany Bay had a revenue cutter to watch the large vessels that frequently put in in distress, and to check the smuggling. She had made no captures, but had been of service in recovering small vessels carried off by convicts, in saving wrecked mariners, and in communicating on Government business with various places along the coast.

A return of trade in Ceylon for the five years ending 1839 is annexed to the file, and reads as below :

	Imports (*Value*).	*Exports* (*Value*).
	£	£
1835	352,076	199,267
1836	411,167	334,519
1837	541,239	326,860
1838	490,083	292,315
1839	510,664	375,608

(The principal article of export trade was cinnamon. From June 1, 1839, to May 31, 1840, 374,530 pounds cinnamon were exported.) A Customs survey of 1839 gives the following description of outports and commerce in Ceylon :

Imports.	Exports.
Jaffna: Paddy, rice, cloth, earthenware.	Madder, tobacco, ebony.
Manar: Paddy, rice, cloth.	Madder, dried fish, gingelly-seed.
Trincomalee: Paddy, rice, cloth.	Beeswax, gingelly-seed, ivory, ironwood.
Batticaloa: Paddy, rice, cloth, iron, brassware.	Beeswax, cocoanuts, ivory, timber.
Muletivu: Paddy, rice, cloth, earthenware.	Beeswax, cocoanuts, jaggery, bark, and timber.

Cap. 17 of 3 and 4 Vict. increased the Customs duties by 5 per cent. on all goods except spirits, corn, and flour, and the drawbacks, bounties, and allowances, in the same proportion. The duty on imported spirits was increased by 4d. a gallon. Cap. 19 removed this impost from timber, and replaced it by a string of additional specific duties. The Passenger Act was extended by Cap. 21 so as to apply to the passenger trade from the West Indies, Bahamas, and Bermuda. By Cap. 56 ships belonging to native princes or states having subsidiary treaties or being in alliance with the East India Company were admitted to the privilege of British ships within the limits of the East India Company's charter.

The Treasury apprised the Board of a despatch from Lord Palmerston, stating that information had been received that the Carlist commander, Cabrera, had sent money to England for the purchase of 20,000 muskets. An order was therefore issued that all shipments of arms should be notified to the Treasury.

The first consignment of fish-oil from the Malabar coast arrived. The quantity was 15 butts only. It was admitted by Treasury order at the low duty (1s. a tun), and directions were issued that all subsequent consignments should be passed at the same rate if caught by his Majesty's subjects.

The first case of removal of coffee from bond for husking purposes occurred at Greenock. (This is a common practice at the present day. The goods are frequently imported in husk, and removed under bond to places where the husk is removed. They are then returned to bond, reweighed, and taken to account for duty at the new weight.)

An order was issued in November, 1840, to the effect that, the Baltic traders and whalers having returned, the Coastguard officers and collectors were to use their best endeavours to obtain able volunteers for the navy.

The Governor-General of Canada informed Lord Russell that the provisions of the Passenger Acts were still in many cases disregarded (see p. 191). He instanced two vessels which had brought emigrants from Westport. They had been seven weeks on the voyage. Provisions ran short, and for a long period the steerage passengers were in a state of semi-starvation. In another case the captain had charged extortionate prices—37s. 4d. a hundredweight for bread which cost 17s. 6d., 3d. a pound for barley which cost 1½d., 'and other things in proportion.' (These matters illustrate the spirit in which the collectors and Emigration officers approached their work, and prove that the average shipmaster is by no means the jovial, open-handed, open-hearted person that song and story have combined to make him.)

The collector of Dominica reported that on April 26, 1840 (Sunday), he went on board three vessels belonging to St. Kitts, St. Lucia, and Dominica, seized their pendants, which they were flying in contravention of Sect. 11, Cap. 13, 4 Wm. IV., and then informed the captains they were liable to a penalty of £50 each. This produced petitions from the terrified shipmasters, which the collector forwarded, with a statement that he had taken bond for the penalties, pending the Board's decision. The Board directed him to cancel the bonds, and to refer to the governor for instructions in future, before seizing pendants or flags. It is evident the penalty was one of a kind frequent in the British Statute-books—a 'bogey' penalty—and the law on the matter one of those peculiarly British laws which shrewd men never dream of enforcing.

It appears that the colonial governors still shared in the proceeds of seizures under the revenue and Navigation laws. On June 5, 1840, the earl of Gosford applied to the Board from Park Place, St. James's, London, for his share of the Montreal seizure proceeds, due to him as governor of Lower Canada. The amount (£85 3s. 1d.) was paid to him.

During 1840 a committee of the Nova Scotian House of Assembly made certain statements to the governor. They recommended that the Nova Scotian Customs and Excise should be amalgamated, and stated that under the existing system, when goods were cleared at landing, three customs and two excise entries were required, and that when goods were warehoused four customs and three excise entries were called for, and that at some of the outports the customs and excise offices were miles apart. They urged that the collectors should be placed under local control, and the London Board's powers abolished. (It appears that in Canada and Newfoundland the customs and excise duties were collected by one staff.) The committee also stated that some of the officers appointed by the home authorities were unsatisfactory, and when the governor asked for proof the following reply was given : ' The House has considered that the statement did not require any evidence in support thereof, the same being well known to many of the members and to the public, and accordingly no evidence was taken by the committee thereon.' The papers were referred to the London Board, who merely marked them ' Read.'

The Roman Catholic vicar of Newfoundland memorialized the Board, stating that he ordered three church organs for the use of various Catholic churches in the colony, that the goods were sent out in a colonial-built ship via Hamburg, and that in consequence of the vessel's having called at Hamburg the Newfoundland customs officers charged him the duty payable upon foreign manufactured organs (£71 0s. 8d.). On inquiry in London, it was found that the master had not cleared his ship for Hamburg, also that the organs had not been entered outwards, nor had the British export duty been paid on them. Still, the Treasury authorized the Board to refund the extra amount paid in Newfoundland. The shipmaster was fined.

Fifteen years had elapsed since the Privy Council for Trade and the Customs Board had been made aware of the startling fact that, although Labrador had been included in many revenue Acts, there was not a single established customs officer on its extensive coast, yet no regular appointment was made there till 1840. True, Mr. Langley (see p. 148) had, much to his own disappointment and detriment, acted as collector for a year or two, and the sheriff who accompanied the judge on his annual visits to Labrador had occasionally attempted to act under instructions from the collector of St. John's, Newfoundland, but the results had been as vague as the systems of appointment. In 1840 the Newfoundland Legislature appointed Mr. Elias Rendall as collector of provincial customs at Labrador, and the collector of St. John's instructed him to levy the imperial duties as well. He was not particularly successful, the British fishermen stationed there declining to pay duty, the reason assigned being that they were not protected in their fisheries. Said one of the fishing agents: 'The Americans who swarm on the coast visit most of these harbours and creeks with goods for sale. Were it possible to enforce a general payment, the British resident would not seek any immunity.'

To show how cautiously the warehousing privileges were extended to ports, we give a summary of the proceedings on the memorial of William Burge, of Falmouth, Jamaica. He informed the Board that the trade of the port in 1838 had been as below:

Tonnage of vessels inward	.. ..	11,457
Tonnage of vessels outward	.. ..	11,688
Customs collected	.. .. ..	£1,764 11s. 2d.

He stated that the Jamaica Assembly had passed a resolution declaring it expedient to establish a bonded warehouse at the port of Falmouth, and that he was prepared to provide such a warehouse, if an Order in Council could be obtained sanctioning the proceeding. The requisite order was issued on March 1, 1840, and the warehouse was opened on October 1.

The amount of customs duties collected in Jamaica for the quarter ending April 5, 1840, shows that trade was increasing fast.

	£	s.	d.	
Kingston and Old Harbour	18,182	13	8	(sterling).
Port Morant	856	15	11	,,
Port Antonio	146	8	2	,,
Port Maria and Annatto Bay ..	663	14	9	,,
Montego Bay and Lucea	4,004	14	11	,,
Savannah-la-Mar and Black River ..	1,645	6	4	,,
Falmouth, Rio Bueno, and St. Anne's Bay	3,626	17	10	,,
	29,126	11	7	,,

It appears that Newcastle, N.S.W., had experienced peculiar vicissitudes. In 1834 a petition, signed by sixty-nine merchants, had been sent to the governor of N.S.W., asking that the customs officer at Newcastle might be allowed to enter and clear vessels. The petition stated that three ships had been laden with wool at Newcastle recently, and that there was a considerable export trade in maize, tobacco, coal, butter, and cheese to Tasmania. The governor allowed the privilege requested. (Previously vessels discharging and loading at Newcastle had been entered and cleared at the head port, Sydney, and all duties had been paid there as well.) The Sydney collector apprised the Board of the governor's action, stating that Hunter's River was the most productive part of the colony, especially with regard to wool, and that the trade of Newcastle was increasing with great rapidity. In 1838 he reported that during the last quarter of 1837 seventy-one vessels, tonnage varying from 14 to 344, had cleared out from Newcastle, the cargoes being maize, coal, sheep, hides, tallow, and wool, but the imports were trifling, as follows:

Spirits : 3 cases, 17 casks.	Sugar : 1 ton, 16 mats.
Tea : 28 packages.	Porter : 1 barrel.
Beef : 40 barrels.	Timber : 38 loads.
Wine : 1 cask.	Flour : 72 bags.

The value of the wool shipped from Newcastle to the United Kingdom in 1837 was £20,000. Soon afterwards the port began to go down. In 1840 the landing-waiter was removed to Sydney, the exportation of wool to the United Kingdom having ceased, and a tide waiter only remained at the port, to look after the coasting trade.

The collector of Colombo reported to the Board that an article had appeared in the *Bombay Courier*, commenting upon a growing practice of 'sailing vessels under more than one flag.' The collector supported this by quoting the case of the *General Wood*, a ship which had been sailing under various flags and names ever since she was built in 1816. He also stated that the provisions of the Navigation Acts were rarely observed in the East India ports. But it appeared upon investigation that there was no law prohibiting a *British* ship from trading under false colours, or with false papers.

The inspector of Waterguard at Liverpool informed the Board that several of his officers had become Socialists, and proceeded to comment upon the matter in the high-flown language so often used by the higher officials whenever they dealt with matters outside the scope of ordinary routine. 'I have read,' he stated, 'several Socialist publications. The doctrines they contain are as blasphemous as they are inimical to the constitution of this country. They tend to equalize all classes of society, and to deny all authority from superiors. These dangerous principles partake of neither religion nor morality. They have substituted a new and specious system of their own, a system contrary in spirit to the queen's proclamation against vice and immorality, contrary in spirit to the Treasury Minute of March 18, 1836, which goes to inculcate good order in Society. This delusion is daily increasing in these parts, and I have felt it my duty to bring it forward. I cannot but look upon this as a most serious matter, for I must doubt the trustworthiness of that officer who denies in principle any control but his own will. Can his oath be depended upon?' The collector, controller, and inspector-general of Liverpool furnished supplementary statements, couched in language equally turgid and ambiguous. They agreed with Mr. Walker that Socialism was 'likely to be attended with the most baneful and pernicious consequences to the community at large, and to man in his social state.'

Now, the Minute quoted by Mr. Walker as inculcating 'good order in Society' had been issued in consequence of an address to the king by the Commons in 1836, praying the discouragement of all *political* associations that held communication by means of secret signs and symbols, or excluded people of a different religion, and had been levelled particularly against Orange Lodges. Yet the Board thought it applicable to the Socialists, and in their covering report to the Treasury they expressed a deadly determination to carry it out. But the Treasury held that the Minute was inapplicable. Yet they desired the

Board to communicate the following message to the Liverpool iconoclasts : ' My Lords learn with the sincerest regret that any officers in H.M. Service have connected themselves with a Society so subversive of morality and religion.'

The first consignment of guano from the Pacific arrived in 1841. The Treasury waived the duty of 5 per cent. *ad valorem* to which the guano would ordinarily have been liable as ' unenumerated goods,' and rated it at 5s. per ton only. Later they allowed preserved turtle to enter duty-free—a privilege which live turtle had always enjoyed. A later Minute announced that the queen, by letters patent under the Great Seal, had been pleased to ' erect ' the islands of New Zealand into a separate and distinct colony. Another directed that Mr. Gray, customs controller at Aberdeen, should be censured for inducing the provost and chief magistrate of that substantial town to apply to the Treasury, praying that Mr. Gray might be appointed to the vacant collectorship.

Although in 1841 the Customs establishment at Port Adelaide was not under the control of the Board, but appointed solely by the governor, the collector managed to gain what may with fairness be called unenviable distinction. On June 29 the French-built vessel *Ville de Bordeaux* anchored in Glenelg Roads. The captain reported her as from St. George's Sound to Tasmania, he being commissioned to buy stock at the latter colony for transport to West Australia, and stated that he had put into Port Adelaide because he had reason to think stock could be procured there more readily. He ordered a number of sheep, and entered his vessel for Bourbon. The officious customs clerk who took his entry thought fit to tell the collector that he had observed that the captain was uneasy while making it, so the collector examined the ship's register and log, made certain inquiries, took it upon himself to detain the vessel under suspicion of contemplated infringement of the Navigation laws, and then apprised the governor, explaining the causes of detention. He stated that the vessel had previously been taken to Sydney in a leaky condition, and that her owners, a French firm located at Bordeaux, made a pretended sale of her at Sydney to one Joubert, a Frenchman, who had been naturalized there as a Britisher. The transfer had not been properly endorsed on the register. She was manned at Sydney by a mixed crew of Englishmen and Frenchmen, and provided with an English captain, and the new captain's name had not been put on the document. And there was an entry in the log which showed that she had previously made an illegal voyage from Lombock (a French settlement) to West Australia. (It is apparent, however, that she had been furnished at Sydney with a register *de novo*, although the document had not been properly completed.)

When the sheep were brought to the quay the man in charge refused to disclose their destination. The collector became still more suspicious, and declared the ship seized. He sent the tide-surveyor to put a tidesman on board, and the captain threatened to pistol the tide-surveyor, but that official got on board with his tidesman, and then the captain put to sea. It appears that the English portion of the crew had not been well treated, and they at once volunteered to overpower the Frenchmen and seize the ship, if the tide-surveyor would order them to do so. That gentleman, however, was not prepared to take the risk just then. According to his subsequent report, the captain went below, destroyed the incriminating entry in the ship's log, and substituted a fresh statement. Then he navigated the vessel off and on, threatening to shoot the officers if they did not consent to leave her. In the end the English sailors rushed aft, overpowered the captain, and took the ship back to the roads. There she remained, and the intending exporter of the sheep sold his flock by auction, getting a poor price, but the collector insisted that this was but a dodge to incense the public against the Customs. If it were, it succeeded, for the public took sides with the captain, and the local press assailed the collector with much vituperation. Mr. Joubert claimed the vessel, and the judge of the Supreme Court allowed his claim, on condition that he gave security for the expenses incurred. The governor of South Australia transmitted an account of the proceedings to the Secretary of State for the colonies, who referred it to the Treasury. It was sent to the Board, and their report on it was singularly perspicuous. Below is a summary :

'The matter should not have been thus referred. South Australia at present a chartered, not a Crown, colony, and the Board have no supervision. Still—

'1. The collector for South Australia not legally empowered to carry out either the Navigation or the Ships' Registry laws.

2. 'Even if thus empowered, has done wrong. *Ville de Bordeaux* arrived *in ballast*, so, even if French, had right to enter port. She cleared out for Bourbon, a French settlement. Collector's statement that she is really for West Australia merely the result of hearsay.

'3. Collector's statement that she has made a previous voyage from a French settlement to West Australia cannot be proved. No Customs in West Australia to prove it.

'4. Collector claims power to condemn vessel and cargo, they not having been claimed by the appellant Joubert within prescribed period. But Joubert's neglect does not enable collector to do an unjust thing, and does not deprive Joubert of power to claim indemnity on an equitable plea.'

The Treasury Minute on this report must have startled the collector. It directed the governor to restore the vessel at once. If sold, her proceeds were to be given to the owners, without any deduction for expenses. If sold, and governor not satisfied as to *bona fides* of claimant, the proceeds were to be sent to the Treasury, and that department would deal with the matter of claim. The collector was censured, and admonished not to deal on his own responsibility with such matters in future, and that the law providing for summary sale of unclaimed seized vessels was intended to prevent unnecessary legal expenses, not to shield unauthorized seizers. The Minute proceeded thus: 'The collector has incurred great personal responsibility by the course which he has pursued, and his want of caution in the transaction may prove the source of much embarrassment to himself and to the colony.'

Undoubtedly the collector had strained matters. (It should be mentioned that when he saw the vessel leave the roads with the customs officers on board he actually seized the bleating innocents that were waiting shipment on the quay, and did not restore them till the vessel was brought back, also, that the value of the *Ville de Bordeaux* was estimated at between £8,000 and £10,000, and that, had he secured her forfeiture, he would have pocketed a very pretty sum.)*

The account of the customs survey of the port of Launceston, Tasmania, in 1841, is rather informative. The customs duties collected during 1840 were £33,727. The tonnage inwards was as follows: ships from the United

* The marginal comments pencilled on the reports by Mr. Dean, the Customs Chairman, are amusing. One of them is worded thus: 'The affair seems to partake of a little robbery, a little piracy, and a little buccaneering' (the difference between buccaneering and piracy he did not explain). 'With the exception of carrying goods from Lombock to West Australia, I can discover no grounds for seizure under the Customs laws. Even on this point you have only the log to help you, and the log would appear to be altogether a fiction. The French Government may demand restitution of the British Government.'

The bad phrasing may be overlooked. Mr. Dean was a remarkable man, extremely clever and industrious, yet eccentric—witness his habit of jotting down little explosive comments on the papers he dealt with. Some of the comments are intensely amusing. For instance, when, in conducting an inquiry, he listened to the statements of an incoherent and unwilling witness, he remarked in pencil: 'What a —— fool this fellow is!'

On another occasion, when reading a verbose statement penned by a Scottish officer who was desirous of initiating a scheme of 'official reform,' and obtaining thereby an increase of his own salary, the observant Dean ornamented the margin of each paragraph with a pencilled 'Hum-m!' till he reached the one that suggested profit to the applicant; then Dean wrote, 'Aha, I thought we should come to this!' and straightway damned the whole scheme.

Kingdom, 4,379 tons; colonial ships, 29,839; foreign, 547. Outward ships for the United Kingdom, 3,521 tons; colonial, 33,275; foreign, 1,136. Value of imports, £303,140; exports, £452,870. In the bonded warehouse were 91,152 gallons spirits; 208,398 pounds tobacco; 4,589 pounds cigars, and 66 casks wine. The staple articles of export were bark, flour, hay, potatoes, whale-oil, bones, cattle, horses, wool (6,161 bales), and sheep (78,028). The surveying collector thought the smuggling was decreasing, the settlers being afraid of the convicts, who gave information whenever they witnessed a run, 'that being the surest way to obtain a ticket of leave.'

Sir William Colebrooke approached the Treasury with a scheme for altering the bonding system in the Leeward Islands. He suggested that importers should be given six months' credit for duties on their goods, to date from the period of entering the goods for home use. Sir William opined that this method would assist traders, and lower the price of commodities. The scheme was referred to the Customs Board, and they reported on it with considerable freedom, pointing out that there were many free warehousing ports in the West Indies at which importers might bond their goods duty-free till required for home use—or bond them for exportation. They hinted that Sir William's propositions were not so clearly worded as they might be. 'Nevertheless, we gather from his communication that he proposes to deliver goods at once into the hands of the importer, without payment of duty, merely taking security for the payment of the same within a stated period.' They proceeded to pooh-pooh the whole suggestion.*

A dispute arose in New Brunswick on the matter of goods for the fisheries. Articles such as biscuit, meat,

* It is evident that Sir William desired to save importers the expense of warehouse rent. Before the system of bonding in warehouse was introduced into Great Britain, the method suggested by Sir William had been in general use, and most of the duties were thus bonded. If an importer paid at importation, he was granted discount.

cordage, hooks, lines, nets, anchors, for use by the fishers, were allowed to be imported duty-free, or warehoused if necessary, and afterwards cleared duty-free. Certain merchants of New Brunswick complained to the Board that in some instances the collector had refused to deliver, duty-free, molasses and sugar warehoused for the fisheries. They had accordingly paid the duty under protest. The collector justified himself by stating that he had charged duty in the cases mentioned because the merchants had failed to furnish satisfactory proof that the goods would be used by the fishermen. He had reason to believe that in the past large quantities of goods had been cleared duty-free for fishery use, and afterwards consumed by the general public. The Board endorsed his action.

Cap. 3, 5 and 6 Vict., Sect. 2, settled a curious point. The lieutenant-governor of Tasmania had by proclamation of February 4, 1829, imposed certain rates of customs in the colony, and an excise on distilled spirits. He derived the authority to do this from Cap. 114, 59 Geo. III., and Cap. 96, 3 Geo. IV. Cap. 83, 9 Geo. IV., made the last-quoted Act perpetual, but provided that, as New South Wales and Tasmania had become separate colonies, the *two* governors should henceforth administer affairs *with the advice of their respective Legislative Councils.* On January 2, 1834, the Tasmanian Council had confirmed the governor's proclamation of 1829. Soon there arose doubts as to whether the duties taken between 1829 and 1834 had been legally collected. In 1842 the matter was adjusted by the Act quoted at the beginning of this paragraph, announcing that the proclamation was legally binding, and indemnifying all concerned in the collection of the disputed duties.

The Anti-Corn-Law League, formed in Manchester in 1838, had become extremely powerful. There had grown up at the same time a disturbing factor of a far different type—Chartism. It does not appear that there was ever any great sympathy between the leaders of the two movements. Such men as Cobden and Bright could scarcely be expected to run in harness with Ernest Jones and Feargus O'Connor. The men of the Manchester school were essentially opportunistic and 'utilitarian.' They had noted the effect of many years of past legislation —legislation directed principally towards the benefit of 'the landed interest.' Legislation performed in the interests of rent had starved the weavers and spinners. They believed that they could bring about a new Britain—a Britain of cotton lords and wizened operatives, cheap bread and dear exports. Britain was to become one gigantic workshop, and to distribute for ever her bales of prints and her cases of machinery to an admiring and unemulative world. (The universal contempt of agriculture displayed in the legislation and literature of the sixties, seventies, and eighties of the nineteenth century was entirely due to the teaching of the Manchester school.)

Yet it must be admitted that something had to be done. The people could be starved no longer. It must be admitted, also, that the thing could not have been *safely* done by any but the Manchester politicians. The temper of the modern British is extremely peculiar; there must be some element of what is called 'practicality' in a movement ere they can be brought to bestow abiding sympathy upon it. Widespread Industrialism—the devotion of masses of people to the production of mean things for everyday use—is responsible for this new phase of the national temper, under which no risks must be taken, but every revolution must have its register and ledger, its dreary diary and misleading statistics. 'We will make work plentiful and bread cheap,' said the Manchester men; and the tame cry captured the lower classes, who were not aware that under rigid Protection their ancestors had cheap bread (and something with it) for centuries and centuries.

The Chartists were altogether different. Such men as Shelley and Byron, men whose names will be honoured when those of Cobden and Bright have been relegated to the list of doctrinaires, would have thrown themselves heart and soul into the Chartist movement—a movement which conveyed promise to the souls of all who refused to have their mouths stopped with cheap bread, and their aspirations limited by a twelve-hour day and the white-washed walls of a factory. One must study the poets of the two systems to achieve suitable comparison. Most of Ebenezer Elliot's verse reminds one of the yelping of a hungry dog, but there is true vehemence, there is a touch of the old elemental fire of revolt, in, 'We're low, we're low, we're very, very low.'

After this little outburst, which may refresh if it fails to convince readers, we proceed to state that though Chartism and Cobdenism marched toward widely divergent goals, their potentialities in disturbance combined to influence the thoughts of the great Conservative statesman of the day, and the result was Cap. 14, 5 and 6 Vict., under which the corn duties were lowered considerably. Below is a comparison :

WHEAT FROM FOREIGN COUNTRIES.

	Previous Duties. £ s. d.	*New Duties.* £ s. d.
When price of British wheat under 51s. a quarter	A sliding scale of duties, rising from £1 16s. 8d. when the price was 50s. and less than 51s., to £2 8s. 8d. if the price went under 39s.	1 0 0
Do., 51s. and under 52s.	1 15 8	0 19 0
Do., 52s. and under 53s.	1 14 8	
Do., 53s. and under 54s.	1 13 8	0 18 0
Do., 54s. and under 55s.	1 12 8	
Do., 55s. and under 56s.	1 11 8	0 17 0
Do., 56s. and under 57s.	1 10 8	0 16 0
Do., 57s. and under 58s.	1 9 8	0 15 0
Do., 58s. and under 59s.	1 8 8	0 14 0
Do., 59s. and under 60s.	1 7 8	0 13 0
Do., 60s. and under 61s.	1 6 8	0 12 0
Do., 61s. and under 62s.	1 5 8	0 11 0
Do., 62s. and under 63s.	1 4 8	0 10 0
Do., 63s. and under 64s.	1 3 8	0 9 0
Do., 64s. and under 65s.	1 2 8	0 8 0
Do., 65s. and under 66s.	1 1 8	0 7 0

WHEAT FROM FOREIGN COUNTRIES (*continued*).

	Previous Duties.			New Duties.		
When price of British wheat 66s.	£	s.	d.	£	s.	d.
and under 67s.	1	0	8			
Do., 67s. and under 68s.	0	18	8	0	6	0
Do., 68s. and under 69s.	0	16	8			
Do., 69s. and under 70s.	0	13	8	0	5	0
Do., 70s. and under 71s.	0	10	8	0	4	0
Do., 71s. and under 72s.	0	6	8	0	3	0
Do., 72s. and under 73s.	0	2	8	0	2	0
Do., 73s. and upwards	0	1	0	0	1	0

WHEAT FROM BRITISH POSSESSIONS OUT OF EUROPE.

Previous Duties.	s.	d.	New Duties.	s.	d.
When price of British wheat under 67s. a quarter	5	0	Under 55s.	5	0
			55s. and under 56s. ..	4	0
			56s. and under 57s. ..	3	0
When price 67s. or more	0	6	57s. and under 58s. ..	2	0
			58s. and upwards ..	1	0

(Proportional rates for other kinds of corn.)

The prohibitions of colonial and foreign malt, and of all foreign and colonial ground corn except wheat meal, wheat flour, and oatmeal, survived.

This important measure was followed by a new copyright Act (Cap. 45, 5 and 6 Vict.). It repealed the copyright Act, Cap. 19, 8 Anne, and the Acts amending it (Cap. 107, 41 Geo. III., and Cap. 156, 54 Geo. III.). The new Act provided as below :

1. The word 'book' to signify every volume or part, pamphlet, sheet of letterpress or music, chart, or plan, separately produced ; the words 'dramatic piece' every play or scenic, musical, or dramatic entertainment ; the word 'copyright' exclusive right of printing and multiplying copies of the above ; the words 'personal representative' every person entitled to rights of administration ; the word 'assigns' every person in whom the author's copyright interest might be vested ; the words 'British Dominions' the United Kingdom, Channel Islands, and all other possessions of the Crown.

2. Copyright to endure for author's life and seven years

longer, or till forty-two years after first publication (if last term the longer). If published posthumously, to endure for forty-two years.

3. If after author's death his assign refused to re-publish, the Privy Council might license any complainant to publish.

4. The usual free copies to be delivered to certain institutions.

5. Copyright might be registered at Stationers' Hall.

6. Actions for piracy to be in the Court of Record, in that part of the dominions in which the offence was committed.

7. Importation of pirated works to be punishable by forfeiture, and fine of £10 and double value of goods. Pirated books might be seized by Customs or Excise.

8. The Act to apply to musical compositions.

9. Seized pirated books to become property of holder of copyright.

10. Registration of copyright necessary before action taken, but copyright to exist even if unregistered.

Such were the main provisions of the new Act. Whether it or any Statute moulded on similar lines could be held just to authors may be worth a few moments thought. The Copyright Acts were the first British Socialistic laws, for they decreed that literary work should not be assignable beyond a certain period. Then it was to become public property. It is curious that literature—the poorest-paid work performed by man—should be treated thus.

Cap. 47, 5 and 6 Vict., amended the Customs laws. It repealed the long-existing prohibition of importation of foreign cattle, sheep, swine, beef, pork, mutton, and lamb, of fish imported in foreign vessels, and of fish of foreign taking. (But in the last case the fish—with certain exceptions—had to be brought from a foreign port ; it might not come direct from the fishing-ground.) It repealed the stipulation for a separate manifest for imported tobacco, and declared bonds entered into by merchants with the Treasury or Customs valid in law. It re-amended the Copyright laws, by enacting *complete* prohibition of books produced in the United Kingdom and reproduced abroad (but the copyright-holder was to apprise the Customs of his rights before such prohibition could be enforced). It abolished the exemption of coastguardsmen and revenue patrolmen from tolls, and gave the Treasury power of amending duties towards reciprocity. It provided for the assaying of gold and silver plate imported for sale. It repealed the previous duties and drawbacks, and granted a new scale, by which the dutiable goods, which had previously been arranged alphabetically, were assorted under nineteen headings for imports and one for exports. The duties were still in many cases preferential with regard to British possessions. The duties on tea, tobacco, silks, and spirits, were still tremendously high. The only export duties were on coal, clay, china stone, cement stone, flint, wool, and skins.

The Act was scarcely passed when it was amended by Cap. 56. Certain new duties on timber were postponed for a year ; the meaning of ' parts,' applicable to regulating the duties on copper ore, was explained to be ' parts of a hundred ' ; the statement that goods of the Channel Islands were to be deemed foreign was qualified so as to read ' goods produced in the Channel Islands from foreign materials '; a misleading parenthesis was corrected ; specimens illustrative of natural history were included in the list of ' exemptions from duty '; the law as to assaying foreign plate was relaxed so as to admit antique plate free of assay ; the export duty on cement stone was repealed, and certain new regulations as to delivery of bonded goods were deferred. These might be called a tolerably large bunch of alterations, and there can be no doubt that they were the result of protests from merchants, which proves that the mind of the high revenue official is not always clear.

The time-honoured Excise survey of tobacco manufacture had been discontinued under an Act of 3 and 4 Vict. The result had been wholesale adulteration, sometimes to the extent of 70 per cent. The Excise control was renewed by Cap. 93, 5 and 6 Vict., and many stringent regulations were reimposed.

Considerable misapprehension had arisen in some of the colonies as to duties leviable under the Act 59, 3 and 4 Wm. IV. There had been in that Act a clause stating that whenever any goods chargeable with duty under its provisions were also chargeable under colonial laws, the duties mentioned in the Act were not to apply except they *exceeded* the duties leviable under the colonial laws, and then only to the amount of such excess. In some of the colonies the local duties had exceeded those under the Act 59, 3 and 4 Wm. IV., yet the colonial legislators had insisted on full collection. Cap 49, 5 and 6 Vict., accordingly, made all such proceedings in the past legal, and imposed a new scale of duties. (The complications in the colonies over the collection of revenue were indeed extraordinary. To them, and to the greed and arrogance of some of the imperial collectors, was due the approach of the abolition of the home control.)

During 1842 the Roman Catholic Bishop of Montreal applied for remission of duty on vestments, etc., imported for religious purposes, and the collector of Montreal, in reporting to the Board on the matter, stated that he did not think the privilege should be granted, as he had reason to believe that if it were similar applications would at once be made by the priests of the seminary of St. Sulpice, Montreal. The Board reported to the Treasury that indulgences of the kind were occasionally extended to indigent priests, but that in this case the applicant was surrounded by an opulent clergy.*

* An application had been made in 1839 by the Catholic clergy of Trinidad, who alleged that similar privileges had been granted to the Catholics of that island ever since 1797. The Board recommended the remission, although the collector's valuation of the articles differed materially from that furnished by the clergy on their entry. For instance, they had valued ten fine Italian

On August 3, 1842, the officers at Halifax, Nova Scotia, seized a number of copies of the *New World*, a New York publication. A copy is appended to the file. It is a curio, being merely a complete reproduction of a novel by Lady Blessington, entitled 'The Lottery of Life.' The motto of the paper is, 'No pent-up Utica contracts our powers, for the whole boundless universe is ours'—a motto distinctively American, and highly expressive of the American publishing methods of that day. The collector stated: 'The importation of this and similar reprints is considerable, and occasions much dissatisfaction to the booksellers of this port, as it greatly interferes with the sale of the English books which are imported from the United Kingdom.'

No doubt the New York publisher had gauged the literary tastes of the Nova Scotians. Their character may be best displayed by a reproduction of the opening and conclusion of Lady Blessington's novel, which contains all of 'The Lottery of Life' that we have found ourselves able to read.

Opening: 'Born of humble but honest parents, I was so fortunate as to attract the notice of Abraham Mortimer, a retired banker.'

Conclusion: 'A letter despatched a few days after to her dear friend, Lady Frances Lorimer, in answer to one from that young lady announcing her approaching nuptials, contained such excellent advice on the danger of young wives exacting attentions only paid during the days of courtship, that it had the best effect on that lady.

---

devotional paintings at £8 the lot. Still, the collector let them pass duty-free on receipt of the Treasury order to that effect, remarking that he preferred doing that to arguing with the Bishop. Soon the clergy imported other articles, and claimed them duty-free, and the governor sanctioned delivery, relying upon the previous Treasury Order. When the Board heard of this, they surcharged the unfortunate collector with the amount payable. In 1844 the priests imported various church ornaments and two casks of wine, but, needless to state, had to pay duty. (The Catholic clergy of the Mauritius claimed remission in 1845, but were refused.)

This judicious counsel considerably lowered the exaggerated and romantic expectations she had previously indulged of the unbroken felicity of wedded lovers, and saved the husband of Lady Frances from the scenes of domestic chagrin that had clouded the conjugal happiness of Lord Henry and Lady Emily Fitzhardinge, during their first entrance as a wedded pair into fashionable life in London.'

It appears from the advertisement list of the *New World* that the other books most in demand, and therefore diligently pirated, were 'Morley Ernstein,' 'Zanoni,' 'The Jacquerie,' 'Summer and Winter in the Pyrenees,' and 'The United Irishmen.'

The traders of St. Kitts and Nevis had petitioned at various periods between 1828 and 1842 that the Customs establishments of those islands should be consolidated, and all traffic between them deemed 'coastwise' trade. The Board had replied that though they were empowered to regulate coastwise traffic in the colonies, their powers did not extend to making intercolonial into coastwise trade, and had pointed out that the customs duties in the respective islands were paid in to separate colonial treasuries. But in 1842 they departed from this decision, and allowed the privilege requested, so far as regarded vessels owned in the two islands.

The sub-collector of Wellington, New Zealand, reported as to the lack of protection of British and colonial trade in his district. He stated that American fishing vessels frequently came close to the shores of Stewart's Island, and traded in contraband with the settlers and natives; also that a colonial schooner brought a cargo of tobacco (duty-paid), and it was found impossible to sell the goods, the Americans having supplied all requirements. He was of opinion that a revenue cruiser should be stationed at Cloudy Bay. The Board merely inscribed the damning word 'Read' on this important epistle.

On July 4, 1842, the governor of Ceylon, in his address to the Council, stated the total revenue for 1841 as £344,463, and announced a deficit of £16,870, which had to be paid out of the balance previously remaining in the public chest.

Cap. 29, 6 and 7 Vict., referred to an Act passed in 1842 by the Legislature of Canada, imposing a duty of 3s. a quarter on all wheat imported into Canada, except from the United Kingdom. It appears this Act had been passed with the view that the United Kingdom should act reciprocally by lowering the duties on Canadian wheat. They were accordingly, by Cap. 29, reduced to 1s. a quarter. Cap. 79 affirmed certain provisions, made by a Convention, regulating the fisheries between Great Britain and France. It enjoined that the French might not fish in the waters between France and the British Islands, except at a distance exceeding three miles from low-water mark. The Board of Trade might draw up by-laws applicable to the fisheries. The British revenue officers were authorized to examine the registry certificates and tackle of British fishing vessels, and to execute warrants granted by justices of the peace on account of infringements. Proceedings against French fishers for offences committed whilst encroaching were to be dealt with by the magistrates of the adjoining counties. Offences committed by the French outside the limits were to be deposed to before the magistrates, and the depositions sent to the British consul at the offender's place of residence. Cap. 84 amended the Customs laws. There had been much fraud, especially in the Port of London, by entering high-duty goods 'on sight,' carrying them away unexamined, and producing for examination low-duty goods made up in similar packages. It was provided under this Act that all 'sight entries' were to be accompanied by a declaration from the importer as to the amount of duty reasonably likely to be due, and that amount was to be deposited before the goods were examined. If on examination it was found that more duty was due, the balance was to be paid before any of the packages were delivered. It was also provided that colonial vessels might deliver in the United Kingdom oil, blubber, etc., of British or colonial taking, at the low rates of duty, as was allowed with British vessels, and that the queen, by Order in Council, might from time to time define the reciprocal export privileges granted to certain foreign States, and specify the colonial ports at which goods might be warehoused for exportation. The Act concluded by repealing the prohibition of exportation of many kinds of machinery. (This last proviso was no doubt incited by two circumstances : 1, The rapid spread of Free Trade principles ; 2, a recent astounding revelation of Customs connivance at evasion of the prohibiting laws. See pp, 261-269.)

On March 21, 1843, lists of copyright works were for the first time sent to the various ports. Only books advised to the Customs by the copyright-holders were included in the lists.

A Treasury Minute of July 25, 1843, stated that certain revenue officers in Ireland had joined Repeal Associations, and warned them to abjure membership at once, on pain of dismissal.

By an Act of 6 Vict. the Legislature of New South Wales had allowed goods of Tasmania and New Zealand to enter New South Wales free of duty. (All Acts passed by this Legislature had to be submitted to one of the imperial Secretaries of State, it being provided by a Statute of 9 Geo. IV. that the king should thus have an opportunity of signifying his approbation or disapproval.) On August 31, 1843, Lord Stanley apprised the governor of New South Wales that the recent Act was disallowed. 'The principle,' he stated, 'of establishing differential duties in favour of particular colonies is so objectionable that Her Majesty's Government cannot consent to any further extension or recognition of such a system. If allowed, it would inevitably give rise to retaliating measures on the part of other colonies, and a system of protection and preferences would gradually be established among the several colonial dependencies of the Empire, by which the operation of commerce would be embarrassed.'

On becoming aware of the nature of this despatch, the Sydney collector took it upon himself to impose the *ad valorem* duty of 5 per cent. on Tasmanian grain imported into Melbourne. (It had been duty-free under *previous* colonial Acts. The Acts had not been clearly worded, and the collector took advantage of their ambiguity.) Both governor and Board supported his action, the latter recommending that the levy should be continued, and the importers be left to take legal action for recovery of the duties if they felt disposed.

An extraordinary squabble amongst customs officers was reported from Kingston, Jamaica. It appears that the trouble started in the Custom-house, several of the participants (Messrs. Elliott, Evans, Davis, and Morphy) coming to blows. The collector admonished the parties concerned, but did not apprise the Board. On June 12, 1843, Davis and Morphy were at a club in Kingston, when Elliott and Evans entered. Elliott observed in staccato tones to his friend, 'Who introduced these blackguards here? Who brought the —— snobs into this place?' Morphy at once struck him with a cane, and a mêlée ensued, all four using their sticks freely, Elliott shouting, as he belaboured Morphy, 'You —— scoundrel! I'll knock out your brains!' and then, as he bestowed similar favours on Davis, who was a mulatto, 'You brute beast, you woolly-headed scoundrel, I can find no brains to knock out in you!' Davis replied, whilst defending himself, to the effect that Elliott's mother had been a camp-follower, and that Elliott's position in the Service was the result of Elliott's sister's good looks and extreme complaisance. Several members of the club intervened, and parted the enraged officials.

Later in the evening Elliott and Evans, armed with stout canes, placed themselves in ambush on the Parade. Perhaps the wine of the island had obscured their faculties, for they fell upon an inoffensive stranger, and gave him an unmerciful drubbing. On discovering their mistake, they begged a thousand pardons, and explained that the drubbing was intended for Morphy.

This quarrel, at first exemplified in wood, was soon transferred to paper, Elliott reporting Davis to the Board for casting aspersions upon the female branch of the Elliott family. The Board directed the collector to censure all concerned.*

During 1843 a person signing himself 'William Large, gentleman, Warren's Place, Cork,' wrote the Board, asking for compensation for certain services which he claimed to have performed as waiter and searcher in Surinam in 1801-02, during the time the place was a British possession. The Customs Solicitor dismissed the claim, stating that all papers connected with Surinam had been lost in the fire that destroyed the London Custom-house in 1814. The Roman Catholic Bishop of Cape Town memorialized the Board, praying that certain materials for church-building, etc., might be admitted to the colony duty-free. The list specified the following goods :

7,312 feet timber.	2,000 feet window-glass.	100,000 bricks.
1,200 slates.	170 gallons oil and turpentine.	Certain altar-pieces.
6½ tons sheet-lead.	1,250 pounds paint.	Certain pictures.
1,860 pounds nails.	3,000 pounds cement.	Certain statues.
8,000 pounds iron bolts, etc.		Certain bells.
		An organ.

All the above were for a church at Cape Town, and there was another list for a church at Grahamstown. The memorial stated that indulgences had been extended to certain Protestant churches, both Dutch and British-colonial. The collector admitted that the governor had remitted certain duties in the past, but reminded the Board that they had pronounced against any subsequent indulgence of the kind. The application was rejected.

The International Copyright Act of 1 and 2 Vict. (amended by Cap. 45, 5 and 6 Vict., see p. 208) was re-

* Undoubtedly the Board made allowance for temperature, and the potency of the cooling drinks used so freely in the West Indies at that time.

pealed, and Cap. 12 of 7 and 8 Vict. provided that works first published abroad might enjoy the privilege of copyright, provided that an Order in Council specified that the copyright privilege should be extended, and on condition that the works were produced in the particular foreign country specified. If published in one foreign country and produced in another, they were to be prohibited from importation into the British dominions, unless the proprietors of the copyright sanctioned such importation. All such privileges were to be reciprocal. Cap. 66 removed many of the restrictions upon aliens. It provided that any person born of a British mother should be capable of holding real or personal estate, that subjects of a friendly State might hold lands, etc., in residence for a term not exceeding twenty-one years, that aliens might become naturalized, and that naturalization should attach to any woman who married a British subject.

Cap. 43, 7 and 8 Vict., amended the Customs laws relating to the Isle of Man. Trade from the United Kingdom to that island, and *vice versa*, was no longer to be deemed foreign. All ships thus employed were to be held coasting ships, yet specific Manx duties were payable on certain goods. Some of these goods might still only be imported from Great Britain, and these were liable to the restrictions applying to foreign goods.

The Board issued instructions to collectors as to carrying out the provisions of Cap. 79, 6 and 7 Vict. (see p. 214). All British fishing-boats were to be numbered in series according to the customs districts to which they belonged, and were to be marked with the initial letters of their respective districts. All derelict fishing-gear, etc., was to be delivered to the Customs, and the collectors were empowered to restore such goods to their owners, and to award the finders salvage.

Incredible though it may seem, up to 1844 the method of taking bottled spirits to account for duty at the outports had been different to that used at London. In the former case the goods had been estimated at 6 reputed quarts to the gallon—an extremely slipshod method. The outport officers were directed by a 'General Letter' of August 27, 1844, to conform to the London practice, under which the quantity per case was estimated by actual measurement of certain bottles.

On June 10, 1844, the collector of Dominica reported that the island was in a state of rebellion, and had been placed under martial law. The coloured people had committed many outrages. The militia had been called out, and had fired on the mob, killing two and wounding several others. Two hundred persons had been taken, and were to be tried by court-martial. The trouble had arisen through a provincial Act enjoining the taking of the census, the coloured people believing that this was a device towards re-enslaving them.

A letter from the Postmaster-General reached the Board, stating that the postmasters at the frontier offices between Canada and the United States had not been supplied with the usual list of British copyright works, and were therefore unable to cope with the introduction of pirated books into Canada. Later he wrote asking that the customs officers in New Brunswick might be instructed to cooperate with the postal authorities there in preventing the smuggling of letters (to evade postage expense) from the United States.*

Major Smith, 'a shipowner and merchant of Port Elizabeth, Algoa Bay,' applied to the Board, representing himself as a trader with Bengal, Mauritius, and the Cape coasts. He stated that he had established a depot on the coast of Kaffraria, and imported goods at Algoa Bay for exportation thither. The collector of Cape Town had called on him for the duties on these goods, although other goods imported at Table Bay for a similar purpose had been delivered duty-free. The major pointed out that the British Government had by treaty disclaimed all

* The incessant complaints as to smuggling, literary piracy, and unfair trading, on the part of Americans, tend to show that commercial morality was even scarcer in the United States than in the United Kingdom.

control of Kaffraria, and that it was preposterous to levy duty on goods imported at Algoa Bay for exportation to an independent State.

Later he found it was necessary to get a licence for the trade, and applied to the governor at Cape Town. The collector recommended that the licence should be granted, on condition that no arms, wines, or spirits were to be landed, and that the duties on the goods were paid. Smith got his licence, and then renewed protest against paying the duty. But the governor enforced payment.

The collector's report on Smith's application was interesting. It described Port Elizabeth as a free warehousing port in the eastern part of the colony—the colony being bounded east and west by the mouths of the Great Fish River and the Unizimkulu. The territory ceded to the Kaffirs lay within the eastern boundary, and the dominance of the British Government had been asserted in the treaty. Till recently there had been only a land trade from Cape Town and Natal to the Kaffir territory. All goods taken thither had been first duty-paid, and the traffic was tolerably extensive, larger quantities of Kaffir produce returning by the same route. Smith's trade by sea to the coast of the territory was a recent venture, and the collector insisted that if goods were allowed to go there duty-free they would be smuggled into Cape Colony. In the end it was decided that no goods should be thus shipped till duty-paid (unless they were products of the colony). The object seems to have been to discourage the traffic, it being thought that an open sea trade would favour the introduction of arms. The Board refused Smith's application. (It appears he was not a merchant and shipowner, after all, but agent for Messrs. Hawkins, of Great Tower Street, London.)

Mr. Furlonge, landing-waiter at Montserrat, caused some little trouble during 1844. He commenced by sending word to the Board that the Hon. I. P. M. Trott, senior assistant judge of the Court of Queen's Bench in Montserrat, had been concerned in extensive smuggling transactions. Later he wrote again, complaining that he had been persecuted by Trott. 'I am now,' he wrote, 'confined in the common jail with a heavy fine, for a trifling assault upon a gentleman who had grossly insulted me. The collector was one of the judges who assented to this cruel persecution.' He proceeded to insinuate that the collector was Trott's intimate friend, and had connived at the latter's frauds. But the Board, no doubt realizing that this was another case of over-indulgence in 'sugar-cane wine,' treated the reports with contempt.

During the same year the President of Montserrat queried the collector for failing to carry out an Act passed by the Montserrat Legislature in 1748. The collector stated that he could not undertake to enforce colonial Acts which were repugnant to the imperial laws. The matter dropped. Below is an extract from the Montserrat Act of 1748:

'Whereas frequent and great losses happen by the clandestine carrying off of the inhabitants and other people, their negroes and substance, from this island, etc.' It proceeded that no vessel might depart till the master had entered into bond of £1,500 that he would carry off no one till authorized by a ticket from the island Secretary's office. The collector was to withhold clearance till the bond had been entered into.

During several years there had been a deal of correspondence on the question of establishing a Customs station at Labrador (see p. 196), an arrangement much desired by some of the settlers in that territory, while others opposed the idea. In 1836 Lord Glenelg had described the situation in a despatch to Captain Prescott, governor of Labrador, stating that the Planters believed they were separate from Newfoundland, and still under the authority of the king in Council, but that this view was not correct, Cap. 27, 49 Geo. III., and 59, 6 Geo. IV., being against it. He also quoted the decision arrived at by a recent Commission, which had stated that the coast of Labrador, east of a line drawn north and south from the harbour of Blanc Gablon, was annexed to the colony of Newfoundland. Lord Glenelg was of opinion that the Labrador settlers could claim to be represented in the Newfoundland Legislature.

In 1843 the Attorney-General for Newfoundland delivered an opinion upon the matter. He recommended the appointment of two customs officers, to remain on the Labrador coast from June to September. He pooh-poohed the idea that the expense would exceed the collection, pointing out that the colonial customs officers were not appointed simply to raise revenue ; they were the enforcers of the Navigation laws and of commercial treaties. He referred to illicit trade on the coast of Labrador, conducted by 'vessels of the United States fitted out for fishing and trading. Against such proceedings,' he observed, 'the customs officers would be some check, and their appointment is, I think, essential for the reasonable and consistent maintenance of the system. At the conclusion of the late war, when peace restored to France, as well as the United States, their privileges of fishery in these parts, the coast of Labrador was resorted to by numerous planters from the settlements of Newfoundland, who during the war had enjoyed the exclusive benefit of fishing between Cape St. John and the straits of Belle-isle.' He proceeded to state that these settlers were supplied with stores from Newfoundland, and returned each year the produce of their fishery. English and Jersey merchants also erected establishments at Labrador, importing their supplies direct from Europe, and carrying their fish and oils direct to European markets. Of late these industries had become depressed, British-taken fish being subjected to heavy duties in foreign countries, and the French and American fisheries being supported by liberal bounties. Thus most of the colonial settlers and English merchants had abandoned their Labrador establishments.

In 1844 the Customs Lawyers in London made a vague and half-hearted report upon the case. They suggested that it was a matter that the governor should deal with, and they thought the appointment of 'transient officers' would be inexpedient. It appears that in the end the governor of Newfoundland decided to appoint officers, and to place a suitable vessel at their disposal. Thus it is clear that at Labrador up to 1845 there was no regular collection of duty, and that the fishing treaties and conventions, and the laws of Navigation, were as nothing.

On May 14, 1844, an American brig was discovered derelict and ashore at Stewart Castle, near Falmouth, Jamaica. Her name was the *Gleaner*, and she had a full cargo of pipes of gin and wine. The lord of the manor impounded her, and soon afterwards the American consul put in a claim. On May 22 a claim was made by the Receiver of Admiralty Droits. Then began a paper war among the claimants three—manorial, national, and departmental. The consul became importunate, and quoted instructions from the American Secretary of State. The collector who held the vessel in custody apprised the Board, and was instructed to keep ship and cargo till the case was decided in the Vice-Admiralty Court of the island. Unfortunately we are unable to discover which claim succeeded.

The matter of trade marks appears to have possessed the minds of the Jamaica customs men at this period. Several detentions took place under the Acts relating thereto. One was of two gold Swiss watches marked 'Tobias, Liverpool,' and another of six gold Swiss watches, with English words on them denoting quality, movement, etc. (Sec. 11, Cap. 47, 5 and 6 Vict.). The Board in this case directed forfeiture of the goods marked 'Tobias, Liverpool,' and release of the other consignment. Another detention was of cheese from New York, marked 'English Dairy.' The importer furnished proof that the cheese was made at an American farm called 'The English Dairy,' so the goods were released.

The Legislature of New Zealand, by Ordinance of

June 20, 1844, had abolished all the old tariff exemptions and preferences, and imposed duties as below :

	£	s.	d.
Spirits, per proof gallon	0	5	0
Leaf tobacco, per pound	0	0	9
Manufactured tobacco, per pound	0	1	0
Cigars and snuff, per pound	0	2	0
Wine	20 per cent. *ad valorem.*		
Malt liquors	15 ,, ,,		
Arms and ammunition ..	30 ,, ,,		
All other goods	5 ,, ,,		

Three firms of merchants protested against paying these duties upon their imports from the United Kingdom. They urged that the ordinance was repugnant to the imperial laws, but the Board sanctioned collection. On September 28, 1844, the Legislature changed round, and produced one of the most striking fiscal ordinances on record, repealing all customs duties, and directing that revenue should be raised solely by a tax on property. The preamble ran : 'Whereas the commerce, agriculture, and general prosperity of New Zealand would be greatly promoted by removing all restrictions on the free intercourse of shipping with its numerous ports and harbours,' etc.

A copy of this Ordinance was forwarded to the Board by the collector of Hobart Town, Tasmania. He had been instructed to send an officer to Auckland, New Zealand, and to pay the officer's salary till he arrived and took up his employment. The bewildered collector asked what he was to do, as there was no employment for the officer to take up. He also bewailed the new measure, stating that it would have an evil tendency upon the revenues of the adjacent colonies. For instance, when goods were cleared duty-free from bond at Hobart Town for shipment to New Zealand, their arrival could no longer be certified, there being no Customs to do the certifying, and thus such goods might be brought back, and run almost with impunity on the coast of Tasmania.

The Ordinance earned the approval of the governor of New Zealand. He stated in his speech at the opening of the Session that the Maoris were anxious for free trade, that their friendship should be secured at any price, that it would be impossible to check smuggling on 3,000 miles of coast, and that the amount of customs previously collected was but £18,000 a year, while the expense of collection was nearly £,5,000.

The Board referred the Ordinance to the Treasury, and directed that the officers sent to New Zealand should remain there. It is not exactly apparent how long the Ordinance endured, but the Customs were soon in operation again. Soon, too, there was a new governor, and a flaming, destructive war with the Maoris.

The imports into Port Adelaide during 1843 had been :

	Value.
From the United Kingdom..	£50,053
From other British colonies	1,680
From foreign countries	25,842

The collector of Hobart Town, Tasmania, in his account to the Board of his survey of Launceston, reported that trade was declining (imports rapidly, exports slowly).

1843.	Value.	1844.	Value.
Imports	£705,260	Imports	£442,988
Exports	439,890	Exports	408,799

The collector of Colombo, in an account of his survey of Galle, stated the value of the trade there at £68,425 (imports) and £25,794 (exports). Most of the goods imported were from the British colonies ; most of those exported went to England. There was much smuggling of spirits and tea from passing vessels, and he suggested that three fast-sailing canoes should be manned and appointed in prevention. He stated that the tide waiters, who were natives, were overworked and badly paid. They had only three nights a week in bed, and their pay was but 18s. a month.

The canoes were procured, and the governor issued an injunction 'To the District Modliars and Fisher Head

Men along the coast' to do their duty in preventing smuggling. During the following year the collector reported that the smuggling had been checked so far as the port of Galle was concerned, but the smugglers had taken to landing their goods 'farther down,' storing them on the coast, and smuggling them from thence 'into the bazaar.' Two of their hiding-places had been discovered, and one contained over 1,000 flasks of spirits.

In closing the portion of this chapter that deals with tariffs and departmental practice, a few remarks should be made on the general aspect of affairs. We furnish an account of the Customs revenue for 1844. (We have had choice of three sets of returns, and find that they all differ slightly ; therefore we can only give the amount as *approximately* correct.) Shillings and pence omitted.

GROSS CUSTOMS REVENUE, 1844.

	£
England	19,993,273
Scotland	1,918,887
Ireland	2,362,826
Total	24,274,986

The cost of collection was about 5·2 per cent. on the gross takings (4·75 in Great Britain, and 9·12 in Ireland). The repayments, drawbacks, etc., amounted to £170,129. Besides the cost of collection and the drawbacks, other charges were made on the revenue—viz., the expenses of quarantine and warehousing establishments, certain amounts in adjustment of light dues, compensation to certain Irish civil servants and to naval officers of the coastguard, payments in support of the civil government of Scotland, etc., besides which about half a million was retained as an outstanding balance. The amount actually paid into the Exchequer was £22,504,821. London's gross return was £11,778,516 ; Liverpool returned £4,487,664 ; Bristol, £1,007,832 ; Hull, £607,963 ; Leith,

£631,926; Glasgow, £551,851; Greenock, £367,465; Dublin, £1,043,466; Belfast, £366,414; Cork, £302,207. *Chester* actually returned £75,985, while the once famous Chichester only accounted for £834. The most 'barren' ports were Aberystwith, with £82, and Campbeltown, with £4 17s. 4d. (*gross*, be it remembered). Manchester, which had been granted bonding privileges, figured in the returns for the first time, with £1,991. Twenty-eight ports in England and Wales, eight in Scotland, and three in Ireland, yielded no 'net'; indeed, on most of them there were deficits. Below is the list of undesirables:

Aberystwith.
Aldborough.
Arundel.
Blackney and Clay (of old a stirring port).
Bridlington.
Bridport.
Cardigan.
Chichester (another famous port of old).
Cowes.
Dartmouth.
Deal.
Faversham.
Fowey.
Gweek.
Harwich.
Llanelly.
Lyme.
Maldon.
Milford.
Padstow.
Poole.
Ramsgate.
Rye.
St. Ives.
Scilly.
Southwold.
Wells (once important).
Weymouth (once important).
Ayr.
Banff.
Campbeltown.
Kirkwall.
Lerwick.
Stornoway.
Stranraer.
Wick.
Baltimore.
Coleraine.
Tralee.

Public opinion was veering towards Free Trade. The Navigation laws, praised by most historians of the eighteenth century as the noblest productions of patriotic foresight, were rapidly falling into disrepute. Much was urged against continuance of even the *disjecta membra* of those assertions of British dominance. They were decried in many quarters as utterly incompatible with the spirit of modern commercial progress, but close scrutiny of many cases arising from them leads to the conviction that much of this outcry was due to a brace of causes—causes likely to escape the notice of the ordinary historian. One was the inherent villainy of many of the administering officials. The other was the greed of certain shipowners, who, improving upon the growing desire for cheaper commodities, wished to cheapen manhood, and to substitute for the sturdy breed by Nature and training fitted to hand, reef, and steer, and to wield boarding-pike and rammer, bandy-legged Lascars, frowsy niggers, and squinting Mongols.

The reports made by Committees of Inquiry into Revenue during the early forties testify to a growing dislike of protective duties. Undoubtedly the chief cause of this was the bad influence of the later Corn laws, an element of evil which, as has been shown, sprang into existence during the last ten years of the eighteenth century. These pages form no suitable lists within which to wage the bitter controversy as to whether Free Trade is or is not completely suitable to the needs of a nation. But, as they have here and there exhibited the dents and rents in the Protectionist panoply, room may be reasonably found for the assertion that many of the arguments by which the country was being converted to Free Trade were utterly specious.

To prove this, quotations must be made from the evidence of two 'experts,' both officials of the Board of Trade. One insisted that certain protective duties then imposed, notably the tax on imported woollens, were useless from a revenue point of view, and unnecessary as instruments of protection. The tax on woollens, said he, brought in little revenue, and was never intended to be anything but protective. But the woollen trade did not need protecting, for the exports of woollens had become vast. Now, any straight-thinking reader will perceive that it is difficult to prove such a statement, especially when the intending prover goes on to argue from it that protective duties do not protect. For the history of the restrictions on the importation of woollens—and, in fact, the whole history of the English woollen manufacturing trade—prove that that trade was for ages systematically fostered at the expense of the foreign purchaser of wool and of the English agriculturist, and the very figures quoted proved that the shutting-out of the foreigner did not prevent the foreigner from buying extensively from the shutters-out. But to sneer at a tax as 'merely protective,' and then repeat the sneer because the tax is unproductive, is highly characteristic of your 'expert.' For it is abundantly clear that a tax on imports, to be genuinely protective, *must* be unproductive.

The other Board of Trade witness made a profound impression upon the Committee that examined him—at least, the report stated thus ; but it is likely that a deal of the praise bestowed on him was due to the fact that, though the initials differed slightly, his and the Chairman's names were similar.

It is easy to perceive that Mr. James Deacon Hume, of the Board of Trade (formerly of the Customs), was a dull disciple of the old Adam and the young Richard. He enunciated the childish maxim that the way to make foreign countries open their markets is to import large quantities of foreign goods. Then the people in the protected foreign countries will find it difficult to 'get their returns,' and will agitate for the removal of their own protective duties, so that their customers oversea may be able to 'pay with goods.' Of course, no merchant in the possession of his wits would ever dream of acting as pioneer in such a venture, unless he intended roguery, but that signifies nothing to an ambitious official who is suffering from too much Adam Smith and too little knowledge of the ways of men. Many such chirping absurdities did Mr. Hume tender to the Committee. But the item most curious was his excursion into the realms of prophecy. 'I feel the strongest confidence,' said he, 'that if we were to give up our protective system altogether it would be impossible for other countries to retain theirs much longer.' Students of the course of events from 1840 to 1910 will be able to judge of Mr. Hume's reliability in the prophetic line. The framers of the final report stated, 'Mr. Hume's words are remarkable.' (Barring their occasionally ungrammatical arrangement, it is hard to detect anything remarkable in them, or in the utterances of his brother official.)

The Committee made many palpable slips in their report. France, for instance, was quoted as an example of a country committed thoroughly to Protection, and unable to obtain importance as a manufacturing centre. Yet the evidence had revealed that the thing most dreaded by British manufacturers of silk, lace, and other fancy goods was French competition. History was at hand to prove that for ages France had supplied us with wines, brandies, and delicacies innumerable, and had dictated the fashion of attire; and her supremacy in many important lines of manufacture had been proved by the circumstance that when all intercourse with her was prohibited thousands of English coast-dwellers had risked the press, the hulks, and the gallows, to flood England with contraband French manufactures! Switzerland was quoted as a country unprotected by tariffs, yet excelling in manufactures. But the secret of Switzerland's success was sedulously concealed: the fact that men, women, and little children drudged in the châlets from dawn to dark at monotonous and soul-paralyzing occupations, for wages that would not have been tolerated in England, even in the blackest days of the old factory system.

We introduce these excerpts and comments mainly to illustrate the absurdity of taking too much notice of interested 'experts,' and of making long doctrinal reports. No doubt the members of this and other Committees meant well. They knew that the country was in a parlous state, that the Customs department was badly officered and, now and then, corruptly administered, that bread was dear, and their occasional excursions into the manufacturing towns had made them familiar with a type of juvenile physiognomy far different from that which elicited the historic '*Non Angli, sed Angeli.*' It was convenient to ascribe all the effects of the manifold villainies of Greed and Unreason to Protection. Children were wailing in the streets ; the wolf of Starvation was at many a door. Any truncheon was good enough to slay Lupus with. And the result ? Good was done—harm here and there, which future legislation may attempt to rectify—but good in the main.

We now furnish an account of the various preventive measures, and some of the remarkable seizures and smuggling episodes, during the period extending from 1826 to 1845.

Early in 1826 the smacks *Fox* and *Lovely Lass* were seized at Portsmouth with tubs of spirits concealed in the spaces between waterline and keel, the concealment being contrived so that access to the goods could not be gained till the vessels were laid ashore.

On the night of February 24, 1827, Lieutenant Digby, of the Coastguard, found about eighty smugglers on the beach at the Devil's Gap, Rottingdean, engaged in signalling to a vessel that was hovering on the coast. They advanced upon him, and he drew his pistol, which flashed in the pan. One of the smugglers knocked him down with a bludgeon, and another disarmed him. Then he was beaten till he became insensible. Two men named May and Palmer were convicted at the Horsham assizes for this offence.

At the same assizes Abraham Cox, a labourer, was charged with attempting to bribe Timothy Harrington, a naval sailor employed on the Coast blockade. Harrington stated that the prisoner approached him on the night of April 1, 1826, while he was on patrol at Newhaven, and offered him a bribe to allow a ' crop ' of tubs to be landed on the following night. Cross-examination elicited that when a seaman made a statement of this kind he was at once relieved from the irksome and dangerous duty of patrolling, so that he should be kept out of the way of the smugglers, and that the patrolmen would do almost anything to obtain this relief. The defence set up was that Harrington was unworthy of credence. Cox was acquitted.

No doubt there was a deal of false testimony and straining of evidence in some of the revenue cases. A poor rustic lad named Hazelgrove was charged with making a fire on the coast at Middleton on January 4, 1827, to signal to smugglers, but it was proved that the fire was lit for other purposes entirely, and the boy was acquitted.

A coral smuggling case was tried in the Exchequer on May 29, 1827. Two Italians, Guecco and Mazzinchi, bought a large quantity of coral, which had been warehoused at the London Docks for exportation, sent it to Rotterdam, and then re-imported the goods, concealed in kegs of butter. They imported five consignments between July, 1824, and July, 1825—in all, nearly 8,000 ounces of coral. One day, while the customs officers were weighing the butter at importation (butter being, of course, liable to a low duty), one of the casks fell and burst, and out rolled a tin containing coral. Mazzinchi promptly turned king's evidence. Guecco was fined £400.

On February 13, 1827, the officers at Roseau, Dominica, seized two sloops and their cargoes because the goods were being landed prior to report of ship. There being no direct evidence of fraud, the seizure was a mere arbitrary enforcement of the strict letter of the law. When the seizure note reached London, the Customs Lawyer reported that the officers had no right to seize the goods, the ship only being liable to forfeiture. On inquiry, it appeared that this could not be rectified, for the Dominican officers had promptly secured condemnation and sale of both ship and goods. All the Board could do was to direct that the net proceeds of the sale of the goods should be paid to the owners. Why, because the officers were either ignorant or greedy, the costs of condemnation and sale should be deducted out of the proceeds of goods illegally seized and perhaps corruptly sold, will be past the comprehension of any plain-thinking person. Yet such was the invariable practice; this is but one case among hundreds. Of course, the aggrieved parties might go to law for damages, and then the whole of the Crown's legal phalanx would be pitted against them, *at no extra expense to any official concerned.*

Fraud was extensive in connection with the shipment of bountied linen, the manufacturers enclosing 'Unions,' a mixture of linen and cotton, in bales of genuine linen, and claiming bounty on the whole. The fraudulent goods were made by means of a 'devil.' Several cases of the kind were discovered during 1827.

The Board altered the regulations with regard to 'head-money' (awards made to officers for capturing smugglers). The £15 previously given for capture and committal, and the £20 for capture and transfer of the offender to the navy, were not to be granted in future, except when *armed* smugglers were captured on the coast.

Early in 1828 the boat *Mary* of Dover was found to have a double bottom and double sides, containing thirty tin cases filled with spirits. In May information was received that the sloop *Farmer's Delight* of Hastings had been sold to a Boulogne merchant for use in smuggling. The barge *Alfred* of London, bound coastwise from Arundel to London with wood hoops, was seized off Birchington by the revenue cruiser *Vigilant.* She had taken on board at sea no less than 1,045 tubs of spirits, which were found beneath the wood hoops.

By Cap. 23 of 10 Geo. IV. the scale of rewards for seizing smuggled silks was substantially increased. The seizing officer was to receive the full value of the goods seized, and half of all penalties recovered. (The duties on silks were increased by the same Act.) The usual strings of information reached the Board, one item containing a description of four vessels which had recently gone into the smuggling trade, and another announcing that foreign silks were extensively imported in bales of rags. The seizures were many ; we quote two or three of the more illustrative cases.

Early in the year the *Lucy* of Fowey was seized at Chichester, with 100 tubs of spirits in her false bottom and sides. In March the barge *Independence* of Kinsale was seized at Galway, with kegs of brandy concealed in her storeroom, and tobacco and cigars in the cabin ceiling. In April a number of cases containing eggs from Jersey were found at Southampton to have hollow sides, with silks packed in the spaces. The trawler *Two Brothers* of Falmouth was advertised as 'wanted' for having sunk 152 tubs of spirits at Coverack. A large quantity of tobacco and tea was found in casks of resin, landed in the Port of London by an American ship during August.

(The following are quoted from the general list of merely 'huge' seizures.)

A boat seized by the Shoreham Coast blockade, with 1,245 gallons spirits and 1,950 pounds tobacco ; and two boats seized at one time by the Arundel Coast blockade with 1,117 gallons spirits, 54 pounds tea, and 2,083 pounds tobacco.

To prove that many consignments went clear, it will be necessary to quote one or two specimens of reliable information. A huge run took place on March 20, 1829, 'between Jew's Gut and the Ness Point.' The goods passed through Lydd at 8 a.m. in twelve carts, escorted by about eighty armed smugglers. (The Lydd people came to the doors and cheered as the cavalcade went clanking by.) A run took place between Winchelsea Watchhouse and Cliff End early on June 5, 1829. Seventy or eighty men, each carrying two tubs, went through Winchelsea about 4 a.m. Another consignment of tubs, numbering ninety, was floated up the Brede Channel the same night, and run at Winchelsea Sluice. On July 23, 1829, a large run of half-ankers took place near Eastbourne, and the goods were loaded in carts *at noon*, and

REVENUE CRUISER 'VIGILANT,' WITH BARGE 'ALFRED' IN TOW.

To face p. 234.

carried inland. 'Midway between Eastbourne and Willingdon,' wrote the informer, 'one cart overturned, and caused some delay.'

On October 1, 1829, a cargo of tubs was run on Romney Sands, and a gang of men carried the tubs inland, and loaded them up on carts. Early on October 2, 1829, a galley, 44 feet long, 4 feet 5 inches broad, and 2 feet 6 inches deep, was rowed through mountains of surf and beached near the 'Ivy Cottage,' on the Shorncliffe station. Her cargo was landed and carried inland, but the boat's back was broken. The Coast blockade found her on the beach at daylight. (A similar run took place near Dungeness, and again the long galley used was swamped and disabled. The carriers were not at hand, and the blockade men found and seized boat and goods, but the crew escaped.) On October 29, twenty large bales, supposed to be tea or silks, were run on Dover Beach, 'near the bathing-machines.' Twelve men were in waiting, who put the bales into a coal-cart, and conveyed them into the town. (A few days prior to this daring run the Dover customs officers had found sixty-five half-ankers sunk near Shakspeare's Cliff.) A *chasse-marée* was sighted hovering off the coast in the Arundel district on October 29. H.M.S. *Cameleon* chased and boarded her, but found nothing. She had no boat, so officers scoured the coast, and found a boat lying derelict. It transpired afterwards that she had landed 200 tubs, and the Frenchmen had assisted to carry them inland.

Desperate resistance was not so frequent as of old, yet it occurred occasionally. One hundred and fifty tubs were run at Cliff End, in the Rye district, on the morning of December 3, 1829. The blockade men arrived just as the tubs had been loaded up. The smugglers, armed with 'bats,'* at once engaged them. Four of the blockade men were badly injured. The run was effected successfully, though several of the 'batmen' were wounded and one killed.

* 'Bat,' a long stick used with both hands.

News reached Thames Street that the collector of Dominica, while searching a house for contraband, was assaulted by a crowd of coloured people, and badly injured. Annexed to the report was a copy of the *Dominican Colonist*, containing the following letter: 'As it is more than probable that the coloured gentry of this island who are in the habit of smuggling are unacquainted with Sec. 54 of the Act 114, 6 Geo. IV., do me the favour of inserting it in your next number. Mr. Evans, some time ago, was thrown overboard by a coloured man while in the execution of his duty, Mr. Constable was beaten and maltreated by another, and within the last few days Mr. Redman suffered similar treatment.'

The officers asked for permission to offer a reward for the discovery of the parties. The Board's minute of reply was rather discouraging: 'We see no grounds to comply with this request.'

Cap. 10 of 11 Geo. IV. and 1 Wm. IV. provided that smugglers who were allowed to escape sentence by joining the navy should receive but half the pay at which they were rated; and if their wives or families became paupers the other part should go to the parish supporting them.

On February 10, 1830, the landing-waiter at Sandy Point, St. Kitts, informed the collector that he had tried to seize a boat that was engaged in smuggling, that a mob collected and stoned him almost to death, and that two of his assailants had been convicted, fined £50 each, and imprisoned for three months.

Certain smuggling cases at the port of Kingston, Jamaica, produced in the end a remarkable decision by the Board—a decision which appears to go beyond the law entirely. Seizures were as plentiful as usual; on June 14, 1830, the officers seized five cases of gin in a house in White Street, Kingston; on July 1, in a house occupied by a Spaniard, they seized forty 'jugs' gin and 400 pounds brown sugar, which had been landed from a schooner from Cuba; and two chests of tea on board the same schooner. In August, 1830, other seizures of gin and wine were made ashore, and in the house of one Hyman Levy the officers found forty-nine barrels of salt, in which were concealed carboys of gin. On the premises owned by one Cohen they found many other barrels of salt, but these had been opened, and the precious carboys disposed of. And one Solomon Lazarus was concerned with Cohen and Levy in importation of said salt and gin. Each Jew protested his innocence and accused his confederates, and the Board directed that proceedings might be waived against Levy if he would pay £100, and *consent to give evidence against the other parties!* He promptly decamped to the United States. Proceedings were waived against Lazarus on his paying £459 penalty and £105 15s. costs. (Levy returned to the island in 1836, and paid a heavy fine.) There was not sufficient evidence to carry proceedings against Cohen.

The United Kingdom smuggling records (second-hand) for 1830 are voluminous. Of course, we can only quote a few cases, which we select as fairly illustrative of the various phases of the trade.

A seizure of a large quantity of eau-de-Cologne was made at one of the outports. The goods had been put into long-necked bottles, the corks covered with gilt foil, and the consignment labelled and entered as champagne.

Books which had been printed prior to 1801 were allowed importation at a much lower rate of duty than was payable upon books printed subsequently (£1 per hundredweight against £5). A large consignment, entered at Dublin as printed prior to 1801, turned out on inspection to be fitted with false title-pages.

A quantity of silks had been smuggled ashore at Rochester, and the receivers were chary of conveying them by road to London, fearing they might be discovered by the mounted patrol; so they had a number of egg-boxes constructed with hollow sides, in which they packed the silks. They imported a cargo of eggs, landed and cleared them, packed them in the silk-lined egg-boxes, and sent them to London by waggon. Someone connected with the business gave information to the Customs, and eggs and silks were seized on arrival.

Repeated information arrived as to the doings of the *Grace* of Gweek. She was stated to have been often at Roscoff, engaged in loading contraband, and to have frequently met French vessels at sea, taken in contraband goods, and landed them near Land's End. Her crew were described as ' the three brothers Carlyon of Coverack, reputed smugglers.'

We quote from the Dover list (April 5, 1829, to June 5, 1830) the seizures made by the officers employed in examining imports and clearing passengers' baggage.

April 6, 1829.—2 pairs silk stockings, 2 lace veils, 1 lace scarf, 132 yards lace.

April 9.—24 pieces of chip (for hats).

April 14.—44 yards silk, 1 silk handkerchief, 1 pair silk braces, 1 silk waistcoat, 1 silk cravat, 3 yards merino, 3 pairs leathern gaiters, 14 pairs leathern gloves, 1 book containing 50 prints, 2 pairs earrings, 6 buttons, 6 metal forks, 1 inkstand, 1 piece porcelain, 5 yards thread lace.

Another seizure of 2 yards velvet, 31 yards silk, 4 silk handkerchiefs, 1 reticule, 12 reels and 21 skeins floss silk, 1 silk band, 1 cushion, 2 worked muslin caps, 5 necklaces, 66 buttons, 1 pair bracelets, 6 snuff-boxes, 3 pairs leathern gloves, 1 book containing 50 prints, 1 piece glass, 3 ounces beads, 2 salt glasses, 4 decanter-stands, 2 pairs earrings, 1 pair eardrops, 1 cream-jug.

Another of 12 yards silk, 3 yards merino, 4 wineglasses, 3 fans, 1 necklace, 4 pairs earrings, 2 glass balls, 5 papers pins, and sundry beads.

April 23.—224 yards silk riband.

April 30.—446 yards blond lace.

May 2.—13 pairs leather gloves.

May 8.—22 yards silk, 2 flasks eau-de-Cologne, 2½ pounds tea.

May 10.—1 clock.

May 13.—16 flasks eau-de-Cologne, 136 yards silk riband.

May 14.—47 yards cotton fringe, 24 flasks eau-de-Cologne, 2¾ pounds tea, 1 trunk.

May 17.—8 pairs silk stockings.

May 19.—1 merino shawl.

May 23.—9½ pounds tea, 6 pairs gloves.

June 10.—3 cambric petticoats.

June 11.—6 cartons manufactured hair.

June 16.—36 packs playing-cards.

June 19.—22 pieces lace.

July 8.—3 musical boxes, 26 musical snuff-boxes, 18 gold watches.

July 11.—14 ounces plain silk, 10 ounces figured gauze, 1 ounce silk gauze, 2 ounces figured silk.

July 13.—7 pounds tea, 7 flasks eau-de-Cologne.

July 15.—46 bottles and 50 flasks perfumery, 4 silk umbrellas.

The list proceeds in much the same fashion up to June, 1830. Now and then larger seizures occur, of which a few appear below.

A seizure of 55 pounds vultures' feathers. Another of 44 yards silk riband, 2,170 'porcelain teeth,' 300 human teeth, and 1 bracelet. Another of 2 silk bonnets, 8 silk dresses, 2 silk aprons, and 2 silk waistcoats. Another of 16 silk dresses, 24 pieces trimming, 4 silk tippets, 26 embroidered caps, 37 embroidered tippets, 42 pieces embroidery, 1 embroidered dress, and 8 bonnets. The list shows seizures of musical instruments, percussion caps, stained paper, ostrich feathers, and many other curios.

The rummaging staff at Dover are credited with three tolerable seizures during the same period—one of a sloop and 27 casks brandy; one of a boat with 789 yards silk and 544 yards riband; and one of a 'raft' of spirits, containing 65 tubs. The Coast blockade at Dover seized during the same period a boat with 14 tubs spirits, a boat with 9 tubs, a four-oared boat with 167 tubs, 4 boats with 32 tubs, 2 boats with 229 tubs, a boat with 47 tubs, a boat with 23 tubs, a boat with 37 tubs, and a boat with 35 tubs, amounting in all to about 1,914 gallons spirits, besides an immense number of 'sunken tubs crept up,' in parcels of from 1 to 10.

Below is a list of large seizures made during 1830-31:

March 22, 1830.—By the Hastings Coast blockade. The boat *Mary*, with 1,706 pounds tobacco and 487 pounds snuff.

March 31.—By the Hastings Coast blockade. The smack *Neptune*, with 2,971 pounds tobacco and 1,389 pounds snuff.

May 29.—By the Margate Coast blockade. 2,439 yards figured silk, 1,265 yards black silk, 3,667 yards coloured silk, 35,825 yards silk gauze, and 4,607 yards Petersham gauze.

June 23.—By the Rochester Coast blockade. The coasting brig *Industry*, with coals, and concealed beneath the coals 1,850 gallons spirits, 2,688 pounds tea, and 41,110 yards silk gauze, which had been taken on board at sea.

September 22.—By the Rochester Coast blockade. The coasting sloop *William*, laden with oats, and 1,974 gallons spirits and 1,203 pounds tea as above.

January 16, 1831.—By the Ramsgate Coast blockade. 3,940 pieces silk gauze, 1,515 ells crape, 5 silk dresses, a velvet skirt, 1,591 pounds tea, and a half-anker of brandy.

An ingenious fraud was discovered at Southampton early in 1831. A consignment of casks of cider from Jersey was examined closely, and the officers found that sections of the upper part of each cask were diagonally 'blocked off,' and that tobacco had been packed in the spaces thus created.

The Coast blockade was abolished in 1831, as previously stated. This force had been established in 1817, for special protection of the coast of Kent and Sussex. The blockade men had made many important seizures, yet the authorities had never imposed implicit confidence in them. The force was practically independent of the Board's control, yet disagreements often occurred between the Board and the Admiralty on account of its proceedings. A committee inquired into the protection of the Revenue in 1821, commented unfavourably upon the constitution and discipline of the force, and urged that it should be governed by the Customs Board. Much correspondence ensued, the Board losing no opportunity of belittling the blockade men, a task in which they were ably supported by several of the collectors at the outports—notably by the collector of Shoreham, whose confidential reports on the matter contained most remarkable statements. He declared that the force was composed principally of 'raw Irishmen,' who had never been on board ship previous to their taking passage for England, and of old and worn-out seamen; that the discipline enforced was barbarous, there being many cases of brutal flogging; and that when seamen were required for the expedition to Navarino in 1829 not one-third of the men were found fit for naval service. (After the Coast blockade was abolished, the Revenue Coastguard took over the duties, and the Board thus regained control of the whole of the preventive service.)

A report made by a revenue spy in May, 1831, seems to show that there had been good reason for suspecting the integrity of the blockade men. It stated that smuggling was suspended in Kent and Sussex since the abolition of the Coast blockade, as the various contraband syndicates were busily studying the methods of the new force, but that at one of the ports the smugglers had actually stolen an eight-oared galley belonging to the Coastguard, and taken her to Calais. A fleet of galleys lay at that port, waiting orders from England. Later came a report from Rye that in consequence of the suspension of smuggling the price of spirits had risen from about 50s. to £4 a tub.

The preventive regulations were strengthened during 1832 by the clauses in Cap. 84 enacting forfeiture of goods fraudulently concealed in packages entered on bill of sight, and liability of unauthorized enterers of goods and of hirers of smuggling parties, and giving power to customs officers to stop and examine vehicles without being liable to action at law if such examination were fruitless. It was also directed that fishing and pilot vessels should be painted black (that they might be readily distinguished from hoverers).

It had become a common practice with smugglers to furnish false information, and to make demonstrations of runs at certain places, in order to lure the preventive men into watching and visiting the places in question. While the guards were thus occupied, genuine runs were made at other places.

There can be no doubt that some of the preventive men were inclined to use weapons with remarkable promptitude. Early in the morning of December 23, 1832, two coastguardsmen named Carter and Lovell, stationed at Weymouth, saw a fore-and-aft vessel hovering off 'the old Sluice.' Then a boat with five men appeared, ploughing through the surf, and beached safely. The coastguardsmen fired a rocket as a signal for assistance, and ran towards her; the smugglers leaped out and escaped. Attached to the boat by a warp were many tubs of spirits. The coastguardsmen loaded their pistols, expecting an attempt at rescue; nor were they deceived, for up came a number of men armed with sticks, who began to cut the tubs loose. One of the men knocked Lovell's cutlass from his hand, and another attacked Carter, who at once opened fire. The smugglers then dispersed, carrying off many of the tubs. Assistance arrived, and the officers collected 65 tubs of spirits, and found two of the smugglers, named Webber and Burt, lying dead on the beach. Mr. Thackeray, the Customs Lawyer who was sent from London to attend the inquest, reported thus on the result: 'The jury came to the best conclusion I have ever known a Dorsetshire jury to do where smugglers were concerned.' The verdict ran thus: 'The deceased, James Webber and George Burt, came by their deaths by being shot with pistol balls by some officers in the service of the Coastguard in the execution of their duty, for the preservation of themselves and to prevent the rescuing of contraband goods which they had seized in the king's name.'

Another and much more desperate mêlée occurred in the Folkestone district. Information having been received by Lieutenant Parry of the Coastguard that a 'forced landing' would be attempted at 'No. 5 Guard,' that officer placed himself in ambush with a party of his men, and soon after nightfall a boat laden with kegs of spirits ran in through the surf. On the officers attempting seizure, about 200 people, armed with clubs and guns, appeared on the beach, and a battle-royal ensued. The smugglers were beaten off, and one of them was killed. Two of the coastguardsmen were badly injured, and Lieutenant Parry received seven severe wounds, all in front. The officers captured the boat and kegs, and took them into Rye, bearing their wounded and the dead smuggler with them. The Admiralty Minute on the papers read thus: 'Inform the Board of Customs and Lieutenant Parry that in approbation of the gallant conduct of the lieutenant their Lordships have promoted him to the rank of commander.'

Another battle-royal took place at St. Leonards. The coastguard, under the command of Lieutenant Palmer, came upon a party engaged in a run, and were at once attacked by a squad of 'batmen,' who beat them most severely; but Palmer and his men killed several of the smugglers, and captured a boat and 46 ankers of brandy. (Palmer was promoted for this and similar services in 1839.)

It must not be thought that all revenue officers were like Messrs. Parry and Palmer. The inspecting commander of Coastguard at Carne, Ireland, was by no means inclined to take risks. On January 26, 1832, he apprised the controller-general of Coastguard that the Carne district was in rebellion. 'The tricoloured flag,' he stated, 'is displayed in open day. . . . The Rev. Mr. Staples, the magistrate, was in conference with me this day, intimating that he was fearful of an attack, and that he should be obliged to call out the revenue police and the Coastguard. At Clonmelly they pulled their priest on Sunday from the altar, set fire to several stacks, houghed cattle, etc. May I request to know, as there is no provision made for naval officers in this service in case of loss of life, whether I am to order a civilian to take charge of the party when called on by a magistrate ?'

The controller-general drew his pen under the concluding lines, and reported to the Board thus : ' An officer who under such circumstances is capable of offering such a suggestion for the purpose of avoiding personal risk is utterly unfit for and unworthy of the office he holds.' The Board referred the papers to the Admiralty. Admiralty Minute : ' Direct his immediate removal. Acquaint the Customs. Nominate Commander Henry Parker.' The most amazing part of the business was that the superseded officer actually wrote the Admiralty, trying to justify his previous letter. He asked : ' When naval officers are called upon to act offensive instead of defensive, are they to be considered as acting afloat, and remunerated in case of wounds ?' He ended with this peculiar statement : ' These are times when it renders it necessary to act with the greatest caution.' He received no reply.

The Admiralty had adopted a method of promoting specially each year from among the coastguard officers one captain, one commander, and one midshipman, for distinguished services, the appointments being made on the recommendation of the Customs Board. We furnish a summary of one of the reports of recommendation.

Report on Commander Langharne : ' Employed for the last eight years in Ireland. Was instrumental in bringing about the capture of the *Elizabeth and Grace* by H.M.S. *Semiramis* on the Irish coast, and the capture of the *Marie Theresa* by H.M.S. *Pike*. In March, 1827, prevented the landing of a large cargo, and captured several persons who were signalling. In October, 1827, again frustrated the plans of the smugglers, earning Board's special approval. In March, 1829, was on leave. A run took place during his absence. Returned, captured the run goods (492 bales tobacco), dispersed a crowd several hundred strong, that attempted rescue. Secured conviction of instigator of run (penalty £10,876 10s. 9d.).'

Report on Lieutenant Neame: 'Fourteen years in coastguard, first at Mersea, Essex. Detected and convicted principal smugglers there. Went to Ireland in 1820; was very successful. Large run in Bray district, February, 1820. Neame and party attacked by several hundreds of the country people. Beat off the rioters, killing and wounding forty or fifty of them, and captured forty bales tobacco, fourteen horses and carts, and nine men, seven of whom were convicted and transported. Afterwards went to Antrim, and reorganized the Coastguard there successfully.'

Report on Midshipman Hay: 'Instrumental in capture of several vessels, and about 2,000 kegs spirits. Saved many shipwrecked people, notably when the *Mary Ann*, East Indiaman, went ashore on the Devon coast in 1827, and when H.M.S. *Echo* was wrecked on same coast in 1831.

'Langharne to captain, Neame to commander, Hay to lieutenant.'

About the middle of 1832 the Treasury approved an arrangement for filling vacancies in a new 'Mounted Guard' appointed for Kent and Sussex, by volunteers from dragoon regiments, at the following rates of pay: Sergeants, 5s. a day; corporals, 4s. 6d.; troopers, 4s., and allowances for the horses. Forage, saddlery, weapons, and veterinary attendance to be paid for by the Crown. (In the following year this force was increased so as to guard the whole of the English coast.)

Another ingenious fraud was discovered by the Southampton officers. A number of coops containing poultry arrived from Guernsey. It was found that the coops had false bottoms, filled with tobacco.

The various Government postal packets were deeply

suspected at this period, and on January 26, 1832, a special rummage was instituted on board the *Messenger* packet, which had arrived at Falmouth from Gibraltar. Below is a list of the contraband goods found :

414 pounds leaf tobacco and 44 pounds cigars under the planking of the coal-hole ; 60 pounds cigars under the plates of the engine-room ; 15 pounds cigars under the cinders in the smith's forge on deck ; 2½ pounds cigars in the starboard paddlebox ; 2¼ pounds cigars under the sails in the sail-room ; 16 pounds leaf tobacco under firewood in the forehold ; 12 glass tumblers under a false sill in the engine-room.

Said the rummagers in their report : 'The officers gave us every assistance, with the exception of the boatswain, who, with the engineers, stokers, and coal-trimmers, acted in a very insubordinate manner, and threw every impediment in our way.'

An important seizure was made on June 13, 1832, by the Newhaven Coastguard. The victim was a vessel named the *New Speedwell*, with 23 pounds cigars, 990 pounds leaf tobacco, 1,095 pounds tobacco-stalk flour, and 12,986 pounds tobacco-stalks (in all nearly 7 tons).

To display the course of smuggling in the West Indian colonies, we quote the following curious list of seizures, made in Dominica in November, 1832 :

1. In a negro hut (for being illegally landed), 2 barrels flour, 1 barrel bread, 1 barrel tar.

2. In the house of François Brown (for being illegally landed), 1 barrel fish. (The above were American goods.)

3. In the house of Frederick Smith (illegally landed), 1 basket anisette, 3 baskets onions, 1 basket oil, 1 pair shoes, 21 snuff-boxes.

4. In the house of Joseph Rolle (illegally landed), 2 baskets anisette, 2 baskets onions, 1 box candles, 18 earthen pots, a firkin of butter, a box of raisins, 6 boxes oil.

5. In the house of Jeanne Rose (illegally landed), 18 drinking-glasses, 1 box eau-de-Cologne, 1 box candles.

6. In the house of Julienne Marceau (illegally landed), 1 box soap, 30 earthen pots. (The above were French goods.)

7. In the house of Charles Melangam (illegally landed), 2 barrels flour, 36 earthen pots.

8. In the houses of Martial Roger, Mordesin de Blanc, and Mariette Bellot (illegally landed), 1 barrel pork, 4 barrels flour, 2 boxes oil, 2 firkins butter.

In the Bay of Colihaut, 13 dozen 'goglets,' 22 firkins butter, 12 boxes oil, 1 bag corn (two canoes used in conveyance).

At Souffriere, 5 barrels flour, 2 barrels pork, 12 dozen claret. (The above were partly French and partly American goods.)

The Board directed forfeiture of goods in all the cases, but declined to authorize prosecution of the smugglers, they being indigent coloured people.

Early in 1833 a number of bales of cotton, which had been delivered into a lighter at Belfast from an American ship, accidentally took fire, and it was discovered during salvage that a large bale of leaf tobacco was concealed within each package of cotton.*

A new system of rafting tubs was discovered at Langstone Harbour. Sixty-three tubs had been lashed together 'in the form of a pile of shot.' Each tub had a sling attached to it, and to each sling was fastened an iron plate weighing about 8 pounds. The upper tiers of tubs were painted white. This raft had grounded in 7 feet of water, yet but three of the tubs were visible, and they from a short distance only. Two grapnels were attached to the raft, so as to be caught by dredging with a 'sweep line.'

On September 13, 1833, the coasting barge *Rebecca*, with a cargo of limestone, arrived at St. Germain's Lake, Plymouth. The coastguardsmen overhauled her, and

* In 1835 a number of barrels of pitch were landed from the same vessel, and it was found that a block of tobacco, weighing 100 pounds, was secreted within each barrel of pitch.

found 211 tubs spirits beneath the limestone. The tubs had been taken on board at sea from a 'hoverer.'

Below are illustrative extracts from the seizure lists of Port Louis and Montreal.

Port Louis, Mauritius.

Quarter ending January 5, 1833.—This includes cigars and straw hats seized on a vessel from Calcutta ; coffee on a vessel from Bourbon ; smoked salmon on a vessel from Salem ; and coffee thrown overboard from a French schooner, and recovered by divers.

Quarter ending April 5, 1833.—Muskets and bayonets found on premises occupied by one Pyton ; loaf sugar and the boat conveying it ; cigars and the boat conveying ; coffee on a ship from Bourbon ; gunpowder and spermaceti on an American ship from Salem.

Quarter ending July 5, 1833.—Arms and gunpowder run ; sundry goods from Calcutta ; sundry goods from Singapore ; cigars and preserved ginger on a ship from Batavia ; arms on a vessel from Bourbon.

(The inhabitants were in a state of excitement over the reinstallation of the unpopular Procurator-General, Mr. Jeremie. This may account for the smuggling of arms and gunpowder.)

Montreal.

December 2, 1833.—Seized on the highway from a non-resident foreigner, 1 horse, 1 sled, 132 gallons of American whisky, and 156 pounds of coffee of the French West Indies.

December 30.—On the premises of I. Mack, innkeeper, 1 bale American bristles.

December 30.—On bank of St. Lawrence (owner unknown), 6 cases of clock movements, 156 dozen boxes of combs, 9 gross of buckles, 1 bridle, 1 horse-collar, 1 saddle, 1 umbrella (all American).

January 16, 1834.—In the street, 'from a non-resident,' 12 pounds of tea.

February 3.—In a cellar under a stable, owner unknown, 1,530 pounds of American tobacco.

February 4.—On premises occupied by N. C. Kurcyan, 1,200 pounds of American tobacco.

February 10.—On premises occupied by P. Darragh, 4 chests of tea, 2 packages of tobacco.

February 15.—On premises occupied by C. Wilkinson, 78 gallons of American whisky.

February 18.—On premises occupied by J. Craig, 1 chest of tea, 4 packages of tobacco.

February 26.—On premises occupied by J. Brown, 1 bag of coffee.

February 27.—On premises occupied by Louis Gareau, 2 chests of tea and 23 pairs of American gloves.

February 27.—On premises occupied by Stephen Franchiri, 2 boxes of tea, 194 pounds of tobacco.

February 28.—On premises occupied by Stephen Dier, 10 kegs of tobacco, 1 bag of coffee.

March 7.—On premises occupied by W. Megill, 2 boxes of tea, 232 pounds of tobacco, and 360 pounds of American butter.

March 26.—'In the cellar of a Frenchman' (name unknown), 2,160 pounds of American tobacco.

March 26.—In a barn owned by one Morrison, 840 pounds of American butter.

During 1833 the collector of St. Kitts forwarded to the Board a deposition made by the master of a colonial sloop, to the effect that in the previous year he had conveyed the Honourable R. W. Pickwoad, judge of the Vice-Admiralty Court, and Lieutenant Hutchinson of the 86th Regiment, 'to the French islands,' that they bought there a considerable quantity of wine and perfumery, that he brought the sloop back to St. Kitts, and landed the goods without the knowledge of the Customs, and that the said goods were surreptitiously conveyed to the Honourable R. W. Pickwoad's residence. Both Pickwoad and Hutchinson denied the charge, and the former wrote the Board, stating that he had previously found it necessary to complain to the Secretary of State as to the conduct of Lieutenant-Colonel Nickle, the officer who administered civil government at St. Kitts, and also that of the Attorney-General for the island, and that those officials had induced the informer to make the statements in question. (Considerable correspondence ensued, ended by a statement from St. Kitts, on February 27, 1835, that Mr. Pickwoad was dead.)

During 1834, by Cap. 13 of 4 and 5 Wm. IV., the practice of sending convicted smugglers to serve for five years in the navy was abolished. The pecuniary penalties prescribed for certain smuggling offences were also abolished, and justices were granted power to imprison offenders instead.

During 1835 the Board received information of a subtle fraud. A quantity of brandy had been cleared duty-free from bond for exportation, carried to sea, transhipped to a coaster; the casks had been placed inside puncheons containing sugar, the consignment landed as British refined sugar removed coastwise, and the brandy thus taken into home consumption free of duty.

Many ingenious 'concealments on the person' were discovered. One man was found to be wearing a corset with eighteen quilted spaces, and a pair of drawers secured at the ankles, carrying in all 24 pounds of tea. Six men were captured wearing waistcoats, 'thigh pieces,' and 'shin pieces.' Two of them had in these receptacles nine parcels of lace each. The remaining four had eight parcels each. Several Deal boatmen were found to be fitted with 'shin pieces,' 'bustles,' 'stays,' 'thigh pieces,' and 'cotton bags to fit the crown of the hat.' Each boatman carried 30 pounds of tea.

A French sloop, laden with a full cargo of tobacco, intended for the coast of Ireland, and carrying an Irish pilot and an Irish supercargo, was driven by storm into Douglas, Isle of Man, and captured.

A petty squabble between merchants and customs

officers in Ceylon led to revelations of much illegal trading in that colony. On September 20, 1835, Messrs. Ackland and Boyd, merchants, landed at Colombo from the barque *Anne*. They had six turkeys with them, and it appears that they went on shore with these birds at a place not approved by the Customs for the landing of baggage and effects. A customs officer saw them land, and insisted upon detaining the turkeys, although turkeys were duty-free, basing his action upon the circumstance that landing had occurred at an unapproved place. Ackland refused to allow him to seize the birds, and sent them back to the ship. The officers then instituted proceedings in the island Courts for obstruction. Ackland was acquitted, and when the report reached London the Board expressed an opinion that the officers had acted unwarrantably. Ackland and Boyd then complained to the Board that entry had since been refused to certain wines, imported by them from Tutticorin. Inquiry elicited that the merchants had been evading the Navigation laws by importing wine from France to Colombo 'for exportation,' transhipping it to Tutticorin, and then importing it thence as goods from a British possession. (Subterfuges of this kind were common during the times of restricted trade.) They pleaded that other merchants were allowed to do this, and indeed it seems, to one who reads between the lines, that Ackland and Boyd's goods would never have been restricted but for that unfortunate affair of turkeys. The Board intimated that a new controller was on his way to Ceylon, and that no doubt he would try to prevent squabbles between merchants and officers, and evasions of the laws of Navigation.

Cap. 60 of 6 and 7 Wm. IV. relaxed to a certain extent the preventive regulations as to size of package and tonnage of importing vessel, allowing spirits to be imported in casks containing not less than 20 gallons, and tobacco or snuff in packages not less than 300 pounds in weight, and reducing the legal tonnage for import ships to 60 tons. It extended the powers of the Board with regard to the granting of general transires for coasting vessels. At the same time it empowered magistrates to deal with *petty* cases of smuggling without an order from the Board. This provision extended merely to cases in which the goods seized, being spirits, did not exceed a gallon, and, being tobacco, did not exceed 6 pounds. The magistrates under such circumstances might inflict fines not exceeding £5, or imprisonment for not more than one month.

In 1836 a steamer trading to London was found to have her paddle-boxes lined so as to contain a considerable quantity of contraband goods. The smack *Tam o' Shanter* was seized by the Coastguard at Padstow, 72 tubs of spirits being found concealed in spaces between the cabin and the outer timbers. She was a coaster, carrying coals.

During March, 1837, a curiously-built boat was found on the beach at Bognor. She had no thwarts, and was flat-bottomed. Her bottom was pierced so that when loaded she would sink just below the surface of the water. A net was found on board, and it was evident that she had been used for running tubs. When loaded, the net had been laced from gunwale to gunwale to keep the tubs in position, and she had then been set adrift. The smugglers had unloaded her, and left her on the beach.

On March 14, 1837, the *Sylvia* revenue cruiser seized the *Good Intent* schooner at Mount's Bay, on account of the following concealments : 26 tubs in false lining near sail-locker ; 138 tubs in a space formed by double bulkheads between hold and cabin ; 26 tubs in the coal-locker, under the coals ; 148 tubs in a space formed by double bulkheads between forepeak and hold ; 21 tubs under flooring of forepeak. The bulkheads and flooring had been newly tarred, so that the odour of the spirits should not be apparent.

On July 1, 1837, the same revenue cruiser took the *Spartan* schooner off Land's End. She had a hollow beam under the cabin floor, and a double bulkhead between the hold and the coal-hole. These spaces were filled with compressed tobacco.

There was considerable smuggling at Sydney ; witness the following seizures :

December 5, 1837.—On the brig *Gazelle,* from Boston, U.S.A., 1,211 pounds of tobacco.

June 9, 1838.—On the *Mary Ann,* of London, 503 pounds of tobacco, 115 gallons of whisky, 45 gallons of geneva.

September 14.—On the ship *Earl Durham,* 478 pounds of tobacco.

November 24.—Found in possession of a dealer at George Street, Sydney (had been shipped from bond for exportation to New Zealand, and afterwards run), 356 pounds of tobacco.

Many seizures were made in the United Kingdom on board Her Majesty's ships. We quote three specimens only :

Portsmouth.—Seventy pounds of tobacco, found concealed between bulkheads on board H.M. cutter *Seaflower,* from Jersey.

Dover.—Sixty pounds of tobacco, 10 packages of cigars, and 2 casks of spirits, found in the engine-room of H.M. Post-Office packet *Widgeon.*

Jersey.—Two hundred and fifty-two pounds of tobacco, part found ashore alongside H.M. Post-Office packet *Dasher,* part in the engine-room (illegal shipment for England).

The collector of Colombo informed the Board that the governor had prohibited the traffic hitherto carried on with passing vessels by the boatmen of Galle. The Board concurred, while hinting that care had better be taken as to the forfeiture of boats engaged in the trade, the law not being fully applicable to such cases.

In 1839 the collector of St. Kitts reported that the customs officer at Sandy Point pursued a smuggling boat, overtook her, and stepped on board to seize certain ankers of gin. The smugglers, named respectively Lammond and Parsons, took the officer by the neck and heels, gave him a couple of swings, and, Lammond calling out 'Now is the time,' threw him into the sea. Then they rowed off with the gin. They were afterwards arrested, and Lammond was sentenced to twelve months imprisonment. Parsons was acquitted—why is hard to discover.

The *Lady de Saumarez* arrived at Southampton from Jersey. Part of her cargo consisted of bundles of laths, and in the middle of each bundle was found a roll of tobacco, weighing about 4 pounds.

A peculiar fraud was discovered at the London Docks. It was the practice to gauge quarter-casks of brandy for duty by the 'diagonal,' a graduated rod being inserted in the bunghole diagonally, so that its end touched the bottom chimb of the cask, and the gallons being read as marked on the rod. A shrewd merchant turned this to account by importing casks the diagonal of which was shortened artificially, the bung stave being depressed, and the heads put in obliquely. By this means he had succeeded in getting his casks through each at 3 gallons less than the actual content (the usual content of a brandy quarter-cask being 29 to 30 gallons).

On November 19, 1839, the tobacco manufacturers of Edinburgh memorialized the Treasury, complaining of the injury done to their business by smuggling, and stating that they had reliable information of a recent transaction at Leith, where over 2 tons of cavendish were landed ; also that they were of opinion that the customs staff at Leith, which had been recently reduced, required strengthening. The Board reported on the petition, stating that they believed smuggling had increased of late. They had recently sent officers to search certain suspected houses in Leith and Edinburgh, and five seizures had been made (356 pounds of cavendish in all). In connection with this paper there is a quotation from the London tobacco brokers' circular, calling attention to the fact that the quantity of tobacco duty-paid during the year ending October 5, 1839, was at least a million pounds less than in the preceding year.

On November 20, 1839, four large cases were landed at one of the London legal quays, from a vessel from Hamburg, and entered on 'sight.' The Customs received information that an attempt would be made to run these goods, and produce four substituted cases for examination. The cases were opened at once, and found to contain about a ton of tobacco and cigars. The goods were not seizable in a strictly revenue sense, being entered on 'sight,' a method of declaring that the contents of the packages are unknown to the importer, but they were seized as infringing the laws of Navigation, being the produce of Asia, imported from Hamburg in a foreign ship.

The following statement appeared in the *Hampshire Telegraph*: 'The Adelaide revenue cutter has recently been twenty-three weeks in this harbour (Portsmouth) refitting, in which time she was recoppered, and supplied from London with a new set of rigging. A continuance of such gross robbery on the Government ought immediately to be remedied, and these craft should be sent to the dockyard for stores and repairs in future. Had this been the case in the present instance the vessel in question would not have been delayed more than ten days or a fortnight.'

A seizure was made at one of the Irish ports of a quantity of English-manufactured arms, packed in large cases, the arms being concealed beneath parcels of snuff-boxes and corkscrews.

The Deal punt *Canning* was seized at Deal. She had been ostensibly engaged in catching shellfish, but was found to have sixteen large tin cases of spirits concealed beneath her bottom boards.

A number of tin cases, each containing 63 pounds tobacco, were found in the water-tank on board an American trader.

An Ordinance of the island of Mauritius, issued on March 2, 1840, had prohibited the importation, culture, or sale of a substance called 'gandia,' formerly much used by the labouring population of that colony. The Ordinance described it as a most pernicious drug, causing furious excitement. Forty-two bales, weighing in all 1,907 pounds, were seized by the collector of Port Louis, but, it being proved that the goods had been shipped at Bengal prior to the issue of the Ordinance, the Board allowed them to be exported.

In 1841 new regulations were issued with respect to British 'open boats,' as below:

	Between Beachy Head and North Foreland.	*On any other part of coast.*	*Along coast.*
Fast rowing-boats might not go more than	4 leagues from coast	6 leagues from coast	20 leagues
Open boats for sailing and rowing, under 15 tons	4 leagues from coast	8 leagues from coast	50 leagues
Open boats for sailing and rowing, 15 tons and above	4 leagues from coast	8 leagues from coast	70 leagues
Decked vessels, under 15 tons	4 leagues from coast	12 leagues from coast	Around coast

(Extra privileges might be granted to fishing-boats if the masters were of good character.)

A vessel which had brought herrings from the Orkneys was seized in the Dunfanaghy district (Donegal), it being found that she had 187 bales of tobacco on board (about 10,000 pounds).

A large seizure of pirated books was made at Kingston, Jamaica, including parcels of volumes under the following titles: 'Nicholas Nickleby,' 'Oliver Twist,' 'Pickwick Papers,' 'Sketches by Boz,' 'Miss Austen's Novels,' 'History of Rome,' 'Smollett's Works,' 'Chitty's Medical

Jurisprudence,' 'The Pathfinder,' 'Moore's Life of Byron,' 'Fielding's Works,' 'Mrs. Hemans' Poetical Works,' etc., etc. This seems to have been a bad case, for the goods were entered 'on sight,' and it was afterwards found that the importer had a complete invoice. But the Board allowed the goods to be returned to the United States.

Below is a copy of the seizure list of Sydney, N.S.W., in 1841:

May 12, 1841.—22 gallons brandy in the Commercial Inn, smuggled thither by the waiter.

102 pounds tobacco near the Queen's Wharf (seized by police).

May 26.—70 barrels beef and pork on the *Lapwing* from New Zealand, entered as 'British.' Had been originally sent from London to New Zealand, but had lost their 'British' privileges through being landed there, New Zealand not being at the time a Crown colony.

June 4.—42 gallons brandy, seized by a civilian in Rushcutter's Bay. (The goods had been landed from a boat belonging to a passing Calcutta trader. The boat escaped with a number of other casks, but was afterwards captured and seized—the casks not found.)

September 4.—13 gallons brandy in a house in Erskine Street, Sydney.

49 cases spirits in a public-house in King Street, Sydney.

September 6.—74 gallons spirits and 60 pounds tobacco in a house in Erskine Street, Sydney. 174 gallons spirits in a public-house in Erskine Street.

September 16.—154 pounds tobacco at Kissing Point, Parramatta River.

November 23.—84 pounds snuff and 6 pounds cigars on the *Lady Raffles*, from New Zealand.

Most of the goods thus seized formed part of a huge run previously made by a notorious smuggler. It appears that a cargo of spirits and tobacco had been shipped duty-free from bond in Sydney for New Zealand, and the smuggler in question had effected the re-landing and distribution of the whole consignment. 'Robert Henderson,' said the report, 'has been long suspected, but living until lately in a wild and extensive harbour twenty-one miles north of Sydney by sea and seventy by land, so many obstacles have presented themselves in the way of detection that nothing before has been brought against him.'

Below is a copy of the seizure list for the Jaffna district, Ceylon, for the first four months of 1841 :

January 25, 1841.—2 shawls, on board a 'dhoney' at Manar.

January 28.—13 skeins silk thread, concealed among rice on a dhoney.

February 1.—32 bags rice, landed without report.

February 7.—14 silk handkerchiefs and 1 silk shawl, for being landed on a Sunday.

February 8.—22 hundredweight of coriander seed and 1 hundredweight of garlic, imported in a vessel of less than the legal tonnage.

March 12.—34 pieces cloth, transhipped without entry.

March 24.—3 chelas and 1 somen (manufactures of India).

April 1.—15 bags rice and a quantity of paddy (transhipped without entry).

April 7.—6 whips, 5 pairs slippers, 17 pieces soap, 32 chowries, 4 shawls, 16 pieces cloth, 40 handkerchiefs, 2 wrappers, 2 looking-glasses, imported in a vessel of less than the legal tonnage.

April 8.—30 pounds coffee (prohibited goods), 7 yards cloth, at Point Pedro (not reported).

April 22.—4 shawls, for being unstamped.

In 1842 the revenue cruiser *Vulcan* seized the French smack *Le Courier* off Weymouth. She had arrived in ballast, and on rummaging her the revenue men found that she was provided with most ingenious 'concealments.' Between the ballast and the keelson was a false keelson, fitted with ten tanks containing spirits, each tank having an aperture leading into the next tank.

The vessel's pump was aft, and within the lining of the pump was a tube that extended from the end tank to the deck. Forward an 'air tube' extended from the deck to the false keelson, and along the tops of the tanks. Filling and emptying might be performed through the pipe that passed up the pump-lining aft (see diagram).

A few weeks later the Weymouth tide-surveyor seized the schooner *Sea Flower* for being fitted up with various elaborate concealments.

There were many seizures of British-made soap at

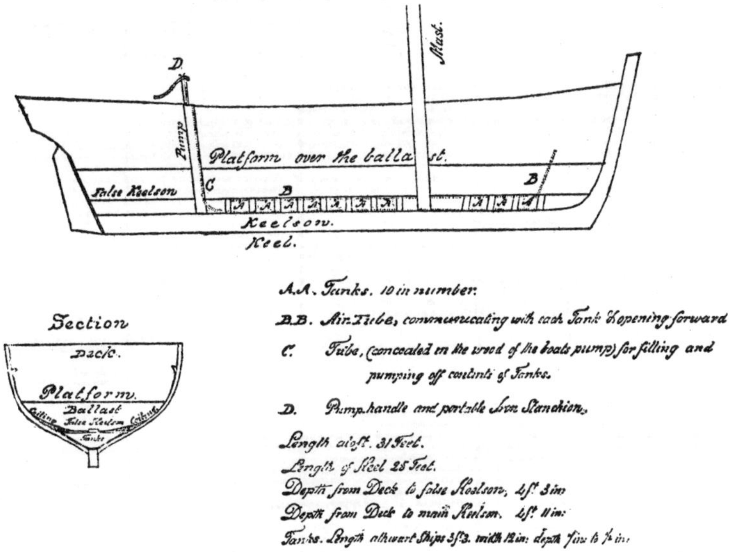

Irish ports in 1842. There was an excise duty on soap manufactured in Great Britain, and when such soap was shipped for Ireland a drawback equal to the duty was paid to the shipper. When this drawback was paid the Excise granted a 'sufferance,' which went with the goods. If the sufferance were not produced in Ireland, the goods were seizable, it being presumed they had been manufactured in Great Britain, and shipped without paying the excise duty.

On the night of December 5, 1842, the officers at St. John, N.B., seized fifteen casks of rum on the highway outside the town. Soon after they were attacked by a crowd of armed people, who tried to rescue the goods. The officers fought their way successfully, and captured four of their assailants.

As population increased in the Australian colonies, smuggling became rife. On May 30, 1842, the commander of the revenue cutter stationed at Sydney reported to the Board his recent cruise to Trial Bay to intercept the *Velocipede*, a schooner which had cleared out from Sydney to New Zealand with a cargo of 100 casks spirits, 59 kegs tobacco, 7 cases cigars, and 1 case snuff, shipped duty-free from bond. The *Velocipede* had been informed against after clearance, as not bound to New Zealand at all, but merely on a cruise, to return in a few days, and run her cargo somewhere between Smoky Cape and the entrance to the McLean River. The cutter's crew sighted her hovering off the coast, boarded her, and found that her cargo was still intact. The master stated he had been to New Zealand, and, finding that there was no sale for his goods, had decided to go to Singapore. (If he had really been to New Zealand and back, he had made a remarkably fast voyage. And why he should have called at Smoky Cape on his way to Singapore was past mortal understanding.)

Nothing could be done. There was no absolute proof that he intended to smuggle, yet there were many grounds of suspicion. For instance, the cutter found a large schooner, belonging to the owners of the *Velocipede*, lying at anchor in Trial Bay. The master stated he had come for a cargo of cedar, but it did not appear that any such cargo was in waiting. Later, too, it was found that the *Velocipede* had hovered on the coast of Broken Bay, and been warned off by fires, lit ashore by confederates who had observed that the revenue men were on the alert. Nothing could be done, but the cutter followed the *Velocipede* along the coast till she lost sight of her in the darkness, and then a gale sprang up, and the cutter returned to Sydney. There is nought to show what became of the *Velocipede*, but it is likely she ran back to Trial Bay, and transhipped her goods into the coasting schooner, or landed them in some secret place where they would be safe till the receivers arrived.

It is evident that the colonial revenue men made many gross blunders. On November 6, 1842, Captain Nagle, of H.M. colonial brig *Victoria*, while lying at Kapiti, Cook's Straits, New Zealand, was informed by certain Maoris that they had witnessed a run of contraband, and that the goods had been taken to a store kept by one Mayhew, a merchant who acted also as American vice-consul. Nagle accordingly went to Mayhew's store, and seized a great roll of tobacco and 200 gallons of rum. He left the goods with the sub-collector of Wellington for condemnation, and then it was found that Mayhew had cleared the rum from bond, and paid the duty on it, and that the tobacco had been imported prior to January 1, 1842, when it was exempt from duty. So the goods had to be restored.

The year 1842 is memorable from a Customs point of view as that in which an immense system of fraud, connived at, and partly suggested, by certain officers of the Port of London, was laid bare. It is necessary to go back a year or two to describe fully the circumstances of the case. It appears that for a considerable time there had been much confidential intercourse between many of the London landing-waiters and certain wealthy city men who were importers of French silks, gloves, and lace. The waiters had the entrée of the merchants' parlours, their wives were frequent purchasers on credit at the merchants' wholesale stores, and able to procure expensive dresses and all kinds of costly frippery for themselves and friends, the goods being charged to them at wholesale prices, and payment rarely pressed for. Some of the waiters kept up most expensive establishments, and were heavily in debt, their bills being backed by their merchant friends. The result was wholesale fraud and unblushing connivance. Of course we can but quote from evidence, but it should be stated that undoubtedly only a few of the frauds committed came to light, and there is every reason to believe that though only a few landing-waiters were exposed and punished, the landing department was, and had for many years been, utterly corrupt, that the superior officials had winked at their subordinates' misdoings and indirectly shared in the proceeds, and that one or two members of the Board were not above suspicion.

The arch-villain of the piece was a landing-waiter named Burnby. The general course of his conduct may be best displayed by a few quotations from his own and his accomplice's confessions. In 1837 he induced a landing-waiter named Homersham to join him in a profitable scheme of connivance, which consisted in allowing prohibited machinery to be exported. As our readers will have gathered, the exportation of many kinds of machinery was forbidden by law, and consequently attempts were frequently made to export such goods surreptitiously, very high prices being obtainable in foreign countries. Burnby and Homersham established an understanding with certain manufacturers and foreign buyers, and no doubt made a deal of money. Soon they gained another connection, the merchants exporting dummy packages, and the officers certifying that the packages contained goods entitled to drawback. In 1839 they connived at the introduction at St. Katherine's Dock of a large quantity of cigars in cases entered as containing marble. In 1840 their proclivities had become so well known that a clerk employed by one of the houses in the City approached Homersham with an inquiry as to whether they 'could do business,' and a fresh arrangement was at once made. The firm imported a large consignment of gloves. Homersham took an exact account of them in his 'rough book,' entering the particulars in pencil. It was quite usual at the time for the landing-waiters to 'give credit,' by examining and delivering goods before the duty was paid. Homersham acted thus with the gloves. As soon as they had reached the warehouse and been dispersed among the other stock, Homersham was apprised. Then he erased the correct account in his rough book, and made a fresh entry of the goods, which showed them at about half the proper quantity. The firm entered them, and paid duty according to the new account, and then divided the amount saved between themselves and the officers concerned. Thus things went merrily on. Soon the waiters came in touch with a large firm of silk importers (afterwards exchequered for £35,000), and then with another firm, so that they seemed to be on the highway to fortune. (Yet it appears that Burnby had lent Homersham much money, probably to make him secure.) They forged entries in the official books, taking the books to the merchant's house for that purpose. In short, they were extremely busy, yet they were merely the worst of a very bad gang. The other waiters were engaged in frauds not quite so extensive and daring—good old time-honoured Customs villainies, such as deliberate undervaluing of *ad valorem* goods, and the 'faking' of Customs tares. Much roguery was practised with goods imported 'on sight,' cases of high-duty goods being entered thus, landed, and swiftly delivered, similar cases of low-duty goods previously landed and duty-paid, but not delivered, being brought into the examination-room. This last trick was done with the connivance of both Customs and dock employés. The Customs and dock officials were on extremely friendly terms; indeed, one of Homersham's sureties was a dock official. This surety was convicted of extensive smuggling, and imprisoned, yet the clerk at the Custom-house, who was supposed to examine into the security of officers' sureties, knew nought of the matter till years later, when the great exposure occurred.

Towards the end of 1841 Burnby, for some reason or other, decided to 'peach,' and made a communication to his brother-in-law, Captain Morgan, late of the Coastguard. Morgan communicated with Sir George Cockburn, and a private meeting took place on November 9, 1841, at the Admiralty: present, Burnby, Morgan, the Chancellor of the Exchequer, and the Chairman of the Customs Board. Burnby made a confession, and inculpated twenty-one landing-waiters and many London merchants. The sneaking villain then proposed, as a means of proving his statements, that packages should be imported, and the inculpated officers allowed to deal with them. This proposal was rejected, but he was put upon duty with several of the officers, with instructions to watch them and report their proceedings. Things went on without any public exposure till 1842, when Burnby induced Homersham to peach. Then a number of landing-waiters were suspended from duty, and it is evident that Burnby was blamed for informing, for things became so uncomfortable between him and his brother officers that he fled to France, but was induced to return and continue his disclosures. A Committee was formed to inquire into the matter; members, Lord Granville Somerset, Mr. Gladstone, Mr. Baring, Mr. Milnes-Gaskill, and Mr. Pringle. Several curious episodes marked the proceedings. For instance, a return was asked for of the quantities of silks and brandies imported from France during the years 1827-1841. The Board of Trade furnished one, showing the quantities shipped in France, according to the French Customs returns, and the quantities landed in the United Kingdom, according to the British Customs returns. The French return of silk showed that during the fifteen years in question 5,344,416 pounds silk manufactures had been exported to the United Kingdom. The British return showed that 2,652,550 pounds only had been received. It would appear, therefore, that more than half the goods had either been smuggled directly, or not taken to account by men of the type of Burnby and Homersham. Yet conclusions must not be formed too rapidly. For, turning to the brandy account, we are confronted by the following statement: From 1827 to 1833 inclusive the account of brandy exported from France to the United Kingdom was much larger than the import account thereof into the United Kingdom. Then—amazing to note—*the proportions varied the other way*. In 1834, 1,747,827 gallons were exported from France, and 2,999,012 gallons (French brandy) imported into the United Kingdom. And thus the imports continued to exceed the exports down to 1841. The Committee made no comment upon this staggering return, except a hint that the *French* account might be wrong. Then why did they publish it in the report?*

Another curious episode. The Committee asked the Chief Jerquer of the Customs to produce his book, in order that they might ascertain the method of checking the landing accounts of goods. The Chief Jerquer was sorry; his book had just been destroyed (it is to be presumed by accident).

The Commissioners of Inquiry found many things to complain of, but the methods of Customs management displeased them most of all. They discovered that though there were nine gentlemen on the Board only two, the Chairman and Deputy-Chairman, had done any work worthy the name. Few personal visits had been made, and seven of the Board had next to no knowledge of the officers they were put to control.† The seven

* Perhaps it is good for the believer in statistics that he has little opportunity of intelligent comparison. Otherwise people would have less faith in Blue-books, and many a long financial oration which has become historical might appear a wind-borne bag of unreliability.

† Next to no knowledge of their official qualities, but the social excellences of certain men were well known to certain Commissioners. The following is from a letter written by a member of the Board to a colleague, with reference to the contemplated special promotion of Mr. ——, of the Coastguard:

'——, you perhaps know, was introduced to ——' (one of the Board) 'by ——, whose brother, the collector of Wells, thought highly of him, and ——, as I think, a little irregularly, induced —— to move him to the Isle of Wight. It was there he became acquainted with ——' (another member of the Board), 'who, I believe, saw a good deal of him, and thought very well of him,

'walking gentlemen' came at eleven (eight months out of the twelve; they were on leave the other four), and left at three. Even the parenthetical sentence 'eight months out of twelve' needs qualification. During that eight months' spell the seven 'lay figures' stayed away on every Monday, and but four of them came during the rest of the week. Thus life was one bright holiday. Yet during the whole of the proceedings the industrious and eccentric Chairman, Mr. Dean, continued to write letters of indignant protest to the Commissioners of Inquiry—letters in which, although he had every chance of obtaining credit by comparison, he almost demanded that scrutiny of the habits and official methods of his colleagues should cease. 'They are gentlemen—men of education,' was his chivalrous contention; 'they should not be subjected to such indignity.' One of his letters to Mr. Gladstone was especially characteristic. It expressed the opinion that the Board's attendance should not be regulated as though they were artisans or schoolboys, yet admitted that men were not made Commissioners of Customs because they possessed any special aptitude. Mr. Dean then proceeded to exhibit his incompetency as a reasoner. He stated that Government should rely more upon men than measures. (Yet it was evident that seven of his colleagues were incompetent, and what self-respecting Government would rely upon incompetent men? And why, in the name of reason, if the character of men was so much more important than the issue of regulations, had the Board in the past relied solely upon regulations—regulations which were admitted to be utterly beyond practice—and never taken the trouble

and when ——'s' (another member of the Board) 'son was about to join Sir R. Stopford's ship at Portsmouth, —— took great notice of him—I believe took him' (the boy) 'into his own house, and was very kind to him—and I am advancing nothing but what I believe to be true by saying that —— has lost no opportunity of ingratiating himself with any members of the Board with whom he may have communicated, and I wish much you could privately hear what Gowland says and thinks of him, who would speak his mind honestly, and is no bad observer of human nature.'

to make themselves acquainted with the officers' methods of work?) What Mr. Gladstone, then in the full tide of his intellectual powers, thought of Mr. Dean's letters is not manifest, but it is possible they may have inspired him with that contempt and dislike of the Customs which he displayed through his subsequent career.

During September, 1843, Mr. Dean's indignation was excited still more by the appearance in the *Times* of two articles headed 'Customs Frauds,' articles which reflected upon the character of certain members of the Board.*

* The articles in question were extremely bitter. The Board were accused of partiality and vindictiveness in their proceedings, both against certain firms which had been concerned in the frauds and the conniving officers. It was stated that the Customs, before entering action, seized the property of the merchants who had offended, and then complicated the proceedings in a remarkable manner. For instance, they arrested the principals of the firm of Candy and Co. several times within an hour, obliging them to secure bail on each occasion, the total sum covered by the several securities amounting to nearly £22,000. They were not satisfied with dismissing the officials implicated; they inquired into the pecuniary circumstances of others, some of whom had given bills upon their property. 'Yet,' stated the article, 'the paper of some of the Commissioners themselves has been about in the market under circumstances not particularly creditable to those parties.' The Board were also accused of resorting to discreditable proceedings and compromises in order to gain information. 'What can we say of a surveyor-general who takes down to his private residence a parcel of dismissed officers, and who, over his own bread and cheese and ale, seeks to worm out of them their secrets? . . . What can be gained by employing Burnby to pump a fellow now in a spunging-house for frauds on the revenue, which he' (Burnby) 'has done by working on his victim's hopes and fears in the daytime, so that he might be primed at night to make the necessary disclosures implicating others?'

The writer insisted that, revengeful and underhanded as their proceedings had been, the Board had taken no judicious steps to remedy the abuses existing in the department. 'Has anything,' he asked, 'been done effectually in the corn trade, where the fraud committed in drawback upon damaged corn is as notorious as the sun at noonday? What has been effected in the tobacco trade, where more cheroots have been smoked in one night than have paid duty in a year? Have the frauds in the export of cloths been probed to the bottom? With the exception of the Chairman and Vice-Chairman, the Commissioners know as much of the affairs passing through their own department as their own washerwomen.'

The Board applied to the editor, demanding the name of the writer; the editor replied that it was known to the Committee of Inquiry. The gallant old official Dean then sent Lord Granville Somerset a letter, declaring that the articles were libellous, and the Board despatched a protest to the Commissioners of Inquiry, stigmatizing the writer of the article as a 'hireling caterer to an able and unprincipled public journal.' (Later they offered to expunge these expressions.)

The inquiry proceeded, and in the end even Mr. Dean

He accused one of the surveyors-general, who had been entrusted with the task of investigating some of the frauds, of direct connivance, especially in the way of screening the informer Burnby, stating that this official had upon one occasion apprised Burnby that a special search of the station under his survey was about to be made, and adjured Burnby to conceal or remove certain incriminating packages; also that the surveyor-general had written to an implicated officer, stating that the officer might send him on as much wine as he could get, 'at the same price.'

He blamed the Board (and not without reason) for conducting their investigations *in camera*, stating that it was only in the Customs that such unfair proceedings were carried on. The defendants, he insisted, did not hear the evidence; the only thing communicated to them was the charge. In Customs investigations the defendant was presumed to be guilty till he proved himself innocent (a diabolical inversion of legal practice common with the higher officials of that day). In some of the cases in question the defendants were impeached *in camera* by the informer Burnby, and tried by an official who was a personal friend of that informer, and the said official made a *secret* report of the proceedings to the Commissioners.

Then he treated his readers to a few paragraphs of lurid scandal. He referred to two high officials who had taken a prominent part in the investigation, and declared that years back, when they were landing-surveyors, they were in the habit of deciding contentions as to the *ad valorem* rates chargeable on certain high-duty goods by spinning a coin on the counter of the 'Ship' tavern, Water Lane. He stated that the Commissioners, with two exceptions, were of no use as business men; that they were entirely in the hands of the surveyors-general (a most damning statement, if his charges against the surveyors-general were even partially correct). He then furnished a comparative statement of the official doings of several members of the Board, and of their private transactions, of which statement we supply a summary, arranged for the convenience of readers:

felt himself compelled to descend from the pedestal of indignant challenge, and to own that there was much need of reformation in the Board Room as well as on the quays. The old hero admitted that he was overcome with mortification at the turn affairs had taken. 'I had a better opinion of the department,' he wrote, and it is likely that his pad was blotted here and there with scalding tears. It is certain that if any man in the department had earned his salary Mr. Dean had. The quantity of work got through by him was simply pro-

---

Official Procedure.	Semi-Official and Private Transactions.
Dismissal of a certain officer for giving a bill on effects.	Drawing bills on each other, and getting them discounted by merchants and wharfingers.
Prosecution of an ordinary smuggler for 50s. worth of contraband.	Release, without inquiry, of an opera-singer's baggage, containing hundreds of pounds' worth of contraband.

(The above, it was stated, were seizures made simultaneously and by the same officers.)

Issue of a report condemning and forbidding the making of purchases by officers at wholesale houses.	Collusion with an inferior officer to purchase goods in the manner reprobated.

(The writer announced that he held the incriminating letters. He even quoted them.)

The articles wound up with a statement that the Board, as constituted, were utterly incompetent. 'The department must have at the helm something more than mere men of family and fashion. We want men of character and talent, who, knowing their duty, have nerve enough to act up to it.'

Thus the *Times*, and though there can be no doubt that the journalist responsible stuck at nothing to make attractive copy, and that he had as suppliers of information one or two of the subtle rascals who had been dismissed, and certain vindictive persons in the department who had considered themselves overlooked by the Board, it is likely most of the statements were true, and that the action of the 'Thunderer' was to a certain extent warrantable. (Sorrow must be expressed for Mr. Dean, that he should have been included, even by the mere circumstance of proximity, in so public and sweeping a censure.)

digious, and may have induced the Commissioners of Inquiry to make the suggestion they did—viz., that a 'Director' and 'Vice-Director,' with a few intelligent subordinates in close touch, would form a better staff of control than (to quote Dean) 'nine gentlemen of birth and education.'

A tremendous outburst of vigilance took place in 1843. The seizures increased in number to an amazing extent, and some of them were exceedingly creditable to the officers concerned. It had become quite evident that smuggling, especially the smuggling of tobacco, had been on the increase for several years. The manufacturers clamoured that the duties might be reduced to 1s. a pound, in order to remove the incentive to smuggling. They protested that they had been placed in the embarrassing position of either throwing themselves into the arms of the smugglers or drifting into bankruptcy. There can be no doubt that they did their very best to 'make a case' for reduction of duty; still, after every allowance has been made for exaggeration on their part, and also on the part of some of the notorious smugglers who about this time furnished much information to the authorities, we come to the conclusion that smuggling had never been so extensive, or carried out with such ingenuity, as between 1835 and 1843.

Early in 1843 a quantity of tobacco, cut in pieces exactly resembling shoe-soles, was seized at Portsmouth. Soon after it was found that alcohol had been extensively imported as turpentine, and passed at the turpentine rate (5s. a hundredweight). The goods were in reality only slightly flavoured with turpentine. After landing, the flavouring matter was removed by distillation, and a pure spirit obtained (strength, 60 O.P.). Information was received of an extensive fraud effected by making up tobacco in rolls resembling 'junk,' and introducing it amid coils of old rope.

The following are a few of the large seizures of tobacco made in 1842-1843:

At London: 1,389, 11,280, 5,242, 1,906, 3,377, 6,030 pounds.
At Holyhead: 7,047 pounds.
At Boston: 2,172 pounds.
At Dover: 2,652 pounds.
At Goole: 11,482 pounds.
At Harwich: 3,340, 7,222, 6,153 pounds.
At Hull: 4,560 pounds.
At Lyme: 2,705 pounds.
At Stockton (Yarm): 5,918 pounds.
At Arundel: 6,174 pounds.
At Exeter: 9,471 pounds.
At Grimsby: 4,161 pounds.
At Plymouth: 3,457 pounds.
At Southampton: 5,922 pounds.
At Kirkaldy: 2,063 pounds.
At Downpatrick: 1,122 pounds.
At Waterford: 28,620 pounds.
At Belfast: 3,042, 3,386 pounds.
Off the Lincolnshire coast, by revenue cruiser *Lapwing*: 9,271 pounds.
In a tugboat at Tynemouth: 8,788 pounds.
Same locality (seized by revenue cruiser *Scout*): 6,153 pounds.
In Holyhead harbour, by the tide-surveyor: Two smacks and 7,047 pounds.

But it must not be thought that the quantities seized bore any appreciable proportion to the quantities run. Indeed, it was stated boldly by many experts that not above a third of the tobacco used in the United Kingdom paid duty. The tobacco goods most frequently smuggled were leaf, negro-head, and cheroots. The smuggling was principally from Holland, Belgium, and Prussia. Information was tendered of one enterprising contrabandist who made a trip every two months from Holland to Belfast, conveying each time 40,000 pounds of tobacco.

Much of the information given came from tobacco manufacturers, who had been compelled by contraband competition to dabble extensively in smuggling and adulteration. Some of the statements made were simply astounding. One eminent firm of London tobacco brokers declared their belief that from 20,000,000 to 25,000,000 pounds of tobacco were smuggled into the United Kingdom every year. A well-known manufacturer stated that he had been approached by a notorious smuggler, who offered to run cargoes at £100 a time, taking all risks. The manufacturer thereupon cleared 49 hundredweight of tobacco duty-free from bond for exportation, and shipped it to Holland. The smuggler followed, took the tobacco on board his lugger, sailed across the North Sea, ran the goods in Deptford Creek, and brought them by cart to the City. This traffic was continued. On one occasion the smuggler had very bad weather, and lost a man overboard. He managed to reach the Thames, but in a distressed condition, and he put into Leigh, Essex. The fishermen of Leigh* helped him to land his cargo (3 tons of tobacco), and carried it on their backs to Rochford, where it was repacked into casks, and then brought by carrier's cart to London.

A certain smuggling syndicate owned several 'hatch-boats,' which were supposed to be engaged in fishing off the North Foreland. The syndicate had a regular 'buyer and packer,' who lived at Rotterdam. He made a practice of buying 20 tons of tobacco at a time, and repacking the goods into small bales. The hatch-boats sailed across, took in cargoes of about 3 tons, covered the goods with fish, and ran them over into Barking Creek. During 1843 about 15,000 pounds were seized from them. Still, they did very well, for they succeeded in running 85,000 pounds safely.

Another syndicate imported herrings from Holland, and landed them in casks at Billingsgate. Along with the herrings they brought an equal number of casks of tobacco. 'A few barrels,' stated the informant, 'are opened in the salesman's presence' (it is to be presumed they had been previously passed by the Customs). 'The smugglers' agent buys the whole consignment.' It was stated that this syndicate had been known to land 15 tons of tobacco during one Saturday afternoon.

At this time there were but few steamers in the coasting trade. That trade, including the huge coal traffic between the North of England and London, was principally carried

* The fishermen of Leigh were incorrigible smugglers, and it is only during recent years that their enterprise in this direction has lapsed. There may still be people in Leigh who remember the doings of 'old ——,' a well-known smuggler, who, if information be correct, right up into the recent eighties, was in the habit of running over to the Continent in his 'bawley,' and bringing back cargoes of contraband goods. It is stated that he was caterer for the light-ships, for many of the river bargemen, and for most of the good people of Leigh.

on by means of small sailing vessels. Between 20,000 and 30,000 coasters and collier brigs came up London river each year. Many of these vessels were engaged in smuggling. Sometimes a coaster would 'break her voyage,' while on her way to London, by running across to the Continent, taking a cargo of tobacco, overstowing the goods with coasting cargo, and then recrossing and proceeding to her destination. But oftener the practice was to run the goods over in a cutter, pick up the coaster at a place agreed upon, and tranship them into her. Much tobacco was smuggled in this way from the Channel Islands into the United Kingdom, Jersey in particular being a notorious place of output of contraband. Information was given of one inhabitant of that island who made fifteen trips in a year, carrying 15 tons of tobacco each time. The goods were transhipped off the Nore into coasting 'billy-boys.' The importing syndicate hired a wharf below Blackwall, at which all the goods were landed safely. Another venture from Jersey consisted of over 20,000 pounds of tobacco, packed in iron-hooped bales, so as to resemble ordinary merchandise, transhipped into a coaster in the Channel, and landed openly in London as coastwise cargo.

A curious statement was made as to a smuggling exploit at Stockton. A vessel loaded oak-bark at Newcastle, left for Stockton, ran over to Rotterdam, took in a great quantity of tobacco, overstowed the goods with bark, and then sailed to Stockton. Vague information as to her proceedings had reached the Stockton Customs, and three officers were put on board on the night of her arrival, to watch her until daybreak. The captain got into the confidence of one of the officers, and bribed him. The other two were made helplessly drunk, and the whole of the tobacco delivered into a lighter before morning. The lighter was taken up the river to Yarm, and the tobacco run into the churchyard. A carrier was engaged, and the whole of the goods were conveyed safely to Sheffield. In the morning the vessel was searched by the Customs, and nought found but oak-bark.

A great deal of tobacco was run ashore from the Pool, London, by the sailors on board the packets and cargo-boats that plied between London and the Continent. The most daring and skilful dealers in this line were the sailors of the General Steam Navigation Company. Most of these men came from the neighbourhood of Folkestone, and were the descendants of incorrigible smugglers. A great part of the goods brought by them was conveyed ashore on the persons of professional 'carriers,' and taken to the dwellings of professional receivers. The most famous receiver of all was 'Mother Gregson.' She had a tobacco-dealer's licence, and kept a chandler's shop in Barking Churchyard, a shop which was practically a 'clearing-house' for smuggled goods. She employed a number of lads (all under sixteen years of age, and therefore immune from prosecution), who did nothing for a livelihood except carry tobacco ashore on their persons from the vessels lying in the Pool and at the London wharves, and tramp with it down to her shop. This juvenile smuggling force was known among the waterside folk as 'Mother Gregson's gang.'* Some idea of the extent to which the conveying of tobacco 'on the person' was carried on may be gleaned from the evidence of a waterside police expert of the time, who stated that, though 210 persons were convicted of this practice in 1842-43, it was his firm conviction that not more than one offender out of a hundred was detected. It should be borne in mind that a practised 'carrier' could convey with ease from 8 to 20 pounds of tobacco on his person (one man was caught carrying no less than 47 pounds). Information was given, after the event, as to an extraordinary venture in this line. The crew of a Dutch vessel

* Mother Gregson was in touch with many City tobacco merchants and shopkeepers. On one occasion a large quantity of tobacco was found at her shop. The goods were undoubtedly contraband, but she escaped by producing false invoices, which said the information, 'she procured at a few hours' notice from some of the most respectable people in the tobacco trade.'

(ten in number) brought 2 tons of tobacco to London, concealed among the cargo on board. They carried this huge quantity ashore upon their persons within a week, making several trips each day. It was stated that the customs officer who was employed to watch the vessel winked at their proceedings, receiving as reward the paltry sum of £3.

There was much smuggling of tobacco-stalks, the goods being used in the illicit manufacture of snuff. Many large manufacturers of snuff dabbled in this business. In 1844 a huge seizure of stalks was made in the Minories by several of the London police. The goods had been landed 'down the river,' and thence conveyed to the premises of an eminent London firm, a firm whose name is a household word with snuff-takers.

Flushing, Rotterdam, Antwerp, Hamburg, Bremen—all these were places where much pains were devoted to the packing and manufacture of tobacco for smuggling into the United Kingdom, principally into the great centre of absorption, London. The quiet and winding creeks and rivers of East Anglia had become favoured running-places, the goods being afterwards taken to London in market-carts and carriers' vans. But London was not the only great smuggling port. Hull ran her very close; indeed, the records of information dealing with the ancient port on the Humber are most picturesque of all. We quote two or three:

1. A billy-boy left the Humber, ostensibly to procure ballast at Spurn Point. She 'ran over,' took in 140 bales of tobacco and stalks, and landed them on the Humber shore without a hitch. 'Part,' said the informant, 'went to ——, part to ——, the rest came to me.'

2. A smack, belonging to Faversham, went foreign, took in 3 tons of tobacco (cut, leaf, and stalks), and landed the goods on the Humber bank close to Hull. 'The shag,' said the informant, 'was brought to me by a truckman, packed in hampers.'

3. The same smack made a second trip, and arrived in

the Humber in a blinding snow-storm, after a terrible passage. She lay off Grimsby a whole day, *close alongside the revenue cutter.* Next morning she got under weigh early, and landed her cargo at Stone Creek. 'I kept the cut tobacco,' said the informant, 'and sent the stalks to Sheffield.'

4. Another vessel landed between 10 and 11 tons in one run on the Holderness coast. 'Any quantity of tobacco,' said the informant, 'may be landed at Hull.'

5. An American smuggling agent approached a Hull manufacturer, and offered to supply him with any desired quantity of smuggled tobacco. 'Leave your warehouse door open,' said the persuasive Yankee, 'and we will take care the tobacco is placed there. If it is seized, we will not ask you for any money; if it goes through safe, we shall ask you 2s. a pound in a banker's bill for two months.'

The Americans were not in 'the trade' as much as formerly, so far as Great Britain was concerned. Their greatest feats of smuggling were performed in Ireland, but even there not to the same extent as during the 1810-1819 period. (It should be remembered that prior to 1819 there had been next to no purely preventive force in Ireland. Then the Irish Coastguard was formed, the first station manned being on the coast of Cork, where great smuggling had been transacted by Americans. It was the opinion of experts that prior to 1819 about 6,000,000 pounds of tobacco had been smuggled annually on the south-western coast of Ireland, and that the ordinary customs staff there had connived at the trade.) Still, great runs took place occasionally on the Irish coast. It was not uncommon, when a run was made, for a thousand or more of the country people to muster, armed with sticks, scythes, and pitchforks, and assist the smugglers. 'Not one of these,' ran the information, 'will incriminate the purchaser.' On p. 277 is an accredited statement of the expenses and proceeds of a run made in Ireland by Americans for an Irish purchaser, and connived at by the Coastguard.

GOODS SHIPPED (60,000 POUNDS TOBACCO).

To	£	s.	d.	*By*	£	s.	d.
Original cost at 4d. a pound ..	1,000	0	0	56,000 pounds tobacco sold at 2s. a pound ..	5,600	0	0
Freight cost at 1½d. a pound—	375	0	0				
Wages of ship's company ..	59	0	0				
Douceurs to ship's company ..	180	0	0				
Interest on ship's cost, depreciation	102	0	0				
Loss on weight of goods	66	0	0				
Loss by 'decoy' (so many bales to be left for the officers to seize)	150	0	0				
Bribe to Coastguard	200	0	0				
Expense of conveyance inland	250	0	0				
Extra expenses (roughly) ..	118	0	0				
	2,500	0	0				
Profit ..	3,100	0	0				
	5,600	0	0		5,600	0	0

(The transaction occupied two months.)

It was stated that many people in the Channel Islands had made large fortunes by smuggling. The supervision of cargo-boats that left Jersey and Guernsey for England was extremely slack, the Jersey and Guernsey officers merely making perfunctory surveys, ostensibly to see that no contraband goods had been shipped. So lax were the searches that in 1842 one Guernsey vessel laden with stone actually brought 12 tons of tobacco, and landed it safely in the Regent's Canal Dock, London. There was much smuggling of tobacco in casks of apples, the Customs scrutiny of the apples on shipment at Jersey being practically nothing more than a journey to obtain a declaration for the Jurat that the apples were the produce of the island. The examination of the goods on their arrival in England was equally slipshod. There was also much smuggling from the Channel Islands into France —information said more than into England.*

It is apparent that the Coastguard in the United Kingdom had for some years been miserably inefficient. The force numbered about 11,000 men, nearly two-thirds of whom were employed afloat. During the five years 1839 to 1843 inclusive this large force seized only 89,691 pounds of tobacco and 4,908 pounds of cigars. Of this the greater part was seized in 1843, through the sudden vigilance inspired by the current inquiries into revenue and revenue fraud.† It should be noted that against this the regular Customs staff had seized, in 1843 alone, 93,000 pounds of cigars and tobacco, while the excise officers had seized over 15,000 pounds as smuggled, and about an equal quantity as adulterated.

Although (thanks to contraband) tobacco must in many places have been tolerably cheap, there was much adulteration—probably resorted to in self-defence by such of the manufacturers as did not deal with smugglers. It should be observed, too, that Mr. Baring's Act, which tacitly permitted the adulteration of tobacco, had been in operation several years. The adulterants used were rhubarb-leaves, foxglove-leaves, brown paper saturated with sarsaparilla, syrup of sugar, powdered chicory-root, glutenized Irish moss, carbonate of potash, sulphate of potash, carbonate of magnesia, carbonate of lime, terra japonica, alum, sand, salt, crude nitrate of ammonia, muriate of potash, and *bread* (this last being cut up with the tobacco).

Other circumstances combined to favour fraud. The

* The manufacture of tobacco in France was granted as a licence by the Crown to various companies, who regulated prices as they chose. The smuggling into France was even worse than that into the United Kingdom. Most of it was across the Belgian frontier, and was performed by dogs specially trained to carry the goods to the various receivers. It appears from a return made in 1830 that in ten years the French revenue officers had killed no less than 40,278 of these dogs.

† Late in 1843 they made three large hauls (on the Lincolnshire coast and off Tynemouth).

regulations, circumlocutory as they were, were terribly imperfect. Leaf tobacco, stripped of the stalk, and imported in a high-dried condition, paid no more than leaf imported with the stalk in, and containing a normal amount of moisture. Thus it became a practice to ship tobacco from bond, duty-free, for exportation to the Channel Islands, dry it till it had lost a third of its weight, and then reimport it promptly for duty. A few weeks after duty had been paid the bales regained their ordinary moisture, and then they were sold to dealers at the normal weights.

The exposures of Customs connivance and rampant smuggling narrated in the last few pages did not fail to discredit certain members of the Board, and several 'retirements' took place. It is possible that the Chairman, Mr. Dean, despite his well-known zeal and efficiency, did not escape blame, for his connection with the department ceased soon afterwards.

Large seizures were still reported from the Colonies. Early in 1843 the *Jane* arrived at Launceston, Tasmania, from Manilla, and landed, amongst other goods, seventeen butts of molasses. Ten of these were transhipped on board the *Westbrook* for Sydney; the other seven were duty-paid as molasses. Several days afterwards a cooper observed a heap of remains of dismantled casks lying in a corner of a wharf at Launceston, and noticed that wooden cleats were nailed to the inside of some of the staves. He told one of the customs officers, who inspected the staves, and came to the conclusion that they were the remains of the casks which had been cleared as containing molasses. He went on board the *Westbrook*, examined the ten casks which had been transhipped, and found a large jar inside each cask, fastened to the inside of the staves by cleats. The ten jars contained 110 gallons of spirits.

On March 25, 1843, a large seizure was made at Sydney, N.S.W. A customs officer observed a dray, loaded with casks and escorted by Lascars, passing along Clarence Street. It stopped near 'the Albion Mills,' and unloading commenced. The officer examined the casks, and found that they contained sugar, with kegs of tobacco inside. He seized horse, dray, and goods, and sent for his surveyor. That official brought a writ of assistance, searched the mills, and found several other casks of sugar containing tobacco. Forty casks were also found in a store hard by. The total amount of tobacco seized was 17,343 pounds. The goods had been landed from the *Duchess of Kent,* a vessel recently arrived from Calcutta, and they had been cleared by the Customs as sugar.

A dispute at once arose between the Solicitor-General for the colony and the customs collector as to whether the vessel was liable to seizure, the Solicitor-General opining that she was exempt, the goods being seized after landing ; the collector that she had been liable to seizure from the moment she reached harbour, the goods having been reported under a false denomination. The case was referred to the Board, who agreed with the Solicitor-General.

It appears that another vessel belonging to the same owners was on her way from Calcutta with a similar consignment. As soon as she arrived she was searched from stem to stern, but the only goods seized were 3,000 cigars, belonging to the captain and not reported, and 80 pounds tobacco, which had been concealed by the Lascar crew. Then one of the passengers came forward, and stated that a sailing-boat had intercepted the ship off Jarvis Bay, and had put a letter on board, upon reading which the captain had directed the Lascars to take off the hatches and throw a number of large casks into the sea. Then the Lascar serang turned informer, and corroborated the passenger's statement, mentioning incidentally that the captain had given the Lascars the 80 pounds of tobacco recently seized as compensation for their trouble in jettisoning the rest. The captain was convicted, but the ship was held exempt from forfeiture, she being outside the limits when the offence took place. No proceedings were entered against the owners ; they became bankrupt.

On October 27, 1843, a Chinaman imported and entered 180,000 cigars at Port Louis, Mauritius. When the officers came to weigh the goods, they found 96 pounds of opium concealed among the cigars. The whole of the goods were forfeited.

In June, 1843, the searcher at Woodbridge Bay, Dominica, received information that goods were to be run in the neighbourhood by a sloop from Martinique. He placed himself in ambush, and soon a boat came ashore laden with contraband goods. He seized her. Then another boat put off from the sloop, making for a distant part of the bay. The searcher pursued and captured her, and found that she was also loaded with contraband. Later he attempted to seize the sloop, but was violently assaulted and repulsed. Proceedings were taken against his assailant in the Court of Grand Session, Dominica, but the grand jury returned 'no true bill,' although the defendant had admitted the offence. The collector reported that this was 'mainly to be attributed to the feeling that exists in the community against revenue officers.' But the Board did not advise any further proceedings.

On May 27, 1843, an officer at Montreal seized a trunk, landed as baggage by 'a non-resident foreigner.' It contained the following works: 'A Guide to Family History,' by the Rev. Fletcher, Finsbury Chapel (399 copies); 'Gallery of British Arts,' by Finden (6 copies); 'Scenery and Antiquities of Ireland,' by N. P. Willis (36 copies); 'Canadian Scenery,' by N. P. Willis (50 copies); 'The Parent's Gift,' by Susan Jowett (5 copies).

It appears that they were seized as landed without payment of duty, not as piracies (Willis and Jowett, we presume, would be American authors). The seizing officer's report stated: 'I found the case had been landed as baggage, with instructions that it should be sent to a tavern in this city. The individual stated that the package had been forwarded here in mistake. As he is known to be engaged in the contraband trade, I did not place any faith in his statement.' The books were forfeited, but the smuggler was not prosecuted. It is evident that books were smuggled extensively from the

United States into the British North American possessions, merely to escape the duty.

Cap. 16 of 7 Vict. declared tobacco-stalks to be tobacco within the meaning of the revenue Acts (this was not to repeal the existing prohibition of their importation), and extended the liability of detention, attaching to persons found on ships that had contraband goods on board, to persons on foreign mail-packets. It also provided that the penalty for an offence against the revenue in which several persons were concerned should attach to each offender, and that smugglers convicted more than once should become liable to imprisonment with hard labour.

The Lieutenant-Governor of St. Vincent wrote to the Treasury, suggesting certain measures for the repression of smuggling in that island. It appears that much gin was run, the coloured people preferring it to the rum manufactured in St. Vincent, and that the Legislative Assembly of the island objected to the appointment of an extra customs officer, they being doubtful whether the finances of the colony would bear the strain, but they recommended that the police should be stimulated by a grant of the whole of the 'officers' share' of reward for seizure. In this recommendation both Board and Treasury concurred.

Dr. Bartlett, editor of the *Albion*, a periodical published at New York, complained to the Treasury through the governor of Jamaica that the Kingston customs officers had seized as piracies several hundred copies of his paper. He forwarded eight specimen copies, and the Customs lawyers thought they did not warrant seizure. But when the Board's notice to release the goods reached Jamaica the collector replied to the effect that some of the copies contained matter entitled 'Life and Adventures of Martin Chuzzlewit,' and other extracts from works which were on his copyright list. Then Dr. Bartlett stated that he had authority to publish 'Martin Chuzzlewit.' All the Customs lawyers continued in the opinion that the papers were not seizable. Things looked rosy for the American editor, till the Customs secretary thought of applying to

Mr. John Murray for an opinion. Mr. Murray's reply was so emphatic that we reproduce it:

'*June* 27, 1844.

'DEAR SIR,

'I now return the numbers of the *Albion*, and enclose for your perusal letters from Mr. Colburn, the publisher, and from Mr. Turner, who is well versed in the law of copyright.

'Were such a paper as the *Albion* published in Great Britain, I should feel myself called upon to bring an action against the publisher of so gross a piracy. I have no doubt I should obtain an injunction. It is little more than a selection of the best articles from our best periodicals, which are copyright as much as any separate volume. I see our paper from *The Quarterly* among others, for which £80 was paid, printed here *in extenso*.'

(Letters were enclosed from Colburn and from Mr. Turner, solicitor to the Society for the Protection of British Literature, stating the papers contained glaring piracies.)

This correspondence was referred to the lawyers, and they at once qualified their original opinion. A Treasury Minute of July 20, 1844, confirmed the seizure.

The sub-collector at Black River, Jamaica, seized fifty-five smuggled Panama hats, and the horse carrying them, on the highway between Black River and Savanna-la-Mar, on December 5, 1844. The goods were escorted by a Spaniard named Juan Ernandez. The sub-collector took Ernandez and the seized goods into the yard of a settlement close by, and asked one George Adams to act as interpreter, Ernandez being unable to speak English. Adams entered into conversation with the Spaniard, but declined to interpret the meaning thereof. Suddenly he and the Spaniard set upon the officer, dragged him across the yard, and threw him with great violence against a gate, injuring him seriously. For this they received twelve months' imprisonment.

It will be seen from a perusal of the foregoing that there had been little or no improvement in commercial morality. Some of the old methods of smuggling had become unfashionable, but they had been replaced by new ones. Concealments on board, transhipment into coasting craft, the running of goods which had been cleared duty-free for export, and the rafting and sinking of tubs of spirits, had become the favourite manœuvres. The old fighting methods had been abandoned. The practice of mustering 'batmen' to protect a run had practically ceased since 1832, when the whole of the preventive men were supplied with firearms, for the smugglers found that the long hard 'bat,' which in the hands of an athletic longshoreman had often overcome dirk and cutlass, was of little use against a loaded musket. Another new phase of the contraband trade was the extensive smuggling of tobacco in preference to spirits.

LIST OF AUTHORITIES.

Revenue legislation : The various Acts quoted in text.

Incidence of duties, etc. : The various books of rates and Service handbooks.

Colonial revenue and smuggling : Antigua, St. Kitt's, 'Reports,' 'Treasury,' Dominica, Jamaica, 'Promiscuous,' Quebec, Newfoundland and New Brunswick, Australia, Tasmania and New Zealand, Nova Scotia, Mauritius, Ceylon, Montserrat, and Montreal files.

British smuggling : London *Times*, March 30 and 31, and May 30, 1827 ; General Letters, 1827, 1828, 1829, 1830, 1831, 1832, 1834, 1835, 1836, 1837, 1839 ; Admiralty Papers, 1832, 1833, 1839 ; Treasury Papers, 1834, 1835, 1839, 1840, 1841, 1842, 1843 ; 'Remarkable Seizures' (Customs Library), 1842.

Departmental regulations : General Letters, 1828, 1829, 1830, 1832, 1833, 1836, 1839 ; Treasury Papers, 1834 ; General Letters, 1840, 1841, 1842, 1843, 1844.

Liverpool : 'Inquiry into Condition and Discipline of Liverpool Customs' (Customs Library) ; General Letters, 1839, 1840.

Theft of public money : 'Robbery of the King's Chest' (Customs Library).

Botany Bay and Broken Bay : 'Curious Board's Papers' (Customs Library).

Carlist purchase of arms, Malabar fish-oil, coffee-husking, and guano : Treasury Letters, January 3, January 16, and May 6, 1840, and September 21, 1841.

Infringement of Passenger Acts : General Letters, 1840.

Seizure of flags : Dominica file.

CHAPTER III

TOWARDS FREE TRDAE

PERUSAL of that portion of the preceding chapter which deals with tariffs and departmental history will have revealed to readers that the duties imposed by the Consolidating Acts of 1833 were in many instances altered during the eleven years following. Other important alterations had been made in the revenue laws, notably the substitution of hard labour for impressment into the navy as a punishment for smuggling, and the removal of the prohibition of exportation of machinery. In 1845 it was considered necessary to issue ten new statutes, re-consolidating the Customs.

The first of the new Acts, Cap. 84 of 8 and 9 Vict., repealed the ten Consolidating Acts of 3 and 4 Wm. IV., as well as fourteen Customs Acts passed subsequently. Cap. 85 regulated the management of the Customs. Cap. 86 recited the usual provisions as to report, entry, times of work, Customs right of search, method of securing *ad valorem* duties, returned goods, ships' stores, certificates for goods entitled to special import privileges, and derelict goods. It also contained the usual list of restricted and prohibited articles. The restricted articles were fish of foreign taking, which might only come in vessels regularly cleared out from foreign ports as traders ; goods from places within the East India Company's charter, which might only come into certain approved ports ; infected hides, etc., which might be prohibited from time to time by Order in Council ; parts of articles, which might only come in packages containing the other component parts ;

tea, which still might only come from the Cape of Good Hope and places eastward towards the Straits of Magellan; gloves, silks, spirits, and tobacco, which were subjected to the restrictions as to tonnage of importing ship, size of package, etc. The goods prohibited without qualification were articles of foreign manufacture marked as the produce of the United Kingdom, pirated books, paper printed on in English, clocks and watches improperly marked, counterfeit money, malt, snuff-work, spirits from the Isle of Man, tobacco-stalks, and tobacco-stalk flour. Arms and ammunition might only be brought under royal licence, and no goods might come from the Isle of Man except foreign corn and flour, and such articles as were produced in the island. (It should be understood that all the above articles, except arms, ammunition, pirated books, infected articles—and silks, gloves, tobacco, etc., in illegal packages—might be *imported and warehoused for exportation*.) With regard to export goods, arms, ammunition, pearl ashes, military and naval stores, and provisions, *might* be prohibited by Proclamation or Order in Council. Exportation of clocks and watches 'without the movements,' and of metal-work inferior to silver and set upon lace, was utterly prohibited. The coasting regulations were also recited. Cap. 87 consolidated the preventive regulations, introducing little that was new, except that it extended to customs officers the powers held by excise officers of search in connection with illicit distillation or brewing, and that it defined the Customs power of search of the person, and granted power to customs officers to execute revenue warrants within the metropolitan police district. The Navigation laws were reaffirmed by Cap. 88, and the laws governing registration of ships by Cap. 89.

Cap. 90 recited the duties. The following articles, previously dutiable, were made free: Agates not set, alkali, alkanet root, bitter almonds, aloes, alum, rough amber, ambergris, amboyna wood, angelica, annatto, antimony, argol, aristolochia, arsenic, asphaltum, un-

Board-Room, Custom House, London.
(Present day.)

To face p. 286.

enumerated balsams, barilla, bark, barwood, basket-rods, beef-wood, unenumerated berries, singing birds, bitumen, judaicum, bladders, bones, boracic acid, borax, certain kinds of bottles, box-wood, brazil-wood, brimstone, bronze works of art, camomile flowers, unrefined camphor, cam-wood, candlewick, canes not mounted, caoutchouc, cardamoms, cassia, castor, unmanufactured chalk, cedar-wood, china-root, chip, cinnabaris nativa, citrate of lime, citric acid, civet, coal, cobalt, cochineal, colocynth, columba-root, copperas, coral, cotton yarn, cream of tartar, rough crystal, cubebs, cutch, divi divi, down, unenumerated drugs, ebony, undressed feathers, flax and tow, flocks, flower-roots, fustic, galls, gamboge, gentian, ginseng, glue waste, grease, greaves, guano, unenumerated gums, gunstocks, gypsum, unmanufactured hair, heath, hellebore, hemp, undressed and unenumerated hides, hides only tanned, hones, hoofs, hoops, horns, indigo, unwrought inkle, unwrought iron—the irons known as cast, bloom, chromate, rod, and hoop—jalap, jet, unset jewels, lemon and orange juice, kingwood, sticklac, lapis calaminaris, lard, shaven latten, lavender flowers—all lead except pig, sheet, and manufactured—leaves of roses, leeches, lentils, litharge, logwood, madder, mahogany, manganese ore, manna, unenumerated manures, bell-metal, moss, mother-of-pearl, musk, myrrh, certain nuts, oakum, ochre, many kinds of oil (including train-oil, etc., of British taking), oilcake, olibanum, olive-wood, orange-peel, orchal, unenumerated ores, orpiment, orris root, unmanufactured painters' colours, palmetto thatch, pink root, pitch, plaster of Paris, platina, chip plait, pomegranate peel, quicksilver, quills, radix, rags, redwood, rhubarb, rosewood, rosin, safflower, saffron, sal, saltpetre, sanguis draconis, Santa Maria wood, sapan wood, sarsaparilla, sassafras, satin wood, saunders, scammony, certain kinds of seeds, senna, shumac—raw, waste, and undyed thrown silk—skins, sponge, stavesacre, unwrought and scrap steel, straw for plaiting, sweet wood, talc, tar, tarras, tartaric acid, teasels, terra japonica, terra sienna, terra umbra, terra verde, tin ore, tincal, tornsal, unmanufactured tortoiseshell, tulip wood, turmeric, the rougher kinds of turpentine, valonia, ancient vases, vermilion, walnut wood, mineral water, beeswax, myrtle-wax, weld, British-taken whale-fins, certain kinds of staves, teak, New Zealand wood, wool, camel yarn, and raw linen yarn. It was also provided that any unmanufactured goods which might be imported subsequently, and which were not specified, either as free or dutiable, in the new tariff, should be free.

The only export duty that survived was on coal exported in foreign ships (4s. a ton).

This tedious list of exemptions is quoted to show the extent to which the tariff was simplified. Most of the articles made free had been previously subjected to nominal duties only, and collection had in many instances been complicated by provisions favouring British shipping. It will be observed that the articles were principally 'raw' products. The momentous duties on lace, manufactured silks, tea, tobacco, wine, and spirits remained unaltered. The rates were still in many instances preferential as regarded goods from British possessions.

Cap. 91 dealt with the warehousing of goods. The Commissioners of Customs might still appoint the tobacco warehouses, providing for them out of the Customs receipts, and levying rent on packages for reimbursement. Warehoused goods on delivery were to be duty-paid at the original landing quantity, except sugar, tobacco, wine, coffee, cocoa, pepper, and corn, on which goods allowance was to be made for natural waste.*

Cap. 92 dealt with bounties on exported goods. The only goods thus favoured were the various kinds of refined sugar.

Cap. 93 regulated the colonial trade on much the same lines as previously. The Board of Customs had power to

* The allowances on wine, coffee, cocoa, and pepper were only granted when the goods were delivered from warehouse for exportation.

transform intercolonial into coasting trade, and the governors to appoint custom-houses. The queen by Order in Council might establish 'limited' as well as free ports. The old provisions as to permission to foreign nations to trade direct with the colonies, bringing only their own products, but carrying goods for export from the colonies to any place, were reaffirmed, with the usual conditions as to reciprocity.

Cap. 94 regulated the trade of the Isle of Man, the duties being as before. The quantities of spirits, tobacco, and cigars which might be imported into the island remained unchanged, and so did the management and application of the duties, except that a repealed grant of harbour duties to the Harbour Commissioners was made good by a grant out of the island Customs.

Among the confidential letters of 1845 we find a curious communication signed 'Strathallan.' It was originally sent to the Treasury, and desired that 'young Burnett' (a customs landing-waiter in Tasmania) might be favoured. It quoted certain statements made to the writer in a letter from Burnett, which represented the colony as a sink of iniquity, a receptacle for rogues and vagabonds from all parts of the world, etc., and attributed this unsatisfactory state of affairs to the measures taken by Lord Stanley for the settlement of the colony.*

For several years the Board had been vexed with complaints from shipowners that British trade to the Mauritius suffered through a practice by French vessels of bringing wine from France, touching at Port Louis, and apprising the wine-merchants there, then going to the adjacent French settlement of Bourbon, and waiting the arrival of craft from Port Louis, into which the wine was transhipped, and then conveyed to Port Louis, where the Customs allowed it to be landed at the low rate as brought in British ships. 'The General Shipowners' Society'

* It is likely the letter had effect. Burnett was made collector of Launceston, Tasmania, by Treasury Warrant of August 22, 1848. (His father was sheriff of Tasmania, and related to a certain noble Scottish family.)

stated that out of 9,332 casks of French wine imported into Mauritius in 1831 nearly two-thirds arrived by this crooked line of traffic. There can be no doubt that this practice was adopted to evade a special Order in Council of 1827, and that it was just a cumbrous way of breaking the regulations; yet, though the correspondence on the matter was voluminous and amazingly intricate, it appears that the Customs lawyers shirked giving a decision. Hair-splittings most microscopic, opinions most contradictory, pervade the papers, yet nothing definite was delivered till 1846, when the Board announced that such traffic was legal.

A list of emigrants, forwarded by the collector of Quebec to the Board in connection with an unfounded charge of infringement of the Passenger Acts, furnishes instructive information as to the usual type of settler in Canada. The vessel concerned left London in 1842, but the investigation did not terminate till 1845. She carried 134 passengers, the greater part being women and children. Of the adults one was a tanner, one a dentist, one a teacher, one a doctor, one a carpenter, four were drapers, four servants, three dealers, and no fewer than twenty-five were farmers. Only three of the farmers were over thirty-five, and all bore distinctive Midland-English names. It is worth a little mental debate as to whether the reduction of the corn duties had anything to do with this preponderance of agriculturists.

Cap. 22 of 9 and 10 Vict. amended the corn laws, providing that the following duties should be paid on foreign wheat till February 1, 1849:

Average Market Price of British Wheat.	Duty Payable. £	s.	d.
Under 48s.	0	10	0
48s., and under 49s.	0	9	0
49s., and under 50s.	0	8	0
50s., and under 51s.	0	7	0
51s., and under 52s.	0	6	0
52s., and under 53s.	0	5	0
53s., and upwards	0	4	0

(Proportionate rates for other corn and for flour and meal.)

On February 1, 1849, these duties were to be abolished, and a tax of 1s. per quarter to be imposed on *all* foreign *corn*, and of 4½d. on every cwt. of foreign flour and meal.

Cap. 23 amended many of the duties leviable under the Consolidating Act of 1845, abolishing those upon animals, bacon, beef, bottles, casts of figures, caviare, cherry-wood, cranberries, cotton manufactures not made up, enamel, gelatine, glue, hay, certain hides, printers' ink, wrought inkle, lamp-black, unenumerated linens not made up, magna grecia ware, manuscripts, maps and charts, mattresses, meat, medals, parchment, partridge-wood, pens, plantains, potatoes, pork, purple-wood, dyed thrown silk, telescopes, unenumerated thread, unenumerated woollens not made up, vegetables, and vellum. It also lowered the duties on many kinds of wood and seeds. Cap. 94 gave power to the Legislatures of the colonies in America and the Mauritius to reduce or repeal the colonial Customs duties. Customs officers were made competent to conduct proceedings in Customs cases, under the direction of the Commissioners. Cap. 102 slightly reduced the duties on colonial spirits.

An anonymous letter reached the Board from Manchester, England, complaining of the customs men at Montreal. It stated that the collector and controller were interested in pushing forward the supposed pending transference to the Colonial authorities of the power of appointing officers, as they were desirous of recommending their own nominees, who were brother 'Odd Fellows.' It went on that when 'the navigation' opened in spring there was always a rush of business at the Custom-house, and that the merchants were much obstructed by the dilatoriness and circumlocution practised by the officers. The complaint was sent to Montreal, and evoked an indignant denial, the officers furnishing an account of the duties taken from May 5 to 31 (the 'busy time') in 1845 and 1846. (Amount in 1845, £79,329 currency; in 1846, £67,580.) The officers stated that nearly all the respectable people of Montreal were 'Odd Fellows'—'the late

Lord Metcalfe was one.' And they sent on a testimonial to their own capacity and alertness, signed by many merchants of Montreal.

The Governor-General of Canada complained to the Treasury that Mr. Jessopp, collector of Quebec, had refused to furnish him with a list of seizures. The Treasury directed Jessopp to comply, but the undaunted collector merely stated that there were no seizures to return, and hinted that the governor should first have applied to the Board. (Jessopp was an old offender in this way. See p. 179.)

The gradual narrowing of the London Customs Board's influence in colonial matters is exemplified by a letter from the Treasury to the Board, dated August 4, 1846. Their Lordships referred to a recent complaint made by the governor of New Brunswick as to appointment of customs officers, and directed the Board to forward all future communications, intended to reach colonial governors, through the Treasury.

The sale of bait to foreign fishermen by certain inhabitants of Newfoundland had become a burning question in the North American colonies, and with the various British firms that continued to send vessels to fish on the Banks. The administration of most of the regulations affecting the Newfoundland fisheries had been for many years vested in the North American customs officers. They supervised the delivery of stores duty-free for the British and colonial fishers' use ; they took charge of foreign vessels seized for encroaching, etc., and either condemned them if no appeal was made, or, if the seizure were disputed, entered the necessary action in the Vice-Admiralty Court of the colony concerned. The sub-collectors along the coast were expected to apprise the proper authorities of any foreign encroachments that came to their knowledge. It appears that the customs men tried their best to enforce the Fishery laws, but were foiled by the apathy and timorousness of the British controlling departments. The treaties between Great Britain and France and the

United States had been drafted vaguely, and without due consideration of the importance of the issues involved. Thus report after report was transmitted of insolent trespass by American fishermen, and of the uninterrupted smuggling of bait, yet little notice was taken. The Board either evaded the issue, being, it appears, dubious as to their powers, or referred the reports to the Treasury or Foreign Office, and those departments were equally cautious. It is evident, too, that colonial feeling on the matter varied considerably. The better class of people in the North American colonies were anxious that British and colonial priority in the fisheries should be preserved. The 'scallawag' class, especially in Newfoundland, revelled in evasion, in the open sale of bait to foreigners, and in welcoming their encroachments, which gave abundant chances of exchanging fish for contraband. There can be little doubt that the annihilation of the ancient British fishing industry on the prolific Banks was due to the milk-and-water policy of the imperial administrators. Evidence on the point may be gleaned in plenty from the Customs files.

In 1844 the governor of Newfoundland asked the Secretary of State whether the provisions of Cap. 26, 26 Geo. III., prohibiting the sale of bait, etc., to foreigners, were still in force, or whether they had been repealed by Cap. 59 of 3 and 4 Wm. IV. and subsequent Acts. The law officers of the Crown had given quite a non-committal opinion, implying that the Act was in force, but that the practice had changed, and hinting that the new principles of Free Trade were against rigid enforcement of such statutes. The Customs lawyers also thought the Act applied, but that its provisions should be enforced by the colonial governors, not by the Customs.

The Newfoundland Assembly forwarded an address to the queen, extolling the Fisheries as a time-honoured nursery of naval seamen, and alluding to the many natural advantages possessed by the colony. They described the population as 100,000, all of British extraction. They valued the annual imports at £800,000, and the exports at £1,000,000. But they bewailed the existing illicit traffic in bait with St. Pierre and Miquelon, stating that it would destroy the local fishery, as the cod were deserting their old haunts, and congregating on the shores of the French islands. The French fishery had increased to nearly 300 square-rigged vessels of from 100 to 400 tons, and a multitude of open boats. The French import of bait from Newfoundland reached 70,000 barrels caplin and 28,000 barrels herring per year. Twenty thousand men were employed in the French fishery, and in 1843 they had caught 1,400,000 quintals of cod, against 1,000,000 quintals caught by British and colonials.*

What was the reply? A tame letter from Lord Stanley to the governor, asking if it would be practicable to carry into effect Cap. 26, 26 Geo. III., and hinting that the Act might be deemed obsolete. The governor, no doubt accepting the hint towards temporizing, replied that it would be inexpedient to enforce the Act, as the (illegal) exportation of bait was *the poor man's trade!* Thus it came about that the Newfoundland legislators were induced to compromise by levying a small duty on exported bait. The whole of the official proceedings seem contemptible.

In 1845 the customs sub-collector at Little Bay reported that little duty could be collected on bait unless cruisers were kept on the coast to enforce compliance with the Act. The Customs lawyers replied that the responsibility lay with the colonial authorities.

In 1846 a cruiser was appointed to supervise the trade in bait, and to check encroachments by the French. To form an opinion of the extent of successful protection of an important industry likely to accrue, one has but to read the instructions given to Commander Oke. He was told that under the existing treaties the French might not

* The British and colonial fishermen complained much of the French system of fishing on the Banks with the 'bultow,' an immense tangle of wires and lines covering a huge space of water.

fish or take bait nearer than three miles from the south-west coast of Newfoundland or east of Cape Ray, and nearer than mid-channel directly between Newfoundland and the French islands. Penalty, forfeiture of ship and tackle. But, to avoid international complications, he was not to seize encroaching vessels. He was to identify them, and then wait on the Commandant of St. Pierre, and desire him to punish the offenders under the French laws. Oke was to carry a pendant and colours, and not to use arms except in self-defence. Thus it will be seen that, if an offending vessel tried to escape identification, he might not even fire an unshotted gun ; that if he desired to board her to see the master's papers, and the crew resisted, he might not sustain his search, for he could not then be said to be acting in self-defence ; and that, whilst assuming the power of enforcing the conditions of a treaty, the legality of any action he might take was to be determined in the end by laws other than those embodied in the treaty. An officer thus hampered would, it may be conceived, read between even the non-committal lines of his instructions, and take care not to bestir himself much.

By Cap. 1 of 10 and 11 Vict. it was prescribed that the reduced duties on corn, meal, and flour imposed by Cap. 22 of the preceding year should be suspended from January to September, 1847. Cap. 2 allowed the importation during the same period of corn, rice, flour, meal, and potatoes in any ships from any country, the Navigation laws notwithstanding ; and Cap. 3 extended the suspension of import duties to buckwheat, maize, and rice. These temporary Acts of relief were passed on account of the partial failure of the home and colonial corn crops. Cap. 23 complicated revenue matters considerably by differentiating the duties on colonial spirits according to country of importation.* This queer statute disarranged collection as below :

* To meet the wishes of West Indian traders. (The Excise duty on home-made spirits varied proportionately.) Differentiation continued, with slight variations, till 1858.

Rum of British possessions within the East India Company's charter, spirits and strong waters of the American colonies, and rum-shrub of the British possessions within the East India Company's charter or in America.	Previous duty: the proof gallon in the United Kingdom, 8s. 10d. Duty under this Act: In England, 8s. 7d.; in Scotland, 4s. 5d.; in Ireland, 3s. 5d.

Under the new arrangement no foreign spirits might be removed from one part of the United Kingdom to another except first warehoused in bond, and when they arrived in the other country they were to be duty-paid at the rate obtaining there. Spirits duty-paid in Ireland were not to be taken to Scotland or England, and no warehoused foreign spirits were to be taken to England from Scotland except by sea.

Cap 64 of 10 and 11 Vict., passed on July 9, 1847, under prospect of another bad harvest, extended the suspension of duty on foreign corn, etc., till March 1, 1848, and Cap. 86 extended the privilege of importation of those articles in any ship from any country till the same date.

The Chairman of the Board (Sir Thomas Fremantle) issued a circular, stating that since his recent appointment he had received many letters from noblemen and gentlemen, soliciting the promotion of certain officials, and that he was convinced these applications had been instigated by the officers concerned.

It appears that up to 1847 the bottles allowed to be used by merchants in taking their duty-free samples of wines and spirits had been smaller at the outports than in London. This is but one instance of the many discrepancies that prevailed in ancient Customs practice.

During 1845 the Board had refused to grant a British register to the British-built ship *Ecuador* (belonging to the Pacific Steam Navigation Company), because certain foreigners held shares in the concern. The Company took proceedings in the Court of Queen's Bench, and the Court directed that a peremptory mandamus should issue, requiring registration of the vessel. This decision was based on the ground that the Company applied in its corporate capacity, on which account the Court could not take notice as to whether the constituent members were foreigners or not. (This seems an extraordinary verdict.) The Board referred the matter to the Privy Council for Trade, asking if it would be necessary to alter the Navigation laws on account of the decision. The Council replied that they did not think any alteration necessary, and directed the Board to notify all the customs collectors, which was accordingly done in 1847.

As this treatise is approaching the period at which the severance of the British and colonial Customs was initiated, we supply a list of the colonies for the year 1847 :

Antigua.
Bahamas.
Barbadoes.
British Guiana.
Bermuda.
Canada.
Cape of Good Hope.
Ceylon.
Dominica.
Gambia.
Grenada.
Jamaica.
Mauritius.
Montserrat.
New Brunswick.
Newfoundland.
New South Wales.
New Zealand.
Nevis.
Nova Scotia.
St. Helena.
St. Kitts.
St. Lucia.
St. Vincent.
Sierra Leone.
South Australia.
Tasmania.
Tobago.
Tortola.
Trinidad.
Victoria.

The establishments of many colonies which are now important were at this time imperfect, large stretches of coast being left unprovided with custom-houses and collectors. Below is an account :

Canada.—A collector at Quebec, a collector at Montreal, sub-collectors at Gaspe and New Carlisle (two ports and two ' outbays ').

New South Wales.—A collector at Sydney (one port only).

South Australia.—A collector at Port Adelaide (one port only).

Victoria.—A collector at Melbourne, a sub-collector at Portland Bay (one port and one outbay).

Tasmania.—A collector at Hobart Town, a sub-collector at Launceston (one head port and one minor port).

New Zealand.—A collector at Auckland, sub-collectors at Wellington, Russell, Akaroa, Nelson, and New Plymouth (one head port and five minor ports).

Cape of Good Hope.—A collector at Cape Town, sub-collectors at Simon's Town, Port Elizabeth, Mossel Bay, and Port Beaufort (one head port and four minor ports).

Ceylon.—A collector at Colombo, sub-collectors at Jaffna, Galle, Trincomalee, and Pantura (one head port and four minor ports).

During 1847, the few imperial duties remaining having been abolished in Nova Scotia, a new official, called the 'Controller of Navigation laws,' was stationed there. This appears to have effected abolition of the Board's control of *revenue* in that colony, and in the following year several other colonies were dealt with similarly. In most instances the imperial staff remained, and took office in the provincial Customs. The new 'Controller's' duties were defined as below:

1. To enforce the surviving Navigation laws.

2. To issue certificates of registry to British and colonial-built ships.

3. To enforce the laws governing colonial commerce—viz., to preserve the exclusive privileges of the numerous 'free ports,' to see that the various Orders in Council that dictated occasional relaxations were not abused, and to grant the certificates for colonial produce exported to other colonies and to the United Kingdom.

4. To assist in the compilation of statistics by furnishing the returns required by the home statists.

5. To compile annual returns for the imperial Parliament.

6. To enforce the Passengers Act, the Merchant Seamens Act, and the consolidated Acts for the suppression of the slave-trade.

Some of the new controllers soon caused trouble: see

the following brief account of the situation at Halifax and Nevis :

Pending arrival of the controller at the former port, the governor appointed an acting controller, who at once began to air his self-importance, insisting that the provincial collectors of customs should send their letters to the colonial Secretary through him (the controller). The Board soon disabused his mind on this point. The real controller arrived (he had been imperial collector at Antigua), and it appears that he made himself more agreeable than his predecessor had done, for the governor gave him the job of collecting the colonial customs at Halifax, but only paid him £300 a year in currency. The Board objected to his taking over the job, hinting that, as his pay from the imperial funds was £600 sterling, the governor was trying to economize at the expense of the United Kingdom. The Treasury were inclined to allow him to officiate, but the Board made a telling and spirited statement, urging that the Navigation laws, under which he acted, were almost amended out of existence, and would soon be repealed, and that he was therefore overpaid already as controller. They reiterated their former hint that the colony proposed to profit at the expense of the United Kingdom, and pointed out that, as provincial collector of Halifax, he would deal with about £60,000 a year, principally collected from distilleries. In the end the Treasury forbade him to accept the additional employment.

The controller at Nevis obtained the job of collecting certain colonial duties, his compensation to be a percentage on receipts, and the Legislature of the island embodied his appointment in an Act, but this did not prevent the Board from insisting that the governor should obtain the sanction of the Treasury. The additional appointment was not sanctioned till 1851, and then it was directed that the sum received by the officer as percentage should be deducted from his pay as controller. He soon resigned the extra employment, stating that his remuneration from it was insignificant. 'Although I have advanced a step in rank, I have lost in pocket.'

Considerable trouble was given during 1847 by Lord Howard de Walden. That nobleman, who had recently assisted in arranging at Lisbon a Treaty of Commerce between Great Britain and Portugal, sent his effects, consisting principally of British goods and the wines of Oporto, direct to Montego Bay, Jamaica, where he had an estate. He went to London and thence to Jamaica, and was much annoyed to find that the articles had been charged with duty as foreign goods. He declined to pay, urging that his effects, being originally British, should be duty-free, and that he should pay no higher duty on his wine than if he had imported it from the United Kingdom. He referred to the share he had taken in the Treaty as a proof that he might claim to understand matters of trade between Portugal and the British possessions. Undoubtedly he was in error, but the Board remitted the duty on his effects, while insisting that he should pay the foreign duty on his wine.

A curious question arose at Kingston, Jamaica. One Watson arrived at that port on July 20, 1847, in command of a cutter called the *Sun*, registered at London. He carried cargo from the Spanish Main, and claimed exemption from tonnage duties because he held a commission from the king of the Mosquito Islands, and his vessel was thus a foreign man-of-war. He stated that he had refrained from cancelling his British register because the Mosquito Government was not recognized by the adjacent states, and he therefore wished to retain the protection of the British flag. The Board decided that he was only entitled to the privileges of an ordinary British trader.

The coast-waiters' boats at Broken Bay and Botany Bay, New South Wales, had up to this time been manned by selected convicts. In 1847 the waiter at Broken Bay apprised the Sydney collector that his boatmen had been apprehended for robbery, and soon afterwards the waiter at Botany Bay sent word that his crew had received their tickets-of-leave and abandoned their occupation. In August the Superintendent of Convicts informed the collector that no more convicts would be supplied. It was accordingly arranged to employ 'free men' at £4 a month (it would seem that wages were low prior to the discovery of gold).

On June 15, 1847, the Treasury transmitted to the Board a revenue Ordinance, recently passed by the Legislature of South Australia, and asked in the usual way whether it contained anything objectionable. The Board pointed out the following imperfections:

1. The Ordinance had prescribed a method of dealing with undervalued *ad valorem* goods similar to that obtaining in the United Kingdom. The Board (perhaps bearing in mind how badly the British system worked) thought the appointment of an expert appraiser would be preferable.

2. The governor and the naval and military officers were allowed drawback of the import duty upon such spirits as they consumed. The Board thought this unusual.

3. The Ordinance tampered with the Navigation laws in a way only allowed to the king in Council.

4. The tariff was extremely complicated, and there were many differential duties.

The Treasury communicated with the governor, upholding the Board's opinions. All the objectionable clauses were removed except the first, which was retained on the strength of a report from the collector of Port Adelaide to the effect that there had been much undervaluing prior to the issue of the Ordinance, but only one case since.

On July 30, 1847, the collector of Hobart Town informed the Board that the Tasmanian revenue sustained loss through the issue of duty-free rum to the troops. He stated that there were 1,500 soldiers, and that each received $\frac{1}{7}$ quart per day (say a total annual issue of 19,500 gallons). Much of the rum was transferred to tavern-keepers, who paid the soldiers for it at the rate of 2½d. a daily ration. The collector mentioned incidentally that an attempt was once made at Sydney to commute the issue of rum at the rate of 1d. a day per man, but that the regiment concerned mutinied. Later he reported to the colonial Secretary that he had news of illicit distillation, and that the spirit thus obtained was mixed with the rum which the troops sold. It is evident he was suspected of a vivid imagination, for nothing was done.

By Cap. 97, 11 and 12 Vict. the sugar duties, which had been arranged so as to decrease annually till a certain rate was reached, were altered so as to reach a still lower rate. Cap. 127 effected a substantial reduction in the duties on unmanufactured copper and on pig and sheet lead.

The various collectors in the United Kingdom were directed to make known to masters of whaling-ships the rewards offered for information as to the *Erebus* and *Terror*, employed under Sir John Franklin.

Precautions had been taken in 1847 to prevent the importation of sheep affected with the 'variola ovis.' In 1848 the collectors were exhorted to special vigilance, as the disease was spreading fast in Norfolk and Suffolk.

During 1832 Anguilla had been made a 'free port,' at the request of the St. Kitts Council of Assembly. In 1848 the council asked the Treasury to abolish the Customs establishment at Anguilla, as it was a drain upon the colony, the expenses greatly exceeding the receipts. Many unreasonable appeals had been made by the colonial Legislatures, but none so unreasonable as this. The establishment had been made against the Board's wish, and it could not have oppressed the colony, for the officers' salaries, the rent of the custom-house, and the expense of the customs boat, were paid out of the United

Kingdom Customs. It is worth noting, too, that the Customs takings *in the Island of St. Kitts* failed to cover the expenses, and the deficit had to be made up annually by the London Receiver-General.

On October 18, 1848, the English brig *Croxdale* arrived at Rio de Janeiro. She had left Liverpool on July 12 with twelve seamen and over 120 passengers. The British consul at Rio inspected her, and found that she carried no medical man; that her medicine-chest was imperfectly supplied; that the master, his son, the mate, and four passengers were down with typhus; that there had been much sickness during the voyage, also two cases of child-birth, in which both mothers and children had died; that the vessel was but 290 tons, and altogether unfitted for her employment; and that the unfortunate passengers (all Irish emigrants) were unclean and dejected. They had been half starved during the voyage, and deprived of lime-juice, though it had been served out to the crew. The Admiralty transmitted this depressing report to the Board (the Customs being considered the department empowered to prosecute). Thereupon arose the usual quibbles, the Customs lawyers urging that it was not a Customs matter, and much correspondence with the Emigration Department took place, till in the end it was arranged that the Customs should prosecute. It seems that the only person responsible was the shipowner, and he but for failing to provide a surgeon. He was prosecuted before the Liverpool justices under sections 18 and 62 of Cap. 112, 7 and 8 Vict., and cast in the mitigated penalty of £33 6s. 8d. Then arose another discussion as to which department should bear the expense of prosecution. This endured till the Treasury directed that the cost should be paid out of the Customs revenue.

On September 11, 1848, three forged £1 notes were foisted upon the Customs at Sydney. The fraud was discovered when they were paid by the Customs into the Bank. It appears that there were many of these in circulation—indeed, two were presented by innocent people at the duty-counter on the following day, but the clerks detected them in time. The governor relieved the clerks from surcharge. (A £1 note converted into a £5 note had been passed in payment of duty at the same Custom-house in 1841.)

The collector of Hobart Town applied to the Board for advice. Under two colonial Acts recently passed the *ad valorem* duty on foreign goods had been raised from 5 to 15 per cent., and all preferential duties had been abolished. Thus the produce of New South Wales, hitherto admitted into Tasmania duty-free, had been made liable to the duty on foreign goods. Nearly all the payments of duty since the passing of the Acts had been made under protest, the merchants insisting that the Acts were not drafted in accordance with the provisions of the imperial Act empowering the governor in Council to make laws for the colony. The defect alleged was absence of statement as to how the duties were to be appropriated. It appears the Council had previously enacted a similarly defective dog tax, and the Judge of the island had decided that it was illegal. (The Board declined to interfere.)

The pertinacity in economizing, characteristic of many officials, was illustrated during 1848 by one of the customs officers of Jamaica. Being on leave in Scotland, he wrote the Secretary of Customs, calling attention to a clause in the agreement between the Admiralty and the Royal Mail Steam Packet Company with regard to the mails, under which clause the Company undertook to carry certain officials (when proceeding on duty) to the West Indies, free of all except mess expenses. 'I would go by an early steamer, as it will make a material difference in expenses, which is an object of moment to me.' He received a curt intimation that he was not entitled to profit by the clause. (The wonder is that so frugal a man had taken leave.)

The Navigation laws were further 'amended' by

Cap. 29 of 12 and 13 Vict.* It is apparent that many people in high administrative positions had become tired of the ancient regulations that had done so much for the achievement and maintenance of British mercantile supremacy, and that had produced and fostered that wonderful exemplar of hardihood, endurance, and nautical dexterity, the ancient British seaman. Readers will have perceived, by inspection of such extracts as have been furnished from the records, that in many instances lawyers and high officials interpreted these statutes in opportunist fashion, and that the customs men who were appointed to enforce them, especially in the colonies, often used the laws in the way that a footpad uses a loaded bludgeon. The public mind was inclined towards general relaxation. 'Free trade and open ports' was the cry. The public eye, in its scrutiny of measures, beholds but two colours: every measure is either black as the pit or white as driven snow, and it is certain that the 'amendments' mentioned captured public approval.

A number of Navigation Acts and parts of Acts were accordingly repealed, and the poor remnant put together in a statute that contained the following provisions:

1. Coastwise trade in the United Kingdom, the Isle of Man, the Channel Islands, and the colonies was still to be conducted in British ships; but if two or more colonies agreed to desire that their mutual trade should be made coastwise, or if any colonial Legislature prayed the queen that its coasting trade should be thrown open to foreign ships, the privileges might be granted by Order in Council.

2. The coastwise trade of India might be thrown open to foreign ships if the Governor-General chose to direct the same by his Order in Council, the document to be laid before the imperial Parliament.

3. To constitute a ship 'British,' she was to be registered. If she was in the coastwise or fishing trade of the United Kingdom, Channel Islands, or Isle of Man, all

* The new Act was to operate from January 1, 1850.

her crew had to be British; if in any other trade, the master and three-fourths of the crew; but there were several insidious exceptions attached to the last proviso.

4. Any natural-born subject of the queen, any holder of papers of naturalization or denization, any person who had served three years on a British ship of war, and *any Lascar from a place within the East India Company's charter,* might be deemed a British seaman. No imaginative person can read certain clauses in this Act without calling to mind the immortal line—

'Here, a sheer hulk, lies poor Tom Bowling.'

The Customs laws were amended afresh by Cap. 90 of 12 and 13 Vict. thus:

A package of imported tobacco legal as to weight might not be made up of illegal internal packages. (This was to combat a recent smuggling practice.)

If any dispute arose between importer and officer as to duty payable, the importer was to deposit the duty demanded, pending action if desired.

Goods discharged from vessels lying afloat, to be taken to a quay for examination, were to be landed promptly.

Persons concerned in importing prohibited or restricted goods were to be liable, even though such goods had not been unshipped.

All corn, meal, etc., was to be duty-paid on importation. (Previously the duties had been allowed to be bonded.)

(Most of the 'amendments' were either legal devices to check recently-discovered methods of fraud, or time-honoured provisions forgotten at the time of re-consolidation.)

During 1849 great public excitement was caused by the murder of Patrick O'Connor, a customs gauger employed at the London Docks. Perusal of O'Connor's official records reveals that he was a usurer, an exploiter of the poor, a man without either morals or scruples—in short, a precious scoundrel. It appears that he engaged with a dock foreman and an adventurer named Fitzgerald in a pretty enterprise. When young Irish labourers came to London for work, they were approached by Fitzgerald, who told them that he had a friend in the Customs who would secure them permanent employment in the docks, purely out of Christian charity, but it was necessary that plump fees should be paid to Fitzgerald. When the money was down the unfortunate fellows were taken on, but in every case the foreman soon found occasion to dismiss them. Meantime O'Connor, Fitzgerald, and the dock bully divided the spoil. One turbulent Irishman attempted to blackmail O'Connor, but the crafty gauger stationed a detective in ambush, and had him arrested. The fellow got twelve months' imprisonment, but the revelations during the trial were of so lurid a nature that the Board declined to promote O'Connor when his turn came.

Meantime he had formed an illicit connection with Mrs. Manning, an attractive and buxom creature, who was married to a railway guard, and whose husband appears to have winked at his wife's flirtations on the condition that O'Connor, who was quite a wealthy person, contributed most of the housekeeping money. Perhaps O'Connor was penurious, for in the end the Mannings laid a deadly trap for him. He was going on leave to Ireland, and they induced him to deposit his trunk, containing valuable securities, etc., at their house in Rotherhithe, and to come and dine with them on the Sunday preceding his departure. On the Saturday they procured a fat goose and other delicacies, and dug a hole under the hearthstone in the kitchen. On the Sunday morning, while Manning basted the goose at the kitchen fire, his wife went upstairs and shot O'Connor through the head. The body was stowed beneath the hearthstone, and the two wretches sat down above it, and dined off the goose and trimmings.

Afterwards they gave up the house, and travelled here and there, disposing of O'Connor's 'paper.' Some little clumsiness caused them to be arrested. O'Connor's absence was noted, and a search was made at the empty house in Rotherhithe. During the search a stray dog entered the kitchen, and began to sniff and whine above the hearthstone. The stone was taken up, and the corpse discovered. Both the Mannings were hanged.

Below is quoted O'Connor's last official letter—an application for promotion:

'HONOURABLE SIRS,

'As there is now a vacancy in the department I belong to, by the superannuation of Mr. Robinson, inspector of gaugers, I beg most respectfully to express my hope that your Honours will not on this as on a former occasion think it right to pass me by in the expected promotion, for whatever offence I may have given your Honours by my having on former occasions long ago brought trouble on myself for repeating a few words told me by a tide-waiter, and not being able then to prove it to your Honours' satisfaction, as I had no writing, and he denied it, and also by lending money to different officers, now most of them out of the Service, and in doing which I had lost the most part of what I had got together after about twenty years of economy and frugal habits.

'I do then respectfully and most humbly intreat your Honours will give every consideration to my case, as I have at all times attended strictly and honestly to my official duties, and never had my honesty questioned. I beg again to repeat my strongest hope that I may be allowed to go forward to the next class of gaugers, and to resume my former position.

'Respectfully submitted by your Honours' most obedient and very humble servant,

'P. O'CONNOR.'

Beneath appears this note in the inspector's handwriting, dated August 20, 1849:

'Mr. P. O'Connor was found dead on the 17th inst., under circumstances that leave but little doubt he has been murdered.'

On July 28, 1849, the governor of the Gold Coast, who was on leave, wrote from Clifford's Inn to the Secretary of State for the Colonies, recommending the establishment of a tariff and of Customs at various ports under his control. (It would seem there was no Customs staff except at Sierra Leone and Gambia. About £20,000 a year was collected at these two ports.) The articles proposed to be taxed at the new ports were spirits, tobacco, gunpowder, and firearms, 'the goods most extensively used.' The proposed duty on firearms was 6d. each, on gunpowder 5s. per 100 pounds, on spirits 3d. a gallon (the governor did not state whether liquid or proof), on tobacco 2d. *a gallon* (evidently the governor meant 'a pound').

The Act dated Cap. 1, 12 Vict., passed by the Legislature of Jamaica, had imposed duties for the period from February 15, 1849, to October 1, 1849. On September 30 (Sunday) a vessel arrived at Kingston from Halifax, N.S., with a cargo of fish, oil, shingles, etc., and reported on the following day. The captain then applied to the collector for a pass, to proceed to sea again; the collector granted it, and the vessel was taken outside the limits of the port. She returned on October 3, and her cargo was entered with the Customs. No new revenue Act had been passed, but the collector made the importers pay duty on the cargo under the old Act, insisting that it had been in force till midnight of October 1, 1849. It seems that the importers, Messrs. Darrell and Barclay, had expected this, and, to enable themselves to raise an objection, had taken the vessel to sea during the 1st, and brought her back when the Act could not be held to operate. They paid the duty—£233 odd—under protest.

The London Customs lawyers held that this trickery did not affect the issue. The vessel came first within the port on September 30, and that circumstance rendered her cargo liable under the Act. The Act did *not* cease, as the collector had maintained, at midnight on the 1st, but at midnight on the 30th. Such was the construction to be placed upon the words 'till October 1.' Still, they were doubtful whether, if the duties had not been paid, they could have been recovered in the colonial Courts. The Board ordered that the duties should be retained, they being due when the vessel first entered port.*

It appears that the merchants of Jamaica were spirited litigants. On December 15 one of them asked the collector to grant him an allowance out of duties paid on certain goods—the goods turning out damaged. The collector declined, stating that the merchant should have claimed the allowance before delivery, so that the Customs might have surveyed the goods and formed an estimate as to their depreciation. The merchant applied to the Board, furnishing a certificate of survey, and insisting that the collector was merely using routine to render the law as to abatement inoperative. The Board, against the advice of their own lawyers, directed the collector to grant the allowance, unless he had good reasons for suspecting the accuracy of the claim.

Other Jamaica merchants asked the Board to inform them as to the precise limits of the port of Kingston (perhaps on account of Darrell and Barclay's case). The collector was directed to inquire, and replied that he had failed to find any specifying document except an island Act (Cap. 39, 8 Vict., reaffirming a provision of the repealed statute, Cap. 39, 41 Geo. III.), which stated that the harbour included the waters 'between the shores in the parishes of Kingston and Port Royal, and the shores in the parishes of Kingston, St. Andrew, and St. Catherine, and the shores in the parishes of Port Royal and St. Catherine, and extending from the head of the harbour to a right line from Gallows Point, in the parish of Port Royal, to the southernmost point of the Twelve Apostles' Battery.'

Cap. 95, 13 and 14 Vict., amended the Customs laws, providing that the rules, orders, and regulations issued

* See p. 313 for another case.

by the Board should be valid until rescinded by the Board, even though the statutes that influenced their issue might no longer be in operation; also that no superannuation allowance granted to a Customs official should be legally assignable. It allowed the importation duty-free of goods from the Channel Islands, provided they were goods of Channel Island growth, or manufactured from materials produced in the Channel Islands, said materials being of a kind not dutiable in the United Kingdom. The importation into the United Kingdom of extracts of coffee, chicory, tea, and tobacco, was prohibited. The only remaining export duty—that of 4s. a ton on coals exported to foreign countries in foreign ships—was repealed.

The Board regularized the system of dealing with small quantities of tobacco and cigars brought by passengers. If the quantity were under half a pound, and the passenger not a frequent traveller, the goods might pass duty-free.

The ways of petty legal practitioners were illustrated by the case of a Liverpool tide-waiter named Thomas. He had been arrested for debt, and the collector advised the Board. It appeared that a London solicitor had apprised Thomas that his wife had been left £154. The various legal expenses swallowed all of the legacy except £23 10s. This remnant Thomas expended. Then the lawyer sent in a bill for 'proctor's charges,' amounting to £20 7s. 2d., sold him up, and threw him into gaol.

The Plymouth tide-waiters petitioned the Board, stating that they were sometimes kept on small foreign craft for preiods ranging from forty to eighty days. (This must have been an utterly barbarous and useless formality.) Thus they suffered in health, and had few opportunities of seeing their families. The Board did not lighten their lot to any great extent. It was merely directed that when a tide-waiter had been on duty *seven successive days and nights* he should be allowed a night's rest before being boarded again!

The inspecting commander of Coastguard at Seafield,

Miltown Milbay, Ireland, reported an extraordinary riot in that locality. The brig *Andrew White*, laden with timber, went ashore on the coast, and the rabble of Miltown Milbay (described by the officer as 'the most unruly population in the kingdom') mustered, on plunder bent, armed with reaping-hooks, hammers, axes, crow-bars, sticks, and stones. The officer asserted that some of the wealthier inhabitants, who desired to profit by the plunder, supplied the mob with whisky. The police and Coastguard did their best, but it seems that the rabble carried off most of the cargo, and that certain responsible citizens purchased it from them.

Part of the correspondence connected with this case is ludicrous. One of the rioters fell and broke his thigh, and then put in a claim for 'salvage'! One of the 'receivers' sent the following modest though garbled petition to the Board :

'The police seized a cross-cut saw of mine which was in care of one of my laborers, and in his absence it was taken by some men who the police found on the shore and also found the saw. I sent to the Sergeant, who said it could not be given without your authority. I will feel obliged your ordering him to return it to me.

'And you will oblige,
'faithfully,
'THOS. H. MORONY.'

On February 19, 1850, the U.S.A. Consul at St. John, New Brunswick, applied to the controller of Navigation laws for enlightenment as to the state of affairs under the recently-amended Navigation Acts. Below are the questions and replies, the latter sanctioned by the Board :

1. 'May American vessels trade coastwise in the provinces ?' Reply : 'No ; but they may trade between province and province, to and from ports provided with custom-houses.'

2. 'May an American vessel from a foreign port trade to a colonial place other than a "free port," or load at

such place for foreign?' Reply: 'She may trade to or from such place if the place be provided with a custom-house.'

3. 'May an American vessel be made British?' Reply: 'Yes; the full conditions of registry, etc., being complied with.'

When the Newfoundland Customs were handed over to the colony, the gauging and testing instruments, stationery, etc., went as well, under stipulation that the colony should pay for them. In 1850 the controller of Navigation laws wrote to the Board thus: 'It will surprise your Honours to learn that, although these articles were actually necessary to the colonial officers, the House of Assembly twice rejected the proposed vote, and it was not until after a third application had been made by the Executive that the amount was granted.'

The Jamaica revenue Act alluded to at p. 309 had been replaced by another statute—a statute drafted rather more carefully, for it provided that the tariff should expire on *December 31*, 1850. It was not passed until several days after the previous Act had determined, but it was made retrospective. Messrs. Scott and Leaycraft, Kingston merchants, refused to pay duty on certain goods imported by them during the interval. Thereupon an American resident, rejoicing in the illustrious name 'Benjamin Franklin,' followed suit. A decree was obtained against Scott and Leaycraft, with costs, in the Vice-Admiralty Court of the island. They gave notice of appeal, but did not persevere. A decree was also obtained, with costs, against Franklin, and he deposited the duty and costs in the Customs chest, stating that he intended to lay his case before the queen. A deal of trouble was gone to in the United Kingdom to provide defence against Franklin's expected appeal, and there was much discussion as to whether the imperial or the island Customs should bear the expense if he carried it into the higher Court. All this, it seems, might have been spared, for there is no record of any further steps taken by him.

Questions from foreign shipowners, as to the purport of the amended Navigation Act, continued to trouble the Board. One, transmitted by the Jamaica collector, was from the British consul at St. Jago de Cuba, asking whether a Spanish vessel might trade as a mail-packet between Cuba and Jamaica. The consul was doubtful on the point, as the Spanish regulations were not reciprocal. The Board told him the vessel might trade, and hinted that the collector might have dealt personally with so simple a matter.*

An account of the finance of the colony of South Australia appears in one of the returns. The total revenue for 1850 was £147,455. Of this, £80,000 was raised by Customs, the duty taken on spirits and tobacco alone realizing £42,000. There was a 'bonded debt' of £15,000. The Customs expenses were extremely moderate. The collector had but £500 a year. The total charges on the Customs establishment were £3,719 for salaries, and £455 for incidents. Another return states the nature of New Zealand products exported from Auckland during 1848-1850: 1848, £15,525; 1849, £27,092; 1850, £45,765. The chief articles exported were cordage, flax, grain, 'houses in frame,' black oil, sperm oil, spars, timber, copper ore, and potatoes. The exports of copper ore had increased in value from £500 in 1848 to £14,887 in 1850; of potatoes, from £121 to £5,780. Another return states the trade and revenue of the port of Geelong in 1850: Imports, £40,883; exports, £359,687; Customs revenue, £11,348. (In 1851 the Geelong return was: Imports, £113,672; exports, £392,950; Customs revenue, £16,037.)

The only revenue Act of 1851 was Cap. 62, 14 and 15

* The best definition of the new state of affairs that we have been able to find is that furnished by the London 'Bench Officers' (Customs) in 1850. They stated that all limitations were removed, save that foreign ships might not trade with or in the Channel Islands, or coast in the United Kingdom and the colonies.

Vict., which reduced the duty on foreign coffee and several kinds of foreign timber. The goods in question, when imported from British possessions, had been previously admitted at low preferential duties. The Act abolished such preference, and made the duties equal.

During 1851 the mayor and burgesses of Cork memorialized the Treasury, stating that the copper coinage in the south-west of Ireland was defective, much bad coin being in circulation, and a number of 'tokens' issued by irresponsible persons. It was suggested that the collector of customs at Cork should be allowed to sell £1,500 worth new copper coin. Copper coin to the value of £500 was sent to the collector at Belfast. The officers were directed to remit in all £2,000 to the Bank of England, to the credit of the Master of the Mint.

The Customs return to the Census officers in 1851 was as below:

	Established Officers.	*Temporary Officers.*	*Superannuated Officers.*
London	1,736	367	408
English outports ..	2,236	533	645
Scotland	528	59	131
Ireland	476	193	177
	4,976	1,152	1,361

Late in 1850 one of the Southampton officers reported to the Board that a sealed bag had been shipped by a vessel for Lisbon 'by a Spanish gentleman.' The bag, he thought, contained letters, but he had not presumed to detain it, although he intimated suspicion that the postal regulations with respect to foreign letters might have been evaded. The Board communicated with the Postmaster-General, who referred to the Spanish minister in London, who in turn applied to the Spanish consul, who denied knowledge of the transaction, and sent an indignant demand for explanation, which the minister transmitted, along with a few severe remarks on his own account, to the departments interested. Early in 1851 it was found that the bag had been sent from the *Portu-*

guese Legation, under the Portuguese Consulate seal, and quite in accordance with official routine.

A Bideford ship cleared out from Westport for the North American colonies with sixty-seven emigrants. She displayed her proper complement of boats when the collector made his inspection, but when she arrived in the colonies the Customs found she was one short. Inquiry was made, and the Westport collector ascertained that the captain borrowed a boat prior to inspection, and returned it 'from sea' after leaving port. The matter was allowed to drop, the vessel having gone into the foreign trade.

On January 17, 1851, the *Emerald Isle*, with emigrants from Sydney to San Francisco, left the former port without Customs sanction. Clearance had been withheld, and a tide-waiter put on board to insure detention, because the Emigration agent had declared the vessel unseaworthy. She took the officer to sea with her. The governor reported the affair to the Privy Council for Trade, and intimated that the colonial law officers opined that no proceedings could be taken, the law being defective on the point at issue. The matter was referred to the London Customs lawyers, who opined differently, pointing out that prosecution might be effectively sustained under the following Acts: Cap. 33, 12 and 13 Vict., against the master, for sailing without the Emigration agent's certificate; Cap. 13, 9 Vict. (New South Wales Act), for sailing without Customs clearance, and also for carrying the officer away. These proceedings should be taken in New South Wales, but if the master came to the United Kingdom, he might be prosecuted under Cap. 87, 8 and 9 Vict. (The vessel was not liable to seizure.)

Meantime the *Emerald Isle* put in to Honolulu, and landed the officer, who in course of time found his way back to Sydney. She proceeded to San Francisco, and her company promptly deserted her, except the chief mate, who after a time succeeded in obtaining fresh hands. She was in England in 1852, and the new captain furnished a statement to the Board, from which it appeared that the previous skipper had not been much to blame, for it was shown that he had an independent survey made at Sydney, under which the ship was declared 'tight, staunch, and strong, and fit to proceed to any part of the world'; that he offered to put the officer ashore along with the pilot, but the officer would not budge; that when he landed the officer at Honolulu he gave him £20 to pay his expenses back; and that the consul at Honolulu surveyed the vessel, and testified to her seaworthiness. The matter was dropped.

The first section of the imperial Act 59, 13 and 14 Vict., had decreed the separation of Victoria and New South Wales. This exercised the minds of the New South Wales Crown lawyers and the collector of Sydney. The lawyers thought that only goods which were *shipped* from Victoria after date of separation should be charged with duty. Otherwise, they held, duty-paid goods shipped—say, in Melbourne—prior to separation, might arrive at Sydney on the day after separation and have to be duty-paid again. (The mere layman might think that it would be an equal hardship if the merchant shipped such goods after separation. In either case he would pay twice.)

On November 1, 1851, the collector of Melbourne informed the Board that the governor had made substantial increases in the pay of all the inferior officials, 'under the present unprecedented circumstances, consequent upon the discovery of gold in this colony.' Many officials of other departments had deserted and made off for the diggings, but the Customs men had pledged themselves to stick to their posts.

During this year the Board of Customs furnished Government with various accounts of large shipments of arms and ammunition to the Cape. The foreign office directed that inquiries should be made as to the ultimate destination of these goods, and the Cape Town collector furnished in reply a statement tending to show that the smuggling of arms and ammunition across the boundary of the colony to the Boers, Kaffirs, 'bastard Hottentots,' and Portuguese, had ceased years ago. Yet he failed to explain satisfactorily the deliveries of gunpowder from the two colonial storehouses, Craig's Tower and Amsterdam Battery, which during three months of 1851 had reached 41,200 pounds. Later he seemed to think that most of this went to the Boers, and was used in protecting their stock and in killing game. 'The Boer and his gun,' he stated, 'are constant companions, and to deprive him of the use of it would undoubtedly be deemed a great grievance.' He also procured statements from vagrant traders, which went to show that if the sale of weapons and powder to natives had ceased it must have ceased rather suddenly. Said one: 'I have seen black people (bastard Hottentots) bartering for gunpowder, giving in exchange corn, skins, ostrich eggs, ostrich feathers, etc. I have seen a trek-ox bought for half a pound of gunpowder, and three oxen for a gun' (worth about five dollars). Another expert stated that twenty Boers bought 1,000 pounds of powder from him in one lot; and another stated that the Boers frequently paid their Kaffir labourers in arms and ammunition. (This man had seen a large quantity of gunpowder run on the coast from a Liverpool vessel.)

Later Earl Grey wrote complaining bitterly of the running of guns, powder, and bar lead to the hostile Kaffirs. Soon came a report from the commander of H.M.S. *Rhadamanthus*, who had been sent to Espiègle Bay and the mouth of the Orange River to investigate. He had found no unauthorized supply on hand, except five barrels of powder intended for blasting purposes, but he had collected much information from Field-Cornet Cornelissen and a trader named Dickson. These concurred in stating that the smuggling of arms, etc., was nearly ended; but Dickson's admissions as to his dealings in the past cause us to think he might still be active, as soon as H.M.S. *Rhadamanthus* departed. Not only did he give details of his own doings, but of certain traffic by missionaries, and of direct landing of guns and powder by European vessels at Angra Pequena and Walwick Bay. There can be no doubt that 'gun-running' was a profitable business, and that many unworthy British merchants made a good thing of supplying weapons to the enemies of their country.

The New Zealand collectors were empowered by the governor to allow tobacco to be mixed in bond with spirits of tar or turpentine, and then delivered duty-free for manufacture into sheepwash.

Provision had been made by treaty in 1819, and ratified by Cap. 54, 59 Geo. III., for reciprocity in commercial arrangements between the United Kingdom and the United States of America, and the United Kingdom and Portugal. Cap. 90, 8 and 9 Vict., had extended reciprocity so as to apply between the United Kingdom and all foreign powers that had entered into similar treaties. Cap. 47, 15 and 16 Vict., conferred still greater elasticity, for it provided that the queen by Order in Council might at any time establish reciprocity as regarded commerce and navigation between the United Kingdom and any foreign power that gave to British goods and shipping the same privileges as to its own, such reciprocity to endure as long as the foreign power continued to grant the privileges, even though no treaty had been entered into. The places that enjoyed Treaty privileges were: Austria, Belgium, Bolivia, Costa Rica, Denmark, the Dominican Republic, 'the Republic of the Equator,' France, the city of Frankfort, Greece, Guatemala, Hanover, the Hanse cities (of Bremen, Hamburg, and Lubeck), Liberia—the Duchies of Mecklenburg-Schwerin, Mecklenburg-Strelitz, Oldenburg, and Tuscany—Mexico, Holland, New Grenada, Turkey, Peru, Portugal—Prussia, and the various states forming the German Commercial Union—Rio de la Plata, Russia, Sardinia, Sicily, Sweden and Norway, the United States of America, Uruguay, and Venezuela.

In 1852 the Board issued directions as to dealing with

a new article of import 'known as Semolina.' It was to be admitted as wheat-meal, at 4½d. a hundredweight duty.

The once famous port of Chichester was made a creek (head port, Arundel) on December 5, 1852.

A Treasury Order of November 29, 1852, directed that all tobacco, except cigars, in the Queen's Warehouse as 'seized,' and all such tobacco seized thenceforward, should be destroyed, instead of being disposed of by auction at the Customs sales. The order stated that it was apparent that the sale of seized tobacco 'led to fraud,' and injured the honest trader, 'by displacing in the market a corresponding quantity of tobacco which would otherwise be entered for home consumption.' (This order, slightly modified, is still in force. Why it should apply only to tobacco is difficult to discover.)

By a Board's Minute of 1852 certain privileges had been granted to merchants of unshipping duty-free goods in the Port of London before and after legal hours without any expense for Customs attendance. Later the merchants of Liverpool asked that the privilege might be extended to that port. The Board replied that the measure was but experimental. The Liverpool merchants applied afresh, declining to consider it 'experimental,' it having been extended to Leith, Kirkcaldy, and Dundee. The Board referred the petitioners to the collector at Liverpool, but they refused to accept the recommendation, and soon the Liverpool Chamber of Commerce moved the Board upon the matter. Then a full report was called for, and the Customs surveyor-general tried his best to make out a case for the preferential treatment of London, stating that the London dock and wharf hours were similar to the Customs hours; that few goods were unshipped in London before and after the usual hours, except into craft, to be cleared by Customs during the legal period; but that at Liverpool nearly all the goods were landed, and required to be cleared at once, and that if the Crown had to pay the officers for the extra attend-dance, great public expense would be incurred. He thought that 'the American portion' of the Chamber of Commerce had inspired the memorial. The request was afterwards granted, and later still one from the Bristol merchants.

During 1850 and 1851 the Customs Board had been considerably embroiled with the directors of the London and St. Katherine's Docks. The trouble arose in 1849,* when information of fraud in connection with 'sweepings' in the St. Katherine's Docks was given privately to the Solicitor. To make things quite clear, it may be necessary to explain the position of a dock company with respect to the Customs. In the first place the dock company was under a heavy bond to the revenue department—a bond liable to be put in suit if any fraud were discovered for which the company might legally be held blamable. The directors were bound to provide all reasonable facilities for the customs men to take account of goods, and might deliver no goods, either dutiable or free, without Customs sanction. In connection with the unpacking, repacking, weighing, etc., of certain kinds of dutiable goods, especially such goods as raw coffee and cocoa, there was frequently an accumulation of 'sweepings'—viz., litter from the various packages—and when the floors were cleared at the end of each day the 'sweepings' were put away by the dock company's servants. In course of time they grew into a large quantity, and it was the practice of the dock company to assume possession, clean them, lot them, and either pay duty on them and sell them, or export them duty-free. In short, they became the company's perquisites, it being held that they could not be justly allotted to the various merchants' goods. It will be evident to readers that if the dock company's officials happened to be astute and unscrupulous people, they had here a chance of committing fraud. In the first

* A case much similar had occurred in 1816, when, acting upon information received, the Customs seized goods to the value of about £12,000 for being found in various places in the London Dock, and not accounted for in the Company's books.

place there could be no exact check on the quantity of 'sweepings' till the period arrived when the bulk was weighed and lotted. During the interval much might be done. 'Sweepings' of dutiable goods might be slyly conveyed from the dock, or used in making up deficiencies in goods which had been taken to account (deficiencies caused by neglect or abstraction). There can be no doubt that something of the kind had been practised pretty freely at the St. Katherine's Dock. A sudden search was made by the Customs on December 4, 1849, and several packages, some containing 'sweepings,' and other goods which had not been entered with the Customs, were seized. Other searches were made during the early part of 1850, and many packages detained. The total value of the goods seized (mostly coffee, indigo, and pepper) was £8,392.

On March 2, 1850, information was tendered as to similar irregularities in the London Dock. Several searches were made, and goods to the value of £10,467 were seized.

The directors of both dock companies displayed great hostility, and combated the proceedings of the Customs in every possible way. It is likely that the searches were conducted in an arbitrary manner, that many of the packages were seized on mere suspicion, and that the Customs Solicitor was a little too masterful and dexterous in his efforts towards securing the conviction of offenders and the inculpation of the dock companies. But the dock directors behaved in obstinate fashion, refusing to accept the slightest blame for what must at all events have constituted gross neglect, championing certain employés of theirs who certainly did not deserve protection, and levelling accusations wholesale against the customs men. They even insisted that large losses discovered upon wines housed in the vaults were due to the bibulous habits of the officers. The Customs Solicitor entered actions in the Exchequer against both companies. The St. Katherine's Dock Company compromised the matter by paying £100, and admitting that great irregularities had prevailed. The London Dock Company fought their case, and, after a verdict had been given which satisfied neither Customs nor company, the latter did the same as the St. Katherine's Dock company had done. Yet, though both companies thus admitted that they were wrong and the Customs right, the latter were not to come off with flying colours.

Fiery articles, denouncing the Customs Board, began to appear in certain journals, and indignation meetings were held at several influential ports. A petition, signed by numerous merchants, was presented to the House of Commons, and a Parliamentary Committee, of which Mr. Gladstone was a member, sat to inquire into Customs matters generally. While this Committee was at work a separate Committee of merchants, elected by the trade, also sat in Charlotte Row, heard much evidence, and forwarded many recommendations to the Parliamentary Committee. Afterwards the proceedings of this self-appointed body were published in a volume, together with many remarkable reflections upon the British Customs, and especially upon the Customs Board.

The number of witnesses called up and examined by the Parliamentary Committee was remarkable. Extremely remarkable, too, was some of the evidence given by the witnesses, especially those who were hostile to the Board. Ship-owners, smack-owners, merchants, lightermen, and wharfingers, joined in complaining bitterly of Customs incompetence, circumlocution, and greed. Some of the complaints appeared justifiable; others were manifestly made by men who had been trying to break the regulations, and who, having failed and suffered, had evolved burning grievances.

The Parliamentary Committee's report was decidedly unfavourable to the Board as constituted. It stated that the Commissioners' holidays were excessive, and recommended that at least one person from the mercantile class and one practical customs officer should be admitted as Commissioners. It proceeded that the inferior officers were shut out unfairly from promotion. There were six classes of these officers, and, although they all entered under educational tests that differed but little, promotion from one grade to another was rare, and none could rise from the five lower classes into the highest. The Committee found fault with the *ad valorem* duties, stating that they produced little and were extremely troublesome, and that the system adopted by the Crown of buying undervalued goods and selling them by auction caused a loss to the public. It was urged that greater powers in the disposal of questions raised should be granted to the higher outdoor officials, as under the method in use vexatious delay was often inflicted on the mercantile community. It was also suggested that in Customs trials, when the duty involved did not exceed £100, a much cheaper tribunal could be found than the Court of Exchequer ; also that the owners of vessels should not be fined for acts of smuggling committed by their employés, except when the fraud was extensive, or the captain or chief officer was implicated. Another reform suggested was the transference of liability for duties on bonded goods from the original importer to the warehouse-keeper, the Customs to give the latter a voucher in all cases of delivery of goods, and the Crown to take stock periodically, so that the then owner of the goods might be made to re-enter them. Simplification of the method of entering free goods was also recommended. Under the system in vogue each entry passed through the hands of nineteen customs officers. The Committee thought all entry of free goods by the separate consignees might be dispensed with, and the ship's report be accepted.*

The Committee commented severely upon certain tactics pursued by the Customs Solicitor in conducting the case against the dock companies. It appears that

* This would have been impracticable, as there would be nothing to make the consignee liable if his goods contained contraband.

during the proceedings six labourers were charged by the Customs as assistants in the assumed frauds. Five of these men were bailed, the other remained in prison three weeks, and was then bailed. Finally the dock company took steps to have them defended. The informations against them were filed by the Customs in December, 1850. Early in 1851 the defending solicitors asked four times for particulars of the informations. These were never furnished, nor were the informations tried, and at the time of the Committee's report in 1852 the defendants were still under bail, the charges against them being for penalties amounting to £10,800 !

Two prominent members of the Board resigned, and it was not deemed necessary to fill up the vacancies. Undoubtedly the Consolidation Act of the following year resulted from the strong agitation against many Customs restrictions that was kept up by the mercantile community. Yet, while this agitation was going on, a huge memorial was presented to the Commons by the shipowners, bewailing the repeal of the bulk of the Navigation laws ! To suit all classes of the commercial community is as hopeless a task as that essayed by Æsop's old wittol, who, in trying to please everybody, pleased nobody, and lost his ass into the bargain.*

The Tasmanian Act 5 of 15 Vict., passed February 19, 1852, for regulating the Customs in that island, stated that the discovery of gold in the neighbouring colonies had raised the price of goods in Tasmania, and made it necessary to increase official salaries. It repealed certain previous revenue Acts, and imposed a tariff upon imported spirits, wine, tobacco, tea, sugar, coffee, dried fruit, hops, and malt liquors.

Up to 1852, the maritime revenue in Victoria had arisen from harbour, entrance, lighthouse, and tonnage dues, and a comprehensive tariff with many *ad valorem* items. In 1851 the dues had produced but £6,501, and the tariff £106,260, of which £91,688 came from spirits,

* See pp. 150, 151, vol. i., 'The King's Customs.'

wine, tobacco, tea, sugar, and coffee. A Victorian Act of 1852 abolished the vexatious dues, and all import duties except upon the six prolific articles.

(These colonial revisions are mentioned to show that the progress of opinion in some of the colonies was similar to that in the United Kingdom.)

Among the Customs 'Plantation' documents for 1852 appear many cancelled commissions from Australia and Tasmania, illustrating the complete severance of colonial Customs control and the home supervision. (The controllers of Navigation laws, etc., still continued to report to the Board upon matters such as trade and copyright.) The Customs in New Zealand completed severance in 1853.

On April 21, 1853, a remarkable debate on Customs reform took place in the House of Commons. The Secretary for the Treasury opened the proceedings by a recapitulation of the circumstances attending the dispute between the Board and the dock companies, and referred to a deputation of City men that had waited on the Chancellor of the Exchequer early in 1853, when it had been promised that matters should be improved and a Customs Consolidation Act passed. He stated that the weighers and tide-waiters might with fairness be admitted to higher appointments, and that certain arrangements had been made in that direction. He described the system previously obtaining as one which seemed 'to savour more of the spirit of Eastern caste than of English freedom.'* On account of the many under-valuations of *ad valorem* goods, it was intended that there should be as few *ad valorem* duties in the forthcoming tariff as possible. Every person who considered himself aggrieved by a Customs seizure, detention, etc., might be allowed to have his case dealt with in open court by one of the

* It cannot be truly said, even at the present day, that any branch of the Civil Service is free from the influence of 'the spirit of caste.' There is a strong prejudice against 'outdoor men.' Talent and energy count for little, unless the exponent be a 'clerk' or a 'University man.'

Commissioners if in London, and at an outport by the collector. The Treasury stated that arrangements would be made allowing the inland carriage of transhipment goods from one port to another, so as to foster British shipping, and predicted that this would work wonders in the way of making the United Kingdom a place of transhipment. He declared that British shipping had increased considerably since the repeal of the Navigation laws in 1850. The Government were also prepared to rescind the prohibition of importing arms in transit, and to allow the transfer of goods in bond. They would abolish the varying warehouse privileges, and make all bonded warehouses subject to the same restrictions (the warehouse-keeper to be responsible for losses). But the Government declined the Committee's suggestion that there should be no entry for duty-free goods except the ship's report, and here the Secretary enlivened his audience by a few anecdotes of smuggling—viz., of the 'oil-cake case' (see p. 347), of tobacco found in casks of potatoes, tubs of butter, tierces of provisions, and barrels of resin; of the 'rape-oil case' (see p. 364); and of a recent capture of the mate of a steamer from Boulogne, who was preparing to walk ashore wearing a corset containing forty watches. (The Secretary produced the corset to his audience. This was probably the first time that a smuggler's panoply had been exhibited in Parliament.) He then told an amusing tale, illustrative of the impudent and false charges occasionally brought against the Customs. A merchant doing business in Holborn employed as receiver a woman who lived near Bedford Row. Eleven cases of smuggled watches were found in her house. After the receiver had suffered and the watches had been sold, the merchant came forward and claimed restoration of the goods, and made abominable and unfounded charges against the seizing officers. For instance, he accused them of wrongfully detaining his personal correspondence, although it had been restored to him long before, and although it furnished evidence that he was not only the importer of the watches seized at Bedford Row, but a patron of the corset-wearing mate of the Boulogne steamer.

The Secretary then proceeded to lay an extra coat of flattery upon the already overlarded James Deacon Hume, consolidator of Customs laws, describing the work done by him as 'one of the greatest mental wonders ever achieved by man!' Then he made cheerful comparison between shipping in 1817 and in 1850; but we will refrain from quoting his statistics, whilst expressing hope that they were correct. Then came a list of exports, which showed that the export trade of Liverpool was more than double that of London, while that of Hull nearly equalled London, and that the shipping of London was less than that of Liverpool. Yet the Customs revenue of London was more than three times that of Liverpool, which, even when we take into account that all exports were free, leaves room for scepticism. But the most remarkable comparison was that between London and Hull.

London's tonnage was 3,289,000; Hull's was 836,000. (It should be remembered that this was a statement on foreign trade, so we may presume coasting ships were not included.) London's exports were of the value of £14,137,000; Hull's, £10,366,000. London's Customs revenue (all from imports) was £11,285,000; Hull's £353,000. Therefore, if the imported goods were at all similar at each port, London's imports would be about thirty-two times the bulk of the Hull imports. London's exports slightly exceeded those of Hull, so we may leave the relative bulk of goods, export and import combined, as 32 to 1. Yet the relative tonnage of shipping was exactly 4 to 1. The Financial Secretary seems to have perceived that there was a discrepancy, but he kept on quoting statistics. It is to be wondered if he had ever given a few moments' thought to the question whether this statistical porridge with which, since the days of Adam Smith, the British voter and member of Parliament had been so liberally dosed, was made of corn or of powdered chaff.

After the Financial Secretary had ended, the member for Bridport criticized his speech, and was severe on the Chairman of the Customs Board, stating that his administration was responsible for the late vengeful proceedings. He said that ninety-four informations were framed against the dock companies, that the case against the London Dock cost the defendants £12,000, and that the only verdict obtained in the Exchequer was one condemning two boxes of sugar. Then he had a slap at the Customs Solicitor. 'A few years before,' said he, 'this solicitor, Mr. Hamel, was an obscure attorney at the inland town of Tamworth. . . . Here was an ignorant and vain man, who said to himself, "I will distinguish myself; I will show by my conduct that I have the talents to justify my appointment,"' etc.

The member for Sunderland took up the cudgels on behalf of Mr. Hamel, stating that gentleman had been Sir Robert Peel's solicitor, and Sir Robert Peel had put him in his present position. Mr. Hamel had been spoken of as an obscure country attorney. Why should a man's original obscurity be a bar to his filling an important office? etc. (Other members defended the Customs Chairman.)

Cap. 95 of 16 and 17 Vict. prolonged indefinitely the provisions of the Act of 1833 (see p. 172) as to government by the East India Company of the territories within their charter. But the Governor-General's previous powers of control were amplified, and it was provided that the imperial Commander-in-Chief should be Commander-in-Chief of the Company's forces in India. (The Company were allowed to increase the number of their European soldiers from 12,200 to 20,000.)

Cap. 106 announced the promised Consolidation and the new tariff. The following goods were still subject to *ad valorem* duties: Agates, boxes, *unenumerated* cotton manufactures, unenumerated embroidery, essence of spruce, extracts (of cardamoms, coculus indicus, grains of paradise, liquorice, nux vomica, opium, Guinea pepper, Peruvian bark, quassia, radix rhataniæ, and vitriol), unenumerated extracts, unenumerated manufactures of hair, iodine, japanned ware, jewels set, hand-made lace, unenumerated leather manufactures, unenumerated linen manufactures, unenumerated musical instruments, foreign ships for breaking up, unenumerated manufactured silks,* gauzes, velvets, and mixtures of silk with other materials, unenumerated wood, unenumerated woollens, and all goods partly or wholly manufactured and not prohibited which had not been mentioned in the tariff list.

The goods liable to specific duties were certain kinds of almonds, almond-paste, apples, arrowroot, pearl barley, baskets, beads except of glass, beer, biscuit and bread, books of editions printed since 1800, certain brass manufactures, gold and silver brocade, bronze manufactures, butter, candles, certain sticks, caoutchouc manufactures, capers, playing-cards, cassia lignea, cassava powder, cheese, cherries, chicory, chinaware, cinnamon, clocks (varying according to value), cloves, cocoa, coculus indicus, coffee, comfits, confectionery, unenumerated copper manufactures, coral négligées and beads, corks (except fishermen's corks), corn, flour, and meal, cotton fringe, gloves, and stockings, currants, daguerrotype plates, dates, dice, unenumerated earthenware, eggs, certain kinds of feathers, figs, fig-cake, artificial flowers, unenumerated raw fruit, ginger, certain kinds of glass, grains of paradise, grapes, gutta-percha manufactures, hats and bonnets, hops, iron and steel manufactures, lace, lead manufactures, enumerated leather manufactures, certain kinds of linen manufactures, liquorice, matches, macaroni, mace, mandioca flour, manna croup, marmalade, medlars, millboards, morphia, enumerated musical instruments, mustard, nutmegs, certain kinds of nuts, nux vomica, certain oils, oilcloth, onions, opium, oranges

* Some manufactured silks, etc., might be charged with either specific or *ad valorem* duties at customs option.

and lemons, paper, pasteboard, pears, pepper, percussion caps, perfumery, pewter manufactures, pickles in vinegar, pimento, gold and silver plate, platting, preserved and French plums, pomatum, potato flour, hair powder and starch, prints and drawings, prunes, quassia, quinces, sulphate of quinine, raisins, rice, sago, salicine, unenumerated sauces, scaleboards, caraway-seeds, semolina, enumerated manufactures of silk, gauze, and velvet, and of silk mixed with other stuffs, soap, soy, spa ware, unenumerated spelter manufactures, spirits, stearine, succades, sugar and molasses, tallow, tapioca, tea, tinfoil and unenumerated tin manufactures, tobacco and snuff, toys, turnery, varnish containing spirit, veneers, vermicelli and macaroni, vinegar, washing-balls, watches (varying according to value), Cologne-water, wine, enumerated wood (except small staves, hoops, teak, waste wood, stringy bark, red and blue gum, green-heart, certain kinds of tree-nails, shovel-hilts, wood for herring barrels, and colonial firewood), woollen carpets, rugs, shawls, scarves, handkerchiefs, and gloves, and worsted yarn for embroidery. On most of these the rates were much reduced. The tea duty was to diminish annually till it reached 1s. a pound in 1856, and several other articles were also subject to diminishing duties—in some cases until they became free. The only preferential rates on colonial goods allowed to remain were those on apples, books, butter, cheese, eggs, unenumerated embroidery, ginger, liquorice paste and powder, caraway-seed, unenumerated silk manufactures, spirits, sugar and molasses, tallow, wine, and wood.

There were no export duties. Drawback was payable at export upon rice cleaned in the United Kingdom, sugar refined in the United Kingdom, tobacco manufactured in the United Kingdom, and wine; and there was an export allowance upon British manufactured plate.

Such articles as had previously been liable to duty in the Isle of Man, and had been made duty-free into the

United Kingdom, became duty-free into the dependency. The duties on two or three of the other articles into the island were increased, but the vexatious licence and quantity regulations were abolished.

The other alterations effected by the Act have been foretold in our account of the Parliamentary debate at pp. 326, 327.

The above scale of duties will appear formidable to readers, yet it is diminutive compared with the previous list.

Below is an account of the ports and creeks of the United Kingdom, as shown in the Customs records of 1853:

Ports.	Subports and Creeks.
First Class.	
Bristol.	Uphill.
Dublin.	Balbriggan, Howth, Wicklow, Arklow, Kingstown.
Glasgow.	Renfrew, Bowling Bay.
Greenock.	Holyloch, Lochgilphead, Oban, Tobermory, Rothesay.
Hull.	Bridlington.
Leith.	Newhaven, Cockenzie, Fisherow, Dunbar, North Berwick, Eyemouth.
Liverpool.	Runcorn.
London.	Gravesend.
Second Class.	
Belfast.	Donaghadee, Larne.
Cork.	Kinsale, Clonakilty, Youghal, Robert's Cove, West Passage.
Newcastle.	Amble.
Plymouth.	Devonport, St. Germains, Calstock.
Southampton.	Lymington, Christchurch.
Waterford.	Passage, Dungarvan, Dunmore.
Third Class.	
Aberdeen.	Peterhead, Stonehaven, Newburgh.
Dundee.	Ferryport-on-Craig.
Exeter.	Topsham, Exmouth, Teignmouth, Seaton.
Gloucester.	Lydney, Beachley.
Limerick.	Tarbert, Kilrush, Clare, Dingle.
Londonderry.	Greencastle.
Portsmouth.	Fareham, Emsworth.

Ports.	Subports and Creeks.
Third Class.	
Sunderland.	Seaham.
Stockton.	Cleveland Point, Middlesbrough.
Whitehaven.	Ravenglass, Millom.
Yarmouth.	Lowestoft, Beccles, Southwold.
Fourth Class.	
Douglas.	Derbyhaven, Peel, Ramsay.
Dover.	Hythe, Sandgate.
Lancaster.	Glasson Dock, Arnside, Ulverston, Ireleth, Angerton, Barrow, Walney, Poulton.
Lynn.	Heacham.
Newry.	Warrenpoint, Newcastle, Ardglass, Killyleagh.
Rochester.	Sheerness, Maidstone.
Shoreham.	Brighton.
Sligo.	Killala, Donegal, Ballyshannon.
Fifth Class.	
Berwick.	Budle Bay, Holy Island, Alnmouth.
Boston.	Wainfleet, Saltfleet, Spalding.
Bridgwater.	Combwich, Minehead, Watchet.
Cardiff.	Aberthaw, Barry, Sully.
Carlisle.	Allonby.
Chester.	Flint, Wepra, Mostyn, Rhuddlan.
Cowes.	Newport, Yarmouth, Ryde.
Dartmouth.	Brixham, Torquay, Salcombe.
Drogheda.	
Dumfries.	Annan, Carsethorn, Barlocco, Kirkcudbright.
Dundalk.	
Falmouth.	St. Mawes, Penryn, Gweek.
Fowey.	Pentewan, Mevagissy, Charlestown, Par, Polkerris, Looe.
Galway.	Clifden.
Goole.	Selby.
Grangemouth.	
Inverness.	Cromarty, Burghead, Findhorn, Lossiemouth, Portmahomack, Fortrose, Fort George, Fort William.
Ipswich.	
Kirkcaldy.	Leven, Largo, Dysart, Burntisland, Anstruther, Pittenweem, St. Andrews, Crail.
Milford.	Little Haven, Nolton, Pembroke, Saundersfoot, Haverfordwest.
Newhaven.	Eastbourne.
Newport.	
Penzance.	

Ports.	Subports and Creeks.
Fifth Class.	
Poole.	Swanage.
Port Glasgow.	
Preston.	Hesketh Bank, Skippool, Freckleton, Lytham.
Ramsgate.	Margate, Sandwich.
Rye.	Hastings.
Shields.	Blyth.
Swansea.	Newton, Oxwich, Penarth, Aberavon, Neath.
Truro.	
Weymouth.	
Sixth Class.	
Arbroath.	
Arundel.	Littlehampton, Chichester.
Ayr.	Girvan.
Baltimore.	Castletownsend, Bear Haven, Bantry, Skibbereen.
Banff.	Fraserburgh, Garmouth, Buckie.
Barnstaple.	Ilfracombe.
Beaumaris.	Holyhead, Amlwch, Conway, Aberffraw.
Bideford.	Appledore.
Borrowstoness.	Brucehaven, Limekilns, Charlestown, Inverkeithing, St. David's.
Bridport.	
Carnarvon.	Pwllheli, Barmouth, Portmadoc.
Chepstow.	
Clay.	Cromer, Mundesley, Wells.
Colchester.	Brightlingsea.
Coleraine.	Portrush, Ballycastle.
Faversham.	Whitstable, Herne Bay, Milton.
Folkestone.	
Gainsborough.	Stockwith.
Grimsby.	
Guernsey.	
Hartlepool.	
Harwich.	Mistley, Walton, Thorpe, Holland.
Irvine.	Troon, Saltcoats, Largs, Ardrossan.
Jersey.	
Llanelly.	Pembrey, St. Clair, Carmarthen.
Maldon.	Burnham, Bradwell, Leigh, Rochford.
Montrose.	Johnshaven.
Padstow.	Port Isaac, Bude, Boscastle.
Perth.	Newburgh, Errol.
Ross.	
Scarborough.	
Scilly.	
St. Ives.	Hayle, Portreath.

PORTS.	SUBPORTS AND CREEKS.
Sixth Class.	
Stornoway.	
Stranraer.	Drummore, Portnessock, Portpatrick.
Westport.	
Wexford.	
Whitby.	Sandsend, Robin Hood's Town.
Wick.	Helmsdale, Thurso.
Wisbech.	Sutton Wash.
Woodbridge.	Aldborough, Orford.
Supernumerary Ports.	
Aberystwith.	Aberdovey, Llansantffraid, Aberayron, New Quay.
Alloa.	Stirling, Kincardine, Kennetpans, Clackmannan, Cambus.
Ballina.	
Campbeltown.	Islay, Tarbert.
Cardigan.	Fishguard, Newport.
Deal.	
Fleetwood.	
Kirkwall.	Stromness, Sanday.
Lerwick.	
Lyme.	
Maryport.	
Strangford.	Killough, Quoile.
Tralee.	
Wigton.	Gatehouse of Fleet, Creetown Garliestown, Port William, Whithorn.
Workington.	Harrington.

Up to 1853 it had been the practice to mark each package of imported goods taken into bond with the initials of the ship and her captain. This had been found inconvenient, and on February 21 the Board instituted the present system of marking the packages with the year and a number denoting the ship, the number being taken from a series corresponding with the arrival of the ships in each year. Thus packages from the first ship in 1854 would be marked $\frac{1854}{1}$, and those from subsequent ships in sequence, and the accounts were to be kept accordingly.

The system of granting 'satisfactions' to detaining

officers after release of goods detained for mere informalities (the ‘ satisfactions ’ taking the form of payments by owners of goods) was discontinued.

The Board announced that, in accordance with the recommendations of the late select Committee on Customs, and the provisions of the recent Consolidation Act, a room had been set apart in the London Custom-house for investigating disputes between officers and the public, and that a Commissioner would attend for that purpose on Tuesdays and Fridays.

Among the 1853 Customs records is a return sent by the controller of Navigation laws in Victoria, which bears striking testimony to the sudden increase of trade consequent upon the discovery of gold in the Australian colonies. Five ports are shown—Melbourne, Geelong, Portland, Port Fairy, and Port Albert. The Customs revenue from imported spirits, tea, wine, tobacco, and coffee was £765,728. Trade as follows:

IMPORTS.

	£
From Great Britain	8,288,226
From British possessions	5,064,844
From the United States	1,668,606
From other foreign States	820,961
	15,842,637

EXPORTS.

	£
To Great Britain	9,875,624
To British possessions	942,741
To the United States of America	19,646
To other foreign States	223,532
	11,061,543

£8,644,529 of the ‘ exports ’ stood under the heading ‘ gold.’ The greater part of the rest was under ‘ wool.’

Repeal of the Navigation laws, so far as the United Kingdom was concerned, was completed by Cap. 5 of 17 Vict., which opened the coasting trade of the United Kingdom and Channel Islands to foreign ships.

Cap. 28 and Cap. 29, 17 and 18 Vict., placed certain temporary imposts upon sugar and molasses, increased the duties on spirits of the British possessions in Scotland, and fixed the sugar duties at a higher rate than had been provided for under the Consolidation Act. It abolished the refining of sugar in bond.

Cap. 77, 17 and 18 Vict., provided that the Governor-General of India might from time to time, with the consent of the East India Company's directors, take under his authority by proclamation any part or parts of the Company's territory.

Cap. 94, 17 and 18 Vict., altered the dates of the financial quarter-days, April 5, July 5, October 10, and January 5, to March 31, June 30, September 30, and December 31, and made the end of the financial year March 31 instead of January 5.

Cap. 122, 17 and 18 Vict., imposed a duty on imported arms and ammunition. (These articles had been previously on the 'prohibited' list, except when imported in transit.) It altered the duties on a few articles, abolishing one or two, and in other instances either reducing them or changing them from *ad valorem* to specific.

Under the provisions of Cap. 73, 16 and 17 Vict., the Board directed the comptroller-general to select 1,500 men from the Coastguard, to serve in the navy.

Great Britain being at war with Russia, the various collectors of customs were authorized to carry out the Order in Council of March 29, 1854, that all Russian vessels in ports of the United Kingdom should be allowed a period within which to load and depart, or if on the way to any port in the United Kingdom should be allowed to enter such port and discharge. Later this was extended to the colonies, and the period warranting entry and discharge was also extended so that all Russian vessels that had left Russian ports prior to May 15, 1854, should be allowed to complete their voyages to the United Kingdom, discharge, and depart.

Messrs. Longmans and Co., publishers, addressed a letter to the Chairman of the Board. They enclosed a communication from an agent in Sydney, urging them to have their books at once put on the Customs list of copyright works. The agent stated that large importations had recently been made of American piracies of Macaulay's works, Ure's 'Dictionary,' and McCulloch's 'Dictionary,' and that these books had not been entered on the list, yet he had succeeded by threats of legal proceedings in inducing the importers to send them back. On investigation, the Board found that the books named *were* on the Customs list.

Later, Longmans transmitted another letter from the agent, stating that a leading article had appeared in the Sydney *Argus*, advocating evasion of the copyright laws, and that a flood of piracies had recently been put on the market; also that things were worse at Melbourne, where the booksellers' shops were full of piratical reprints. The controller of Navigation laws at Sydney (who was also collector of customs) was communicated with, and stated that all books which could be identified from the Customs list as piracies were detained and destroyed. He forwarded an account, from which it appeared that many such books had been seized, and a deal of indecent literature as well.

The conclusion of the Board's correspondence with the colonies is marked by a quaint series of papers dealing with applications made by the controller of Navigation laws, Halifax, Nova Scotia. On July 20, 1854, he asked the Board to recommend him for an additional office—that of Government Accountant in the colony. (Evidently he anticipated the speedy lapse of his own office.) The Board declined. Early in 1855 he wrote again, referring to his approaching retirement, and asking to be made collector of customs at Kirkwall, Scotland, at a salary equal to the pension due him on retirement, 'thereby effecting a saving to Her Majesty's Government, and relieving me from the great depression I feel on being totally unemployed.' 'The late M.P. for the Orkneys,' he continued, 'was a relation of my wife's, and her family connections still reside and have much influence there.' In spite of the delicate hint thus conveyed, the Board refused his request. He wrote again, evidently determined to acquire something beyond his mere pension, and asked the Board to give him the office table. Even this request was refused, and he retired, no doubt with a string of burning grievances.

The account of smuggling from 1845 to 1847 inclusive has had to be collected from various sources. As hinted in our 'Introduction,' there is but little first-hand material prior to 1848. From 1848 onward the hand of the foolish destroyer has been to some extent fettered, and thus we are enabled to furnish extracts from original memoranda—the *actual* reports of seizures and proceedings. As usual, we can only find space for a few, and these must be reported as briefly as possible.

Early in 1845 the Plymouth officers seized forty-two tins containing tobacco—the tins being soldered and painted so as to resemble ordinary red bricks—in casks of pitch imported from that hotbed of smuggling, Jersey.

During May in the same year the Liverpool officers seized a large quantity of tobacco, concealed in hollowed deal ends on board an American ship.

A vessel arrived at London from Jersey with a number of empty casks as deck cargo. The casks were found to have two sets of staves, the spaces between the staves being packed with cigars.

The collector of St. Andrews, New Brunswick, reported that he had information that goods were often smuggled into the town at night, concealed under hay and straw in carts, and he desired instructions as to whether the British revenue law, which empowered customs officers to stop carts on suspicion, and exempted them from liability if such suspicion proved groundless, applied to the colonies. The Board replied that it did not, and advised him not to stop any carts unless he was certain that they contained smuggled goods.

On October 19, 1845, the tide-surveyor at St. John's, Newfoundland, attempted to seize a lighter containing a large quantity of tobacco. The owner of the lighter instructed his men to resist seizure, with the result that the tide-surveyor and his subordinates were violently assaulted. It afterwards turned out that the tobacco was duty-paid. The Board refused to sanction prosecution of the tide-surveyor's assailants.

On January 6, 1846, the customs tide-waiter stationed at St. George's, Charlotte County, New Brunswick, visited certain mills in the neighbourhood, to search for smuggled goods. He made several seizures, and then one of the owners menaced him with a loaded gun, and forced him to abandon search. The Board declined to sanction proceedings against the offender, but recommended the officer to apply to the provincial authorities.

On December 9, 1846, Madame Souliè, an actress, landed at Port Louis, Mauritius, and, on her baggage being examined, seizure was made of the following 'French goods': 29 pairs stays, 31 pieces ribbon, 28 pieces silk trimmings, and 2 pieces lace. The lady petitioned the governor as follows:

'EXCELLENCE,

'La soussignée "Veuve Souliè," artiste dramatique, a l'honneur d'exposer bien humblement. Que dans un voyage qu'elle a fait a Bourbon, elle a reçu en paiement quelques objets de mode de mince valeur, pour son usage personnel comme artiste. Que ces objets sont indispensables a l'exposante comme artiste, que n'ayant jamais en l'intention de les vendre, etc.

'ROSALIE SOULIÈ.'

But the officers insisted that the goods had been concealed in false bottoms in Rosalie's trunks, and the

Revenue Cruiser chasing Smuggler by Night on the Kentish Coast.

To face p. 340.

governor declined to interfere. On which the lady petitioned afresh : 'Ces objets sont des articles de mode indispensables à une actrice qui obligée d'avoir un grand nombre de costumes pour ses rôles.' She protested that she put them in 'les derniers compartiments de ma malle de voyage,' to prevent their being damaged.

The collector's report to the Board seemed to show that Madame Rosalie might have been devoid of fraudulent intention, for it appeared that the so-called 'false bottoms' occupied the greater portions of the trunks, and the goods were examined on 'baggage sufferance' (a form of entry generally held to be non-committal). Yet the collector sold the goods before making his report. The Board directed that the net proceeds of the sale should be given to the lady (which was tantamount to acknowledging that they did not hold her to blame). But the collector was unable to secure the lady's receipt for the moneys till 1848, 'in consequence of the illness of the party alluded to.' He stated that he had not deducted the duties from the gross proceeds, as he thought the party had been 'injured and greatly inconvenienced' by the seizure. The London lawyers hinted that the duties were due, and that the collector should be surcharged ; but the Board remitted the duties. (It appears that the seizure was a scandalously harsh proceeding, that may have utterly ruined the unfortunate actress.)

The Mauritius officers were extremely zealous in the detection of opium-smuggling. Below is an account of several cases, extending over a period of three years. On December 9, 1844, a landing-waiter at Port Louis apprised the collector that he had seized a large quantity of opium in a store kept by two Chinamen, and that the Chinamen had offered him £80 as a bribe to ignore the concealment. The Chinamen were prosecuted in the V.A. Court, fined £200 and costs, and the £80 offered as a bribe was declared forfeited. The opium was sold for exportation, to be shipped either to Indian ports, where its importation was not prohibited, or to Great Britain, for manufacturing into morphine. The Chinamen prayed the governor to relieve them from two-thirds of the penalty, but he declined, so they paid the fine and the enormous costs. Then the collector made a subtle suggestion to the Board that the £80 offered as bribe should be given to the seizer, and that a third of the £200 fine should be given to the collector, to compensate him for his trouble in prosecuting. The Board considered this modest request, awarded the seizer his proper share of the fine, ordered the £80 to be paid in to the Crown's account, and gave the collector nothing. The Chinaman who landed the goods was captured soon afterwards, and fined £100 and costs. He went to prison in default, and the Queen's Proctor, who had prosecuted (the collector declining to officiate in this case), sent in a bill of costs to the Customs for £165 18s. 11d., £61 of which was under the heading of 'Registrar's fees.' The prisoner memorialized the governor, stating that he employed a lawyer to defend him, and that the lawyer charged him £140, which he had paid. It appears the poor fellow's health had broken down in prison. He produced the lawyer's receipt for the costs, and the governor released him. (The papers connected with this seizure convey ghastly impressions to the reader. It is manifest that the case was 'loaded' by the seizing officer. No proceedings could be taken against a mere *importer* of opium; the goods had to be landed and deposited for use ere action could be taken, so the seizer, who had been informed of the arrival of the opium from Calcutta, had allowed it to be unshipped, and watched it to its destination. When this is considered, along with the brazen extortions of the Mauritius lawyers, one is inclined to think that the officers and lawyers should have been imprisoned instead of the Chinamen.)

In 1847 a vessel arrived at Port Louis from Calcutta. She had two screwed and hooped bales of cotton on deck, and when the officers opened these they found in each a large tin case containing opium. As the goods were seized prior to landing, no proceedings could be taken, but the opium was sold for exportation. Soon after a Chinaman was caught on a vessel from Pondicherry with twenty boxes and three bladders of opium.

A squabble arose over the proceeds of sale, the officers insisting that the goods should be assessed for the purpose of award at 40s. a pound, although they fetched but 16s. a pound. The Board dealt summarily with the matter, giving the greedy fellows one-third of the *actual sale price.*

Later, one of the officers made a report which fills the reader with irksome suspicions. He stated that he was informed that a quantity of opium had been deposited on his premises. He made for home, and on his way observed his own servant in the company of a Chinaman. The men were carrying a trunk, and he found in the trunk forty-four boxes of opium. The colonial law officers held that there was not enough evidence to convict either servant or Chinaman, but the opium was condemned. (A reasonable opinion is that the officer found it on board ship, and sent it home by his servant, intending to sell it privately, and, becoming fearful that he might have been observed, charged the servant with the offence, and inculpated the first unlucky Chinaman he could get hold of. Things quite as villainous were done in the colonies in those golden days.)

The seizing officer fought tooth and nail for assessment at 40s. a pound, but the Board were firm. Then he applied to the governor for a further award, but was told no grant for that purpose could be made out of the colonial funds. After studying the practice of the Mauritius lawyers and officials, one is inclined to doubt which could be the worse, removal of all restrictions upon the importation of the drug, or the employment of such a set of sharks to detect it.

The collector of St. John, New Brunswick, reported detention of a number of pirated copies of 'The Emigrants,' consigned to Messrs. McMillan, booksellers, at

St. John. He suggested leniency, the importers having searched the 'prohibited' list prior to importing the books from Boston, U.S.A. (The list containing the entry did not arrive till after the order was sent.) The copyright was held by Mr. John Murray. McMillan petitioned the Treasury, but without avail, the Customs lawyers insisting upon the forfeiture of the books, and stating that the Treasury had no control in the matter of prohibition under copyright.

The Board, by their General Letter of October 2, 1848, sent to all ports of the United Kingdom, announced that several flagrant cases of collusion between informers and seizing officers had been brought to light. In future, whenever an officer received information, he was to communicate the informer's name confidentially to the collector if at an outport, to the Solicitor if at London. All rewards to informers were to be paid through collectors or the Solicitor, and they were to satisfy themselves that the persons claiming such rewards were the actual informers.

During 1848 the Jersey officers began to entertain profound suspicion with regard to the *Eliza*, a cutter belonging to that island. On November 30, 1848, Richard Butt, master of the *Eliza*, was induced to make a statement as to his recent misdoings. It appeared that on June 8, 1848, he cleared from Jersey for France, but instead of proceeding thither went to Bonne Nuit Bay, Jersey, and took in a quantity of spirits in kegs, and about 2½ tons of tobacco-stalks, cigars, and snuff. He then proceeded to Fishguard Bay, but was signalled to keep off for a time. About eleven at night he crept in and ran his cargo, then went over to France, took in sheep, and conveyed them to Jersey. On September 22 he left St. Heliers without clearance, proceeded to Greve de Lecq, took on board 5 tons of leaf tobacco, snuff, and cigars, and a number of bags of tea and cases of spirits, sailed to Fishguard Bay, ran the goods, then took in stone ballast, and made for Jersey. On the way home he was met by a revenue cruiser, and the captain boarded him, and found he had no papers. Butt explained this by stating that he had piloted a vessel down Channel. He reached Jersey, and claimed his pay from the syndicate that had employed him. Instead of paying him, according to agreement, at the rate of £50 a ton, they gave him but £10. His deposition concluded thus : ‘ In consequence thereof, as well as for other misunderstandings between deponent and the above parties, he has considered it a duty which he owes himself to make the present declaration.’

The persons composing the syndicate absconded, but in 1849 one of them wrote from France, offering to become an approver. His offer was accepted, but it does not appear that any of the other principals were captured. (The cutter was condemned in the Exchequer.) Several of the receivers suffered. The excise officers of Haverfordwest heard of the transactions, and instituted a search in the neighbourhood. They seized two horses and a waggon, conveying two large casks addressed to a person living in Farringdon Market, London, to be forwarded by rail from Bristol. The casks contained tobacco stowed beneath layers of bones, the goods having been repacked thus after landing. On the following day they found a quantity of tobacco in a hay-loft, but the total quantity seized (1,408 pounds tobacco and 32 pounds snuff) was a mere fragment of that originally run.

Many other remarkable cases appear in the 1848 record ; see below :

March 8.—Two horses, a waggon, and 912 pounds tobacco, seized by excise officers at York Railway Station (goods landed at Goole).

In May.—The *Jane and Nancy*, seized off Stonehouse, after she had thrown her cargo overboard (sixty bales tobacco—say 3,000 pounds).

July 16.—Information received of a run of 1,008 gallons spirits at Penryn.

October 30.—968 pounds tobacco and 180 pounds stalks seized in a storehouse at Plymouth.

November 30.—224 pounds tobacco seized on board the *Good Intent* at Fowey. (All the ship's company implicated.)

December 2.—195 pounds tobacco and cigars found on board a ship at Liverpool, concealed in tins of biscuit.

On September 4, 1848, the coastguard at Salcombe observed a boat entering the harbour at nightfall. They went off to board her, and she at once headed for the shore, and her occupants, two men and a woman, jumped out and took to their heels. One escaped, the other two were captured. The boat contained thirty bales of tobacco-stalks, weighing 1,598 pounds. The man taken was Richard Pepperell, probably the most daring and notorious smuggler in the West of England. He escaped after capture, by jumping from a window three stories high, but was retaken, convicted, and imprisoned in default of paying a fine of £100. The woman was acquitted on the plea of her being a passenger. (We shall have occasion to describe other transactions in which Pepperell was concerned.)

A seizure reported on March 24, 1848, from Auckland, New Zealand, throws light upon the methods of bartering for contraband in the colony. One Henry Atkins was captured with 138 pounds tobacco, which he had obtained from an American vessel lying at the Great Barrier, in exchange for nine hogs. On December 9 in the same year a smack was seized with 86 pounds tobacco on board, which the master had bought from an American whaler. On January 9, 1849, the Auckland officers seized ninety-one casks wines and spirits, landed without entry from the American ship *Robert Pulsford*. This last seizure appears to have been unjust, for the goods were shown on the ship's manifest; but the magistrates, perhaps influenced by Uncle Sam's general record as a smuggler, condemned the goods, and the Board refused to intervene, though appealed to by the shipowners. The authorities were not always so severe. In November, 1848, the collector at Russell, New Zealand, had seized a large quantity of tobacco at a whaling settlement near Wanganui. The goods were removed to the Custom-house at Russell, and the owners were prosecuted and fined £100. For some reason or other the governor remitted the penalty, and soon afterwards unknown adventurers broke into the Custom-house at night and carried off the goods. It was found that they had been originally run from an American whaler, and when this vessel came into port the collector detained her, and placed a tide-waiter on board. As soon as darkness fell the Yankee skipper began to get his vessel under weigh, so the tide-waiter went ashore and apprised the collector, who at once went off in a boat and asked the captain what he was doing. The captain answered, 'Guess I'm goin',' and shot off into the night. Even then there was not an end of the trouble. In June, 1849, a Maori found a large case of tobacco concealed in the scrub near the whaling settlement. He mustered his tribe, who divided the tobacco and made off. Then the finder reported the matter to the collector, doubtless expecting a reward. (The papers close with a pathetic statement from the collector that he has lost his original action, lost the reward he expected, lost the goods, lost all chance of making the American skipper pay, lost the whole of a second seizure except the package, been put to expense which he cannot charge to the Customs account, and is now derided and persecuted by the whalers and settlers.)

During 1849 a French smack was seized at Plymouth with tanks of spirits concealed between double bulkheads, and a huge seizure of compressed snuff was made by the London officers, the goods being made up as 'oil-seed cake,' and packed with the genuine article. Thieves broke into the Custom-house at Newry, and stole 607 pounds tobacco. On April 21, 1849, about 2½ tons of tobacco were found floating off the Essex coast.

The following illustrative cases of seizures are quoted from the 1849 papers :

March 3.—Horse, cart, and 993 pounds tobacco, seized by excise officers and police near Shield Row, Durham.

May 3.—122 pounds tobacco, seized on a ship in Leith Roads.

May 16.—150 tubs spirits, seized in Portsmouth Harbour, while being towed by the steam tug *Royal Charter*.

May 24.—96 tubs spirits, found sunk off Challaboro', Devon.

May 25.—128 pounds tobacco, seized on a ship at Liverpool (concealed in casks of biscuit).

July 30.—74 tubs, 31 flagons, and 8 half-flagons spirits, seized on a vessel in the Itchen River (concealed under concrete along the keelson).

October 15.—799 pounds of tobacco-stalks, seized on a vessel off Challaboro', Devon. (The incorrigible Pepperell was concerned in this case. He had just been released from prison ; see p. 346.)

October 29.—Cutter *Lion* and 335 gallons spirits, seized at Jersey.

October.—1,038 pounds tobacco, seized at the Eastern Counties railway station, London. (The goods had been landed at Woodbridge, Suffolk, and forwarded by rail, packed in hampers and advised as fish.)

November 18.—The *Deux Amis* and 1,189 pounds tobacco and cigars, seized at Jersey. (The goods were intended for illegal exportation to France.)

November 27.—168 pounds tobacco, seized in a cab outside the Liverpool docks.

November.—1,096 pounds tobacco, seized at Newry on a vessel from Quebec. (Goods packed in 24 casks flour.)

December 10.—The *Aide de Famille* and 370 pounds tobacco, seized at Alderney. (Goods for illegal exportation to France.)

The largest seizure that we find in 1849 is that made by the *Vigilant* revenue cruiser in Sea Reach (Thames), on December 13. The *Vigilant's* crew boarded an ordinary sailing-barge, the *Charlotte,* took off her hatches, and found in the hold a number of casks, containing in all 14,402 pounds tobacco. This seizure was returned as 'made without information,' but we think it strange that a boy who was employed on the barge, and who was exempted from proceedings because he was under sixteen, bore the same Christian and surname as the mariner on the *Vigilant* who suggested that the barge should be searched. The following awards were made to the seizers: To the master of the *Vigilant,* £431; gunner, boatswain, carpenter, and steward, £86 each; five mariners, £30 each; seven boys, £21 each; and £6 to the ship's company as 'head-money.'

The seizure report from Falmouth for the period extending from November 12 to 30, 1849, is quite remarkable, and bears testimony to the industry and skill of the rummaging officers. We reproduce it:

Two pounds tobacco seized ashore from a seaman; 50 pounds tobacco and 1 pound tea, seized on board the *Alchemist* (vessel detained and fined); 13 pounds tobacco, seized on board the *Aghios Spiridion* (vessel detained and fined); 22 pounds cigars and 9 pounds tobacco, seized on board the *Peppina* (vessel detained and fined); 8 pounds cigars on a further search of the *Peppina;* 2 pounds cigars and 3 pounds tobacco on board the *Susan;* 9 pounds cigars, seized on board the *Vasilachi;* 4 pounds cigars, seized on board the *Parraghia Evangelistica;* 46 pounds cigars and 162 pounds tobacco on a further search (vessel detained and fined); 82 pounds tobacco seized on board the *Alexandra* (vessel detained and fined). Five of the above were Greek vessels.

The gradual transference of Customs control to the various colonial Governments is made apparent in the seizure records of the time by a tendency on the part of the London Customs lawyers to 'unload' many of their responsibilities. Thus, when a seizure of sixteen cases tobacco was made at Quebec on November 8, 1849, on board the schooner *Niger*, from Cape Breton, the case was dealt with by the provincial Government, the goods being restored on condition that the defendant paid the duty and costs, and 10 dollars as a 'satisfaction' to the seizing officer. When an account of the case was sent to Thames Street, the Solicitor remarked upon the papers that it was no longer necessary to report Canadian seizures to the Board. (He meant 'revenue seizures': cases under the Navigation and Fishery laws were still reported.)

Seizure notes continued to flow in from the Antipodean colonies. Below is the list from Port Adelaide, October 24, 1849, to May 1, 1850: 160 pounds tobacco, concealed in an imported case of crockery; 168 pounds tobacco, concealed in an imported cask of soda; a quantity of rings and fancy wares, and two trunks of boots, not reported; 2,500 cigars, seized at a wharf; 60 pounds cigars, seized in a shop; 20 pounds cigars, seized on board the *Amicas*; 181 pounds cigars, concealed in imported packages of hops.

The regulations as to boats, etc., were remodelled by Board's circular of April 26, 1850 (in consequence of the provisions of Secs. 16 and 17, Cap. 90, 12 and 13 Vict.). In their new form they stood thus:

Class.	Scope of Traffic.
Open boats and vessels under 15 tons.	Only 4 leagues seaward between Beachy Head and North Foreland. On the rest of the coast, 8 leagues seaward. Along the coast, 50 leagues.
Open or half-decked boats above 15 tons.	Only 4 leagues seaward between Beachy Head and North Foreland. On other coasts, 12 leagues seaward. Along the coast, 80 leagues.
Decked vessels under 40 tons, and *all* vessels less than 170 tons, whose length is to the breadth greater than 3 feet 6 inches to 1 foot (except steam vessels).	Only 4 leagues seaward between Beachy Head and North Foreland. On other coasts, except in the Irish Sea, only 12 leagues.

No vessel less than 170 tons might carry arms for resistance in excess of two muskets to every five men. (Any vessel might have one carriage gun, without shot, for signalling.) The maximum number of men and boys as crew was stipulated.

Below are a few remarkable seizures made in the United Kingdom during 1850 :

January 24.—The cutter *Mary*, seized off Shields with 7,187 pounds tobacco-stalks and 323 pounds tobacco.

February 14.—70 tubs spirits, seized ashore at Babbicombe, Devon.

February 23.—A large quantity of adulterants, seized on a tobacco manufacturer's premises at Bristol.

March 21.—A French cutter, captured off Lulworth, after she had thrown her cargo overboard during chase.

March 29.—The *Rob Roy* cutter, seized off Shields with 8,210 pounds tobacco.

April 2.—589 pounds tobacco, found in a cave near Marsden Rock, in the Shields district.

May 14.—412 pounds tobacco, seized at Leeds. (The goods had been imported in cases of glass at Goole.)

May 23, 25, *and various subsequent dates.*—About 8,000 pounds tobacco-stalks, seized at Bristol and Aberthaw. (Run by the schooner *Wave*, and afterwards captured by search. Probably only part of the consignment).

July 12 *and* 13.—An immense quantity of coffee and sugar, seized at Liverpool for having been tampered with while in bond. (Connected with the famous 'Duncan Stewart' case.)

August 3.—The French lugger *Georges*, captured in the English Channel after she had run her cargo. (Crew convicted.)

August 8.—The smack *Zoe*, with 3,098 pounds tobacco-stalks, seized in Dartmouth Harbour.

August 27.—170 gallons spirits, seized in an outhouse at Goldhanger, Essex.

October 1.—The oyster-smack *Rival*, seized in Chichester harbour, while towing 13 tubs spirits.

November 1.—160 pounds cigars, seized by excise officers at Monkwearmouth railway station.

Several seizures were made in Scotland of smuggled silks which were being hawked by pedlars, and at Deal no less than three important seizures of tobacco which had been brought on board Belgian pilot-cutters. The largest seizure we find in the 1850 file is that made on September 13, on board the sloop *Sarah and Susannah*, at Goole. This vessel arrived with a cargo of flints, and the master produced his cargo-book, which showed that he had taken them in at Ramsgate. It was soon manifest that he had since made a trip oversea, for beneath the flints the officers found 15,452 pounds of tobacco and tobacco-stalks. The captain absconded. His wife, who was on board during the voyage, the mate, and the solitary seaman who formed the 'crew,' were arrested. The lady was acquitted, it being held that she had acted under her husband's influence. The mate and sailor were convicted, and while in prison they gave information which led to the arrest of the master, and the financier of the venture, a person living at Yarmouth.

On March 31, 1850, the principal coast officer (Customs) at Brighton saw four tubs floating at some distance from the shore. The weather was so rough that the coastguardsmen refused to launch their boat, but the plucky officer induced four fishermen to get a boat out, put to sea, with a tide-waiter as coxswain, and secured the tubs, which contained spirits. He then asked the Board that the fishermen might be paid for the risk and trouble, and concerning this request there was almost as much discussion and circumlocution, between the Solicitor and the Accountant-General, as though demand had been made for the whole of the contents of the Treasury. In the end the fishermen got 10s. each for risking their boat and lives.

The case of Mr. Hyams furnishes proof of the extraordinary persistency of the Jewish race in cases where money's worth is concerned. Hyams landed at Folkestone on October 20, 1850, and omitted to declare certain new articles of apparel which were distributed in his baggage. The officers detained them, and Hyams proceeded to bombard the Board with explanations and petitions. Then he applied to Baron Lionel de Rothschild, who was good enough to refer the matter to Mr. Spring Rice at the Treasury. An exhaustive investigation was held by the Board, and the seizure was confirmed. Mr. Hyams, when the inquiry was concluded, expressed himself satisfied. A few days after he fired a parting shot in the shape of a letter, charging the officers with misrepresentation.

It is possible that the Folkestone officers may have been extremely strict, for just previous to the detection of Mr. Hyams the following letter had reached the Board:

'FOLKESTONE, KENT,
'*September*, 1850.

'MY LORDS AND GENTLEMEN,

'I beg most earnestly to call your Lordships' attention to the character, cast, disposition, and deportment of the men engaged here by the Customs as tide-waiters, rummagers, and boatmen; the latter are blackguardly, insolent, and abusive, and the former appear to be the very refuse of God's creation—uncultivated, unclean, and obscene, both in their conduct, address, and manner; indeed, they are the very scum of the community, a perfect disgrace to your Lordships, as well as to Her Majesty's Service.

'These men assume and take upon themselves more than they are either authorized or entitled to do in their capacity as underlings, and to this there appears to be neither bounds nor check, as they continue in the daily practice of heaping abuse and calumny on all those whose lot or business calls them to travel between this country and the Continent; they are also meddling, offensive, and atrociously wicked, and are each and every one of them addicted to the vile practice of smoking while on duty, etc., etc.

'Your Lordships' most obedient servant,
'A TRAVELLER AND SOJOURNER
IN HER MAJESTY'S SERVICE.'

Sad to state, this stirring appeal, fortified as it was by a choice 'derangement of epitaphs,' failed to secure the dismissal of the Customs staff.

Among many curious items in the various seizure lists for 1850 we observe one at Dover of seventeen turkeys seized for not being reported, appraised value £5 4s., duty 5s. 2d., and a petition by a seaman of the *Washington Irving*, an American vessel lying at Liverpool. 150 pounds tobacco had been found on board, and the ship's officers put the blame upon the petitioner, who was fined £100, and imprisoned in default. He stated that the charge against him was the result of conspiracy, he being the only Britisher in the crew. He asked the Board to release him, stating that if this were granted he would 'in future years pray for the welfare of this Great Realm and its Sovereign.'

Whenever a native of Deal was convicted of smuggling it was the practice of the inhabitants of that town to sign a huge memorial to the Treasury, describing him as a respectable citizen, a devoted husband, a tender father, and, so far as the smuggling was concerned, a victim of delusive appearances. It may be mentioned also that it was the invariable custom of the Treasury to refuse to release him, but it does not appear that this in any way discouraged the worthy burgesses. One of these futile petitions was forwarded in 1850 on behalf of the crew of the galley *Lucy Long*, who had been in the habit of using cigars as ballast. It was backed up by Lord Clarence Paget, who stated that he had been instigated by 'a large and respectable portion of his constituents, of all shades of political opinion.'

In August, 1850, the tide-surveyor at Bristol received information of an intended run. He impressed a yawl and two fishermen, went afloat, and seized the *Henri*, a French cutter, with 6,632 pounds tobacco and stalks on board. The Board awarded £456 for this seizure, £228 of which went to the tide-surveyor, and £9 for division between the yawl-owner and the two fishermen. The fishermen complained to the Rev. Mirehouse, vicar of St. George's, and he reported the facts of the case to the Treasury, making it evident that the men had rendered most valuable assistance. The Board directed the officers to pay the men an additional £20.

On December 12, 1850, certain excise officers found under a hedge in front of a house near Penypistill, Pembrokeshire, two cellars, containing in all sixteen bales of tobacco-stalks. Later they searched a farmer's premises, and found a cellar in the garden, beneath a bed of leeks, and another beneath the stable. These contained twenty-two bales. Total quantity seized, 2,153 pounds. The officers stated these seizures were made without information, but on inquiry it became apparent that this was false. The magistrates refused to convict, stating that there was no proof that the party charged had put the goods in the cellars.

During the same year two excise officers found a tub of spirits in a fishmonger's shop in Lower Thames Street, London, and a letter from Lymington, Hants, sent as invoice. They wrote under a feigned name to the sender, and ordered five tubs more, then proceeded to Lymington, watched his premises, and found that he was being supplied by 'the ——s,' a notorious family of smugglers. After watching for some time they made a search, and found the five tubs they had ordered. They then summoned to their assistance the excise supervisor of the district, the men of the coastguard, and a constable, and proceeded to search the houses occupied by the ——s. The search was fruitless as regarded contraband, but the officers persevered until they reached the cottage occupied by 'Old ——,' a well-known desperado. Here they were richly rewarded indeed. They forced an entrance, one of the London excisemen, armed with a naked sword, leading the charge. Old —— was at the top of the staircase, provided with several utensils full of filth, which he discharged upon the heads of the revenue men. Undaunted by this unsavoury fusillade, the leading excisemen rushed up the stair and gained the landing. Then —— graciously permitted the search to proceed. 'The scene indoors,' stated the chief officer of coastguard in his report, 'was too disgusting to be described.' Old —— was exchequered for his complicity in the smuggling, and imprisoned, but speedily released by Treasury Order. This clemency may have been the result of a memorial sent to the Board of Excise, signed by the mayor of Lymington and several justices of the peace, in which the officers were stigmatized as *agents provocateurs*, who had 'inveigled and tricked' —— and others into defrauding the revenue. The smuggler's note to the London fishmonger may be found interesting :

'Sir,

'12 pr. of Soles—if Cod is very cheap send. I have not received any orders this week we have got so many Herring boats heare. I have' [sent one] 'as a sampal the price is £3 10s. You must mix it in this way. A large pan put 4 quarts and a pint of nice clean water. Tipe out about half the spirits and mix it well and then put 4 quarts and 1 pint more of water and ad the other spirits you will find it quite strong enough. Should you like 2 more I can send them. It will make altogether 22 quarts of Hollands the longer kept the better it gets you may look out for it tomorrow morning.'

(The tub was sent in a hamper, packed with fish.)

Extraordinary tactics on the part of seizing officers, both at home and in the colonies, were frequently brought to the notice of the Board. A case in which Mr. Munro, the collector of Tortola, was implicated, cannot well be passed over ; it displays so fully the crooked dealings of some of the colonial officials. The collector had informed the Board that wrecks frequently occurred on the shores of Anegada, and that the Anegadians made a practice of laying hands upon the goods that came ashore, and smuggling them into the foreign islands adjacent. On January 26, 1850, an American brig, with a valuable cargo, went on the shoals, and although all the cargo was salved, only a part of it reached the Tortola Custom-house. The collector informed the Board that this was due to the obstinacy of the captain, who had refused to pay for a customs officer to guard the wreck.

It should be mentioned that Munro had previously given the Board much trouble. In 1846 he had been charged by one of his subordinates with buying two wrecked ships, and then repairing and selling them, with importing goods without paying duty, and with infringing the rules which prohibited customs officers from interfering in elections. The President of the island, Mr. Hay, had censured him, and the Board had concurred. But Munro had in a way got even with the President, by proving that the latter had illegally exempted himself from paying provincial tonnage dues, and by detecting him in a smuggling transaction, and making him pay the duty on the goods. The President had thereupon summoned Munro before the Privy Council of the island, but Munro stuck to his guns and to the duty, although one of the members of the Council accused him openly of having condoned a smuggling transaction in which he (the member) had taken part. After much mud had been thrown on both sides the matter was allowed to drop, and it might be thought that Mr. Munro would be more careful in future. But a study of the Anegada wreck case reveals that he could not refrain from meddling.

The most convincing and amusing portion of the Anegada report was the American captain's statement. He deposed that after the goods salved had been put in the

Tortola Custom-house he took up his quarters at an hotel. He had not been there long ere 'a stout loquacious individual' called on him, and 'in a soft and insinuating manner' warned him against putting his affairs in charge of one of the ordinary shipping agents, stating that the said agents would render but 'a Flemish account' of the wrecked goods, and leave him with scarcely enough money to pay his passage home. The stranger also suggested that Munro should be made agent, as he would do the work free of charge. All this, the oily interviewer explained, in the way of Christian charity. 'I tell you what it is, sir,' replied Captain Jacob A. Cobb, 'your advice is too disinterested for me,' and with that escorted him to the door. There the captain observed a gentleman waiting outside, undoubtedly Munro. Captain Cobb also accused Munro of allowing the inhabitants of Tortola to plunder the wrecked goods after they had been put in the Queen's Warehouse. 'For the first two or three days,' he stated, 'there was a grand jubilee at Tortola.' It was admitted that a considerable quantity of wine had been consumed, but the agent chosen by the skipper came to Munro's rescue, and stated that the wine was distributed as samples, to induce bidding at the sale. The President of the island sent the captain's complaint to the Treasury, but could not refrain from displaying some little vindictiveness, which probably assisted in securing Munro's partial exoneration. The matter fizzled out in the end, after discrediting everyone concerned except the unfortunate captain, who, it seems, had merely escaped the winds and waves to fall into peril from the fangs of a nest of harpies.

Two Mauritius merchants cleared 48 hogsheads of brandy duty-free from bond, for exportation from Port Louis to Madagascar. The goods were shipped, and during the night the parties concerned emptied twenty-three of the casks, removed the contents ashore, and filled the casks with water. The officers heard of this too late to capture the run goods, but they went on board and seized the balance. Action was entered against the merchants in the Vice-Admiralty Court of the island, and the bond entered into for due exportation of the goods was adjudged forfeited, but it does not appear that the merchants were made liable to any other penalty. The sureties were unable to pay, and the Customs lawyers in London made severe remarks upon the collector's neglect to inquire into the sufficiency of the sureties before accepting the bond.

Below are a few of the important seizures made in the United Kingdom during 1851 :

January 6.—2,643 pounds tobacco seized at Liverpool, concealed behind false bulkheads in master's state-room, on board the *Warrior* from New York.

March 6.—The *Linnet* (coaster), seized at Southampton, with 6,165 pounds tobacco-stalks.

March.—A large quantity of tobacco and snuff seized at Jersey and Shoreham, concealed in hollow chimbs of casks of cider.

May 9.—468 pounds tobacco and 9 gallons spirits, seized at Yarmouth, concealed on board a foreign trader.

May 29.—The hatch-boat *Fanny*, with 7,395 pounds tobacco, seized near the Galloper Light.

June 4.—200 pounds tobacco, seized by the police at Dublin.

June 29.—An open boat and 621 pounds tobacco-stalks, seized off Salcombe. (Pepperell's wife implicated.)

July 3.—Horse, van, and 649 pounds tobacco-stalks. seized at St. Budeaux.

July 4.—654 pounds tobacco, seized by excise officers in a wood near Eggbuckland, Devon.

July.—98 bales tobacco-stalks (say about 5,000 pounds), seized near Tamerton Folliott, Devon. (Seizing officer censured for suppressing the fact that he had received information.)

September 24.—The smack *Defiance*, seized at the Nore by the revenue cruiser *Fly*, with 6,152 pounds tobacco.

September 27.—A galley and 79 tubs spirits, seized off Selsea.

November 30.—124 tubs spirits, found floating off Langstone harbour.

December 16.—4,488 pounds tobacco, seized at 'Fox's Barn,' Nacton, Suffolk. (A run of more than twice that quantity had been made previously at Trimley.)

December 26.—A French 'tub-boat,' seized off Portland, with 75 tubs and 1 flagon spirits.

A huge run of tobacco-stalks took place early in the year in the vicinity of Brixham. The customs officer stationed at that cosy port came to hear of the transaction, and instituted a search. He found fifty-nine bales in a carrier's stable, thirty-nine buried in a garden belonging to a local shipwright, and twenty-nine in a hayloft and stable at a farm in the neighbourhood. Total quantity seized = 6,619 pounds.

On March 13 the coastguard at Deal seized twenty-four stone bottles of spirits, which a boatman was trying to run. The boatman drew a knife, and made desperate attempts to stab the chief coastguard officer. He was overpowered, and then his mother and sisters attempted to rescue him. They behaved like veritable Amazons, seizing the officers by the hair, throwing them down, and violently assaulting them. The boatman was convicted, and imprisoned for six months. One of the women was acquitted; the others were sent to gaol for six months each, without hard labour.

On April 3 the *Stag* revenue cutter observed the *Duck* of Portsmouth (a vessel supposed to be exclusively in the coasting trade) cruising off the French coast. After a long and exciting chase she was captured, and her master was found to be one Crasweller, of Hayling Island, a notorious smuggler, who had been convicted in 1845 and 1848. 'During chase,' the *Stag's* commander reported, 'her manœuvres indicated the time of throwing overboard her cargo, although the distance was too great for occular (*sic*) demonstration.' He brought the *Duck* into

Cowes, and laid her ashore. Then something peculiar was detected in the conformation of the lower timbers, and a close search revealed that she had a false bottom, in which were thirty-six tubs brandy.

The case of *La Comête*, which 'came to a head' in 1851, is worth special notice. During 1848 the vice-consul at Zeeland had sent news of this vessel. She had been on a smuggling trip to the north of Scotland, cleared £1,000 by the run, and was lying at Flushing ready to depart for the same bourne with 6,000 pounds leaf tobacco. It is likely that she was an English vessel, for her original name had been *Helena Maria*, afterwards altered to *Venus*, then to *Phênix*.

The Board apprised the officers on the east coast, and on the north coasts of Scotland and Ireland. The vessel left Flushing, but soon returned with part of her cargo, the rest having been seized during the operation of running. She filled up and left again, this time under the name *La Comête*, with a bogus clearance for Sweden. On February 13, 1849, she was driven dismasted into Whitby, and at once reported her cargo as for Sweden. The packages were of legal size, so nothing could be done. After refitting she returned to Flushing, apparently for orders, for she soon sailed again under the name *Planet*. She continued her voyages during 1849 and 1850, till, on April 27, 1851, she was sighted within the limits off St. Abb's Head, and captured by a revenue cruiser. On this occasion she was *La Comête*. All her crew were convicted at Leith. A 'bill of suspension and liberation' was put in by the defendants, but the Court of Justiciary refused it on a bare formality, for not being entered in the Court of Exchequer. It appears that had the bill been properly entered two of its objections to conviction would have been valid: (1) That the evidence against the prisoners had not been reduced to writing; (2) that though counsel put in a special written statement of certain evidence for the defence, the justices wrongfully rejected it. The vessel was condemned with her cargo (5,868 pounds leaf and 1,468 pounds stalks). The informer received as reward £303.

On September 29 the revenue cruiser *Adder* detained a French lugger off the Isle of Wight. The lugger had thirty-three bales of tobacco on board, and several empty wrappers similar to those surrounding the bales were found, and this was regarded as evidence that she had disposed of part of her cargo. She had a manifest for the tobacco, and a clearance from Dunkirk for Morlaix. She was taken into Cowes, and then released, it being found that the packages of tobacco were of the weight specified as 'legal' by the Customs laws. Her master applied for compensation through the French consul at London, and his request was referred to the Board by the Foreign Office, with an order that the preventive officers were to be directed to refrain from seizing 'on unfounded suspicion' vessels belonging to a friendly power. The Customs lawyer stated in reply that there could be no doubt that the vessel had been engaged in smuggling, and that her French clearance had been obtained, and the goods packed legally, with a view to defence by quibble if seized. He insisted that the captain of the *Adder* had full right to detain her and examine her cargo, but should not have taken her to Cowes for that purpose. Still, the master of the lugger was not entitled to compensation.

The conduct of Edward Smith, a coastguardsman stationed at Felpham, Devon, was made the subject of an inquiry during 1851. It appears that on the morning of August 30 Smith informed his superior officer that whilst on duty on the coast he found several tubs of spirits at low-water-mark, and that as he was approaching them several men sprang upon him, wrenched his loaded pistol from him, bound him hand and foot, and then carried off the tubs; that he wriggled himself partially free, and then cut his bonds with a knife. The inspecting commander placed him under arrest, but on September 4 allowed him to go for a walk on parole. It appears Smith provided himself with a loaded pistol, and on his return exhibited it empty, stating that he had met one of the men who assaulted him, and had chased the fellow some distance and fired after him. The offender was actually arrested soon after, and imprisoned for six months, notwithstanding which the inspecting commander persisted in charging Smith with connivance, and pursued the charge with venomous bitterness ; but a Court of Inquiry acquitted the poor fellow, and cleared his character most effectively.

Seizure records continued to arrive from certain colonies during 1850-1852. Among many others may be noted the following :

May 28, 1850.—459 pounds tobacco, seized at Hawke's Bay, New Zealand, on premises occupied by 'Yankee Smith.' Defendant absconded. The collector stated in his report that the principal portion of the coast was entirely unprotected, and that there were many facilities for smuggling.*

July 20, 1850.—659 pounds tobacco and 16,000 cigars, seized at Port Adelaide, in a tavern kept by Salvador Guadici. The goods had been cleared duty-free from bond for exportation to Swansea by a vessel belonging to Aberdeen, Scotland, and then run 'on the coast below the harbour mouth,' and removed to Guadici's premises. Master, mate, and receiver, each fined £100. Ship released on proof of owners' innocence, but it appears that her detention cost them £232.

September 19, 1851.—860 pounds tobacco, seized at Abercrombie Battery, Fort George, Mauritius, 'hid among aloe-trees.'

October 1, 1852.—(A 'mixed' venture) 3 cases wine, 1 case tinned salmon, 1 case cocoa paste, 14 pounds tobacco, 24 shirts, a suit of clothes, and a box of arrowroot, seized 'on the shore at Hobson's Bay,' Melbourne.

* During 1851 Mr. Carkeek, collector of Wellington, New Zealand, reported to the governor that the master of a vessel from Havana landed a full cargo on the coast without Customs cognizance, and then came to Wellington and tendered the duty!

October 13, 1852.—298 pounds tobacco, seized at Geelong, concealed on board a vessel from Liverpool.

Same Date.—326 pounds tobacco, also concealed on a vessel from Liverpool.

November 10.—351 pounds tobacco, seized at Melbourne, concealed in 19 imported casks of oranges.

Early in 1852 a large seizure of tobacco was made at London, on a vessel loaded with granite from Guernsey. The tobacco had been packed in tins containing about 20 pounds each, and stowed amid the cargo.

Another ingenious fraud was detected in the same port. Casks and circular tins had been imported, containing rape-oil, and it was found that the sides of the packages were double, and that the spaces thus created were packed with tobacco-stalk flour.

Three trunks containing effects, which had been put on board ship at Guernsey for conveyance to London, were found by the Guernsey officers to have double sides, the spaces containing cigars.

A ship which had discharged her foreign cargo, and been cleared by the Customs at Limerick, was found by the officers at Kilrush to be fitted up with large and ingeniously contrived places of concealment. She was seized and condemned. From the investigations afterwards held it appeared probable that immense smuggling had been carried on from this vessel.

Below are a few other cases in 1852 :

May 14 *and* 15.—Two horses, a waggon, 1,512 pounds tobacco, 577 pounds stalks, 138 pounds snuff, and 47 pounds cigars, seized at Ross, Herefordshire, by excise officers ; 29 pounds tobacco, seized at Swansea, in a house occupied by one of the parties concerned in the above.

May 20.—A smack and 494 pounds tobacco, seized off Southwold.

June 5.—The lugger *Earl Grey*, with 300 pounds tobacco and 900 pounds stalks, seized at Deal.

June 18.—250 pounds tobacco, seized at Sunderland, concealed in a ship's hold.

June 22.—The smack *Mary*, seized off Hayling Island, with 14 tubs of spirits concealed in lining of hold.

September 2.—1,290 pounds tobacco-stalks, seized in an inn-yard at Southampton.

September 8.—10 tubs spirits, seized at Brixham, after being hauled ashore and then drawn up a sewer.

The following cases appear remarkable :

On the night of January 11, 1852, a Glasgow tide-waiter, whilst going on duty, observed a man carrying a heavy package from the quay and up Finnerton Street. He followed, but lost sight of his quarry. Returning, he stumbled over two sacks of tobacco lying in the street near a public-house. He procured assistance, searched the public-house, and found two other sacks of tobacco. A further search revealed another sack in a coal-bunker near the door, and seven packages more in a press—in all 704 pounds. A shopkeeper who lived near, and the publican's servant, were prosecuted for 'being concerned' (they had tried to conceal the goods from the officers during search). The servant was acquitted, and the shopkeeper convicted, the magistrates recommending him strongly to the mercy of the Board. The public-house keeper, a woman, was then prosecuted, but the magistrates held the case 'not proven,' and 'assoilzied' her. Mr. Muirhead, the local lawyer employed by the collector, reported : 'There is scarcely a chance for the Crown's ever carrying a conviction before the justices here.'

On August 19, 1852, two well-dressed men visited the police-station at Margate, and stated that they were excise officers from London in chase of 'two ruffians who were escaping from the country,' that they had reason to believe the 'ruffians' had got on board a smack that was hovering off the Margate coast, that they had engaged a boat and four watermen to pursue her, and required a policeman to go with them. A policeman was provided, and away the party went, and picked up the smack beyond the limits of Ramsgate port, seven miles from land. The strangers jumped aboard, and one of them took off the hatches. A pungent smell arose from the hold, and the Margate boatmen at once perceived, to their disgust, that they had been deluded into assisting in the capture of a cargo of contraband. The vessel was the *Marie* of Dunkirk, with 6,000 pounds of tobacco on board. She had a French crew, but in the forecastle were two stalwart Englishmen, who spoke the true Deal dialect. The Margate boatmen refused to assist in navigating the vessel into port, whereupon the two stout Deal men offered to do so, and became at once most friendly with their captors. To such an extent did cordiality prevail that, a small public-house on the coast coming in sight, the excise officers asked the boatmen to pull ashore and obtain a gallon or two of beer. Off came the beer, and the seizing officers passed it round and round, till the sunburnt faces of the French crew, the Deal 'spotsmen,' and the Margate boatmen, grew red as the sun on a frosty evening, and even the rubicund countenance of the policeman acquired a deeper tinge. And thus they proceeded merrily into Ramsgate harbour, where the two seizers placed smack, cargo, and prisoners under the charge of the customs collector, announcing themselves respectively as Mr. R——, excise officer of Rochester, and Mr. S——, excise officer of Stepney. The prisoners were charged, and the magistrates, not being quite certain as to their powers, communicated through the collector with the Thames Street lawyer, who instructed them that the goods were liable to forfeiture, and so was the vessel, but the Frenchmen must be released, the seizure having been made beyond the three-mile limit. The two Deal men were liable, being English, and the seizure being made within four leagues of the land. But there was a quibble as to the vessel. By a recent case of the kind it had been shown that the aspect of international law should be studied in connection with seizures afloat. Therefore the *Marie* must be deemed liable to forfeiture so as to legalize prosecution of the two Deal men, and after they had been prosecuted forfeiture might be waived. The Deal men were convicted accordingly.

Soon afterwards a notorious Margate smuggler called on the Customs solicitor at Thames Street, and told him he had an idea this was a collusive seizure. The solicitor was impressed, and began to look into the matter, and several corroborating suspicions at once entered his mind. First, the tobacco seized was of wretched quality. Second, R——, the chief seizer, was a native of that stronghold of smuggling, Deal, and connected by marriage with several well-known receivers. Third, R—— had stated that he had never seen either of the two Deal men before, yet it turned out that he had kept a tavern in Beach Street, Deal, prior to entering the Excise, and one of the 'spotsmen' had been his potboy. And it was well known that there were many hardy longshoremen in Deal who, if their wives and families were looked after, would think nought of doing six months in gaol for a bribe of £20. Fourth, the *Marie* had been fooling about many hours off Margate, as though to invite seizure. Fifth, R—— and S—— admitted they had received information, but refused to furnish the informer's name. They alleged that he lived near West Malling, and they implied that he was so extremely sensitive and timorous that the slightest suggestion of publicity would destroy his efficacy as an informer for ever. So the Customs lawyer induced the Board of Excise to look into the matter. The Excise Commissioners were inclined to support their officers. They thought it possible the informer might have acted collusively in luring the smack over to be seized, or might even have financed the venture, it appearing that the expense of hiring the vessel, buying the almost worthless tobacco, and bribing the two Deal men to go to gaol, would amount to but £210, and the informer's share of the seizure-money to £300.* But they would not admit that the officers acted collusively.

* This shows the amount of forethought expended in framing the revenue laws of the period, and the regulations as to seizure awards.

The Customs lawyer merely kept the papers by him, knowing well that the knaves concerned would soon begin to show their hands. First came an application from R—— that the awards might be made as early as possible, for he had already advanced his informer £53, and had spent £11 in expenses (including, no doubt, the amount disbursed off the North Foreland for beer). The lawyer asked for the informer's name. R—— stated the man was one Woodward, generally living at Malling. The lawyer sent for the old Margate smuggler who had first enlightened him, and that hoary rascal intimated an opinion that a dummy informer would be put up if things grew desperate, and that he wouldn't be surprised if that there dummy turned out to be his old pal D—— of Deal, well known as a smuggler, and of old well acquainted with R——.

Meantime the four Margate boatmen who had rowed R—— off to the smack, having incurred some depreciation of self-esteem by being tricked into assisting in the execution of the law, thought they might as well have a share in the profits, and sent in an urgent petition. So did the policeman. The seizing officers protested against these claims, but the Customs Board gave the policeman £5, and the four boatmen £2 10s. each—*these amounts to be deducted from the officers' shares when the latter were paid.*

Soon the pretended informer wrote, signing himself 'Woodward,' and asking for his reward. He stated that people were beginning to suspect him, and that it was not safe for him to show himself in the street. The lawyer asked him to call at his office in Thames Street, and placed the old Margate smuggler in concealment. Just as the informer finished his tale, and reiterated his claim as 'Woodward,' he received a heavy slap from behind, and, turning round, found himself confronted by a grinning ancient, who exclaimed in husky tones: 'Wot cheer, D——, old boy! How is things headin' just now?' It does not appear that the informer was at all discomposed, or that any hint was made of proceedings against him. It may be safely assumed that he at once 'owned up,' and that Deal and Margate went from the Custom-house arm-in-arm, and straight into the most convenient tavern.

It might be thought that R—— would hear of this, and cease his solicitations, but it is likely that D—— merely told him a string of lies, for he continued to pester the Customs Board with requests for compensation and awards. The Board made no reply. The papers connected with this extraordinary case conclude with a note by the lawyer in June, 1854, thus :

'The difficulty I have had in dealing with these papers is at an end by a circumstance which confirms my view of the case. I find that R—— has defrauded the Excise and decamped.'*

(Nothing appears as to what became of S——. Probably he was quite unaware that R—— had taken him into an arranged case.)

During 1852 information reached the Board that a Grimsby oyster-boat called the *Lord Rivers* had run across to the French coast. Her captain was one Mimmack, a desperate smuggler belonging to Saltfleet, Lincolnshire. Orders were sent to the eastern and southern ports, and revenue cruisers went in search of her. She was found off Dunkirk, with nothing on board except a number of empty cigar-boxes. During the rest of the year she was closely watched and repeatedly searched, and nothing discovered that would justify her detention, yet it seems she must have been smuggling all the time. On January 28, 1853, she was searched off Dover, and found to have what the officers deemed 'a false stem,' the

* We have seen a good many sets of papers in which some of the reports suggest collusion in seizures, but none quite so remarkable as this case. It is clear that the distances from the shore, etc., were studied out by R——, so that the Frenchmen should escape and the ship be released ; that he bribed two of his old acquaintances to suffer imprisonment, and another to personate the informer if necessary ; and that he expected to secure his own promotion, and a tolerable surplus after expenses were paid.

interior of which smelt strongly of spirits. She was detained, but it appearing that such peculiarities of structure were common in vessels of the kind, and there being no actual proof that she had been smuggling, release was granted. In February, however, a person concerned gave startling information as to the doings of Captain Mimmack and his crew, from which it appeared that this little craft, though scarcely ever out of the hands of the revenue men, had carried on a steady traffic in contraband. She was therefore seized, but the crew were not prosecuted.

Early on the morning of March 10, 1853, a policeman detained three horses and two carts near Woodbridge for conveying 1,231 pounds tobacco and 2,541 pounds stalks. Inquiries were made, and it was found that the goods had been landed on the bank of the Orwell from a small vessel called the *Susan*. The vessel was captured with her master and crew, and several persons residing near Bungay were arrested on suspicion of being concerned. One of the crew made a statement, describing the whole of the proceedings, the departure from England, the taking-in of the goods at Flushing, the run, etc. The rest of the crew and the driver of the carts were convicted. After release from gaol the crew made statements still further implicating the Bungay receivers, but the Customs solicitor was indisposed to take proceedings, and recommended that certain moderate sums which had been offered by the accused as compositions should be accepted. 'Perhaps drawing their capital would do more to cripple their smuggling operations than incarceration.' He thought a conviction might be obtained, but it would be by contaminated evidence, which would 'subject the Crown to the usual observations on such occasions.' (It is apparent that Mr. Hamel had been rendered more cautious by the proceedings of the Parliamentary and Charlotte Row Committees. See pp. 324-325 and 329.) The Board concurred.

The proceedings of the police in this case were not exactly creditable, neither were those of the collector of

Woodbridge. The police returned the seizure as made without information, whereas the seizing constable's attention had been called to the conveyances by a local post-office clerk who was going to work. The police appear to have done their best to 'bluff' him out of participation, but the Board, deeply experienced in the ways of seizing officers, refused to be hoodwinked, and compensated the clerk liberally. The Woodbridge customs men, no doubt annoyed that the police handed the seized goods over to the Excise, did their best to squeeze themselves into the seizure, but without avail.

On March 12, 1853, the smack *Ariel* was searched off Ramsgate, and 2 pounds tobacco and seven packs of playing-cards seized. A petty seizure, it may be thought, and little did the revenue men deem that she had just discharged a cargo into the Deal lugger *Mary*, which vessel was making for London river. An hour later the *Mary* was sailing past the Reculvers, when she was boarded by the coastguard, who found that she was carrying 1,615 pounds tobacco-stalks.

Information was given to the authorities that the *John and Susannah* of Lowestoft had gone oversea for a cargo of tobacco. On April 30, 1853, the coastguard seized her off Whitby with 5,165 pounds tobacco. 'Immediately on the discovery being made,' wrote the seizing officer, 'the master, James Blasey, jumped overboard and tried to drown himself, but was rescued by my men. He was very refractory and troublesome.' Quite a remarkable number of people tried to squeeze themselves into this case, some professing to have given information, others to have assisted the seizing officers. The excise officer at Ipswich claimed on the former ground, but was rapped over the knuckles. The real informer pestered the Board with complaints and begging letters. This miserable traitor's appeals for money remind us of the methods of Rogue Riderhood. After receiving £5 as 'pecuniary relief,' £11 8s. as 'share of forfeiture,' £50 3s. 2d. as 'subsistence,' £1 as 'railway expenses,' and £50 as 'gratuity,' he wrote to say that his life was in danger from the smugglers. The Board offered to pay his expenses if he would emigrate, but it seems that was not in his line. He replied thus:

'HONOURABLE GENTLEMEN in writing to your Honourable board I beg to state that my wishes are in all respects willing to do the best that ever lay in my power to give any information to your Honourable board that may come in my way and I do Flatter myself that by exerting my powers to do so that I can be of greater service than perhaps Gentlemen you really think I know a great many smuggling parties all along the west coast and can do more than you are aware of providing I had the means to set me up in the world and I think either Portsmouth or Southampton the most suitable places for me to do anything in as I am in danger here with thanks for the suggestion cannot at my age and with a sick wife think of emigrating but should be happy if I could provide a Liveing by industry in any place,' etc., etc.

(Imagine him 'flattering' himself upon the possession of such accomplishments!)

During September, 1853, the suspicions of the coastguard at Lowestoft were excited by the sudden absence of a noted smuggler. A look-out was kept. The absentee returned as suddenly as he had left, and it was suspected that he had been oversea to arrange a run. On September 16 a lugger was observed hovering off the coast. The inspecting commander of the Coastguard hired a steam tug, went in chase, and captured the lugger about twelve miles from shore. She was *L'Abondance* of Dunkirk, laden with 7,380 pounds tobacco. The captain stated that he took the tobacco in at Flushing, the shipment being supervised by an Englishman, and that the Englishman had come over in the lugger, and been landed on the previous night. Five hundred francs were to be paid for the trip. Two boys, one aged fifteen and the other twelve, who were on board, were released by the Customs as 'under age.' The captain and the rest of the crew were convicted and imprisoned.

The French consul at once approached the Board, pointing out that three of the men imprisoned were under eighteen, and 'poor, uneducated fishermen, without any will of their own.' The Board declined to intervene, and then the French ambassador memorialized Lord Clarendon on the men's behalf, who moved the Treasury to refer the matter to the Board. The Customs solicitor then stated that it was a common practice to 'man these vessels, as they term it, with boys,' so as to minimize the number of convictions, and that there was every reason to believe that the French fishermen had understood fully that they were embarking in a contraband transaction. He also pointed out that the English spotsman was still at large, and that if he were arrested after the crew had been released it would be difficult to secure identification. Later the consul petitioned afresh, urging that the captain had been made 'the dupe of some designing Englishman,' but the Board stood firm.

The spotsman, whose name, curiously enough, was Mantrip, was arrested and convicted. The inspecting commander had returned the seizure as made without information, but he soon had to amend his report, for a letter reached the Board, furnishing proof that the seizure was entirely due to information furnished by the writer. The informer was rewarded with a grant of £300.*

It is likely that there were other informers in the locality, for on the night of October 14, 1853, the yawl *Sophia* was seized in Lowestoft harbour, with 5,170 pounds tobacco.

Information reached Dublin on March 2, 1854, that the *Mutiné* of Cherbourg would attempt a run. The

* Undoubtedly 70 per cent. of the larger seizures made in the old days were due to information. Many officers, despite the Board's orders to the contrary, made secret arrangements with their informers, and it was only when the latter found themselves likely to be defrauded of the wages of infamy that they appealed to the Board.

coastguard and police were put on the alert, and on the night of March 8 two policemen observed a brace of suspicious-lookingmen lurking on the coast near Baldoyle. They interrogated the lurkers, and, finding nothing to warrant arrest, allowed them to depart. Soon afterwards the policemen fell across seventeen bales of tobacco. Later a Dublin customs officer was informed that tobacco-stalks had been landed at Rocky Island. Search was made, and 105 bales were found. This made the total quantity seized 6,681 pounds.

On May 21, 1854, a boat belonging to the Queenborough Oyster Company was searched in the Medway by the coastguard, and 2,481 pounds tobacco found on her.

On the night of May 25 the tide-surveyor of Ramsgate observed two suspicious characters on a mud-lighter in the harbour. He went on board, and found in the hold forty-two bales of tobacco, weighing in all 2,123 pounds, which had been run during the evening by a French lugger, and put in charge of the lightermen for transmission to the receiver. The lighter belonged to the Harbour Trustees, and they were directed to enter into a bond of £200 pending investigation of the case. The lighter was afterwards released and the bond cancelled, it appearing that the Harbour Trustees had no cognizance of the attempted fraud.

On November 10 a Norwegian barque arrived at Shields from Drammen, and the customs rummagers found 459 pounds tobacco concealed amid the battens that formed her cargo. Several of the seamen were convicted, and the ship was released on a fine of £5 only. The captain, in applying for her release, furnished a copy of an agreement entered into in Norway between himself and each member of the crew. Below is an extract :

'I, Andrew Hansen, promise to conduct myself as a brave and honest Norwegian sailor . . . and to act in accordance with the Norwegian laws, most especially the law of 28th July, 1824, respecting smuggling and fraud, not taking anything on shore or on board without the captain's knowledge and consent.'

To show the extent to which smuggling had been carried on in the creeks and rivers of East Anglia,* we must travel a few months beyond the announced scope of our treatise. Early in 1855 the excise officers seized 1,400 pounds tobacco at Wenhaston, near Halesworth, on premises occupied by a well-known smuggler. The occupier was convicted and imprisoned, and while in gaol implicated two other persons residing in the neighbourhood of Halesworth, but requested that their arrest might be delayed till he had induced one of them to pay him £60, the amount of a loan for which he held a promissory note. He failed to obtain payment, so the men were arrested and convicted. Then a clergyman living near forwarded to the Board the following letter, received from a parishioner :

'REV. SIR,

'Smuggling has been carried on within the parish of Wenhaston—and Mr. —— at its head—I should say for about twenty-five years, during which period he has done well. The duties of the excise officers and those of the coastguard are unknown to me ; I cannot say much thereon—I do wonder how it can have lasted so long—runs have been made time after time, landed, conveyed about night and day, for a long period, and a fortune saved, and his race unbroken now.

'—— has ships, a wherry, the public-house at the harbour mouth of Southwold, horses, carts, and his own men by his side—in fact, every facility to accomplish his object.

'We have had the goods by Southwold up the river to the bridge, unloaded there, taken to several places (not a few to Dunwich) sent off by the carrier to Ipswich,

* It is evident from the records that the bulk of the smuggling was transferred from Kent and Sussex to the Eastern Counties in 1831.

then by train to London, while another portion has been driven by his own man and horses to Mr. ——, draper, Norwich, who is his brother-in-law.

'I believe all the goods of late have been landed between Lowestoft and Gorleston—something far from being right there, that is, I think so—and from information I can obtain much has gone away without coming to Wenhaston—the last lot came home, a portion of which was taken by the Excise at ——s, but the quantity left, I think, on the Monday night before the seizure, and I have but little doubt was driven by his brother-in-law to London, and I expect left at Mr. ——s. This man was once with —— at Wenhaston, and his father now lives at Dunwich.

'When you arrive in London, I do hope you will refuse to give in my name. —— has said he shall have it in three months, and he should like him to be shot in the road. His man —— says they have obtained it before, and shall have it again by payment of a fee.* Should the gentleman demand my name, I must decline giving any further information. Should, however, it be left in your hands quietly I will try to put down that disgraceful traffic which I consider has long been a pest to the parish, and the existing officers under Government have not been able to extinguish it.'

The worst that can be said of high tariffs, severe preventive regulations, and the disbursement of 'blood-money,' is that they encourage the inherent meannesses of hypocritical people. It would be safe to assert that the person who sat quiet for twenty-five years while contraband traffic was rampant all round him refrained from joining in the traffic merely because he had not sufficient courage, and blossomed out as an anonymous informer when he knew that the law was on his enemy's

* The old smuggler king had circulated a report that informers' names might be obtained on payment of a fee at the Custom-house, and had hinted that discovery would be followed by vindictive retribution.

track. The study of smuggling literature forces one to the grim conclusion that the average man is not by any means more likely than the average woman to shut his mouth and mind his own business when his neighbour is in trouble.

The aim of this treatise has been mainly annalistic, but the incidental research has unearthed much that may be informative to the student of fiscal doctrine. Many thinkers hold that fiscal science occupies too much of the average man's attention, and that the spectacle of a group of ordinary citizens, equipped with journals and statistics, discussing a second-hand proposal of tariffs, is not particularly cheering. It has been pungently said that there is nothing so easy as imposing taxes ; that the fools and madmen of all ages have been adepts at that disastrous exercise, and that the really wise man—the man who deserves a golden statue and the worship of posterity—is he who abolishes a tax. Yet, while national expenditure continues, many taxes must be imposed and collected, and a few workday hints on origin and system may be useful.

The public is now divided into two parties, and, to describe the position in a broad way, it will be sufficient to state that they differ as to the system of collection. The Tariff Reformers desire to revert to the old method under which most foreign articles were taxed, and it must be admitted that most of the arguments used to support their idea are as ancient as the method recommended. The Free Traders also use many well-worn formulæ, under which they claim for their system every virtue under Heaven. It is not wise to intervene abruptly, for it is becoming apparent that many of the disputants do not desire to be told the naked truth ; they prefer listening to platitudes that support 'The Programme.' Yet the truth is the truth, whether it be welcome or no, and what is termed 'far-fetched and iconoclastic reasoning' to-day may furnish maxims for the school-children of a hundred years hence.

It follows that a few bald remarks upon method, etc., may be of more immediate service than the most profound reasoning. 'Such were the favoured tactics at such a date; mark their result,' may go far, when the most symmetrical arguments fail. As contentious stuff will now and then creep in, it may be wise to preface the matter with a closer definition of the attitudes of the two antagonistic parties.

The Free Trader pleads that his system, as exemplified in Great Britain and nowhere else, confines the Customs levies to a few productive articles—articles which he contends are not absolute necessaries. He goes on to state that the revenue is by this method collected accurately and cheaply, and that the mere means of existance are not in any way curtailed. He announces that his system compares favourably with all that differ—viz., with the systems used everywhere except in the United Kingdom—that it is of all systems least oppressive of the poor, and that it does not in any way injure the home producer, but rather stimulates production, and increases the sale of British goods in foreign markets. He points triumphantly around him, indicating in succession the British baker distributing cheap bread, the sporadic evidences of great wealth, and the standard of living (admittedly higher in some respects than under the old system of Protection). These, he states, are the results of Free Trade, and of Free Trade only.

The Tariff Reformer protests that under Free Trade the United Kingdom has been made a 'dumping ground' for low-priced foreign goods; that we open our markets to the foreigner and he shuts us out from his; that in consequence most of the articles used in the United Kingdom are of foreign production; that many once flourishing British lines of business have thus been destroyed, and that others are tottering to a fall. He claims that Tariff Reform, by shutting out many of the articles now imported, would stimulate production in the United Kingdom, and reduce the present ghastly list of unemployed.

It may be easy to show that both of the disputing parties are partially wrong, without proving each to be misled past redemption. Every system, except Thuggee and Sweating, has its advantages as well as its defects. If the misstatements of the advocates of each party be brought under observation, the residue may be left alone, for Truth should need no bolstering up.

QUESTIONS TO BE CONSIDERED.

1. Does the history of Customs duties show that they are necessarily oppressive ?

Perhaps the best way of finding an answer will be to look into the question of the rich man's contribution to Customs revenue. If it be found that he pays, or has paid in the past, his just proportion, it may be admitted that Customs duties are no more oppressive than other forms of taxation. What is the proportion that the rich man should in justice pay ? According to reason, according to practice with regard to the impost on incomes, most of the poor should be exempt or lightly taxed. Few rich men will venture to dispute this publicly. He who inherits wealth inherits its just responsibilities. He who makes money by speculation or business enterprise may be allowed perhaps to ascribe one-tenth of his success to personal excellence—the rest is the result of luck, or of the labour of others. Luck is an acknowledged factor, for every successful speculator or business man knows at least a dozen quite as skilful and energetic as he who have either made little or lost much. Earnest, moderately-paid clerks and salesmen are the ministering angels of fortune, while its very foundation is cheap labour. This being acknowledged, the old and new methods of collection may be examined with profit.

Previous to 1303 the Customs levies were 'The Ancient Custom' on exported wool, 'Prisage,' and 'The Maltolte.' The first was light, and could not to any extent have oppressed even the English agriculturist, except that the regulations of enforcement were rather irksome. There was an insatiable foreign demand for English wool, and when such is the case the last buyer pays all. (There is at present an insatiable demand for tea and tobacco in the United Kingdom, and, as neither article can be produced here at a profit—as, to put it another way, there is no home-produced supply to compete with the foreign, the consumer in the United Kingdom pays all the duties on those articles. Were we dependent upon the United States for supplies of a peculiar kind of corn which we could not do without, and the United States levied an arbitrary export tax on all such corn shipped to Great Britain, undoubtedly the British consumer would pay the tax.) As to Prisage, which was on imported wine, the poor drank ale, except during those amazing periods when the Gascon vintners flooded the south of England with cheap wine. The Maltolte was an occasional heavy tax, usually levied on exported wool. When, as may have happened on rare occasions, this was applied to imported food-stuffs, the poor suffered, for it appears that food-stuffs were not imported extensively except in times of stress.

From 1303 to the commencement of Edward III.'s *actual* sway the following changes were introduced and maintained: (1) a slight increase in the duty on exported wool; (2) Butlerage, as a substitute for Prisage, on aliens' wines only; (3) a slight tax (protective) on imported cloth; (4) 3d. in the pound on goods imported by aliens (protective).

From the beginning of Edward III.'s actual domination, to the inception of Tunnage and Poundage during the same reign, there were repeated heavy imposts on exported wool, enforced in a way that must have plagued producers. A duty was levied on exported cloth, and, as the English cloth industry was at the time in a struggling condition, it is likely that the producer paid this tax.

From the institution of Tunnage and Poundage to the end of Elizabeth's reign the additional levies were: Tunnage, on imported wine; Poundage, on denizens' merchandise. (Thus nearly all merchandise was taxed.) The Maltolte on wool became the permanent 'Subsidy.' Arbitrary imposts were laid upon wine by the Tudors.

From the accession of the Stuarts to the revolt of the Long Parliament there was much corrupt farming of Customs, and many monopolistic licences to import, export, etc., were granted. The added burdens were: many additions to the 'official values' of poundage goods, taxes on exported ale, and tremendous occasional impositions upon tobacco. The growth of the English cloth industry, combined with the heavy and complicated restrictions, had well-nigh stopped the legal exportation of wool.

From 1641 to the end of the Protectorate certain increases were made in the official values of imported goods, and the import-excise was instituted. Customs farming was abolished, and Customs collection purified. The Navigation Act was imposed, and the exportation of wool prohibited. (The Puritans were bitter Protectionists.)

During the period from the Restoration to the beginning of William III.'s reign the Navigation Act, and the Act prohibiting the exportation of wool, were recast and reaffirmed. The Customs duties were farmed till 1671. Tunnage was collected on wines, and Poundage levied at 5 per cent. on the official values of nearly all import and export goods, under what was called 'The Old Subsidy.' The Coinage Duty was instituted. Several imposts were levied, including the tonnage rates on French vessels, an extra tunnage on wine, and an extra rate of poundage on certain imported goods. Duties on a 'sliding scale' were put on imported corn. Yet it is unlikely that up to

1688 the poor suffered to any noteworthy extent by Customs duties, and it appears that bread and provisions were cheap.

From 1688 to 1791 the Customs duties became heavier and heavier, the most startling increases being made during the reigns of William and Anne, when there appeared in rapid succession 'The second 25 per cent. on French goods,' 'The New Subsidy,' 'The fifteen per cent. on Muslins,' the abominable special duties on salt, 'The one-third Subsidy,' 'The two-thirds Subsidy,' and many other 'permanent' taxes. The sliding scale upon corn was maintained. The Customs tariff became tremendously complicated, till to some extent rectified by the Consolidating Act of 1787. Bread and other food-stuffs did not become permanently dear till near the end of the century.

After 1791 the combined effects of immense increases in the corn duties, of war and the reckless subsidizing of foreign allies, of the growth of urban population, and the enclosure of common lands, were made terribly manifest. How the poor contrived to exist may to many folk of the present day appear a riddle. Yet there were certain ameliorating circumstances. Although for a long period the importation of cattle, etc., had been prohibited, meat was not dear. Fish was sold at a price which at the present day would be considered amazingly cheap. So was fruit, especially in the rural districts. Beer was cheap, and tolerably pure. The duties on tea, tobacco, and many kinds of spirits were enormous, but at least one-third of the trade in those articles was duty-free (witness the smuggling records). The duties were not collected as now with deadly accuracy. The rich paid more in proportion than the poor. The most oppressive Customs duties of old were those on corn, salt, and sugar, and the corn duties were not oppressive except from 1795 to 1845. Even during those sad fifty years most other absolute necessaries (meat, fish, vegetables, fruit, ale, milk, and the rougher wearing stuffs) were sold at reasonable prices. Tea and tobacco were not esteemed absolute necessaries. Many thousands, especially among the rural folk, drank ale at breakfast *from pure choice.* Smoking was not a universal habit. The foreign spirit consumed by the lower classes was Plantation rum, usually a sound and wholesome article, that thoroughly deserved its nickname 'Nelson's blood,' and this was admitted *at highly preferential rates.* Many of the articles, both raw and manufactured, scheduled as dutiable in the old tariff lists, produced next to nothing in the way of Customs, the taxes operating as prohibitions, yet the home-raised or home-made goods identical were not dear. (One striking instance may be quoted — the almost prohibitive apple duty. Apples were exceedingly cheap in the south of England.) The high silk and lace duties were taxes on luxury, and, when not evaded, were paid by the rich. The great evil of most of the old duties (leaving out of consideration those on salt and sugar and the later duties on corn) lay in complicated and erratic collection, and in the smuggling generated. The dishonest trader was given too many chances, compared with his more honest neighbour.

If we refer to the present Customs tariff, we shall find that the poor pay out of all fair proportion. The principal producing factors are tea, tobacco, spirits, and sugar. Many a working man's wife consumes more tea than a duchess. The duty on tea is not graded in proportion to value. Many a working man smokes more tobacco than a duke. (The duke's *disbursements* for tobacco must not be taken into account ; his personal consumption is the true item of comparison.) All tobacco is rated alike so far as quality goes ; the primest product of Virginia pays no more in leaf than the worst of German growth. Belgian cigars pay the same duty as the choicest Havanas. Many a working man consumes more spirits than the average millionaire. The duty on the commonest Egyptian spirit is the same per proof gallon as that on the finest French cognac.* And it is idle to

* Except that the better kinds of spirit are more frequently imported in bottle, and bottled spirits are liable to a slight surtax.

urge that the working man should not smoke or drink. Merely *high* taxation will not keep the poor from drinking and smoking, and if taxation were made prohibitive in this respect smuggling or illicit distillation would at once be resorted to, and the tariff would have to be remodelled. And no class should have the power to tax the *tastes* of others. Nothing is so profoundly immoral as to save one's pocket by taxing a neighbour's so-called vices, for the world is made up of fallible beings, and the true mission of the fiscal reformer is to understand this, and legislate accordingly.

It follows that the Customs tariff of the present day oppresses the poor, for we are in this so much inferior to our fathers, that the nerve-shaking herbs, tobacco and tea, have become absolute necessaries. The sugar tax is directed at the very hearts of the poor, for the children of the poor are inveterate sugar-consumers. Tea, tobacco, and sugar are all purely foreign articles ; there is no home competition in initial production, and the poor pay on those articles disproportionately to their means. The Customs tariff of to-day is the offspring of the early Victorian desire for cheapness of collection. There is no justice in it. It shuts out next to nothing that Patriotism would wish to be manufactured at home, and, as regards its being paid by the consumer, one might think Adam Smith had devised it, merely to justify his own doctrinal flounderings—merely to be able to say : 'I told you that all import taxes were paid by the consumer, and I have provided you with a tariff that will support my argument.'

2. Is it unwise to 'tinker' with Customs duties ?

Undoubtedly. A tax may be antagonistic to pure justice and reason, yet have a kind of merit because people have become used to it, and therefore pay it without much reluctance. It has always been a peculiar trait of the English to pay cheerfully moderate indirect taxes, and this because such taxes are not brought home with startling effect to the payer's mental consciousness. 'Tinkering' with Customs taxes, by making slight additions, irritates the public, for the goods are usually bought in small quantities at short intervals, and every purchase of an ounce of tobacco, a dram of spirits, or a parcel of tea or sugar, reminds the buyer of that which he would willingly forget. This is especially the case when the goods have been previously overtaxed, and the addition actually limits consumption, thus inspiring annoyance and producing no additional revenue, and also when the additional duty is so arranged that the consumer is charged an extra halfpenny on every small purchase, of which but one farthing goes to the revenue and the other to the dealer.

Another objectionable product of 'tinkering' is the dislocation of trade that ensues. For months prior to the annual announcement merchants are fretting and fuming over probabilities. Many an order is delayed, and many a parcel, purchased on mere speculation, remains long upon the dealer's hands. But, while speculators are thus occasionally injured, the bulk of the loss falls upon the consumer. Enterprising firms have been known to net many thousands of pounds by well-judged ventures on Budget possibilities. Till within recent years, it was actually a Customs practice to make special provision as to staff and hours of attendance, in order to enable merchants to indulge to the full their mania for speculation! It is bad enough for the public to be fleeced by keen-witted adventurers, but the matter becomes maddening when the public has to pay overtime to its own servants, that they may assist the process.

3. Are *ad valorem* duties preferable to specific?

Were it possible to infect the mercantile world with sincerity, and to enrol as customs officers none but conspicuously self-sacrificing and efficient persons, an *ad valorem* tariff would be eminently preferable. It would ease the poor, who consume the cheaper articles, and surtax the luxuries imported by the rich. Its chief fault lies in the uncertainties of collection. If we are to believe the Tariff Reformers, the United Kingdom depends more upon imports than any other country in the world. A 'reformed' tariff would not *instantly* check importation, and it is not contended, even by the most violent declaimer, that a reformed tariff would shut out more than a portion of foreign articles. Therefore the present customs men, who have no deep training in the estimation of values, would be suddenly called upon to check a multitude of declarations, or the department would have to employ many highly-paid 'experts.' (Men of insight and common sense would probably prefer the ordinary customs man, whom contact has endowed with a *rough* knowledge of merchandise, to the average conceited and pedantic 'expert.') In either case it is conceivable that many difficulties would arise. Merchants would import goods and declare them at lower than the actual values, much delay and many detentions would occur, and be it known that there are ways of indirectly intimidating overworked officials. As to the danger of corruption, it is certain that the customs officers of the United Kingdom are the most incorruptible in the world, and this is due to—(1) the competitive test for admission into the lower grades, (2) permanence of employment; (3) the absence of *ad valorem* duties. There could be no blacker history than that of the British landing-officers of the early part of the nineteenth century, were it possible, by merely inspecting records, to gauge the extremities of official depravity. It is undeniable that, even with the present staff and under the improved modern methods, a system of *ad valorem* duties would produce a plentiful stock of temptations.

At the same time *ad valorem* duties would assist towards one consummation—a consummation which every Tariff Reformer* avows is next his heart—the shutting out of

* It is to be hoped that the avowal is sincere. The tactics of some of the noisiest of the Tariff Reformers tend to show that the end aimed at is an all-round rise in the price of goods.

some of the 'cheaper and nastier' foreign goods, the flimsy and often putrid rubbish which at present is cast so plentifully upon our shores, to the utter degradation of many British handicrafts and industries. (Even unscrupulous dealing would assist in this, as it did of old, when the aim of the ordinary merchant was to import goods of the highest possible value, and enter them at the lowest rate that the Customs would allow.) Perhaps this may explain why most of the articles made by our ancestors were so much more worthy and enduring than those constructed at present, why paper of 1710 is still as good as new and ink of the same date as brilliant as ever, why ancient furniture is so majestic and substantial and ancient cutlery so perfect in material and finish, and why grandfather's clock ticks so musically and keeps so firm a grip upon the flying seconds. It might even be held to explain the continuance during bygone centuries—due, perhaps, to the self-reliant 'Englishness' engendered—of a certain rough idea of picturesque beauty. Why was it that the early Victorian period teemed with dowdyism? Why does a peasant's cottage of a hundred years back, though steeped in ruin and decay, convey a certain charm to the artistic eye? Will age, or ivy, or sweet natural surroundings, ever thus endow a cottage of the sixties? Will the pork-pie hat and crinoline of the sixties ever be reproduced on canvas, as artists of the present day reproduce the trappings of the Georgian era? It is to be hoped, if we are to have Tariff Reform, that, if it fails in everything else that it has promised, it may make us a little more genuinely *English* than we have been during the past seventy years.

4. May Customs duties be adjusted so as to genuinely foster certain home manufactures?

Undoubtedly this was done in the past. The English woollen industry was simply built upon Protection. As soon as the old export wool duties reached the dignity of a

'Subsidy,' they began to protect the English cloth manufacturer. English, and later Irish, agriculture suffered by the system, but the cloth manufacturer, probably the greatest commercial tyrant that ever existed, prospered exceedingly. The extent to which the duties acted protectively towards the manufacturers is shown by their becoming almost unproductive, years before the exportation of wool was prohibited, and by the vast increase in the exportation of English cloth in the latter end of Elizabeth's reign and the beginning of James I. (Prohibition of the exportation of wool was a device to check 'owling,' which practice was encouraged by the French and Flemings in their desire to hamper the English cloth manufacturers.) The high duties on foreign woollens were also protective. The old 'aliens' duties'—surtaxes on goods imported by foreigners—and the extra levies on goods brought in foreign ships, combined with the Navigation laws in building up the British merchant navy, a distinctive kind of protection, of which the third factor might be existing in a modified form at the present day, but for the clumsiness of the pedants who drafted the Acts incidental, and the innate rascality of some of the administering officials. The preferences given of old to fish, oil, and blubber of British taking, and the privileges granted to the Newfoundland fisheries, were of immense benefit to the industries concerned. It is useless to argue that some of the concerns alluded to prosper now without protection. Difficulty lies as much in the way of establishing as of maintaining a trade. Certain industries now followed in the United Kingdom would not have attained importance but for protection. Of course, the protective idea was often enforced to the extent of absurdity, but freaks of that kind occur in connection with every system. Fools occasionally obtain powers of administration, but that does not utterly invalidate. It may be repeated that many commercial enterprises were stimulated and preserved of old by means of Customs enactments. Whether this was good or no for other ventures, or for the public generally, is outside the present consideration.

Another striking instance of the effect of Protection is the immense and disproportionate growth of London as a centre of shipping. It cannot be shown that London possesses many natural advantages as a port. In the old days the whole of the East India Company's trade was confined to London, and the great city was thus artificially made, not only a hive of British and colonial traffic, but a vast centre of transhipment. Many other kinds of valuable goods were only allowed to be imported into London. As soon as the privileges were abolished the trade of London began to lose its extraordinary eminence. It is likely that most of the modern schemes for the restoration of London's commercial prosperity may prove abortive, merely because the planners have not sufficiently borne this in mind.

It may be pointed out that even the modern tariff contains certain protective items. The surtax on wines and spirits imported in bottle has doubled the bottling of wines and spirits in the United Kingdom. A higher duty is levied on cigars than on tobacco, on manufactured tobacco than on leaf, on manufactured cocoa and coffee than on raw. If these were not intended to act protectively, why were they thus arranged ? It is certain that they *do* act in that way.

5. Is there any weight in the objection to a comprehensive Customs tariff, that it would multiply officials ?

It is likely that we are already overdone with bureaucratism. The average official, after all, is but an average man, with a few extra limitations and a certain dexterity in routine. It must not be thought that the customs men of the present day are worse than other civil servants ; indeed, there is a kind of maritime freshness in the work performed by some of them that has a highly redemptive tendency. As in the days of Adam Smith, they are the most adaptive of revenue officials. There is little that is hidebound in their methods. They do not possess that mechanical hardness that distinguishes the 'inland revenue men,' nor have they much of the astounding priggishness that exists here and there in 'the West End departments.' Yet an army of them would scarcely be a desirable institution. It cannot be too often repeated that we have already far too many officials and institutions, far too many smug people who worry the world from behind desks. It is possible that the genuine English spirit, the subtle essence which has done everything that has bestowed credit on the national name, does not traverse extensively the atmosphere of officialdom. Somehow, we have not done particularly well since the Germanizing of England set in. One thing is certain, the effective supervision of *ad valorem* transactions could not be achieved by purely clerical means. The man would have to be 'on the spot'—to handle the goods. Much would have to be left to the judgment of the 'waterside officer,' or things would soon go wrong. Strong-minded and clever men would be needed in plenty, to do the actual landing work.

6. Can anything be urged in extenuation of the present craze for statistics ?

Little. Faith in statistics appears to be but a form of superstition. It is likely that most of the statistics of commerce, gathered prior to the last ten years, were quite incorrect. This statement will not particularly disconcert such people as hold that incorrect figures are better than none ; therefore it may be best not to embellish the page with many specimens, but to mention casually that even accredited statements of payments into the Exchequer frequently differ, now to the extent of a million or two, then to the tune of seventeen shillings and sixpence ha'penny ; that some of the old statements of tonnage, imports, exports, etc., though quoted in Parliamentary speeches and perpetuated in tables, will not bear common-sense consideration ; that for many, many years our import trade with various countries was estimated according to *ports of shipment instead of places of production ;* that the values furnished often depend on the whim of a mere office-boy ; that one huge item was left out of the export return for many years, and when this was pointed out by a layman the omission was not by any means immediately rectified ; that—but space is limited, and there are folk to whom cold fact is uncomfortable. All old statistics should be dealt with cautiously. It has been suggested that statistics should not be collected *continuously* as now, but at long intervals, as the Census is taken, and then thoroughly. Accurate collection is next to impossible when the uncountable mercantile army is always being pestered for returns, but if statistics were taken every seven years proper arrangements could be made. It is to be assumed that there are men in the country who could make interesting and instructive speeches, and assist in governing the nation, without long lists of figures in front of them.

7. Would Tariff Reform cause a considerable rise in the price of commodities ?

Hard to say. To be effective, according to the plea of its advocates, it should shut out many foreign manufactures, and stimulate British production. It appears likely that in its early stage it would increase prices by raising the reward of labour. People with fixed incomes would then suffer. The price of imported raw material might not be particularly affected, especially such raw material as foreigners compete to supply us with. The trade of a nation is much like individual trade. When a manufacturer is pestered by bagmen who sell raw material, he is usually able to dictate his own terms, but if many manufacturers have to resort to one centre of supply the position is reversed. Broad theories may not with success be applied to commercial matters.

One circumstance deserves reference—the amazing insincerity at present displayed in argument. It is not at all uncommon to hear an ardent 'Reformer' applaud his system as a means of obviating unemployment, and almost in the same breath assert that the unemployed are unemployable. The mercantile man—and Tariff Reform is essentially a mercantile idea—is avowedly opportunistic, and every agitation that he pioneers should be regarded with profound caution. It is for that vast body of people who possess fixed incomes to consider at once whether they are actually willing to pay for a period more money for certain articles than they have done in the past. If patriotism will carry them through the ordeal, no more need be said upon this point. But they should think deeply upon the matter, and weigh carefully the 'bagman' portion of the Tariff Reform arguments.

The apparently 'blunt' style of the foregoing remarks may require explanation. It is due merely to lack of space, and the consequent necessity of curtness. Be it understood that the statements are founded upon long and arduous study of almost every kind of record connected with the older British Customs practice. There are few branches of research more dry and complicated, at the same time fuller of pitfalls into which even the most careful may stumble, than this particular one. Therefore all idea of being dogmatic must be disclaimed. The above deductions may be proved to be wrong. Still, they have been formed cautiously, and should at the present juncture be found interesting. Above all, the 'prophetic' position must be disclaimed. The old records relating to Customs legislation and debate teem with prophecies, yet it would be difficult to quote one prophecy in twenty that was fulfilled. Few subjects are so poorly understood as this of Customs tariffs—this upon which men argue from morn to dewy eve. Hard is the task to form a decision upon any of its vital points—at least, a decision that will stand the test of close thought and common sense. This may be because the subject itself is so repellent to naturally intelligent men, for after all there is a touch of spoliation in every kind of impost. This opinion, coming as it does from customs officers, may seem strange, yet there is something in it. If men would devote as much mental effort to the reduction of national expenditure as they do to the creation of taxes, the world would be all the better for the change.

LIST OF AUTHORITIES.

Revenue legislation : The various Acts quoted in text.

Incidence of duties, etc. : The various Customs handbooks.

Colonial revenue and smuggling : Australia, Tasmania, and New Zealand, Quebec, Mauritius, Newfoundland and New Brunswick, St. Kitts, Jamaica, 'Promiscuous,' Cape of Good Hope, and Nova Scotia Files ; General Letters, 1848.

Departmental regulations : General Letters, 1847, 1848, 1850 ; General Orders, 1853.

Ships' Registry : Privy Council Letter, 1847.

Commercial reciprocity : General Orders, 1852.

First Importation of Semolina : General Orders, 1852.

Chichester : General Orders, 1852.

Parliamentary proceedings : Hansard, April 21, 1853 (Commons).

British smuggling : General Letters, 1845, 1848, 1849, 1850 ; General Orders, 1852 ; 'Remarkable Seizures,' 1848, 1849, 1850, 1851, 1852, 1853, 1854, 1855.

CHAPTER IV

CUSTOMS LITERATI: PEACH; DOYLE; ALLINGHAM

Peach.

CHARLES WILLIAM PEACH was born in 1800 at Wansford, Northamptonshire. It appears that he was appointed to the Revenue Coastguard in 1824 through the influence of Lord Westmoreland. After several removals he was stationed at Gorran Haven, near Mevagissey, Cornwall, and remained there till 1845, when, at the intercession of Dr. Buckland, Sir Robert Peel appointed him to the Customs at Fowey. It is evident that he had been in the 'Mounted Guard' during his stay at Gorran Haven, for the notice of his appointment stands thus in the Establishment Book: 'Charles Wm. Peach, Mounted Guard, appointed Searcher, etc., Treasury Warrant 10th February, 1845.' He was removed to Peterhead as sub-controller in 1849, under Treasury Warrant 16th November. In 1853, by Treasury Warrant of 27th August, he was made controller at Wick, and remained in that office at a salary of £150 a year till 1861, when he was 'retired' with several other officers, on account of reductions rendered necessary by the Commercial Treaty with France. The Board's Minute of August 15, 1861, authorizing this proceeding, gives his age as sixty, his years of service as thirty-seven and seven-twelfths, and his retiring allowance as £130 a year.

An idea of his attainments may be best gleaned from the following extracts from the *Athenæum*'s obituary notice (No. 3,046, pp. 362, 363):

'Peach's taste for collecting was first awakened while on the coasts of Dorsetshire and Devonshire, where he soon acquired an intimate knowledge of the marine fauna of the south of England. His frequent shiftings were in many respects of considerable advantage to him. They gave him a wider range for his observations, and brought him into contact with scientific enthusiasts, from whom he obtained much useful knowledge and the loan of books. In return Peach was able to provide specimens which helped to clear up many points in natural history. Amongst others he was enabled to supply the Rev. Mr. Layton, of Catfield, Norfolk, with the bones required to complete the elephant found in the well-known "Forest Bed" of Norfolk, which is now in the British Museum. While at Gorran Haven Peach began to direct his observations to geological phenomena, and to cultivate his powers of observation. It was not long before he detected fossils in rocks previously regarded as destitute of organic remains. He at this time made one of the chief discoveries of his life in finding lower Silurian fossils in the rocks of Cornwall, which before that time were considered to be azoic. This discovery was of great value to Sir Henry de la Beche, who was then engaged on the Government Geological Survey, as it furnished him with a basis for mapping the rocks of south-western England.

'The British Association met at Plymouth in 1841, and to that meeting Peach communicated his first scientific paper, "On the Organic Remains of Cornwall." He became a member of the British Association, of the Devon and Cornwall Natural History Society, and of the Royal Cornwall Polytechnic Society. In 1843 he furnished to the Polytechnic Society a "Synopsis of the land and fresh-water shells, starfishes, sea-urchins, coralines, alcyonites, sponges, and marine algæ," which was printed in the "Transactions" for that year. This paper bore testimony to his industry, his habits of observation, and to his excellent self-training. After the

Plymouth meeting most of the eminent geologists and many of the naturalists who attended it proceeded into Cornwall. The Polytechnic Society at Falmouth was the centre of this gathering, and Charles Peach became their guide to many of the points of geological interest in the west of Cornwall. Peach thus formed an acquaintance with several men of eminence, which became, by his genial nature, a lifelong friendship. For many years he was a regular contributor to each of the three county societies of Cornwall, and his zeal received in many ways substantial recognition.

'All this time * this remarkable man never received more than £75 a year, and £30 for the keep of a horse. When it is remembered that Peach married in 1829, and had a family of seven sons and two daughters, it will be matter of surprise how he was enabled to maintain his intellectual pursuits amid the struggles of his everyday life.

'Peach was promoted to Peterhead in 1849, and to Wick in 1853. Here his duties were onerous; he had to measure large quantities of timber imported for the herring trade, and he was appointed Receiver of Wreck, which gave him the charge of 180 miles of coast. It was while on one of these journeys that he made the discovery of fossils in the altered rocks of the Highlands, which in Sir Roderick Murchison's hands afforded the key to the elucidation of the structure of that region.

'Mr. Peach formed a friendship with Robert Dick, and worked with him in the Old Red Sandstone fossils, and a living geologist has said of his labours in this field that Peach has done "more, indeed, than all other geologists put together." . . . It is pleasant to find that he was not without rewards which were gratifying to so simple-minded a man, who ever worked for the love of truth. The Prince Consort presented him with Professor Macgillivray's "Natural History of Deeside and Bræmar." The Council of the Geological Society of London in 1859

* During his stay at Gorran Haven.

awarded him the Wollaston fund for his discoveries in the rocks of Devonshire and Cornwall. In 1875 the Royal Society of Edinburgh gave him the Neill prize for excellence in natural history. The Royal Cornwall Polytechnic Society at two of their annual meetings gave him their silver medal for the arrangement and collection of zoophytes from the Cornish coast, and a bronze medal for a collection of algæ. Besides the above, Peach received numerous presents of books from natural history societies, and some small grants of money to enable him to pursue his investigations.

'Mr. Peach died in Edinburgh, on the 28th of February, in the 86th year of his age, respected by a large circle of scientific friends.'

Doyle.

Sir Francis Hastings Charles Doyle was born at Tadcaster, Yorkshire, in 1810. He was descended from an ancient Irish family, which had produced several military officers, all highly distinguished for personal courage.

He acquitted himself well at Eton and Oxford, and among his college intimates were many who afterwards became illustrious (Mr. Gladstone may be mentioned conspicuously). He was called to the Bar in 1837, but it is evident that he was unsuccessful, or that the occupation was not congenial, for in 1845 Sir Robert Peel made him Assistant-Solicitor of Excise. In 1846 he was appointed Receiver-General of Customs. A circular sent by the Customs Secretary to the collectors and controllers at various ports, and worded as follows, appears among the Customs records :

'*July 25th*, 1846.

'GENTLEMEN,

'Sir Francis Hastings Doyle, Bart., having been appointed Receiver-General and Cashier of Her Majesty's Customs in the room of William Boothby, Bart., deceased, I have it in command to acquaint you therewith, in order that your letters and remittances may be addressed and made payable to Sir Francis Hastings Doyle, in like manner as they were to his predecessor.'

Sir Francis, in his 'Reminiscences,' deals humorously with the matter of his Customs appointment. He writes: 'I was kind enough to accept it. I need hardly say that by so doing I gave up all hopes of legal or Parliamentary distinction, resting content with a safe and respectable mediocrity.' He had scarcely taken over the office ere one of the clerks absconded with £270, which sum the new Receiver-General had at once to make up out of his own pocket.*

Sir Francis was made Commissioner of Customs in 1870, in place of R. W. Grey, Esq., deceased. His fellow-Commissioners were Sir T. F. Fremantle, F. Goulburn, G. C. L. Berkeley, and F. Romilly, Esqs. He vacated office in 1883, being succeeded by Viscount Sudley, and died in 1888.

He was well known in his day as a poet, his chief productions being 'Miscellaneous Poems' (1834), 'The Two Destinies' (1844), 'Œdipus, King of Thebes' (1849), and 'The Return of the Guards, and other Poems' (1866). He succeeded Matthew Arnold as Professor of Poetry at Oxford in 1867, and published 'Lectures on Poetry' in 1869. He was re-elected in 1872, and received the distinction of D.C.L. when he resigned the Professorship in 1877.

Much of his verse deals with military incidents. He appears to have held as exalted an opinion of the British Army as Mr. Kipling does at the present day. He translated much verse, and his 'Lectures' display great powers of appreciation and much poetic enthusiasm. Yet it cannot be maintained that he was a great or even a skilful poet. He had an unfortunate knack of breaking down in the last line of a stanza, and many of his best efforts are marred by curious slips into bathos. These

* Later the Treasury refunded the money.

lapses are quite inexplicable, for he had been highly educated. If it be borne in mind that he was a life-long dabbler in the Castalian spring, and a Professor of Poetry at Oxford, they will appear unpardonable.

Below are a few specimens. The first is from 'The Return of the Guards, etc.,' and it should be pointed out that in his preface Sir Francis admitted that his object in publishing the verses was to obtain the vacant Professorship.

'Yes, they return ; but who return ?
The many or the few ?
Clothed with a name, in vain the same,
Face after face is new.'

Take the first stanza of 'The Doncaster St. Leger' ·

'The sun is bright, the sky is clear,
Above the crowded course,
As the mighty moment draweth near
Whose issue shows the horse.'

From 'The Private of the Buffs' :

'Last night among his fellow-roughs
He jested, quaffed, and swore—
A drunken private of the Buffs,
Who never looked before.'

The following extraordinary verse occurs in 'The Foster-Brother' :

'No fairer maid throughout the land than Gwennolak was seen,
The daughter of a noble house, a maiden of eighteen.
Dead the old lord, her father ; dead two sisters, and her mother.
Her father's wife was left, but of her own blood breathed no other.'

Yet he wrote 'The Loss of the Birkenhead,' which contains really fine lines :

'The brave who died,
Died without flinching, in the bloody surf ;
They sleep as well beneath that purple tide
As others under turf.

'They sleep as well, and, roused from their wild grave,
Wearing their wounds like stars, shall rise again,
Joint-heirs with Christ, because they bled to save
His weak ones, not in vain.'

Even in this, his best poem, he could not eliminate the fatal bathotic termination :

> ' That those whom God's high grace there saved from ill,
> Those also, left His martyrs in the bay,
> Though not by siege, though not in battle, still
> *Full well had earned their pay !!!*'

It is all very strange, especially when one reads his appreciative notice of Newman's ' Dream of Gerontius.'

His ' Reminiscences ' are interesting. They are the reminiscences of a fine old Tory, a man hot-blooded, observant, and humorous. It appears that he entertained an unbounded regard for Gladstone until the latter went over to the Liberal camp. When in 1880 Gladstone reassumed office at the head of a large majority, his old college friend sent him a blunt and characteristic letter, openly taunting the statesman with his change of principles. Thus wrote the then Commissioner of Customs :

' You are about to become the strongest Prime Minister that has been seen for many years. You are now an advanced and ever-advancing Liberal. Do you recollect, forty years ago and more, speaking to me thus : " A Scotch Tory is worse than an English Whig, a Scotch Whig is worse than an English Radical, and a Scotch Radical worse than the Devil himself !" And now, because Scotland has surrendered herself to that sulphureous element, you quote poor Lady Nairne's verses only to misapply them, and make her call this infernal region of yours " The Land o' the Leal !" '

Even Dr. Johnson was not a more strenuous upholder of what may with justice be called the heroic old English Toryism. Sir Francis's hatred of the average official political economist was remarkable, and distinctly laudable. ' Misplaced thrift,' said he—' the thrift, for instance, of that narrow-minded skinflint Joseph Hume, upon whom Mr. Gladstone showered his praises the other day, to flatter the people of Aberdeen—is simply the worst form of extravagance.'

Sir Francis, like Johnson and Borrow, had an unaccountable antipathy to Scotsmen, and an ardent admiration of English institutions, sports, and rural life. The average man finds little difference between Lowland Scots and Yorkshiremen, yet Sir Francis loved the latter race as much as he disliked the former. There can be no doubt that he was highly eccentric. Many anecdotes that prove this survive in the department, but it appears that he was extremely popular in the Service, both with subordinates and fellow-Commissioners.

His account of an interview with Gladstone just before the passing of one of the Reform Bills illustrates the great statesman's profound distrust of civil servants. 'I say,' said Sir Francis, 'among other roughs, are you going to let me have a vote now ?'* Gladstone replied with great vehemence : 'Never, until universal suffrage is reached ; never, with my consent, shall a civil servant go to the poll !'

Allingham.

William Allingham was born at Ballyshannon, Donegal, in 1824, and appointed to the Customs in 1846. His official record runs thus :

Appointed principal coast officer, Donegal, March 16, 1846.
Appointed sub-collector, Ramsay, Isle of Man, July 3, 1849.
Appointed sub-collector, Ballyshannon, October 28, 1849.
Appointed controller, Coleraine, September 14, 1853.
Resigned, February, 1854.
Reappointed as controller, New Ross, June 19, 1854.
Appointed sub-collector, Ballyshannon, June 3, 1855.
Appointed clerk, fifth class, Examiner's office, London, October 1, 1862.
Appointed principal coast officer, Lymington, May 8, 1863.
Final resignation accepted under Board's Order of June 18, 1870.

It appears he had written some verse, and contributed to the London magazines, prior to his appointment, and he states in his diary that when he went to Belfast in

* Civil servants were at that time disabled from voting.

1846 to be instructed in Customs work he 'talked to the clerks about literature and poetry in a way that excited some astonishment.'

He continued to write, and found little difficulty in attracting the attention of the leading literary men of the day. He visited London on several occasions, and interviewed Leigh Hunt, Carlyle, Thackeray, Coventry Patmore, Rossetti, and other 'lions.' Later he became acquainted with Tennyson, and the intimacy was only severed by death.

He published 'Poems' in 1850, and 'Day and Night Songs' in 1854. His first resignation of office was a step towards taking up literature as a profession, but the attempt was not successful. It is stated that he received a grant of £60 a year in 1864 in acknowledgment of his literary merits, and that this was afterwards made £100. He published 'Laurence Bloomfield in Ireland'—his longest piece of verse—in 1864, and 'Fifty Modern Poems' in 1865. He edited one or two anthologies, and contributed much, both in prose and verse, to the magazines. After his final resignation he became sub-editor of *Fraser's Magazine*, and editor in 1874, retaining the office till 1879. He died in 1889.

Allingham must have been a man of engaging manners and amiable disposition, to attract as he did the friendship of so many distinguished men, for his literary powers, especially in verse, were extremely meagre. More tiresome poetry than his would be difficult to find, even among the verse produced by his contemporaries, Eliza Cook and Miller the basket-maker. His work is quite destitute of invention, and often extremely bathotic, and his constructive faculty may with justice be described as contemptible. Some of his verses are altogether absurd, almost rivalling the inimitable banality produced by that older Customs official Congreve :

> 'Speak, speak your desire ;
> I'm all over fire ;
> Say what you require.
> I'll grant it. Now let us retire.'

A few quotations from Allingham's verse should be highly convincing :

'Autumnal sunshine spread on Irish hills,
Imagination's brightening mirror fills,
Wherein a horseman on a handsome grey
Along the high road takes his easy way.'

'My Lady Harvey comes of Shropshire blood:
Stately, with finished manners, cold of mood.
Her eldest son is in the Guards ; her next
At Eton. Her two daughters—I'm perplext
To specify young ladies—they are tall,
Dark-haired, and smile in speaking. That is all.'

'Along the winding road to Lisnamoy
The drover trudges and the country boy.'

'Flee from London, good my Walter! boundless jail of bricks and gas,
Care not if your Exhibition swarm with portrait and Gil Blas.'

The following, from 'The Abbot of Innisfallen,' reveals Allingham at his most bathotic :

'Low kneeled that blessed Abbot,
When the dawn was waxing bright ;
He prayed a great prayer for Ireland,
He prayed with all his might.

'Low kneeled that good old Father,
When the sun *began to dart ;*
He prayed a prayer for all mankind,
He prayed it from his heart.'

The utter deeps of deadly dulness are sounded in the following :

'Peasant cots with humble haggarts, mansions with obsequious groves :
A spire, a steeple, rival standards which the liberal distance loves
To set in union : There the dear but dirty little town abides :
And you and I come home to dinner after all our walks and rides.'

'Learning can nourish Wisdom, when good food
Is quietly digested, but too oft
Unfit, ill-cook'd, or overloaded meals
Lie crude, and swell the belly with wind, or breed
Dull fat, mistook for portliness and strength.'

From 'Blackberries' :

'I never write from personal spite
So much as a single word ;
When hot I feel 'tis public zeal,
Which may seem to you absurd.'

And :

> ' I heard the dogs howl in the moonlight night,
> And I went to the window to see the sight :
> All the dead that ever I knew
> Going one by one and two by two.'

How such preposterous stuff ever attained publication, how it passed the reviewers, how it went into several editions, and why in the British Museum Catalogue the title ' Poet ' distinguishes William Allingham of Ballyshannon from William Allingham who wrote a treatise on fistula, must be left to our readers' merciful consideration. A more vital matter of debate intrudes. William Allingham, ' Poet,' was sub-editor of *Fraser's* for five years, and editor for another five. No doubt reams of verse were submitted for his inspection. It is unlikely that he was fitted to judge poetry, who deliberately wrote and published the drivel quoted. The decay of English liking for verse, and the suicidal leanings of some of our real modern poets, may be easily accounted for, if within the last thirty years there have been many such editors and sub-editors.

The most interesting thing done by Allingham is his ' Diary,' a mass of jottings, principally about his distinguished friends. It is evident that he was not destitute of humour, though his verse in a way implies that he was. He wrote : ' I have been an official all my life without the least turn for it. I never could attain a true official manner, which is highly artificial, and handles trifles with ludicrously disproportionate gravity.' He uttered another capital ' aside ' upon the futility of the Victorian methods of ' improving ' the working classes. ' Cloudy, but warm. Institution. Take the chair at Penny Reading. Any use ?' He quoted with evident relish Leigh Hunt's remark upon Robert the Obscurantist : ' Shakspere and Milton wrote plainly, the Sun and Moon write plainly : why can't Browning ?' He told of Edward Fitzgerald, that gin-soaked, tobacco-scented, shabbily-dressed bundle of genius and humour, that he kept a rough book in which he recorded all the ' howlers ' he came across. The book was labelled ' Half-hours with the Worst Authors,' and Allingham was surprised that it was never published. It is likely that he would have found himself figuring in it, to an extent that would have surprised him still more.

APPENDIX

ILLUSTRATIVE DOCUMENTS

No. 1. *Certified copy, made in* 1671, *of the report made in* 1559, *by Amadas and Trevanion, of their survey of Plymouth, Looe, Fowey, Truro, Penryn, Mount's Bay, St. Ives, and Padstow.*

'TO THE RIGHT HONBLE LORDS AND BARONS OF OUR SOVRAIGNE LADY THE QUEEN'S TIES EXCHQR THEIR MOST HUMBLE WILLIAM AMADAS CUSTOMER OF THE PORTS OF PLYMOUTH AND FOWEY IN THE COUNTYS OF DEVON AND CORNWALL AND JOHN TREVANYON COMPTROLL' THERE WITH ALL REV'RENT SUBMISSION AND DOE MAKE OUR SUITE TO YOUR HONORS AS FOLLS ON, ETC.

'Whereas our said most dread Soveraigne Lady the Queen by her Letters patents hath assigned and appoynted us with divers others in the said Lres patents nominated to veiw and pruse* Limit and appoynt all such Places and Creekes to the said Ports belonging where a Customer Comptroll' and Searcher or their Deputys have been Resident by the space of tenne yeares before the Act in that behalfe made at the Parliament begun at Westminster the three and twentieth of January in the first yeare of the Raigne of our said Soveraigne Lady Elizabeth by the Grace of God of England France and Ireland Queen Defender of the Faith &c., and there Prorogued till the five and twentieth of the same month and then and there holden kept and continued untill the Disolution of the same being the eight of May then next ensueing as in the same Act with the same Lres Patents hereunto annexed more at large appeareth. By virtue whereof wee the said William Amadas and John Trevanyon named in the said Comiĉon†

* View and peruse. † Commission.

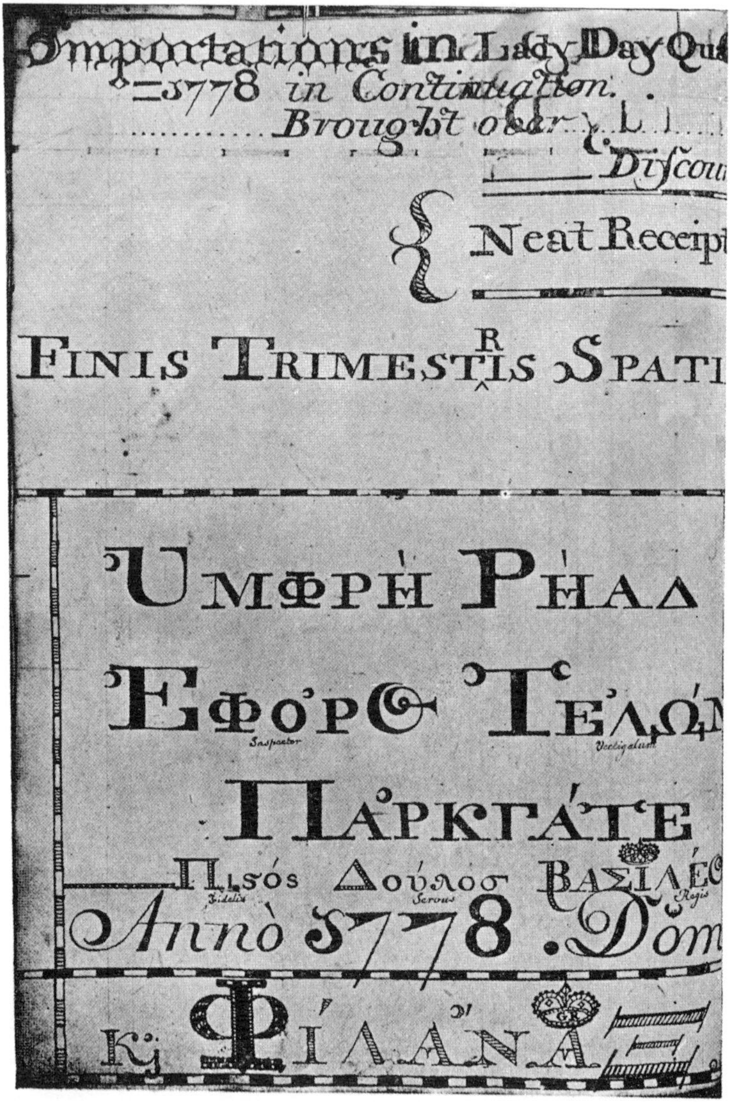

SPECIMEN PAGES FROM REGISTER KEPT BY HUMPHREY READ, DEPUTY-CONTROLLER, PARKG

This curious document is in the Customs Library. (It will be seen that little duty was taken.)

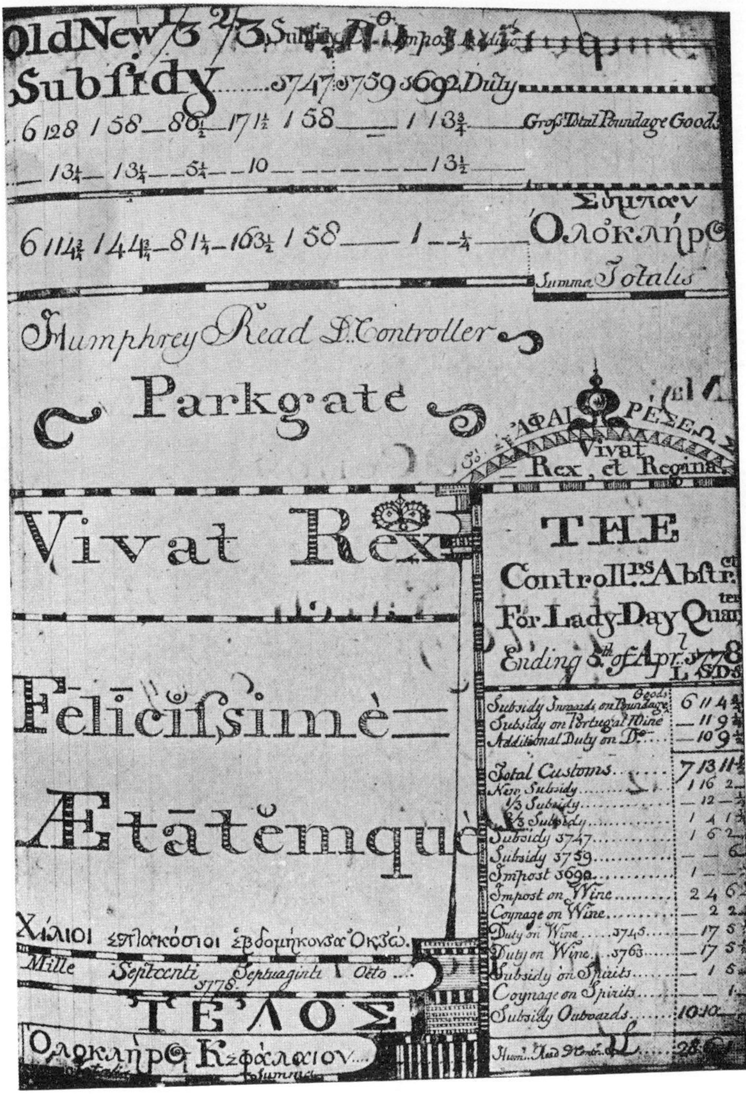
Old New 1/3 2/3 Subsidy Additional Impost ...
Subsidy .... 3747 3759 3692 Duty
6 12 8 1 5 8 — 8 8½ — 17 1½ 1 5 8 — 1 1 3¾ — Gross Total Poundage Goods
— 13¼ — 13¼ — 5¼ — 10 — — 13½ —
Συλλαβών
6 11 4¾ 1 4 4¾ — 8 1¼ — 16 3½ 1 5 8 — 1 — ¼ — Ολόκληρο
Summa Totalis
Humphrey Read D. Controller
Parkgate
Vivat Rex, et Regina
Vivat Rex
THE
Controll.rs Abstract
For Lady Day Quarter
Ending 5th of Apr. 1778
L S D

	L	S	D
Subsidy Inwards on Poundage Goods	6	11	4¾
Subsidy on Portugal Wine	—	11	9
Additional Duty on Do.	—	10	9
Total Customs	7	13	11½
New Subsidy	1	16	2
1/3 Subsidy	—	12	—
2/3 Subsidy	1	4	1
Subsidy 3747	1	6	2
Subsidy 3759	—	—	6
Impost 3692	1	—	—
Impost on Wine	2	4	6
Coynage on Wine	—	2	2
Duty on Wine 3745	—	17	5
Duty on Wine 3763	—	17	5
Subsidy on Spirits	—	1	5
Coynage on Spirits	—	—	1
Subsidy Outwards		10	10
Hum. Read D. Contr.	28		

Felicissimè
Ætatèmque
Χίλιοι επτακόσιοι εβδομήκοντα Οκτώ
Mille Septcenti Septuaginti Octo 1778
ΤΈΛΟΣ
Ολόκληρο Κεφάλαιον
Totalis Summa

Between pp. 406-7.

have veiwed and p[r]used the said Ports Places and Creekes and have Limitted and Appoynted heereunder written to bee open Places of Charging and Discharging of wares and M'chandizes as well comeing from the p[r]tes* of beyond the Seas into the said Ports Places and Creekes as goeing out of the same according to the tenor of the Statute aforesaid in manner and forme following (that is to say)

'Att the Port and Towne of Plymouth the Key† there comonly called Hawkins his Key is appoynted for the only Place of Lading and unlading charging and Discharging of all wares and m'chandizes that hereafter shall be Laden and unladen charged and Discharged within the said Port containing in Length by the waters side seaven score foot and in breadth six score foot.

'Item at the Towne of Lowe the Key there comonly called the Towne Key is appoynted (etc., etc.) containing in Breadth forty foot and in Length three score foot.

'Item at the Towne and Port of Fowey the Key there is appoynted (etc., etc.) containing in Length five hundred foot and in breadth six score foot and bounded on the South side with a key comonly called Burlaces his Key And on the North side with a Key there comonly called Trevarrock's Key.

'Item at the Towne of Truroe the key there comonly called the Towne Key is appoynted (etc., etc.) containing in Length five hundred foot and in breadth one hundred foot.

'Item at the Towne of Penryn the Key there is appoynted (etc., etc.) containing in Length three hundred foot from the North end of the Bridge there comonly called the Colledge Bridge to a Courtlage called Summer Court and in breadth twenty foot. And soe likewise from the South end of the said Bridge unto an Oake directly over against the said Summer Court in Length other three hundred foot and in breadth other twenty foot.

'Item at Mount's Bay the Key of Penzance is appoynted (etc., etc.) containing in Length fower hundred and twenty foot and in breadth sixteen foot.

'Item at the Towne of St. Ives the Key there comonly called the Towne Key is appoynted (etc., etc.) containing in Length two hundred and fower foot and in breadth fourteen foot.

'Item And at the Towne of Paddistowe the Key there commonly called the Towne Key is appoynted (etc., etc.) containing in Length eight hundred foot and in Breadth sixteen foot.

* Parts. † Quay.

'All which p'misses* wee have here certiffied unto yo[r] Hon[ors] according to the tenor of the said Lres Patents of Comicon to us amongst others directed. In Witness whereof wee the said William Amadas and John Trevanyon to these p'sents have sett our Seales the last day of August in the first yeare of the Raigne of our said Soveraigne Lady Elizabeth by the Grace of God Queen of England France and Ireland Defender of the Faith,' &c.

No. 2. *Extracts from the Book of Rates,* 1660 (*Old Subsidy*), *showing the divisions and rating for Customs of foreign cloth, linen, leather, and iron.* (*The Customs 'values' are shown. Divide by twenty for the duty, the rate being* 5 *per cent. on the value. N.B.—For linens, add half the duty thus obtained, there being a special impost on them.*)

		£	s.	d.
'All manner of woollen cloths imported, per yard		8	10	0†
Cloaks of felt, the piece		2	0	0
Coverlets of Scotland, the piece		0	15	0
Callicoes imp[d], the piece		0	10	0
Flannel, the yard		0	1	8
Frise of Ireland, the yard		0	0	9
Cambricks, the piece (13 ells)		2	0	0
Canvas	Dutch and Hessian (120 ells)	3	10	0
	French (narrow) ,,	6	0	0
	,, (broad) ,,	15	0	0
	Packing ,,	2	10	0
Damask	Holland tabling the yd.	1	0	0
	,, towelling ,,	0	7	0
	Silesia tabling ,,	0	4	0
	,, towelling ,,	0	1	4
Diaper	Holland tabling ,,	0	9	0
	,, towelling ,,	0	3	0
	Silesia tabling ,,	0	3	4
	,, towelling ,,	0	1	4
Lawns	French, the piece	1	10	0
	Silesia ,, (4 to 8 yds.)	0	10	0
Linen cloth of the Netherlands, the ell		0	5	0
Do.	Drilling and duck (120 ells)	2	0	0
Do.	Danish, the ell	0	1	8
Do.	Hambro and Silesia (broad) (120 ells)	10	0	0
Do.	,, ,, (narrow) ,,	8	0	0
Do.	Hinderlands and Russian (narrow) (120 ells)	2	8	4
Do.	Irish (120 ells)	2	0	0
Do.	Dowlas (106 ells)	5	0	0
Do.	Minsters (linens) (1,500 ells)	56	13	4
Do.	Oxenbrigs ,, ,,	60	0	0

* Premises.

† Of course utterly prohibitive.

			£	s.	d.
Linen cloth	Polonias, Ulsters, Hanovers, Lubecks, Westphalias, Harfords, and all other narrow cloths of Dutchland and the East Country* ..	120 ells	4	0	0
Leather ..	Basils, the dozen		20	0	0
	Spanish, the doz skins		5	0	0
	Danish ,, ...		2	0	0
	Turkish and East India, the doz skins		2	0	0
Iron ..	Amys, Spanish, Danish, Swedish, the ton		7	0	0
	Small chimney backs, each		0	6	8
	Large ,, ,, ,, ...		0	13	4
	Kettle bands, the cwt.		2	0	0
	Fire irons, the gross		0	10	0
Iron Hoops, the cwt.			1	6	8'

English cloth paid on exportation a specific duty (3s. 4d. on each short cloth if exported by denizens, 6s. 8d. if by aliens. A short cloth was 28 yards in length and 64 pounds in weight). English leather manufactures paid ½d. a pound, English iron 16s. a ton (value £16), English linen 6d. the 40 ells.

No. 3. *Copy of Bill of Entry* (*No.* 5), *showing imports and exports, London, June* 30, 1660, *with ports of shipment and destination, importers' and exporters' names, and lists of ships entered inward and cleared outward.*

'LONDON, IMPORTED, JUNE 30, 1660.

Barbados.	Nico. Enos	25	casks sugar.
	Peter Lear	33	
	Fran. Raines ..	51	
	Paul Allestry ..	87	
	John Miller	36	
	Nath. Whitfeild ..	2	
	Hen. Barton ..	9	
	Rich. Alie	109	
	Rich. Batson ..	15	
	Tho. Crisp	2	
	Tho. Chevely ..	70	
	George Lock ..	2	
	Hen. Grigg	20	
	,, ...	4	bags cottons.
	James Watkins ..	11	
	Sam. Osborn ..	28	bags ginger.
Hambro.	Na. Lownds ..	54	barrels plates.
	John Claypole ..	4	fats iron wyer.
	Tho. Tyte	40	C.† ells Germany linen.
	Wil. Williams ..	60	,, oxenbrigs.‡
	Godf. Lee	58	,, ,,
	Rob. Gore	20	,, ,,
		2400	l§ Dutch yarn.

* (All German and Dutch linen not above three-quarters and a half broad accounted 'narrow.')

† 40 C. = 4,000. ‡ A kind of linen. § Pounds.

Virginia.	John Hatch	..	6 hhds tobacco.
	Wil. Hebb ..	..	8 ,, ,,
	Rich. Audley	..	10 ,, ,,
	Rob. Skelton	..	7 ,, ,,
	Job Sayer ..	..	10 ,, ,,
Hambro.	Cha. Deering	..	86 C.* steel.
Flushing.	Edw. Dethick	..	570 ells linen.
	Peter Roys ..	..	2000 pantiles.
Rochel.	Hen. Allen ..	..	21 tuns vinegar.
Amsterdam.	Tho. Dava ..	..	3 tuns linseed oyl, 5 fats iron wyer, 2 barrels anotto.
	Rich. Baker	..	13 tuns trayn oyl.
Burdeaux.	Tho. Fincham	..	6 tuns spirits, 8 tuns vinegar.
Hambro.	Tho. Bellingham	..	30 C. ells minsters, 8 barrels smalts, 30 C. ells inderlens.†
Amsterdam.	Jacob Balde	..	2 fats drest hemp, 20 C. hemp
Galipoly.	Ra. Lee ..	..	6 tuns oyl, 2 tuns argol.
France.	John Lethulier	..	80 quarters barly.
Cane‡	James Corcellis	..	15 C. ells canvas.
	Law. Martel	..	260 reames paper.
Harlem.	Wil. Somers	..	13 dozen incle.§
Rochel.	John Marishal	..	10 tuns French wine.
Yarmouth.	Wil. Perkins	..	7 ,, ,, ,,‖

'SIX SHIPS ENTERED INWARDS.

The Prosperous, John Tomson, @ Dublin.
The Constant Rebecca, Jer. Stilgo, @ Stockholm.
The Orenge Tree, Geo. Agenor, @ Berbadoes.
And three ships from Norway.

'EXPORTED, JUNE 30, 1660.

Amsterdam.	Peter Mathews	..	10 serges.
Hambro.	Gerd. Hockle	..	59 ,,
	,, ,,	..	6 cloth rashes.
Rotterdam.	Wil. Cargel ..	..	25 serges.
	,, ,, ..	..	4 bearskins.
	,, ,, ..	..	14 otterskins.
	(An illegible entry.)		
Deip.¶	Hen. Whitead	..	4 serges.
	Wil. Spiller ..	..	20 ,,
	Edw. Ware ..	..	7 ,,
	,, ,, ..	..	3 dozen calve skins.
	John Remington	..	20 Spanish cloths.
	,, ,,	..	64 double bays.**
	Edw. Barkley	..	109 dozen hose.
Genoa.	John Dowse	..	25 ,, ,,
	Dan. Edwards	..	20 minikin bays.
Barbadoes.	Isaac Barrow	..	10 C. wrought iron.
	James Blar ..	..	2 short cloths.
Smirna.	John Rand	..	12 ,, ,,
	,, ,,	..	6 long ,,

* Cwt. † Minsters and Hinderlands, certain kinds of linen.
‡ Canet, or Cannes? § Inkle.
‖ Liable to the London surtax when removed from an outport.
¶ Dieppe. ** A kind of West-country cloth.

Dort.	Edw. Tidcomb	..	30 short cloths.
	,, ,,	..	4 long ,,
Legorn.	Tho. Goodyear	..	220 perpetuanos.*
Smirna.	Ralph Lee ..	..	5 fodder lead.
Roan.†	James Burton	..	3 ,, ,,
	Steph. Bolton	..	4. C. verditor.
St. Mallo's.	Hen. Oliver ..	..	120 dozen jumps.‡
Russia.	John Cliffe ..	..	336 lb. cloth shreds.
Burdeaux.	Mich. Clipsham	..	90 firkins butter.
Ireland.	John Wright	..	486 lb. Virginia tobacco.
Guinny.§	Tho. Bell ..	..	38 C. copper bars.
	,, ,, ..	..	17 C. brass rings.

'Foreign Goods Exported by Certificate.

Russia.	John Gourney	..	7 C. olibanum.
Legorn.	John Welden	..	10 C. red earth.
Hambro.	,, ,,	..	30 ,, ,, ,,
	Tho. Sanders	..	43 C. panellis sugar.
	Ph. Graxty ..	..	4 ,, ,, ,,
Amsterdam.	Nich. Cook ..	..	890 lb. mohair yarn.
	Law. Sawcer	..	1117 calicos.
Rotterdam.	Roger Scattergood	..	707 ,,
Roan.	John Dickins	..	7000 lb. cotton wool.‖
	,, ,,	..	300 ,, ,, yarn.
Deip.	Law. Sawcer	..	50 pieces bengal stuffs.
New England.	Edw. Mytton	..	52 birding-pieces.¶
Barbadoes.	Isaac Barton	..	200 ells canvas.

'Ships Cleared Out.

The Peter, Wil. Buckley, for St. Vallery.
The Hope, And^r Lehot, for Roan.
The Gift of God, Rob. Deneale, for Deip.'

No. 4. *Order of Embargo upon vessels carrying naval stores (during war with Holland,* 1665). *From Letter-Book of Wells.*

'Whereas dureing the present warr wth the Dutch his Maties service doth necessarily require extraordnary supply of Navall p'vitions for the timely p'viding whereof all good & lawfull meanes are to bee made use of: these are therefore in pursuance of a warr^t from his Royall Highnesse James Duke of Yorke Ld High Admirall of England &c to will & require you y^t when any shipps or vessells wherein there shall bee any p'vitions or stores necessary for his Maties Navy shall bee sent

* A kind of cloth or linen? † Rouen. ‡ Query. § Guinea. ‖ Raw cotton. ¶ Fowling-pieces.

into any Port or Creek within the limits of yo[r] Port of Lynn & its memb[rs] by any private man of warre you take espetiall care to send notice of the same to me by the first opportunity to the end y[t] care may bee taken for the buying of the same of the true proprietor at the Markett price: And you are not to suffer the said p'vitions or stores to be carried out of such port or creek or to bee any waies disposed of untill you shall receive direccons concerning the same from me & in case by accident any other shipp or vessell shall be brought or come into any port or Creek within yo[r] said limits or jurisdiccon whose lading or any considerable pt thereof shall consist of Navall p'vitions you are to cause the same to be stoppt and detained untill further order and to give notice thereof to me and for so doeing this shall be yo[r] Warr[t]. Given under my hand and seale at Raigneham this 3[d] day of Jan[y], 1665.

'TOWNSHEND.

'To the Mayor of the towne of Lynn Regis & to the offic[rs] of his Ma[ties] Customs there.'

No. 5. *Form of Master's declaration at report inward of an English ship from Malaga,* 1678. *From the Letter-Book of Wells.*

'You doe affirme and sweare that you are the person whose name is subscribed hereunto, that you are Master of the shipp whereof you now make entry, and that there hath been no other Master dureing this voyage, that the said shipp is English-built, and that all the owners of the said shipp are English, that the number of the Marriners of the said shipp's Company are 18 Englishmen and 4 forreigners, that shee took in her present lading in the Port of Malaga, that the entry now tendered by you containes a just accompt of the Burthen, contents, and ladeing of the said shipp with the particular marks, numbers, quantities, and contents of every parcell of goods therein laden, as also of the names of the merchants to the best of your knowledge: And that you have not broken bulke nor delivered any goods out of the said shipp, since her ladeing in the said Port of Malaga: And in cause you finde any other goods not mencꝯoned in this entry you will give the Principall Officer notice thereof before the delivery thereof out of the said shipp.'

No. 6. *Order in Council issued at accession of James II., reaffirming the repeal of aliens' duties on goods the product of the English realm* (*January* 22, 1685-86). *From the Letter-Book of Wells.*

BY THE KING'S MOST EXCELLENT MAJ^TIE & THE LORDS OF HIS MAJ^TIE'S MOST HONOR^BLE PRIVY COUNCELL.

'Uppon reading ye Peticon of Sr Peter Vandeputt & others on behalfe of themselves & severall other merchants of the City of London, setting forth that whereas by an Act in the twelfth yeere of the Raigne of his late Maj^tie, entituled, a Subsidy granted to the King of Tonnage & Poundage & other sumes of money payable uppon merchandise exported & imported it was enacted among other things y^t of every £ value of any of the native comodities of this Realme, or Manufacture wrought of such Native Comodities, to bee carried out of this Realme by any Merchant Aliens, according to the value of the Booke of Rates therein mentioned and referred unto, there should be paid unto his said Matie the sum of two shillings, being double as much as any natives paid, wch said Act the Parliam^t afterwards uppon mature deliberation finding to bee p'judicially to hinder the exportation of the native woollen manufactures, leade, tinn, & fish, did by an Act for taking off Aliens' Dutys uppon Comodities of the growth p'duct & Manufacture of the Nation, repeal so much thereof as did concerne any Custome or Subsidy uppon any of the native Comodities of this kingdome, to bee exported out of this Realme, payable by any Merchant Alien made Denisen, or other stranger or Alien, over and above the Custome & Subsidie payable by his Maj^ties naturall-born Subjects: Ever since the making of wch said Act merchant Aliens & strangers & theire factors have paid no more Custome for any of the Native Comodities exported by them out of this Realme (Coales excepted) than his Maties naturall-borne Subjects have done, by which the Petitioners conceived y^t that the Trade of the woollen Manufacture & of the Native Comodities had beene much encouraged & the Revenue of the Crowne not thereby lessened.

'Further (by their said Peticon) humbly representing, y^t of late the Comission^rs & Offic^rs of his Maj^ties Customes, uppon the grant of the Customes as they were settled the twelfth yeere of his Maties Reigne, require from all Merchant strangers and Aliens the double duty in the said Act mencõned, which if continued would p'bably lessen the exportation of the native goods of the growth of this kingdome, and most certeinely remove part of the trade from the hands of the faire trading Merchants, his Maties good subjects who justly pay his Maj[ties] Customes (not onely for themselves but as factors) into the hands of slight persons & unfaire traders, who make little scruple of Defrauding his Maj[ty] and colouring Strangers goods, to the great p'judice of the Petitioners' trade: Praying y[t] his Maj[ty] would give direc̄c̄on to take no other Customes from Merchant Aliens & Strangers or their factors, for goods exported of the native p'duct of this kingdome, then were payable by the Statute of the twenty-fifth of his late Maj[ties] Reign. And upon heareing the Comissioners of his Maj[ties] Customes thereuppon, his Maj[ty] was pleased to declare his Royall pleasure in favour of the Petitioners,' &c., &c.

(The Order proceeds to state that the king will take no more of aliens than of denizens upon such goods exported, as in the latter part of his predecessor's reign, and this although his Subsidy was granted at the rates laid down in the early part of said reign.) 'And if his Maj[ty] shall hereafter finde cause to alter his Royall pleasure, he will give timely notice thereof, to the end that noe person may be surprised.

'Whitehall, Treasury Chambers, 28th January, 1685. Lett the Comissioners for his Maj[tie] take care y[t] the Order of Councell whereof the within written is a true coppie bee duly complied with according to his Maj[ties] Royall Pleasure therein declared.

'ROCHESTER.'

No. 7. Collector and controller of Yarmouth to Board, June 3, 1689.

'HON[BLE] SIRS,

'There is brought into this port by Capt. Fitzpatrick, Comander of their Ma[tys] Frigott the *Lark*, a privatere belonging to Dunkirk. The Sayles and Runing Rigging we have taken into Custody, and the men, being 21 in number, he put on shore on Satturday last. Our Towne Goale being not capable of receiving soe many p'sons wee were forced to desire the assistance of a Justice of the Peace in the County to comitt them to the County Goale at Norwich, w[ch], according to yo[r] order of the 30th Aprill last, wee give you accompt thereof.

'Wee have given order for the men to have twopence a day allowance for y[e] p'sent & if yo[r] Hon[rs] shall think fitt to abate of that, or allow more, shall observe yo[r] orders.

'Wee find ye Majistrates of this port verry ready to assist us as farr as lies in their powre, but canot comit any p'son to ye County Goale w^th^out the assistance of a Justice of ye Peass in ye Country, soe that it will be the more charge to theire Ma^tys^. If yor Hon^rs^ shall think fitt to allow thereof, wee shall p'ceed as wee have done.

'Three of ye p'sons in ye privatere above menc̃oned being Sweeds,* formerly taken by the French, & were forced to goe into the s^d^ privatere, the Capt has taken into theire Ma^ts^ Service ye 2nd Inst.'

No. 8. Seizure Note (Irish Customs), 1699.

'July 17th, 1699. Seised by Alexand^r^ Erwin, in a passeng^rs^ bundle, on board the *Seafarer* of Livp^le^,† Henry Ballintin M~r~, one pce of Black Sarge,‡ and sent to the Store the 18 of July, 1699, the Ship being Outward Bound, and it not Entred.

'A^x^ ERWIN.'

No. 9. Board to Surveyor of Wells, demanding explanation as to a certificate of English taking of fish, irregularly granted. From the Letter-Book of Wells.

'MR. GOODWIN,

'We have before us a p'mitt dated in y^r^ Port ye 6th Novemb' last signed by y^r^ selfe ye Custo^r^ and Collr & by Mr. Isaackston ye Comp^t^ for 5900 English Caught fish in ye True-love of Wells Robt Pin for Newcastle, wch wee are informed was sent after ye vessell to Scarborough when ye fish was under ye hands & examination by ye officers of y^t^ Port, which wee take to bee a very irregular proceeding of yrs, & expect you give us satisfaction how you came to grant the said Permitt, what ground you had for soe doeing, & what knowledge you had of the takeing and loading ye said fish, & give us an Acc^t^ of all circumstances of ye case that might induce you to y^r^ granting ye said Permitt, for that wee are credibly informed ye said fish was never in y~r~ Port : Wee rest,

'Y^r^ loveing friends,
T. NEWPORT.
C. GODOLPHIN.
SAM. CLARKE.
ROB^T^ HENLY.

'Cust° Ho. London
24th *Decr* 1700.'

* Swedes. † Liverpool. ‡ Serge.

No. 10. *Statement of the average prices of middling wheat from 1697 to 1820, of the duties actually leviable under the 'sliding scale' when wheat was at the prices shown, and of the balance of imports and exports of corn food-stuffs, from 1697 to 1794. Compiled by the Authors from official returns and the various Books of Rates.*

Periods.	*Prices of wheat per statute quarter.*	*Duty actually leviable on imported wheat.*	*Excess in quarters of imports of corn food-stuffs over exports.*	*Explanatory remarks.*
	£ s. d.	£ s. d.		
5 years ending—1701	2 2 8	0 18 0	139,866	This included the duty under the 'New Subsidy.'
6 years ending—1707	1 5 11	0 19 9	289,304	This included the duties leviable under the '⅓ and ⅔ Subsidies' (discount deducted).
4 years ending—1711	2 9 9	0 16 7	299,367	The duty less because the price exceeded 44s.
1715	1 17 8	0 19 9	453,986	
1719	1 13 1	,,	485,852	
5 years ending—1724	1 8 10	,,	532,732	
1729	1 17 7	,,	216,643	
1734	1 5 9	,,	468,244	
1739	1 10 10	,,	597,462	
1744	1 8 7	,,	446,378	
1749	1 7 9	19s. 9d. till 1747; £1 1s. 9d. 1747-49	932,593	Duty higher in and after 1747. Increased by the '1747 Subsidy.'
1754	1 10 5	1 1 9	1,080,077	
1759	1 16 2	,,	273,805	
1764	1 10 7	,,	696,117	

Periods.	*Prices of wheat per statute quarter.*	*Duty actually leviable on imported wheat.*	*Excess in quarters of imports of corn food-stuffs over exports.*	*Explanatory remarks.*
5 years ending—	£ *s.* *d.*			
1769	2 3 2	Duty free under temporary Acts of relief.	223,184	
1774	2 7 9	Do. till 1773. In 1773-74, 16s. 11d.	276,206	1773-74, duty less because price exceeded 44s.
1779	2 0 9	1774-78, £1 1s. 9d. 1779, £1 2s. 10d.	290,595	1779, duty higher because increased by an impost of 5 per cent. on proceeds.
1784	2 5 9	1779-81, 17s. 10d.	185,906	Price exceeded 44s.
		1782-84, 18s. 8d.		Duty increased in 1782 by another impost of 5 per cent. on proceeds. (Discounts abolished in 1781.)
		£ *s.* *d.*		
1789	2 3 3	1 4 3	198,716	Price low. The duty is as levied on cheap wheat before 1779=£1 1s. 9d. *plus* two imposts of 5 per cent. and the amount previously allowed as discount. (N.B.—Consolidation Act of 1787 raised the limit price from 44s. to 48s.)
•1794	2 7 2	1 4 3	1,145,584	The sliding scale altered in 1791. Limit price raised from 48s. to 50s.

Periods.	Prices of wheat per statute quarter.	Duties actually leviable on imported wheat.		Explanatory remarks.
		From foreign countries.	From British Plantations.	
	£ s. d.	£ s. d.	£ s. d.	
1795	3 14 2	0 0 6	0 0 6	'The second low duty.' Price above 54s. a quarter for foreign and above 52s. for Plantation wheat.
1796	3 17 1	,,	,,	
1797	2 13 1	0 2 9	0 0 6	Two temporary imposts of 5 per cent. each on proceeds during 1797. Not added here to duty on Plantation wheat because result fractional. Duty 'first low duty' for foreign. Price between 50s. and 54s. (foreign), but above 52s. (Plantation).
1798	2 10 3	0 2 9	0 2 9	'First low duty' for both. Plantation limit 48s. to 52s.
1799	3 7 6	0 0 6	0 0 6	'Second low duty' for both.
1800	5 13 7	0 0 6	0 0 6	
1801	5 18 3	,,	,,	
1802	3 7 5	,,	,,	
1803	2 16 6	,,	,,	
1804	3 0 1	1 4 3	,,	Sliding scale altered. High duty chargeable on foreign wheat when under 63s.; on Plantation when under 53s.
1805	4 17 10	0 0 6	,,	
1806	3 19 0	,,	,,	
1807	3 13 3	,,	,,	N.B.—From 1803 to 1814 the 'temporary war duties' were levied, as well as the duties shown, at gradually increasing rates. These would make the 1804 duty on foreign corn about £1 7s. 4d. and the 6d. duty leviable at other periods from 7d. to 8d.
1808	3 19 0	,,	,,	
1809	4 15 7	,,	,,	
1810	5 6 2	,,	,,	
1811	4 14 6	,,	,,	
1812	6 5 5	,,	,,	
1813	5 8 9	,,	,,	
1814	3 13 11	,,	,,	
1815	3 4 4	Prohibited	Prohibited	By the Act of 1815 foreign wheat was prohibited from use for home consumption when the price was under £4 a quarter, and Plantation wheat when the price was under 67s. (The goods might be imported and warehoused, but not delivered for home use.) If wheat were at the prices quoted or above, it was duty free.
1816	3 15 10	,,	Duty free	
1817	4 14 9	Duty free	,,	
1818	4 4 1	,,	,,	
1819	3 13 0	Prohibited	,,	
1820	3 5 7	,,	Prohibited	

Of course, the duties in this return are made to fit the average prices shown, and the same rule applies to the prohibitions, etc. For instance, it does not follow that *none* except the 'first low duty' was paid in 1798, or that imported corn was prohibited from home use through *the whole* of 1820. The scale is merely illustrative, not absolute, as to the particular periods covered.

The reader should refer to pp. 1 to 8. He will perceive that high corn prices did not obtain till nearly the end of the eighteenth century, and that when they were firmly established only nominal duties were actually *collected*. Undoubtedly the alterations in the sliding scale in 1791 and 1804 helped to raise prices, and the wicked prohibitions under the Act of 1815 helped to keep them high. But from 1795 to 1815 high prices were more the result of an increase in population, the crowding of towns, war, and the incidental hampering of oversea traffic, etc., than of high duties. It will be observed that when the strain of actual war was removed the deadly contrivance of occasional prohibition was effected. This was purely a device to keep up rents.

No. 11. *Extracts from 'Instructions to Scottish Collectors, 1707.' (This book contains the whole scheme of Customs as performed in England, and applied to Scotland after the Union, with specimens of all the documents used by collectors.)*

'1. You are to behave your self in a sober and discreet Manner, so as to give no occasion of Scandal or just Complaint.

'2. You are not for your Self, nor for any other Person, directly nor indirectly to be concerned in Trade, Merchandise, or Shipping.

'3. You are not to keep any Ale-House, Tavern, or House of Entertainment to divert you from the performance of your Duty and the Attendances of Her Majesties Service, in the Imployment wherewith you are intrusted, as the Law directs.

'4. You are to keep your Residence in the Port where you are appointed Collector, and not to leave the same and your District.

'7. In every Thing and Matter relating to the Duty of a Collector, you are to behave yourself with Prudence and

Circumspection, that Her Majesties Revenue may not suffer any Diminution, nor any Law relating to the Import and Export of Goods be violated or infringed.

'27. That you may have a clear Idea and perfect Knowledge of the several Branches of Her Majesties Revenue committed to the Management of the Commissioners of Her Customs, and which consequently fall within your Collection, you are to consider the following Scheme, wherein you will find the Duties and Impositions, the Acts of Parliament, and the Pages in the Book of Rates thereto relating ranged in their proper Classes as follows :

Branches of the Revenue.	*Acts of Parliament.*	*Page in the Book of Rates.*
Customs { Subsidy outwards ..	12 Charles 2d commencing	1
Customs { ,, inwards ..		
Customs { Petty-Custom ..		
Customs { Additional Duty ..		
Customs { Composition on Petty Seizures ..		
New or further Subsidy ..	9 and 10 William and Mary	514
One-Third Subsidy	2 and 3 Anne, since the Book of Rates	
Two-Thirds ,, ...	3 and 4 Anne, since the Book of Rates	
Impost on Wines and Vinegar	1st James 2d	334
Impost on Tobacco	1st James 2d	338
Impositions, 1690	2 William and Mary	366
Impositions, 1692	4 and 5 William and Mary	379
New Duty on Whale-Finns ..	9 and 10 William 3	572
New Duty on Coffee, &c. ..	3 and 4 Anne, since the Book of Rates	
New Additional Duty on Coffee, &c., and drugs ..	3 and 4 Anne, since the Book of Rates	
Second 25 per Cent. on French goods	7 and 8 William 3	442
Covnage ..	18 Charles 2d	292
Prysage ..	12 ,,	1
Butlerage ..	,, ,,	205
Excise on Salt { Inwards ..	5 Anne, by the Act for the Union	
Excise on Salt { Outwards ..		

THIS IS THE FOUNDATION AND RULE OF YOUR BUSINESS.

'31. You are to observe an Act 5th Anne, Cap 27, Intituled, An Act for continuing several Subsidies, and for ascertaining the Wine Measure, &c., whereby the Law directs that a tun of Wine is to contain 252 Gallons, each Gallon consisting of 231 cubical Inches, so that for collecting the duties on Wines you and the Officers imployed about the Customs are to study the Art of Gaging, wherein the Officers of the Excise will give you some Information when desired, with their Conveniency.*

'33. With these Gentlemen who have the Inspection of your District, you may concert the Signals which they are to give to your Waiters and Tydesmen, and which the latter are to return for conveying speedy Information of any Ship or Vessel hovering on the Coast, or for the discovery of any other illegal Design.'

'The instructions conclude thus:

'You are to take Notice that the Laws which are now the Standard of Trade and Duties have been constructed with very great Tenderness towards the fair Trading Merchants, with great Encouragements to Industry, and that the severities intended are for the prevention of Frauds, which can only be committed by Men of bad Principles, and destructive to the Common good, who by eluding the Law would render the Supplies Ineffectual, &c.

'By these Laws you are entrusted with the Administration of Oaths, which you are to Execute with Reverence, in a decent manner, that the people who Swear may consider the Consequence of an Oath, in Attesting the Omniscient God to be the Judge of their Deposition.

'**** You have an Essential Encouragement from the

* Defoe, in his 'History of the Union of Great Britain,' states as follows: 'Considering the Ignorance for the most part of their officers' (of the Scottish Excise) 'in the Art of Gauging, and in the new methods of taking the Worts and making a Charge, considering the Difficulty of satisfying and convincing the People who were to pay the Duty, that they had no wrong done them, no Duty' (this in reference to the excise duty on ale) 'was ever settled with so little Noise.'

(It would seem from this that the Scottish customs men would not gain much assistance from the excisemen during the first few years after the Union.)

He also states thus: 'At the beginning the People thought every Seizure of prohibited Goods a Violence upon their Properties, and clamoured at the English and the Union, as if the Union had been made not to bring them under good Government, but to leave them without Government. Upon this Notion they fell to running of Brandy in particular at that prodigious Rate that some thousands of small Casks of Brandy was in Spight of all the Vigilance of Officers secretly supposed to be put on Shore out of the first Dutch Fleet that came to Scotland after the Union, and when the Officers made Seizure of several Parcels the Rabbles by violence rescued them again.' (See also 'The King's Customs,' vol. i., pp. 163, 164.)

Reasonable Hopes of such further Advancement as you shall be found capable of, upon the Representation of your Behaviour to the Lord High Treasurer of Great Britain, who is a Lover of Method and an Encourager of Virtue,' &c.

Specimens from the Instructions. 1. An entry for Plantation tobacco—20,000 lbs. (The duty is 1^{d} a lb under the Old Subsidy, with a discount of 5 per cent. for prompt payment: under the New Subsidy the same less discount, with another discount of 2½ per cent.: under the ⅓ Subsidy, ⅓ of the New Subsidy charge minus the discount, with another discount of 4½ per cent.: under the Additional Duty branch the Old Subsidy less the discount, with another discount of 7½ per cent.: under the Impost 3^{d} a lb. with a discount of 8 per cent. and another discount of 10 per cent. on the net. Complicated as this document may appear it is as nothing compared with entries during the early part of Geo. 3 reign.)

'LEITH. *25 June, 1707.*

'In the *William* of Leith, George Smith Master, from Virginia, John Stuart Merchant.

			£ s. d.
Fifty Hogsheads of Tobacco containing Twenty Thousand Pounds Weight			83 06 08
(Signed) John Stuart		Discompt 5 per cent. ..	04 03 04

	£ s. d.	£ s. d.		
			Old Subsidy ..	79 03 04
New Subsidy ..	79 03 04	77 03 09	New Subsidy ..	77 03 09
Disct 2½ p Cent.	01 19 07			
⅓ Subsidy ..	25 14 07	24 11 06	⅓ Subsidy ..	24 11 06
Disct. 4½ p. Cent. for prompt payment ..	01 03 01			
Additional Duty	79 03 04	73 04 07	Additional Duty	73 04 07
Disct. 7½ p. Cent.	05 18 09			
Impost ..	250 00 00		Impost ..	207 00 00
Disct. 8 p. C. ..	20 00 00			*£461 3 2'
	230 00 00	207 00 00		
Disct. 10 p. c. for prompt payment	23 00 00			

* If the goods were bonded the payments would be: O.S., £79 3s. 4d.; N.S., the same; ⅓ Subsidy, £26 7s. 9d.; A.D., £79 3s. 4d.; Impost, £250; Total, £513 17s. 9d. Only one discount would be allowed, that on the Old Subsidy, which branch would be paid before the goods were put in bond. (The bonding would be in the merchant's own warehouse.)

Entry for Deals, Tar, and Sables.

'Leith. 25th *June*, 1707.

'In the *Thomas* of Leith, John Gibson Master, from Drammen; Thomas Stirling, Merchant.

	£ s. d.
TS. Sixty Hundred Norway Deals	15 00 00
Twenty Lasts Tar	2 10 00
T S. Ten Timber Sables containing forty skins each Timber	15 00 00
	32 10 00
Discount at 5 per cent. ..	01 12 06
Old Subsidy ..	30 17 06
New Subsidy ..	30 17 06
⅓ Subsidy ..	10 05 10
⅔ " ..	20 11 08
Impost 1690 ..	28 02 06
Impost 1692 ..	15 04 08¼
	£135 19 8¼

	£ s. d.
Impost 1690 on Deals	30 00 00
Discount at 6¼ per cent.	1 17 06
	£28 2 06
Impost 1692 on Tar ..	01 05 00
Sables	15 00 00
	16 05 00
Discount at 6¼ per cent.	01 00 03¾
	£15 04 08¼

Thomas Stirling.'

(Note that in the above the system of discounting differs. From 1707 to 1780 the methods gradually grew more complicated, till few officers could be found able to deal with the whole of the varying duties chargeable on goods.)

No. 12. *Board to collector and controller of Blackney, as to the new Quarantine Act applying to pilots. From the Letter-Book of Blackney.*

'Gentlemen,

'The Rt Hon the Lords Comm^{rs} of her Maties Treas^{y} a Lett^{r} from my Lord Dartmouth with one of his Lord^{p} from the Lords of the Adm^{ty} wherein they propose that Pilots goeing on board Ships that come from Places infected should perform Quarantain in the said ships, because the little boats they usually sail in cannot bear ye sea in bad weather, and my Lord Dartmouth having signified her Maties pleasure to have this method observed, you are in pursuance of their Lordps Directions to take care that her

Ma[ties] pleasure therein signified be duly complyed with accordingly: And you are further to take notice that it is her Ma[ties] pleasure (as their Lord[ps] have acquainted us) that the officers of the Customs and ye command[rs] and other Officers of her Ma[ties] ships should be assisting to each other in y[e] due performance of y[e] Quarantain

'YOUR LOVING FRIENDS.

'Custom H°, London.
19th December 1710.'

No. 13. *Extracts from Scottish Board's Minutes.*

'16th *Jan[y]*, 1723/4.

'The Moderator of the Presbytery of Stranraer having made a complaint to ye Board by his letter of ye 13th inst. against James Welsh, Tidesman, in that district, who for ill deportment had been excommunicated & afterwards imprisoned by ye Civill magistrate, from whence he had made his Escape & thereby render'd himself incapable of doing duty for the future: the Commissioners direct that he be dismist ye Service.'

'28th *Feby*, 1723/4

'The Commrs proceeded on ye examination they yesterday began with respect to ye information given by Geo Laverock, and Thomas Grier, tidewaiter at Leith, being accordingly interrogated in relation to a charge that was against him of suffering a considerable quantity of paper to be run out of Fowler's ship from Holland in April last, he confess'd that he had conniv'd at that fraud, for w[ch] he had rec[d] of Mr. Marjoribanks, Merch[t], a Guinea, and some shillings in silver.

'Thomas Morehouse, also tidewaiter at Leith, was also charg'd with having, in concert with James Phelean, W[m] Moncrieff, & ye said Laverock, suffer'd 14 hhds of wine to be run from on board ye *Neptune*, John Nairn master, from Bilbao, in Feby, 1718-9: as reward for which Laverock said he got 4 guineas for his share & supposes ye others receiv'd as much.

'That Morehouse, Phelean, & he ye said Laverock, finding a box of Hungary water bottles in ye same ship, under ye cabin sole, they bargain'd wth ye Master to carry it on shore, w[ch] they did accordingly in their pockets to James Lundie's

No. 14. Statement illustrating the method of dividing the proceeds of Customs seizures in the early part of the eighteenth century.

Goods.	*Cause of Forfeiture.*	*Distribution of Proceeds.*
Tobacco	For being planted in Great Britain	$\frac{1}{3}$ to Crown ; $\frac{1}{3}$ to seizer ; $\frac{1}{3}$ to the poor.
,, ...	,, ,, imported in illegal packages	$\frac{2}{3}$,, $\frac{1}{3}$,,
Cattle	,, ,, imported (importation prohibited)	$\frac{1}{2}$ to seizer (hide and tallow) ; $\frac{1}{2}$ to the poor (rest of carcase).
Ships	For importing cattle	$\frac{1}{2}$ to seizer ; $\frac{1}{2}$ to the poor.
Plantation goods	For being landed prior to deposit of duty	$\frac{3}{4}$ to Crown ; $\frac{1}{4}$ to seizer.
African goods	For irregularities as to ships or trade	$\frac{1}{3}$,, $\frac{1}{3}$,, $\frac{1}{3}$ to the African Co.
Alamodes or lustrings ..	For being imported otherwise than into London	$\frac{2}{3}$,, $\frac{1}{3}$,,
East India goods ..	For being imported by unlicensed persons	$\frac{1}{4}$ to seizer ; $\frac{3}{4}$ to the East India Co.
,, ,, ,, ...	For being landed without directors' warrant	$\frac{2}{3}$ to Crown ; $\frac{1}{3}$ to seizer.
Popish books	For being imported (prohibited)	$\frac{1}{3}$,, $\frac{1}{3}$,, $\frac{1}{3}$ to the poor.
Fish (other than stockfish or live eels)	,, ,, ,, by aliens	$\frac{1}{2}$ to seizer ; $\frac{1}{2}$ to the poor.
Wool	,, ,, exported	$\frac{1}{3}$ to Crown ; $\frac{2}{3}$ to seizer.
,, ...	,, ,, imported from Ireland	$\frac{1}{2}$ to seizer ; $\frac{1}{2}$ to encouragement of Irish linen industry.
All goods seized by men-of-war		$\frac{1}{4}$ to Crown ; $\frac{1}{4}$ to commander ; $\frac{1}{4}$ to the officers ; $\frac{1}{4}$ to the crew.
All other goods seized ..		$\frac{1}{2}$ to Crown ; $\frac{1}{2}$ to seizer.

house, where they deliver'd them, and rec[d] about twenty shillings for that service.

'That on board ye same ship ye abovenam'd officers, finding a parcell of french gloves & playing cards, they deliver'd ye same back to ye Master for a piece of money, but ye informant Laverock does not remember ye sume : but ye said Morehouse firmly insisting upon his innocency and ignorance of ye whole, notwithstanding Laverock, who was present, mention'd severall other circumstances to enforce his assertion & bring ye other to confession : yet as it was to no purpose, & ye board having good grounds from all ye concurring circumstances to look upon him as a person deeply guilty, and unfitt to be trusted for ye future, they resolved to dismiss him from ye Service.'

'Tuesday, 7th July, 1724.

'James Phelean, late tidewaiter at Leith, having made severall discoveries to ye Board of considerable frauds committed at that port, ye Soll[r] is to pay him a guinea now & subsist him at ye rate of five shillings a week from this date till further order.

'George Laverock, late tidewaiter at Leith, having made a complaint to ye Board that John Jack & John Alexander, weighing porters at Leith, had abused and assaulted him, by reason of his having discovered severall frauds committed by ye officers at that port : the Comm[rs] direct that the said two officers be dismist.'

'Wednesday, 10th February, 1724/5.

'The Board having rec[d] advice from ye officers at Stranraer by their letter dated ye 6th inst that a ship of about 60 tons burthen was come in there, having on board of her one John Somervil of Glasgow & Ben· Cross of London, two masters of ships, together with 4 Sailors & 2 boys, w[ch] said Somervil & Cross had at different times been taken by a Pyrate of 22 guns, who about a month ago gave them this ship, chiefly laden with oyle and fruit, w[ch] vessel, by ye arms on her stern, appears to be a French one : The Commrs thereupon direct that my Lord Townshend have ye copy of ye said letter sent him, and that in ye mean time ye officers at Stranraer be directed to keep trusty tidesmen on board said ship, & to suffer no goods whatsoever to be taken on shore without first receiving ye Board's directions.'

'Wednesday, 3rd March, 1724/5.

'The Commrs having recd letters from ye officers in Orkney & Caithness, relating to ye pyrate ship lately taken in ye Orkneys, and it appearing by ye affidavits therein contain'd that severall merchants and others have been concern'd in trading with ye said pyrate & supplying her with necessaries and some ammunition : The Board immediately communicated ye contents of ye said letters to Mr. Grahame ye Judge Admirall & Mr. Sinclair his Majesty's Sollicitor, & it being a matter that immediately concerns ye former's office, such orders were dispatch'd by him as were found necessary upon that occasion, & sent under cover of ye Board's letter to ye officers at Inverness, to be by them forwarded by Express to ye respective places the Judge Admirall's severall warrants were directed to.'

No. 15. *Scottish Board's Minutes on various acts of resistance of the revenue authorities,* 1735-36.

'Friday, 13th June, 1735.

'Ordered : That Mr. Armour : Assistant Sollicitor, do without loss of time make up an account of his disbursements upon any matters under his direction & lay the same before the Board without any further delay & particularly the charges incurred on a prosecution before the Baillie of Cuningham agt sundry persons for breaking open the Custom House of Irvine in July 1733.

'The Surveyor-Genl and collector of Inverness to be directed forthwith to send up copys of the severall warrants of commitment of the Officers of the Customs & three Soldiers who are imprisoned in Relation to the deceas'd Hugh Fraser, mercht there, who was killed by one of the soldiers when out in the King's boat to protect the officers, and Letters being to go from my Lord Advocate & the Sherriff to admit them all to bail except McAdam, one of the soldiers who is charged with having killed Fraser. The Surveyr Genl and Collector is to become surety for them and to defray the charge thereof, & likewise agreeable to the Sheriff's letter to get McAdam liberated from the Stocks or Irons, so that he may only Remain in prison in an open & free manner till he is tryed by due Course of Law, and the said Surveyr Genl & collector are in the mean time to furnish him with comfortable Subsistance, & to acquaint the Commander of the Troops that the Board will protect him.'

(It appears that Fraser was killed in attempting a rescue, and the magistrates committed the Customs men and soldiers concerned to prison pending trial, and loaded McAdam with irons. Both he and the others received the royal pardon. It is evident that the troops had been sent to Inverness in consequence of the collector's complaint, quoted at pp. 230, 231, vol. i., 'The King's Customs.')

'*Thursday, 2nd Octobr, 1735.*

'Mr. Armour having acquainted the Board that there will be occasion for Mr. Townson, land-wr, and the boatmen of Inverness (now here) to attend again to give evidence in the Court of Admiralty in the Cause against McKinnen and others, for assaulting them, &c., and they being apprehensive that in case of their return to Inverness, they may be hindred from being here in time to give their evidence, the Commrs direct,' &c.

(It is likely that the officers feared they would be prevented by force if they returned to Inverness, so they were put on duty at Aberdeen, and the Aberdeen boatmen sent to Inverness.)

'*Friday, 3rd Octobr.*

'The collector of Dundee having acquainted the Board that James Young and James Laird, tidesmen, who had been boarded on ye ship *Good Intention* from Norway, were in the night time deforc'd by the mate & ship's crew, & a considerable quantity of goods run out of her, a prosecution,' &c., &c.

'*Monday, 6t Octobr.*

'The Board being acquainted that Robert Bryson, Shipmatr, is pursuing Mr. McGill, Tide Surveyor at Kirkaldy, for the Subsistence of a party of Soldiers station'd on board the said Bryson's ship, Mr. Armour is to take care to defend Mr. McGill at the Crown's Expence.'

(The soldiers had been quartered on the ship, and the captain brought an action to recover the cost of their keep.)

'*Wednesday, 26th Novembr, 1735.*

'The collector of Kirkaldy has leave to come hither (to Edinburgh) for six days, and John William Cosens, Tidesman there, for Twelve days.'

(The Custom House at Kirkaldy had been broken into, and a sum of money stolen. Cosens was suspected of connivance.)

'*Thursday, 22nd Jan.* 1735/6.

'Mr. Armour having this day reported: That from the examination of the severall persons who were Guilty or accessory to the breaking open and stealing a sum of money out of the Custom House at Kirkaldy, & particularly one Wilson, that there is good ground to believe John William Cosens, Tidesman, has been in the knowledge of the Robbery, and discovered the place where the money was lodged, but that there is not sufficient evidence for proseeuting him criminally, in which his Majtys Sollr Genl, Mr Areskine' (Erskine) 'concurring, the Board agreed to his being forthwith dismist the Service, &c. The precognitions taken at Kirkaldy, and by his Majtys said Sollr Genl were put into Mr Armour,s hands, for him to proceed against Millar and Hunter.'

(It is just possible that the generally-accepted account of Wilson's theft of Customs money from the Kirkaldy collector at Pittenweem may be incorrect. It is evident that Wilson—whose execution caused the Porteous riots—was charged with robbing the Kirkaldy Custom-house.)

'*Friday, 9th March,* 1735/6.

'A Petition of Robert Hay, collector of Kirkaldy, to the Lords Commrs of the Treasury, praying Relief touching the Loss of £96 12s. 7½d. Stole out of the Custom House, was this day delivered in at the Board, and read together with their Ldps. reference thereupon.'

No. 16. *Board's Letter to the collector and controller of Hull, apprising them of a smuggling vessel's arrival on the coast,* 1735-36. *From the Letter-Book of Hull.*

'Gentlemen,

'Inclosed you will receive Extract of a letter from Mr. Southgate, Commander of a vessell in the service of Wells, dated 11th inst: Representing that a Brigantine belonging to Berwick, William Wilkinson, master, from Burdeaux, laden with Wine and Brandy, being hovering upon that Coast, and that it appears to him the said Cargoe is intended to be run in this Kingdom, and as the said vessell sailed for the Yorkshire Coast with a design to run her cargoe: We direct you to give Notice thereof with a description of the Vessell to the severall officers belonging to your Port, with directions to keep a careful look out for the said Vessell and to use their utmost endeavours to prevent her running any Goods, giving us an acco[t] of your Proceedings.

'Your loving Friends,

'J. STANLEY, J. EVELYN, B. FAIRFAX, R. CORBET.

'16th *March*, 1735/6.'

No. 17. *Order sent by the Customs Secretary to all English ports.*

'17th, *Jany*, 1740.

'Mr. Thomas Cartwell, an Officer at the port of Rye, having been lately murdered, and a Corporal and three Dragoons, whom he took to his assistance, very much wounded by the Smuglers, and a Considerable Quantity of Tea, which had been seized, rescued from them :

'You are to acquaint all the Officers at your Port that when ever they shall go out to make seizures they are to take care to have a sufficient Military force wth them, in case there are any forces quartred in y[r] Parts, for which purpose they are to wait upon the Commanding Officer and acquaint him with the nature of the Service, & consult him as to the force necessary for their assistance, that the Service may not suffer in the manner it has done on the late occasion, which I have in Command to signify to you.'

No. 18. *Extracts from the 'Coast Cocket Book' of Dartmouth,* 1745, *showing coastwise traffic from various ports.*

[Cover.] 'The Port of Exeter.

'A Blank Book containing six leaves for the Customers and Comptrollers within Dartmouth, a member thereof.* Of all goods and merchandises to be carried between port and port and for certificates from the Feast of the Nat[y] of our Lord God Anno 18 Regni Regis Georgii Secundi untill the Feast of St. John the Baptist then next following that is to say for the space of half a year.

'DARTMOUTH.'

* A member of Exeter.

[Within.] 'In the *Alexander* of Dartm[h], David Reeves Mr., pr. Cocq[t], 29th November last. Dan Caudewell & Co.

'4 trusses c[t] 1540 ells German & Russia & 45 yards Brit[h] Linnen.
20 casks ct 760 galls spirits.
6 hhds 3 casks 1 truss 2 boxes sugar.
2 pipes with staves.
2 dozen empty rundletts.
6 empty Pipes.
1 hhd glass and earthenware.
2 tons lead & shott.
3 bags & 1 pocket Hops.
43½ sacks Seeds.
3 butts 2 puncheons 3 barr[ls] oil.
3 boxes 1 bottle 2 parcells 1 cake 4 bags 2 bask[ts] 3 barr[ls] oilmen's ware.
4 trusses 1 bundle haberdashery.
3 tons hemp.
30 cases Hard sope.
1 box 1 pottmanteau apparell.
2 barr[ls] 1 bask[ett] 1 box tin-monger's ware.
1 truss household goods.
2 half hhds 1 barrell porter.
3 topmasts, 3 yards, 4 tons cordage.
40 empty casks.
½ ton Cheese.
3 casks ct 80 galls Spirits.
12 quarters beans.
20 barrells Tarr.
2800 pipe-staves (From London).'

'4th *March*, 1744/5.

'In the *Postboy* of Cowes Mich[s] Grigg Mr., pr. Cocq[t] 11th ultimo. Turnpenny & Co.

'2 Tons Barr Iron.
3 hampers, 1 bundle Ironware.
43 casks ct 1400 galls British Brandy.
1 cask ct 108 galls Rum.
1 caskett Snuff.
27 Crates Earthenware.
10 hhds 1 tierce refined Sugar.
½ butt Currants.
2 hhds Musco[d°] Sugar.
½ ton Barr Iron.
6 Boxes Tyn plates.
37 dozen Bottles.
1 box 4 Crates Glass & Earthen ware.
23 bags, 22 half bags Nails.
5 cwt. Shearmoulds.*
½ ,, Steel.
40 barr[ls] Tarr.

landed at Plymouth:

2 hhds musco[d°] Sugar.
10 hhds lump Sugar
35 bags Nails.
2 hampers Ironware.
½ butt Currants.
1 baskett Ironware.
2 pkges Glass (From Bristol).'

(Only six vessels arrived during the half-year with general cargo. Five of these were from London, one from Bristol. Three vessels arrived from Newcastle with coals, three from Sunderland, two from Swansea, and one from Llanelly. Ten vessels arrived from Milford with culm. One vessel left for Exeter carrying 14 puncheons duty-paid rum, with 2 casks brandy, 4 casks geneva, and 22 casks of rum. These last were seized goods, condemned in the Exchequer, and sent to Exeter for sale. She carried also 7 hogsheads cider, 2 chests lemons and oranges, and 3 casks blubber. Seven vessels left for London, the total of

* Planks used in shipbuilding.

their cargoes being 30 'pack-cloths' wool, which equals 97½ hundredweight; 1 pipe, 798 hogsheads, 3 puncheons, and 85 half-hogsheads cider; 35 quarters malt; 48 quintals dry Newfoundland codfish, 16 bales serges; 842 quarters oats; 100 quarters barley; and 3 sailors' chests.)

Copy of cocket for 10 packages wool carried coastwise from Dartmouth to London.

'Know all Men by these Presents that we, *John Andrews of Dover in the County of Kent, Marriner, and Saml Windeatt, of Berry Pomroy in the County of Devon, Fellmonger*, are firmly bound unto our Sovereign Lord *George the Second* in the Sum of *Five Hundred and Forty-six Pounds* of good and lawful money of Great Britain, to be paid to our said Lord the King, his heirs and successors, to which certain Payment well and truly to be made We bind ourselves and every of us jointly and severally for and in the whole our Heirs, Executors, Administrators, and Assigns, and every of them by these Presents: Sealed with our Seals dated the *twenty-fifth* day of January in the *eighteenth* year of the Reign of our Sovereign Lord *George the Second*, by the Grace of God, &c.

'The Condition of this Obligation is such. That if *Ten pack-cloths at Thirty-two hundred and two quarters of a hundred w^t Raw British Wooll Consigned to Samuel Ruggles of Bocking in Essex* mentioned in an Entry made in the Custom House in the Port of *Dartmouth* the Day of the date above written in the name of *Saml Windeatt* and laden in the Ship or Vessel called the *Endeavour of Dov^r Jno Andrews Mr for Lond^n* be discharged and laid on land in the aforesaid Port of *London*, or in some Port or Creek within Great Britain, or any of the Dominions thereof, and in no other Place, and if the aforesaid *John Andrews* shall within six months next after the day of the date hereof bring a true Certificate from the Officers of His Majesty's Customs of the Port, Creek, or Place, where he shall happen to discharge or land the said Goods, certifying that the said Goods are there discharged and laid on the Land, unto the Officers of His Majesty's Customs in the said Port of *Dartmouth*: That then this present obligation to be void, or else to remain and be in full Force and Virtue.

'Sealed and Delivered in the presence of

'WM. COWELL. JOHN ANDREWS.
THOS. SKINNER. SAML WINDEATT.'

Certificate of Landing of the above Goods.

'London. Know ye that Samuel Windeatt hath landed in this port ten Cloaths raw wool marked numbered and weighing as on the back hereof. Containing Thirty-three hundred three quarters and seven pounds weight,

Coast. out of the *Endeavour*, Mr. John Andrews, from Dartmouth, as by Cocq[t] thence, dated 25th Jany 1744: What security you have taken in that behalf you may release: Given by the officers of the Great Customs, dated 20th February, 1744. Eighteenth year King George the Second.

'H. LEWIS, Cust[mr]. T. PLAYER, D. Compt[r].'

(Document endorsed with coastwaiters' account of reweighing. This document went to Dartmouth with the cocket. The Dartmouth officers then endorsed the cocket, and cancelled the bond.)

No. 19. *Scottish Board's Minute on a 'relanding' of dutiable goods, which had been shipped for foreign parts (a kind of smuggling prevalent in Scotland).*

'*Wednesday*, 10th *April*, 1745.

'The Collector and Comptroller of Anstruther having transmitted to the Board a copy of a report made there the 19th of last month by James Redlay, master of the ship *Ann & Cathrine*, of Leith, for Hamburgh in Germany : viz. :

Goods loaded at Leith.
40 tons coals.

Loaded at Anstruther.
103 Ankers containing 988 gallons of brandy.
2 ,, ,, 19 ,, ,, geneva.
1 box ,, 74 lbs Bohea tea.
2 cannisters ,, 20 ,, ,,

*Reported at Leith for foreign Parts.
1 Anker & 3 half-ankers of foreign spirits.
2 Casks of sugar.
5 bundles of tea.
2 ,, coffee berries.*

* The master had entered Leith with foreign spirits, sugar, tea, and coffee, probably shipped in England. He then loaded coals at Leith, and went to Anstruther, where he took in brandy, geneva, and tea. He cleared out for foreign, and two days later the ship was found at Burntisland, with nothing on board but coals.

'And acquainted them the said Master sailed from thence the same day he made the above report, and Mr. James Patterson, tide surveyor at Leith, having informed the Board that the said ship came into Burntisland harbour on the 21st of the said month at 12 o'clock at noon, having only coals on board, and the Sollicitor having reported that the master should be prosecuted for treble the value of the goods run, upon the statute 8th Ann: Resolved, that the Sollicitor do proceed accordingly.'

No. 20. Scottish Board's Minute upon conduct of one Porteous, a tidewaiter (possibly a relative of the subject of the Porteous Riots).

'*Tuesday, 30th April, 1745.*'

'The Commissioners having considered the charge given by their order to Francis Porteous, Tidewaiter at Leith, founded upon a complaint signed by Mr. James Patterson, tide-surveyor at Leith, John* Anderson & Thomas Vernon, Land-carriage waiters at the City gates of Edinbr, then acting as tidewaiters at Leith, that the said Francis Porteous, being stationed on the 24th instant upon the *Janet* of Leith, John Watt Master, loaded with wine, he left his duty and went on shoar with the Master and several of the Sailors to drink with them, and returned the worse for Liquor.

'That he Spirited up the Sailors against the said Anderson & Vernon, who were joined with him on Duty on board the said Vessel, and threatened to throw them over Board: And having likewise considered the said Porteous's answers to the said Charge, the observations of the Collector and Comptroller of Leith thereupon, and he having advanced nothing Satisfactory in his Vindication, and the Collector and Comptroller having reported that he is a dangerous Officer, and further, he having been formerly guilty of Sundry Misdemeanours in the Execution of his Duty, and excused upon promises to be exact and diligent in doing his duty for the future: Resolved, that he be dismissed, and his Deputation called in to be cancelled.'

* Anderson and Vernon had previously complained of one John Cunningham, that he had repeatedly beaten and assaulted them.

No. 21. Various Minutes by the Scottish Board, exemplifying the effect on Customs business, etc., of the rebellion in 1745.

'Monday, 9th September, 1745.

'Mansfeldt Cardonnel, Esq., in the Chair.

'The Secretary laid before the Board a letter from Mr. Lowe with the warrant of the Lords of the Treasury for—

'Alexander Shank, Surveyor of the Customs at Kirkaldy.'

(The report breaks off here, and no further record appears till November 29, 1745. Gardiner was defeated at Collbrig on September 16. The Pretender occupied Holyrood on the 18th, and left early in November. It appears that the Commissioners of Customs left off work some time before the city was captured, and did not resume till some time after the Pretender was across the Border and well on his way to Derby.)

'Friday, 29th November, 1745.

'Richard Somers, Esq., in the Chair.

'Received several letters and directed answers thereto.

'Monday, 2nd December, 1745.

'John Campbell, Esq., in the Chair.

'The Commissioners considered the several letters received during the Interuption of Business by the Rebels Entering the Town, and directed answers to such Ports as the Rebels are not in possession of.

'Tuesday, 3rd December, 1745.

'John Campbell, Esq., in the Chair.

'The Commissioners received a letter from Mr. Scrope, with a copy of one from the Duke of Newcastle, signifying his Majesty's pleasure that Directions should be sent to the officers of the Customs in the several ports to stop and search all Soldiers which shall arrive from Holland, whether they have passes or discharges from the respective regiments in the service of the States-General, to which they may have belonged, or not, and to detain them in safe custody till further orders, there being reason to apprehend that many of them have deserted with a design to pass into this kingdom in order to join the Rebels.

'*Thursday, 19th December, 1745.*

'Richard Somers, Esq., in the Chair.

'Received the establishments for the officers employed in the Customs and Salt Duty for Michaelmas quarter, 1745, warranted by the Lords Commissioners of the Treasury.

'The Rebels having retreated back into Scotland, and being within a few days' march of this Town, and Business thereby interrupted; The books and papers belonging to the Custom House, formerly lodged in the Castle, and brought down from thence after the Rebels evacuated this town, are again to be carried up for Security.'

(No further entry appears till February 12, 1745-46.)

'Lord Rosse in the Chair' (none else present except Somers).

'Ordered that the several officers have notice to bring from the Castle the Books and Papers belonging to their respective offices, deposited there for Security during the Rebellion.

'That a Circular letter be sent to the several ports, requiring the principal officers to enquire in the most expeditious, particular, full, and impartial manner, into the Conduct and Behaviour of the Inferiour Officers, during the Unnatural and Horrid Rebellion, and to report the same to the Board without delay.'

(Work went on as usual. The Battle of Culloden was fought on April 16.)

'*Wednesday, 9th April, 1746.*

'Alexander Arbuthnot, Esq., in the Chair.

'The Supervisor of the Salt Duty at Prestonpans having transmitted to the Board an account of the Officers and Watchmen in that collection who continued to act under the Rebels, the same was returned for the Collector and Supervisor to give the matter in Charge to the respective Officers, and to send it back with the Officers' answers, and their observations, for the Consideration of the Board.

'*Tuesday, 6th May, 1746.*

'John Campbell, Esq., in the Chair.

'The Lord Justice Clerk having transmitted to the Board a Memorial and paper, a part containing sundry regulations and directions for discovering such persons as have been concerned in the Rebellion, and desired them to give directions accordingly to all the officers under their management: Resolved: That a copy of the said Memorial and separate Paper be sent to all the ports.

'*Thursday, 15th May, 1746.*

'Alexander Arbuthnot, Esq., in the Chair.

'The Commissioners having received sundry affidavits against James Rannie, King's Couper at Leith, that he was aiding and assisting to the Rebels, particularly by Pressing Persons, by virtue of an order from the Young Pretender's Secretary, to drive their Baggage, and it further appearing that he has not produced a certificate of his qualifying to the Government according to law, though frequently required so to do, and he having been formerly suspended for neglect of duty: Resolved, that the said James Rannie, for the above reasons, be dismissed till he clears himself before proper judges, to the satisfaction of the Board, &c.'

(On June 18, 1746, the Board resolved that proceedings should be taken against certain persons who acted as sellers of the goods in the King's Warehouse, and others who received money for the said sales and handed it over to the rebels. On July 10 they dismissed thirteen officers at Prestonpans for having acted under the rebels. Many other officers were charged.)

'*Monday, 28th July, 1746.*

'Mansfeldt Cardonnel, Esq., in the Chair.

'The Lord Justice Clerk having by a letter of this date signified to the Board that he has received intelligence that the Pretender's Son has left the Highlands and is come towards the Coast in order to make his escape, and desired the Board to give orders to the officers at all the ports, except those north of Dundee, to lay an embargo on all shipping, &c. &c.'

(On August 11 the Board allowed James Robertson £2 10s. 'for entering in a Book lists of Persons concerned in the Rebellion.')

'*Monday, 4th August*, 1746.

'Richard Somers, Esq., in the Chair.

'The Lord Justice Clerk having signified to the Board that the Information that the Pretender's Son had left the Highlands and was come towards the Coast to make his Escape by Shipping proves uncertain, and desired that the Embargo laid in consequence of the said Information may be taken off: Resolved, that directions be immediately sent to the several Ports accordingly.

'*Wednesday, 8th October*, 1746.

'John Campbell, Esq., in the Chair.

'The Right Honorable the Earle of Albemarle Commander in Chief of his Majesty's Forces in Scotland having signified that he has received Information that many of the Rebels of the first Rank are still lurking upon the East Coast of Scotland waiting the opportunity of Escaping in some Vessel from the Ports on the said Coast, and desired the Board to give directions to the several officers of the Customs stationed at those ports in the strictest manner to search all Outward Bound vessels of whatever Size, least any Rebels should be concealed on them, and also to make Inquiry where such Rebels may be lurking in order to their being apprehended, &c.

'*Thursday, 18th December*, 1746.

'Lord Rosse in the Chair.

'Considered the Petition of Mr. James Patersone, Tide Surveyor at Leith, setting forth his Services during the late Rebellion, and Copys of the certificates annexed of the Generals, Sir John Cope, Handasyde, and Guest, Admiral Byng, and his Majesty's late Advocate and Sollicitor General, of those Services to the Government. The Board are of opinion it is not in their Power to Reward him out of the Revenue, but resolve to Present Mr. Patersone to the Lords of the Treasury for the first suitable Vacancy.

'*Thursday, 29th January*, 1746-7.

'Richard Somers, Esq., in the Chair.

'The Collector and Comptroller of Borrowstoness having in their letter of the 23rd instant given the Board an Account of some Rebels being apprehended on board a Ship bound for Holland, the same was laid before the Justice Clerk the 25th instant.'

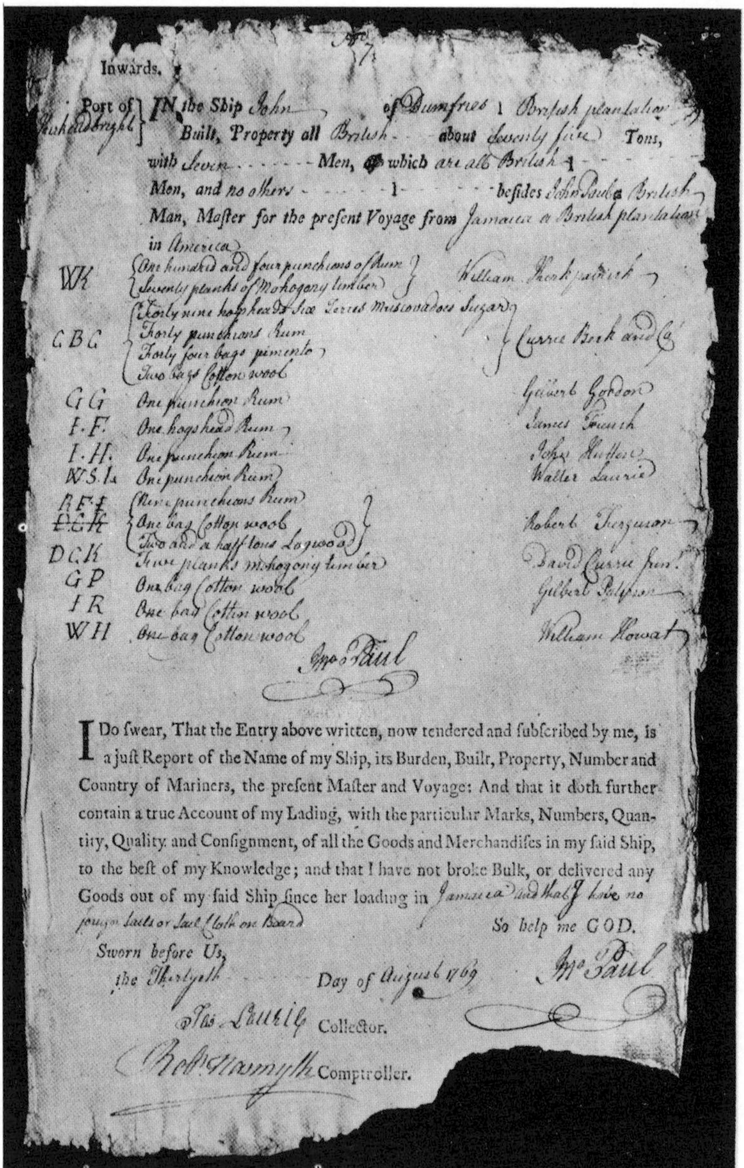

Inwards.

Port of Kirkcudbright } IN the Ship John of Dumfries, British plantation Built, Property all British about seventy five Tons, with Seven Men, of which are all British Men, and no others besides John Paul a British Man, Master for the present Voyage from Jamaica a British plantation in America

Marks	Goods	Consignees
WK	One hundred and four puncheons of Rum; Seventy planks of Mahogany timber	William Kirkpatrick
CBC	Forty nine hogsheads Six Tierces Muscovadoes Sugar; Forty puncheons Rum; Forty four bags pimento; Two bags Cotton wool	Currie Beck and Co.
GG	One puncheon Rum	Gilbert Gordon
IF	One hogshead Rum	James French
IH	One puncheon Rum	John Hutton
WSL	One puncheon Rum	Walter Laurie
RF	Nine puncheons Rum; One bag Cotton wool; Two and a half tons Logwood	Robert Ferguson
DCK	Two planks Mahogany timber	David Currie Junr.
GP	One bag Cotton wool	Gilbert Paterson
IR	One bag Cotton wool	
WH	One bag Cotton wool	William Howat

Jno. Paul

I Do swear, That the Entry above written, now tendered and subscribed by me, is a just Report of the Name of my Ship, its Burden, Built, Property, Number and Country of Mariners, the present Master and Voyage: And that it doth further contain a true Account of my Lading, with the particular Marks, Numbers, Quantity, Quality and Consignment, of all the Goods and Merchandises in my said Ship, to the best of my Knowledge; and that I have not broke Bulk, or delivered any Goods out of my said Ship since her loading in Jamaica and that I have no foreign sails or sail Cloth on Board

So help me GOD.

Sworn before Us, the Thirtyeth Day of August 1769

Jno. Paul

Thos. Laurie Collector.

Robt. Nasmyth Comptroller.

FACSIMILE OF REPORT OF THE 'JOHN,' OF DUMFRIES. JOHN PAUL ('PAUL JONES'), MASTER (1769).

To face p. 439.

'*7th April*, 1909.

'The signatures which appear on the reports of the *John*, of Dumfries, are those of a person much celebrated in naval history. John Paul was born at Kirkbean in 1747. His father, John Paul, had three other sons, one of whom, William Paul, was adopted by an elderly Scotsman named Jones, who had settled in Virginia. John Paul, senior, died in 1767, and was buried in Kirkbean churchyard, his son John erecting a tombstone to his memory.

'John Paul, junior, went to sea at an early age, and eventually became captain of the *John*, of Dumfries (by Buell erroneously called the *John* of Kirkcudbright). This vessel belonged to Currie, Beck, and Co., a Scottish firm of shipowners located at Whitehaven. (Buell gives the title of the firm as "Donald Currie, Beck, and Co.," and makes reference to a vessel named the *Grantully Castle*, of which John Paul eventually became master. It must not, however, be thought that this was the source of the firm of to-day that bears the name of "Donald Currie," and has recently had a ship called the *Grantully Castle*. Inquiries have elicited that the firm of Donald Currie and Co. is quite modern.)

'On one of the voyages indicated in the accompanying reports, John Paul had occasion to strike a mutinous sailor. On arrival at the Plantations the man died, and John Paul was tried at Tortola for the offence and acquitted. On his arrival at Whitehaven he was again put upon trial and acquitted. One of the reports (1769) bears endorsement to the effect that the *John* went on to Whitehaven to complete discharge. (Buell states that she was at Whitehaven in 1770; and the reports show that after the 1770 trip John Paul was no longer master. Therefore, it may have been that the vessel, *in 1770*, after discharging her cargo at Kirkcudbright, went to Whitehaven to load or to complete loading.)

'The accounts of John Paul's career in 1771 differ. Buell states that he became captain of the *Grantully Castle*, trading to Lisbon, Madeira, East Indies, and the Plantations, but in the "National Dictionary of Biography" it is stated that he spent a considerable period of that time in smuggling between the Isle of Man and the Solway Firth. It appears he was in Virginia in 1773, and found that his brother William had but a few hours to live. William had succeeded to the estate left by Jones, and in the will was a provision that John should succeed to the estate at William's death, on condition that he assumed the name of Jones. Thus he became a Virginian planter, and thenceforth signed himself "Paul Jones."

'When the War of Independence broke out, "Paul Jones" joined the American Navy, and eventually became captain of the *Ranger*. His exploits as a naval commander are well known and quite extraordinary. There can be no doubt that he possessed talent, courage, and sincerity in their highest and most original forms, but he is stated to have been exceedingly hasty and irritable, and much disposed to quarrel. When he left the American Navy he secured a command in the Russian, which he had to resign, evidently through the jealousy and undermining tactics of other Russian commanders.

'He had, for some reason or other, a deadly hatred of the British, whom he repeatedly stigmatizes in his letters as an arrogant and faithless race; and it is noticeable that most of his depredations were committed near the scenes of his boyhood. But he was ardently attached to the French, and they repaid his attachment by many favours and much "lionizing." He died in Paris, of dropsy of the heart, in 1792, and was buried in Père la Chaise, "in a shroud, without uniform or trappings of any kind." Principally through the instrumentality of President Roosevelt, his remains were removed to America in 1905, and interred in the crypt of the chapel of the Naval Academy at Annapolis.

'He is described as about 5 feet 7 inches in height, exceedingly swarthy, but with handsome features, and remarkably well built.'

(The above has been extracted from the Customs Library Memoranda.)

No. 22. Extracts from 'The Annual Register' (1782 *to* 1802).

'*Feb.* 15*th*, 1782.

'Yesterday was tried, before the Earl of Mansfield in the Court of King's Bench at Guildhall, a cause of general concern. A merchant of Flushing brought an action against a merchant of this city for the recovery of the amount of three bills of exchange given by the defendant for tea sold to the plaintiff, and delivered at Ostend to the defendant's order: the defence was that the tea never came to the defendant's hand, but was seized as run goods, therefore the plaintiff was liable to the loss: the defendant went upon two other points of law, namely, that the plaintiff could not apply for justice, as the act of selling the tea was a fraud upon the revenue: also that if the tea had actually been delivered the plaintiff was not entitled to recover. The noble judge in his charge to the jury remarked that Flushing and Ostend were the most famous ports for smuggling. If the jury considered the tea to be sold for the purpose of being smuggled to England they would find for the defendant. He observed that the East India ships were the only bottoms of conveyance of tea to England*: besides it was proved that the plaintiff kept boats and horses to convey tea to the coast of England. The jury found for the defendant, and thereby made the notes void.

'*Jany.* 10*th*, 1785.

'The following facts relative to the seizing and burning of the smugglers' boats may be depended on: advice was sent to Mr. Pitt that the severity of the season had occasioned the smugglers to lay up their craft, and a fine opportunity offered for the destroying them if sufficient force could be procured to intimidate the smugglers from attempting a rescue. Mr. Pitt sent to the War Office, and required a regiment of soldiers to be at Deal on a certain day. He was told it could not be complied with. His answer was it must, and a regiment was immediately marched. But the commanding officer found on his arrival that the people of the town, having some intimation of the business, had advised the publicans to pull down their signs, in order that the soldiers might have no quarters. They took the advice, and no quarters were to be had. A large barn at a small distance presented itself as an eligible place, and the quartermaster rode off to the landlord, who refused to let it on any other terms than for two years certain. The officer took it, marched the men in, and then with very much difficulty procured them some provisions. The next day Lieut. Bray received orders to prepare some cutters to hover off the beach, and the soldiers were all drawn out. The inhabitants, not imagining what was going to be done, thought the cutters were to embark

* The East India Company, and persons licensed by them, were the only parties allowed by law to land tea. It is evident from the context that the plaintiff was an Englishman living at Ostend, who undertook to illegally land tea, and to convey it to the warehouses of London merchants.

the soldiers in, but to their surprise orders were given to the men to burn the boats, and, the force being so great, the inhabitants were obliged to remain silent spectators, and dared not attempt a rescue.

'*Sept.* 4*th*, 1787.

'*Leeds.*—The captain of the Swedish ship seized at Hull a few days ago for having a quantity of wool on board* has now made an open confession, and impeached several people in that neighbourhood, who it seems have carried on a large trade in this iniquitous practice for some time past. The mate of the ship has declared upon oath that he believes every Swede or Danish vessel that comes into the port of Hull smuggles wool abroad every voyage, both captain and crew being concerned in this business, and although the quantity in each ship is but trifling yet when it comes to be considered that there are twenty or thirty ships of those two nations which make three or four voyages to Hull annually, the wool smuggled even from the above port becomes considerable. Two other ships were also seized on Saturday last at Hull, with wool.'

(Most of the 'owling' was done with the produce of Lincolnshire, Kent, and Sussex.)

'*June*, 1788.

'Mr. Tankard, a king's officer at Dartford, in consequence of an information, stopped the mail coach from Dover, and demanded from the guard the key of the trunk on which he sat. Being refused, he broke the trunk open, and two letter bags, with the brass labels 'Dover bags,' were found filled with lace. The coach and horses were seized.

'*Novr.* 29*th*, 1802.

'It may be recollected that about four years ago Johnson, the notorious smuggler, and another, were apprehended for obstructing and ill-using some revenue officers on the Sussex coast, and were committed to the New Gaol in the Borough to take their trial, but effected their escape in the most daring way, and remained at large notwithstanding £500 reward was offered for their apprehension. The first time Johnson

* For exportation (prohibited). It is apparent that English wool commanded a much higher price abroad than in England (see pp. 380, 387, 388).

was heard of after his escape was at the time the expedition to the Helder was meditated by Government, when he made an offer of his services to accompany the expedition, as from his smuggling connexions he had gained a complete knowledge of the Dutch coast : Government accepted of his services, and granted him a full pardon on his promise never to be again concerned in the smuggling trade. Johnson acquitted himself in this undertaking so much that he became a great favourite with several of the ex-ministers, and with the late Sir Ralph Abercrombie in particular. He afterwards contracted debts to the amount of £11,000, was arrested, and lodged in the Fleet prison nearly six months ago, where he remained. It appears before he became an inhabitant of the Fleet that in his pecuniary difficulties he again had recourse to smuggling, and he was capitally indicted on very strong grounds. Johnson, aware of these circumstances, turned his thoughts once more to making his escape, which he effected, notwithstanding he was confined in a strong room with two doors, or rather a double door, such as are generally fixed to the chambers in Inns of Court. At the top of each door was a panel instead of glass. It was by forcing out these two panels and creeping through the holes of them that Johnson was enabled to reach the gallery, and from thence the high wall that surrounds the prison, which it was impossible for him to have done without accomplices, as the panel of the outer door, it appears, had been forced from without. On his coming to that part of the wall next to Fleet Street, he found a rope ladder, which his friends on the outside had provided for him, and placed there agreeable to their plan. In the evening he arrived in a chaise and four on the coast of Brighton, where a lugger was in waiting for him in which he embarked, and arrived at Calais on his way to Flushing, after landing at Dieppe. He had a severe wound in the thigh, which he related to have received in the following manner : He had got on the top of the last wall that separated him from the street, 70 feet from the ground : a lamp was placed in the wall at some distance beneath the place where he was. He let himself down the wall exactly over the iron bar, and when he was forced to give up his hold he stretched his legs so as to fall astride. He had taken every precaution, and fell across the bar without overturning or hurting himself, but as he could not guard against an additional piece of iron it caught his thigh above the knee, and ripped it up almost to the top. At this moment he heard the watchman crying the hour, and had so much fortitude as to remain astride in that situation, bleeding most abundantly, till the watchman had gone his round without perceiving him. Immediately after he had the resolution to let himself down at all hazards.'

No. 23. *Statement of Net Produce of Plantation Customs in* 1784.

(New Brunswick, Port Roseway in Nova Scotia, and Cape Breton, had only been provided with Customs establishments during the current year. Therefore their accounts do not appear in the statement. Return from Tortola also not forthcoming.)

Colony.	*Net after charges of management paid.*	*Deficit.*	*Remarks.*
	£ s. d.	£ s. d.	
Jamaica		504 18 6	
Barbados ..	553 11 4		
Antigua	145 6 11¾		
St. Kitts ..	387 8 2		
Montserrat ..	81 17 3		
Nevis	33 6 8		
Newfoundland ..		354 4 8¼	
Grenada		208 9 7¾	
St. Vincent's ..		86 9 6¾	
Dominica ..		56 1 1¾	
Bahamas ..	81 16 6		
Bermuda ..	272 11 1¾		
Nova Scotia ..	36 18 11		
St. John's Islands		67 8 11	
Quebec		310 16 9¾	
		1,588 9 3¼	
		4 7 8¼	Balance accruing to the imperial revenue
	1,592 16 11½	1,592 16 11½	

(The above statement signed by ' J. Mills, for the Receiver-General: Joshua Powell, for the Controller-General: and J. Dalley, Supervisor of Payments.')

No. 24. *Extracts from statement of the charges upon coal bought coastwise to the port of London during the latter part of the eighteenth century.*

'This examinant saith: That he is one of the two clerks to the 15 sea-coal meters for the City of London, and has been so for 24 years; he and the other clerk are appointed by them, and do all the official business except that all the warrants and duplicates are signed by one coal meter, and they hold a Board once every month, January excepted. He understands the appointment of the sea-coal meters is vested in the Corporation of the City of London, and the office, when vacant, is sold for the term of 21 years, by public auction, in the Chamber of London, for the benefit of the City: they have sold for upwards of £6000, and the last was sold for about £5300, besides which every coal meter pays an annual sum of £100 to the Chamber of London. The purchaser must be a freeman of London, and in case of his demise the term is vested in his representatives.

'EDWARD MILLSOM.

'*Nov.* 1*st and* 2*nd*, 1784.'

(The charges were: 1s. 2d. per chaldron (36 bushels, weighing, say, 30 hundredweight). This sum was paid at the meter's office; 10d. of it went to the City as 'Orphans' Duty,' 3d. was divided among the meters, who were sinecurists, and the other 1d. went to their deputies, who did the actual measuring. Then the following duties were payable at the Custom House: 3s. and 2s. a chaldron as 'Coast Duties,' and further sums under the 'Church-building Duty,' only payable in the port of London, and the imposts of 1779 and 1782. Thus the total charges per chaldron were about 9s. 4d.)

No. 25. *Extracts from a statement made by the official who acted as deputy to the London Collector outwards during the latter part of the eighteenth century.*

'This examinant saith: That he is *chief* deputy to the duke of Manchester, who is the collector of the Customs outwards in the port of London. The collector holds his office by patent, for life: he executes no part of the business.

'The collector is paid by a salary and fees: his salary is

£276 13s. 4d. a year, inserted in his patent: the fees are received by the deputy and paid over to the chief deputy, for the use of the collector: they amounted last year to about £1855.

'This examinant also saith: That he himself has no salary, but is paid by the deputy, out of the fees he receives from merchants,* £360 a year, and by the deputy of the Coast business, out of the like fees, £88 4s. 0d. a year, and from the Receiver of the Trinity Lights £9 9s. 0d.

'J. MELLER.'

'*June* 16, 1785.

No. 26. *Specimens of documents used in the payment of Customs duties just prior to the Consolidation of* 1787.

ENTRY FOR SIXTY PAIRS BELLOWS.

Branches.	*Value of Parcel.*	*Duty.*
	£ *s.* *d.*	£ *s.* *d.*
Old Subsidy	10 0 0	0 10 0
New ,, ...	10 0 0	0 10 0
⅓ ,, ...	3 6 8	0 3 4
⅔ ,, ...	6 13 4	0 6 8
Subsidy 1747	10 0 0	0 10 0
Duty on Hides, &c.	45 0 0	2 5 0
Additional Duty on Hides, &c.	45 0 0	2 5 0
	130 0 0	
Impost, 1779	6 10 0	0 6 6
,, 1782	6 10 0	0 6 6
	143 0 0	7 3 0

(Explanation: The Old Subsidy value is the value as set in 1660. The duty on the old, new, ⅓, and ⅔ subsidies, and the Subsidy 1747 is at the rate of 5 per cent. on the value. The Duty on Hides, etc., is at the rate of 15 per cent. on the *genuine value* (£15) as declared by the importer. So is the Additional Duty on Hides, etc. The Imposts, 1779 and 1782, are at the rate of 5 per cent. on the total duties payable previous

* It is stated that the Collector's office was a sinecure, and evident that the chief deputy's was one as well.

to 1779. N.B.—The discounts for prompt payment had been abolished in 1781. Otherwise this document would have been almost unexplainable.)

STATEMENT OF DUTY PAYABLE ON TWENTY REAMS FRENCH ROYAL PAPER.

Branches.	*Value of Parcel (Document).*			*Duty.*		
	£	s.	d.	£	s.	d.
Old Subsidy	20	0	0	1	0	0
New ,, ...	20	0	0	1	0	0
⅓ ,, ...	6	13	4	0	6	8
⅔ ,, ...	13	6	8	0	13	4
Subsidy 1747	20	0	0	1	0	0
,, 1759	20	0	0	1	0	0
Impost 1692	100	0	0	5	0	0
French Duty	100	0	0	5	0	0
Duty on Soap, Paper, &c. ..	280	0	0	14	0	0
Add[l] Duty ,, ..	140	0	0	7	0	0
Duty on Paper, 1784 ..	140	0	0	7	0	0
	860	0	0			
Impost 1779	43	0	0	2	3	0
,, 1782	43	0	0	2	3	0
	£946	0	0	£47	6	0

(Explanation: The duty under the old, new, ⅓, ⅔, 1747, and 1749 subsidies is at the rate of 5 per cent. on the value as set in 1660. The Impost, 1692, is at the special rate of 25 per cent., the goods being French. The French Duty is the same. The Duty on Soap, Paper, &c., is a specific rate per ream according to quality = 10 reams atlas at 16[s], and 10 reams super royal at 12[s] = in all £14. The Additional Duty is half this. The Duty on Paper, 1784, is a specific rate per ream = 10 Atlas at 10[s], and 10 super royal at 4[s] = £7 in all. The imposts are at the rate of 5 per cent. on the produce of all duties previous to 1779.)

*No. 27. An account of the quantities of tobacco and snuff seized in England, Ireland, and Scotland in each year from 1789 to 1825 inclusive.**

Year.	England—		Scotland—		Ireland—	
	Lbs. tobacco.	*Snuff.*	*Lbs. tobacco.*	*Snuff.*	*Lbs. tobacco.*	*Snuff.*
1789	401,710	36,909	128,980	4,297	153,838	154
1790	149,964	19,943	79,426	2,303	209,981	328
1791	177,449	20,310	291,812	4,260	306,292	715
1792	144,563	8,937	89,408	2,168	233,054	247
1793	156,528	1,489	81,806	2,009	80,092	369
1794	137,868	4,896	50,922	2,231	39,216	18
1795	96,073	5,935	66,284	2,272	20,596	
1796	164,295	9,989	114,565	747	44,066	
1797	112,178	3,618	15,091	410	606	
1798	86,584	2,836	5,277	19	7,763	6
1799	92,182	4,702	4,091	101	31,542	83
1800	121,685	1,557	283,276	1,046	95,879	90
1801	133,752	3,235	5,254	130	62,138	
1802	108,134	10,016	24,167	28	83,907	147
1803	134,846	1,341	7,060	1,246	239,955	141
1804	117,597	1,527	2,276	1,860	237,987	46
1805	181,209	947	13,786	908	115,358	146
1806	43,601	606	3,928	1,969	195,267	407
1807	102,955	738	31,592	629	112,109	259
1808	21,607	2,867	3,422	621	120,119	140
1809	6,466	1,086	2,752	1,270	15,196	147
1810	21,862	360	2,136	462	50,640	73
1811	39,964	170	1,850	387	17,741	77
1812	99,871	383	1,312	759	52,905	154
1813	3,313	519	534	454	5,222	126
1814	4,331	855	723	270	6,099	77
1815	18,026	578	1,039	125	32,723	9
1816	18,005	2,941	930	248	22,314	35
1817	51,985	1,254	1,195	148	59,219	77
1818	64,295	521	6,007	352	43,884	93
1819	28,461	760	3,481	531	201,239	165
1820	73,247	1,445	35,415	1,850	883,971	179
1821	73,298	548	22,418	2,219	424,823	138
1822	72,378	3,338	80,914	5,026	525,466	12
1823	98,748	11,633	14,113	189	254,991	31
1824	97,969	12,509	1,884	579	282,035	60
1825	100,970	6,287	1,373	13	234,119	39

* This is not a complete account, yet it is the only one available. From 1789 to 1814 the English account does not include the London Customs seizures, the records previous to 1814 being destroyed by fire. From 1789 to 1797 the Irish account does not include the Excise seizures in Ireland, the records having disappeared.

(Remarks : The Irish record for 1797 and 1798 was affected by the rebellion. Undoubtedly the whole record for 1813 and 1814 was rendered imperfect by the burning of the London Custom-house. The immense increase in the seizure records of Ireland in 1819 and 1820 marks the establishment of the Coastguard. For the previous ten years smuggling on the south and west coasts of Ireland, by Americans especially, had been vast and unchecked. Note also the increase in the English and Scottish records in 1820-22. The English Coast Blockade was established in 1817, and the Scottish Coast-guard in 1819-20. *The rewards to seizing officers were increased* in 1820. All these new arrangements appear to have left their mark upon the seizure records.)

No. 28. *Comparison from two accredited authorities of separate statements of Customs payments into Exchequer* (*Great Britain*, 1802-06 ; *United Kingdom*, 1822-26).

(' No. 1 ' is accompanied by elaborate explanations as to the various disbursements from the gross receipts. ' No. 2 ' is quoted from a Parliamentary Return. The quoter heads it as a statement of ' Customs yield to the Exchequer,' which, if it means anything, must signify the actual payments into the Exchequer. Yet he states that the expenses of collection have not been deducted ! We have therefore deducted the said expenses from his account. It will be seen that if his statement had been accepted as a return of actual payments, the discrepancies would have been still more pronounced. It should also be stated that the account from which we have extracted ' No. 2 ' goes back to 1692, yet states that the returns for 1692-1706 are for Great Britain. It is to be assumed that ' England ' was meant.)

Year ending January 5 in—	*No.* 1.	*No.* 2.	
	£		£
1802			8,758,184
		Deduct charges of collection	523,588
	5,871,200		8,234,596
1803			7,698,958
		Deduct ..	549,614
	6,058,626		7,149,344

Year ending January 5 in—	*No. 1.*	*No. 2.*		
	£			£
1804				8,158,494
		Deduct	..	555,965
	7,179,620			7,602,529
1805				9,424,711
		Deduct	..	566,999
	8,357,871			8,857,712
1806				10,129,634
		Deduct	..	614,913
	9,084,458			9,514,721
1822				12,734,560
		Deduct	..	1,479,587
	10,582,762			11,254,973
1823				12,958,101
		Deduct	..	1,547,486
	10,663,616			11,410,615
1824				13,854,536
		Deduct	..	1,567,779
	11,498,762			12,286,757
1825				13,519,151
		Deduct	..	1,462,096
	11,327,741			12,057,055
1826				18,749,076
		Deduct	..	1,504,703
	16,541,524			17,244,373

No. 29. *Copy of Scottish Board's Minute of February* 1, 1813, *showing material for indictment of smugglers.*

'Ordered that the Solicitor do prosecute the Persons concerned in these transactions, as proposed by Mr. Menzies, viz.:

'John Miller, Master of the *Hercules* of Glasgow, upon the Act 8th Ann, Cap. 7, Sec. 17, for the penalty of treble the value of 80 gallons of Rum, for having been assisting or otherwise concerned in unshipping the same without payment of

No. 30.—Comparative statement of duties levied on brandy and rum, tobacco, tea, and wine: 1803 to 1854.

Articles.	1803.	1826.	1834.	1845.	1854.	*Explanatory Remarks.*
Brandy and Rum (The rates on most other spirits were higher.)	Brandy, single, per gallon, 13s. 10d. Rum, single, 11s. 1d.	Brandy, per proof gallon, £1 2s. 6d. Rum, 8s. 6d.	Brandy, per proof gallon, £1 2s. 6d. Rum, 9s.	Brandy, per proof gallon, £1 2s. 10d. Rum, 9s. 4d.	Brandy, per proof gallon, 15s. Rum, into England, 8s. 2d. Rum, into Scotland, 6s. Rum, into Ireland, 4s. 4d.	'Single' means underproof. Overproof spirits were called 'double.' The rates from 1826 onward are per proof gallon. The rum rate is that levied on Plantation rum, which was preferentially treated.
Tobacco	British possessions: leaf, per pound, 1s. 7d. Spanish, 4s. 8d. Cigars (not shown).	British possessions: in America, leaf, per pound, 3s. 9d. Russia, Turkey, E. I. Co.'s possessions, 4s. Any other place, 6s. Cigars, 18s.	British possessions in America: leaf, per pound, 2s. 9d. Any other place, 3s. Cigars, 9s.	All kinds of leaf, per pound, 3s. 1d. Cigars, 9s. 5d.	All kinds of leaf, per pound, 3s. 1d. Cigars, 9s. 5d.	
Tea	Under 2s. 6d. a pound, 60 per cent. *ad val.* 2s. 6d. and above, 90 per cent.	At or under 2s. a pound, 96 per cent. Above 2s., 100 per cent.	Bohea, per pound, 1s. 6d. Congou, etc., 2s. 2d. Souchong, etc., 3s.	All kinds, per pound, 2s. 2d.	All kinds, per pound, 1s. 6d.	
Wine	French, per gallon, 10s. 4d. Spanish and Portuguese, 6s. 10d.	French, per gallon, 7s. 3d. Cape, 2s. 5d. All other wines, 4s. 10d.	Cape, per gallon, 2s. 9d. All other wines, 5s. 6d.	Cape, per gallon, 2s. 10d. All other wines, 5s. 9d.	British possessions, per gallon, 2s. 10d. All other wines, 5s. 9d.	

Fractions of a penny disregarded. Readers who desire to authenticate these figures must bear in mind that the duties for 1803 include the 'temporary war duties,' but not the 'Convoy duty.' Whenever there was a privilege granted to goods brought in British ships, the preferential rate has been used. When an Excise duty was levied as well as a Customs duty, the two rates have been totalled. The rates shown for tobacco and wine in 1845 and 1854, and for tea in 1845, include the 'additional 5 per cent. duty.'

duties: on the Act 9th Geo. 2*, Cap. 25, Sec. 23, for the like penalty, in respect the said Rum was put out of the said vessel within the distance of 4 leagues of the coast of this kingdom: on the Act 26th, Geo. 3, Cap. 40, Sec. 8, for the penalty of £200 for breaking bulk within the said distance from the coast: and on his bond granted pursuant to the Act 26th Geo. 3, Cap 40, Sec 15.†

'The Mate of the said vessel upon the Act 26th, Geo. 3, Cap. 40, Sec. 8, for the penalty of £200 for breaking bulk: and on his smuggling bond given pursuant to the 15th Section of the said Act.

'Robert Russel, weaver, in Kilbride, who brought the Rum in his boat to Little Cumbrae, and afterwards conveyed the same to Kilbride, on the Act 8th Ann, Cap. 7, Sec. 17, for the penalty of treble the value of the Rum, for having been assisting or otherwise concerned in the unshipping thereof without payment of duties: for the like penalty in respect the Rum knowingly came into his hands, after being so unshipped: under the Act 9th, Geo. 2, Cap. 25, Sec. 23, for the like penalty of treble value for having been aiding and assisting or otherwise concerned in receiving the said Rum after being so unshipped within 4 leagues of the coast.

'Robert Barbour, farmer, in Yonderfield, in the lands of Arniel, and his sons Humphry and William Barbour, on the Act 38th, Geo. 3‡, Cap. 89, Sec. 8, for the penalty of treble the value of the 50 bolls of Irish salt, for being concerned or employed in unshipping, landing, removing, or putting the same on shore, without payment of duties: and for the like penalty in respect the said salt knowingly came to their hands after being so unshipped.'

No. 31. *Copy of a certificate of registry (de novo) as granted to a ship built in the British Plantations. Date, March* 15, 1815.

'In pursuance of an Act passed in the twenty-sixth year of the reign of King George the Third, intituled: an Act for the further Increase and Encouragement of Shipping and Navigation:

'*William Fryer of Wimborne in the County of Dorset, and*

* Known as the 'First Act of Indemnity.' See vol. i., p. 212.
† Known as the 'Manifest Act.' See vol. i. p. 326.
‡ See vol. i., p. 404.

Robert Pack of the town and County of Poole, Merchants, having taken and subscribed the Oath required by this Act and having sworn that *they are* sole owners of the Ship or Vessel called *Eagle* of *Poole* whereof *William Stickens* is at present Master, and that the said Ship or Vessel was *built at Barrington in Nova Scotia in the year* 1801, *as appears by a certificate of a former Register granted at St. John's, Newfoundland,* 22nd *Oct*[r] 1814: *No.* 69 *now delivered up, and cancelled and the said vessel registered* de novo *at this Port, in pursuance of the Act of* 27 *Geo.* 3. *Cap.* 19: and *John Stansmore, tide-surveyor,* having certified to us that the said vessel is *British Plantation built* has *one* Deck and *two* Masts; that her length from the Fore Part of the Main Stem to the After-part of the Sternpost aloft is 56 *feet* her breadth at the broadest part, above the Main Wales 17 *feet* her height *in the hold* 8 *feet,* and admeasures $64\frac{63}{94}$ Tons: that she is a *square-sterned Schooner with rise quarter-deck,* has no Gallery, and *no figure*-Head, and the said subscribing owner having consented and agreed to the above Description and Admeasurement, and having caused sufficient Security to be given, as is required by the said Act, the said *Schooner Eagle* has been duly registered at the Port of *Poole.*

'Given under our hands and seals of office, at the Custom House in the said Port of *Poole,* &c., &c.'

No. 32. *Copy of 'Libel' exhibited in the Vice-Admiralty Court, Jamaica, by the naval officer who seized the American brigantine 'Union' for trading in the Plantations contrary to the Navigation laws.*

'JAMAICA.

'Malcolm *qui tam v*[s] The brigantine *Union.*

'In the Court of Vice-Admiralty.

'Charles Malcolm, Esquire, late Commander of His Majesty's Ship *Sybelle* as well for and on behalf of our Sovereign Lord the King as for and on behalf of himself the said Charles Malcolm and his Officers, Seamen, Marines, and Mariners.

against

A certain Brigantine or Vessel called the *Union* whereof one Allen Putnam late was or pretended to be Master her Tackle Furniture and Apparel and certain Goods, Wares, and

Merchandize. To wit: Twenty-six hogsheads and seventy-two boxes of Fish, eighty boxes of Soap, fifty boxes of Candles, forty-nine barrels of Beef, three hundred barrels of Flour, seven bales of Sheeting, a quantity of Lumber, twenty-two barrels of Potatoes, 5 boxes of Nails, one hundred and thirty Shooks, and three thousand Hoops, laden in and on board her.

'Be it remembered that on the twenty-second day of February in the fifty-ninth year of the Reign of our Sovereign Lord George the Third, by the Grace of God of the United Kingdom of Great Britain and Ireland King and of Jamaica Lord Defender of the Faith and so forth (&c.), came Charles Malcolm Esquire (&c.) by John Lynch one of the Proctors of this Honourable Court and the true and lawful Procurator and Proctor of him the said Charles Malcolm (&c.) in this behalf prosecutor against a certain Brigantine called the *Union* (recapitulation of cargo, etc.) To wit, at the Parish of Port Royal in the County of Surry and said island of Jamaica and within the jurisdiction of this Honourable Court the said island of Jamaica then and now being an island plantation or colony in America belonging to and in possession of His Majesty and the said Charles Malcolm late Commander as aforesaid on the behalf aforesaid by his Proctor aforesaid doth article allege and propound and say that after the making and passing of a certain Act of Parliament made and passed in the twelfth year of the Reign of His late Majesty King Charles the Second intitled 'An Act for the Encouraging and Increasing of Shipping and Navigation' and also after the making and passing of a certain other Act of Parliament made and passed in the seventh and eighth years of the Reign of His late Majesty King William the Third intitled 'An Act for preventing Frauds and regulating Abuses in the Plantation Trade' and before the day of exhibiting this Libel To wit on the fifteenth day of February in the year of Our Lord One Thousand Eight Hundred and Nineteen and whilst the said Charles Malcolm was Commander of His Majesty's ship *Sybelle* he the said Charles Malcolm as such Commander as aforesaid did seize as forfeited to and for the use of our said Sovereign Lord the King and of himself the said Charles Malcolm his officers (&c.) the said Brigantine or Vessel called the *Union* (recapitulation of cargo, etc.). For this, To wit that whereas after the making and passing of the Acts of Parliament aforesaid and before the day of exhibiting this Libel (&c.) certain goods wares and merchandizes To wit (recapitulation) were imported in the said Brigantine or Vessel called the *Union* into the island of Jamaica To wit into the port of Port Royal in the parish of (&c.) and within the jurisdiction (&c.) the said Brigantine or Vessel called the *Union* not being of the Built* of England or of the Built of Ireland or the said Colonies or Plantations and wholly owned by the People thereof or any of them and Navigated with the Master and three-fourths of the Mariners of the said places only and the said Brigantine or Vessel not having been taken as Prize and Condemnation thereof made in one of the Courts of Admiralty in England Ireland or the said Colonies or Plantations and not being navigated by the Master and three-fourths of the Mariners English or of the said Plantations as aforesaid and whereof the property did belong to Englishmen contrary to Law and to the form and effect of the aforesaid Statutes in such case made and provided whereby and by force of the said several Statutes or one of them the said Brigantine or Vessel called the *Union* (recapitulation) became and were and are forfeited and lost One Moiety thereof to the use of our said Sovereign Lord the King and the other Moiety thereof to the use of the said Charles Malcolm his Officers Seamen Marines and Mariners.

'Whereupon and upon all and singular the premises the said Charles Malcolm (&c.) by his Proctor aforesaid humbly prays that the said Brigantine or vessel called the *Union* (&c.) may be confiscated and adjudged forfeited and lost one half thereof (&c.) and that this libel may be received.

'William Burge (Attorney-General).
Lynch (Proctor).'

N.B.—Many irritating repetitions have been left out in our copy (see the parentheses).

No. 33. *Extract from a petition furnished by Tortola merchants*, 1815.

(Forty-five of the principal merchants of St. Thomas, West Indies, petitioned the British Rear-Admiral, Sir P. C. Durham, that St. Thomas might still be the place of rendezvous for West Indiamen waiting to be convoyed to

* Build, invariably expressed as 'Built' in the old Statutes.

Great Britain, although the island had ceased to be a British possession. On hearing of this the merchants of Tortola put forward a counter-petition, as below :)

'SIR,

'On the restoration of the Danish islands, St. Thomas becoming thereby a foreign colony, we were firmly persuaded that Tortola would again be the place of rendezvous. Our hopes were kept alive notwithstanding that merchants of St. Thomas addressed your Excellency. We had not the slightest apprehension that a foreign port would be preferred to Tortola, where from 300 to 400 sail have frequently been accommodated, but we cannot conceal the astonishment and regret we have felt on reading a copy of your answer to the merchants of St. Thomas, and this day seeing a part of the fleet pass this port on their way to that island. We had relied on one paragraph in which your Excellency had assured the Gentlemen of St. Thomas that you would do everything in your power to grant their request, 'if the planters of the different islands should start no objection.'

'As another fleet will be collected before the Double Insurance takes place, we cannot, without forgetting our duty as British subjects to be jealous of our privileges, refrain from submitting remarks on the injurious effect likely to be produced to the British revenue, trade, and subjects. First, as to the revenue: we will suppose a fleet of 200 sail anchor in the roads and harbour of St. Thomas, with a boat from every second ship on shore every day, being little short of 400 sailors, who will furnish themselves with East India goods, gin, tobacco, and other contraband articles, to be smuggled into England.'

(The petitioners then assume that one or more of the merchantmen may be run ashore at St. Thomas.)

'—and discharge and repair damages. The expense must be paid for by the sale at that foreign port of part of her sugars, the duties whereon are lost to his Majesty, whereas no such loss would accrue if the rendezvous was at a British port. We refer your Excellency to the Act of 12 Chas. 2nd.

'The provision trade from Ireland and our North American colonies would receive material injury. Captains of vessels and passengers, from Demerara down to Tortola, knowing that St. Thomas is to be the rendezvous, and that they can there purchase provisions of the American States from 30 to

50 per cent. less than Irish or British-American, would take in their stores at that port, thereby carrying an alarming influx into a foreign island.

'There are many situations in which vessels may be placed, if suffered to rendezvous there, calculated to affect their policies of insurance. And, should any sudden change take place in the politics of Europe while a British fleet was lying in a Danish port, consequences might be serious.

'It may be asserted that the flesh and vegetable markets at Tortola do not equal those at St. Thomas. This is not absolutely the case: beef, mutton, pork, poultry, and vegetables are produced here in great abundance, and a notice of one or two days of the expectation of a Convoy is quite sufficient. These islands contain a great number of poor but industrious inhabitants. As British subjects they certainly have superior claims over foreigners. Many of them have supplied themselves with articles they expected to sell to the fleet.

'We trust that your Excellency will direct the next fleet to assemble at and sail from the Harbour of Tortola. Our utmost and united exertions will be used to render every service and accommodation to the ships, which we trust will be found to equal what they have ever experienced at St. Thomas.'

(The above proves that the art of mercantile advertisement was almost as well understood a hundred years ago as now. Below is an extract from the Rear-Admiral's reply:)

'GENTLEMEN,

'I am in receipt of your petition, with your admirable calculation, which nothing can equal but the exorbitant charges, &c., which I know from experience the Squadron has met with in many instances at Tortola.

'I consider the anchorage of St. Thomas far superior to that of Tortola, which port I shall never make the rendezvous when it can be avoided.'

The indomitable merchants of Tortola sent the correspondence to the Board of Customs.* Board's Minute thereon:

'The parties to be acquainted that this is not a matter that comes under the cognisance of this Board.'

* Evidently thinking that the Board might put the Navigation laws into operation against the Rear-Admiral.

No. 34. *Extract from a petition against customs officers' fees* (1816).

'Virgin Islands, Tortola.

'To the Right Honourable the Comm[rs] of Customs.

'The humble petition and memorial of sundry inhabitants of the Virgin Islands, who are owners of small boats and vessels under tonnage: Sheweth: That, by the docket of fees established by the Commissioners sent out from England in the year 1812 or thereabouts, small boats from ten to twelve tons burthen are required to pay to the different officers of the Customs the sum of six dollars, equal to the sum of two pounds nine shillings and sixpence Tortola currency, for a non-objection note in ballast, and a further sum of two shillings at the Revenue fort.

'That the owners of the boats of the description aforesaid are persons possessing very little or no property, and many of them with large families to support, and that to be done through no other channel than by the employment of their said boats.

'That this description of boats are most commonly employed to carry passengers and letters through the Virgin Islands, and to and from the adjacent Danish islands: That many of the said boats, being decked for safety from the high seas that run between these islands, are compelled to take registers, and to pay at the Custom-house thirteen-and-a-half dollars, and to his honor the President four dollars . . . .

'That one of your memorialists is the owner of a small boat of ten tons burthen, which boat is employed by the deputy postmaster at St. Croix* to convey the letters which come through the English post-office to this island, and from hence to St. Croix: That at St. Croix he does not pay one farthing for Custom-house fees, but at this port is compelled to pay six dollars, which is nearly a moiety of the sum which your memorialist receives for the voyage, out of which sum three persons are paid wages as seamen, exclusive of providing them with provisions.

'Your petitioners therefore humbly pray your Honors to take their situation into your serious consideration' (etc., etc.).

(Eleven signatures.)

(No relief afforded.)

* Danish colony.

No. 35. *Précis of a petition sent to the King by Trinidad merchants, praying relief on account of the forfeiture of their goods for duties and law costs, the said merchants having objected to pay duties, levied according to Spanish law as operating in the island before it became a British colony. (Probable date,* 1820.)

'TO THE KING'S MOST EXCELLENT MAJESTY IN COUNCIL.

'The humble petition and appeal of Mess[rs] Edgar, Lyon, and Fleming of the island of Trinidad, merchants, Mess[rs] Walrond, Edmonstone, and Co. of the same place, merchants, and Mess[rs] Clarke and Co. of the same place, merchants: most humbly sheweth:

'That in the month of December, 1814, your petitioners were severally concerned in the importation into Trinidad, in British vessels navigated according to law, of certain manufactured goods from Scotland, upon which a duty of 3½ per cent. *ad valorem* was charged by the officers of the Customs in that colony, and in order to procure entry of the same your petitioners were obliged to give their several promissory notes for the amount of the duty on the said articles in which they were interested: your petitioners Messrs. Edgar, Lyon, and Fleming, and Walrond, Edmonstone, and Co. two several notes for the sum of 1712 dollars and for the sum of £785 10s. currency respectively, your petitioners Messrs. Duncanson, Clarke, and Co. for the sum of £350 currency.

'That your petitioners, being advised that the demand of the said duties was unwarranted and illegal, respectively refused to pay the said promissory notes when they became due, whereupon Henry Fuller, Esq., H.M. Attorney Gen[l] of the said island, upon the 3rd Feb. 1815, commenced proceedings against your petitioners in the Tribunal of the Intendant according to the forms of Spanish law. Your petitioners were cited to appear before the Escribano of the said Court. An order was issued to seize the goods of your petitioners to the value of the said sums and costs.

'That execution was levied upon the goods of your petitioners, and the same remained sequestered, after which your petitioners were cited to shew cause why final judgment should not be pronounced against them.

'That your petitioners prayed to be allowed copies of certain ordinances of 1783, 1786, 1794, and 1796, relating to the payment of duties, issued by the Spanish Government, which were in force at the time of the surrender of the colony to the British arms in February, 1797.

'That copies of the Ordinances of 1783 and 1786, and certain Ordinances of 1795 and 1796, were furnished to your petitioners, but they were unable to obtain copies of certain other Ordinances of 1796, regulating by whom and under what circumstances the said duty was to be payable, and they prayed permission to prove by oral testimony the manner in which the duty had been levied: viz., upon foreign goods imported in foreign bottoms at the time when the colony remained in possession of the Spaniards.

'That H.E. the Governor, exercising the office of Intendant, gave judgment, allowing the said Ordinances to be received in evidence, but rejecting the prayer of the petition for leave to adduce the other evidence tendered as above.

'That your petitioners, conceiving themselves aggrieved, presented a petition to the Governor, praying leave to appeal to your most gracious Majesty in Council.

'That the said Attorney Gen[l] presented a petition to the said Court, in opposition, in which he insisted on the legality of the said demands.

'That H.E. the Governor gave judgment, directing execution to be carried into effect against the goods seized, that the same should be sold, and that the Attorney Gen[l] should enter into bond on behalf of the Crown to make restitution in case the said judgment should be reversed, and admitting the appeal upon the usual securities.

'That the goods were sold for the payment of the said promissory notes, amounting to £1991 10s. currency, with taxed costs amounting to £1066 19s. 6d., the amount of which was received by the Treasurer of the said island of Trinidad.

'Your petitioners pray that the said decree may be reversed and annulled, and that a day may be appointed to hear the said appeals, and that Henry Fuller, Attorney Gen[l] for the island of Trinidad, do appear and attend the hearing thereof, and that your Majesty will be pleased to grant to your petitioners such other relief as to your Majesty shall seem meet.'

(Unfortunately there is no information as to how the colonial Hampdens fared, for the Board disowned connection with the case, pointing out that the 3½ per cent. duty was purely colonial. The 3½ per cent. duty had been abolished, so far as British *linen and cotton goods* were concerned, by a Privy Council Order of November 27, 1815. It would be interesting to know whether there was really any legal authority for the continuance of a Spanish duty, after the date of British occupation, and also whether the original duty was levied on *all* kinds of goods, or, as the appellants claimed, merely on foreign goods in foreign ships. It is apparent that the legal costs, as usual, were monstrous, and that the Crown lawyer was determined to secure them.)

No. 36. *Documents connected with the clearance of a British vessel (foreign-built, evidently taken as prize and then given a British Register) with a cargo of spirits and molasses from one British colony to another. Date* 1820.

(1. Licence. 2. Entry of goods outwards. 3. Certificate of clearance. 4. Certificate that 4½ per cent. duties paid. 5. Master's bond that goods shall not be landed contrary to Navigation laws. 6. Certificate of origin of goods. 7. Master's bond that such part of cargo as consists of spirits shall not be landed in the Isle of Man. 8. List of crew [missing from file].)

No. 1.

'*Saint Christopher.*

'Whereas it has been represented to us by Roger Woodburne of the said island Merchant that it is his wish to export from the same direct to the islands of Malta and Gibraltar on board the brig *Superior* Andrew Cook master the following articles being of the growth produce and manufacture of the said island That is to say eighty puncheons of rum fifty puncheons of molasses thirty puncheons of rum shrub eight hogsheads and seven tierces of muscovado sugar amounting in value to the total sum of two thousand one hundred and forty-seven pounds ten shillings sterling money of Great Britain. And whereas he has therefore requested us to grant him a Licence for that purpose we do hereby grant him the said Roger Woodburne a permission or Licence to load the said articles on board the said brig *Superior* bound direct to the island of Malta and Gibraltar aforesaid. He with the said Andrew Cook master of the said brig having given the security required by law.

'Given under our hands and seals of office at the Custom House, Basseterre, this 13th day of November, 1820, in the first year of His Majesty's reign.

'C. Woodley, Collector.
W. H. Male, Controller.'

No. 2.

'St. Christopher, 16th *Novem.*, 1820.

'On Board the *Brig Superior, Andrew Cook*, Master, for *Gibraltar*.

Roger Woodburne.

'*Marks*.

W Nos 1/15	8 Hogsheads Sugar at 1400 is 11200	
	7 Tierces —do— at 800 is 5600	
	16800 lbs.	
W 1/80	80 puncheons Rum at 90 is 7200 *gallons*.	
W 1/50	50 puncheons Molasses at 90 is 4500 *gallons*.	
W 101/130	30 puncheons Shrub at 90 is 2700 *gallons*.	

Sugar duty 756 *lbs*.			
Rum and Shrub duty 445½ *galls*.	@ 2s. 9d. ..	..	£61 5 1½
Molasses duty 202½ ,,	,, 2s. ..	..	20 5 0
			£81 10 1½

'*Jno Hasell, Junr*
Actg Searcher

To the Waiters and Searcher.

'*C. Woodley*, Collector.
W. H. Male, Controller.'

(Authors' Note.—The duties were the '4½ per cent.' The sugar duty was taken in kind; the rum and molasses duties were commuted. The searcher's examination is shown on the back of the document.)

No. 3.

'*Saint Christopher*.

'These are to certify all whom it may concern that *Andrew Cook* master or Commander of the *brig Superior* burthen *246* tons, mounted with *no* guns, navigated with *12* men, *foreign* built, and bound for *Gibraltar*, having on board'

(Here follows recapitulation of cargo)

'hath here entered and cleared his said vessel according to law.

'Given under our hands and seals (etc.).

'*C. Woodley, Collr.*
W. H. Male, Contr.'

No. 4.

'*Saint Christopher.*

CUSTOM HOUSE, *Basseterre.*

'These are to certify, That the *brig Superior*, *Andrew Cook* master, for *Gibraltar* hath here loaden and taken on board'

(Recapitulation of cargo)

'for which his Majesty's Duty of Four-and-Half per Cent. hath been here fully answered and paid.

'Given under (etc.).

'*C. Woodley, Collr.*
W. H. Male, Contr.'

No. 5.

'*Saint Christopher.*

'These are to certify all whom it doth concern, that'

(Recapitulation as to master, vessel, destination, and cargo)

'and hath here given bond with *one* sufficient surety in the sum of *Two Thousand Pounds* with condition That all Rum which shall be laden on board the said ship shall not be landed at any part of Europe to the northward of Cape Finisterre, except Great Britain or Ireland, and that all other non-enumerated goods (except Rum) so laden on board thereof shall not be landed at any port of Europe to the northward of Cape Finisterre, except in Great Britain, Ireland, Jersey, or Guernsey. And these are further to certify that it appears by the original Register now produced to us that the above-mentioned ship was registered at *Liverpool* the *11th* day of *August 1816.*

'Given under (etc.).

'*C. Woodley, Collr.*
W. H. Male, Contr.'

(AUTHORS' NOTE.—Readers may be referred to Sec. 30, Cap. 52, 6 Geo. 3; Cap. 2, 7 Geo. 3; and Sec. 3, Cap. 28, 9 Geo. 3.)

No. 6.

'*Saint Christopher.*

'These are to certify that proof has been produced to us by affidavits, agreeable to the Act 4 Geo. 3, Cap. 15, that the undermentioned goods and merchandize, now shipped on board the *brig Superior*, *Andrew Cook* master, bound for

Gibraltar, are of the growth, produce, or manufacture of the British Colonies :'

(Recapitulation of cargo and details of registry.)

'Given under (etc.).

'*C. Woodley, Collr.*
W. H. Male, Contr.'

No. 7.

'*Saint Christopher.*

'These are to certify'

(Details as to master, ship, cargo, etc.)

'and hath also here given Bond with *one* sufficient surety in the sum of *Two Thousand Pounds* with condition that the said *Rum, Shrub*, or any part thereof, shall not be carried to or landed in the Isle of Man.

'Given under (etc.). *C. Woodley, Collr.*
W. M. Male, Contr.'

(AUTHORS' NOTE.—See Cap. 39, 5 Geo. 3 for the above. One document is missing from the file—the list of men, furnishing names, station, ages, stature, etc. This was issued so that the collector at port of arrival could satisfy himself that the proper number of 'King's subjects' were employed.)

No. 37. *List of Fees charged on Customs transactions by the officers at Kingston, Jamaica, up to* 1821.

By the Collector.	£	*s.*	*d.*
On entering a vessel with cargo from Europe	10	1	3
,, endorsing a British consul's manifest (for wine carried as cargo)	2	15	0
,, clearing vessel outwards for Europe (with cargo) ..	15	16	3
,, granting a new register (if required)	5	6	8
,, endorsing as to change of master or owner (if required)	1	15	0
,, Certificate to cancel bonds	0	12	6
,, Licence and bond if negro slaves carried as passengers ..	1	6	8
,, Certificate if carrying liberated negroes	1	6	8
,, Special manifest if tobacco carried as cargo	1	15	0
,, 'Sea Letter' for one voyage (if required)	1	15	0
Collector's total charges ..	42	10	0
Controller's charges (at ⅓ the collector's rate)	14	3	4
Tide-surveyor's charges on entry and clearance	2	13	4
Landing-surveyor's do.	2	13	4
Waiters and searchers (usually four in number) each £2 13s. 4d.	10	13	4
	£72	13	4

N.B.—The above is the *maximum* amount, leviable by the officers for their own emolument, on the kind of vessel that yielded most profit, when every impostable transaction possible took place. It will be seen, however, that if a vessel merely entered and cleared from Europe, the collector could charge £25 17s. 6d., the controller £8 12s. 6d., and six other officers £2 13s. 4d. each. Total, £50 10s.

The entry and clearance fees chargeable on vessels with cargo from a British colony (without any special transaction) were: collectors, £8 5s. 10d.; controllers, £2 15s. 3d.; other officers, £16. Total, £27 11s. 1d. Coasting drogers paid 7s. 6d. to the collector and 2s. 6d. to the controller for entry and clearance, and no more. If a vessel arrived with a cargo of goods taken as prize (a frequent occurrence), she had to pay special fees of £2 15s. to the collector and 15s. to the controller for a 'permit to land cargo.'

No. 38. *Gross receipt of Customs,* 1823 *to* 1838 *inclusive, with cost of collection (departmental statistics).*

Date.	*England.*		*Scotland.*		*Ireland.*	
	Gross.	*Cost per cent.*	*Gross.*	*Cost per cent.*	*Gross.*	*Cost per cent.*
	£		£		£	
1823	12,695,004	$7\frac{5}{8}$	891,409	$16\frac{1}{20}$	1,918,455	$23\frac{7}{8}$
1824	12,689,690	$7\frac{1}{2}$	953,837	$14\frac{7}{8}$	1,847,630	$19\frac{7}{8}$
1825	16,713,756	$5\frac{7}{8}$	1,512,960	$10\frac{1}{4}$	2,140,934	$17\frac{1}{5}$
1826	17,252,350	$5\frac{19}{20}$	1,299,351	$11\frac{5}{8}$	2,031,222	$17\frac{2}{5}$
1827	17,627,949	$5\frac{3}{4}$	1,376,044	$10\frac{5}{8}$	2,005,057	$16\frac{1}{2}$
1828	17,642,362	$5\frac{13}{20}$	1,376,001	$10\frac{1}{20}$	1,590,347	$19\frac{5}{8}$
1829	17,524,138	$5\frac{7}{20}$	1,372,089	$9\frac{3}{4}$	1,675,609	$18\frac{1}{8}$
1830	17,984,549	5	1,520,791	$8\frac{1}{4}$	1,579,183	$17\frac{1}{8}$
1831	16,688,586	$5\frac{5}{8}$	1,479,904	$7\frac{1}{2}$	1,477,448	$17\frac{7}{8}$
1832	16,689,751	$6\frac{1}{16}$	1,477,913	$7\frac{3}{5}$	1,516,908	$16\frac{5}{8}$
1833	15,724,967	$6\frac{9}{16}$	1,338,513	8	1,511,701	$16\frac{3}{10}$
1834	17,922,158	$5\frac{1}{2}$	1,441,393	$7\frac{1}{5}$	1,755,368	$13\frac{2}{5}$
1835	19,602,726	$5\frac{1}{8}$	1,529,996	$6\frac{5}{8}$	2,016,176	$12\frac{1}{4}$
1836	20,334,650	$4\frac{3}{4}$	1,587,648	$6\frac{3}{10}$	2,036,738	$11\frac{4}{5}$
1837	19,335,474	$4\frac{15}{16}$	1,626,291	$6\frac{3}{16}$	1,945,849	$12\frac{1}{4}$
1838	19,592,846	$4\frac{15}{16}$	1,666,398	$6\frac{3}{10}$	1,951,636	12

No. 39. *Scottish Board's Minute of August* 20, 1821.

'Read the report of the Solicitor on letter from Rear-Admiral Otway, with copy of one from Capt. Melville of the

Earl Moira cruiser, stating an unsuccessful attack by a boat's crew upon a smuggling lugger, in which one of the mariners was killed and two severely wounded.

'Ordered: Copies to be transmitted to Lerwick and Kirkwall, with directions to the officers to use every means in their power for obtaining information respecting the crew of the smuggling lugger, the port to which she belongs, and such other particulars as may lead to the discovery of the persons on board of her who were concerned in the attacking, killing, and wounding the mariners belonging to the *Earl Moira*.'

No. 40. *Irish Customs Board's advertisement of seized tobacco for sale in May*, 1824. (*The Cork record probably includes the goods seized in* 1822 *on the 'Peru,' at Kinsale, see pp.* 118-120). *Only the sound tobacco was sold; therefore the advertisement does not enlighten as to the full amount of tobacco seized.* (*Much of the 'Peru's' cargo was damaged.*)

NOTICE TO IMPORTERS OF TOBACCO.

'The Commissioners of Customs hereby give Notice that it is their intention to offer for sale, to Importers of Tobacco *only*, all Seized Tobaccoes in Store worth the duties, and which may have been legally condemned at the Ports of

Dublin ..	about	9,200 lbs.		Londonderry	about	15,000 lbs.
Cork ..	,,	185,000 ,,		Sligo ..	,,	600 ,,
Belfast ..	,,	100,000 ,,		Strangford ..	,,	12,000 ,,
Galway ..	,,	40,000 ,,		Waterford ..	,,	8,400 ,,
Limerick ..	,,	147,000 ,,				*

and to receive Tenders for the purchase of the same, on or before the first day of July next.

'And they further give Notice that the Sampling will commence on the 20th May, at which time every facility will be given the Merchants to view the same, as no claim will be admitted on account of the Tobaccoes being considered inferior to the Samples.

'Purchasers must either warehouse the Tobaccoes so purchased, according to law, or take them away in ten days after they shall be declared, paying down the purchase money, or† purchase money and duty as the case may be,

* Total between 230 and 231 tons.

† (Purchase money if the goods were to be warehoused; purchase money and duty if they were for immediate clearance.—AUTHORS.)

at the same time, otherwise the Board's agreement to the proposal to be null and void.

'As the Tobacco that may be purchased under the conditions of this Advertisement will be considered exactly in the same situation as if it had that day been regularly imported by the Merchant who makes the purchase, the purchasers must bear the expense attending removing, unwarehousing, warehousing, cooperage, and porterage.

'No proposal will be taken into consideration if the price offered be less than two pence per lb. exclusive of the Duties, and the proposal must have reference to each specific lot, as well as the marks and numbers of the several casks of which it is composed.

'Sealed proposals, with the words "Tenders for Tobacco" endorsed thereon, to be sent addressed under cover to the Secretary of the Board of Customs, Custom House, Dublin, on or before Twelve o'clock at noon on Thursday, the first July, after which time no tender will be received.

'By order of the Commissioners,

'C. I. A. MACLEAN,

'*Secretary.*'

'CUSTOM HOUSE, DUBLIN.'

No. 41. *Specimen of Colonial reports of seizure and subsequent proceedings*, 1824.

'CUSTOM HOUSE, ST. VINCENT.

'HONOURABLE SIRS,

'We have the honour to acquaint you that a seizure was made on the 2nd inst. by Messrs. Hodder and Billinghurst, of the sloop *Dandy* belonging to this port, and her cargo, consisting of 40 firkins and 4 ½-firkins butter, 69 boxes candles, and 18 cases oil, the whole being French property and prohibited.

'Information was received by the above officers that the *Dandy* (a suspected vessel) was in the Bay of Barmuallie, about 12 miles leeward of Kingstown, and that two or three persons were on shore endeavouring to effect a sale of her cargo. The officers proceeded (about sunset) in their boat, and fell in with the sloop one mile and a half from the shore, apparently beating to windward.

'The Attorney-General had no doubt as to the legality of their having so acted. The information was filed on the

16th. The goods have been appraised and sold under an order from the Court of Vice-Admiralty as perishable articles, and also the vessel.

'On the part of the prosecution the evidence will be respectable, and positive as to the intention to smuggle; it will also, we presume, be positive that they did come to an anchor that evening in violation of S. 18, Cap. 44, 3 Geo. IV.

'We beg to state that the goods belonged to two Frenchmen, passengers on board, who will probably be induced to enter a claim, under the impression that as nothing was landed the going into a port does not constitute importation. Their only excuse was to get a supply of water (having left Martinique only 36 hours) and that their destination was the Gulph of Paria.

'GEO. HUSKISSON, *Coll^r^.*
RICH^D^ ARRINDALE, *Cont^r^.*

	Appraised value in currency.			*Amount sold for.*		
	£	*s.*	*d.*	£	*s.*	*d.*
Sloop	82	10	0	97	0	0
Butter	168	0	0	261	4	9
Candles	138	0	0	156	6	6
Oil	22	10	0	31	9	9
	411	0	0	546	1	0

'Since the above was written we have been informed that a Mr. Lamotte, one of the passengers, having procured security, intends to put in a claim. He is a native and resident of Grenada, whose connexions are French, at Martinique.'

(Later report.)

'We have now to inform you that the Claimant (Etienne Lamotte) clandestinely withdrew from this island, and has not since been heard of. The sureties, becoming responsible in the sum of £60 sterling, were called on for payment. A monition was served, which has had the effect of bringing them to a promise of payment at an early day.

'From the heavy charges attending the prosecution of seizures in this colony, we submit the expediency of a revision of the colonial docket under which such charges are made.

'The present system cannot but operate as a discouragement to the officers, and severely indeed would it have been felt by them in the above case, had it been otherwise decided.'

No. 42. Notice offering reward for discovery of certain smugglers who had resisted and assaulted the customs men at Swanage.

'*13th November*, 1827.

'Whereas it has been humbly represented to the King that in the Evening of Wednesday the 19th of September last an outrageous assault was committed at Swanage, in the County of Dorset, upon the Persons of the Chief Officer and Crew while employed at their Duty in the said place in the Prevention of Smuggling, by a gang of about 70 Smugglers, most of whom were armed with Fire Arms, Swords, and Swingles, and that the said Chief Officer and Several of the Crew were severely wounded:

'His Majesty, for the better discovering of the Offenders concerned in the commission of this Outrage, is hereby pleased to offer His most gracious pardon to any one or more of them, present at and aiding in such Outrage (save and except those who actually assaulted and beat the Chief Officer and his Crew) who shall discover his or their accomplice or accomplices therein so that he or they may be apprehended and brought to justice.

'LANDSDOWNE.

'And the Commissioners of His Majesty's Customs do hereby offer a Reward of

£200

'to any Person or Persons who shall make such discovery (save and except as aforesaid), the same to be paid by the Collector of His Majesty's Customs, at the said port of Poole, on the Conviction of the Offenders or any of them.

'T. WHITMORE,
'*Secretary to the Commissioners of Customs.*'

No. 43. *Statement of the average annual emoluments of Plantation customs collectors (salaries and fees) during the five years ending January* 5, 1826 (*the date at which fees were abolished*).

Port.	*Amount per year of salaries and fees (salaries nominal).* £	s.	d.
Kingston, Jamaica*	6,525	11	4
Morant Bay "	881	10	6
Port Antonio "	823	6	2
Annatto Bay "	700	0	0
Port Maria "	758	2	9
St. Anne's "	459	18	10
Falmouth "	1,329	15	0
St. Lucea "	589	3	2
Montego Bay "	1,980	12	7
Savannah-la-Mar "	853	8	10
Bridgetown, Barbados	2,343	8	10
Oistens "	152	10	0
Speights "	417	8	11
Hole Town "	157	11	8
Antigua	1,835	17	7
St. Kitts	1,011	1	6
Nevis	504	4	6
Montserrat	352	0	0
Tortola	493	15	2
Grenada	1,839	1	0
St. Vincent	1,603	9	3
Dominica	1,057	14	0
Trinidad	2,392	5	9
Tobago	1,481	10	0
St. Lucia	1,291	4	4
Demerara†	5,219	8	7
Berbice	940	0	0
Nassau	789	13	4
Turk's Island	745	10	0
Exuma	103	9	4
Crooked Island	114	4	2
Bermuda	906	15	1
Newfoundland	1,928	1	11
Nova Scotia	2,013	15	0
Cape Breton	383	8	7
St. John, New Brunswick	3,210	9	11
St. Andrew's "	732	0	7
Prince Edward's Island	386	7	10
Quebec‡	4,261	15	1

* The Kingston controller made £2,551 7s. 5d.; the tide-surveyor, £1,067 19s. 7d.

† The Demerara controller made £1,766 9s. 5d.; the first clerk, £400; the second clerk, £366 13s. 4d.; the third clerk, £250; the three landing-waiters £1,021 4s. 11d. each.

‡ The Quebec controller made £2,098 14s. 10d.; the two landing-waiters £1,015 1s. 5d. each.

The total annual amount of the Plantation Customs emoluments

No. 44. *Licence granted by the Customs Board to a vessel (armed) to trade as a whaler (Southern Fishery),* 1828.

'Licence (No. 56513.)

'By the Commissioners for managing and causing to be levied and collected His Majesty's Customs.

'Value. *Three Thousand Pounds.*

'Suffer the *Ship* or vessel called the *Coronet* of *London John Kenney* master *Carvel* built *ninety-four* feet *eleven* inches long *twenty-five* feet *six* inches broad *two hundred and seventy-five* 3/94 tons, with a *standing* bowsprit *Armed with eight guns, six nine and twelve-pounders, thirty muskets, thirty pistols, thirty cutlasses, thirty rounds of powder and ball* whereof *Francis Deacon of Russell St. Bermondsey and others, are* owners, intended to be employed in *the Southern Whale Fishery*, to pass without any Lett, Hindrance, Seizure, or Molestation, provided it shall appear by certificate on the back hereof from the collector, controller, or other proper officer of the Customs that the said Owners have given security to their satisfaction as required by law. Given under our hands, &c.'

No. 45. *Customs officers at Montego Bay, Jamaica, to London Board, announcing negro insurrection,* 1831-32.

'*Jan.* 13*th*, 1832.

'Honourable Sirs,

'It is our painful duty to inform your Honors of the rebellion of the negroes of this parish, the destruction of the greater number of its country-houses and their properties by fire, much loss of life in several skirmishes between the military and the insurgents, as also by the execution of many of the leaders of the rebellion, martial law having been duly proclaimed on the last day of the year.

'It appears that some insurrections have taken place in other parishes, but the principal seat of the rebellion is in this, where the insurgents first commenced by firing several country-houses about 10 or 12 miles to leeward of this town, on the night of the 27th ult.

---

was £115,990 19s. 8d., divided amongst 243 officials. The total net amount remitted to the imperial Exchequer for the year ending January 5, 1826, was £15,032 15s. 6d. Thus, for every £1 gained by the Exchequer nearly £7 15s. was paid in salaries and fees to officials.

'We have reserved this letter to send by the Export Packet Post, that we might communicate the latest intelligence to your Honors, and we rejoice to state that the present appearances are much more favorable, several estates' negroes having returned quietly to work, many having surrendered, fires comparatively of rare occurrence, and hopes (but not very sanguine) are entertained of a speedy and entire suppression of the revolt.

'The headquarters of the Commander-in-Chief, Sir Willoughby Cotton, are in this town, and three vessels of war, under Commodore Farquhar, are in the harbour. No reasonable apprehension is entertained of an attack, but the utmost vigilance is required to guard against the prowling incendiary, as most of our servants are negro slaves, and our houses are principally built of wood.

'It is not, however, our province to enter into the general detail of this unhappy rebellion, but we beg leave to narrate such circumstances as relate more particularly to this office. On the first appearance of revolt your officers wrote to the Custos and Magistracy, dispensing with the legal exemption from the civil and military employment, and offering their services in whatever situation they might be thought most useful, out of office hours. We have accordingly been appointed Storekeepers of provisions for the troops, and the Magistracy having guaranteed the payment or satisfaction of duty on flour in bond, we have suffered delivery to the Commissariat in some instances without payment to the colonial Receiver General. In other cases, that officer being at an outport with his company of militia, we have rec[d] the duties ourselves, which we shall hand over to him on his return. We have also been required not to clear any vessel from this port, as they would afford a refuge for women and children in the event of emergency (and indeed most nights till lately they have been completely crowded), but this restriction has been dispensed with as regards droging vessels, and we now clear out large vessels on special order to that effect from the Commander of the Forces or the Commodore. When the danger of fire was more imminent, the regular troops not having arrived, we selected the more valuable documents of this office, and deposited them in a case for immediate removal to a vessel in the harbour in the event of alarm, and after the business of the day they are again deposited in the same case, and as the collector's clerk sleeps in a room adjoining the office, they would instantly be conveyed on board a sloop lying off the Custom House wharf.

'The above are the principal occurrences relating more especially to this department, to which we may be permitted to add that all your officers are at their posts, and we trust that the official duties have been correctly performed.

'We have the honor to be,

'Your most obedient Servants,

'JOHN ROBY, *Collector.*
N. ASHBY, *Controller.*'

Board's minute, 10th March, 1832:
'The Board approve.'

No. 46. *Extract from a statement as to obstruction of customs officers,* 1834 (*illustrative of the state of popular feeling in Tortola*).

'VIRGIN ISLANDS,
'TORTOLA.

'Augustus McCleverty, customs boatman, sworn, declares:

'Between 5 and 6 last evening Mr. Richardson, searcher, ordered the Customs boat to take him to Sea Cow Bay. We went towards "Jimmy Duff's Bottom"; there was nothing there. Mr. Richardson said "Pull towards Mr. Littsom's place"; we pulled off there but could see nothing. Mr. Richardson said "We'll go back"; while we were in the act of turning the boat one of the hands sung out that there was a boat just coming in. Mr. Richardson said "Boys, we will board, and see what she is." Boat still stood into the bay, and we pulled up to her. Mr. Richardson hailed and directed them to heave to; they immediately jibed and stood before the wind. We pulled alongside. Mr. Richardson said "Augustus, get on board." I went on board, and Eneas Pickering jumped out of the hold and said "—— —— you, you have no business here; I'll put you overboard," and did attempt it. I told him I was ordered to come on board; he said he did not care a ——, he would put himself out of the way, and hauled his wind and stood to the southward. He then said "—— —— it, put her about, put Augustus on board his boat." I said "Luff, or you'll run our boat down"; he said "—— —— it, draw her away." The hands in the Custom-house boat pulled her quickly and just crossed our bow. He then luffed up again, apparently with the intention of running the Custom-house boat down, so much so that the jib boom obliged Mr. Richardson to stoop to avoid it. Our boat managed to get alongside. Eneas said, " Augustus, I order you to get into your boat," which I immediately did. Dunbo, one of the hands in our boat, still held on to the vessel, and Edward Lloyd, one of the hands on board the said vessel, said " There is a bill forward : chop his —— hands off." A man came forward and took up something and made a chop at Dunbo which struck the boat. We tried to get alongside the second and third time, but the force opposed was too great : every time we went alongside they chopp'd at us.'

(Prosecution was instituted against Lloyd. The judge summed up in favour of a conviction, but the jury acquitted the prisoner. Crown costs, £23 5s. 9d. currency.)

No. 47. Official statement of life-saving services rendered by the Coastguard on the east coasts of England and Scotland (8th December, 1835, to April, 1836). Summarised.

8th *December*, 1835.—John Gregory, coastguardsman, stationed at St. Andrews, Fifeshire, leaped into the sea and saved the life of a local pilot. The Humane Society presented Gregory with an acknowledgment on vellum.

17th *January*, 1836.—The *Janet* of St. Andrews drove ashore at the mouth of Elie Harbour, Fifeshire. Lieut. Randall of the Coastguard and his men boarded her through a tremendous surf, saved the crew, and afterwards by extraordinary exertions saved the vessel and cargo. Thanked by the Board and the Admiralty. (Randall had frequently been thanked for daring conduct, having personally rescued over 30 people.)

17th *February*, 1836.—The *Janet and Agnes* wrecked off Scarborough. The coastguard saved four of the crew. The rest were drowned.

18th *Feby*, 1836.—The *Janet* of Scotland drove ashore near Pakefield, Suffolk. Coastguard rescued the crew. Vessel broke up directly afterwards.

Same date.—The same coastguardsmen rescued the crew of the *Venus* of Weymouth, getting a hawser on her and bringing the men off by repeated trips in a small boat. (At this time 15 vessels were ashore ' within a short distance.' The crews of all were saved by the coastguardsmen and fishermen.)

Silver medal to Coastguard Lieutenant Joachim, and a money reward to his crew.

Same date.—The *William Parker* of North Shields dashed to pieces against a cliff near Bridlington. The Coastguard saved the crew, hauling them up the cliff by ropes.

5th *March*, 1836.—The *London Packet* of Aberdeen went on the rocks off Peterhead. The Coastguard rescued crew and passengers just before the vessel broke up.

8th *April*, 1836.—The *Tyne* of Newcastle went ashore on a reef in Spey Bay. The Coastguard rescued the crew and saved ship and cargo.

No. 48. *Form of receipt given to the Dominican collector of customs by persons who received from him as apprentices negroes captured on slavers.*

'Received from the Hon'ble Symonds Bridgwater, collector of the Customs' (number) 'African apprentices, which I promise to feed and provide for agreeably to the Orders in Council, and for whom I promise to enter into any Indenture or Security required. I further promise to furnish the collector, in the course of ten days, with the particulars below mentioned of each apprentice, and I shall consider such promise as binding as if such Indenture or Security had actually been signed or given.

'1. His or her African name.
2. The name by which to be called in future.
3. The sex.
4. Age.
5. Height or stature.
6. Marks or peculiarities of feature.
7. Place of nativity.
8. Colour.

'ROSEAU, *May*, 1837.'

(The indenture alluded to was made between the collector and the person to whom the negro was apprenticed. It stated the term of apprenticeship, and the trade to which the negro was to be put, and that such negro should be properly fed, clothed, and doctored, baptized, and instructed in the Christian faith. The collector to have power to visit and interrogate the apprentice, nor was the latter to be removed by sea without Customs licence, or to be put to field labour if a female. If the master died before expiration of term the indenture became void. The penalty on the master for infraction was double the amount for which the negro would sell if a slave.)

No. 49. *Memorial presented to the Controller-General of Coastguard in* 1838 *by John Hatch, chief officer of Coastguard, St. Margaret's Bay.*

'HUMBLY SHEWETH,

'That your memorialist has served upwards of six years in the Royal Navy, as volunteer of the first class, midshipman, and master's mate, on board H.M. ships *Apelles*, *Barfleur*, *Nemure*, and *Ferret*, for which he encloses copies of certificates and testimonials.

'He was twice stranded (near Margate in December, 1808, and on the coast of France near Boulogne in May, 1812, when the *Apelles* was captured by the enemy). He at the Flushing expedition served as orderly to Sir Richard Keats, and was intrusted by him with despatches to General Hope. He was capsized in the *Apelles* jolly-boat off Dungeness in November, 1810, when the master, surgeon, and one seaman were drowned. He has been maimed twice (in the *Barfleur* near Toulon in 1813, and in the *Ferret* near Brest in 1815), the last time severely, at the capture of a fort, a man-of-war brig, cutter, and seven sail of merchant vessels, when your memorialist had charge of a boat.

'He has served nearly eighteen years as chief officer in the Coast Guard Service. He has made some seizures, and has had full charge of four vessels in distress, which were conveyed to places of safety by the coastguard: viz. the brig *Hugh* of Belfast, from Denmark, with a cargo of sugar—she was boarded between Portnessoch and the Mull of Galloway—she had two feet of water in her hold, and her rudder unshipped—all the crew left except the mate and two men: the sloop *Firth of Forth*, with a cargo of herring, on shore in the bay of Luce, totally abandoned by her crew: a sloop belonging to Limekilns with a cargo of lime, on fire near Burgh Head: and the Russian ship *Fathers Landa*, on shore near St. Margaret's Bay, and your memorialist does humbly hope that his servitude in the navy may entitle him to the same pay as mates of the navy of the present day are now to receive when appointed chief officers in the Coastguard Service.

'And your memorialist as in duty bound will ever pray.'

(Hatch encloses laudatory statements from naval officers Oliver, Dougal, Sir Edward Berry, Maitland, Stirling, Campbell, Prosser, Hellard, and Parry, also from the owner of the brig *Hugh*, the customs collector of Stranraer, the late M.P. for Galloway, the 'proprietor of Burghead,' and the Cromarty magistrates. It is to be trusted that this formidable backing secured him the extra pay desired.)

No. 50. *Application by James Brooke, afterwards Rajah of Sarawak, that his yacht 'Royalist,' lying at Table Bay on her way to the Indian Archipelago, should enjoy the 'exemption from report and clearance' usually granted to vessels of the Royal Yacht Squadron*, 1839.*

'THE HONORABLE THE COMMISSIONERS OF HER MAJESTY'S CUSTOMS.

'SIRS,

'Mr. Field, the collector of customs of this colony, having thought it his duty to enter my vessel at the Custom House, I have to beg the exemption from the dues, usually granted to yachts under similar circumstances. I have been given to understand likewise that no orders respecting yachts belonging to the Yacht Squadron have been received at the Custom House, and that in consequence all yachts arriving here must be considered in the light of merchant vessels. May I further request you will take the subject under your consideration and forward the necessary orders, should you be of opinion that the privileges of yachts of the Squadron extend to this colony as well as to our colonial possessions in the Mediterranean.

'I have the honor to be, Sirs,

'Your obedient Servant,

'J. BROOKE.'

'YACHT 'ROYALIST,' R.Y.S.,
TABLE BAY, CAPE OF GOOD HOPE,
20th March, 1839.'

Board's minute, June 14, 1839:

'Applicant to be informed that the collector of the Cape would appear to have acted correctly on the occasion in question, and that the Board cannot comply with this request.'

* Brooke was bound for Borneo, on his celebrated expedition against the Dyak pirates.

No. 51. *Customs notice, posted at Sydney, New South Wales,* 1841.

'NOTICE.

'Whereas

SMUGGLING

to a considerable extent is known to have been carried on in the Harbour of Port Jackson, and at other places along the Coast of this Colony, both by Persons commanding vessels and Persons residing on shore, who in other respects are considered respectable: And whereas it would appear, from the circumstance of no information having ever been given of such transactions, that it is not generally known that the Person giving information is entitled to a Reward, without having his Name divulged:

'Notice is hereby given, that any Person giving information to the Collector or other officer of Customs of any Spirits, Tobacco, or other dutiable goods being concealed on board any vessel, or having been put into any other vessel (either within or without the Harbour) or having been landed without payment of Duty, so as to lead to the seizure of such Goods, he or she will be entitled to one-third of whatever sum may accrue to the seizing officer from the sale of such Goods, however large it may be: and the name of the Party will not be suffered to transpire.

'J. GIBBES, *Collector.*'

'CUSTOM HOUSE, *August 6th*, 1841.'

No. 52. *Jersey smuggler's confession.*

'ISLAND OF JERSEY.

'The Deponent, ——, late master of the *Eliza* of this port, declareth that on the morning of the 8th June last, instead of proceeding to St. Germains (France) for whence she had cleared on the 6th proceeding, she went to Bonne-nuit Bay in this Island, the owner, ——, being on board, as well as —— of Bembridge, Isle of Wight, and ——, residing here, the two latter forming with myself the crew, and there took in from a boat which came alongside several times about two & a half tons of tobacco stems, spirits in casks, segars, and snuff, which Deponent had agreed with the above —— and a Mr. ——, tobacconist, of this place, to take to Wales, at the rate of fifty pounds per ton, but not to be paid for above two tons, two shares of which as master I was to receive, one-third each to the crew; and the other one-third for the vessel*; that we sailed the said night, —— remaining on board, and arrived at a bay to the eastward of that of Fishguard, near Cardigan, the afternoon of the 5th day, that —— proceeded on shore, with ——, and found that we had gone too far to the eastward, we then proceeded to Fishguard Bay, where —— landed at daybreak, and after some time requested us to keep off until the evening, which we did, running in at about 11 o'clock that evening, when he came off with five or six men in a boat, and took the goods in four or five trips on shore, he remaining on shore after the first trip, as also —— and ——, to assist in conveying the goods to a store close by, early the following afternoon we left, leaving him at Fishguard, and went to St. Germain, where we took in thirty-two sheep, and returned to this Island on the 29th following, accounting to the officers here for her long absence that we had been benipped at St. Germain. That we were not boarded or spoken by any English revenue officer, cutter, or boat, during our absence. That since that return five pounds were paid to myself and five to my wife, by Mr. ——, who has also paid five to —— (on account) being the whole that I have as yet received.

'That at about 3 a.m. of the 22nd Sept. last, when I left St. Helier's New Harbour without a clearance, we, being the aforenamed —— and —— in lieu of ——, on board as crew, proceeded to or near Grève de Lecq, and there found a large boat at anchor waiting for us, with goods which we took on board, being about five tons (some being obliged to be put in the cabin of our vessel) of leaf tobacco in bales from thirty-six to forty pounds each, snuff in bales and segars in boxes, and several bags of tea and cases of spirits. —— had left this island by *Sir Francis Drake*, Plymouth steamer, the same morning, on his way to Fishguard Bay, where I was instructed to meet him. We sailed the same morning, viz. the 22nd, and landed in our boat, manned by ——, the night of the 25th, at Fishguard, the boatmen returning on

* This is rather confusing, but it is likely that he was to get £66 13s. 4d., each of the crew one-third of the remainder, and the remaining £11 odd was to defray expenses of vessel.

board. I found that —— had not yet arrived there: after some time I found one of the men concerned in former transaction and returned on board with him and five or six others in a shore boat, and they or some of them in seven or eight trips to the shore landed all the tobacco, &c. Early next morning we got under weigh and proceeded to an adjacent bay to the westward, and there took in some stones for ballast, the vessel being too light for working, and returned to this Island on the evening of the 29th following; on our way home, say the 28th, we were boarded in Mount's Bay by a boat belonging, the Deponent believes, to the *Sylvia* revenue cutter, to the officer of which Deponent stated, to account for his being there without papers, that he had piloted a vessel down Channel. That for this trip, which Deponent had agreed with the aforenamed —— was to be paid at the rate of former trips, but not for more than four tons, he has as yet received nothing, and that in consequence thereof, as well as for other misunderstandings between Deponent and the above parties, he has considered it a duty which he owes himself to make the present declaration.

'Signed and declared before us at Custom House, Jersey, this 30th day of Novr. 1848.

'(Signed) —— ——

'G. B. RADFORD, *Pl Offr.*
JAs RIDER, *Contr.*'

No. 53. *Report made by the actual seizer of the Charlotte*, 1849.

'I am Mariner of the *Vigilant* revenue cruiser. On the evening of the 13th December instant I was one of the hands sent in a boat from the cutter to board a vessel seen coming up the river Thames. When we got near her I perceived her to be a barge. When the boat got alongside I with the rest of the boat's crew went on board. She had a quantity of straw on deck. I helped to remove some of the straw abaft the mast, and got to the main hatch, which was lifted up. I, with one hand, got into her hold, and by the light of the lanthorn saw there were some casks in it. I heard the gunner, who was on deck, ask what was in the casks, and heard somebody answer Tallow

'I then heard the gunner say he must see what was in them, and also heard someone answer, "You have got a good Prize."

'The gunner then came into the hold, and' (I) 'saw him take off a piece of tin which was nailed over a hole in one of the casks, there was a piece of wood under it.

'I then came on deck and with William Matson went into the barge's cabin, one of the men belonging to the barge followed us into the cabin, and he said "It's no use." I observed "How is that?" He said, "What is our loss is your gain."

'I asked him what they had got in the casks, he answered Leaf Tobacco, I then asked him how much there was, he said between nine and ten tons as far as he knew.

'I went on deck after that.

'The gunner then ordered me and three other hands to go into the boat and acquaint Captain Gowlland.

'Signed in my presence this 17th day of December, I. Moore Hodder, Coll^{r} (Rochester).

'FREDERICK FRENCH.'

No. 54. *Précis of papers connected with a large seizure, made 'on rummage,' at Liverpool, in* 1850.

'(To the Collector and Controller, Liverpool):

'RIVER INSPECTOR'S OFFICE.

'GENTLEMEN,

'I beg to report that yesterday afternoon, on rummaging the barque *Warrior* from New York, we discovered beneath the master's stateroom, behind a false bulkhead, 11 bales of leaf tobacco, weighing net 1380 lbs, and also a quantity of lumps of foreign manuf^{d} tobacco, weighing net 1263 lbs: total, 2643 lbs net.'

(Proceeds that master, both mates, and an apprentice, arrested.)

'They were charged before Edward Rushton, Esq., this day, when the master, first mate, and apprentice were remanded, to await the directions of the Honble Board. The magistrate being satisfied that the second mate had no guilty knowledge of the transaction, he was discharged.

'WILLIAM JAGO.'

(London Customs Solicitor's report on above):

'The vessel and tobacco are liable to forfeiture, and the parties to detention and prosecution before the justices for the penalty of £100 each, under Sections 3, 53, and 88, Cap. 87, 8/9 Vict.'

(Board's minute):

'Retain the goods as a seizure: proceed against the parties: keep hands on the vessel.'

(Master and mate imprisoned, the apprentice acquitted, it being thought he was coerced into assisting. Collector and controller call on Jago to state whether the master is able to maintain himself while in prison.)

'GENTLEMEN,

'I beg to report that I have to-day seen the above-named individual. He informs me that the whole of his property consists in an eighth part of the *Warrior*, and that his pay as master of that vessel has ceased, and that he is therefore not in circumstances to support himself in prison.

'WILLIAM JAGO.'

(Maintenance allowance accordingly. Six other part owners, natives of Drogheda, apply to Board, asking for release of their vessel.)

(Board's minute):

'Adverting to the quantity of tobacco seized, the Board do not see fit to release the vessel from seizure, and direct that she be returned into the Court of Exchequer for condemnation.'

(Owners apply to Treasury, quoting cases of two vessels owned by others, seized and afterwards released. Board state that in one case quoted the owners gave information leading to seizure: in the other only 980 pounds were found, and the vessel released on payment by owners of £100. They suggest release of *Warrior* on payment of £400. Owners fail to pay. Vessel condemned, and sold for £625.)

No. 55. *Advertisement offering reward for apprehension of a smuggler*, 1851 (*see* *p.* 352).

'TEN POUNDS
REWARD.

Whereas
SAMUEL NORTON,
late Master of the
Sloop *Samuel & Susannah* of Goole,
who stands charged with
SMUGGLING

Absconded from Goole on the 13th of September last. He is about 5 feet 5 inches high, dark eyes, rather roundshouldered, and a little bowlegged. He is about 35 years of age.

'All reasonable expenses, independent of the above Reward, will be paid on his apprehension, by immediately communicating with Mr. George Cordukes, Superintendent Constable, Goole, who holds a warrant against him.

'There cannot be a doubt of his conviction, as the *Vessel and Goods were condemned in the Exchequer in Michaelmas Term last.*

'GOOLE, 19*th* *day of May*, 1851.'

No. 56. *Suffolk smuggler's confession*, 1852.

(A large quantity of tobacco had been seized in a barn. Supposed to be only part of a quantity run. The 'spotsman' deposed as below):

'About the month of September, 1851, I met a person named —— at the *Lion* publichouse in Ipswich. I had been engaged with him in a smuggling transaction about May in the same year. He said to me that he wished I could get a vessel that would carry 5 or 6 tons, and he would give me £1 a bale, meaning that that was the sum he would pay me for every bale of tobacco I could smuggle into this kingdom. I told him I thought I could. In consequence of this conversation I saw a man named —— who owned a vessel called the *Neptune*, and having ascertained from him that I could have his vessel I again saw —— in the month of October following, at the *Mulberry Tree* publichouse in Ipswich, when I told him that I could get a vessel that was going to Lowestoft, and would return with empty cement barrels and sacks, and would then go over to Nieuport. He then gave me a letter directed to Mr. —— a tobacco merchant (English) at Nieuport. The *Neptune* cleared out for Lowestoft, myself acting as pilot. On arriving there I went to the *Suffolk Arms*, where I met —— who asked me when I should be able to start. I answered " tomorrow," and he then said, " Well, make the best of your way." I sailed from Lowestoft on a Friday, and arrived at Nieuport in the course of the next day, when I handed Mr. —— the letter from ——. When he opened it he said that he could not pay me £100 (as desired) but he would guarantee that it should be paid as soon as the tobacco was on the walls—meaning the embankment or river wall of the Orwell—as soon as we were there. And in the course of that day the *Neptune* received 200 bales into her (one or two of which I cut open for the purpose of procuring samples for —— to sell by), which I and the crew assisted in loading, and sailed the same night for the river Orwell. It was agreed between myself and —— that the cargo was to be landed at a place in that river called Trimley Sluice (where I and he assisted in landing a similar cargo of 80 bales in the May preceding). I arrived in the Orwell in the course of the following Sunday afternoon, and sailed till we came abreast of Trimley Sluice, when two of the *Neptune's* crew rowed me ashore in the boat, and the vessel went up as far as Collinor ' (?) ' Point. I went on to the *Ship* inn at Levington, kept by —— to get assistance to remove the bales when landed. In my way thither I met Lord Alfred Paget and his gamekeeper, the latter of whom bid me good-day. From the *Ship* I went to ——'s mill, and there I found —— in company with the occupier, to whom I gave the samples, and with whom we sat and smoked, the conversation between us being generally the best time and under what circumstances we should remove the bales, and the miller said he would go down with his horse and cart and assist, and I then left for that purpose, leaving —— in ——'s house. On arriving at the marsh I saw the bales laid out in scores. I saw horses and carts, belonging to —— ——, ——, ——, ——, and ——: four of these carts with 100 bales altogether, with which they drove away. Two of the said carts, viz. ——'s, and another, returned twice, and were loaded with the remainder of the bales. I accompanied them to a farm belonging to a person named —— at Bucklesham, where I assisted in unloading the bales into the loft of a stable belonging to him. The miller told me that he had received 100 of the bales. I and —— went to the miller's house and slept there that night, and —— asked me whether the goods were all right and I told him they were, and he desired me at breakfast-time to meet him at the *Mulberry Tree* in Ipswich in a day or two. I accordingly went there on the Wednesday evening following, and received from him a £50 Bank of England note, which I changed at the Yellow Bank at Ipswich, first endorsing my name thereon.

'In the course of two or three days afterwards I received from him at the *Mulberry Tree* another £50 note, which I changed at the Yellow Bank, endorsing my name as before.

'On each of these occasions I paid the master of the *Neptune* £40 at the *Union Jack* publichouse, on account of the services of his vessel, himself, and crew.

'In the course of a few days afterwards I saw —— at the *Victoria Arms* publichouse in Ipswich, on which occasion the master of the *Neptune* was in company with us, and I saw —— pay him two £50 notes.

'Within a month afterwards I received from —— 50s. at the *Mulberry Tree* for my share in bringing over the bales.

'The vessel *Neptune* was seized at Emsworth in Sussex, and I received a letter from —— to a Mr. ——, an innkeeper and butcher at Southwick, Sussex, on the subject, and —— gave me £3 or £4 to defray my expenses in going there.'

(This has been selected as remarkable, on account of the deadly particularization and conclusiveness of the narrative. It will be seen that for bringing over about 12,000 pounds of tobacco the receivers paid as below:

	£	s.	d.
To the spotsman	22	10	0
To the master and crew	180	0	0
To the owners of the carts, etc.—say ..	25	0	0
	227	10	0

The goods would cost in Nieuport—say, 1s. a pound = £600. Roughly, other expenses included, £850 for the cargo. At 3s.

a pound—a very moderate price, duty-paid—the goods would fetch £1,800. It is likely the spotsman thought himself underpaid, whence the information.)

No. 57. Précis of papers connected with a seizure in the Medway, 1854.

Statement of William Coulls, chief Customs boatman at Standgate Creek:

'I was afloat on duty in the river Medway on the morning of Sunday the 21st May instant, about ½ past 3 o'clock in the morning, when I observed a half-decked boat ½ a mile north-east of Standgate Creek. I was then boarding several vessels passing up the Medway, and I let the boat I had just observed get up the river some distance before I made towards her, when she had made about a mile further up the river, and made towards her for about 10 minutes, when I came alongside her. At this time Charles Jennings, a boatman, and James West, also a boatman, were with me. On coming alongside the suspicious-looking boat I found —— and —— on board, and asked them what they had got in their boat, when they answered, "Oysters for Chatham." I went on board and examined her, and on going under the hatches I found that she had no oysters on board, but there were one or two old sails and several coils of rope, on removing which I found several canvas bales, with the number "40" on each, and suspecting that they contained tobacco I called my boatman on board. I detained the boat, which is named the *Charity*, and proceeded with her to the coastguard station at Standgate Creek. On finding the bales I said to the prisoners, "You have very good oysters in." —— asked me if I was satisfied. I told him I was, when he said "Take her, for I have had enough trouble with her," and in the course of a few minutes afterwards he told me he had come over Nieuport Bar with a reef in her mainsail. On examining the contents of the boat I found 62 bales in her, 61 of which contained unmanfd leaf tobacco, and 1 bale, that had been opened, containing manufd shag tobacco, the whole of which I conveyed with the boat *Charity* to the Custom House at Rochester, and delivered the same to the controller. The prisoners I placed on board the *Shamrock* revenue cutter.'

(Both smugglers committed for six months in default of paying a fine of £100 each.)

Their memorial, sent from prison, to the Board:

'The Humble Petition of —— and ——, inhabitants of Queenborough, now confined in Maidstone jail, sheweth:

'That your petitioners very imprudently violated the Law of the Land, in being guilty of smuggling, which step they not only exceedingly regret, but promise in future not to be guilty of a like offence.

'Your petitioners will feel very grateful to your Honourable Board if you will extend to them a similar act of clemency as to others who have been placed in a like position.

'Your petitioners humbly represent to your Honourable Board that they have already been in prison for three months, and that their present distressing position is aggravated by the fact that their wives and children are entirely dependent upon them for support. The case of your petitioner ——'s wife is of a very affecting character, inasmuch as she is greatly afflicted.

'Trusting that your Honourable Board will take your petitioners' case into your merciful consideration, &c.

'We, the undersigned inhabitants of Queenborough, beg cordially to support the prayer of the above petitioners.'

(Here follow the signatures of the mayor, the incumbent, the churchwardens, and many others.)

(Board's minute):

'The request cannot be complied with.'

(Then the incumbent addresses the Board privately):

'GENTLEMEN,

'I have taken pains to inquire of several influential persons in this place regarding the former character and conduct of —— and —— the petitioners who seek at your hands remission of part of their sentence of imprisonment for smuggling, and I find that previous to their being guilty of that act they were regarded as respectable and industrious men. I have been incumbent of this place for only three months, and therefore am unable of my own knowledge to speak of them, but the above testimony is that of persons whom I can trust, and who are of known integrity in my parish. I can therefore conscientiously express a hope that you will kindly listen to the prayer of their petition.

'I am, Gentlemen, yours faithfully,

'GEORGE D. THOMSON, B.A.'

(Board's minute):

'The applicant to be informed that, adverting to the magnitude of the offence of which the parties were guilty, the Board cannot direct their release.'

No. 58. *Précis of papers connected with a seizure in Ireland (Co. Donegal), showing method of charging expenses, subsistence, etc.*

'13th *March*, 1855.

'SIR,

'I beg leave to acquaint you that on the night of the 10th instant a seizure of 8 cwt of tobacco, with the man, horse, and cart by which it was being conveyed, was made by the Revenue Police stationed at Church Hill, in the Letterkenny road, 24 miles inland. It appears that the man ——, apprehended in charge of it, is from the neighbourhood of Derrybeg, and I have every reason to conclude that this seizure is the remaining portion of the tobacco landed from the *Betsy* and *Nora Creina*, as reported in my letter of the 11th Novr last, enclosing the deposition of James ——, and which tobacco, having been concealed in the adjacent mountains, escaped the strict search made by the Coastguard and Revenue Police at the time. It evidently follows from this and the three previous seizures made by the Coastguard and Constabulary that the smugglers have been baffled in all their attempts to secure the tobacco after it was landed, the whole of which I am credibly informed has now been seized, &c, &c.

'FRANCIS COLLINS,

'*Inspecting Lieutenant.*

'TO THE COMPTROLLER OF COASTGUARD
LONDON.'

(Board's minute):

'Retain the goods, horse, and cart, as a seizure: Proceed against the party for the penalty of £100.'

(Below is the return invariably made at the time in such cases, both in Ireland and Great Britain):

'Name, residence, and occupation of the Party	—— —— of Derrybeg, carman.
Offence committed, description and quantity of goods ..	Carrying 867 lbs. tobacco.
Date when offence committed ..	9th March, 1855.
Place where	Drumlurga parish, Kilmainham, Co. Donegal.
When, and by whom, arrested ..	9th March, 1855. Lieut. Robert Newcomen, 9th Revenue Police.
When, and before whom, convicted	T. Patterson, J. M. Beers, J. Chambers, and J. Fleming, Esqs., J.Ps at petty sessions in Letterkenny, 28th March, 1855.
Amount of Penalty, &c. ..	£100. Imprisonment for 9 months, unless he shall sooner pay same.
Where sent, or in what custody	Lifford Gaol.
Of what Country, &c.	Subject of her Majesty.
Apparent age	50.
Apparent state of bodily health	Good.
Whether married or single ..	He will not state.
Number of children depending on him	Do.
General Character	Not known.
Whether convicted of Smuggling before	No information as to this has been obtained.'

(It is likely that the prisoner gave a wrong name.)

PRÉCIS OF PROCEEDS, EXPENSES, ETC.

	£	s.	d.		£	s.	d.
'Horse and cart sold for	7	17	6	Prosecuting solicitor's charges	5	4	0
(Tobacco destroyed)				Justices' clerk ..	1	3	6
Loss to Crown by seizure	26	13	0*	Messengers	0	3	6
				Keep of detained horse (14 days) ..	0	17	6
				Customs officers' travelling charges ..	3	1	0
				Support of prisoner while in jail, 134 days at 6d. a day ..	3	7	0
				Paid to officers as reward	19	14	0
				Paid to officers as headmoney ..	1	0	0
	34	10	6		34	10	6'

(In connection with this case there was much amusing discussion as to whether the grant of 6d. a day was payable in the case of an Irish prisoner. Most of the official experts thought that it was only payable in Great Britain, and that the Irish rate was 4½d. a day, but, a precedent being furnished, the charge was passed. N.B.—In other records the *English* rate is shown as 7d.)

* This is quite a moderate item. The larger the seizures, of course he larger the grants of reward.

ADDENDA

(ILLUSTRATIVE DOCUMENTS, see pp. 439-440.)

No. 21A. *Extract from Scottish Board's Memoranda, September 20, 1779, containing deposition made by captain of revenue cruiser, as to movements of squadron commanded by Paul Jones.*

(The account states that on September 16, 1779, the Board were informed that the squadron, which had been viewed off Dunbar on the 14th, appeared off the Isle of May. Captain Brown, of the *Princess Royal* cutter, was ordered to reconnoitre, and, if the ships belonged to the enemy, he was to 'fire three guns, quick,' as a signal to an armed King's ship then lying in Leith Roads, also to fly a jack at his masthead as an additional signal.)

'And Mr. Brown having proceeded agreeably thereto and returned to Leith at half-an-hour after eleven o'clock on Friday morning' (the 17th) 'his declaration was taken in the Presence of the Honble Capt. Napier, Regulating Officer, and George Clerk Maxwell & Adam Smith, Esq^rs^, Commissioners of the Customs, which is as follows:

'"Mr. Brown, commander of one of the Customhouse Cutters, having received orders from the Commissioners of the Customs to reconnoitre the Ships coming up the Firth, made sail this morning, and at Daybreak found himself within Pistol Shot of a fifty Gun French Ship,* upon which he tacked about, and afterwards retook a prize they had taken in the Mouth of the Firth, but a French twenty-four Gun Frigate immediately made up, and obliged him to abandon

* Undoubtedly *Le Bon Homme Richard*.

the Prize: they brought on Shore a Boy from the Prize, who says they put four soldiers, four Men, & two Officers on board him. The French Squadron consists of a fifty Gun Ship, a twenty four Gun Frigate, and a Brig mounting ten Guns. The Ships sail ill, and they say they are determined to come up to Leith Road. The Commander of the fifty Gun Ship is said to be acquainted with the Coast. Both the fifty Gun Ship and Frigate are painted Black. The fifty Gun Ship has a White Bottom and very clumsy mast head. The Boy says seven sail of them sailed in Company *: they went north † the length of Shetland, and returned separated in a Gale of Wind, some Days ago, from the rest of the Squadron. 17th September, 1779." '

(The Memoranda proceed that Adam Smith and Clerk Maxwell transmitted this deposition by express at 2.15 p.m., September 17, to the Treasury, London, and ordered the three revenue sloops on the east coast to be placed under the direction of the Commander-in-Chief. It is evident from the Memoranda that the British Government had been informed promptly of Jones's previous movements, even of his setting out from France, and that the revenue cruisers all round the British coast were on the look-out, manned and armed 'to the fullest extent,' and ready to assist the British fleet. It is quite evident, too, that Captain Brown was a smart and reliable sailorman, and that the Scottish Customs Commissioners were alive to their responsibilities.)

* Probably including prizes.

† Along the west coast of Ireland, and around the north of Scotland?

INDEX

ILLUSTRATIVE DOCUMENTS

PRESS NOTICES OF VOLUME I. OF THE KING'S CUSTOMS

FROM THE EARLIEST TIMES TO THE YEAR 1800.

Demy 8vo. 10*s.* 6*d. net.*

'Messrs. Atton and Holland must be congratulated on having made the most of their exceptional sources of information in producing an entertaining as well as an historically interesting work.'—*Outlook.*

'The authors have shown great industry and judgment in the collection and utilization of material, the enormous extent of which must have made the task of selection one of considerable difficulty.'—*Morning Post.*

'Every chapter has its list of authorities cited at its close, and where practicable opens with a clear statement of principal Statutes affecting the period under consideration. Thus the general reader will find the course of legislation and procedure made intelligible, stage by stage, as becomes a popular history. . . . Extremely instructive, and often full of entertainment.'—*Westminster Gazette.*

'A popular history of "The King's Customs" was much needed, and Messrs. Henry Atton and Henry Hurst Holland are to be congratulated upon the exhaustive work which they have produced. It provides an extremely interesting "account of maritime revenue and contraband traffic in England, Scotland, and Ireland from the earliest times to the year 1800." . . . The whole volume is of engrossing interest.'—*Dundee Advertiser.*

'It will undoubtedly be a good thing if some of those who argue loudest either for or against Tariff Reform will familiarize themselves with this book—a process that will have the effect of preventing some from wasting their eloquence and of encouraging others to back up intrinsically sound arguments by the evidences of history.'—*Evening Standard.*

'A most interesting account of maritime revenue and contraband traffic in the United Kingdom from the earliest times to the year 1800.' —*Daily Mail.*

'The authors . . . had full access to Departmental materials in its preparation. These materials . . . are, as a rule, dry and bare of the sap and spirit of human interest. Mr. Atton and Mr. Holland have, however, the art of setting the skeleton together, bone and bone, and clothing them with flesh and blood, and even giving them touches of romantic colouring.'—*Scotsman.*

'A book of unique character, well conceived, and ably executed.'—*Birmingham Gazette.*

'All sorts of odd and interesting information can be gleaned from "The King's Customs." . . . It is no mere dry register of facts, but is a lively record which its authors have every reason to describe as "popular."'—*Sunday Times.*